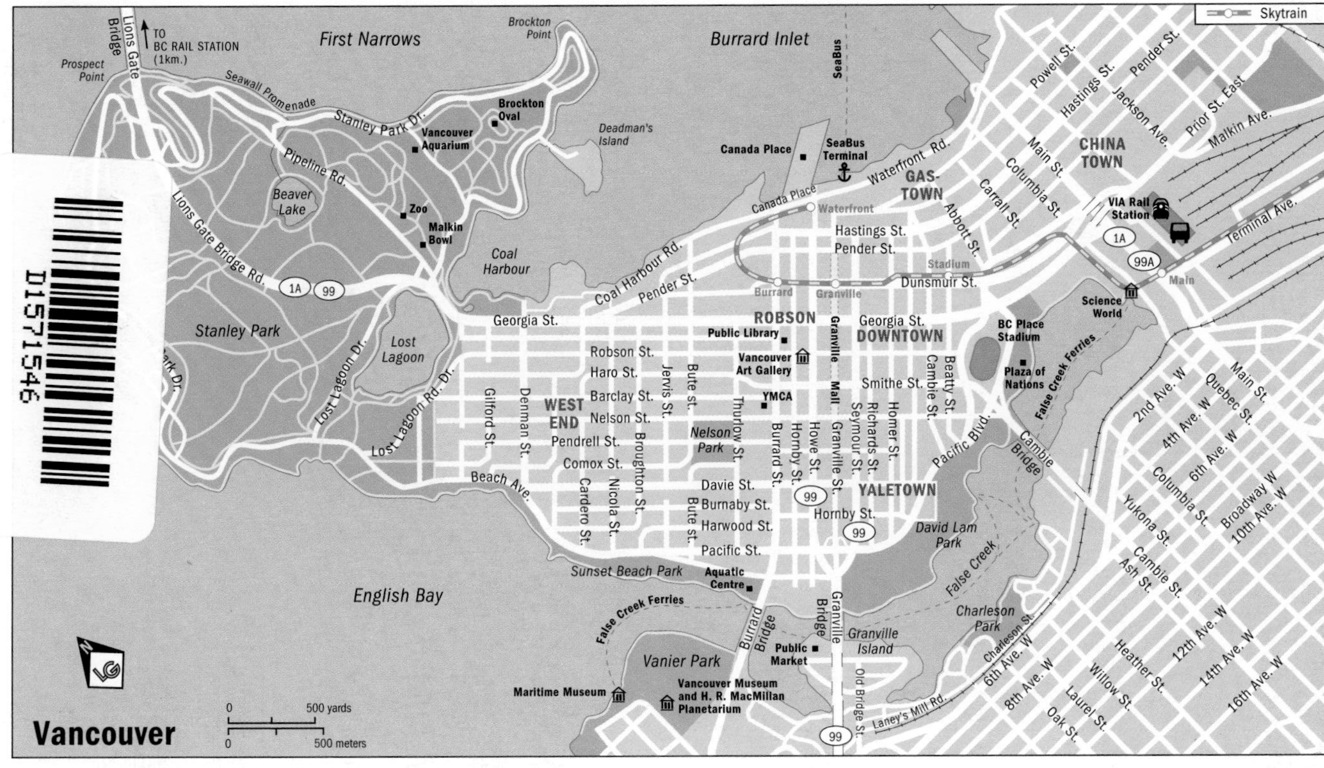
Vancouver
Skytrain
First Narrows
Burrard Inlet
English Bay
SeaBus
Lions Gate Bridge
TO BC RAIL STATION (1km.)
Prospect Point
Brockton Point
Seawall Promenade
Stanley Park Dr.
Brockton Oval
Vancouver Aquarium
Deadman's Island
Pipeline Rd.
Beaver Lake
Zoo
Malkin Bowl
Coal Harbour
Lions Gate Bridge Rd.
1A
99
Stanley Park
Lost Lagoon
Lost Lagoon Dr.
Lost Lagoon Rd. Dr.
Canada Place
SeaBus Terminal
Waterfront Rd.
GAS-TOWN
CHINA TOWN
Powell St.
Hastings St.
Pender St.
Jackson Ave.
Prior St. East
Malkin Ave.
Main St.
Columbia St.
Carrall St.
Abbott St.
VIA Rail Station
Terminal Ave.
99A
Main
Waterfront
Stadium
Burrard
Granville
Coal Harbour Rd.
Pender St.
Hastings St.
Dunsmuir St.
Georgia St.
ROBSON
DOWNTOWN
Public Library
Vancouver Art Gallery
Granville Mall
Robson St.
Haro St.
Barclay St.
Nelson St.
Pendrell St.
Comox St.
WEST END
Gilford St.
Denman St.
Jervis St.
Bute st.
Broughton St.
Nicola St.
Cardero St.
YMCA
Thurlow St.
Nelson Park
Burrard St.
Hornby St.
Howe St.
Granville St.
Seymour St.
Richards St.
Homer St.
Smithe St.
Cambie St.
Beatty St.
YALETOWN
Davie St.
Burnaby St.
Harwood St.
Pacific St.
Hornby St.
Beach Ave.
Sunset Beach Park
Aquatic Centre
BC Place Stadium
Plaza of Nations
Science World
False Creek Ferries
Pacific Blvd.
Cambie Bridge
David Lam Park
False Creek
Charleson Park
Charleson St.
Granville Bridge
Burrard Bridge
Granville Island
Public Market
Vanier Park
Maritime Museum
Vancouver Museum and H. R. MacMillan Planetarium
Old Bridge St.
Laney's Mill Rd.
2nd Ave. W
4th Ave. W
6th Ave. W
8th Ave. W
Broadway W
10th Ave. W
12th Ave. W
14th Ave. W
16th Ave. W
Quebec St.
Yukona St.
Cambie St.
Ash St.
Heather St.
Willow St.
Laurel St.
Oak St.
0
500 yards
500 meters

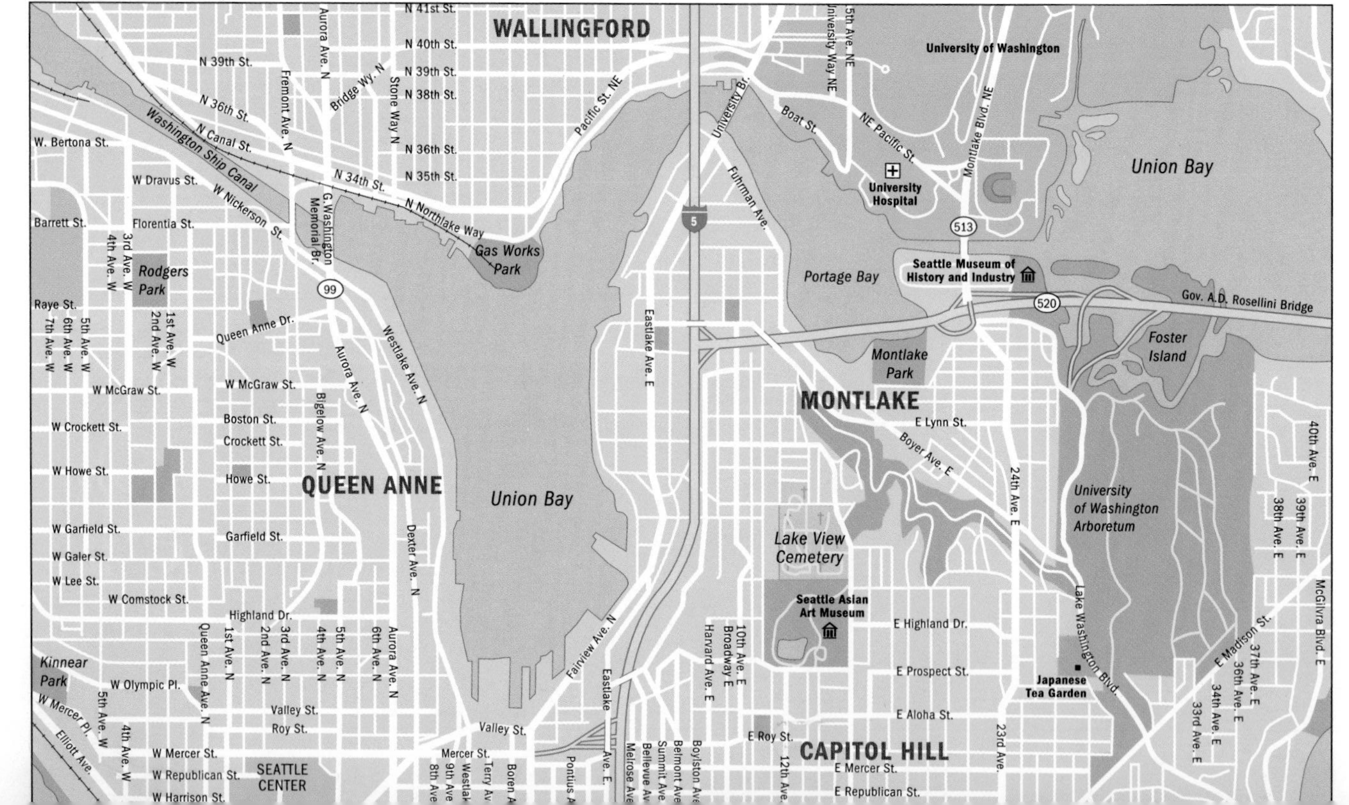

WALLINGFORD
QUEEN ANNE
MONTLAKE
CAPITOL HILL
SEATTLE CENTER
University of Washington
University Hospital
Seattle Museum of History and Industry
Seattle Asian Art Museum
Japanese Tea Garden
Union Bay
Portage Bay
Gas Works Park
Rodgers Park
Kinnear Park
Montlake Park
Foster Island
Lake View Cemetery
University of Washington Arboretum
Gov. A.D. Rosellini Bridge
Washington Ship Canal
G.Washington Memorial Br.
University Br.
99
5
513
520
N 41st St.
N 40th St.
N 39th St.
N 38th St.
N 36th St.
N 35th St.
N 34th St.
N Canal St.
N Northlake Way
Pacific St. NE
NE Pacific St.
Boat St.
University Way NE
15th Ave. NE
Montlake Blvd. NE
Fuhrman Ave.
Fremont Ave. N
Aurora Ave. N
Bridge Wy. N
Stone Way N
W. Bertona St.
W Dravus St.
W Nickerson St.
Barrett St.
Florentia St.
Raye St.
7th Ave. W
6th Ave. W
5th Ave. W
4th Ave. W
3rd Ave. W
2nd Ave. W
1st Ave. W
Queen Anne Dr.
W McGraw St.
W Crockett St.
W Howe St.
W Garfield St.
W Galer St.
W Lee St.
W Comstock St.
W Olympic Pl.
W Mercer Pl.
Elliott Ave.
W Mercer St.
W Republican St.
W Harrison St.
McGraw St.
Boston St.
Crockett St.
Howe St.
Garfield St.
Highland Dr.
Bigelow Ave. N
Westlake Ave. N
Dexter Ave. N
Queen Anne Ave. N
1st Ave. N
2nd Ave. N
3rd Ave. N
4th Ave. N
5th Ave. N
6th Ave. N
Valley St.
Roy St.
Mercer St.
8th Ave
9th Ave
Westlak
Terry Av
Boren A
Pontius A
Fairview Ave. N
Eastlake Ave. E
Eastlake Ave. E.
Melrose Ave
Bellevue Av
Summit Ave.
Belmont Ave
Boylston Ave
Harvard Ave. E
Broadway E
10th Ave. E
12th Ave.
E Roy St.
E Mercer St.
E Republican St.
E Aloha St.
E Prospect St.
E Highland Dr.
E Lynn St.
Boyer Ave. E
24th Ave. E
23rd Ave.
Lake Washington Blvd.
E Madison St.
33rd Ave. E
34th Ave. E
36th Ave. E
37th Ave. E
38th Ave. E
39th Ave. E
40th Ave. E
McGilvra Blvd. E

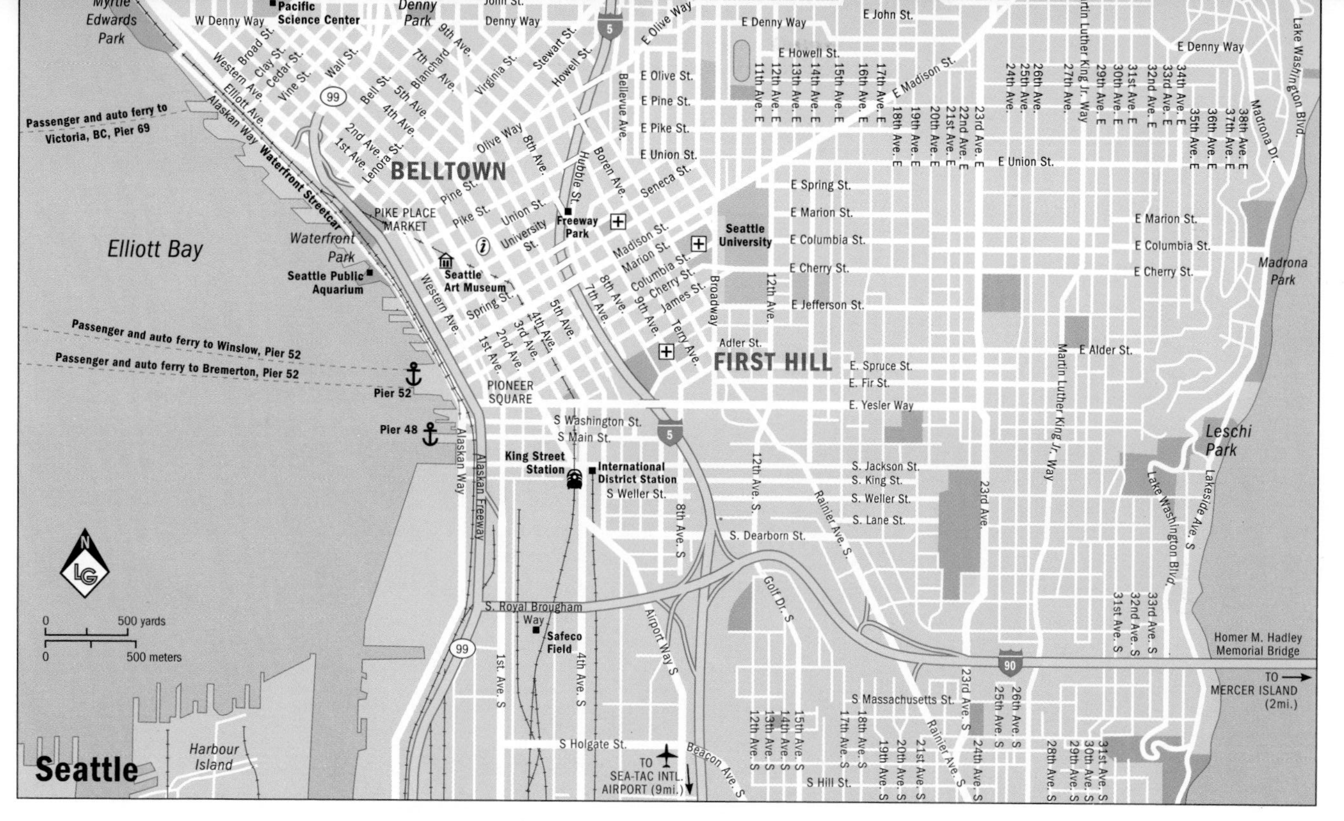

Seattle
Myrtle Edwards Park
W Denny Way
Pacific Science Center
Denny Park
Denny Way
John St.
E Olive Way
E Denny Way
E John St.
E Howell St.
E Denny Way
Lake Washington Blvd.
Madrona Dr.
Broad St.
Clay St.
Cedar St.
Vine St.
Wall St.
Western Ave.
Elliott Ave.
Alaskan Way
Waterfront Streetcar
99
Bell St.
5th Ave.
Blanchard St.
7th Ave.
9th Ave.
Virginia St.
Stewart St.
Howell St.
4th Ave.
2nd Ave.
1st Ave.
Lenora St.
Olive Way
8th Ave.
Bellevue Ave.
Hubble St.
Boren Ave.
Seneca St.
E Olive St.
E Pine St.
E Pike St.
E Union St.
11th Ave. E
12th Ave. E
13th Ave. E
14th Ave. E
15th Ave. E
16th Ave. E
17th Ave. E
18th Ave. E
19th Ave. E
20th Ave. E
21st Ave. E
22nd Ave. E
23rd Ave. E
E Madison St.
24th Ave.
25th Ave.
26th Ave.
27th Ave.
Martin Luther King Jr. Way
29th Ave. E
30th Ave. E
31st Ave. E
32nd Ave. E
33rd Ave. E
34th Ave. E
35th Ave. E
36th Ave. E
37th Ave. E
38th Ave. E
E Union St.
Passenger and auto ferry to Victoria, BC, Pier 69
BELLTOWN
Pine St.
Pike St.
Union St.
University St.
PIKE PLACE MARKET
Freeway Park
Seattle University
E Spring St.
E Marion St.
E Columbia St.
E Cherry St.
E Jefferson St.
E Marion St.
E Columbia St.
E Cherry St.
Madrona Park
Elliott Bay
Waterfront Park
Seattle Public Aquarium
Seattle Art Museum
Western Ave.
Spring St.
Madison St.
Marion St.
Columbia St.
Cherry St.
James St.
8th Ave.
7th Ave.
9th Ave.
Terry Ave.
Broadway
12th Ave.
Passenger and auto ferry to Winslow, Pier 52
Passenger and auto ferry to Bremerton, Pier 52
1st Ave.
2nd Ave.
3rd Ave.
4th Ave.
5th Ave.
Adler St.
FIRST HILL
E. Spruce St.
E. Fir St.
E. Yesler Way
E Alder St.
Martin Luther King Jr. Way
Pier 52
PIONEER SQUARE
Pier 48
S Washington St.
S Main St.
5
Leschi Park
King Street Station
International District Station
S Weller St.
S. Jackson St.
S. King St.
S. Weller St.
S. Lane St.
12th Ave. S.
Rainier Ave. S.
23rd Ave.
Lake Washington Blvd.
Lakeside Ave. S
Alaskan Way
Alaskan Freeway
8th Ave. S
S. Dearborn St.
N
LG
Golf Dr. S
S. Royal Brougham Way
Safeco Field
Airport Way S
0
500 yards
0
500 meters
99
1st. Ave. S
4th Ave. S
31st Ave. S
32nd Ave. S
33rd Ave. S
Homer M. Hadley Memorial Bridge
90
TO MERCER ISLAND (2mi.)
S Massachusetts St.
23rd Ave. S
25th Ave. S
26th Ave. S
12th Ave. S
13th Ave. S
14th Ave. S
15th Ave. S
17th Ave. S
18th Ave. S
19th Ave. S
20th Ave. S
21st Ave. S
Rainier Ave. S
24th Ave. S
28th Ave. S
29th Ave. S
30th Ave. S
31st Ave. S
S Holgate St.
Harbour Island
TO SEA-TAC INTL. AIRPORT (9mi.)
Beacon Ave. S
S Hill St.

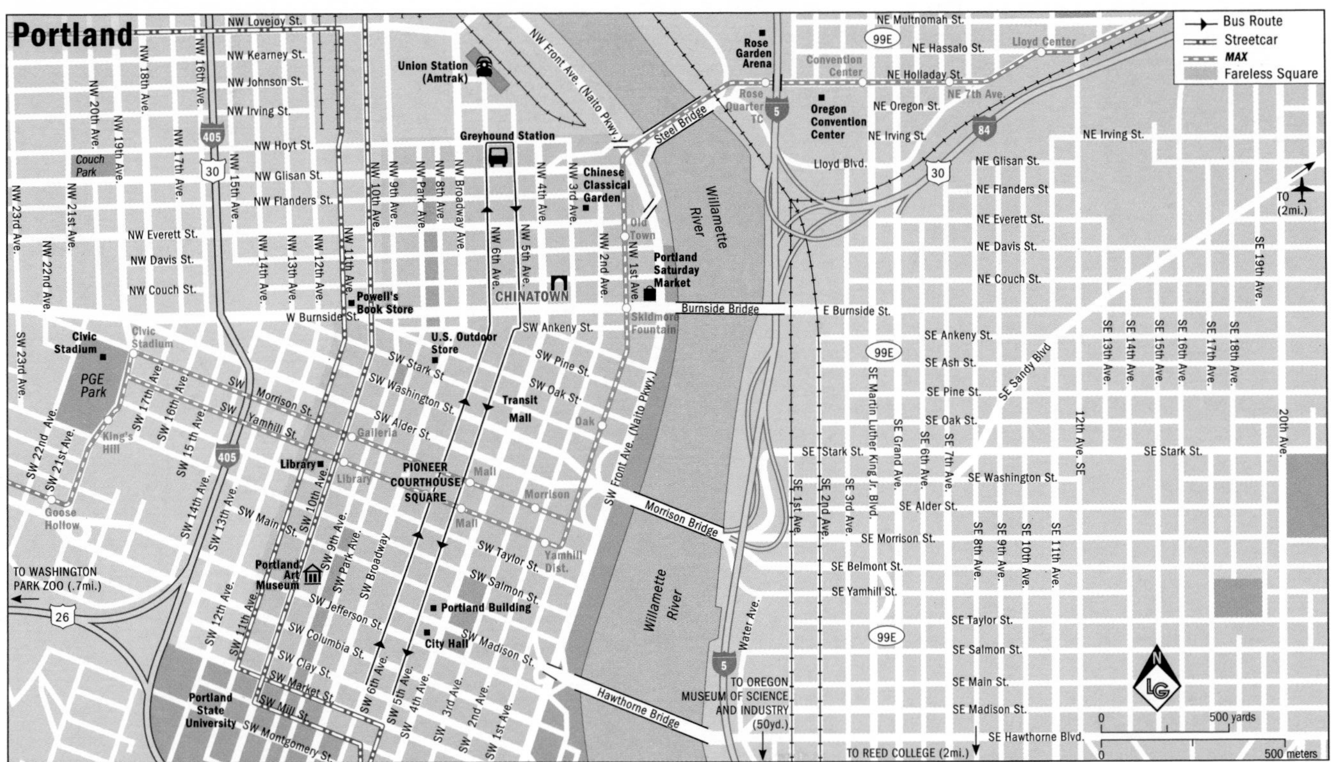
Portland
Bus Route
Streetcar
MAX
Fareless Square
Union Station (Amtrak)
Greyhound Station
Chinese Classical Garden
Portland Saturday Market
CHINATOWN
Powell's Book Store
U.S. Outdoor Store
Transit Mall
PIONEER COURTHOUSE SQUARE
Library
Portland Art Museum
Portland Building
City Hall
Portland State University
Civic Stadium
PGE Park
Couch Park
Rose Garden Arena
Oregon Convention Center
Willamette River
Steel Bridge
Burnside Bridge
Morrison Bridge
Hawthorne Bridge
TO WASHINGTON PARK ZOO (.7mi.)
TO OREGON MUSEUM OF SCIENCE AND INDUSTRY (50yd.)
TO REED COLLEGE (2mi.)
TO (2mi.)
500 yards
500 meters
NW Lovejoy St.
NW Kearney St.
NW Johnson St.
NW Irving St.
NW Hoyt St.
NW Glisan St.
NW Flanders St.
NW Everett St.
NW Davis St.
NW Couch St.
W Burnside St.
E Burnside St.
NW Front Ave. (Naito Pkwy.)
SW Front Ave. (Naito Pkwy.)
SW Ankeny St.
SW Pine St.
SW Oak St.
SW Stark St.
SW Washington St.
SW Alder St.
SW Morrison St.
SW Yamhill St.
SW Taylor St.
SW Salmon St.
SW Main St.
SW Madison St.
SW Jefferson St.
SW Columbia St.
SW Clay St.
SW Market St.
SW Mill St.
SW Montgomery St.
NE Multnomah St.
NE Hassalo St.
NE Holladay St.
NE Oregon St.
NE Irving St.
Lloyd Blvd.
NE Glisan St.
NE Flanders St
NE Everett St.
NE Davis St.
NE Couch St.
NE 7th Ave.
SE Ankeny St.
SE Ash St.
SE Pine St.
SE Oak St.
SE Stark St.
SE Washington St.
SE Alder St.
SE Morrison St.
SE Belmont St.
SE Yamhill St.
SE Taylor St.
SE Salmon St.
SE Main St.
SE Madison St.
SE Hawthorne Blvd.
SE Sandy Blvd
Water Ave.
SE 1st Ave.
SE 2nd Ave.
SE 3rd Ave.
SE Martin Luther King Jr. Blvd.
SE Grand Ave.
SE 6th Ave.
SE 7th Ave.
SE 8th Ave.
SE 9th Ave.
SE 10th Ave.
SE 11th Ave.
12th Ave. SE
SE 13th Ave.
SE 14th Ave.
SE 15th Ave.
SE 16th Ave.
SE 17th Ave.
SE 18th Ave.
SE 19th Ave.
20th Ave.
NW 1st Ave.
NW 2nd Ave.
NW 3rd Ave.
NW 4th Ave.
NW 5th Ave.
NW 6th Ave.
NW Broadway Ave.
NW 8th Ave.
NW Park Ave.
NW 9th Ave.
NW 10th Ave.
NW 11th Ave.
NW 12th Ave.
NW 13th Ave.
NW 14th Ave.
NW 15th Ave.
NW 16th Ave.
NW 17th Ave.
NW 18th Ave.
NW 19th Ave.
NW 20th Ave.
NW 21st Ave.
NW 22nd Ave.
NW 23rd Ave.
SW 1st Ave.
SW 2nd Ave.
SW 3rd Ave.
SW 4th Ave.
SW 5th Ave.
SW 6th Ave.
SW Broadway
SW Park Ave.
SW 9th Ave.
SW 10th Ave.
SW 11th Ave.
SW 12th Ave.
SW 13th Ave.
SW 14th Ave.
SW 15 th Ave.
SW 16th Ave
SW 17th Ave
SW 21st Ave.
SW 22nd Ave.
SW 23rd Ave.
Old Town
Skidmore Fountain
Oak
Morrison
Yamhill Dist.
Mall
Galleria
Library
Civic Stadium
King's Hill
Goose Hollow
Rose Quarter TC
Convention Center
Lloyd Center
405
30
26
5
84
99E

■ THE RESOURCE FOR THE INDEPENDENT TRAVELER

"The guides are aimed not only at young budget travelers but at the indepedent traveler; a sort of streetwise cookbook for traveling alone."

—*The New York Times*

"Unbeatable; good sight-seeing advice; up-to-date info on restaurants, hotels, and inns; a commitment to money-saving travel; and a wry style that brightens nearly every page."

—*The Washington Post*

"Lighthearted and sophisticated, informative and fun to read. [Let's Go] helps the novice traveler navigate like a knowledgeable old hand."

—*Atlanta Journal-Constitution*

"A world-wise traveling companion—always ready with friendly advice and helpful hints, all sprinkled with a bit of wit."

—*The Philadelphia Inquirer*

■ THE BEST TRAVEL BARGAINS IN YOUR PRICE RANGE

"All the dirt, dirt cheap."

—*People*

"Anything you need to know about budget traveling is detailed in this book."

—*The Chicago Sun-Times*

"Let's Go follows the creed that you don't have to toss your life's savings to the wind to travel—unless you want to."

—*The Salt Lake Tribune*

■ REAL ADVICE FOR REAL EXPERIENCES

"The writers seem to have experienced every rooster-packed bus and lunar-surfaced mattress about which they write."

—*The New York Times*

"A guide should tell you what to expect from a destination. Here Let's Go shines."

—*The Chicago Tribune*

"[Let's Go's] devoted updaters really walk the walk (and thumb the ride, and trek the trail). Learn how to fish, haggle, find work—anywhere."

—*Food & Wine*

LET'S GO PUBLICATIONS

TRAVEL GUIDES

Alaska 1st edition **NEW TITLE**
Australia 2004
Austria & Switzerland 2004
Brazil 1st edition **NEW TITLE**
Britain & Ireland 2004
California 2004
Central America 8th edition
Chile 1st edition
China 4th edition
Costa Rica 1st edition
Eastern Europe 2004
Egypt 2nd edition
Europe 2004
France 2004
Germany 2004
Greece 2004
Hawaii 2004
India & Nepal 8th edition
Ireland 2004
Israel 4th edition
Italy 2004
Japan 1st edition **NEW TITLE**
Mexico 20th edition
Middle East 4th edition
New Zealand 6th edition
Pacific Northwest 1st edition **NEW TITLE**
Peru, Ecuador & Bolivia 3rd edition
Puerto Rico 1st edition **NEW TITLE**
South Africa 5th edition
Southeast Asia 8th edition
Southwest USA 3rd edition
Spain & Portugal 2004
Thailand 1st edition
Turkey 5th edition
USA 2004
Western Europe 2004

CITY GUIDES

Amsterdam 3rd edition
Barcelona 3rd edition
Boston 4th edition
London 2004
New York City 2004
Paris 2004
Rome 12th edition
San Francisco 4th edition
Washington, D.C. 13th edition

MAP GUIDES

Amsterdam
Berlin
Boston
Chicago
Dublin
Florence
Hong Kong
London
Los Angeles
Madrid
New Orleans
New York City
Paris
Prague
Rome
San Francisco
Seattle
Sydney
Venice
Washington, D.C.

COMING SOON:

Quick Trips France
Quick Trips Italy
Quick Trips Spain
Road Trip USA

PACIFIC NORTHWEST

Benjamin G. Wells Editor
Robert J. Dubbin Associate Editor
Ankur Ghosh, Diane Lewis Update Editors

Researcher-Writers
Posy Busby
Carleton Goold
James Pinto
Greg Schmeller

Nathaniel Brooks Map Editor
Abigail Burger Managing Editor

St. Martin's Press New York

HELPING LET'S GO If you want to share your discoveries, suggestions, or corrections, please drop us a line. We read every piece of correspondence, whether a postcard, a 10-page email, or a coconut. **Address mail to:**

Let's Go: Pacific Northwest
67 Mount Auburn Street
Cambridge, MA 02138
USA

Visit Let's Go at **http://www.letsgo.com,** or send email to:

feedback@letsgo.com
Subject: "Let's Go: Pacific Northwest"

In addition to the invaluable travel advice our readers share with us, many are kind enough to offer their services as researchers or editors. Unfortunately, our charter enables us to employ only currently enrolled Harvard students.

Distributed outside the USA and Canada by Macmillan.

ISBN: 0-312-31994-0

First edition
10 9 8 7 6 5 4 3 2 1

Let's Go: Pacific Northwest is written by Let's Go Publications, 67 Mount Auburn Street, Cambridge, MA 02138, USA.

ABOUT LET'S GO

GUIDES FOR THE INDEPENDENT TRAVELER

Budget travel is more than a vacation. At *Let's Go,* we see every trip as the chance of a lifetime. If your dream is to grab a knapsack and a machete and forge through the jungles of Brazil, we can take you there. Or, if you'd rather enjoy the Riviera sun at a beachside cafe, we'll set you a table. If you know what you're doing, you can have any experience you want—whether it's camping among lions or sampling Tuscan desserts—without maxing out your credit card. We'll show you just how far your coins can go, and prove that the greatest limitation on your adventure is not your wallet, but your imagination. That said, we understand that you may want the occasional indulgence after a week of hostels and kebab stands, so we've added "Big Splurges" to let you know which establishments are worth those extra euros, as well as price ranges to help you quickly determine whether an accommodation or restaurant will break the bank. While we may have diversified, our emphasis will always be on finding the best values for your budget, giving you all the info you need to spend six days in London or six months in Tasmania.

BEYOND THE TOURIST EXPERIENCE

We write for travelers who know there's more to a vacation than riding double-deckers with tourists. Our researchers give you the heads-up on both world-renowned and lesser-known attractions, on the best local eats and the hottest nightclub beats. In our travels, we talk to everybody; we provide a snapshot of real life in the places you visit with our sidebars on topics like regional cuisine, local festivals, and hot political issues. We've opened our pages to respected writers and scholars to show you their take on a given destination, and turned to lifelong residents to learn the little things that make their city worth calling home. And we've even given you Alternatives to Tourism—ideas for how to give back to local communities through responsible travel and volunteering.

OVER FORTY YEARS OF WISDOM

When we started, way back in 1960, Let's Go consisted of a small group of well-traveled friends who compiled their budget travel tips into a 20-page packet for students on charter flights to Europe. Since then, we've expanded to suit all kinds of travelers, now publishing guides to six continents, including our newest guides: *Let's Go: Japan* and *Let's Go: Brazil.* Our guides are still annually researched and written entirely by students on shoe-string budgets, adventurous travelers who know that train strikes, stolen luggage, food poisoning, and marriage proposals are all part of a day's work. Even as you read this, work on next year's editions is well underway. Whether you're reading one of our new titles, like *Let's Go: Puerto Rico* or *Let's Go Adventure Guide: Alaska*, or our original best-seller, *Let's Go: Europe*, you'll find the same spirit of adventure that has made *Let's Go* the guide of choice for travelers the world over since 1960.

GETTING IN TOUCH

The best discoveries are often those you make yourself; on the road, when you find something worth sharing, please drop us a line. We're Let's Go Publications, 67 Mt. Auburn St., Cambridge, MA 02138, USA (feedback@letsgo.com).

For more info, visit our website: www.letsgo.com.

HOW TO USE THIS BOOK

The first four chapters of this book are designed to familiarize you with the Pacific Northwest and prepare you to visit. **Discover** covers the highlights of this sprawling region. **Life & Times** gives a thumbnail sketch of the area's history and culture. The chapter after that breaks down all the travel **Essentials** you'll need. **Alternatives to Tourism** offers detailed information on working, studying, or volunteering in the Pacific Northwest. Our coverage of the region begins in **Oregon,** traveling up the US Pacific Coast until we reach **Washington.** From there, our coverage enters Canada via **British Columbia,** making a detour to visit **Alberta** before taking a deep breath and heading into the wilds of the **Yukon Territory.**

PLANNING YOUR TRIP

2 MONTHS BEFORE. The first chapter, **Discover the Pacific Northwest,** contains highlights of the region; it includes Suggested Itineraries that can help you plan your trip, whether you want to hike the Canadian Rockies or stick to a single Oregon beach. The **Essentials** section contains practical information about traveling in the US and Canada, and can help you create a budget, make reservations, rent a car, renew your passport, and more.

1 MONTH BEFORE. Take care of insurance and write down a list of emergency numbers and hotlines. Make a list of packing essentials and shop for anything you are missing, such as camping gear or weather-appropriate clothing. Read through the coverage and make sure you understand the logistics of your itinerary (mileage, catching trains and buses, etc.). Make any reservations for camping, hostels, hotels, and B&Bs, along with any required bus, plane, boat or car reservations.

2 WEEKS BEFORE. Leave an itinerary and list of contact phone numbers with someone at home. Take some time to peruse the **Life & Times** of the Pacific Northwest, with info on history, culture, flora and fauna, recent political events, the entertainment industry, and more.

PRICE RANGES & RANKINGS

Let's Go ranks all establishments in this guide by value; the best places get a thumbs-up (☒). With every food and accommodation listing, you'll find a marker indicating a price range, as follows (in either US or Canadian dollars). For a more detailed breakdown of what these ranges imply as far as services, amenities, quality, etc., are concerned, see the table on p. xiv.

PACIFIC NW	❶	❷	❸	❹	❺
ACCOMMODATIONS rate per person per night	$1-15	US$16-30	$31-50	$51-80	$81+
FOOD price of main dish	$1-5	$6-10	$11-15	$16-20	$21+

A NOTE TO OUR READERS The information for this book was gathered by *Let's Go* researchers from May through August of 2003. Each listing is based on one researcher's opinion, formed during his or her visit at a particular time. Those traveling at other times may have different experiences since prices, dates, hours, and conditions are always subject to change. You are urged to check the facts presented in this book beforehand to avoid inconvenience and surprises.

CONTENTS

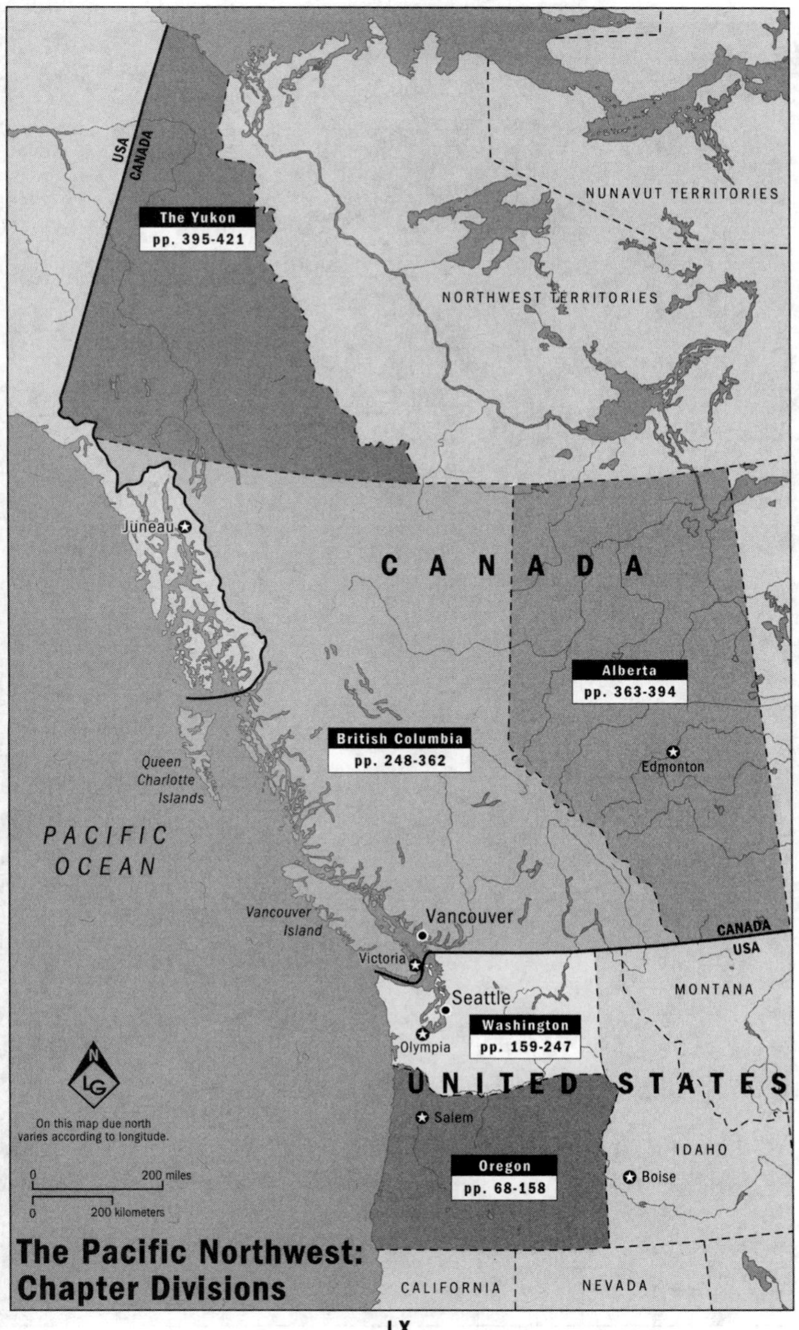
USA
CANADA
The Yukon
pp. 395-421
NUNAVUT TERRITORIES
NORTHWEST TERRITORIES
Juneau
CANADA
Alberta
pp. 363-394
British Columbia
pp. 248-362
Edmonton
Queen Charlotte Islands
PACIFIC OCEAN
Vancouver Island
Vancouver
CANADA
USA
Victoria
MONTANA
Seattle
Washington
pp. 159-247
Olympia
N
LG
UNITED STATES
Salem
On this map due north varies according to longitude.
IDAHO
Oregon
pp. 68-158
Boise
0
200 miles
0
200 kilometers
The Pacific Northwest: Chapter Divisions
CALIFORNIA
NEVADA

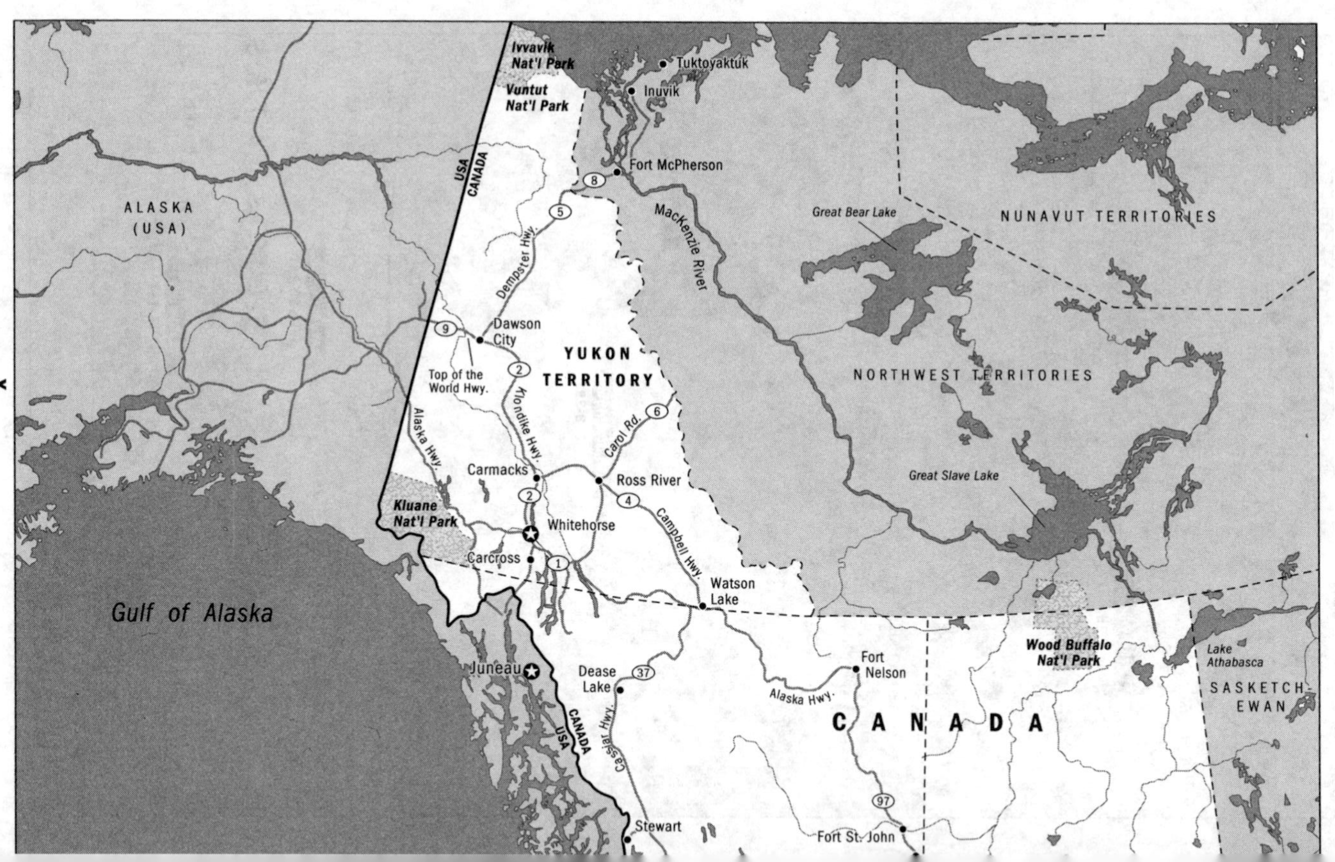

Ivvavik Nat'l Park
Vuntut Nat'l Park
Tuktoyaktuk
Inuvik
Fort McPherson
USA
CANADA
ALASKA (USA)
8
5
Dempster Hwy.
MacKenzie River
Great Bear Lake
NUNAVUT TERRITORIES
NORTHWEST TERRITORIES
9
Dawson City
Top of the World Hwy.
2
YUKON TERRITORY
Klondike Hwy.
Alaska Hwy.
Carol Rd.
6
Carmacks
Ross River
4
Campbell Hwy.
Kluane Nat'l Park
Whitehorse
Carcross
1
Great Slave Lake
Watson Lake
Gulf of Alaska
Juneau
Dease Lake
37
Cassiar Hwy.
Fort Nelson
Alaska Hwy.
CANADA
Wood Buffalo Nat'l Park
Lake Athabasca
SASKETCHEWAN
97
Stewart
Fort St. John

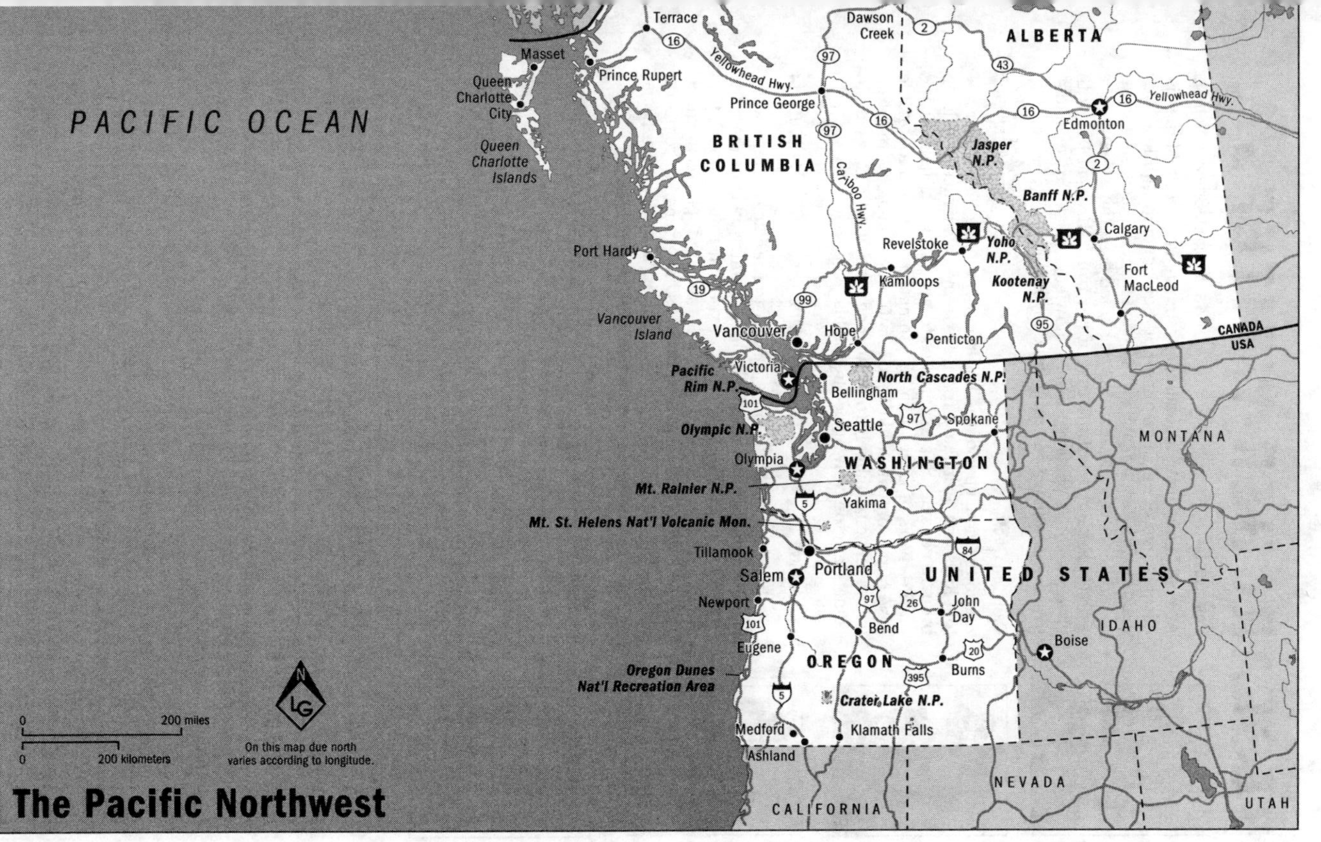

The Pacific Northwest

RESEARCHER-WRITERS

Posy Busby *Washington, British Columbia*

An avid hiker, biker, and outdoorswoman, Posy brought the discerning eye of an Environmental Science and Public Policy major to Washington and BC. Moving from the biggest of cities to the remotest of forests, Posy handled everything Seattle, the North Cascades, and the rest of her route threw at her with cheery aplomb, using her inside knowledge as an Oregon native to send back polished, insightful copybatches.

Carleton Goold *Oregon, Washington*

A two-time member of the US Junior National Whitewater Slalom Kayaking team and a former extreme kayak racer, Carleton brought considerable experience to bear in the mountains and on the rivers of Oregon and Washington. Not even a horrible case of poison oak could keep him from pursuing his research with a tenacity unlikely to be matched at *Let's Go* for years to come. Carleton truly made Oregon his own.

James Pinto *Washington, British Columbia, Alberta*

Fresh off his cross-country journey to the Pacific Northwest, James immediately took to the backcountry and got the most out of every park he visited. An expert at finding both little-known hiking routes and gorgeous (and free) places to camp, James used his extensive wilderness experience to focus on what he considered the true allure of the Pacific Northwest, and the result is expanded insider coverage in several major areas.

Greg Schmeller *British Columbia, Yukon Territory*

A native of Oregon, Greg drove his trusty steed to the farthest reaches of the Yukon and back, shrugging off engine failures, flat tires, and dead batteries along the way with extreme competence. His series of morality plays became the stuff of office legend, and did indeed inspire us to "secure him monies." Not even a charging moose could stop Greg, who was the definition of hard core during his 7-week odyssey.

CONTRIBUTING WRITERS

Ben Davis researched Oregon for *Let's Go: USA 2004*.

Matt Heid has researched for *Let's Go* in Alaska, the Yukon, Europe, and New Zealand. He is also the author of the guides *101 Hikes in Northern California* and *Camping and Backpacking the San Francisco Bay Area* (both available from Wilderness Press).

ACKNOWLEDGMENTS

THE TEAM THANKS Abi for catching our many mistkaes, all of our proofers, Nitin and Ariel, Nathaniel for not letting us forget about maps, and Trader Joe's for their high quality standards. We'd also like to thank Neil Diamond and Robert Goulet, for reasons they're aware of.

WELLS THANKS the best team of researchers in the series—you guys made our job infinitely easier. Many thanks to Abi, our amazing ME, for saving our book by catching every time we messed up, and Dubbin for saving me from technological hell—not to mention making me laugh like the idiot that I am. Nathaniel, for improving our maps 1000 times and being a great guy. Team California, team Southwest, and team USA—the best group of people I could think of working with. You guys kept me (relatively) sane this summer. Thanks to 4A Hingham St. for not evicting me when I was never around, and LG for keeping an eye on me and at least trying to make sure I ate, slept, and left the basement occasionally. 44 JFK for always giving me somewhere to go and people to hang out with when I actually left the office. Digamma. Mom, Dad, John, and Dan, for putting up with me all summer and for the past 20 years—you guys always help me keep things in perspective. And Shilla, for giving me all the love and support I could ask for and then some—you made this the best summer of my life. I love you.

ROB THANKS his group of wicked awesome researchers. Sarah, James, Carleton, Catherine, Greg and Posy: I know it's hard to put 3 months of travel into guide form, but I'll be impressed forever by the job you guys did. Innumerable thanks go to Abi for her care and meticulousness, to Than for his candor and mappiness, to Nitin and Ariel for their willingness to let me throw things at them (selflessness), Eli for somethingorother, Mrs. Wells for her thoughtfulness, and Larry Coker. Special hugs and kisses for my friends at the Harvard Lampoon. This book would never have been finished without Joe Hickey. Thanks to Shilla for making Ben sound funny when he answered the phone, and to Ben for being a heap and half of fun to work with, not to mention the greatest technological computer genius who has ever walked the earth. Up high To Brian, Marty, Ari, and especially Frank: sorry this book kept me in debtor's prison at the end of things. Nicole, I need to take you to some of these places. You're the only person I can think of who would make them more beautiful than they already are. Mom, Dad, Jeff, Andy, and Emmit: I missed you this summer—to the extent that I can dedicate anything, this book is for you guys. Tonight's winning lotto numbers are: ❸❺❷❶❸❹

NATHANIEL THANKS My superstar RWs, who took cartography in stride and went right on redefining the term hardcore. J-Dawg for keeping me ramen-free. N-Dawg for the occasional loan of his letter and last, but not least, the doughty duo who helmed A&P to greatness: Wells and Dubbin, collectively the man.

Editor Benjamin G. Wells
Associate Editor Robert J. Dubbin
Update Editors Ankur Ghosh, Diane Lewis
Map Editor Nathaniel Brooks
Managing Editor Abigail Burger
Typesetter Eduardo L. Montoya

PRICE RANGES >> PACIFIC NW

Our researchers list all establishments in this guide in order of value; their favorite places get the Let's Go thumbs-up (☒). Since the best value isn't always the cheapest price, we have a system of price ranges for quick reference (price ranges are in either US or Canadian dollars). For **accommodations,** we base the range on the cheapest per night rate for a solo traveler. For **food,** we base it on the average price of a main course. Below we list what you'll *typically* find at the corresponding price range.

ACCOMMODATIONS	RANGE	WHAT YOU'RE LIKELY TO FIND
❶	$1-15	Camping; most dorm rooms, such as HI or other hostels or university dorm rooms. Expect bunk beds and a communal bath; you may have to provide or rent linens.
❷	$16-30	Upper-end hostels or small hotels. You may have a private bathroom, or there may be a sink in your room and communal shower in the hall.
❸	$31-50	A small room with a private bath. Should have decent amenities, such as phone and TV. Breakfast may be included in the price of the room.
❹	$51-80	Similar to ❸, but may have more amenities or be in a more touristed area.
❺	$81+	Large hotels or upscale chains. If it's a ❺ and it doesn't have the perks you want, you've paid too much.

FOOD	RANGE	WHAT YOU'RE LIKELY TO FIND
❶	$1-5	Mostly street-corner stands, pizza places, or fast-food joints. Rarely ever a sit-down meal.
❷	$6-10	Sandwiches or low-priced entrees. You may have the option of sitting down or getting take-away.
❸	$11-15	Mid-priced entrees, possibly coming with a soup or salad. Tip will bump you up a couple of dollars, since you'll probably have a waiter or waitress.
❹	$16-20	A fancier restaurant or steakhouse. Either way, you'll have a special knife. Few restaurants in this range have a dress code, but some may look down on t-shirt and jeans.
❺	$21+	Food with foreign names and a decent wine list. Slacks and dress shirts may be expected.

DISCOVER THE PACIFIC NORTHWEST

From the dense, misty rainforests of Oregon to the last desolate, treeless island in northern BC, North America's northwest coast is a land of staggering natural beauty. Along the coast, sharp young peaks soar skyward from the water's edge, spilling pieces of glacier into the ocean at their bases. Human settlements of varying sizes and degrees of polish mark the spots where rivers meet the coast, pointing the way to the country's interior. There, peaks give way to sometimes arable land, desert, tundra, and more mountains, peppered with more cities and towns.

For thousands of years, human settlement in the region has relied on natural resources. In the last two hundred years, human activities have significantly impacted the land—enthusiastic logging, mining, and fishing proved the land isn't inexhaustible—but the birth of the environmental spirit in the late 20th century is revitalizing the region's natural charm. That spirit (visible in the adoption of sustainable practices by resource-based industries) and the explosive growth of tourism (dependent on the beauty of the region's forests) have helped modern governments see old-growth forests as something more than raw lumber.

While you are assured of seeing many visitors wherever you go, with a minimum of effort you are just as able to lose the crowds. For example, while Banff National Park, in the Rockies, welcomes five million visitors a year, the right dayhike—or a visit to one of the park's lesser-known neighbors—is all it takes to find solitude. For those overwhelmed by the boundless backcountry, welcoming hostels, quirky communities, and laid-back cities anchor the wilderness.

Winter visits promise hundreds of miles of skiing, snowboarding, snowshoeing, and snowmachining out of snow-bound cities. Farther south along the coast, winter is more wet than white, and the litany of snow sports is restricted to higher elevations.

However audacious it is to cram this many miles of coast and this deep an interior into a single book, the present attempt is culled from what our researchers insisted they would do again if they could turn around and do their trips over. The sample itineraries that follow are intended to help you picture what your own trip might look like. For practical trip-planning resources, including campground reservation numbers, road reports, climate charts, Internet resources, and preferred outdoor publishing companies, see the **Essentials** (p. 17) chapter, and begin thumbing through the rest of *Let's Go: The Pacific Northwest.*

WHEN TO GO

Tourist season (summer) in the US and Canada runs from late May to early September, from the Victoria Day (Canada)/Memorial Day (US) long weekend to the Labour/Labor Day long weekend. Off season accommodations may be cheaper and much less crowded, but the sights you traveled so far to see may also be closed, and camping is not nearly as pleasant in the colder, damper winter conditions. The coastal cities are justly famous for rain, which pours down

FACTS & FIGURES

OREGON (OR): FOR THE YOUNG & "SPIRITED."

Best place to feel the spirit: Portland, the city with more microbreweries than any other.

Deepest lake in the US: Crater Lake.

Deepest river gorge in North America: Hell's Canyon.

WASHINGTON (WA): BETTER THAN CALIFORNIA.

Number of wineries in 1981: 19. Number of wineries in 2001: 160.

Though (grrr) second to Cali in US wine production, Washington has more awards than any other global wine region. And they have daily sunlight 2hr. longer than California.

BRITISH COLUMBIA (BC): THERE ARE BEARS HERE.

British Columbia's rank among the film and TV production centers in the world: 3.

Total land area of California: 400,000 sq. km.

Total land area of British Columbia: 950,000 sq. km. Booyah!

Number of films shot in British Columbia in year 2000: 192.

ALBERTA (AB): "STRONG & FREE"...& HITTING ITS GROOVE.

No. 1 export: oil. No. 2 export: marijuana. No. 3 export: Do you need anything else?

No. 1 import: Fritos.

Km of road: 180,000. Km of paved roads: 31,000. Km of pipelines for oil: 184,000.

YUKON (YT): YES, YUKON.

Lowest temperature ever recorded in Canada: -62.8°C (northwest of Kluane Lake).

Most famous resident: Jack London.

Close runners-up: Klondike Kate and the Yukon Dancehall Girls (Diamond Tooth Gertie, Mollie Fewclothes, Nellie the Pig, Ethel the Moose, and Snake-hips Lulu).

10 months of the year. The ocean keeps coastal temperatures moderate year-round. In Portland and Vancouver, a few snow days a year are the norm, but the white stuff doesn't stick around for long. To the east of the coastal mountains, expect less precipitation, warmer summers, and colder winters. The same variation is experienced up north, only on a shifted scale—winters in the interior are bitterly cold, while summers are decidedly cool. As in the south, things are more even on the coast, with plenty of rain (called liquid sunshine by some coastal residents).

NATIONAL HOLIDAYS

On national holidays, many sights and all banks and government offices will be closed, and transportation may run on restricted schedules.

2004	2005	US HOLIDAY
Jan. 1	Jan. 1	**New Year's Day**
Jan. 19	Jan. 17	**Martin Luther King, Jr. Day**
Feb. 16	Feb. 21	**Presidents' Day**
May 31	May 30	**Memorial Day**
July 4	July 4	**Independence Day**
Sep. 6	Sep. 5	**Labor Day**
Oct. 11	Oct. 10	**Columbus Day**
Nov. 11	Nov. 11	**Veterans Day**
Nov. 25	Nov. 24	**Thanksgiving**
Dec. 25	Dec. 25	**Christmas Day**

2004	2005	CANADIAN HOLIDAY
Jan. 1	Jan. 1	**New Year's Day**
Apr. 9	Mar. 25	**Good Friday**
Apr. 12	Mar. 28	**Easter Monday**
May 24	May 23	**Victoria Day**
July 1	July 1	**Canada Day**
Sep. 6	Sep. 5	**Labour Day**
Oct. 11	Oct. 10	**Thanksgiving**
Nov. 11	Nov. 11	**Remembrance Day**
Dec. 25	Dec. 25	**Christmas Day**
Dec. 26	Dec. 26	**Boxing Day**

THINGS TO DO

ON FOOT

The vast scenic lands the Pacific Northwest provide hikers with limitless opportunities. Known for its natural beauty, impressive landscape, and sparkling clean waters, this region is arguably the most desirable place in North America to hit the trails. The national, provincial, and state parks provide some of the best and most varied hiking anywhere and are well-staffed, well-maintained, and well worth it. Reading the **Outdoor Activities** sections of a few parks should give a sense of the possibilities. Popular destinations often limit the number of visitors, campsites may be hard to secure, and crowds will surely be on hand, one need not be in a designated park to enjoy the outdoors in the Northwest. Trails through virgin lands more beautiful than you can imagine abound. Contact the visitors center in your specific area for more info on how to break fresh ground. Experienced hikers may wish to consider the following multi-day (month) hikes:

CHILKOOT TRAIL. This three- to five-day (33 mi./53km) hike starts in Skagway, AK, and passes through a range of dramatic climates, terrain, and vegetation, both above and below treeline, on its way through the interior. Originally a trade route protected by the Tagish and Tlingit people, the trail was the route to the Interior during the Yukon gold rush of the 1890s.

PACIFIC CREST TRAIL. This 2650 mi./4260km trail stretches from California's border with Mexico to Washington's border with Canada. First explored in the 1930s, the system of trails is now a federally protected Scenic Trail that takes five to six months to hike. Pick up the trail in any of the national parks along the range or in the Columbia River Gorge (see p. 90). The Pacific Crest Trail Association (PCTA) maintains the trail and sells comprehensive trail guides, videos, and PCTA mouse pads on its website. (☎916-349-2109; www.pcta.org. Call 888-728-7245 for free info pack or trail condition report.)

WEST COAST TRAIL. This spectacular trail winds through 48 mi./77km (five to seven days) of coastal forest and beach along the Pacific Ocean in the Pacific Rim National Park on the west coast of Vancouver Island. Reservations are necessary to hike the trail. (See p. 280 for info.)

ON WATER

Rivers, lakes, and ocean throughout the Northwest provide kayakers, canoeists, surfers, and plenty of rafters with more than enough opportunity to exercise their paddling urges. **Rafting** is the most accessible water sport to novices, and is wildly popular in both the US and Canada. Most of Oregon's commercial trips float on the beautiful **Rogue** (see Grants Pass, p. 128) and **Deschutes** (see Bend, p. 137) rivers. Interior BC offers adrenaline rush runs on **Adam's River** (p. 302), in the Shuswap. In Jasper, two rivers present prime rafting: the **Athabasca** and the faster **Sunwapta** (p. 388). Expect professionalism from a rafting outfit. If the rafts have patches, the life jacket supply is sparse, or the paddles are different shapes and sizes, you may want to take your business elsewhere.

Kayaking in the region's rivers and oceans couldn't be finer (unless the water were a little warmer). The small boat allows almost unlimited access to the coastline, and is perfect for investigating small coves and inlets and losing the cruise ship crowd. The West Coast of Vancouver Island, particularly **The Broken Islands,** (p. 282), is a popular place to explore by kayak.

THE LOCAL STORY

TOP 10 FESTIVALS

1. Yukon Storytelling Festival. Swap tall tales in over 20 languages in Whitehorse, YT (p. 395).
2. Oregon Shakespeare Festival (Ashland, OR; p. 130). The biggest, baddest Bard-related party in the land. Reserve your tickets yesterday.
3. Calgary Stampede. Cowboys and cowgirls rule Calgary, AB (p. 369) during the world's biggest rodeo.
4. Dawson City Music Festival (p. 411). Three days of unforgettable tunes in the heart of the Yukon.
5. International Days. Stewart, BC and Hyder, AK (p. 353) celebrate independence with free events.
6. Edmonton Fringe Festival (p. 363). One of the globe's hottest indie theater events, in Canada's self-proclaimed "Festival City."
7. Portland Rose Festival (p. 70). What's in a name? Not just roses but alpacas, car races, outdoor concerts, and the world's largest kids' parade.
8. Bumbershoot. Fantastic, freaky alt-art in the fantastic, freaky alt capital of the Northwest (Seattle; p. 159).
9. Nanaimo Marine Festival (p. 286). On your mark, get set, float! Canada's best (only) bathtub race.
10. Commissioner's Potlatch. Celebrate First Nations culture and more in the Yukon capital (p. 395).

Long Beach and **Cox Beach,** in Pacific Rim National Park (p. 280), offer sweet surf rides in BC. The best medicine for the icy Pacific is to bear inland to the many **hot springs.** An ideal place to warm up or to soothe aching muscles, this natural phenomenon is a favorite pastime. For a start, try **Cougar Hot Springs** in Eugene, OR (p. 122), **Canyon Hot Springs,** in Revelstoke, BC (p. 317), or **Hot Springs Cove** in the Pacific Rim National Park in BC (p. 280).

Nothing makes a better combination in the Northwest than water and wind. The gods smiled fondly on **Columbia River Gorge** (p. 90), blessing it with a river, gracing it with steep canyons, and consecrating it with a howling wind. Out of this, the **windsurfing** cult arose. Although the Gorge is eminent in the minds of windsurfers, other sites abound, by virtue of good breeze off the Pacific and moderate weather.

ON SNOW

The skiing and riding (snowboarding) in the northern Rockies, the Cascades, and Coast range are some of North America's best. The biggest and best mega-resort is **Whistler-Blackcomb,** p. 267, a 1½hr. drive north of Vancouver, BC, which draws nearly two million international visitors per year. Most remarkable about the skiing, though, is that many great areas are only minutes from urban centers. Hostels in Washington, Oregon, Alberta, and BC all offer ski-and-stay packages. **Fernie Alpine Resort** (p. 315), is working to gain the title of megalith; with its new expansion, the resort now covers more than 2500 acres. The sleeper resort to watch is **Powder Springs Resort** (p. 317), in Revelstoke. With the largest vertical drop in North America and the interest of an Austrian family that already owns 36 resorts in Europe, it may only be a matter of time until Powder Springs becomes another Whistler. Good news for snowboarders across North America: ski hills have finally accepted that riders are here to stay. **Cross-country skiing** tends to get overshadowed by its vertical counterparts in the Northwest, but dump tons of snow on beautiful hiking trails, and what do you get but miles and miles of pristine skiing trails.

ON CRACK

In the past decade, outdoor sports have battled to top the thrill that plain old Mother Nature provides. Pain often seems to be a requisite for the rating of extreme. The **Ski to Sea Race** (p. 192) in Bellingham, WA, on Memorial Day weekend, is the mother of all relays with skiing, running, canoeing, and kayaking stages covering the terrain from Mt. Baker to Bellingham Bay. Defy gravity in Nanaimo, BC at the **Bungy Zone** (p. 286), and defy it again at the **Skaha Bluffs, BC** (p. 307), with phenomenal rock climbing. Firefighters train to sky-dive into forest fires at the **Smoke Jumpers Base** (p. 232), between Winthrop and Twisp, WA. You can off-road on the **Sand Dunes** (p. 110), along the coast of Oregon or **ski sans snow** (p. 330), in August on the sandy bluffs of the Nechako Cutbanks, in Prince George, BC.

CULTURAL HIGHLIGHTS

NATIVE CULTURE

The Northwest is home to some of the finest exhibits of Native American and First Nation (the preferred terms for the indigenous people of the US and Canada, respectively) culture on the continent, and is the birthplace of some of their most popular traditions, such as potlatch, cedar carving, and long houses. While native cultures in the Northwest have not entirely escaped the persecution that have encountered throughout North America, many tribes and customs still thrive. Major museums in the region are the **Royal British Columbia Museum** in Victoria, BC (p. 270); the **Museum of Anthropology** in Vancouver, BC (p. 261); and the **Museum at Warm Springs,** OR (p. 143).

BREWERIES & VINEYARDS

Up and down the coast of Washington and Oregon, small companies turn out unique beverages that have won more awards per liter than any state in the Union. The wine counter-culture is on the upswing—wine bars are cropping up and wine tastings are becoming an institution. In Washington and Oregon, **Spokane** (p. 244), **Salem** (p. 118), and **Lopez Island** (p. 203), have more than their fair share of vintners. In the fertile crescent of Interior BC, **Kelowna** (p. 303), and **Penticton** (p. 307), harbor prize-winning vintages. Stop by Kelowna for the **Okanagan Wine Festival** in October. A must-see for true connoisseurs is the **Shallon winery** in Astoria (p. 94), where you can sample rarities such as lemon meringue pie wine. Beer rules the roost in Oregon: visit the **Oregon Brewers Guild** (p. 70) in Portland (the city with the highest number of microbreweries in the United States) and the **Rogue Ale Brewery** (p. 109), in Newport.

LET'S GO PICKS

BEST RACES: The **Chuckwagon Derby** and the **bathtub** race highlight tests of brawn and skill during Klondike Days in Edmonton, AB (p. 363).

BEST BICYCLE RIDE: Through breathtaking glaciers from Jasper to Banff along the **Icefields Parkway** (p. 387).

BEST BOOKSTORE: Cavernous **Powell's City of Books** swallows patrons in hallowed book-lined walls (p. 80).

BEST ANIMAL ENCOUNTERS: Get intimate with buffalo skeletons at **Head-Smashed-in Buffalo Jump,** AB (p. 376) to learn how a native tribe could destroy a herd of buffalo in an afternoon.

BEST PLACE TO FIND ALLIGATOR SKIN BOOTS: Undoubtedly,**The Stampede** in chilly Calgary, AB where locals celebrate their rough-and-tumble heritage (p. 369).

SUGGESTED ITINERARIES

OREGON (2 WEEKS) Any journey through Oregon should begin and end in **Portland** (4 days). Visitors could wile away weeks in this phenomenal city that combines cosmopolitan flare, crunchy outdoors, and youthful money. After satisfying the city dweller in you, embark on the open road to venture into the **Columbia River Gorge** (2 days), where you can trade the car in for a surfboard and let loose on windsurfing heaven. Venture into the hot interior, visiting the **John Day Fossil Beds** (1 day), where fossilized remains of tropical rainforests defy the naked eye. The unusual landscape continues at **Klamath Falls,** where **Crater Lake** plunges to a depth of 1932 feet (1 day). Unfortunately, it's forbidden to swim in the lake. Withdrawing from the rugged outdoors, stop in at **Ashland** (2 days) to sample some of the country's best Shakespeare. Gradually meander back up the coast to Portland on US 101, with stops to play in the sand and surf (2 days), making sure to ride the waves at **Oregon Dunes,** a mecca for sand-surfing.

WASHINGTON (3 WEEKS) The jewel in Washington's crown is undoubtedly the Emerald City—misty, alt-rocking **Seattle** (1 week). Head south to **Mt. Rainier National Park** (4 days), home to the most technical climb in the continental US and a multitude of fantastic views and dayhikes. Jump on a ferry and plan for several days hopping between the **San Juan Islands** (5 days) and their many beautiful beaches. This archipelago is perfect for kayaking. Touch base in Seattle to provision for a journey to **Mt. Baker** (3 days). A mecca for skiing in the winter, it provides gorgeous vistas, challenging hikes, and breathtaking drives for summer visitors. A final must-see stop is the **Olympic National Park** (5 days), an outdoor-lover's playground; true solace can be found within its rugged boundaries.

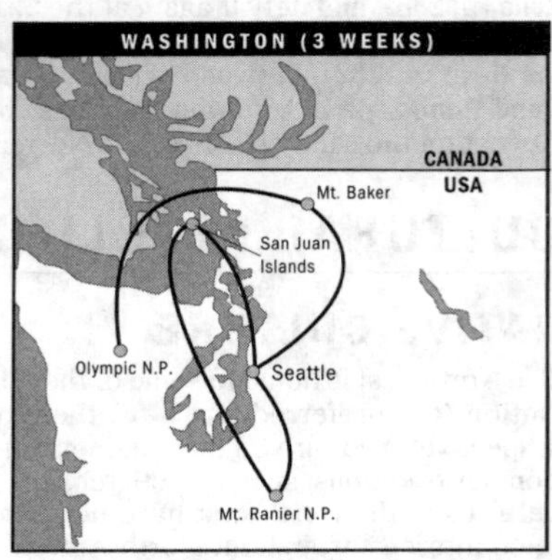

BRITISH COLUMBIA & ALBERTA (4 WEEKS) When discovering western Canada, there is no better starting point than British Columbia's biggest metropolis, **Vancouver** (5 days), which features a variety of sights and exciting nightlife. After you've had enough of the big city, trek out to **Whistler** (4 days); don't forget to pack the skis. Together with Blackcomb, these sister mountains provide some of North America's best downhill runs. Start the National Parks escapade in **Revelstoke** (2 days), a favorite with hikers and bikers, before heading to **Banff** (3 days) and **Jasper National Parks** (3 days). The **Icefields Pkwy.** accesses major portions of both parks. While hiking is the premier activity, climbing, kayaking, and rafting also keep the outdoor-lover satisfied. Strike west on the Yellowhead Hwy. to **Bella Coola.** Stay overnight here before hopping on a ferry to **Port Hardy** (2 days), on the northern tip of Vancouver Island. Meander to the southern tip, and visit the **Pacific Rim National Park** (3 days). Perched on the sea, this park has an entirely different landscape than the inland parks. Meander down Hwy. 19, stopping in towns such as **Campbell River** and **Nan-**

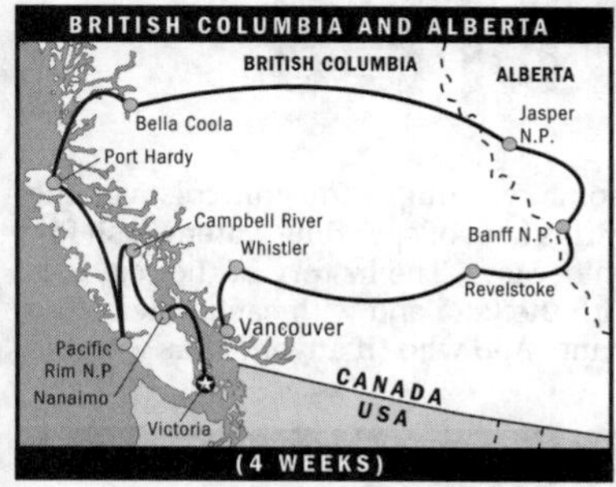

aimo (2 days). Finally, allow at least four days for **Victoria,** at the southern tip of the island. In the most British-feeling city in British Columbia, you'll definitely want to experience high tea.

DESOLATION (2-3 WEEKS) The Northwest is inundated with tourists for the summer. All it takes to get away is a car and the backroads. Fly into **Edmonton, AB** to overstep Calgary's mobs, and go north. Cut across the Alberta/British Columbia border and sojourn in **Dawson Creek, BC.** Get on board the **Alaska Hwy., BC** to get the scenic overhaul of northern BC. Stop in towns like **Fort Nelson, BC** for eats and shut-eye only: the drive *is* the attraction. **Whitehorse, YT** is the biggest town you'll see after leaving Edmonton. Make a final stop in **Dawson City, YT** to provision for the drive up the

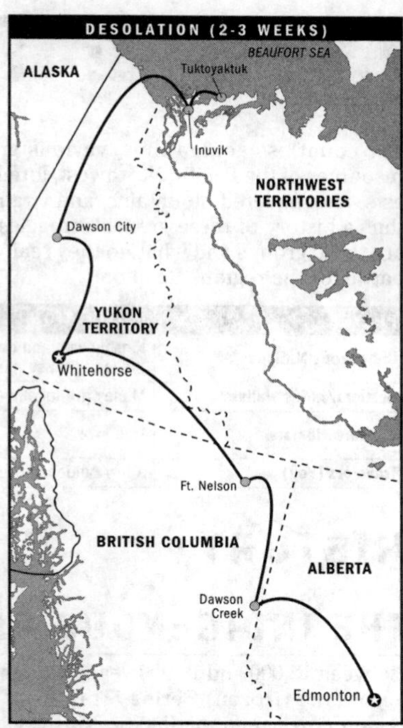

Dempster, YT. The 12hr. drive on brutal gravel is bound to torment tires. At the end of the road is **Inuvik, YT,** where you can stop and dip your toes into the Beaufort Sea. Flightseeing to **Tuktoyaktuk, YT** brings you within sight of the polar caps.

LIFE & TIMES

For countless generations, various groups have fought for control over the resources of the Pacific Northwest, lured by this land of sparkling waters, lush forests, unconquered mountains, and virgin wilderness. The history of the region is thus a history of these groups' struggles with the land and with each other. Who are these groups and what do they really want? And who (if anyone) has won the battle for the region? Read on:

PLAYER	MOTIVATION	WEAPONS/ASSETS
Indigenous Nations	Kinship with and deep respect for the land that supports them	First dibs
Settlers/Industrialists	Money (exploitation)	Big guns, little mercy
Conservationists	True love	1) Lobbyists and legislation 2) Chaining themselves to trees
Travelers (You)	A few (undeniably awesome) thrills	*Let's Go: Pacific Northwest*

HISTORY

THE INDIGENOUS PEOPLE

Between 12,000 and 16,000 years ago, a group of nomadic hunters bravely traipsed across the (frozen) Bering Strait from Siberia into present-day Alaska and the region now called the Pacific Northwest. True to popular imagination, many did live in igloos, use dogsleds for transport (commemorated in Alaska's **Iditarod** race), and sustain themselves by hunting whales and other sealife. They depended on the land and its inhabitants, and treated them all with great respect: for example, in the Yupik tribe, the first time a young man caught a seal, he freed it to secure good luck in catching more seals in the future.

The diverse groups that inhabited the region during this time—among them the Aleutians, Yuits, Inuits, and Eskimos—were distinguished from one another both by their mythologies and their languages, although the **Inuit** language stood as a common tongue. Several basic phrases in Inuit include:

ENGLISH	INUIT	ENGLISH	INUIT
How are you?	*Qanuipit?*	I am hungry	*Kaaktunga*
I am fine.	*Qanuingittunga*	What is it?	*Una suna?*
What is your name?	*Kinauvit?*	I am sick.	*Aaniajunga*
I want to take your picture.	*Ajjiliurumajagit*	I have to use the W.C.	*Quisuktunga*
Thank you.	*Qujannamiik*	Where am I?	*Namiippunga?*
You're welcome.	*Llaali*	I want to go fishing.	*Iqalliarumajunga*

Another common bond among these groups was the land. The rich supply of salmon and halibut sustained these communities, and daily life centered around fishing. The economy of coastal groups focused around three main subsystems, all related to fish: fishing, construction of plank houses for smoking and drying fish, and later transportation, which provided access to the fish. Almost all native groups adjusted their lifestyles according to the season, moving between different settlements that favored the harvesting of available game, fish, and living materials. The coastal culture, prevalent throughout much of the Northwest, was one of waterside villages of cedar plank houses, wooden sculptures, massive dugout canoes, and **potlatch festivals** (see p. 11).

Although large-scale potlatch festivals no longer occur, another remnant of the native culture remains a defining aspect of the Pacific Northwest: the totem pole. Particularly noticeable in British Columbia, the totem pole peppers parks, sites, and tourist shops (see **Five Things...About Totem Poles,** p. 13).

EUROPEAN ARRIVAL

The indigenous tribes and the land of the Pacific Northwest enjoyed an amiable relationship that was upset by the arrival of the Europeans, who came in from Russia first via Alaska. The most notorious European figures include:

EXPLORER	YEAR	NATIONALITY	CLAIM TO FAME
Francis Drake	16th century	English	Circumnavigated the globe; claimed Oregon for the English and affectionately described the coast as wrapped in "vile, thicke, and stinking fogges."
Vitus Bering	1741	Danish, working for Russia	Led the Russians to the Aleutian Islands.
Aleksei Chirko	mid-18th century	Russian	Explored Alaska; brought reports of seals and skilled hunters to Russia, which catalyzed an interest in the fur trade.
Juan Perez & Bruno Heceta	1774-75	Spanish	Claimed Nootka Sound for Spain and re-initiated European interest in the region.
James Cook	1778	English	Searched for a polar trade route; voyaged from Oregon to Alaska's westernmost tip.
George Vancouver	1792	English	Cartographer who accompanied Cook and mapped out the Pacific Northwest. Island and big city in BC named after him.
Alexander Mackenzie	1793	English	Completed an overland exploration of the Pacific Northwest.

Early Russian explorers eagerly recognized the value of trading with the skilled Aleut hunters they encountered in the region. The Aleuts eagerly parted with their otter pelts for beads that, while common to the Russians, the Aleuts saw as portals for spirits. A short while after Britain increased its trading activity in the south, a permanent Russian settlement was established on Alaska's Kodiak Island. By the time of Vancouver's voyage, the Russians had gained control of the Arctic seal hunt, eliminating the need to trade with the Aleuts and other native Alaskans; already, a small population of Aleuts had been relocated from the Pribilof Islands, a rich seal breeding ground. In 1799, the **Russian-American Company** was established in Sitka, in present-day Alaska, and its brokerage clout was felt as far south as California. The Russians' aggressive imposition upon the Native Alaskans incited the **Tlingit,** a powerful coastal nation, to raze the Russians' settlement and massacre nearly every inhabitant in 1802. Two years later, the Russians returned to bombard the Tlingit fort. The Tlingit withdrew from the area after 10 days' fighting exhausted their ammunition.

Prior to this intense conflict, the Europeans considered the indigenous nations autonomous and profitable trading partners. But the coast had become a lucrative asset for a number of well-armed and well-organized outsiders. During the coming decades, it would be bargained for among England, Russia, and the US, while indigenous people would be forced out of partnerships in the coastal economy.

EIGHT THINGS YOU DIDN'T KNOW ABOUT THE OREGON TRAIL:

1. One in ten people died traveling it.
2. Oxen or mules (not horses) were the animals of choice for the wagons.
3. Because their wagons were already too full, the emigrants could not sit inside them and be pulled along by the oxen. Most of them walked. Barefoot.
4. The biggest killer on the trail was cholera.
5. As trees and fuel for the fire became scarce around 1849, when the trail got crowded, travelers resorted to using buffalo dung to get their fires going.
6. Some travelers had to wait for up to two hours for a buffalo stampede to pass.
7. Most people began their journeys by loading their wagons with over a ton of cargo, but within one day of their journey, the precious possessions would be thrown out.
8. Two hundred would-be travelers signed up to ride in the wind-wagon, a forerunner of the airplane, but the contraption never got off the ground.

HOW THE WEST WAS WON

Trade, according to most Europeans, was mutually beneficial: Europeans took valuable furs and pelts, and natives received weapons with which they could defend themselves and their property. Sadly, the Europeans also brought less welcome gifts with them: smallpox, venereal infections, and other contagious diseases. Ultimately, this trade crippled the indigenous people's power.

LEWIS & CLARK. As more people streamed into western Washington and Oregon in the middle of the 19th century, Europeans and natives had to compete not only against one another, but also against the United States. As US President Thomas Jefferson sensed the British beginning to take hold of the region, he organized the first US overland exploration of the West, headed by Meriwether Lewis and William Clark. Jefferson sent the Lewis and Clark expedition out in 1804 with political, scientific, and commercial goals (including the declaration of American sovereignty in the uncharted region), believing that the nation that controlled the fabled Northwest Passage would control the continent's destiny. The team traveled from St. Louis to the Pacific Ocean and back, returning in 1806 with information about plants, animals, rivers, mountains, and native cultures. While the team did not find a northwest passage, its safe return and promising discoveries encouraged many families to migrate west.

OREGON & THE OREGON TRAIL. Hundreds departed for the West along the famed Oregon Trail. The trail extended from Independence, Missouri to the mouth of the Columbia River and took four to six months to travel. While the Trail offered settlers the opportunity to stake claims in unexplored lands, it also posed great risks. The journey was often filled with the hardships, like poor equipment, illness, and attacks from natives. To provide for families on the frontier and the establishment of communities, the **1862 Homestead Act** made 160 acres of land available for free to any married man who would live on and cultivate the land for five years. The same act barred the ownership of land by non-whites. The argument by natives that this was their land, and therefore not the government's to give away, failed to sway those in power. Settlers created a provisional government in 1843, lobbied for territorial status in 1848, and joined the Union as Oregon 11 years later.

HOW THE WEST WAS DOMESTICATED. Gold and oil discoveries along the West Coast in the late 19th century also supported settlement in the Northwest. These finds not only encouraged the development of cities surrounding the gold and oil but also helped supplying towns grow. For example, gold in the Klondike in 1895 drew thousands to the interior of what would be staked out as the Yukon Territory three years later. Seattle and Skagway proudly lay claim to their roles as the Klondike's outfitters. The San Francisco gold rush precipitated the building of Portland, which was well positioned to supply the California town with timber and wheat. Only one territorial acquisition of the period was considered unsound. When Russia offered the sale of Alaska (which included part of the Yukon) to the US in 1867, the icy expanse was considered a depleted resource (nicknamed "Seward's Folly" after US Secretary of State William Seward, who purchased the future oil field). It was not until years later, when the oil fields were discovered, that Seward was celebrated for purchasing the territory for a piddling $0.02 per acre.

By the end of the 19th century, indigenous culture was dying rapidly. The number of newcomers flooding the land and governmental intervention forced the native peoples onto small reservations. The indigenous nations were devastated by disease, enslavement, murder, and the strain of relocation. They had begun to develop new economic patterns more dependent upon white American and British manufactured goods. Traditional means for fishing using canoes and spears were replaced by gasoline engines, power gears, and navigation with tables, compasses, and charts. Even the aggressive warrior tribes of Northwest Coast Indians never mounted a major war against the Europeans. Intimidated by the vulnerability of their coastal villages to naval gunfire, the Native Alaskans had no choice but to share the land. Unfortunately, there peaceful response was not reciprocated, and the situation turned uglier for the indigenous people.

THE LOCAL STORY

ALL WORK NO PLAY: POTLATCH

Potlatch festivals were an opportunity for Native American and First Nations villagers to exchange and display wealth, to celebrate important transitions such as adoptions or aging, and to enact stories and history. Derived from a traditional Chinook word meaning "gift" or "giving," the potlatch was a feast marking an important event in a person's life and required that the host lavishly give of himself, even if he had no resources for daily living. The amount one gave increased the respect he garnered from the community. At intertribal potlatches, rival chiefs might destroy hundreds of blankets and canoes just to demonstrate the excesses of their wealth. Banned for some time by both US and Canadian governments as part of a policy of integration, potlatch festivals are now starting to make a comeback.

POLICY TOWARD NATIVE PEOPLE

While tribes farther east were exiled from their traditional land, the indigenous people of the Pacific Northwest seem to have retained their home court advantage. While not victims of the **Kill and Banish the Indians** policy of the 16th, 17th, 18th, and early 19th centuries, they couldn't escape the **Destroy the Indians' Culture** policy of Canada and the **Take the Indians' Land** policy of the US.

UNITED STATES. From the birth of the United States until 1924, when Congress granted Native Americans citizenship, US policy consisted of a series of broken promises of land. Laws such as the **Indian Removal Act** left little doubt of the government's intentions and led to the Cherokee's forced relocation—known as the **Trail of Tears.** Conditions improved slightly with President Roosevelt's 1934 **Indian Reorganization Act,** by which indigenous communities were recognized as tribes and directed to create their own constitutions. The effect of this policy was mitigated by a subsequent reversal of policy in **Operation Relocation** (1952), in which large groups of Native Americans were relocated from reservations into cities. The gesture had an unexpected effect as, for the first time in generations, Native Americans who lived off reservations began to recognize themselves as an ethnic group against the backdrop of mainstream society. This marked the beginning of a modern native revival.

CANADA. The Canadian policy toward the First Nations was not any more just or kind. The **1876 Indian Act** gave the government complete control over every person that it declared to be Indian. Children were separated from their families, forbidden to speak with their siblings, and even prohibited from speaking their native language. Those who refused to submit to this policy were severely punished, and many children were physically and sexually abused. Adults were taught methods of farming untenable in many of the regions where they were attempted, and traditions of community life were disallowed. A few rights were granted after World War II, and in 1969, presaging the trend toward euphemism, the government ended the policy of **assimilation** in favor of a new policy of **integration.** By the time residential schools were closed, some as late as the 1970s, an entire generation had been raised in isolation from their land and weakened by alcoholism, poverty, and the neglect of their traditions.

Since the 1970s, tribes in both countries have been making slow gains as the descendents of their conquerors grant them more autonomy. Much of their culture is gone forever, as are most native tongues, but for many tribes in the Pacific Northwest, now is a time of renewal.

INDIGENOUS PEOPLE TODAY

Native Americans have recently begun to assert their rights more forcefully.

NEGOTIATING. First Nations (the indigenous people of Canada) and Native American (the indigenous people of the United States) tribes have once again begun to flourish as independent communities. Some indigenous people live on reservations within sight of cities; others have settled land claim negotiations and are living on their traditional territory and resurrecting their customs. Most indigenous communities that are federally recognized reservation tribes in the US, or administered under the Indian Act in Canada, are allowed hunting and fishing rights, as well as the right to use specified lands for ceremonial purposes. Some communities seek first and foremost to preserve the cultural heritage of their traditional lands. In British Columbia, for example, Haida tribesmen oversaw the use of ancient village sites in the disputed territory of the Queen Charlotte Islands and lobbied heavily for its preservation from logging. After the federal government purchased the land, the Haida's role in the stewardship of the spectacular **Gwaii Haanas National Park Reserve** became officially recognized.

1960S. Throughout the 1960s, Native Alaskans watched with increasing frustration as the federal and state governments divvied up vast tracts of land that the Inuit, Aleut, Tlingit, Haida, and Athabasca had claims upon. After the discovery in

FIVE THINGS YOU NEVER SHOULD HAVE LEARNED ABOUT TOTEM POLES

Because they are wrong:

1. The totems in the Pacific Northwest are thousands of years old.
The oldest date from 1835, and most are under 100 years old.

2. Totem pole carving is a disappearing art form.
After a bout in the earlier half of the 20th century in which authentic totem building virtually vanished, totem carving experienced a renaissance in the latter half.

3. Totems were built to be worshiped.
Totems stand for particular people and ideas, but they are not objects of worship.

4. The totem poles in Stanley Park (see p. 261) are fake.
They are actually authentic and among the most valuable totems in the world.

5. Totem poles were used to ward off evil spirits.
A popular myth, but a myth nonetheless.

Totem poles are storytellers: in their images, they recount tales of families, clans, and individuals, reflecting the family-oriented organization of the tribes.

1968 of immense oil deposits in the Beaufort Sea on Alaska's northern coast, Native Alaskans increased pressure to settle the claims that had been so long ignored and sought a share in the anticipated economic boom.

1971. The US government finally made some degree of peace with Native Alaskans, state and federal courts, and environmental groups by passing the **Alaska Native Claims Settlement Act.** Sixty thousand Native Alaskans received a total of one billion dollars and 40 million acres of land.

1993. Yukon First Nations negotiated a settlement for self-government and land claims under a general framework known as the Umbrella Final Agreement.

1997. In the **Delgamuukw** decision of 1997, the Supreme Court of Canada allowed the Wet'suwet'en and Gitksan to cite ceremony and oral tradition to prove that their use of disputed lands preceded the arrival of Europeans.

1998. Negotiations continue over issues of self-government and the right to self-determination. In August of 1998, after years of talks between government officials and the **Nisga'a** band of northern British Columbia, representatives signed a controversial landmark treaty granting the Nisga'a a form of self-government and control over natural resources in 1940 sq. km of their traditional lands.

1999. The Supreme Court of Canada instructed the government to revise the Indian Act so that communities, and not the government, have the power to allow non-residents to vote in elections. It also passed Bill C-49, or the **First Nations Land Management Act,** which created a framework for First Nations to develop their own land-use laws. Most dramatically, on April 1, 1999, the Canadian government split the Northwest Territories in half and granted the densely Inuit-populated eastern portion, **Nunavut** ("Our Land"), self-government.

2001. On April 21, an association of tribes signed an agreement with the state of Alaska which would lay the ground rules for future dialogue between the groups. The agreement said little that was earth-shattering, but it did affirm the right of the tribes to form their own governments and conduct their own affairs.

CONTEMPORARY CULTURE

CONSERVATION & HARVEST

Political entities in the Northwest strive to compete and to protect their independent interests within the framework of federal legislation. Inevitably, negotiations don't go smoothly. The central political tensions are between conservation and harvest, where **harvest** is synonymous with jobs, and **conservation** is synonymous with tradition. These are particularly difficult to balance in Oregon and Washington, home to the most federally- and state-protected land in the United States. The outright challenge of co-managing renewable resources is exacerbated in British Columbia and the Yukon by the involvement of vast quantities of land in territorial disputes with First Nations. The work of co-managing the resources that these states and provinces share—like the Pacific salmon fishery—has been the most dramatic and drawn-out subject of reconciliation.

Policies of environmental stewardship emerged in response to a variety of pressures, from civic consciousness to political activism. Oregon has led the pack in reform, beginning in 1967, when the **Oregon coast** was preserved for free and uninterrupted use by the public. Moreover, Oregon's 1971 **Bottle Bill** was the first recycling refund program in the US.

On the animal front, Washington and Oregon's **spotted owl** has remained a symbol of conflict between conservationists and industrialists after vast tracts of the bird's old-growth forest habitat were protected. On Vancouver Island, residents rallied to save the **endangered marmot;** efforts culminated with a "Marmot-aid" benefit concert. A vociferous battle has also been fought over the gray whale, an interesting case in which the government waited until 1937 to ban commercial harvesting of these creatures. In many cases, indigenous communities lead conservation efforts, suspending their hunting and trapping before sluggish government wheels begin to roll toward curbing industries. An interesting twist on this situation occurred with the **Makah whale controversy.** In the 1990s, when the endangered gray whales had rebounded to a viable population, the Makah people applied to the International Whaling Commission, with US support, for a cultural exemption to the continuing ban. The five-whale allowance granted to the Makah enraged conservationists, but regardless, Makah returned to the ceremonial and subsistence hunt in 1999 among protest and publicity.

WILD THINGS

The wildlife in the Pacific Northwest is one of the region's biggest draws. Some of the critters running around the area include:

CARIBOU. Better known in the popular imagination as reindeer, the caribou were made to travel over land. These animals cover more ground each year (3000 mi.) than any other mammal, and they can get up to speeds of over 50 mph, making them faster than any car on the Dempster highway (see p. 417).

MOUNTAIN GOATS. Unlike the fast-moving caribou, mountain goats move at a more deliberate pace. This can cause problems in the **Canadian Rockies** (see p. 376), where traffic stands still every time a tour bus sights one. Male goats ("billies") crawl on their bellies when they are pursuing a female goat ("nannies").

GRAY WOLVES. If the billies spent less time on their bellies, they might have better luck evading the gray wolves, who are their natural predators (see p. 212). To catch a glimpse of these elusive and cunning creatures, check out **Wolf Haven International** in Olympia (see p. 188).

BLACK BEARS. Though mother black bears will jealously guard their cubs, adult male and female bears are never together except to breed. In fact, as soon as breeding is over, the male bear leaves the female to raise the cubs. One of the best places to see black bears in the Pacific Northwest is in **Banff National Park** (see p. 378), where rangers keep a running tally of sightings in the area.

BALD EAGLES. The emblem of the United States, this majestic bird is unique to North America. Though the population once dwindled due to hunting and pesticides, the bald eagle has staged a promising comeback.

FOOD & DRINK

The Pacific Northwest has tastes that vary drastically from one region to another, but in all cases, cities and cultures cling tenaciously to their distinctive flavors. Here are some of the foods and drinks you'll find in your travels:

BANNOCK IN BRITISH COLUMBIA. Though there's no single traditional recipe, bannock generally takes the form of a biscuit-like cake made from flour, lard, and honey. Some varieties incorporate local delicacies such as salmon. Invariably, everyone who makes it considers theirs the best.

HALIBUT & SALMON. In close proximity to the arctic waters these fish frequent, many cities in the Pacific Northwest are known for superior seafood. Halibut and salmon are in everything, from fish fries to tacos.

MICROBREWS IN OREGON. Portland is the microbrewery capital of North America, and has the beer to prove it. One establishment in Seaside tries to cram as much alcohol as they can into the largest possible beer (see p. 109).

CULTURE & THE ARTS

Years ago, cities like Vancouver were middle-class port towns with burgeoning counter-cultures. In the years since, their popularity has exploded and the entire Pacific Rim seems to have breached its humdrum roots: tourists have poured in, technological industries have expanded, and resource-driven industries are grinding to a halt under environmental pressures. Yet none of the communities of the Northwest stray far from their origins—port towns remain port towns, and the festivals that first brought communities together continue to do so. The laid-back lifestyle of the Northwest results from this seamless blending, and residents' love for the land is expressed in its aggressive defense.

MUSIC & THEATER. Music lovers wouldn't hesitate to say that **Seattle** stole the show from California at the close of the millennium. As the birthplace of **Jimi Hendrix** and the cradle of grunge, it's undeniable that rock's greatest influences emanate from the Northwest. Artists who hit it big in the 90s included Pearl Jam, Nirvana, Alice in Chains, and Soundgarden, who pioneered the **grunge** sound and its studied flannel-and-fussed-hair look. Today, rock still reigns supreme in Seattle at the **Experience Music Project,** which opened in June 2000. Although prowling record executives signing garage bands to contracts have departed Seattle, the Northwest has been identified as a breeding ground for **riot-grrrl** rock and **guitar-timbre** bands. Seattle also has a **repertory theater** community third in size only to those of Chicago and New York, and its **opera** is internationally renowned.

VISUAL ARTS. Some of the continent's oldest art forms can be found in the Pacific Northwest, and the cedar **masks, totems,** and **longhouses** of indigenous coastal nations have long been recognized as some of the world's most notable artistic achievements. Native carving is a versatile art that entwines religious and cultural heritage. **Bill Reid** (1920-1998), a Haida carver and Vancouver native, was one of many artists celebrated for revitalizing communities through carving, dance, song, and potlatch, all forms suppressed during the last hundred years.

Government support reflects the public's commitment to the arts. Portland and Seattle, for example, funnel a 1% tax on capital improvements into the acquisition and creation of public art. While government cutbacks have compromised the health of famed centers for arts in Western Canada, artist communities and colonies are alive and thriving among the San Juan and Gulf Islands of Washington and British Columbia and in small towns like Atlin, BC. Where government comes up short, philanthropists step in: in 1998-9, the Patrons of Northwest Civic, Cultural, and Charitable Organizations, or **PONCHO,** had its best year yet, dispensing $2 million in Puget Sound. (Since 1962, the group has poured $21 million into the region's arts organizations.)

Several major **films** have used the Pacific Northwest as a backdrop:

MOVIE	DIRECTOR	YEAR	LOCATION
Atanarjuat (Fast Runner)	Zacharias Kunuk	2001	The world's first Inuit film, from Nunavut
Mystery Alaska	Jay Roach	1999	Banff National Park, BC (p. 378)
Independence Day	Roland Emmerich	1996	Grants Pass, OR (p. 128)
Free Willy	Simon Wincer	1993	Cannon Beach, OR (p. 101)
Singles	Cameron Crowe	1992	Seattle, WA (p. 159)
The Goonies	Richard Donner	1985	Astoria, OR (p. 94)
Indiana Jones & Temple of Doom	Steven Spielberg	1984	Grand Coulee Dam, WA (p. 241)
The Shining	Stanley Kubrick	1980	Timberline Lodge, OR (p. 87)
One Flew Over the Cuckoo's Nest	Milos Forman	1975	Salem, OR (p. 118)
Call of the Wild	William Wellman	1935	Mt. Baker Lodge, WA (p. 195)

FESTIVALS

DATE	NAME & LOCATION	DESCRIPTION
July 1	**Canada Day** All over Canada	Typically quiet Canada struggles with an irresistible urge to whoop it up for the anniversary of Confederation.
July 4	**Independence Day** All over the US	Fireworks, fireworks, beer, fireworks, beer, beer, fireworks, hot dogs and hamburgers on the grill, and some fireworks.
mid-July	**Oregon Country Fair** Eugene, OR	Arsty-Craftsy folk and earnest crystal-worshippers converge on Eugene to eat, play, discuss sustainable energy, and hug.
mid-July	**Calgary Stampede** Calgary, AB	One of the biggest rodeos in the world; international contestants, hundreds of thousands of visitors, and many cows.
mid-July	**Folk Music Festival** Vancouver, BC	The Woodstock of the West. Folkies from around the world strap on their Birkenstocks and jam.
late July	**Rhythm & Blues Festival** Winthrop, WA	Just what its name says. Ample rhythm and plentiful blues invade a self-proclaimed wild Western town.
early Sept.	**Bumbershoot** Seattle, WA	Seattle's block party for the arts draws hundreds of thousands of groovesters to watch every sort of big-name act, from R.E.M. to the Indigo Girls to Modest Mouse.
Feb.-Oct.	**Shakespeare Festival** Ashland, OR	That's a lot of drama. Enough that accommodations fill up a year in advance, and tickets are often sold for more than three times face value. Reserve your place early.

ESSENTIALS

FACTS FOR THE TRAVELER

ENTRANCE REQUIREMENTS

Passport (p. 19). Required for all visitors to the US and Canada.

Visa (p. 19). Generally required for all visitors to the US and Canada, but requirement can be waived.

Work Permit (p. 20). Required for all those planning to work in the US or Canada.

Driving Permit (p. 48). Required for all those planning to drive.

EMBASSIES & CONSULATES

CONSULAR SERVICES ABROAD

Contact the nearest embassy or consulate to obtain information regarding the visas and permits necessary to travel to the United States and Canada. Listings of foreign embassies within the US as well as US embassies abroad can be found at www.embassyworld.com. A US **State Department** web site provides contact info for key officers at US overseas stations: www.state.gov/www/about_state/contacts/keyofficer_index.html. The Canadian Ministry of Foreign Affairs is at www.dfait-maeci.gc.ca/dfait/missions/menu-e.asp.

US CONSULATES & EMBASSIES

Australia, Moonah Pl., **Yarralumla** (Canberra), ACT 2600 (☎02 6214 5600; fax 6273 3191, www.usembassy-australia.state.gov). **Other Consulates:** MLC Centre, Level 59, 19-29 Martin Pl., **Sydney,** NSW 2000 (☎02 9373 9200; fax 9373 9184); 553 St. Kilda Rd., P.O. Box 6722, **Melbourne,** VIC 3004 (☎03 9526 5900; fax 9525 0769); 16 St. George's Terr., 13th fl., **Perth,** WA 6000 (☎08 9202 1224; fax 9231 9444).

Canada, 490 Sussex Dr., **Ottawa,** ON K1N 1G8 (☎613-238-5335; fax 688-3101; www.usembassycanada.gov). **Other Consulates:** 615 Macleod Trail SE, Room 1000, **Calgary,** AB T2G 4T8 (☎403-266-8962; fax 264-6630); 1969 Upper Water St., Purdy's Wharf Tower II, suite 904, **Halifax,** NS B3J 3R7 (☎902-429-2480; fax 423-6861); 1155 St. Alexandre St., **Montréal,** QC H3B 3Z1 (mailing address: P.O. Box 65, Postal Station Desjardins, **Montréal,** QC H5B 1G1. ☎514-398-9695; fax 398-0702); 2 Place Terrasse Dufferin, B.P. 939, **Québec City,** QC G1R 4T9 (☎418-692-2095; fax 692-4640); 360 University Ave., **Toronto,** ON M5G 1S4 (☎416-595-1700; fax 595-0051); 1095 West Pender St., 21st fl., **Vancouver,** BC V6E 2M6 (☎604-685-4311)

Ireland, 42 Elgin Rd., **Ballsbridge,** Dublin 4 (☎01 668 8777 or 668 7122; fax 668 9946; www.usembassy.ie).

New Zealand, 29 Fitzherbert Terr., **Thorndon,** Wellington (☎04 462 6000; fax 478 1701; http://usembassy.org.nz). **Other Consulate:** 23 Customs St., Citibank Building, 3rd fl., **Auckland.**

South Africa, P.O. Box 9536, Pretoria 0001, 877 Pretorius St., **Pretoria** (☎27 12 342-1048; fax 342-2244; http://usembassy.state.gov/pretoria). **Other Consulates:** Broadway Industries Center, **Heerengracht,** Foreshore (mailing address: P.O. Box 6773,

Roggebaai, 8012), **Cape Town** (☎021 421-4280; fax 425-3014); 303 West Street, Old Mutual Building, 31st fl., **Durban** (☎031 305-7600; fax 305-7691); No. 1 River St., Killarney (mailing address: P.O. Box 1762, Houghton, 2041), **Johannesburg** (☎011 644-8000; fax 646-6916).

UK, 24 Grosvenor Sq., **London** W1A 1AE (☎0207 499 9000; fax 495 5012; www.usembassy.org.uk). **Other Consulates:** Queen's House, 14 Queen St., **Belfast,** N. Ireland BT1 6EQ (☎01232 328 239; fax 01232 248 482); 3 Regent Terr., **Edinburgh,** Scotland EH7 5BW (☎0131 556 8315; fax 557 6023).

CANADIAN CONSULATES & EMBASSIES

Australia, Commonwealth Ave., **Canberra** ACT 2600 (☎02 6270 4000; www.dfait-maeci.gc.ca/australia); 111 Harrington St., Level 5, **Sydney** NSW 2000 (☎02 9364 3000); 123 Camberwell Rd., Hawthorn East, **Melbourne** VIC 3123 (☎03 9811 9999); 267 St. George's Terr., **Perth** WA 6000 (☎08 9322 7930).

Ireland, 65 St. Stephen's Green, **Dublin** 2 (☎01 478 1988).

New Zealand, 61 Molesworth St., 3rd fl., **Thorndon,** Wellington (☎04 473 9577).

South Africa, Reserve Bank Bldg., St. George's Mall St., 19th fl., **Cape Town** 8001 (☎021 423 5240); 1103 Arcadia St., **Hatfield,** Pretoria 0083 (☎012 42 3000).

UK, 30 Lothian Rd., **Edinburgh,** Scotland EH2 2XZ (☎0131 220 4333); Canada House, Trafalgar Square, **London,** SW1Y 5BJ (☎0207 258 6600).

US, 1251 Ave. of the Americas, **New York,** NY 10020 (☎212-596-1658); 550 S. Hope St. 9th fl., **Los Angeles,** CA 90071 (☎213-346-2700); 2 Prudential Plaza, 180 N. Stetson, Ave., Ste. 2400, **Chicago,** IL 60601 (☎312-616-1860); 501 Pennsylvania Ave. NW, **Washington,** D.C. 20001 (☎202-682-1740).

CONSULAR SERVICES IN THE US & CANADA

IN WASHINGTON, D.C. (US)

Australia, 1601 Mass. Ave. NW, 20036 (☎202-797-3000; www.austemb.org).

Canada, 501 Penn. Ave., 20001 (☎202-682-1740; www.canadianembassy.org).

Ireland, 2234 Mass. Ave. NW, 20008 (☎202-462-3939; www.irelandemb.org).

New Zealand, 37 Observatory Circle, 20008 (☎202-328-4800; www.nzemb.org).

UK, 3100 Mass. Ave., 20008 (☎202-588-6500; www.britainusa.com/consular/embassy/embassy.asp).

South Africa, 3051 Massachusetts Ave., 20008 (☎202-232-4400; usaembassy.southafrica.net).

IN OTTAWA, ONTARIO (CANADA)

Australia, 50 O'Connor St. #710, K1P 6L2 (☎613-236-0841; www.ahc-ottawa.org).

Ireland, 130 Albert St. #700, K1P 5G4 (☎613-233-6281).

New Zealand, 99 Bank St. #727, K1P 6G3 (☎613-238-5991; www.nzhcottawa.org).

UK, 310 Summerset St., K2P 0J9 (☎613-230-2961; www.britain-in-canada.org).

US, 490 Sussex Dr., K1P 1M8 (☎613-238-5335; www.usembassycanada.gov).

South Africa, 15 Sussex Dr., K1M 1M8 (☎613-744-0330; www.docuweb.ca/SouthAfrica/).

DOCUMENTS & FORMALITIES

PASSPORTS

REQUIREMENTS. All non-Canadian and non-American citizens need valid passports to enter the US and Canada and to re-enter their countries. Returning home with an expired passport is illegal and may result in a fine. US citizens can enter Canada (and vice versa) with proof of citizenship and a photo ID—a driver's license and birth certificate should suffice.

NEW PASSPORTS. Citizens of Australia, Canada, Ireland, New Zealand, the United Kingdom, and the United States can apply for a passport at any post office, passport office, or court of law. Citizens of South Africa can apply for a passport at any Home Affairs office. Any new passport or renewal applications must be filed well in advance of the departure date, although most passport offices offer rush services for a very steep fee.

PASSPORT MAINTENANCE. Be sure to photocopy the page of your passport with your photo, as well as your visas, traveler's check serial numbers and any other important documents. Carry one set of copies in a safe place, apart from the originals, and leave another set at home. Consulates also recommend that you carry an expired passport or an official copy of your birth certificate in a part of your baggage separate from other documents.

If you lose your passport, immediately notify the local police and the nearest embassy or consulate of your home government. To expedite its replacement, you will need to know all information previously recorded and show ID and proof of citizenship. In some cases, a replacement may take weeks to process, and it may be valid only for a few months. Any visas stamped in your old passport will be irretrievably lost. In an emergency, ask for immediate temporary traveling papers that will permit you to re-enter your home country.

VISAS, INVITATIONS, & WORK PERMITS

VISAS. Citizens of some non-English speaking countries and South Africa need a visa—a stamp, sticker, or insert in your passport specifying the purpose of your travel and the permitted duration of your stay—in addition to a valid passport for entrance to the US. Canadian citizens do not need to obtain a visa for admission to the US; citizens of Australia, New Zealand, and most European countries (including the UK and Ireland) can waive US visas through the **Visa Waiver Program.** Visitors qualify if they are traveling only for business or pleasure (*not* work or study), are staying for fewer than **90 days,** have proof of intent to leave (e.g. a return plane ticket), possess an I-94W form (arrival/departure certificate issued upon arrival), and are traveling on particular air or sea carriers. See http://travel.state.gov/vwp.html for more information. For stays of longer than 90 days in the US, all travelers (except Canadians) must obtain a visa.

In Canada, citizens of some non-English speaking countries and South Africa also need a visitor's visa if they're not traveling with a valid green card. Citizens of Australia, Ireland, New Zealand, the United Kingdom, and the United States do not need a visa. All visitors to Canada must possess a valid passport in order to enter the country. Visas cost US$50, CDN$75, and can be purchased from the **Canadian Embassy** in Washington, DC Monday to Friday between 9am and noon. US citizens can take advantage of the **Center for International Business and Travel (CIBT),** which secures visas to almost all countries for a varying service charge (☎800-925-2428).

WORK PERMITS. Admission as a visitor does not include the right to work; to obtain employment, one needs a work permit. Entering the US or Canada to study requires a special visa. For more information, see **Alternatives to Tourism** (p. 58).

IDENTIFICATION

Travelers should always have two or more forms of identification with them, including at least one photo ID; a passport and a driver's license or birth certificate is usually adequate. Never carry all your forms of ID together; split them up in case of theft or loss, and keep photocopies of them in your luggage and at home.

TEACHER, STUDENT & YOUTH IDENTIFICATION. The **International Student Identity Card (ISIC),** the most widely accepted form of student ID, provides discounts on sights, accommodations, food, and transport; access to a 24hr. emergency help line (in North America call ☎877-370-ISIC; elsewhere call US collect 715-345-0505); and insurance benefits for US cardholders (see **Insurance,** p. 28). The ISIC is preferable to an institution-specific card (such as a university ID) because it is more likely to be recognized and honored abroad. Applicants must be degree-seeking students of a secondary or post-secondary school and must be at least 12 years old. Because of the proliferation of fake ISICs, some services (particularly airlines) require additional proof of student identity, such as a school ID or a letter signed by your registrar and stamped with your school seal.

The **International Teacher Identity Card (ITIC)** offers teachers the same insurance coverage as well as similar but limited discounts. For travelers who are 25 years old or under but are not students, the **International Youth Travel Card** (**IYTC;** formerly the **GO 25** Card) also offers many of the same benefits as the ISIC.

Each of these identity cards costs US$22 or the equivalent. ISIC and ITIC cards are valid for roughly one and a half academic years; IYTC cards are valid for one year from the date of issue. Many student travel agencies (see p. 40) issue the cards, including STA Travel in Australia and New Zealand, Travel CUTS in Canada, usit in the Republic of Ireland and Northern Ireland, SASTS in South Africa, Campus Travel and STA Travel in the UK, and Council Travel and STA Travel in the US. For a listing of issuing agencies, or for more information, contact the **International Student Travel Confederation (ISTC),** Herengracht 479, 1017 BS Amsterdam, Netherlands (☎+31 20 421 28 00; fax 421 28 10; istcinfo@istc.org; www.istc.org).

CUSTOMS

Upon entering the US or Canada, you must declare certain items from abroad and pay a duty on the value of those articles if they exceed the allowance established by the US or Canada's customs service. Note that goods and gifts purchased at **duty-free** shops abroad are not exempt from customs duties; "duty-free" merely means that you need not pay a sales tax in the country of purchase. Upon returning home, you must similarly declare all articles acquired abroad and pay a duty on the value of articles in excess of your home country's allowance. In order to expedite your return, make a list of any valuables brought from home and register them with customs before traveling abroad, and be sure to keep receipts.

MONEY

CURRENCY & EXCHANGE

The currency chart below is based on August 2002 exchange rates between local currency and Australian dollars (AUS$), Canadian dollars (CDN$), Irish pounds (IR£), New Zealand dollars (NZ$), South African Rand (ZAR), British

CUSTOMS DECLARATIONS. Entering the **US** as a non-resident, you are allowed to claim US$100 of gifts and merchandise if you will be in the country for 72hr. *Residents* may claim $400 worth of goods. If 21, you may bring in 1L of wine, beer, or liquor. 200 cigarettes, 50 cigars (steer clear of Cubans), or 2kg of smoking tobacco are also permitted. Entering **Canada,** visitors may bring in gifts, each of which may not exceed CDN$60 in value. Residents who have been out of the country for 24hr. may claim CDN$50 exemption. After 48hr. they may claim CDN$200, and after 7 days CDN$750. If you are of the legal drinking age in the province, and have been out of the country for 48hr. or more, you may bring in 1.5L of wine, 1.14L of liquor, or 24 355mL bottles of beer or ale. You may also bring in 200 cigarettes, 50 cigars, 200 tobacco sticks, or 200g of manufactured tobacco.

pounds (UK£), US dollars (US$), and European Union euros (EUR€). Check the currency converter on financial websites such as www.bloomberg.com and www.xe.com.

As a general rule, it's cheaper to convert money in the US or Canada than at home. While currency exchange will probably be available in your arrival airport, it's wise to bring enough foreign currency to last for the first 24 to 72 hours of a trip.

If you use traveler's checks or bills, carry some in small denominations (US$50 or less) for times when you are forced to exchange money at disadvantageous rates, but bring a range of denominations since charges may be levied per check cashed. Store your money in a variety of forms; ideally, at any given time you will be carrying some cash, some traveler's checks, and an ATM and/or credit card.

US DOLLARS	
CDN$1 = US$0.63	US$1 = CDN$1.58
UK£1 = US$1.53	US$1 = UK£0.65
EUR€1 = US$0.97	US$1 = EUR€1.03
AUS$1 = US$0.53	US$1= AUS$1.87
NZ$1 = US$0.45	US$1 = NZ$2.20
ZAR1 = US$0.10	US$1 = ZAR10.40

CANADIAN DOLLARS	
US$1 = CDN$1.58	CDN$1 = US$0.63
UK£1 = CDN$2.42	CDN$1 = UK£0.41
EUR€1 = CDN$1.53	CDN$1 = EUR€0.66
AUS$1 = CDN$0.84	CDN$1= AUS$1.19
NZ$1 = CDN$0.72	CDN$1 = NZ$1.39
ZAR1 = CDN$0.15	CDN$1 = ZAR6.58

TRAVELER'S CHECKS

Traveler's checks are one of the safest and least troublesome means of carrying funds. American Express and Visa are the most widely recognized brands. Many banks and agencies sell them for a small commission. Check issuers provide refunds if the checks are lost or stolen, and many provide additional services, such as toll-free refund hotlines abroad, emergency message services, and stolen credit card assistance. They are readily accepted throughout the Pacific Northwest. Ask about toll-free refund hotlines and the location of refund centers when purchasing checks, and always carry emergency cash.

American Express: Checks available with commission at select banks and all AmEx offices. US residents can also purchase checks by phone (☎888-887-8986) or online (www.aexp.com). AAA (see p. 48) offers commission-free checks to its members. Checks available in US, Australian, British, Canadian, Japanese, and euro currencies. Cheques for Two can be signed by either of 2 people traveling together. For purchase locations or more information contact AmEx's service centers: in the US and Canada ☎800-221-7282; in the UK ☎0800 521 313; in Australia ☎800 251 902; in New Zealand ☎0800 441 068; elsewhere US collect ☎801-964-6665.

Visa: Checks available (generally with commission) at banks worldwide. For the location of the nearest office, call Visa's service centers: in the US ☎800-227-6811; in the UK 0800 89 50 78; elsewhere UK collect 020 7937 8091. Checks available in US, British, Canadian, Japanese, and euro currencies.

Travelex/Thomas Cook: In the US and Canada call ☎800-287-7362; in the UK call 0800 62 21 01; elsewhere call UK collect 1733 31 89 50.

CREDIT, DEBIT, & ATM CARDS

Where they are accepted, credit cards often offer superior exchange rates—up to 5% better than the retail rate used by banks and other currency exchange establishments. Credit cards may also offer services such as insurance or emergency help, and are sometimes required to reserve hotel rooms or rental cars. Credit cards are generally accepted in all but the smallest businesses in the US and Canada. **MasterCard** and **Visa** are the most welcomed; **American Express** cards work at some ATMs and at AmEx offices and major airports.

ATM cards are widespread in the US and Canada. Depending on the system that your home bank uses, you can most likely access your personal bank account from abroad. ATMs get the same wholesale exchange rate as credit cards, but there is often a limit on the amount of money you can withdraw per day (around US$500), and unfortunately computer networks sometimes fail. There is typically also a surcharge of US$1-5 per withdrawal.

Debit cards are a relatively new form of purchasing power that are as convenient as credit cards but have a more immediate impact on your funds. A debit card can be used wherever its associated credit card company (usually Mastercard or Visa) is accepted, but the money is withdrawn directly from the holder's checking account. Debit cards often also function as ATM cards and can be used to withdraw cash from associated banks and ATMs throughout the US and Canada. Ask your local bank about obtaining one.

The two major international money networks are **Cirrus** (to locate ATMs in the US, call ☎800-424-7787 or check www.mastercard.com) and **Visa/PLUS** (to locate ATMs in the US call ☎800-843-7587 or check www.visa.com). Most ATMs charge a transaction fee that is paid to the bank that owns the ATM.

GETTING MONEY FROM HOME

If you run out of money while traveling, the easiest and cheapest solution is to have someone back home make a deposit to your home bank account. Failing that, consider one of the following options.

WIRING MONEY. It is possible to arrange a **bank money transfer,** asking a bank back home to wire money to a bank in the US or Canada. This is the cheapest way to transfer cash, but it's also the slowest, usually taking several days or more. Note that some banks may only release your funds in local currency, potentially sticking you with a poor exchange rate; inquire about this in advance. Money transfer services like **Western Union** are faster and more convenient than bank transfers, but also much pricier. Western Union has many locations worldwide. To find one, visit www.westernunion.com, or call in the US ☎800-325-6000, in Canada ☎800-235-0000, in the UK ☎0800 83 38 33, in Australia ☎800 501 500, in New Zealand ☎800 270 000, or in South Africa ☎0860 100031. To wire money within the US by credit card (Visa, MasterCard, Discover), call ☎800-225-5227. Money transfer services are also available at **American Express** and **Thomas Cook** offices.

US STATE DEPARTMENT (US CITIZENS ONLY). In dire emergencies only, the US State Department will forward money within hours to the nearest consular office, which will then disburse it according to instructions for a US$15 fee. If you wish to use this service, you must contact the Overseas Citizens Service division of the US State Department (☎202-647-5225; nights, Sundays, and holidays ☎202-647-4000).

COSTS

Factoring in the high costs of gas (ranging from US$1 to US$2 depending on the region) is a must. Before you go, spend some time calculating a reasonable per-day **budget** that will meet your needs.

STAYING ON A BUDGET. A bare-bones day in the Pacific Northwest (camping or sleeping in hostels/guesthouses, buying food at supermarkets) would cost about US$30-40; a slightly more comfortable day (sleeping in hostels/guesthouses, eating one meal a day at a restaurant, going out at night) would run US$ 50-70. For a luxurious day, the sky's the limit. Also, don't forget to factor in emergency reserve funds (at least US$200) when planning how much money to bring.

TIPS FOR SAVING MONEY. Some simpler ways include searching out opportunities for free entertainment, splitting accommodation and food costs with other trustworthy fellow travelers, and buying food in supermarkets rather than eating out. If you plan on staying in hostels, you may want to bring a sleepsack to save on sheet charges, and do your **laundry** in the sink (unless you're explicitly prohibited from doing so).

TIPPING & BARGAINING

In the US and Canada, it is customary to tip waitstaff and cab drivers 15-20%, but do so at your discretion. Tips are usually not included in restaurant bills. At the airport and in hotels, porters expect a tip of at least $1 per bag to carry your baggage. Except in extremely rural regions where native culture may permit it, bargaining is generally frowned upon and fruitless in the Pacific Northwest.

SAFETY & SECURITY

PERSONAL SAFETY

EXPLORING. What crime there is in the Pacific Northwest is concentrated in urban areas. To avoid unwanted attention, try to blend in as much as possible. Familiarize yourself with your surroundings before setting out, and carry yourself with confidence; if you must check a map on the street, duck into a shop or restaurant. If you are traveling alone, be sure someone at home knows your itinerary, and never admit that you're traveling alone.

SELF DEFENSE. There is no sure-fire way to avoid all the threatening situations you might encounter when you travel, but a good self-defense course will give you concrete ways to react to unwanted advances. **Impact, Prepare, and Model Mugging** can refer you to local self-defense courses in the US (☎800-345-5425). Visit the website at www.impactsafety.org for a list of nearby chapters. Workshops (2-3hr.) start at US$50; full courses run US$350-500.

EMERGENCY = 911. For emergencies in the US and Canada, dial **911.** This number is toll-free from all phones, including coin phones. In a very few remote communities, 911 may not work. If it does not, dial 0 for the operator and request to be connected with the appropriate emergency service. In national parks, it is usually best to call the **park warden** in case of emergency. *Let's Go* always lists emergency contact numbers.

ESSENTIALS

TRAVEL ADVISORIES. The following government offices provide travel information and advisories by telephone, by fax, or via the web:

Australian Department of Foreign Affairs and Trade: ☎13 00 555135; faxback service 02 6261 1299; www.dfat.gov.au.

Canadian Department of Foreign Affairs and International Trade (DFAIT): In Canada and the US call ☎800-267-8376, elsewhere call ☎+1 613-944-4000; www.dfait-maeci.gc.ca. Call for their free booklet, *Bon Voyage...But.*

New Zealand Ministry of Foreign Affairs: ☎04 439 8000; fax 494 8506; www.mft.govt.nz/travel/index.html.

United Kingdom Foreign and Commonwealth Office: ☎020 7008 0232; fax 7008 0155; www.fco.gov.uk.

US Department of State: ☎202-647-5225, faxback service 202-647-3000; http://travel.state.gov. For *A Safe Trip Abroad,* call ☎202-512-1800.

DRIVING. If you are using a **car,** learn local driving signals. Children under 40 lb. should ride only in a specially-designed carseat, available for a small fee from most car rental agencies. Study route maps before you hit the road, and if you plan on spending a lot of time driving, you may want to bring spare parts. If your car breaks down, wait for the police to assist you. For long drives in desolate areas, get a cellular phone and a roadside assistance program (see p. 48). Be sure to park your vehicle in a garage or well-traveled area, and use a steering wheel locking device in larger cities. **Sleeping in your car** is one of the most dangerous (and often illegal) ways to get your rest. For info on the perils of **hitchhiking,** see p. 51.

TERRORISM. In light of the September 11th, 2001 terrorist attacks, there is an elevated threat of further attacks throughout the US and Canada. A terrorist attack would likely target a popular landmark; however, the threat is neither specific enough nor of great enough magnitude to warrant avoiding tourist attractions or certain regions. Monitor developments in the news and stay on top of any local, state, or federal terrorist warnings. In addition, prepare yourself for additional security checks in airports and avoid packing any sharp or dangerous objects in your carry on luggage—they will be confiscated faster than you can blink.

FINANCIAL SECURITY

PROTECTING YOUR VALUABLES. There are a few steps you can take to minimize the financial risk associated with traveling. First, **bring as few belongings with you as possible.** Second, buy a few combination **padlocks** to secure your belongings either in your pack or in a hostel or train station locker. Third, **carry as little cash as possible.** Keep your traveler's checks and ATM/credit cards in a **money belt**—not a "fanny pack," which will make you look like a huge, robbable doofus—along with your passport and ID cards. Fourth, **keep a small cash reserve separate from your primary stash.** This should be about US$50 sewn into or stored in the depths of your pack, along with your traveler's check numbers and important photocopies.

CON ARTISTS & PICKPOCKETS. In large cities **con artists** often work in groups, and children are among the most effective. Beware of certain classics: sob stories that require money, rolls of bills "found" on the street, mustard spilled (or saliva spit) onto your shoulder to distract you while they snatch your bag. **Don't ever let your passport or bags out of your sight.** Beware of **pickpockets** in city crowds, especially on public transportation. Also, be alert in public telephone booths: If you must say your calling card number, do so very quietly; if you punch it in, make sure no one can look over your shoulder.

ACCOMMODATIONS & TRANSPORTATION. Never leave your belongings unattended; crime *can* occur in hostels and hotels. Bring your own **padlock** for hostel lockers, and don't ever store valuables in any locker.

Be particularly careful on **buses** and **trains;** horror stories abound about determined thieves who wait for travelers to fall asleep. Carry your backpack in front of you where you can see it. When traveling with others, sleep in alternate shifts. When alone, use good judgment in selecting a train compartment: never stay in an empty one, and use a lock to secure your pack to the luggage rack. Try to sleep on top bunks with your luggage stored above you (if not in bed with you), and keep important documents and other valuables on your person. If traveling by **car,** don't leave valuables (such as radios or luggage) in it while you are away.

DRUGS & ALCOHOL

If you carry **prescription drugs** while traveling, it is vital to have a copy of the prescriptions to present at US and Canadian borders. The importation of **illegal substances** into the Canada or the US is highly risky, and a punishable offense. Border guards of both countries have unlimited rights to search your baggage, your person, and your vehicle. They will seize vehicles on the spot that are found to be involved in smuggling even small quantities of illegal substances. US border guards can also ban you on the spot from re-entering the country for years. If you are not a US citizen, you may have no right to appeal such decisions. Away from borders, police attitudes vary widely, but the old standards—marijuana, LSD, heroin, cocaine—are illegal in every province and state.

In the US, the drinking age is 21; in Canada it is 19, except in Alberta, Manitoba, and Québec, where it is 18. Drinking restrictions are strict; the youthful should expect to be asked to show government-issued identification when purchasing any alcoholic beverage. Drinking and driving is prohibited everywhere, not to mention dangerous and idiotic. Open beverage containers in your car will incur heavy fines; a failed breathalyzer test will mean fines, a suspended license, and possibly imprisonment. Most localities restrict where and when alcohol can be sold under restrictions known as "blue laws." Sales usually stop at a certain time at night and are often prohibited entirely on Sundays.

HEALTH

Common sense is the simplest prescription for good health while you travel. Fortunately, both the US and Canada have excellent health care systems, although medical facilities may be sparse in remote areas.

BEFORE YOU GO

In your **passport,** write the names of any people you wish to be contacted in case of a medical emergency, and list any allergies or medical conditions. Matching a prescription to a foreign equivalent is not always easy, safe, or possible, so carry up-to-date, legible prescriptions or a statement from your doctor stating the medication's trade name, manufacturer, chemical name, and dosage. While traveling, be sure to keep all medication with you in your carry-on luggage. For tips on packing a basic **first-aid kit** and other health essentials, see p. 29.

IMMUNIZATIONS & PRECAUTIONS

Travelers over two years old should make sure that the following vaccines are up to date: MMR (for measles, mumps, and rubella); DTaP or Td (for diphtheria, tetanus, and pertussis); OPV (for polio); HbCV (for haemophilus influenza B); and HBV (for hepatitis B).

USEFUL ORGANIZATIONS & PUBLICATIONS

The US **Centers for Disease Control and Prevention** (**CDC;** ☎877-FYI-TRIP; toll-free fax 888-232-3299; www.cdc.gov/travel) maintains an international travelers' hotline and an informative website. The CDC's comprehensive booklet *Health Information for International Travel*, an annual rundown of disease, immunization, and general health advice, is free online or US$25 from the Public Health Foundation (☎877-252-1200). Consult the appropriate government agency of your home country for consular information sheets on health, entry requirements, and other issues for various countries (see the listings in the box on **Travel Advisories,** p. 24). For information on medical evacuation services and travel insurance firms, see the US government's website at http://travel.state.gov/medical.html or the **British Foreign and Commonwealth Office** (www.fco.gov.uk).

For detailed information on travel health, including a country-by-country overview of diseases (and a list of travel clinics in the USA), try the **International Travel Health Guide,** by Stuart Rose, MD (US$19.95; www.travmed.com). For general health info, contact the **American Red Cross** (☎800-564-1234; www.redcross.org).

MEDICAL ASSISTANCE ON THE ROAD

Medical care in both the US and Canada is world-class and widespread. In more remote regions, finding doctors can be difficult and expensive. If you are concerned about obtaining medical assistance while traveling, you may wish to employ special support services. The *MedPass* from **GlobalCare, Inc.,** 6875 Shiloh Rd. East, Alpharetta, GA, 30005-8372. (☎800-860-1111; fax 678-341-1800; www.globalems.com), provides 24hr. international medical assistance and medical evacuation resources. If your regular **insurance** policy does not cover travel abroad, you may wish to purchase additional coverage (see p. 28).

Those with medical conditions (such as diabetes, allergies to antibiotics, epilepsy, heart conditions) may want to obtain a **Medic Alert** membership (first year US$35, annually thereafter US$20), which includes a stainless steel ID tag, among other benefits, such as a 24hr. collect-call number. Contact the Medic Alert Foundation, 2323 Colorado Ave, Turlock, CA 95382, USA (☎888-633-4298; outside US ☎209-668-3333; www.medicalert.org).

ONCE IN THE PACIFIC NORTHWEST

ENVIRONMENTAL HAZARDS

Heat exhaustion and dehydration: Heat exhaustion can lead to fatigue, headaches, and wooziness. Avoid it by drinking plenty of fluids, eating salty foods (e.g. crackers), and avoiding dehydrating beverages (e.g. alcohol and caffeinated beverages). Continuous heat stress can eventually lead to heatstroke, characterized by a rising temperature, severe headache, and cessation of sweating. Victims should be cooled off with wet towels and taken to a doctor.

Sunburn: If you are planning on spending time near water or in the snow (which might be unavoidable), you are at a higher risk of getting burned, even through clouds. If you get sunburned, drink more fluids than usual and apply an aloe-based lotion.

Hypothermia and frostbite: A rapid drop in body temperature is the clearest sign of overexposure to cold. Victims may also shiver, feel exhausted, have poor coordination or slurred speech, hallucinate, or suffer amnesia. **Do not let hypothermia victims fall asleep.** To avoid hypothermia, keep dry, wear layers, and stay out of the wind. When the temperature is below freezing, watch out for frostbite. If skin turns white, waxy, and cold, do not rub the area. Drink warm beverages, get dry, and slowly warm the area with dry fabric or steady body contact until a doctor can be found. While the entire region gets extremely cold in the winter, Northern Canada is especially frigid.

High altitude: Allow your body a couple of days to adjust to less oxygen before exerting yourself. Note that alcohol is more potent and UV rays are stronger at high elevations.

INSECT-BORNE DISEASES

Many diseases are transmitted by insects—mainly mosquitoes, fleas, ticks, and lice. Be aware of insects in wet or forested areas, especially while hiking and camping; wear long pants and long sleeves, tuck your pants into your socks, and buy a mosquito net. Use insect repellents and soak or spray your gear with permethrin (licensed in the US for use on clothing). **Lyme disease** is a bacterial infection carried by ticks and marked by a circular bull's-eye rash of 2 in. or more. Later symptoms include fever, headache, fatigue, and aches and pains. Antibiotics are effective if administered early. Left untreated, Lyme can cause problems in joints, the heart, and the nervous system. **Ticks**—responsible for Lyme and other diseases—can be particularly dangerous in rural and forested regions. Be on the lookout for them while camping or hiking in any part of the Pacific Northwest. If you find a tick attached to your skin, grasp the head with tweezers as close to your skin as possible and apply slow, steady traction. Removing a tick within 24hr. greatly reduces the risk of infection. Do not try to remove ticks by burning them or coating them with nail polish remover or petroleum jelly.

ESSENTIALS

FOOD- & WATER-BORNE DISEASES

Prevention is the best cure: be sure that your food is properly cooked and the water you drink is clean. When camping, purify your water by using a water filtration system, bringing it to a rolling boil, or treating it with **iodine tablets;** note however that some parasites such as *giardia* have exteriors that resist iodine treatment, so boiling is more reliable. Always wash your hands before eating or bring a quick-drying purifying liquid hand cleaner.

Traveler's diarrhea: Results from drinking untreated water or eating uncooked foods. Symptoms include nausea and bloating. Try quick-energy, non-sugary foods with protein and carbohydrates to keep your strength up. Over-the-counter anti-diarrheals (e.g. Imodium) may counteract the problems. The most dangerous side effect is dehydration; drink 8 oz. of water with ½ tsp. of sugar or honey and a pinch of salt, try uncaffeinated soft drinks, or eat salted crackers. If you develop a fever or your symptoms don't go away after 4-5 days, consult a doctor. Consult a doctor immediately for treatment of diarrhea in children.

Parasites: Microbes, tapeworms, etc. that hide in unsafe water and food. **Giardiasis,** for example, is acquired by drinking untreated water from streams or lakes. Symptoms include swollen glands or lymph nodes, fever, rashes or itchiness, and digestive problems. Boil water, wear shoes, and eat only cooked food.

OTHER INFECTIOUS DISEASES

Rabies: Transmitted through the saliva of infected animals; fatal if untreated. By the time symptoms (thirst and muscle spasms) appear, the disease is in its terminal stage. If you are bitten, wash the wound thoroughly, seek immediate medical care, and try to have the animal located. A rabies vaccine, which consists of 3 shots given over a 21-day period, is available but is only semi-effective.

Hepatitis B: A viral infection of the liver transmitted via bodily fluids or needle-sharing. Symptoms may not surface until years after infection. A 3-shot vaccination sequence is recommended for sexually-active travelers, and anyone planning to seek medical treatment abroad; it must begin 6 months before traveling.

Hepatitis C: Like Hepatitis B, but the mode of transmission differs. IV drug users, those with occupational exposure to blood, hemodialysis patients, and recipients of blood transfusions are at the highest risk, but the disease can also be spread through sexual contact or sharing items like razors that may have traces of blood on them.

AIDS, HIV, & STIS

For detailed information on **AIDS** in the Pacific Northwest, call the US Centers for Disease Control's 24hr. hotline at ☎800-342-2437, or UNAIDS, the Joint United Nations Programme on HIV/AIDS (☎22 791 3666; fax 22 791 4187).

Sexually transmitted infections (STIs) such as gonorrhea, chlamydia, genital warts, syphilis, and herpes are easier to catch than HIV and can be just as deadly. **Hepatitis B** and **C** can also be transmitted sexually (see above). Though condoms may protect you from some STIs, oral or even tactile contact can lead to transmission. If you think you may have contracted an STI, see a doctor immediately.

INSURANCE

Travel insurance generally covers four basic areas: medical/health problems, property loss, trip cancellation/interruption, and emergency evacuation. Although your regular insurance policies may well extend to travel-related accidents, you may consider purchasing travel insurance if the cost of potential trip cancellation/interruption or emergency medical evacuation is greater than you can absorb. Prices for travel insurance purchased separately generally run about US$50 per week for full coverage, while trip cancellation/interruption may be purchased separately at a rate of about US$5.50 per US$100 of coverage.

Medical insurance (especially university policies) often covers costs incurred abroad; check with your provider. **Canadians** are protected by their home province's health insurance plan for up to 90 days after leaving the country; check with the provincial Ministry of Health or Health Plan Headquarters for details. **Homeowners' insurance** (or your family's coverage) often covers theft during travel and loss of travel documents up to US$500.

ISIC and **ITIC** (see p. 20) provide basic insurance benefits, including US$100 per day of in-hospital sickness for up to 60 days, US$3000 of accident-related medical reimbursement, and US$25,000 for emergency medical transport. Cardholders have access to a toll-free 24hr. helpline (run by the insurance provider **TravelGuard**) for medical, legal, and financial emergencies overseas (US and Canada ☎877-370-4742, elsewhere call US collect ☎+1 715-345-0505). **American Express** (US ☎800-528-4800) grants most cardholders automatic car rental insurance (collision and theft, but not liability) and ground travel accident coverage of US$100,000 on flight purchases made with the card.

INSURANCE PROVIDERS. **Council** and **STA** (see p. 40) offer a range of plans that can supplement your basic coverage. Other private insurance providers in the US and Canada include: **Access America** (☎800-284-8300); **Berkely Group/Carefree Travel Insurance** (☎800-323-3149; www.berkely.com); **Globalcare Travel Insurance** (☎800-821-2488; www.globalcare-cocco.com); and **Travel Assistance International** (☎800-821-2828; www.europ-assistance.com). Providers in the **UK** include **Columbus Direct** (☎020 7375 0011). In **Australia,** try **AFTA** (☎02 9375 4955).

PACKING

Pack lightly: lay out only what you absolutely need, then take half the clothes and twice the money. If you plan to do a lot of hiking, also see the section on **Camping & the Outdoors,** p. 32.

LUGGAGE. If you plan to cover most of your itinerary by foot, a sturdy **frame backpack** is unbeatable. (For the basics on buying a pack, see p. 35.) Toting a **suitcase** or **trunk** is fine if you plan to live in one or two cities and explore from there, but a very bad idea if you're going to be moving around a lot. In addition to your main piece of luggage, a **daypack** (a small backpack or courier bag) is a must.

CLOTHING. Dressing in layers is the best way to handle the variable climate in the Pacific Northwest. No matter when you're traveling, it's always a good idea to bring a **warm jacket** or wool sweater, a **rain jacket** (Gore-Tex® is both waterproof and breathable), sturdy shoes or **hiking boots,** and **thick socks. Flip-flops** or waterproof sandals are must-haves for grubby hostel showers. You may also want to add one outfit beyond the jeans and t-shirt uniform, and maybe a nicer pair of shoes if you have the room. If you plan to visit any religious or cultural sites, remember that you'll need something besides tank tops and shorts to be respectful.

CONVERTERS & ADAPTERS. In the US and Canada, electricity is 220 volts AC, which is incompatible with the 220/240V appliances found in most other countries. Appliances from anywhere outside North America will need to be used with an **adapter** (which changes the shape of the plug, price varies) and a **converter** (which changes the voltage, $20).

TOILETRIES. Toothbrushes, cold-water soap, talcum powder (to keep feet dry), deodorant, razors, tampons, and condoms are all readily available in the US and Canada. If you wear **contact lenses,** bring an extra pair as well as back-up glasses. Also bring a copy of your prescription in case you need emergency replacements.

FIRST-AID KIT. For a basic first-aid kit, pack bandages, pain reliever, antibiotic cream, a thermometer, a Swiss Army knife, tweezers, moleskin, decongestant, motion-sickness remedy, diarrhea or upset-stomach medication (Pepto Bismol or Imodium), an antihistamine, sunscreen, insect repellent, burn ointment, and a syringe for emergencies (get an explanatory letter from your doctor).

FILM. Camera stores are common in the Pacific Northwest, and supplies should be available. Less serious photographers may want to bring a **disposable camera** or two rather than an expensive permanent one. Always pack film in your carry-on luggage, since higher-intensity X-rays are used on checked luggage.

OTHER USEFUL ITEMS. For safety purposes, you should bring a **money belt** and small **padlock.** Basic **outdoors equipment** (plastic water bottle, compass, waterproof matches, pocketknife, sunglasses, sunscreen, hat) may also prove useful. **Quick repairs** of torn garments can be done on the road with a needle and thread; also consider bringing electrical tape for patching tears. If you want to do laundry by hand, bring detergent, a small rubber ball to stop up the sink, and string for a makeshift clothes line. Other things you're liable to forget include an umbrella, sealable **plastic bags** (for damp clothes, food, shampoo, and other spillables), an **alarm clock,** safety pins, rubber bands, a flashlight, earplugs, garbage bags, and a small **calculator.**

IMPORTANT DOCUMENTS. Don't forget your passport, traveler's checks, ATM and/or credit cards, and adequate ID (see p. 20). Also check that you have any of the following that might apply to you: a hosteling membership card (see p. 30), driver's license (see p. 20), travel insurance forms, or rail or bus pass (see p. 44).

ACCOMMODATIONS

HOSTELS

Hostels are generally laid out dorm-style, often with large single-sex rooms and bunk beds, although some offer private rooms for families and couples. They sometimes have kitchens and utensils for your use, bike or moped rentals, storage areas, and laundry facilities. There can be drawbacks: some hostels close during

ONLINE BOOKING One of the cheapest and easiest ways to ensure a bed for a night is by reserving online. Our website features the **Hostelworld** booking engine at www.letsgo.com/resources/accommodations. Hostelworld offers bargain beds everywhere from Ashland to Zaireeka with no added commission.

certain daytime "lockout" hours, have a curfew, don't accept reservations, impose a maximum stay, or, less frequently, require that you do chores. In the Pacific Northwest, a bed in a hostel will average around US$15-20.

HOSTELLING INTERNATIONAL

Joining the youth hostel association in your own country (listed below) automatically grants you membership privileges in **Hostelling International-American Youth Hostels (HI-AYH),** a federation of national hosteling associations. HI hostels are scattered throughout the Pacific Northwest, and are typically less expensive than private hostels. Many accept reservations via the **International Booking Network** (Australia ☎02 9261 1111; Canada ☎800-663-5777; England and Wales ☎1629 58 14 18; Northern Ireland ☎1232 32 47 33; Republic of Ireland ☎01 830 1766; NZ ☎03 379 9808; Scotland ☎8701 55 32 55; US ☎800-909-4776; www.hostelbooking.com). HI's umbrella organization's web page (www.iyhf.org), which lists the web addresses and phone numbers of all national associations, can be a great place to begin researching hosteling in a specific region.

Most HI hostels also honor **guest memberships**—you'll get a blank card with space for six validation stamps. Each night you'll pay a nonmember supplement (one-sixth the membership fee) and earn one guest stamp; get six stamps, and you're a member. Most student travel agencies (see p. 40) sell HI cards, as do all of the national hosteling organizations listed below. All prices listed below are valid for **one-year memberships** unless otherwise noted.

Australian Youth Hostels Association (AYHA), Level 3, 10 Mallett St., Camperdown NSW 2050 (☎02 9565 1699; fax 9565 1325; www.yha.org.au). AUS$52, under 18 AUS$16.

Hostelling International-Canada (HI-C), 400-205 Catherine St., Ottawa, ON K2P 1C3 (☎800-663-5777 or 613-237-7884; fax 237-7868; info@hostellingintl.ca; www.hostellingintl.ca). CDN$35, under 18 free.

An Óige (Irish Youth Hostel Association), 61 Mountjoy St., Dublin 7 (☎830 4555; fax 830 5808; anoige@iol.ie; www.irelandyha.org). EUR€15, under 18 EUR€5.

Youth Hostels Association of New Zealand (YHANZ), P.O. Box 436, 193 Cashel St., 3rd Floor Union House, Christchurch 1 (☎03 379 9970; fax 365 4476; info@yha.org.nz; www.yha.org.nz). NZ$40, under 17 free.

Hostels Association of South Africa, 3rd fl. 73 St. George's St. Mall, P.O. Box 4402, Cape Town 8000 (☎021 424 2511; fax 424 4119; www.hisa.org.za). ZAR45.

Scottish Youth Hostels Association (SYHA), 7 Glebe Crescent, Stirling FK8 2JA (☎01786 89 14 00; fax 89 13 33; www.syha.org.uk). UK£6.

Youth Hostels Association (England and Wales) Ltd., Trevelyan House, 8 St. Stephen's Hill, St. Albans, Hertfordshire AL1 2DY, UK (☎0870 870 8808; fax 01727 84 41 26; www.yha.org.uk). UK£12.50, under 18 UK£6.25, families UK£25.

Hostelling International Northern Ireland (HINI), 22-32 Donegall Rd., Belfast BT12 5JN, Northern Ireland (☎02890 31 54 35; fax 43 96 99; info@hini.org.uk; www.hini.org.uk). UK£10, under 18 UK£6.

Hostelling International-American Youth Hostels (HI-AYH), 733 15th St. NW, #840, Washington, D.C. 20005 (☎202-783-6161; fax 783-6171; hiayhserv@hiayh.org; www.hiayh.org). US$25, under 18 free.

REGIONAL HOSTEL INFORMATION IN WESTERN CANADA

HI British Columbia Region: #402-134 Abbott St., Vancouver, BC V6B 2K4 (☎800-661-0020 or in BC 800-663-5777 or 604-684-7111; fax 604-684-7181; www.hihostels.bc.ca) web site offers online reservations.

HI Southern Alberta Region: 1414 Kensington Rd. NW #203, Calgary, AB T2N 3P9 (☎403-283-5551; www.hostellingintl.ca/Alberta). Online reservations and info on ski-and-stay packages at ski areas in the Rockies.

HI Northern Alberta Region: 10926-88 Avenue Edmonton, AB T6G 021 (☎780-432-7798; www.hostellingintl.ca/Alberta). Online reservations and info on northern Alberta.

OTHER TYPES OF ACCOMMODATIONS

HOTELS, GUESTHOUSES, & PENSIONS

Hotel singles in the Pacific Northwest cost about US$45-70 per night, doubles US$65-95. You'll typically have a private bathroom and shower with hot water, although cheaper places may offer shared bath. If you make reservations in writing, indicate your night of arrival and the number of nights you plan to stay. Not all hotels take reservations, and few accept traveler's checks in a foreign currency.

BED & BREAKFASTS (B&BS)

For a cozy alternative to impersonal hotel rooms, B&Bs (private homes with rooms available to travelers) range from the acceptable to the sublime. Rooms in B&Bs generally cost US$40-70 for a single and US$60-90 for a double in the Pacific Northwest. For more info on B&Bs, see **Bed & Breakfast Inns Online,** P.O. Box 829, Madison, TN 37116 (☎615-868-1946; info@bbonline.com; www.bbonline.com), **InnFinder,** 6200 Gisholt Dr. #100, Madison, WI 53713 (☎608-285-6600; fax 285-6601; www.inncrawler.com), or **InnSite** (www.innsite.com).

CAMPING & THE OUTDOORS

For those with the proper equipment, camping is one of the least expensive and most enjoyable ways to travel through the Pacific Northwest. Camping opportunities in this predominantly rural region are boundless, and many are accessible to inexperienced travelers. Generally, private campgrounds have sites for a small fee and offer even the most inexperienced campers safety and security. Campsites in national parks and other scenic areas vary widely in price (some are free, others as much as private campgrounds) but require more experience than camping at a campground, since there are rarely as many people around. An excellent general resource for travelers planning on camping or spending time in the outdoors is the **Great Outdoor Recreation Pages** (www.gorp.com).

USEFUL PUBLICATIONS & RESOURCES

A variety of publishing companies offer hiking guidebooks to meet the educational needs of novice or expert. For information about camping, hiking, and biking, write or call the publishers listed below to receive a free catalog.

The Milepost, 619 E Ship Creek Ave., Anchorage, AK 99501 (☎800-726-4707 or 706-722-6060; www.themilepost.com). An annual trip planning publication—best for home turf Alaska, but also useful in British Columbia, Alberta, and the Yukon.

Sierra Club Books, 85 Second St., 2nd fl., San Francisco, CA 94105, USA (☎415-977-5500; www.sierraclub.org/books). Publishes general resource books on hiking, camping, and provides advice for women traveling in the outdoors, as well as books on hiking in British Columbia, The Pacific, and The Rockies.

The Mountaineers Books, 1001 SW Klickitat Way, #201, Seattle, WA 98134, USA (☎800-553-4453 or 206-223-6303; fax 223-6306; www.mountaineersbooks.org). Over 400 titles on hiking, biking, mountaineering, natural history, and conservation.

Wilderness Press, 1200 Fifth St., Berkeley, CA 94710, USA (☎800-443-7227 or 510-558-1666; fax 558-1696; www.wildernesspress.com). Over 100 hiking guides/maps, with dozens for destinations in the Pacific Northwest.

Woodall Publications Corporation, 2575 Vista Del Mar Dr., Ventura, CA 93001, USA (☎800-323-9076 or 805-667-4100; www.woodalls.com). Woodall publishes the annually updated *Woodall's Campground Directory* (US$22).

NATIONAL PARKS

National parks protect some of the US and Canada's most precious wildlife and spectacular scenery. The parks also offer activities such as hiking, skiing, and snowshoe expeditions. Most have backcountry camping and developed campgrounds; others welcome RVs, and a few offer opulent living in grand lodges.

Entry fees vary from park to park. In US parks pedestrian and cyclist entry fees tend to range from US$2-10, while vehicles cost US$5-20. National parks in the US offer a number of passes. The **National Parks Pass** (US$50 a year) admits the bearer and accompanying passengers in a vehicle (or family members where access is not by vehicle) entry into most US parks. For an additional $15, the Parks Service will affix a **Golden Eagle Pass** hologram to your card which will allow you access to sites managed by the US Fish and Wildlife Service, the US Forest Service, and the Bureau of Land Management. The **Golden Age Passport** ($10 one time fee), available to those 62 or older, and the **Golden Access Passport,** free to travelers who are blind or permanently disabled, allow access to US national parks and 50% off camping and other park fees. Passes are available at park entrances.

CAMPING RESERVATION NUMBERS. Reservations Northwest (☎888-755-6900 or 206-935-1055; www.reservationsnorthwest.com) books campsites at many Oregon and Washington state parks (no reservation fee). The Oregon state parks info line (☎800-452-5687; www.prd.state.or.us) and its Washington equivalent (☎800-233-0321; www.parks.wa.gov) provide info on all state parks, including those not listed with the reservations center, and can refer callers to the agencies responsible for all other campsites in the state. The National Recreation Reservation service partners with the **US Forest Service (USFS)** to offer a reservations line (☎877-444-6777; www.reserveUSA.com) for selected campgrounds in national forests in Washington and Oregon. For info on USFS campgrounds, cabins, and fire lookouts in Washington and Oregon not listed with the nationwide network, contact **Nature of the Northwest,** 800 NE Oregon St. #177, Portland, OR (☎503-872-2750; www.naturenw.org). **BC Discover Camping** (☎800-689-9025 or 604-689-9025; www.discovercamping.ca) reserves sites at many of the BC provincial parks (CDN$12-20 per night; reservation fee CDN$6.42 per night for first 3 nights). For info on other, non-reservable provincial park campsites, call ☎250-387-4550. **Supernatural British Columbia** (☎800-663-6000; www.hellobc.com) can refer you to private campgrounds throughout BC.

ESSENTIALS

The **Western Canada Annual Pass,** available for both individuals and groups, offers a similar deal at Canadian national parks in the four western provinces (CDN$35, seniors over 64 CDN$27, ages 6-16 CDN$18, groups of up to seven adults CDN$70, groups of up to seven which include at least one senior $53).

Let's Go lists fees for individual parks and contact information for park visitors centers (check the index for a complete listing). Every national park in the US and Canada has a web page, accessible from www.nps.gov or http://parkscanada.pch.gc.ca, which list contact info, fees, and reservation policies.

US Forest Service, Outdoor Recreation Information Center, 222 Yale Ave. N, Seattle, WA 98109 (☎206-470-4060; www.fs.fed.us).

Parks Canada, 220 4th Ave. SE Room #550, Calgary, AB T2G 4X3 (☎800-748-7275; fax 292-4408; www.parkscanada.pch.gc.ca).

STATE & PROVINCIAL PARKS

In contrast to national parks, the primary function of state and provincial parks is usually recreation. Prices for camping at public sites are usually better than those at private campgrounds. Don't let swarming visitors dissuade you from seeing the larger parks—these places can be huge, and even at their most crowded they offer opportunities for quiet and solitude. Most campgrounds are first come, first serve, so arrive early. Some limit your stay and/or the number of people in a group. For general information, contact:

Alberta Park and Protected Areas, 9820 106 St., 2nd fl., Edmonton, AB T5K 2J6 (☎780-427-7009; fax 427-5980; www.gov.ab.ca/env/parks.html).

British Columbia Ministry of Environment, Lands, and Parks, P.O. Box 9338, Stn. Prov. Govt., Victoria, BC V8W 9M1 (☎250-387-1161; www.elp.gov.bc.ca/bcparks).

Oregon State Parks and Recreation Department, 1115 Commercial St. NE, Suite 1, Portland, OR 97301 (☎800-551-6949 or 503-378-6305; fax 503-378-5002; www.prd.state.or.us).

Washington State Parks and Recreation Commission, 7150 Cleanwater Lane, P.O. Box 42650, Olympia, WA 98504, info ☎800-233-0321; www.parks.wa.gov).

Yukon Parks and Outdoor Recreation, Box 2703, Whitehorse, YT Y1A 2C6 (☎867-667-5648; fax 393-6223).

US NATIONAL FORESTS

If national park campgrounds are too developed for your tastes, **national forests** provide a purist's alternative. While some have recreation facilities, most are equipped only for primitive camping; pit toilets and no running water are the norm. (See **Camping Reservation Numbers** p. 33, for reservations.) For general information, including maps, contact the **US Forest Service, Outdoor Recreation Information Center,** 222 Yale Ave. N, Seattle, WA 98109 (☎206-470-4060; www.fs.fed.us).

Backpackers can enjoy specially designated **wilderness areas,** which are even less accessible due to regulations barring vehicles (including mountain bikes). **Wilderness permits** (generally free) are required for backcountry hiking.

Many trailhead parking lots in Oregon and Washington National Forests require a Trail Park Pass ($3 per day per vehicle; annual pass for two vehicles $25). Passes are available at area outfitters and convenience stores, but not at trailheads.

The US Department of the Interior's **Bureau of Land Management (BLM)** offers a variety of outdoor recreation opportunities on the 270 million acres it oversees in ten western states, including camping, hiking, mountain biking, rock climbing, river rafting, and wildlife viewing. Unless otherwise posted, all public lands are open for recreational use. Write the Washington/Oregon office (☎503-952-6002) at 1515 SW 5th Ave., P.O. Box 2965, Portland, OR 92208 for a guide to BLM campgrounds, many of which are free.

WILDERNESS SAFETY

THE GREAT OUTDOORS

Stay warm, stay dry, and stay hydrated. The vast majority of life-threatening wilderness situations can be avoided by following this simple advice. Prepare yourself for an emergency, however, by always packing raingear, a hat and mittens, a first-aid kit, a reflector, a whistle, high energy food, and extra water for any hike. Dress in wool or warm layers of synthetic materials designed for the outdoors; never rely on cotton for warmth, as it is useless when wet.

Check **weather forecasts** and pay attention to the skies when hiking, since weather patterns can change suddenly. Whenever possible, let someone know when and where you are going hiking—either a friend, a hostel owner, a park ranger, or a local hiking organization. Do not attempt a hike beyond your ability—you may be endangering your life. See **Health,** p. 25, for information about outdoor ailments and basic medical concerns.

BEARS WILL EAT YOU

If you are hiking in an area which might be frequented by bears, ask local rangers for information on bear behavior before entering any park or wilderness area, and obey posted warnings. No matter how irresistibly cute a bear appears, don't be fooled—they're powerful and unpredictable animals that are not intimidated by humans. If you're close enough for a bear to be observing you, you're too close. If you see a bear at a distance, calmly walk (don't run) in the other direction. If it seems interested, back away slowly while speaking to the bear in firm, low tones and head in the opposite direction or toward a settled area. If you are attacked by a bear, get in a fetal position to protect yourself, put your arms over the back of your neck, and play dead. In all situations, remain calm, as loud noises and sudden movements can trigger an attack.

Don't leave food or other scented items (trash, toiletries, the clothes that you cooked in) near your tent. Bear-bagging—hanging edibles and other good-smelling objects from a tree out of reach of hungry paws—is the best way to keep your toothpaste from becoming a condiment. Bears are also attracted to any perfume, as are bugs, so cologne, scented soap, deodorant, and hairspray should stay at home. For more information, consult *How to Stay Alive in the Woods*, by Bradford Angier (Macmillan Press, US$8).

CAMPING & HIKING EQUIPMENT

WHAT TO BUY...

Good camping equipment is both sturdy and light. Camping equipment is generally more expensive in Australia, New Zealand, and the UK than in North America.

Sleeping Bag: Most sleeping bags are rated by season ("summer" means 30-40°F at night; "four-season" or "winter" often means below 0°F). They are made either of **down** (warmer and lighter, but more expensive, and miserable when wet) or of **synthetic** material (heavier, more durable, and warmer when wet). Prices range US$80-210 for a summer synthetic to US$250-300 for a good down winter bag. **Sleeping bag pads** include foam pads (US$10-20), air mattresses (US$15-50), and Therm-A-Rest self-inflating pads (US$45-80). Bring a **stuff sack** to store your bag and keep it dry.

Tent: The best tents are free-standing (with their own frames and suspension systems), set up quickly, and only require staking in high winds. Low-profile dome tents are the best all-around. Good 2-person tents start at US$90, 4-person at US$300. Seal the seams of your tent with waterproofer, and make sure it has a rain fly. Other tent accessories include a **battery-operated lantern,** a **plastic groundcloth,** and a **nylon tarp.**

Backpack: Internal-frame packs mold better to your back, keep a lower center of gravity, and flex adequately to allow you to hike difficult trails. **External-frame packs** are more comfortable for long hikes over even terrain, as they keep weight higher and distribute it more evenly. Make sure your pack has a strong, padded hip-belt to transfer weight to your legs. Any serious backpacking requires a pack of at least 4000 in^3 (16,000cc), plus 500 in^3 for sleeping bags in internal-frame packs. Sturdy backpacks cost anywhere from US$125-420—and this is one area in which it doesn't pay to economize. Fill up any pack with something heavy and walk around the store with it to get a sense of how it distributes weight before buying it. Either buy a **waterproof backpack cover,** or store all of your belongings in plastic bags inside your pack.

Boots: Be sure to wear hiking boots with good **ankle support.** They should fit snugly and comfortably over 1-2 pairs of wool socks and thin liner socks. Break in boots over several weeks first in order to spare yourself painful and debilitating blisters.

Other Necessities: Synthetic layers, like those made of polypropylene, and a **pile jacket** will keep you warm even when wet. A **"space blanket"** will help you to retain your body heat and doubles as a groundcloth (US$5-15). Plastic **water bottles** are virtually shatter- and leak-proof. Bring **water-purification tablets** for when you can't boil water. Although most campgrounds provide campfire sites, you may want to bring a small **metal grate** or **grill** of your own. For those places that forbid fires or the gathering of firewood, you'll need a **camp stove** (the classic Coleman starts at US$40) and a propane-filled **fuel bottle** to operate it. Also don't forget a **first-aid kit, pocketknife, insect repellent, calamine lotion,** and **waterproof matches** or a **lighter.**

...AND WHERE TO BUY IT

The mail-order/online companies listed below offer lower prices than many retail stores, but a visit to a local camping or outdoors store will give you a good sense of the look and weight of certain items.

Campmor, 28 Parkway, P.O. Box 700, Upper Saddle River, NJ 07458, USA (US ☎888-226-7667; elsewhere US ☎+1 201-825-8300; www.campmor.com).

Discount Camping, 880 Main North Rd., Pooraka, South Australia 5095, Australia (☎08 8262 3399; fax 8260 6240; www.discountcamping.com.au).

ESSENTIALS

Eastern Mountain Sports (EMS), 1 Vose Farm Rd., Peterborough, NH 03458, USA (☎888-463-6367 or 603-924-7231; www.shopems.com).

L.L. Bean, Freeport, ME 04033 (US and Canada ☎800-441-5713; UK ☎0800 891 297; elsewhere, call US ☎+1 207-552-3028; www.llbean.com).

Mountain Designs, 51 Bishop St., Kelvin Grove, Queensland 4059, Australia (☎07 3856 2344; fax 3856 0366; info@mountaindesigns.com; www.mountaindesigns.com).

Recreational Equipment, Inc. (REI), Sumner, WA 98352, USA (☎800 426-4840 or 253-891-2500; www.rei.com).

YHA Adventure Shop, 14 Southampton St., Covent Garden, London, WC2E 7HA, UK (☎020 7836 8541; www.yhaadventure.com). The main branch of one of Britain's largest outdoor equipment suppliers.

CAMPERS & RVS

Renting an RV will always be more expensive than tenting or hosteling, but it's cheaper than staying in hotels and renting a car (see **Rental Cars,** p. 47), and the convenience of bringing along your own bedroom, bathroom, and kitchen makes it an attractive option, especially for older travelers and families with children.

Rates vary widely by region, season (July and August are the most expensive months), and type of RV. Rental prices for a standard RV are around US$1000-1400 per week. It always pays to contact several different companies to compare vehicles and prices.

ENVIRONMENTALLY RESPONSIBLE TOURISM

The idea behind responsible tourism is to leave no trace of human presence behind. A campstove is the safer (and most efficient) way to cook. If you must make a fire, keep it small and use only dead branches or brush rather than cutting vegetation. Make sure your campsite is at least 150 ft. (50m) from water supplies or bodies of water. If there are no toilet facilities, bury human waste (but not paper) at least four inches (10cm) deep, but not more than eight inches (20cm), and 150 ft. or more from any water supplies and campsites. Always pack your trash in a plastic bag and carry it with you until you reach the next trash receptacle. For more information on these issues, contact one of the organizations listed below.

Earthwatch, 3 Clock Tower Place #100, Box 75, Maynard, MA 01754, USA (☎800-776-0188 or 978-461-0081; info@earthwatch.org; www.earthwatch.org).

International Ecotourism Society, 28 Pine St., Burlington, VT 05402, USA (01) (☎802-651-9818; fax 802-651-9819; ecomail@ecotourism.org; www.ecotourism.org).

National Audubon Society, Nature Odysseys, 700 Broadway, New York, NY 10003 (☎212-979-3000; fax 212-979-3188; webmaster@audubon.org; www.audubon.org).

Tourism Concern, Stapleton House, 277-281 Holloway Rd., London N7 8HN, UK (☎020 7753 3330; fax 020 7753 3331; info@tourismconcern.org.uk; www.tourismconcern.org.uk).

ORGANIZED ADVENTURE TRIPS

Organized adventure tours offer another way of exploring the wild. Activities include hiking, biking, skiing, canoeing, kayaking, rafting, climbing, and going on photo safaris and archaeological digs.

Specialty Travel Index, 305 San Anselmo Ave., #313, San Anselmo, CA 94960, USA (☎800-442-4922 or 415-459-4900; fax 415-459-9474; info@specialtytravel.com; www.specialtytravel.com). Tours worldwide.

AmeriCan Adventures & Roadrunner, P.O. Box 1155, Gardena, CA 90249, USA (☎800-TREK-USA or 310-324-3447; fax 310-324-3562; UK ☎01295 756 2000; www.americanadventures.com). Organizes group adventure camping and hostelling trips (with transportation and camping costs included) in the US and Canada.

KEEPING IN TOUCH

BY MAIL

DOMESTIC RATES

In the **United States,** first-class letters sent and received within the US take 1-3 days and cost $0.37; **Priority Mail** packages up to 1 lb. generally take two days and cost $3.85, up to 5 lb. $7.70. **All days specified denote business days.** For more details, see www.usps.com. Letters sent and received within **Canada** take two to four days and cost CDN$0.48; Xpresspost packages take less time and rates for this service can be calculated at http://www.canadapost.ca/personal/tools/rc/res/bin/rcres_ultrawide-e.shtm. For additional information, see www.canadapost.ca.

SENDING MAIL HOME FROM THE US & CANADA

Airmail is the best way to send mail home from the US and Canada. **Aerogrammes,** printed sheets that fold into envelopes and travel via airmail, are available at post offices. Write "par avion" or "air mail" on the front. Most post offices will charge exorbitant fees or simply refuse to send aerogrammes with enclosures. **Surface mail** is by far the cheapest and slowest way to send mail. It takes one to three months to cross the Atlantic and two to four to cross the Pacific—good for items you won't need to see for a while, such as souvenirs or other articles you've acquired along the way that are weighing down your pack. Check with the closest post office to find out about postage rates to your home country.

SENDING MAIL TO THE US & CANADA

Mark envelopes "air mail" or "par avion," or your letter or postcard will never arrive. In addition to the standard postage system whose rates are listed below, **Federal Express** (Australia ☎13 26 10; US and Canada ☎800-247-4747; New Zealand ☎0800 73 33 39; UK☎0800 12 38 00; www.fedex.com) handles express mail services from most home countries to the US, as well as within the country; for example, they can get a letter from New York to Los Angeles in 2 days for $9.95, and from London to New York in two days for UK£25.80.

RECEIVING MAIL IN THE US & CANADA

There are several ways to arrange pick-up of letters sent to you by friends and relatives while you are abroad. Mail can be sent via General Delivery to almost any city or town in the US or Canada that has a post office. Address General Delivery letters as in the following example:

Butch EMMIT
General Delivery
Portland, OR 97204 USA

The mail will go to a special desk in the central post office, unless you specify a post office by street address or postal code. Bring your passport or other photo ID for pick-up. If the clerks insist that there is nothing for you, have them check under your first name as well. *Let's Go* lists post offices in the Practical Information section for each city and most towns.

American Express's travel offices throughout the world offer a free Client Letter Service (mail held up to 30 days and forwarded upon request) for cardholders who contact them in advance. Address the letter in the same way shown above. Some offices will offer these services to non-cardholders (especially AmEx Travelers Cheque holders), but call ahead to make sure. Let's Go lists AmEx office locations for most large cities in Practical Information sections; for a complete, free list, call ☎800-528-4800.

BY TELEPHONE

CALLING HOME FROM THE US & CANADA

A **calling card** is probably your cheapest bet. Calls are billed collect or to your account. You can frequently call collect without even possessing a company's calling card just by calling their access number and following the instructions. *Let's Go* has recently partnered with ekit.com to provide a calling card that offers a number of services, including email and voice messaging. Before purchasing any calling card, always be sure to compare rates with other cards, and to make sure it serves your needs (a local phonecard is generally better for local calls, for instance). For more information, visit www.letsgo.ekit.com.

You can often also make **direct international calls** from pay phones, but if you aren't using a calling card, you may need to drop your coins as quickly as your words. Where available, prepaid phone cards (see below) and occasionally major credit cards can be used for direct international calls, but they are still less cost-effective. (See the box on **Placing International Calls** (p. 38) for directions on how to place a direct international call.)

PLACING INTERNATIONAL CALLS. To call the US or Canada from home or to call home from the US or Canada, dial:

1. The **international dialing prefix.** To dial out of out of **Canada** or the **US,** 011; **Australia,** dial 0011; the **Republic of Ireland, New Zealand,** or the **UK,** 00; **South Africa,** 09.
2. The **country code** of the country you want to call. To call **Canada** or the **US,** 1; **Australia,** dial 61; the **Republic of Ireland,** 353; **New Zealand,** 64; **South Africa,** 27; the **UK,** 44.
3. The **city/area code.** *Let's Go* lists the city/area codes for cities and towns in the US and Canada opposite the city or town name, next to a ☎. If the first digit is a zero (e.g., 020 for London), omit the zero when calling from abroad (e.g., dial 20 from Canada to reach London).
4. The **local number.**

CALLING WITHIN THE US & CANADA

The simplest way to call within the country is to use a coin-operated phone; local calls cost US $0.35 in the United States and CDN$0.25 in Canada. **Prepaid phone cards,** which carry a certain amount of phone time depending on the card's denomination, usually save time and money in the long run, although they often require a US$0.25 surcharge from pay phones. These cards can be used to make both international and domestic calls.

TIME DIFFERENCES

The Pacific Northwest covers several time zones, anywhere from 7 to 9 hours ahead of **Greenwich Mean Time (GMT)**. Both the US and Canada observe daylight savings time, so clocks are set forward one hour in the spring and backward one hour in the fall.

3AM	4AM	5AM	7AM	NOON	10PM
Anchorage, AK	Vancouver Seattle Portland Los Angeles	Calgary Edmonton Denve	Toronto Ottawa New York	London (GMT)	Sydney Canberra Melbourne

BY EMAIL & INTERNET

Though in some places it's possible to forge a remote link with your home server, in most cases this is a much slower (and thus more expensive) option than taking advantage of free **web-based email accounts** (e.g., www.hotmail.com and www.yahoo.com). Travelers with laptops can call an Internet service provider via a **modem.** Long-distance phone cards specifically intended for such calls can defray normally high phone charges; check with your long-distance phone provider to see if it offers this option. **Internet cafes** and the occasional free Internet terminal at a public library or university are listed in the **Practical Information** sections of major cities.

GETTING TO THE PACIFIC NORTHWEST

BY PLANE

When it comes to airfare, a little effort can save you a bundle. If your plans are flexible enough to deal with the restrictions, courier fares are the cheapest. Tickets bought from consolidators and standby seating are also good deals, but last-minute specials, airfare wars, and charter flights often beat these fares. The key is to hunt around, to be flexible, and to ask persistently about discounts. Students, seniors, and those under 26 should never pay full price for a ticket.

COMMERCIAL AIRLINES

Airfares to the US and Canada peak over the summer; in addition, during national holidays (see p. 2), it becomes especially expensive and difficult to travel. Otherwise, flight prices remain steady throughout the year. Midweek (M-Th morning) round-trip flights run US$40-50 cheaper than weekend flights, but they are generally more crowded and less likely to permit frequent-flier upgrades. Not fixing a return date ("open return") or arriving in and departing from different cities ("open-jaw") can be pricier than round-trip flights. Patching one-way flights together is the most expensive way to travel. Flights between capitals or regional hubs in the Pacific Northwest—such as Portland (OR), Seattle (WA), and Calgary (AB)—will tend to be cheaper.

If the Pacific Northwest is only one stop on a more extensive globe-hop, consider a round-the-world (RTW) ticket. Tickets usually include at least five stops and are valid for about a year; prices range from US$1200-5000. Try **Northwest Airlines/KLM** (US ☎800-447-4747; www.nwa.com) or **Star Alliance,** a consortium of 22 airlines including United Airlines (US ☎800-241-6522; www.star-alliance.com).

The commercial airlines' lowest regular offer is the **APEX** (Advance Purchase Excursion) fare, which provides confirmed reservations and allows "open-jaw" tickets. Generally, reservations must be made seven to 21 days ahead of departure, with seven- to 14-day minimum-stay and up to 90-day maximum-stay restrictions. These fares carry hefty cancellation and change penalties (fees rise in summer). Book summer APEX fares early; by May you will have a hard time getting your desired departure date. Use **Microsoft Expedia** (msn.expedia.com) or **Travelocity** (www.travelocity.com) to get an idea of the lowest published fares, and then use the resources outlined here to try and beat those fares.

The following chart shows a range of sample round-trip fares between various destinations and some major airport hubs in the Pacific Northwest, with origins listed on the left and destinations listed on top. Be forewarned that airline prices change frequently; these are just guidelines.

(ALL PRICES IN US$)	PORTLAND	SEATTLE	CALGARY
Most North American Locations	$250-650	$250-650	$300-750
UK & Ireland	$600-1000	$550-950	$650-1100
Sydney, Australia	$1100-1500	$1000-1400	$1300-1700
Auckland, New Zealand	$1250-1600	$1200-1600	$1300-1700
Cape Town/Johannesburg	$800-1200	$750-1150	$650-1050

BUDGET & STUDENT TRAVEL AGENCIES

While knowledgeable agents specializing in flights to the Pacific Northwest can make your life easy and help you save, they may not spend the time to find you the lowest possible fare—they get paid on commission. Travelers holding **ISIC and IYTC cards** (see p. 20) qualify for big discounts from student travel agencies. Most flights from budget agencies are on major airlines, but in peak season some may sell seats on less reliable chartered aircraft.

usit world (www.usitworld.com). Over 50 **usit campus** branches in the UK, including 52 Grosvenor Gardens, **London** SW1W 0AG (☎0870 240 1010); **Manchester** (☎0161 273 1880); and **Edinburgh** (☎0131 668 3303). Nearly 20 **usit NOW** offices in Ireland, including 19-21 Aston Quay, O'Connell Bridge, **Dublin** 2 (☎01 602 1600; www.usitnow.ie), and **Belfast** (☎02 890 327 111; www.usitnow.com). Offices also in Athens, Auckland, Brussels, Frankfurt, Johannesburg, Lisbon, Luxembourg, Madrid, Paris, Sofia, and Warsaw.

Council Travel (www.counciltravel.com). Countless US offices, including branches in Atlanta, Boston, Chicago, L.A., New York, San Francisco, Seattle, and Washington, D.C. Check the website or call ☎800-226-8624 for the office nearest you. Also an office at 28A Poland St. (Oxford Circus), **London,** W1V 3DB (☎0207 437 7767). *As of May, Council had declared bankruptcy and was subsumed under STA. However, their offices are still in existence and transacting business.*

CTS Travel, 44 Goodge St., **London** W1T 2AD, UK (☎0207 636 0031; fax 637 5328; ctsinfo@ctstravel.co.uk).

STA Travel, 7890 S. Hardy Dr., Ste. 110, Tempe AZ 85284, USA (24hr. reservations and info ☎800-781-4040; www.sta-travel.com). A student and youth travel organization with over 150 offices worldwide (check their website for a listing of all their offices), including US offices in Boston, Chicago, L.A., New York, San Francisco, Seattle, and Washington, D.C. Ticket booking, travel insurance, railpasses, and more. In the UK, walk-in office 11 Goodge St., **London** W1T 2PF or call ☎0207 436 7779. In New Zealand, Shop 2B, 182 Queen St., **Auckland** (☎09 309 0458). In Australia, 366 Lygon St., **Carlton** Vic 3053 (☎03 9349 4344).

Travel CUTS (Canadian Universities Travel Services Limited), 187 College St., **Toronto,** ON M5T 1P7 (☎416-979-2406; fax 979-8167; www.travelcuts.com). 60 offices across Canada. Also in the UK, 295-A Regent St., **London** W1R 7YA (☎0207 255 1944).

STANDBY FLIGHTS

Traveling standby requires considerable flexibility in arrival and departure dates and cities. Companies dealing in standby flights sell vouchers rather than tickets, along with the promise to get to your destination (or near your destination) within a certain window of time (typically 1-5 days). You call in before your specific window of time to hear your flight options and the probability that you will be able to board each flight. You can then decide which flights you want to try to make, show up at the appropriate airport at the appropriate time, present your voucher, and board if space is available. Vouchers can usually be bought for both one-way and round-trip travel. You may receive a monetary refund only if every available flight within your date range is full; if you opt not to take an available (but perhaps less convenient) flight, you can only get credit toward future travel. Carefully read agreements with any company offering standby flights as tricky fine print can leave you in a lurch. To check on a company's service record in the US, call the **Better Business Bureau** (☎212-533-6200). It is difficult to receive refunds, and clients' vouchers will not be honored when an airline fails to receive payment in time. One established standby company in the US is **Whole Earth Travel,** 325 W. 38th St., New York, NY 10018, USA (☎800-326-2009; fax 212-864-5489; www.4standby.com) and Los Angeles, CA (☎888-247-4482), which offers intracontinental connecting flights within the US or Europe that cost US$79-139.

TICKET CONSOLIDATORS

Ticket consolidators, or **"bucket shops,"** buy unsold tickets in bulk from commercial airlines and sell them at discounted rates. The best place to look is in the Sunday travel section of any major newspaper, where many bucket shops place tiny ads. Call quickly, as availability is typically extremely limited. Not all bucket shops are reliable, so insist on a receipt that gives full details of restrictions, refunds, and tickets, and pay by credit card (in spite of the 2-5% fee) so you can stop payment if you never receive your tickets. For more info, see www.travel-library.com/air-travel/consolidators.html.

TRAVELING FROM THE US & CANADA

Travel Avenue (☎800-333-3335; www.travelavenue.com) searches for best available published fares and then uses several consolidators to attempt to beat that fare. Some consolidators worth trying are **Interworld** (☎305-443-4929; fax 443-0351); **Pennsylvania Travel** (☎800-331-0947); **Rebel** (☎800-227-3235; travel@rebeltours.com; www.rebeltours.com); **Cheap Tickets** (☎800-377-1000; www.cheaptickets.com); and **Travac** (☎800-872-8800; fax 212-714-9063; www.travac.com). Yet more consolidators on the web include the **Internet Travel Network** (www.itn.com); **Travel Information Services** (www.tiss.com); **TravelHUB** (www.travelhub.com); and **The Travel Site** (www.thetravelsite.com). Keep in mind that these are just suggestions to get you started with research; *Let's Go* does not endorse any of these agencies.

TRAVELING FROM THE UK, AUSTRALIA, & NEW ZEALAND

In London, the **Air Travel Advisory Bureau** (☎0207 636 5000; www.atab.co.uk) can provide names of reliable consolidators and discount flight specialists. From Australia and New Zealand, look for consolidator ads in the travel section of the *Sydney Morning Herald* and other papers.

BORDER CROSSINGS

ENTERING CANADA FROM THE US. Though a passport is not specifically required to cross the Canadian border, proof of citizenship is, and so it pays to bring identification to avoid annoying delays. Don't be surprised if authorities ask to search your car.

ENTERING THE US FROM CANADA. In the wake of September 11, count on a search of your car and a thorough examination of your identification papers. It pays to have your passport handy, as well as any other identification you can muster. It also goes without saying that potentially hazardous materials or items you have purchased should be left behind (or not purchased in the first place) under these circumstances.

GETTING AROUND THE PACIFIC NORTHWEST

BY TRAIN

By locomotive is one of the most scenic ways to tour the US and Canada, but keep in mind that air travel is much faster, and often much cheaper, than train travel. As with airlines, you can save money by purchasing your tickets as far in advance as possible, so plan ahead and make reservations early. It is essential to travel light on trains; not all stations will check your baggage.

AMTRAK. (☎800-872-7245; www.amtrak.com.) The only provider of intercity passenger train service in most of the US. Their informative web page lists schedules, fares, arrival and departure info, and takes reservations. Discounts on full rail fares are given to: senior citizens (15% off), students with a Student Advantage card (15% off; call 877-2JOINSA to purchase the $20 card; www.studentadvantage.com), travelers with disabilities (15% off), children ages 2-15 accompanied by an adult (50% off up to two children), children under two (free for one child), and US veterans (10% off with a VeteransAdvantage membership card). "Rail SALE" offers online discounts of up to 90%; visit the website for details and reservations.

VIA RAIL. (☎888-842-7245; www.viarail.ca.) Amtrak's Canadian equivalent offers **discounts** on full fares: students 18-24 with ISIC card (35% off full fare); youth 12-17 (35% off full fare); seniors 60 and over (10% off); ages 11 and under, accompanied by an adult (free). Reservations are required for first-class seats and sleep car accommodations. "Supersaver" fares offer discounts between 25-35%. The **Canrail Pass** allows unlimited travel on 12 days within a 30-day period on VIA trains. Between early June and mid-October, a 12-day pass costs CDN$658 (seniors and youths CDN $592). Off-season passes cost CDN$411 (seniors and youths CDN$370). Add CDN$33-$56 for additional days of travel. Call for information on seasonal promotions such as discounts on Grayline Sightseeing Tours.

BY BUS

Buses generally offer the most frequent and complete service between the cities and towns of the US and Canada. Often a bus is the only way to reach smaller locales without a car. *Russell's Official National Motor Coach Guide* ($17.30 including postage) is an invaluable tool for constructing an itinerary. Updated

each month, *Russell's Guide* has schedules of every bus route (including Greyhound) between any two towns in the US and Canada. Russell's also publishes two semiannual supplements that are free when ordered with the May and December issues; a *Directory of Bus Lines and Bus Stations*, and a series of route maps (both $8.40 if ordered separately). To order any of the above, write Russell's Guides, Inc., P.O. Box 278, Cedar Rapids, IA 52406 (☎319-364-6138; fax 365-8728). For those who want someone else to do the itinerary planning for them, **Contiki Travel** (☎1-888-CONTIKI; www.contiki.com) runs comprehensive 8-9 day bus tours starting at $825. Tours include accommodations, transportation and some meals.

GREYHOUND

Greyhound (☎800-231-2222; www.greyhound.com) operates the most routes in the US. Schedule information is available at any Greyhound terminal or agency, on their web page, or by calling them toll-free.

Advance purchase fares: Reserving space far ahead of time ensures a lower fare, but expect a smaller discount during the busy summer months. For tickets purchased more than 14 days in advance, fares anywhere in the US will be no more than $109 one-way. Fares are often reduced even more for 21-day advance purchases on many popular routes; call for up to the date pricing or consult their web page.

Discounts on full fares: Senior citizens (10% off); children ages 2-11 (50% off); students with a Student Advantage card (up to 15% off); travelers with disabilities and special needs and their companions ride together for the price of one. Active and retired US military personnel and National Guard Reserves (10% off with valid ID) and their spouses and dependents may take a round-trip between any 2 points in the US for $179. With a ticket purchased 3 or more days in advance during the spring and summer months, a friend can travel along for free (some exceptions).

Ameripass: Call ☎888-454-7277. Allows adults unlimited travel through the US for 7 days ($209 for adults, $188.10 senior citizens and students with valid ID); 10 days ($259, $233); 15 days ($319, $287); 21 days ($369, $232); 30 days ($429, $368); 45 days ($469, $422); or 60 days ($599, $539). Passes that allow travel through the US and Canada are for 15 days ($399, $359 student and senior); 21 days ($439, $395); 30 days ($499, $449); 45 days ($569, $512); 60 days ($639, 575). For travel exclusively through western US and Canada, there is a 15 day pass ($299, $269) and a 30 day pass ($399, $359). Children's passes are half the price of adult passes. The pass takes effect the 1st day used.

International Ameripass: For travelers from outside the US. A 4-day pass to travel through the US is $135; a 7-day pass ($185, $166 students with a valid ID and senior citizens); a 10-day pass ($239, $215); 15-day pass ($285, $257); 30-day pass ($385, $347); 45-day pass ($419, $377); 60-day pass ($509, $458). Travel through the US and Canada for 15 days runs ($339, $305); 21 days ($389, $350); 30 days ($449, $404); 45 days ($499, $449); 60 days ($559, $503). The western US and Canada pass is available for 15 days ($299, $269); or 30 days ($399, $359). Call ☎888-454-7277 for info. International Ameripasses are not available at the terminal; they can be purchased in foreign countries at Greyhound-affiliated agencies. Telephone numbers vary by country and are listed on the web page. Passes can also be ordered at the web page, or purchased in Greyhound's International Office, in Port Authority Bus Station, 625 Eighth Ave., New York, NY 10018 (☎800-246-8572 or 212-971-0492; intlameripass@greyhound.com).

GREYHOUND CANADA TRANSPORTATION

Greyhound Canada Transportation, 877 Greyhound Way, Calgary, AB T3C 3V8 (☎800-661-8747; www.greyhound.ca) is Canada's main intercity bus company. The web page has full schedule info.

Discounts: Seniors (10% off); students (25% off with an ISIC; 10% off with other student cards); a companion of a disabled person free; ages 5-11, 50%; under 4 free. If reservations are made at least 7 days in advance, a friend travels half off. A child under 15 rides free with an adult.

Canada Pass: Offers 7, 10, 15, 21, 30, 45, and 60 day unlimited travel from the western border of Canada to Montreal on all routes for North American residents, including limited links to northern US cities. 7 day advance purchase required. 7-day pass (CDN$249, $224 for students); 10-day pass (CDN$319, CDN$287); 15-day pass (CDN$379, CDN$341); 21-day pass (CDN$419, CDN$377); 30-day pass (CDN$449, CDN$404.10); 45-day pass (CDN$535, $482); 60-day pass (CDN$599, CDN$539). The Canada Plus Pass includes coast to coast travel and is slightly more expensive.

GREEN TORTOISE

Green Tortoise, 494 Broadway, San Francisco, CA 94133 (☎800-867-8647 or 415-956-7500; www.greentortoise.com; tortoise@greentortoise.com), offers a more slow-paced, whimsical alternative to straightforward transportation. Green Tortoise's communal "hostels on wheels"—remodeled diesel buses done up for living and eating on the road—traverse the US on aptly named Adventure Tours. Prices include transportation, sleeping space on the bus, and tours of the regions through which you pass, often including such treats as hot springs and farm stays. Meals are prepared communally and incur an additional food charge. Cross-country trips run February to October between Boston or New York City and San Francisco, Los Angeles, or Seattle (14 days; $429, plus $131). Prepare for an earthy trip; buses have no toilets and little privacy. Reserve one to two months in advance; deposits ($100) are generally required. Many trips have space available at departure. Reservations can be made over the phone or through the web.

BY CAR

ROAD CONDITIONS. Both **Oregon** (☎800-977-6368 or 503-588-2941; www.tripcheck.com) and **Washington** (☎800-695-7623 or 206-368-4499; www.smarttrek.org) have comprehensive web sites with live traffic cameras and up-to-date reports on construction and snow conditions in mountain passes. In **British Columbia,** check the web site www.th.gov.bc.ca/th. The site has links to road conditions in **Alberta** and the **Yukon** as well.

Carry emergency **food and water** if there's a chance you may be stranded in a remote area. A cell phone is the perfect companion on a road trip, but beware of spotty coverage in rural areas. Always have plenty of **gas** and check road conditions ahead of time (see **Road Conditions,** below), particularly during winter. The huge travel distances of North America will require more gas than you might at first expect. To burn less fuel, make sure your tires have enough air.

Be sure to **buckle up**—seat belts are required by law in almost every region of the US and Canada. The **speed limit in the US** varies considerably from region to region and road to road. Most urban highways have a limit of 55 mph (88km per hr.), while the limit on rural routes ranges from 60-80 mph (97-128km per hr.). The **speed limit in Canada** is generally 50km per hr. in cities and towns, and 80-110km per hr. (50-68 mph) on highways.

DRIVING PERMITS

If you do not have a license issued by a US state or Canadian province or territory, you might want an **International Driving Permit (IDP).** While the US allows you to drive with a foreign license for up to a year and Canada allows it for six months, the IDP may facilitate things with police if your license is not in English. You must carry your home license with your IDP at all times. It is valid for a year and must be issued in the country of your license, and you must be 18 to obtain one.

Australia: Contact your local Royal Automobile Club (RAC) or the National Royal Motorist Association (NRMA) if in NSW or the ACT (☎08 9421 4444; www.rac.com.au/travel). Permits AUS$15.

Ireland: Contact the nearest Automobile Association (AA) office or write to the UK address below. Permits EUR€5. The Irish Automobile Association, 23 Suffolk St., Rockhill, Blackrock, Co. Dublin (☎01 677 9481), honors most foreign automobile club memberships (24hr. breakdown and road service ☎800 667 788; toll-free in Ireland).

New Zealand: Contact your local Automobile Association (AA) or their main office at Auckland Central, 99 Albert St. (☎ 9 377 4660; www.nzaa.co.nz). Permits NZ$10.

South Africa: Contact the Travel Services Department of the Automobile Association of South Africa at P.O. Box 596, 2000 Johannesburg (☎11 799 1400; fax 799 1410; http://aasa.co.za). Permits ZAR28.50.

UK: To visit your local AA Shop, contact the **AA Headquarters** (☎0870 600 0371), or write to: The Automobile Association, International Documents, Fanum House, Erskine, Renfrewshire PA8 6BW. For more info, see www.theaa.co.uk. Permits UK£4.

AUTO CLUBS

Membership in an auto club, which provides free emergency road-side assistance 24 hours per day, is an important investment for anyone planning to drive on their vacation. AAA and CAA have reciprocal agreements, so a membership in either is good for road service in Canada and America.

American Automobile Association (AAA). (Emergency road service ☎800-222-4357) Offers free trip-planning services, road maps, guidebooks, 24hr. emergency road service anywhere in the US, limited free towing, commission-free traveler's checks from American Express with over 1,000 offices scattered across the country. Discounts on Hertz car rental (5-20%), Amtrak tickets (10%), and various motel chains and theme parks. AAA has reciprocal agreements with auto associations of many other countries, which often provide you with full benefits while in the US. Membership hovers between $50-60 for the first year and less for renewals and additional family members; call ☎800-564-6222 to sign up.

Canadian Automobile Association (CAA). (Emergency road service ☎800-222-4357) 1145 Hunt Club Rd. #200, Ottawa, ON K1V 0Y3. Affiliated with AAA, the CAA provides nearly identical membership benefits. Basic membership is CDN$63 and CDN$32 for associates; call ☎800-564-6222 to sign up.

Mobil Auto Club. (Information ☎800-621-5581; emergency service ☎800-323-5880) 200 N. Martingale Rd., Schaumbourg, IL 60174. Benefits include locksmith reimbursement, towing, roadside service, and car-rental discounts. $7 per month covers you and another driver.

RENTING

Car rental agencies fall into two categories: national companies with hundreds of branches, and local agencies that serve only one city or region. National chains usually allow you to pick up a car in one city and drop it off in another (for a hefty charge, sometimes in excess of $1000), and by calling their toll-free numbers, you can reserve a reliable car anywhere in the country. Generally, airport branches have more expensive rates. All branches except Hertz charge those aged 21-24 an additional fee, but policies and prices vary from agency to agency. If you're 21 or older and have a major credit card in your name, you may be able to rent where the minimum age would otherwise rule you out.

Alamo (☎800-462-52663; www.alamo.com.)

Enterprise (☎800-736-8222; www.enterprise.com.)

Dollar (☎800-800-4000; www.dollar.com.)

Thrifty (☎800-367-2277; www.thrifty.com.)

Budget (☎800-527-0700; www.budget.com.)

Hertz (☎800-654-3131; www.hertz.com.)

Most rental packages offer unlimited mileage, although some allow you a certain number of miles free before the charge of $0.25-0.40 per mile takes effect. Quoted rates do not include gas or tax, so ask for the total cost before handing over the credit card; many large firms have added airport surcharges not covered by the designated fare. Return the car with a full tank unless you sign up for a fuel option plan that stipulates otherwise. And when dealing with any car rental company, be sure to ask whether the price includes insurance against theft and collision. There may be an additional charge for a **collision and damage waiver (CDW),** which usually comes to about $12-15 per day. Major credit cards (including MasterCard and American Express) will sometimes cover the CDW if you use their card to rent a car; call your credit card company for specifics.

Bolder travelers to the Pacific Northwest will want to access some areas that are simply not accessible without a four-wheel drive (4WD) vehicle. If you plan on off-roading it, make sure the vehicle you rent can handle the strain; don't endanger yourself in the interest of saving a few bucks. Cheaper cars tend to be less reliable and harder to handle on difficult terrain, and less expensive 4WD vehicles in particular tend to be more top heavy, making them more dangerous when navigating particularly bumpy roads.

DRIVING PRECAUTIONS. When traveling in the summer, bring substantial amounts of **water** (a suggested 5L of water per person per day) for drinking. If radiator fluid is steaming, turn off the car for 30min.—never pour water over the engine to cool it. If you plan to drive in snow, you should also carry a **shovel, traction mats** (burlap sacks or car floor mats make a good substitute in a bind), and **sand** or **kitty litter.** For long drives to unpopulated areas, register with police before beginning the trek, and again upon arrival at the destination. Check with the local automobile club for details. When traveling for long distances, make sure tires are in good repair and have enough air, and get good maps. A **compass** and a **car manual** can also be very useful. You should always carry a **spare tire** and **jack, jumper cables, extra oil, flares, a torch (flashlight),** and **heavy blankets** (in case your car breaks down at night or in the winter). If you don't know how to **change a tire,** learn before heading out, especially if you are planning on traveling in deserted areas. Blowouts on dirt roads are exceedingly common. If you do have a breakdown, **stay with your car;** if you wander off, there's less likelihood trackers will find you. **Sleeping in a vehicle parked on the highway or in the city is extremely dangerous**—even the most dedicated budget traveler should not consider it an option.

CAR INSURANCE

Some credit cards cover standard insurance. If you rent, lease, or borrow a car, and you are not from the US or Canada, you will need a **green card,** or **International Insurance Certificate,** to certify that you have liability insurance and that it applies abroad. Green cards can be obtained at car rental agencies, car dealerships (for those leasing cars), some travel agents, and some border crossings.

BY BICYCLE

Before you rush onto the bike paths of the Pacific Northwest, remember to make a few preparations. **Bike helmets** are required by law in most of the region and are essential safety gear. A good helmet will cost about $40 to buy; get help to ensure a correct fit. A white headlight and red taillight (and not just reflectors) are likewise both required and indispensable. **Anybody's Bike Book** ($12) provides vital info on repair and maintenance during long-term rides.

Bikeways Local Network (www.bikeways.com/maps2/mapsframe.htm). A compilation of road and cycling maps in British Columbia. Key in route planning.

The Bicycling Visitor's Guide to Seattle (www.cascade.org/visitors_guide.html). Bike routes and information on cycling in and around Seattle.

Oregon Department of Transportation (☎503-986-3556; www.odot.state.or.us/techserv/bikewalk). *Oregon Bicycling Guide* and *Oregon Coast Bike Route Map* outline bike routes and campgrounds. (Free; order phone.)

Adventure Cycling Association, P.O. Box 8308-P, Missoula, MT 59807 (☎800-755-2453 or 406-721-1776; fax 721-8754; www.adv-cycling.org). A national, nonprofit organization that maps long-distance routes and organizes bike tours for members. Membership $30 in the US, CDN$35 in Canada, US$45 overseas.

The Canadian Cycling Association, 702-2197 Riverside Drive, Ottawa, ON K1H 7X3 (☎613-248-1353; www.canadian-cycling.com). Sells maps, books, and guides to regions of Canada and the Pacific Coast. Pick up *The Canadian Cycling Association's Complete Guide to Bicycle Touring in Canada* (CDN$24).

BY FERRY

Along the Pacific Coast, ferries are an exhilarating and often unavoidable way to travel. Ferry travel can become quite expensive, however, if you bring a car along. The web site www.ferrytravel.com provides schedules for **Washington State Ferries, BC Ferries,** and seven independent companies. Information about fares, reservations, vehicles, and schedules often varies with the season. Consult each ferry company when constructing your itinerary in order to clear up any additional questions before finalizing your plans.

BC Ferries (☎888-223-3779 in BC, 250-386-3431 outside BC; fax 381-5452; www.bcferries.bc.ca/ferries). Passenger and vehicle ferry service throughout coastal BC. Service is frequent and reservations are recommended on the longer routes through the **Inside Passage** and **Discovery Coast Passage,** and to the **Queen Charlotte Islands.** Heavy traffic on weekends, particularly in the summer.

Black Ball Transport, Inc. (in Victoria ☎250-386-2202, fax 386-2207; in Port Angeles ☎360-457-4491, fax 457-4493; www.northolympic.com/coho). 2-4 ferries daily between **Port Angeles** and **Victoria.** 90min. $7.50 each way, car and driver $29.50, motorcycle and driver $17.50. Bicycles $3.50 extra. Reservations not accepted.

Victoria Clipper, 2701 Alaskan Way, Pier 69, Seattle, WA 98121 (☎800-888-2535, in Seattle 206-448-5000, in Victoria 250-382-8100; www.victoriaclipper.com). Daily passenger service between **Seattle, WA** and **Victoria, BC.** 2-3hr. $66 one-way, round-trip $79-109 (order 14 days in advance for best prices); bike $10 each way.

Washington State Ferries, 801 Alaskan Way, Seattle, WA 98104 (in Seattle ☎206-464-6400 or in Victoria 250-381-1554; www.wsdot.wa.gov/ferries). Ferries to **Sidney, BC,** and throughout **Puget Sound.** No reservations, except for travel to the **San Juan Islands** or **British Columbia.** Service is frequent, but traffic is heavy—especially in summer, when waits of over an hour to board a ferry are not uncommon. Fares fluctuate but stay reasonable. Bikes $10.

BY THUMB

Let's Go urges you to consider the risks and disadvantages of hitchhiking before thumbing it. Hitching means entrusting your life to a stranger who happens to stop beside you on the road. While this may be comparatively safe in some areas of Europe and Australia, it is **NOT** in most of North America. We do **NOT** recommend it. Don't put yourself in a situation where hitching is the only option.

That said, if you decide to hitchhike, there are precautions you should take. **Women traveling alone should never hitch in the United States.** Refuse a ride if you feel in any way uncomfortable with the driver. If at all threatened or intimidated, ask to be let out no matter how uncompromising the road looks. Have a **back-up plan** in case you get stranded or face an emergency. Carrying a cellular phone for emergency use is a good idea, although coverage is spotty in some isolated areas. In rural areas, hitching is reportedly less risky than in urban areas. Many people hitchhike in the North, but it is not unusual to get stranded on a sparsely traveled route. All states prohibit hitchhiking while standing on the roadway itself or behind a freeway entrance sign; hitchers more commonly find rides near intersections where many cars converge and well-lit areas where drivers can see their prospective rider and stop safely. Hitchers riding across the **USA-Canada border** should be prepared for a series of queries about citizenship, insurance, contraband, and finances, and for an auto inspection. Walking across the border avoids the hassle.

SPECIFIC CONCERNS

WOMEN TRAVELERS

Women exploring on their own inevitably face some additional safety concerns, but it's easy to be adventurous without taking undue risks. If you are concerned, consider staying in hostels which offer single rooms that lock from the inside or in religious organizations with rooms for women only. Stick to centrally located accommodations and avoid solitary late-night treks or metro rides.

Always carry extra money for a phone call, bus, or taxi. We can't repeat it enough: **Hitchhiking** is never safe for lone women, or even for two women traveling together. When on overnight or long train rides, if there is no women-only compartment, choose one occupied by women or couples. Look as if you know where you're going and approach older women or couples for directions if you're lost or uncomfortable. Generally, the less you look like a tourist, the better off you'll be. Dress conservatively, especially in rural areas. Trying to fit in can be effective, but dressing to the style of an obviously different culture may cause you to be ill at ease and a conspicuous target. Wearing a conspicuous **wedding band** may help prevent unwanted overtures. Your best answer to verbal harassment is no answer at all; feigning deafness, sitting motionless, and staring straight ahead at nothing in particular will do a world of good that reactions usually don't achieve.

For general information about being a female traveler, contact the National Organization for Women (NOW), 733 15th St. NW, Fl. 2, Washington, DC 20005 (☎202-628-8669; www.now.org), which has branches across the US.

TRAVELING ALONE

There are many benefits to traveling alone, including independence and greater interaction with locals. On the other hand, any solo traveler is a more vulnerable target of harassment and street theft. As a lone traveler, try not to stand out as a tourist, look confident, and be especially careful in deserted or very crowded areas. If questioned, never admit that you are traveling alone. Maintain regular contact with someone at home who knows your itinerary. For more tips, pick up *Traveling Solo* by Eleanor Berman (Globe Pequot Press, US$17) or subscribe to **Connecting: Solo Travel Network,** 689 Park Road, Unit 6, Gibsons, BC V0N 1V7, Canada (☎604-886-9099; www.cstn.org; membership US$35). **Travel Companion Exchange,** P.O. Box 833, Amityville, NY 11701, USA (☎631-454-0880, or in the US 800-392-1256; www.whytravelalone.com; US$48), will link solo travelers with companions with similar travel habits and interests.

OLDER TRAVELERS

Senior citizens are eligible for a wide range of discounts on transportation, museums, movies, theaters, concerts, restaurants, and accommodations. If you don't see a senior citizen price listed, ask, and you may be delightfully surprised. The books *No Problem! Worldwise Tips for Mature Adventurers*, by Janice Kenyon (Orca Book Publishers; US$16) and *Unbelievably Good Deals and Great Adventures That You Absolutely Can't Get Unless You're Over 50*, by Joan Rattner Heilman (NTC/Contemporary Publishing; US$13) are both excellent resources. For more information, contact one of the following organizations:

ElderTreks, 597 Markham St., Toronto, ON M6G 2L7 (☎800-741-7956; www.eldertreks.com). Adventure travel programs for the 50+ traveler.

Elderhostel, 11 Ave. de Lafayette, Boston, MA 02111 (☎877-426-8056; www.elderhostel.org). Organizes 1- to 4-week "educational adventures."

The Mature Traveler, P.O. Box 15791, Sacramento, CA 95852 (☎800-460-6676). Deals, discounts, and travel packages for the 50+ traveler. Subscription$30.

Walking the World, P.O. Box 1186, Fort Collins, CO 80522 (☎800-340-9255; www.walkingtheworld.com). Organizes trips for 50+ travelers.

BISEXUAL, GAY, & LESBIAN TRAVELERS

American cities are generally accepting of all sexualities, and thriving gay and lesbian communities can be found in most cosmopolitan areas. Most college towns are gay-friendly as well. However, homophobia can still be encountered almost anywhere. The more rural you get, the more rampant it is likely to be. Listed below are contact organizations, mail-order bookstores, and publishers that offer materials addressing some specific concerns. **Out and About** (www.planetout.com) offers a bi-weekly newsletter addressing travel concerns and a comprehensive site addressing gay travel concerns.

Gay's the Word, 66 Marchmont St., London WC1N 1AB, UK (☎20 7278 7654; www.gaystheword.co.uk). The largest gay and lesbian bookshop in the UK, with both fiction and non-fiction titles. Mail-order service available.

Giovanni's Room, 1145 Pine St., Philadelphia, PA 19107, USA (☎215-923-2960; www.queerbooks.com). An international lesbian/feminist and gay bookstore with mail-order service (carries many of the publications listed below).

International Lesbian and Gay Association (ILGA), 81 rue Marché-au-Charbon, B-1000 Brussels, Belgium (☎+32 2 502 2471; www.ilga.org). Provides political information, such as homosexuality laws of individual countries.

ESSENTIALS

TRAVELERS WITH DISABILITIES

US federal law dictates that all public buildings must be handicapped-accessible, and recent laws governing building codes have made disabled access more the norm than the exception. Businesses, transportation companies, national parks, and public services must assist the disabled in using their facilities. However, traveling with a disability still requires planning and flexibility.

Those with disabilities should inform airlines and hotels of their disabilities when making reservations; some time may be needed to prepare special accommodations. Call ahead to restaurants, museums, and other facilities to find out if they are handicapped-accessible. **Guide dog owners** should inquire as to the quarantine policies of each destination country.

FURTHER READING.

Spartacus International Gay Guide 2002-2003. Bruno Gmunder Verlag (US$33).

Damron Men's Guide, Damron Road Atlas, Damron's Accommodations, and *The Women's Traveller*. Damron Travel Guides (US$14-19). For more info, call ☎800-462-6654 or visit www.damron.com.

Ferrari Guides' Gay Travel A to Z, Ferrari Guides' Men's Travel in Your Pocket, and *Ferrari Guides' Inn Places.* Ferrari Publications (US$16-20). Purchase the guides online at www.ferrariguides.com.

Gayellow Pages USA/Canada, Frances Green. Gayellow pages (US$16). They also publish smaller regional editions. Visit Gayellow pages online at www.gayellowpages.com.

In the US, both Amtrak and major airlines will accommodate disabled passengers if notified at least 72 hours in advance. Amtrak offers a 15% discount to physically disabled travelers (☎800-872-7245,TDD/TTY 800-523-6590).

If you are planning to visit a national park or attraction in the US run by the National Park Service, obtain a free **Golden Access Passport,** which is available at all park entrances and from federal offices whose functions relate to land, forests, or wildlife. The Passport entitles disabled travelers and their families to free park admission and provides a 50% discount on all campsite and parking fees.

USEFUL ORGANIZATIONS

Mobility International USA (MIUSA), P.O. Box 10767, Eugene, OR 97440, USA (☎541-343-1284, voice and TDD; www.miusa.org). Sells *A World of Options: A Guide to International Educational Exchange, Community Service, and Travel for Persons with Disabilities* (US$35).

Society for the Advancement of Travel for the Handicapped (SATH), 347 Fifth Ave., #610, New York, NY 10016, USA (☎212-447-7284; www.sath.org). An advocacy group that publishes free travel information and the travel magazine *OPEN WORLD* (US$18, free for members). Annual membership US$45, students and seniors US$30.

TOUR AGENCIES

Directions Unlimited, 123 Green Ln., Bedford Hills, NY 10507, USA (☎800-533-5343). Books individual and group vacations for the physically disabled; not an info service.

The Guided Tour Inc., 7900 Old York Rd., #114B, Elkins Park, PA 19027, USA (☎800-783-5841; www.guidedtour.com). Organizes travel programs for persons with developmental and physical challenges in the US and Canada.

MINORITY TRAVELERS

Racial and ethnic minorities sometimes face blatant and, more often, subtle discrimination and/or harassment, although regions in the US and Canada differ drastically in their general attitudes toward race relations. Verbal harassment is now less common than unfair pricing, false information on accommodations, or inexcusably slow or unfriendly service at restaurants. The best way to deal with such encounters is to remain calm and report individuals to a supervisor, and establishments to the Better Business Bureau for the region (the operator will provide local listings). Contact the police in extreme situations. *Let's Go* always welcomes reader input regarding discriminating establishments.

In larger cities, African-Americans can usually consult chapters of the Urban League and the **National Association for the Advancement of Colored People (NAACP)** (www.naacp.org) for info on events of interest to African-Americans.

TRAVELERS WITH CHILDREN

Family vacations often require that you slow your pace, and always require that you plan ahead. If you rent a car, make sure the rental company provides a car seat for younger children. **Be sure that your child carries some sort of ID** in case of an emergency or in case he or she gets lost. Finding a private place for **breast feeding** is often a problem while traveling, so plan accordingly.

Museums, tourist attractions, accommodations, and restaurants often offer discounts for children. Children under two generally fly for 10% of the adult airfare on international flights (this does not necessarily include a seat). International fares are usually discounted 25% for children from two to 11.

For more information about traveling with children of all ages, consult one of the following books:

Backpacking with Babies & Small Children, Goldie Silverman. Wilderness Press (US$10).

How to take Great Trips with Your Kids, Sanford and Jane Portnoy. Harvard Common Press (US $10).

Have Kid, Will Travel: 101 Survival Strategies for Vacationing With Babies and Young Children, Claire and Lucille Tristram. Andrews McMeel Publishing (US$9).

Kidding Around Portland. Deborah Cuyle (US$8).

Adventuring with Children: An Inspirational Guide to World Travel and the Outdoors, Nan Jeffrey. Avalon House Publishing (US$15).

Trouble Free Travel with Children, Vicki Lansky. Book Peddlers (US$9).

DIETARY CONCERNS

Vegetarians should have no problems getting by in the Pacific Northwest. *Let's Go* consistently tries to list vegetarian-friendly establishments and grocery stores. The North American Vegetarian Society, P.O. Box 72, Dolgeville, NY 13329 (☎518-568-7970; www.navs-online.org), publishes information about vegetarian travel, including *Transformative Adventures, a Guide to Vacations and Retreats* (US$15), and the *Vegetarian Journal's Guide to Natural Food Restaurants in the US and Canada* (US$12). For more information, visit your local bookstore or health food store, and consult *The Vegetarian Traveler: Where to Stay if You're Vegetarian*, by Jed and Susan Civic (Larson Publications; US$16).

Travelers who keep kosher should contact synagogues in larger cities for information on kosher restaurants. Your own synagogue or college Hillel should have access to lists of Jewish institutions across the nation. If you are strict in your observance, you may have to prepare your own food on the road, especially as the towns you visit become more remote. A good resource is the *Jewish Travel Guide*, by Michael Zaidner (Vallentine Mitchell; US$17).

OTHER RESOURCES

Listed below are books and web sites that can serve as jumping off points for your own research beyond what *Let's Go* can offer.

TRAVEL PUBLISHERS & BOOKSTORES

Hippocrene Books, Inc., 171 Madison Ave., New York, NY 10016, USA (☎718-454-2366; www.hippocrenebooks.com). Publishes foreign language dictionaries and language learning guides.

Hunter Publishing, 470 W. Broadway, Fl. 2, South Boston, MA 02127, USA (☎617-269-0700; www.hunterpublishing.com). Has an extensive catalog of travel guides and diving and adventure travel books.

Rand McNally, P.O. Box 7600, Chicago, IL 60680, USA (☎847-329-8100; www.randmcnally.com), publishes road atlases.

Adventurous Traveler Bookstore, P.O. Box 2221, Williston, VT 05495, USA (☎800-282-3963; www.adventuroustraveler.com).

Bon Voyage!, 2069 W. Bullard Ave., Fresno, CA 93711, USA (☎800-995-9716, from abroad 559-447-8441; www.bon-voyage-travel.com). They specialize in Europe but have titles pertaining to other regions as well. Free newsletter.

Travel Books & Language Center, Inc., 4437 Wisconsin Ave. NW, Washington, D.C. 20016, USA (☎800-220-2665; www.bookweb.org/bookstore/travelbks/). Over 60,000 titles from around the world.

WORLD WIDE WEB

Almost every aspect of budget travel is accessible via the web. Within 10 minutes at the keyboard, you can make a reservation at a hostel, get advice on travel hotspots from other travelers who have just returned from the Pacific Northwest, or find out exactly how much a train from Portland to Seattle costs.

Listed here are some budget travel sites to start off your surfing; other relevant web sites are listed throughout the book. Because website turnover is high, use search engines (such as www.google.com) to strike out on your own.

ART OF BUDGET TRAVEL

How to See the World, www.artoftravel.com. A compendium of great travel tips, on everything from cheap flights to self defense to interacting with local culture.

Rec. Travel Library: www.travel-library.com. A fantastic set of links for general information and personal travelogues.

Lycos, cityguide.lycos.com. General introductions to cities and regions throughout the US and Canada, with by links to applicable histories, news, and local tourism sites.

INFORMATION ON THE PACIFIC NORTHWEST

CIA World Factbook, www.odci.gov/cia/publications/factbook/index.html. Tons of vital statistics on the geography, government, economy, and people of the US and Canada.

MyTravelGuide, www.mytravelguide.com. Country overviews, with everything from history to transportation to live web cam coverage of the US and Canada.

Geographia, www.geographia.com. Highlights and culture of the US and Canada.

Atevo Travel, www.atevo.com/guides/destinations. Detailed introductions, travel tips, and suggested itineraries.

World Travel Guide, www.travel-guides.com/navigate/world.asp. Helpful practical info.

PlanetRider, www.planetrider.com. For the US and Canada, this website has a subjective list of links to the "best" websites covering regional culture and tourist attractions.

WWW.LETSGO.COM Our website, www.letsgo.com, now includes introductory chapters from all our guides and a wealth of information on a monthly featured estination. As always, our website also has info about our books, a travel forum buzzing with stories and tips, and additional links that will help you make the most of a trip to the Pacific Northwest

. hike through the rugged landscape of the 'acific Northwest offers an affordable and xhilarating travel experience unlike any ther. Some equipment tips:

ootwear: Your feet are the single-most important omponent of your total hike experience. Appro-riate hiking footwear provides stability and upport for your feet and ankles while protecting nem from the abuses of the environment. Mid-veight hiking boots are a good all-around hoice. Stability over uneven ground is nhanced by a stiffer sole and higher ankle col-ar—good for travel along rugged trails. A good t is the most important feature: your toes hould not hit the front of your shoe when you're oing downhill, your heel should be locked in lace inside the shoe, and there should be a min-num of extra space around your foot. When lac-ng, leave the laces over the top of your foot nstep) loose but tie them tightly across the nkle to lock the heel down. All-leather footwear asts longer, has a good deal of natural water esistance, and will mold to your feet over time. 'ootwear made from synthetic materials or a abric/leather combination are lighter and heaper, but not as durable. Some boots have Gore-Tex, making them waterproof (but less reathable). Expect to pay $100-200 for a good air of boots. Blisters are almost always caused y friction due to repetitive foot movement (slip-age) inside the shoe. Buying shoes or boots that t properly and taking a minimum of 1-2 weeks o break them in will make a huge difference in lister prevention. If the heel is slipping and blis-ering, try tightening the laces across the ankle.)amp feet blister more easily: avoid moisture-etaining cotton socks and try wearing a fast-vicking synthetic liner sock if you have sweaty eet. If you notice a blister developing, stop nmediately and apply adhesive padding (such s moleskin) over the problem spot.

urvival: A map of the area and a simple compass re critical for not getting lost. Carry at least 1L f water (2L is preferable) and drink regularly to void cramps and dehydration. Always be pre-ared for the unexpected night out. Carrying vaterproof matches, a headlamp/flashlight, xtra clothes, and extra food will keep you varm and comfortable. A whistle is a powerful distress signal and can save your life if you become immobilized. Bring a basic First Aid Kit: an over-the-counter painkiller; a 2-4" wide elastic bandage for wrapping sprained ankles, knees, and joints; and bleeding wound treatment (antibiotic ointment, sterile gauze, adhesive and wrap-around bandages, and medical tape).

Pack: The best packs will have a padded waist belt that allows you to carry pack weight on your hips and lower body rather than shoulders. When trying on packs, loosen the shoulder straps, position the waist belt so that the belt rests on top of your hips, and then tighten the shoulder straps. Ideally, the straps will attach to the pack slightly above (and off) the shoulders, preventing the pack weight from being borne by the easily-fatigued muscles of your shoulders and back. For day hikes, a pack with a capacity of 1-2000 cu. in. (16-32L) is recommended.

Clothing/Rain Gear: Go synthetic. Cotton clothing absorbs a lot of moisture and dries slowly, leaving a wet layer next to your skin which conducts heat away from your body, increasing the risk for hypothermia, especially in cool, windy conditions. Nylon and polyester are the most common synthetic materials, absorb little moisture, and dry extremely fast. While waterproof rain gear does not breathe and traps your sweat next to your body while you hike, it's the cheapest—you should be able to find a jacket for $25-50. When shopping, don't buy a water-resistant nylon windbreaker. Fully waterproof nylon jackets will have an impervious coating on the inside, with all the seams taped. Traditional rubber rainwear also works well and is cheaper, but heavy and bulky. A poncho is the bare-bones option, costs very little (less than $20), is lightweight and compact, but will not keep you dry in a heavy downpour. Waterproof/breathable rain gear is impervious to liquid water, but allows water vapor (sweat) to pass through to the outside. In hot, humid conditions, waterproof/breathable jackets don't work. Gore-Tex is still considered the best waterproof/breathable barrier, but there are a variety of similar products which perform admirably. A laminate barrier is a preferable coating, which can rub off with use. Expect to pay a lot for the comfort these jackets provide ($100-300+).

Matt Heid has researched for Let's Go *in Alaska, the Yukon, Europe, and New Zealand. He is also the author of* 101 Hikes in Northern California *and* Camping and Backpacking the San Francisco Bay Area *(both available from Wilderness Press).*

ALTERNATIVES TO TOURISM

When we started out in 1961, 1.7 million people in the world were traveling internationally; in 2002, nearly 700 million trips were made, projected to be up to a billion by 2010. Nearly 1.5 million tourists came to the Pacific Northwest in 2002, continuing the steady growth in the number of visitors each year. The dramatic rise in tourism has created an interdependence between the economy, environment, and culture of many destinations and the tourists they host, particularly in a region as sensitive and dependent upon its surroundings.

Two rising trends in sustainable travel are ecotourism and community-based tourism. **Ecotourism** focuses on the conservation of natural habitats and using them to build up the economy without exploitation or overdevelopment. **Community-based tourism** aims to channel tourist dollars into the local economy, by emphasizing tours and cultural programs that are run by members of the host community and that often benefit disadvantaged groups.

For many rural towns in the Pacific Northwest, the influx of visitors each summer has become a yearly economic event as regular as the salmon runs, generating jobs and a source of income. Yet others see a slow erosion of local culture in the wake of these tourists, as national corporations trickle in to make money off of the region's tourism boom. Conservationists are concerned over the impact of increased use on once-isolated national parks, forests, and wildlife refuges. Native cultures too, hold an ambiguous outlook upon the impacts of tourism. With the opening up of rural villages as a travel destination, natives gain economic benefits from locally owned tour operations. At the same time, they worry about the overuse of subsistence-use land and the access of subsistence harvests by non-natives, the replacement of local travel businesses with larger, resource-rich companies from out of town, and the potential loss of traditional culture.

Those looking to **volunteer** in the efforts to resolve these issues have many options. You can participate in projects from maintaining trails in old-growth forests of spurce to constructing community centers in rural villages, either on an infrequent basis or as the main component of your trip. Later in this section, we recommend organizations that can help you find the opportunities that best suit your interests, whether you're looking to pitch in for a day or a year.

There are any number of other ways that you can integrate yourself with the communities you visit. **Studying** at a college or language program is one option. Many travelers also structure their trips by the **work** that they can do along the way—either odd jobs as they go, or full-time stints in cities where they plan to stay for some time. Other possibilities abound in the major cities, such as Portland (OR), Seattle (WA), and Vancouver (BC). For more on volunteering, studying, and working in the Pacific Northwest and beyond, consult Let's Go's alternatives to tourism website, **www.beyondtourism.com**.

VOLUNTEERING

Though the US and Canada are considered wealthy in worldwide terms, there is no shortage of aid organizations to benefit the very real issues the region does face. Like all places in the world, it must contend with poverty and hunger, but also problems such as conservation and Native American/First Nations issues.

A NEW PHILOSOPHY OF TRAVEL

We at *Let's Go* have watched the growth of the 'ignorant tourist' stereotype with dismay, knowing that the majority of travelers care passionately about the state of the communities and environments they explore—but also knowing that even conscientious tourists can inadvertently damage natural wonders, rich cultures, and impoverished communities. We believe the philosophy of **sustainable travel** is among the most important travel tips we could impart to our readers, to help guide fellow backpackers and on-the-road philanthropists. By staying aware of the needs and troubles of local communities, today's travelers can be a powerful force in preserving and restoring this fragile world.

Working against the negative consequences of irresponsible tourism is much simpler than it might seem; it is often self-awareness, rather than self-sacrifice, that makes the biggest difference. Simply by trying to spend responsibly and conserve local resources, all travelers can positively impact the places they visit. Let's Go has partnered with **BEST** (**Business Enterprises for Sustainable Travel,** an affiliate of the Conference Board; see www.sustainabletravel.org), which recognizes businesses that operate based on the principles of sustainable travel. Below, they provide advice on how ordinary visitors can practice this philosophy in their daily travels, no matter where they are.

TIPS FOR CIVIC TRAVEL: HOW TO MAKE A DIFFERENCE

Travel by train when feasible. Rail travel requires only half the energy per passenger mile that planes do. On average, each of the 40,000 daily domestic air flights releases more than 1700 pounds of greenhouse gas emissions.

Use public mass transportation whenever possible; outside of cities, take advantage of group taxis or vans. Bicycles are an attractive way of seeing a community first-hand. And enjoy walking–purchase good maps of your destination and ask about on-foot touring opportunities.

When renting a car, ask whether fuel-efficient vehicles are available. Honda and Toyota produce cars that use hybrid engines powered by electricity and gasoline, thus reducing emissions of carbon dioxide. Ford Motor Company plans to introduce a hybrid fuel model by the end of 2004.

Reduce, reuse, recycle–use electronic tickets, recycle papers and bottles wherever possible, and avoid using containers made of styrofoam. Refillable water bottles and rechargable batteries both efficiently conserve expendable resources.

Be thoughtful in your purchases. Take care not to buy souvenir objects made from trees in old-growth or endangered forests, such as teak, or items made from endangered species, like ivory or tortoise jewelry. Ask whether products are made from renewable resources.

Buy from local enterprises, like street vendors. In developing countries and low-income areas, many people depend on the "informal economy" to make a living.

Be on-the-road-philanthropists. If you are inspired by the natural environment of a destination or enriched by its culture, join in preserving their integrity by making a charitable contribution to a local organization.

Spread the word. Upon your return home, tell friends and colleagues about places to visit that will benefit greatly from their tourist dollars, and reward sustainable enterprises by recommending their services. Travelers can not only introduce friends to particular vendors but also to local causes and charities that they might choose to support when they travel.

Most people who volunteer in the region do so on a short-term basis, at organizations that make use of drop-in or once-a-week volunteers. These can be found in virtually every city, and are referenced both in this section and in our town and city write-ups themselves. The best way to find opportunities that match up with your interests and schedule may be to check with organizations such as **United Way** or **Americorps** (a US version of the Peace Corps), which both work with local organizations to promote community service at the grassroots level (see below). Visit web sites such as www.planetedu.com, www.volunteermatch.com, and www.volunteerabroad.com, as well as the ones listed below to begin your search.

More intensive volunteer services may charge you a fee to participate. These costs can be surprisingly hefty (although they frequently cover airfare and most, if not all, living expenses). Most people choose to go through a parent organization that takes care of logistical details and frequently provides a group environment and support system. There are two main types of organizations—religious and non-sectarian—although there are rarely restrictions on participation for either.

ENVIRONMENT & CONSERVATION

With the Pacific Northwest's wealth of wildlife, forests, mountains, tundra, and waters, it is essential that we not only admire and enjoy nature, but also take care to maintain and pass on its pristine state. The following organizations all offer volunteer opportunities that conserve the wilds in the Pacific Northwest.

National Park Service, 1849 C St., NW, Washington, D.C., 20240 (☎202-208-6843; www.nps.gov/volunteer). **Volunteers-in-Parks** program partcipants work in National Parks and all other national lands in a range of capacities, from nature guide to maintenance. A list of parks currently seeking volunteers is on the web site. National Parks that are part of the **Artists-in-Residence** program offer a chance for artists, writers, and composers to live and work inside the park.

USDA Forest Service: Pacific NW Region, P.O. Box 3623, 333 SW First Ave., Portland, OR 97208-3623 (☎503-808-2971; www.fs.fed.us/r6). Volunteer in a range of capacities, from desk jobs to more exciting tasks in the outdoors. Flexible duration, ranging from one-time to full year; part-time or full-time. Option to live in national forest in summers. Part-time and full-time jobs also available. No fee.

Parks Canada National Volunteer Program, 25 Eddy St., 4th floor, Hull, Quebec, CA K1A 0M5 (coordinator.volunteer@pc.gc.ca; www.parkscanada.ca). The Canadian equivalent of the National Park Service accepts volunteers for parks, historical sites, and marine conservation areas. Canadian applicants should contact the specific parks in which they are interested. Foreign applicants should write to the address above or email to obtain a questionnaire. Deadline for summer and autumn placement is Dec. 1 of the preceding year; deadline for winter and spring placement is June 30.

Student Conservation Association, 689 River Rd., P.O. Box 550, Charlestown, New Hampshire 03603 (☎603-543-1700; fax 603-543-1828; www.thesca.org). Begun in Olympic National Park, the SCA allows you to live and work in public lands and other natural and cultural resources for 3-12 months. Projects include conservation, archaeology, backcountry management, forestry, and more. All expenses paid intership; possible scholarship. Contact the **SCA Northwest Office,** 1265 S. Main St., #210, Seattle, WA 98144 (☎206-324-4649, fax 324-4998).

Earthwatch, 3 Clock Tower Place, Suite 100, Box 75, Maynard, MA 01754 (☎978-461-0081; www.earthwatch.org). Places volunteers in 1-3 week research programs with scientists to promote conservation of natural environments. Average program cost $1600.

BEFORE YOU GO Before handing your money over to any volunteer or study abroad program, make sure you know exactly what you're getting into. It's wise to get the name of **previous participants** and ask them about their experience, as some programs sound much better on paper than in reality. Also, make sure the program itself is able to answer the following **questions:**

-Will you be the only person in the program? If not, what are the other participants like? How old are they? Will you interact with them?

-Is room and board included? If so, what is the arrangement?

-Is transportation included? Are there any additional expenses?

-How much free time will you have? Will you be able to travel?

-What kind of safety network is set up? Will you still be covered by your home insurance? Does the program have an emergency plan?

Yoho National Park, Box 99, Field, British Columbia, Canada VOA IGO (☎604-343-6324; http://www.worldweb.com/ParksCanada-Yoho). One of Canada's many aforementioned individual parks, Yoho offers a variety of outdoors volunteer projects. Call for information on program availability and participation fees.

ABORIGINAL ISSUES

While outsiders are not openly unwelcome in rural villages and communities, natives prefer to be aided by their own professionals, educators, and activists. Nonetheless, some programs, chiefly museums and activities centers, gladly accept volunteers. These offer a good opportunity to interact at a deeper level with native cultures, people, and history.

Visions Service Adventures, 110 N 2nd St., P.O. Box 220, Newport, PA 17074 (☎717-567-7313; www.visions-adventure.org). Summer programs immerse students into native Ahtna villages, where they participate in construction projects, outdoors adventures, and cultural exploration. Must be 14-18. $2800-3800.

Volunteer Alberta, Kahanoff Centre, 1202 Centre Street SE, #1170, Calgary, AB T2G 5A5 (☎403-266-5200 or 877-915-6336; www.volunteeralberta.ab.ca). Association of voluntary organizations throughout the province, with listings of groups and individuals looking for volunteer services in fields ranging from aboriginals to the arts.

Volunteer BC, 207 W Hastings St., #302, Vancouver, BC V6B 1H7 (☎604-873-5877; www.vcn.bc.ca/volbc). Similar to Volunteer Alberta, but for British Columbia.

COMMUNITY DEVELOPMENT

The organizations listed below are chiefly concerned with the typical urban issues. They work to alleviate poverty, feed the hungry, aid the sick, mentor the young, and other community-oriented service projects to create a healthy environment.

Americorps, 1201 New York Ave., NW, Washington, D.C., 20525 (☎202-606-5000; www.americorps.org). The domestic equivalent to America's Peace Corps, Americorps places US citizens in community development programs throughout the US for a 10 month or 1-year term. Open only to US citizens or permanent residents. Expense paid. Visit their web site to search for programs in the Pacific Northwest.

Big Brothers Big Sisters (www.bbbsa.org in the US, www.bbbsc.ca in Canada). Mentor a child in any major city in the region. Canada's organization is organized by province.

Habitat for Humanity, 500 W Intl Airport Rd., Suite E, Anchorage, AK 99518 (☎907-272-0800; www.habitat.org). A coalition dedicated toward constructing homes for the needy. Visit their website to search for other local offices in Alaska.

Northwest Harvest, P.O. Box 12272, Seattle, WA 98102 (☎206-625-0755 or 800-722-6924, fax 625-7518; www.northwestharvest.org). Washington's largest food bank (based in Seattle), providing food bank services for the entire state. Volunteers needed for everything from faxing to forklifting.

Oregon Food Bank, P.O. Box 55370, 7900 NE 33rd Dr., Portland, OR 97238-5370 (☎503-282-0555; www.oregonfoodbank.org). Similar to the WA food bank above.

Red Cross, 431 18th St., NW, Washington, D.C., 20006 (☎202-303-4498; www.redcross.org). The Red Cross aims to disturb communities as little as possible by respecting local customs while carrying out their missions. Also contact the **Canadian Red Cross** (www.redcross.ca) for more information.

United Way, 701 North Fairfax St., Alexandria, VA 22314 (☎703-836-7112; www.unitedway.org). A network of local chapters dedicated to community service. For **United Way of Canada**, visit www.unitedway.ca.

Volunteers for Peace, 1034 Tiffany Rd., Belmont., VT 05730 (☎802-259-2759; www.vfp.org). Arranges placement in American and Canadian work sites with wide range of projects. Membership required for registration. Average cost US$200-400 for 2 weeks to 4 months, depending on program.

STUDYING

Study abroad programs range from basic language and culture courses to college-level classes, often for credit. In order to choose a program that best fits your needs, you will want to research all you can before making your decision—determine costs and duration, as well as what kind of students participate in the program and what sort of accommodations are provided.

In programs that have large groups of students who speak the same language, there is a trade-off. You may feel more comfortable in the community, but you will not have the same opportunity to practice a foreign language or to befriend other international students. For accommodations, dorm life provides a better opportunity to mingle with fellow students, but there is less of a chance to experience the local scene. If you live with a family, there is a potential to build lifelong friendships with natives and to experience day-to-day life in more depth, but conditions can vary greatly from family to family.

International students studying in the US and Canada must have student visas. See **Visa Information,** p. 65, for more information. Students must prove sufficient financial support, and be in good health (see **Entrance Requirements,** p. 17).

UNIVERSITIES

If you are currently studying as an undergraduate and would like to get credit for schoolwork completed in the US or Canada, check with universities in your home country to see if they offer exchanges with particular North American schools. Most university-level study-abroad programs are meant as language and culture enrichment opportunities, and therefore are conducted in the native language of the country. Those relatively fluent in English may find it cheaper to enroll directly full-time in a university in Alaska or the Yukon, although getting college credit may be more difficult. For non-English speaking students, many colleges and schools offer English as a second language courses.

A good resource for finding programs that cater to your particular interests is www.studyabroad.com, which has links to various semester abroad programs based on a variety of critera, including desired location and focus of study. The following is a list of organizations that can help place students in university programs abroad, or have their own branch in the Pacific Northwest.

NORTH AMERICAN PROGRAMS

Association of Commonwealth Universities (ACU), John Foster House, 36 Gordon Sq., London WC1H OPF (☎+44 020 7380 6700; www.acu.ac.uk). Publishes information about Canada's Commonwealth universities.

Council on International Educational Exchange (CIEE), 7 Custom House St., 3rd floor, Portland, ME, 04101 (☎800-407-8839; www.ciee.org/study) sponsors work, volunteer, academic, and internship programs in the United States and Canada.

International Association for the Exchange of Students for Technical Experience (IAESTE), 10400 Little Patuxent Pkwy. Suite 250, Columbia, MD 21044-3519, USA (☎410-997-2200, www.aipt.org). 8- to 12-week programs in Canada for college students who have completed 2 years of technical study. US$25 application fee.

International Student Exchange Program (ISEP), 1616 P St. NW, Suite 150, Washington, D.C., 20036 (☎202-667-8027; www.isep.org). A network of over 230 universities in 35 countries, ISEP allows students of participating institutions to study afforadably internationally at member universities. Students pay their normal tuition and board to their home university and study full-time at their host school from one term to two years.

School for International Training, College Semester Abroad, Admissions, Kipling Rd., P.O. Box 676, Brattleboro, VT 05302 (☎800-336-1616, or 802-257-7751 from outside the US and Canada; www.sit.edu). Semester- and year-long programs in the US and Canada run US$10,600-13,700. Also runs the **Experiment in International Living** (☎800-345-2929; www.usexperiment.org), 3-5 week summer programs that offer high-school students cross-cultural homestays, community service, ecological adventure, and language training. Costs range US$1900-5000.

PROGRAMS IN THE PACIFIC NORTHWEST

Thanks to government subsidies, tuition at Canadian schools is generally affordable. Although foreign students pay more than Canadian citizens, the total cost can be less than half of the tuition for American schools.

Oregon and Washington have innumerable liveral arts, community, professional, and technical colleges. Unfortunately, tuition costs are high in the United States and a full course of undergraduate study entails a four-year commitment. The state university systems are usually very affordable for residents of those states, but expensive to outsiders. Community and technical colleges cost less.

Many institutions of higher learning in the Pacific Northwest belong to the **National Student Exchange**, a network of univiersities in the US, Canada, and Puerto Rico. (Check the website for a list of all participating universities.) It allows students of member institutions to spend up to one year at any other member school. Policies may vary depending on your home institution, but usually students pay the same tuition that they would at their resident university, and all credits are transferrable. (☎800-478-1823; www.nse.org.)

Association of Commonwealth Universities (ACU), John Foster House, 36 Gordon Sq., London WC1H OPF (☎+44 020 7380 6700; www.acu.ac.uk). Publishes information about Commonwealth institutions including the University of British Columbia, University of Alberta, and Athabasca University, among others.

ALTERNATIVES TO TOURISM

University of Alberta Faculty of Graduate Students and Research (FGSR), Edmonton, Alberta, Canada (see website for phone contact information and correct street address, which varies with department. http://gradfile.fgsro.ualberta.ca/international.)

University of Oregon Office of International Programs (OIP), 5209 University of Oregon. Room 330 Oregon Hall, Eugene, OR 97403-5209, USA (☎541-346-3206, http://oip.oregon.edu). International students with F-1 or J-1 visas can enroll in one of the many programs offered. Check the website for details and admissions information.

University of Washington, 1410 NE Campus Parkway, Box 355852, Seattle, Washington 98195-5852, USA. (☎206-543-9686; www.washington.edu/students/uga/in). Website offers information for international students seeking to apply. Open M-F 8am-5pm.

LANGUAGE SCHOOLS

Language schools are a good alternative to university study if you desire a deeper focus on the language or a slightly less-rigorous courseload. These programs are also good for younger high school students that might not feel comfortable with older students in a university program. Many universities offer **English as a Second Language (ESL)** classes for international or non-native speakers of English as part of its courses, though these may be limited to certain campuses. Some institutions also offer courses and degrees in the native languages of the First People of Canada and Native Americans. Some good programs include:

Oregon State University English Language Institute (ELI), 301 Snell Hall, Corvallis, OR 97331-1632, USA (☎541-737-2464; http://www.orst.edu/dept/eli). Specifically addresses the needs of both teens and adults. US$75 application fee.

University of British Columbia English Language Institute (ELI), 2121 West Mall, Vancouver, BC, Canada V6T 1Z4 (☎604-822-1555; http://www.eli.ubc.ca). Services include both long- and short-term programs; ELI can also set visiting students up with accommodations.

University of Washington International and English Language Programs, 5001 25th Ave. NE, Seattle, WA 98105, USA (☎206-543-2320; http://www.esl.washington.edu/international). Offers certificate programs for international students with the proper visa credentials. Not all classes are for credit, see website for details.

CLASSROOM OUTDOORS

Studying in the Pacific Northwest is not just about pouring over books, attending lectures, and typing away at papers. Alaska gives you the chance to learn through doing, and adventure becomes just as educational as that heavy textbook you never opened.

IslandWood, 4450 Blakely Ave. NE, Bainbridge Island, WA 98110 (☎206-855-4300; www.islandwood.org). This sustainably-designed 255-acre campus in Puget Sound provides summer and weekend programs for children and adults about nature education and community/environmental stewardship. They offer a 10-month on-site intensive teaching certification for graduate students as well as teacher training for others looking to further their skills in that field.

National Outdoor Leadership School, 284 Lincoln St., Lander, WY 82520 (☎307-332-5300; www.nols.edu). Summer sessions at their 30-acre Pacific Northwest headquarters in Conway, WA teach outdoor leadership, canoeing, kayaking, mountaineering, and backpacking. Suggested application 3 months in advance. Prices $2000-7000. Financial aid and scholarships possible. Certain colleges accept credit.

Sojourns in Nature, P.O. Box 153, Lowell, VT 05847 (☎802-744-2392; www.sojournsinnature.com). Two week programs in the outdoors provide instruction in nature photography and hands-on experience. Undergraduate credit available if accepted by students' home institutions. $2700.

WORKING

VISA & WORK PERMIT INFORMATION.

All foreign visitors are required to have a **visa** if they are planning a stay of more than 90 days (180 days for Canadians), or if they intend to work or study in the US or Canada. In addition, travelers must provide proof of intent to leave, such as a return plane ticket or an **I-94** card. To obtain a visa, contact a US embassy or consulate. Foreign students who wish to study in the US must first be admitted to a school, then apply for either an **M-1 visa** (vocational studies) or an **F-1 visa** (for students enrolled full-time in an academic or language program). Students who wish to study in Canada need a student authorization (IMM 1208) plus the appropriate tourist visa. **To obtain a visa,** contact a US or Canadian embassy or consulate. See **Essentials,** p. 17, for a list of US and Canadian consulates in English-speaking nations, and see p. 19 for more on obtaining visas. Or, check http://travel.state.gov/links.html for US listings and www.dfait-maeci.gc.ca/world/embassies/menu-en.asp for Canadian listings worldwide. **Visa extensions** are sometimes attainable with a completed I-539 form; call the Bureau of Citizenship and Immigration Service's (BCIS) forms request line (☎800-870-3676) or get it online at http://www.immigration.gov. See http://travel.state.gov/visa_services.html and www.unitedstates.gov for more information.

A **work permit** (or "green card") is also required of all foreigners planning to work in the US. Your employer must obtain this document, usually by demonstrating that you have skills that locals lack. Friends in the US can sometimes help expedite work permits or arrange work-for-accommodations exchanges. **To obtain a work permit,** fill out the I-765 form from the BCIS, follow all other instructions, and return it to your regional BCIS service center. Processing may take up to 90 days. Recent security measures have made the visa application process more rigorous, and therefore lengthy. **Apply well in advance of your travel date.** The process may seem complex, but it's critical that you go through the proper channels—the alternative is potential deportation.

As with volunteering, work opportunities tend to fall into two categories. Some travelers want longterm jobs that allow them to get to know another part of the world as a member of the community, while other travelers seek out short-term jobs to finance the next leg of their travels. In the Pacific Northwest, short-term jobs are easier and more abundant than long-term jobs. With the arrival of summer comes tourists and hundreds of tourism related jobs in hotels, lodges, tour operations, outfitters, and restaurants. Summer also brings the salmon runs, creating a huge labor demand in fishing and seafood processing, though these jobs could potentially be long-term as well. Some other long-term jobs to consider are in the service industry, one of the fastest growing industries in the state, but with comparatively low wages. Other options are in the transportation industry and business. As in the rest of America, school districts have a teacher shortage, but this is difficult as a mandatory state certification requires tests and several specified classes, and generally takes a few months or more.

All foreign visitors intending to work in the US and Canada must first obtain a work permit (see p. 65). To apply, you must first find a job and be sponsored by an employer, but several organizations such as Council Exchanges or BUNAC will help you obtain a work permit without having a job (see below).

Even if you already have a job lined up before arriving in the region, it is wise to carry at least US$1000 with you, more if you still need to find employment. Cost of living in the Pacific Northwest is expensive. Rent for a 1-bedroom apartment averages $600 but expect a wide range of values. Consider living in a tent city if only working temporarily. Seattle ranks up their with New York and San Francisco among the more expensive US cities to live in. But don't let this scare you—the region is young and growing and has plenty to offer to those adventurous at heart. Work side by side with experienced fishermen to bring in the latest run of salmon, guide kayak excursions through narrow fjords, or help run one of the region's many campgrounds. Minimum wage is around US$7.

A good option is to read the classified sections of major newspapers. In Canada, you can visit www.jobsetc.ca, which provides job listings, techniques on finding a job, advice, and various links. Another Canada-oriented possibility is **ActiJob** (☎888-907-1111; www.actijob.com), where job-hopefuls can post and update their resumes, search for employers, and browse a frequently-updated list of openings.

LONG-TERM WORK

If you're planning on spending a substantial amount of time (more than three months) working in the region, search for a job well in advance. International placement agencies are often the easiest way to find employment and obtain a work permit. **Internships,** usually for college students, are a good way to segue into working abroad, although they are often unpaid or poorly paid (many say the experience, however, is well worth it). Be wary of advertisements or companies that claim the ability to get you a job abroad for a fee—often times the same listings are available online or in newspapers, or even out of date. It's best, if going through an organization, to use one that's somewhat reputable. Some good organizations include:

Parks Canada, 25 Eddy St., 4th floor, Hull House, Quebec, CA K1A 0M5 (www.parkscanada.ca). Gives information for full-time, part-time, and seasonal jobs in the national parks of Canada. Though it has no actual listings, it directs visitors to other Canadian employment web sites. Also, visit individual national parks and ask directly.

Council Exchanges, 52 Poland St., London W1F 7AB, UK (☎44 020 7478 2000; US 800-407-8839; www.councilexchanges.org) charges a US$300-475 fee for arranging visas and short-term working authorizations (generally valid for 3-6 months) and provides extensive information on different job opportunities in the U.S. and Canada. Must be at least 18 and a full-time student.

BUNAC, 16 Bowling Green Lane, London EC1R 0QH, UK (☎020 7251 3472; US 203 264 0901; www.bunac.org). Same services as Council Exchanges, similar prices.

AU PAIR WORK

Au pairs are typically women, aged 18-27, who work as live-in nannies, caring for children and doing light housework in foreign countries in exchange for room, board, and a small spending allowance or stipend. Most former au pairs speak favorably of their experience. Drawbacks often include long hours of constantly being on-duty and the somewhat mediocre pay. Au pairs in the US can generally expect to receive $140 in spending money every week, as well as $500 toward studying at a local college or institution. Much of the au pair experience depends on the family you're placed with. Try one of the following agencies: **Childcare International, Ltd.,** Trafalgar House, Grenville Pl., London NW7 3SA (☎+44 020 8906 3116; fax 8906-3461; www.childint.co.uk); **InterExchange,** 161 Sixth Ave., New York, NY 10013 (☎212-924-0446; fax 924-0575; www.interexchange.org); **Au Pair in America,** 37 Queen's Gate, London SW7 5HR, UK (☎+44 020 7581 7322; fax 7581 7345; www.aupairinamerica.co.uk).

SHORT-TERM WORK

Traveling for long periods of time can get expensive; therefore, many travelers try their hand at odd jobs for a few weeks at a time to make some extra cash to carry them through another month or two of touring around. Potential odd jobs you might try your hand at include working at a small cafe or restaurant, adventure outfitters, tour operators, or most popularly, working in a fish cannery or processing plant. Another favorite is to work at a hostel in exchange for free or discounted room and/or board. Most often, these short-term jobs are found by word of mouth. Many places are always eager for help, even if only temporary. *Let's Go* tries to list temporary jobs when possible; look in the practical information sections of larger cities, or check out the list below for some short-term jobs in popular destinations.

NW Hospitality.net (www.nwhospitality.net). An online database of hospitality (mostly restaurant) jobs in the region.

SummerJobs.com (www.summerjobs.com) lets you search by location for jobs all over the Pacific Northwest.

Resort Jobs, (www.resortjobs.com). Not only seasonal listings for the tourist season, but a few long term jobs as well in resorts and other tourism-oriented establishments.

International Association for the Exchange of Students for Technical Experience (IAESTE), 10400 Little Patuxent Pkwy. Suite 250, Columbia, MD 21044, (☎410-997-3068; www.iaeste.org). Arranges 8-12-week programs in the US and Canada for college students in technical and scientific majors. US$25 application fee.

ECO-TOURS

Many tour operators and agencies will try to sell you their travel packages, convincing you that theirs is the best way to see the region. However, these companies may not always be concerned with eco-tourism and giving back to locals. Before you sign up with any of them, check their business policies and their guidelines. Below are a few good resources to consult when planning a community-friendly trip. Listed also are outfitters who run tours specifically designed to comply with the principles of eco-tourism and sustainable travel.

BC Wilderness Tourism Association, P.O. Box 1483, Gibsons, BC V0N 1V0 (☎604-886-8755; www.wilderness-tourism.bc.ca). Before your trip, visit their web site for listings of locally-run tourist services and businesses in BC and beyond that focus on eco-tourism and sustainable travel. Search by keyword or location.

G.A.P. Adventures, 19 Duncan St., Suite 401, Toronto, Ontario M5H 3H1 (☎800-465-5600 US and Canada only; fax 416-260-1888; www.gapadventures.com). Small group organized travel with emphasis on adventure and responsibility toward local communities. Average price $1800.

Oceanic Society, Fort Mason Center, Building E, San Francisco, CA 94123 (☎415-441-1106; fax 415-474-3395; www.oceanic-society.org). Naturalists lead journeys in the region for whale-watching, wildlife sightings, and natural history. $2800.

OREGON

OREGON FACTS & FIGURES

Capital: Salem. **Area:** 98,386 sq. mi. **Population:** 3,421,399.
Motto: "She flies with her own wings." **Nickname:** Beaver State.
State Animal: Beaver. **State Fish:** Chinook salmon. **State Dance:** folk dance.
State Rock: Thunderegg (a.k.a. geode). **State Shell:** Oregon Hairy Triton.

"Discovered" by Lewis and Clark on their overland expedition to the Pacific Ocean, Oregon soon became a hotbed of exploration and exploitation. Lured by plentiful forests and promises of gold and riches, entire families liquidated their assets and sank their life savings into covered wagons, corn meal, and oxen, high-tailing it to Oregon (on the infamous "Oregon Trail") in search of prosperity and a new way of life. This population of outdoors-enthusiasts and fledgling townspeople joined the Union in 1859, and has ever since become an eclectic mix of tree-huggers and suave big-city types. Today, Oregon remains as popular a destination as ever for backpackers, cyclists, anglers, beachcrawlers, and families alike.

The wealth of space and natural resources that supported the prospectors and farmers of old continues to provide the backbone of Oregon today: four out of ten Oregonians are involved in some way in the most diversified agricultural center in the US. More than half of Oregon's forests lie on federally owned land, hopefully preserving them for future generations of outdoor explorers, but 80,000 workers depend on an timber industry that is threatened by over-logging, by the Endangered Species Act, and by disputes over ownership of the remaining land and rights. Nevertheless, Oregon deserves its environmentalist reputation, having created the country's first recycling refund program and spearheaded wide-scale preservation of coastline for public use.

The caves and cliffs of the coastline are a siren's song to Oregon's most precious non-natural resource: tourists. For those in search of big city life, Portland's laid-back and idiosyncratic personality—its name was determined by a coin toss (the flip side would have christened it "Boston, Oregon")—draws the microchip, mocha, and music crowds, while the college town of Eugene embraces hippies and Deadheads from around the West. From excellent microbrews to snow-capped peaks, a visit to Oregon is still worth crossing the Continental Divide.

HIGHLIGHTS OF OREGON

CRATER LAKE NATIONAL PARK (p. 144) protects a placid, azure pool in the maw of an ancient and enormous volcano.

HIGH DESERT MUSEUM in Bend (p. 137) bolsters appreciation for nature.

COLUMBIA RIVER GORGE (p. 90) cuts a stunning chasm.

ASHLAND'S SHAKESPEARE would make Will proud (p. 134).

CANNON BEACH'S (p. 101) silky soft stretch of sand is the ultimate getaway.

DUNE BUGGIES gear it up in Oregon Dunes National Recreation Area (p. 110).

PERUSE Portland's Rose Garden to see why it's dubbed the City of Roses (p. 70).

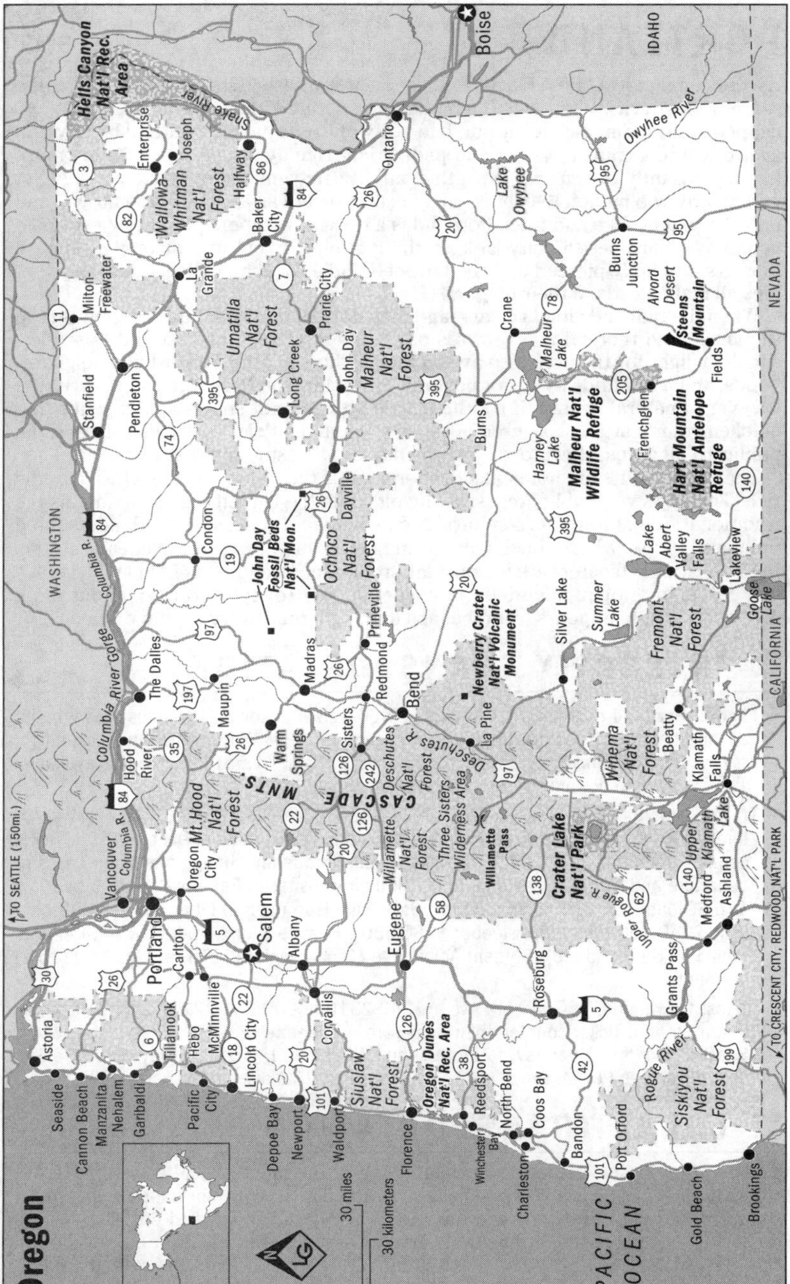
Oregon
30 miles
30 kilometers
TO SEATTLE (150mi.)
WASHINGTON
IDAHO
NEVADA
CALIFORNIA
PACIFIC OCEAN
TO CRESCENT CITY, REDWOOD NAT'L PARK
Boise
Hells Canyon Nat'l Rec. Area
Snake River
Wallowa-Whitman Nat'l Forest
Umatilla Nat'l Forest
Malheur Nat'l Forest
Ochoco Nat'l Forest
John Day Fossil Beds Nat'l Mon.
Mt. Hood Nat'l Forest
CASCADE MNTS
Deschutes Nat'l Forest
Willamette Nat'l Forest
Three Sisters Wilderness Area
Willamette Pass
Newberry Crater Nat'l Volcanic Monument
Crater Lake Nat'l Park
Winema Nat'l Forest
Fremont Nat'l Forest
Siuslaw Nat'l Forest
Oregon Dunes Nat'l Rec. Area
Siskiyou Nat'l Forest
Malheur Nat'l Wildlife Refuge
Hart Mountain Nat'l Antelope Refuge
Steens Mountain
Alvord Desert
Owyhee River
Lake Owyhee
Malheur Lake
Harney Lake
Summer Lake
Lake Abert
Goose Lake
Upper Klamath Lake
Columbia R.
Columbia River Gorge
Deschutes R.
Upper Rogue R.
Rogue River
Astoria
Seaside
Cannon Beach
Manzanita
Nehalem
Garibaldi
Tillamook
Pacific City
Hebo
Lincoln City
Depoe Bay
Newport
Waldport
Florence
Reedsport
Winchester Bay
North Bend
Coos Bay
Charleston
Bandon
Port Orford
Gold Beach
Brookings
Portland
Vancouver
Oregon City
Carlton
McMinnville
Salem
Albany
Corvallis
Eugene
Roseburg
Grants Pass
Medford
Ashland
Klamath Falls
Hood River
The Dalles
Maupin
Warm Springs
Madras
Sisters
Redmond
Bend
Prineville
La Pine
Beatty
Silver Lake
Lakeview
Valley Falls
Condon
Dayville
John Day
Long Creek
Prarie City
Burns
Crane
Frenchglen
Fields
Burns Junction
Stanfield
Pendleton
Milton-Freewater
La Grande
Baker City
Enterprise
Joseph
Halfway
Ontario
30
26
6
22
18
20
101
5
126
38
42
199
58
138
62
140
97
242
35
84
197
19
74
395
11
7
82
3
86
95
78
205

PORTLAND ☎503

As a recent spate of "Best Places to Live" awards attests, Portland is no longer the secret it once was. With over 200 parks, the pristine Willamette River, and snow-capped Mt. Hood in the background, the City of Roses basks in natural beauty. An award-winning transit system and pedestrian-friendly streets make it feel more like a pleasantly overgrown town than any traffic-jammed, dirty metropolis. Yet with nearly two million residents, a respectable set of skyscrapers downtown, and industry giants Nike and Intel, Portland is a thriving component of the West Coast economy. Nor does the city lack anything in big-city cultural diversity: hippies, hipsters, the body-pierced and the tattooed, indie rockers, college kids, and yuppies all make Portland their home.

When the rain and clouds clear—and they do, in summer—outdoors lovers reap the visual and recreational rewards of the nearby Oregon Coast and Cascades. Ample delight for the eyes also awaits those who walk the flower-lined neighborhoods, and a brief ride by car or light rail to Washington Park totally immerses the traveler in natural beauty. If it's the plastic arts and not snow-capped peaks that quicken your heart, rest assured of satisfaction in the Pearl District's galleries, the public art all across downtown, and the numerous restaurant displays.

The culinary arts are not neglected here, nor is their enjoyment exclusive to the rich. The city's venerable orchestra, the oldest in the United States, maintains the traditional side of Portland's cultural scene. In the rainy season, Portlanders flood pubs and clubs, where musicians often strum, sing, or spin for cheap or free. Improvisational theaters are in constant production, and the talented and/or brave can chime in at open-mic night, in vogue all over town. And throughout it all, America's best beer pours from the taps in the microbrewery capital of the U.S.

INTERCITY TRANSPORTATION

Flights: Portland International Airport (☎460-4234) is served by almost every major airline. The airport is connected to the city center by the **MAX Red Line,** an efficient light rail system. (38min.; every 15min. daily 5am-11:30pm; $1.55) Taxis are also available, with flat rates to downtown (see Local Transportation, below).

Trains: Amtrak, 800 NW 6th Ave. (☎273-4866; reservations ☎800-872-7245 or through www.amtrak.com), at Irving St. in historic Union Station, built in 1896. Ticket counter open daily 7:45am-9pm. Ticket prices frequently change based on dates of departure and arrival, so be sure to check their website. To **Eugene** (2½hr.; 5 per day; $16-20 one-way, $38-45 round-trip); **San Francisco** (19hr.; 1 per day; $81-92 one-way, $150-160 round-trip, sleeper $280-330); **Seattle** (4hr.; 4 per day; $23-36 one-way, $56-65 round-trip). Student Advantage (15%), senior (15%), and military (15%) discounts.

Buses: Greyhound, 550 NW 6th Ave. (☎243-2310 or 800-231-2222), at NW Glisan by Union Station. Ticket counter open 5am-1am. To **Eugene** (2½-3½hr., 9 per day, $14); **Seattle** (3-4½hr., 9 per day, $21); **Spokane, WA** (7½-11½hr., 4 per day, $40.50). Student Advantage (15%), senior (10%), and military (10%) discounts. Lockers $5 per day.

LOCAL TRANSPORTATION

The award-winning **Tri-Met bus system** is one of the most logically organized and rider-friendly public transit systems in America. The downtown **transit mall,** closed to all traffic but pedestrians and buses, lies between SW 5th and 6th Ave., where over 30 covered passenger shelters serve as stops and info centers. Southbound buses stop along SW 5th Ave., northbound along SW 6th Ave. Bus routes are col-

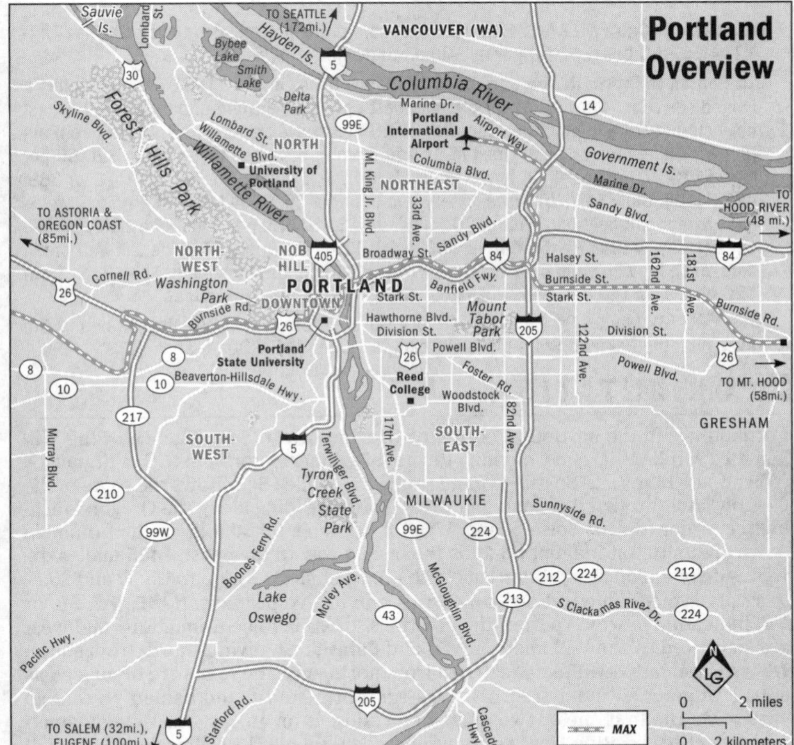

ored according to their **service areas,** each with its own whimsical insignia: red salmon, orange deer, yellow rose, green leaf, blue snow, purple rain, and brown beaver. Most of downtown is in the **Fareless Square,** where all public transportation is free. (Anywhere north or east of 405, west of the river, and south of Irving St.) For directions and fares outside this zone, see **Public Transportation,** below.

Most downtown streets are **one-way.** The city's **Smart Parks** are common and well marked. (Near Pioneer Sq. \$0.95 per hr., \$3 per hr. after 4hr., \$2 after 6pm, max. \$12; weekends \$5 per day.) Parking is cheaper farther from city center. **Tri-Met** is the best bet for day-long excursions downtown.

Public Transportation: Tri-Met, 701 SW 6th Ave. (☎238-7433; www.tri-met.org), in Pioneer Courthouse Sq. Open M-F 7:30am-5:30pm. Several information lines available: **Call-A-Bus** info system ☎231-3199; fare info ☎231-3198; TDD info ☎238-5811. Buses generally run 5am-midnight with reduced schedules on weekends. All buses and bus stops are marked with 1 of 7 symbols and offer public bike racks. Fare \$1.25-1.55, ages 7-18 \$0.95, over 65 or disabled \$0.60, free downtown. All-day pass \$4; 10 fares for \$10.50. **MAX** (☎228-7246), based at the Customer Service Center, is Tri-Met's light-rail train running between downtown, Hillsboro in the west, and Gresham in the east. Clean and convenient, the MAX keeps pace with technology—electronic signs tell when the next train's coming at many stops. A new line serves the airport from the main line's "Gateway" stop (see above). Transfers from buses can be used to ride MAX. Runs M-F about 4:30am-1:30am, Sa 5am-12:30am, Su 5am-11:30pm.

Taxis: Radio Cab (☎227-1212), $2.50 base, $1.80 per mi. **Broadway Cab** (☎227-1234), $2.50 base, $1.80 per mi. Airport to downtown $25-30.

Car Rental: Crown Rent-A-Car, 1315 NE Sandy Blvd. (☎230-1103). Although it has a limited selection, Crown is by far the cheapest option for anyone under 25. 18-21 must have credit card and proof of insurance. 22-25 must have credit card. Transport from airport available upon request. Open M-Sa 9am-5pm or by appointment. From $20-60 per day, $110-275 per week. **Rent-a-Wreck,** 1800 SE M.L. King Blvd. (☎233-2492 or 888-499-9111). Older cars. Will occasionally rent to under-25. Open M-F 7:30am-5pm, weekends by appointment only. From $20-30 per day, $110-150 per week, with 100-150 free mi. per day. **Dollar Rent-a-Car** (☎800-800-4000), at airport. Must be 25 with credit card, or be 21 with proof of insurance and pay a $20 per day surcharge. Open 24hr. From $20 per day, $140 per week, unlimited mileage. Extra 15% airport fee.

AAA: 600 SW Market St. (☎222-6777 or 800-222-4357), between Broadway and 6th Ave., near the Portland State University campus. Open M-F 8:30am-5pm.

ORIENTATION

OREGON

Portland lies in the northwest corner of Oregon, near the confluence of the Willamette (wih-LAM-it) and Columbia Rivers. **I-5** connects Portland to San Francisco (659 mi., 11-14hr.) and Seattle (179 mi.; 3-3½hr.), while **I-84** follows the route of the Oregon Trail through the Columbia River Gorge, heading along the Oregon-Washington border toward Boise, Idaho. West of Portland, **US 30** follows the Columbia downstream to Astoria, but **US 26** is the fastest way to the coast. **I-405** makes the west side of a loop around Portland with I-5, and links the loop to US 30 and 26.

Every street name in Portland carries one of five prefixes: **N, NE, NW, SE,** or **SW,** indicating in which part of the city the address is to be found. East and west are separated by the Willamette River, and **Burnside St.** divides north from south. **Williams Ave.** marks off plain ol' north from northeast. The roads are organized as a grid: in general, numbered *avenues* run north-south, and named *streets* go east-west. The first one or two digits of an address on an east-west street generally reflect its position relative to numbered streets: 3813 Killingsworth St. will be near 38th Ave.

The principal unit of urban measurement in Portland is the neighborhood, so here are a few of the major ones. Close to the city center, **Northwest** Portland is home to **Chinatown** and most of **Old Town,** which holds the highest concentration of Portland's nightclubs and bars. **Nob Hill** and **Pearl District,** the recently revitalized homes to most of Portland's beautiful people as well as many of the chic-est shops in the city, are found further north, while **Washington Park** is found further west. **Forest Park** is a huge wooded area that stretches along the river. **Southwest** Portland includes downtown, the southern end of Old Town, and a slice of the wealthier **West Hills** area. **Portland State University** fills a large space south of the city center. **Southeast** Portland contains parks, factories, local businesses, residential areas of several socioeconomic brackets, and a rich array of cafes, stores, theaters, and restaurants, particularly around **Hawthorne Blvd.** east of SE 33rd St. **Reed College,** with its wide green quadrangles and brick halls, lies deep within the southeast district at the end of **Woodstock Ave.** (some might say appropriately), which has a distinct culture of its own. **Northeast** Portland is highly residential, but has pockets of activity; areas around **Killingsworth** and **Alberta St.** east of 99 East are currently undergoing gentrification as "hipsters" and restaurants flock to a once seedy area. The Northeast does not have any accommodations, so venturing out is a little more difficult. Some of the northeast's biggest draws are near the river, and include the Lloyd Center Shopping Mall and the Oregon Convention Center. The north of Portland is mostly residential, and receives next to no tourist traffic.

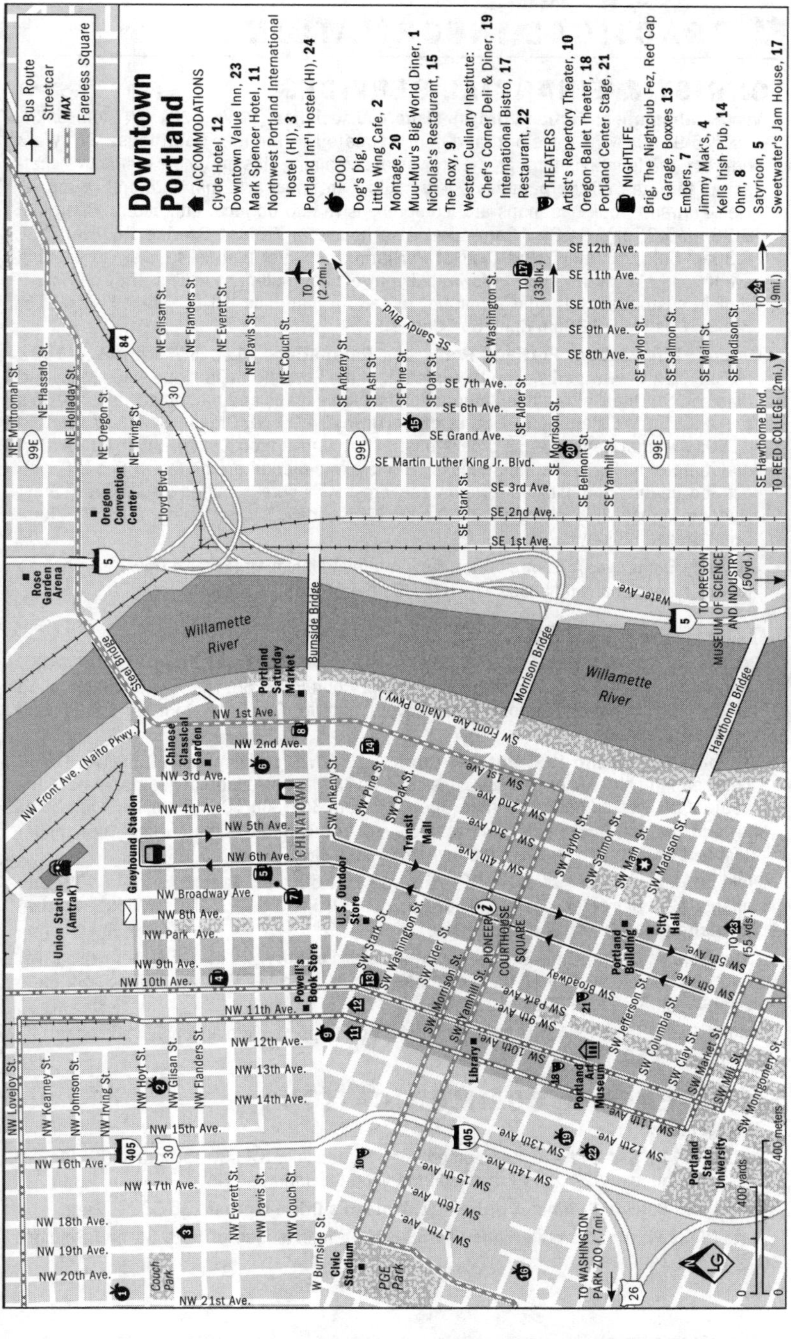

Downtown Portland

Bus Route
Streetcar
MAX
Fareless Square

ACCOMMODATIONS
Clyde Hotel, **12**
Downtown Value Inn, **23**
Mark Spencer Hotel, **11**
Northwest Portland International Hostel (HI), **3**
Portland Int'l Hostel (HI), **24**

FOOD
Dog's Dig, **6**
Little Wing Cafe, **2**
Montage, **20**
Muu-Muu's Big World Diner, **1**
Nicholas's Restaurant, **15**
The Roxy, **9**
Western Culinary Institute: Chef's Corner Deli & Diner, **19**
International Bistro, **17**
Restaurant, **22**

THEATERS
Artist's Repertory Theater, **10**
Oregon Ballet Theater, **18**
Portland Center Stage, **21**

NIGHTLIFE
Brig, The Nightclub Fez, Red Cap Garage, Boxxes **13**
Embers, **7**
Jimmy Mak's, **4**
Kells Irish Pub, **14**
Ohm, **8**
Satyricon, **5**
Sweetwater's Jam House, **17**

PRACTICAL INFORMATION

TOURIST & FINANCIAL SERVICES

Visitor Information: Portland Oregon Visitors Association (POVA), 701 SW Morrison St. (☎275-9750; www.travelportland.com). Located in Pioneer Courthouse Sq. Walk between the fountains through the crowds of screaming kids and more distinctive characters to enter. All the pamphlets you could want, plus a 12min. interpretive movie. Free *Portland Book* has maps and comprehensive info on local attractions. Open M-F 8:30am-5:30pm, Sa-Su 10am-4pm. Also houses a **Tri-Met Service Counter** (M-F 8:30am-5:30pm) and **Ticket Central Portland,** a counter that sells tickets to sporting events and almost any show in town, plus day-of-show half-price tickets. They only serve walk-in customers, but offer a number to call for half-price ticket availability (☎275-8358). Open M-F 9:30am-6pm, Sa 10am-2pm.

Outdoor Information: Portland Parks and Recreation, 1120 SW 5th Ave. #1302 (☎823-2223; www.parks.ci.portland.or.us), in the Portland Building between Main and Madison St. Offers a wealth of information including maps and pamphlets on Portland's parks. Open M-F 8am-5pm. **Nature of Northwest,** 800 NE Oregon St. #117 (☎872-2750; www.naturenw.org), 2 blocks east of the Convention Center on NE 7th Ave. A multitude of hiking maps, guidebooks, and raw information are on tap at this U.S. Forest Service-run shop. Pick up a Northwest Forest Pass here, required for parking in most National Forests in Washington and Oregon ($5 per day, $30 annually). Open M-F 9am-5pm. Closed holidays.

Currency Exchange: A **Thomas Cook's** can be found inside of Powell's Travel (see below) for any money-changing needs. Open M-F 9am-5:30pm, Sa 10:30am-2pm.

LOCAL SERVICES

Bookstore: See **Powell's City of Books,** p. 80. **Powell's Travel Store** (☎228-1108). Adjacent to the **Tourist information** in Pioneer Courthouse Sq. Has a vast array of road maps, hiking maps, guidebooks, and travel literature. Open M-F 9am-7pm, Sa 10am-6pm, Su 10am-5pm.

Outdoors Equipment: U.S. Outdoor Store, 219 SW Broadway (☎223-5937). Found between Pine and Ankeny Streets, this store has a huge selection of gear for almost any outdoor activity, summer or winter. Open M-F 9am-8pm, Sa 10am-6pm, Su noon-5pm.

Gay and Lesbian Info: Portland's best resource for queer info is the biweekly newspaper **Just-Out** (☎236-1252), available free around the city.

Tickets: Ticketmaster (☎224-4400). Surcharge $1.50-7.75. **Fastixx** (☎224-8499) Surcharge $2-3 per order plus an additional $1 per ticket ordered. Also try **Ticket Central Portland** (see **Tourist Services,** above).

Laundromat: Springtime Thrifty Cleaners and Laundry, 2942 SE Hawthorne Blvd. (☎232-4353). 150 ft. from the Hawthorne hostel. Open M-F 7:30am-9pm, Sa-Su 8am-8pm. Wash $1.25, dry 25¢ per 10min.

Public Pool: Call 823-5130 for a list of 14 public pools. Admission $2.50; under 17 swim for $1.50.

EMERGENCY & COMMUNICATION

Emergency: ☎911.

Police: 1111 SW 2nd Ave. (non-emergency response ☎823-3333; info ☎823-4636; lost and found ☎823-2179), between Madison St. and Main St.

Crisis and Suicide Hotline: ☎655-8401. **Women's Crisis Line:** ☎235-5333. 24hr.

Late-Night Pharmacy: Walgreens (☎238-6053), intersection of 39th St. and Belmont St. Open 24hr.

Hospital: Legacy Good Samaritan, 1015 NW 22nd St. (☎413-8090; emergency 413-7260), between Lovejoy and Marshall. **Adventist Medical Center,** 10123 SE Market St. (☎257-2500).

Internet Access: Found at the elegant and distinguished **library,** 801 SW 10th Ave., between Yamhill and Taylor. 1hr. free access. Open Tu-Th 9am-9pm, F-Sa 9am-6pm, Su 1-5pm. **Internet Arena,** 1016 SW Taylor St. (☎224-2718), across the street from the main library. $6 per hr., minimum $2. Open M-F 11am-8pm.

Post Office: 715 NW Hoyt St. (☎800-275-8777). Open M-F 7am-6:30pm, Sa 8:30am-5pm. **Postal Code:** 97208.

ACCOMMODATIONS

Although Marriott-esque hotels dominate downtown and smaller motels are steadily raising their prices, Portland still welcomes the budget traveler. Two Hostelling International locations provide quality housing in happening areas. Prices tend to drop as you leave the city center, and inexpensive motels can be found on SE Powell Blvd. and the southern end of SW 4th Ave. All accommodations in Portland fill up during the summer months, especially during the Rose Festival, so make your reservations early.

OREGON

HOSTELS & MOTELS

Portland International Hostel (HI), 3031 SE Hawthorne Blvd. (☎236-3380), at 31st Ave. across from Artichoke Music. Take bus #14 to SE 30th Ave. Lively common space and a huge porch define this laid-back hostel. Kitchen, laundry. Recently-installed wireless Internet access for those with laptops is free; "conventional" Internet is $1 per 10min. The $1 all-you-can-eat pancakes are a big bonus. Fills early in summer. Reception daily 8am-10pm. Check-out 11am. 34 beds and a tent yard for overflow. Dorms $15, nonmembers $18. Private rooms $41-46. ❶

Northwest Portland International Hostel (HI), 1818 NW Glisan St. (☎241-2783) at 18th Ave. Centrally located between Nob Hill and the Pearl District. Take bus #17 down Glisan to corner of 19th Ave. This snug Victorian building has a kitchen, lockers, laundry, and a small espresso bar. 34 dorm beds (co-ed available). Reception 8am-11pm. $14-16 plus tax, with a $3 fee for nonmembers. Two private doubles, $40-50. ❶

McMenamins Edgefield, 2126 SW Halsey St. (☎669-8610 or 800-669-8610), in Troutdale. Take MAX east to the Gateway Station, then Tri-Met bus #24 (Halsey) east to the main entrance. This beautiful 38-acre former farm is a posh escape that keeps two hostel rooms. On-site brewery and vineyards, plus 18-hole golf course ($8-9, $1 club rental), and several restaurants and pubs. Offers many activities, including 2-day rafting trips ($140). Lockers included. Call ahead during summer (but no reservations for the hostel). Reception 24hr. 2 single-sex dorm-style rooms with 12 beds each ($20 plus tax) are the budget option. Singles $50 with breakfast, 2 queen double $95-$105. ❷

The Clyde Hotel, 1022 SW Stark St. (☎517-5231; www.clydehotel.com), west of 10th Ave. Take MAX to SW 10th Avenue, walk towards Burnside St. Built in 1912, the charming and historic Clyde has kept all its furniture in the original style, from Victorian tubs to bureau-sized radios. Continental breakfast included. Reception 10am-9pm, front desk open 24 hr. Reservations recommended. Rooms (double or queen) $60-110, two-room suites $110-190 (for 2-4 people). Off-season rates about $10 less. ❷

The Mark Spencer, 409 SW 11th Ave., (☎800-548-3934; www.markspencer.com). Since 1907, self-proclaimed "Portland's Boutique Art Hotel" has housed the *Phantom of the Opera* cast and many other groups on tour. Continental breakfast included, plus free tea and cookies 4:30pm-7pm daily. Coin-op and valet laundry, cable TV, kitchens in every room, phones with data ports. Check-in 4 pm. Check-out noon. Summer reservations recommended one month in advance. Queens $90 summer, $80 off-season. ❸

Downtown Value Inn, 415 SW Montgomery St. (☎226-4751), at 4th Ave. Take bus #12 or #19 to the corner of 5th Ave., or follow signs to the city center and Montgomery. An inexpensive option with clean, recently remodeled rooms. Pizza hangout/pub downstairs. Phones, cable TV, laundry; microwaves in some rooms. Reception 24hr. Check-out 11am. Reservations recommended. Singles from $50; doubles from $60; rooms with jacuzzi $70. ❷

FOOD

Portland ranks high nationwide in restaurants per capita, and dining experiences are seldom dull. Downtown and the NW districts tend to be expensive, but restaurants and quirky cafes in the NE and SE quadrants offer great food at reasonable prices. For some reason (perhaps a cosmic one) depictions of The Last Supper seem to be a seal of approval for some of the best restaurants in Portland: be on the look-out for Christ and His apostles.

PEARL DISTRICT & NOB HILL

Trendy eateries line NW 21st and 23rd St. **Food Front,** 2375 NW Thurman St., a small cooperative grocery, has a superb deli and a wonderland of natural foods, fruit, and baked goods. (☎222-5658. Open daily 8am-9pm; winter 9am-9pm.)

OREGON

Muu-Muu's Big World Diner, 612 NW 21st Ave. (☎223-8169), at Hoyt St. Bus #17. Where high and low culture smash together. Artful goofiness—the name of the restaurant was drawn from a hat—amidst red velvet curtains and gold upholstery. Brutus salad, "the one that kills a caesar" $6, 'shroom-wich $7.50. Open M-F 11:30am-1am, Sa-Su 10am-2am. ❷

Little Wing Cafe, 529 NW 13th Ave. (☎228-3101), off Glisan. Bus #17. The food is arranged nearly as well as the gallery of beautiful ceramic art on the walls. Sandwiches include the Eggplant Supreme ($6). Dinner entrees run about $12. Open M-Th 11:30am-4pm and 5:30-9pm; F-Sa 11:30am-4pm and 5:30-10pm. ❸

DOWNTOWN & OLD TOWN

The center of town and tourism, Southwest Portland can get expensive. Street carts offer an array of portable food and bento boxes (lunches of meat or vegetables on a bed of rice), making it easy to grab a quick, healthy meal. Ethnic restaurants also peddle cheap eats on Morrison St. between 10th and 11th Ave. A 24hr. **Safeway** supermarket is behind the PAM (see **Sights,** p. 78), 1025 SW Jefferson St.

Western Culinary Institute (☎223-2245) would leave the Frugal Gourmet speechless. The ratio of cooks to patrons in these restaurants is extraordinarily high, with the culinary students rotating between restaurants and duties. WCI has 4 eateries, each catering to a different budget niche, all of them reasonable. **Chef's Diner ❶,** 1239 SW Jefferson, opens mornings to let cheerful students serve, taste, and discuss sandwiches, the breakfast special, or the occasional all-you-can-eat buffet ($5). Open Tu-F 7am-noon. **Chef's Corner Deli ❶,** 1239 SW Jefferson, is good for a quick meal on-the-go. Enormous sandwiches go for $1.25. Open Tu-F 8am-6:30pm. Moving up the price scale, the elegant **Restaurant ❹,** 1316 SW 13th Ave., serves a classy 5-course lunch ($10) rivaled only by its superb 6-course dinner (Tu, W, and F, $20). Reservations recommended. Open Tu-F 11:30am-1pm; dinner 6-8pm. **International Bistro ❸,** 1701 SW Jefferson, serves cuisine from a different region of the world every week, at prices that range just below those at Restaurant.

The Roxy, 1121 SW Stark St. (☎223-9160). Giant crucified Jesus with neon halo, pierced wait staff, and quirky menu. The owner's collection of signed celebrity photos graces the booths; Slash (from Guns N' Roses) and other celebs have been known to stop by. Visiting the Dysha Starr Imperial Toilet seems like an important thing to do, if only because of its name. Quentin Tarantuna Melt $6.25, coffees and chai about $1-3. An ideal post-movie or after-bar stop. Open Tu-Su 24hr. ❷

Dogs Dig Vegetarian Deli, 212 NW Davis St. (☎223-3362). Vegetarian and vegan sandwiches and soups in a tiny storefront adorned with bad jokes and snapshots of every dog in Portland. Soup and sandwich $5, burrito $2.50. Open M-F 9am-5pm. ❶

SOUTHEAST PORTLAND

Anchored at happening Hawthorne Blvd., Southeast Portland is a great place to people-watch and tummy-fill. Eclectic eateries with exotic decor and economical menus hide in residential and industrial neighborhoods. **Safeway** is at 2800 SE Hawthorne, at 28th Ave. (☎232-5539; open daily 6am-midnight). Bring cash to SE Portland restaurants, since many of the best do not accept credit cards.

Nicholas's Restaurant, 318 SE Grand Ave. (☎235-5123), between Oak and Pine opposite Miller Paint. Bus #6 to the Andy and Bax stop. Phenomenal Mediterranean food in an authentic atmosphere. The meat, vegetarian, or vegan mezzas ($7.75) are fantastic deals for both quality and quantity (might feed two). Sandwiches $5-$6. Open M-Sa 10am-9pm, Su noon-9pm. ❶

Montage, 301 SE Morrison St. (☎234-1324). Take bus #15 to the East end of the Morrison Bridge and walk under it. Where straight-laced, mainstream Portlanders enter a beautifully surreal land of dining. While seated Last-Supper style underneath a macaroni-framed mural of that famous meal, try oyster shooters ($1.75) and huge portions of jambalaya ($10.50 chicken, $14.50 gator). The popular mac and cheese is a cheaper option ($5). Open M-Th 11:30am-2pm and 6pm-2am, F 11:30am-2pm and 6pm-4am, Sa 6pm-4am, Su 6pm-2am. ❷

Delta Cafe, 4607 SE Woodstock Blvd. (☎771-3101). The decor is typical Portland: pastoral paintings in one room, voodoo dolls and a lone, framed Chewbacca (the wookie) portrait in the other. 40 oz. Pabst Blue Ribbon comes in champagne bucket, $3. Po' Boy Samwiches, $4-7. Open M-F 5pm-10pm, Sa-Su noon-10pm. ❶

Cafe Lena, 2239 SE Hawthorne Blvd. (☎238-7087). Bus #14. A fixture of the breakfast scene. Open Tu 8am-midnight, W-Th 8am-9:30pm, F-Sa 8am-10pm, Su 8am-3pm. ❷

Barley Mill Pub, 1629 SE Hawthorne Blvd. (☎231-1492). Bus #14. A smoky temple to Jerry Garcia. The hearty burgers are upbeat, yet mellow, like the man himself. McMenamins beer and 20 other kinds on tap ($3-4). Happy Hour M-F 4-6pm. Open M-Sa 11am-1am, Su noon-midnight. ❷

Cup and Saucer, 3566 SE Hawthorne Blvd. (☎236-6001). Ask Chef Karen to cook you a famous garden scramble any time of day. Ani DiFranco has been spotted here, and the staff promises that you'll at least hear her on their stereo. Open daily 7am-9pm. ❷

NORTHEAST PORTLAND

The northeast is distant from any hostel, but the food is worth a short trip. Places to eat line Broadway and Alberta east of the river, and other pockets of commerce produce good eats for Portland's most residential area.

Vita Cafe, 3024 NE Alberta St. (☎335-8233). Huge portions of "comfort food," with an emphasis on vegetarian and vegan fare, but carnivores can find sustenance as well. American, Asian, Mediterranean, and "Mexican Fiesta." M-F 11am-10pm, Sa 8am-10pm, Su 8am-3pm. ❷

Chez What? 2203 NE Alberta St. (☎281-1717). A strange fascination with poodles, especially pink ones, is the visual theme. Good hearty eating is the gustatory one. The dreadlocked staff create a mellow scene (but a peppier environment waits just next door at **Whatever?!** lounge). Curly Tom's Hippy Eggs, $7. M 8am-3pm, T-Sa 8am-1am, Su 9am-3pm. ❷

CAFES

Although locals sometimes complain that cafes are where trendy Portlanders try excessively hard to be cool, the decor, delicious food, and caffeine of these establishments still make them great places to make an appearance.

Palio Dessert & Espresso House, 1996 SE Ladd St. (☎232-9214), on Ladd Circle. Bus #10 stops right in front of the cafe, or walk south 3 blocks on SE 16th Ave. from Hawthorne. This tranquil cafe offers Mexican mochas ($2.50) and espresso mousse ($4). Bring a book and enjoy the outside seating, or mosey over to the park next door. Open M-F 8am-11pm, Sa-Su 10am-11pm. ❶

Pied Cow Coffeehouse, 3244 SE Belmont St. (☎230-4866). Bus #15. Sink into velvety cushions in this quirky and friendly Victorian parlor, or puff a hookah in the garden outside. Espresso drinks $1-3, cakes about $4. Open M-F 4pm-1am, Sa-Su noon-1am. ❶

Coffee Time, 712 NW 21st Ave. (☎497-1090). Sip a cup of chai ($2-3) while watching locals play chess. The intelligentsia mingle on the couches; bohemians chill to music in the parlor. Lattes $2-3. Coffee time is nearly all the time (Open daily, 6am-3am). ❶

Rimsky Korsakoffeehouse, 707 SE 12th Ave. (☎232-2640), at Alder St. Bus #15 to 12th St., then walk 2 blocks north. Unmarked and low-key, this red Victorian house is a hidden gem with a frenzy of desserts. Ask for a "mystery table." Live classical music nightly. Open Su-Th 7pm-midnight, F-Sa 7pm-1am. ❶

OREGON

SIGHTS

Parks, gardens, open-air markets, innumerable museums, and galleries bedeck Portland. For $1.25, Bus #63 delivers passengers to at least 13 attractions. Catch the best of Portland's dizzying art scene on the first Thursday of each month, when the Portland Art Museum and small galleries in the Southwest and Northwest stay open until 8pm. For more info, contact the **Regional Arts and Culture Council,** 620 SW Main St. #420 (☎823-5111), across from the Portland Centre for the Performing Arts, or grab the *Art Gallery Guide* at the Visitor's Center.

DOWNTOWN

Portland's downtown centers on the pedestrian and bus mall, which runs north-south on 5th and 6th Ave. between W Burnside Blvd. on the north end and SW Clay St. on the south. On the **South Park Blocks,** a cool and shaded park snakes down the middle of Park Ave., bordered on the west by **Portland State University (PSU).** The area is accessible by any bus from the Transit Mall; once there, set out on foot.

PORTLAND ART MUSEUM (PAM). PAM sets itself apart from the rest of Portland's burgeoning arts scene on the strength of its collections, especially in Asian and Native American art. The Northwest Film Center (see Cinema, p. 83) shares space with the museum, and shows classics, documentaries, and off-beat flicks almost every day. *(1219 SW Park, at Jefferson St. on the west side of the South Block Park. Bus #6, 58, 63. ☎226-2811. Dial ext. 4245 for info on new exhibits. Open Tu-Sa 10am-5pm, Su noon-5pm, and until 8pm for Th and Fri in summer. $10, seniors 55+ and students $9, under 19 $6, under 5 free; special exhibits may be more.)*

PIONEER COURTHOUSE SQUARE. The still-operational **Pioneer Courthouse,** at 5th Ave. and Morrison St., is the centerpiece of the **Square.** Since opening in 1983 it has become "Portland's Living Room." Tourists and urbanites of every ilk hang out in the brick quadrangle. During late July and most of August, **High Noon Tunes** (p. 83) draws music lovers in droves. *(701 SW 6th Ave. Along the Vintage Trolley line and the MAX light-rail. Events hotline ☎223-1613. Music W noon-1pm.)*

NO ROOM FOR MUGGERS In 1948, a hole was cut through the sidewalk at the corner of SW Taylor St. and SW Naito Pkwy. (Front St.). It was expected to accommodate a mere lamp post, but greatness was thrust upon it. The streetlamp was never installed, and the 24-inch circle of earth was left empty until noticed by Dick Fagan, a columnist for the *Oregon Journal*. Fagan used his column, "Mill Ends," to publicize the patch of dirt, pointing out that it would make an excellent park. After years of such logic-heavy lobbying, the park was added to the city's roster in 1976. At 452.16 square inches, Mill Ends Park is officially the world's smallest. Locals have enthusiastically embraced it, planting flowers and hosting a hotly contested snail race on St. Patrick's Day.

5TH AVENUE ARCHITECTURE. The most controversial structure downtown is Michael Graves's **Portland Building,** 1120 SW 5th Ave., on the mall. This assemblage of pastel tile and concrete, the first major work of postmodern architecture built in the US, has been both praised as PoMo genius and condemned as nothing more than an overgrown jukebox. Walking underneath, look out for the giant pitchfork-wielding woman, *Portlandia*, reaching down from above: she's the second largest hammered copper statue in the U.S. Nearby, the **Standard Insurance Center,** 900 SW 5th Ave., between Salmon and Taylor, strokes the libido with **The Quest,** a sensual white marble sculpture commonly known as "Five Groins in the Fountain."

OLD TOWN & CHINATOWN

The section of downtown above SW Stark running along the Willamette River comprises **Old Town.** Although not the safest part of Portland (avoid walking alone here at night), Old Town has been revitalized in recent years by storefront restoration, and new shops, restaurants, and nightclubs. On weekends, **Saturday Market** draws all of Portland for food, crafts, hackey-sacks, and live entertainment. Just west of Old Town the arched **China Gates** at NW 4th Ave. and Burnside provide an entrance to a Chinatown that, apart from a few restaurants and shops, seems more about business than Asian culture.

SHANGHAI TUNNELS. Downtown's waterfront district is laced with a complex web of underground passages known as the **Shanghai tunnels.** Urban lore has it that seamen would get folks drunk, drag them down to the tunnels, and store them there until their ship sailed. Forced aboard and taken out to sea, these hapless Portlanders would provide a free crew. Unfortunately, all entrances to the tunnels are in private businesses; fortunately, **Portland Underground Tours** guides trips through the historic passageways. *(☎622-4798. Adults $11, children under 12 $6.)*

CLASSICAL CHINESE GARDENS. The newest addition to Portland's long list of gardens, this city block makes up the largest Ming-style garden outside of China. The large pond, winding paths, and ornate decorations invite a relaxing, meditative stay. Ignore the skyscrapers and warehouses looming over the garden's walls, and you'll think you were back in a simpler time when relaxation was done properly. A tea house also offers a chance to experience authentic Chinese tea for $4-5. *(NW 3rd and Everett; ☎228-8131. Open Apr.-Oct. 9am-6pm., Nov.-Mar. 10am-5pm. $6; seniors, students, and children 6-18 $5; under 6 free.)*

PEARL DISTRICT

Opposite the North Park Blocks, between NW 8th and Park Ave., the Pearl District buzzes. Stretching north from Burnside to I-405 along the river, this former industrial zone is packed with galleries, loft apartments, and warehouses-turned-office buildings. Stores and cafes make the area welcoming despite its boxy architecture.

POWELL'S CITY OF BOOKS. The largest independent bookstore in the world, Powell's is a must-see for anyone who gets excited about the written word. If you like to dawdle in bookshops, bring a sleeping bag and rations. Nine color-coded rooms house books on everything from criminology to cooking. The atmosphere is more like a department store than a bookstore, but the sheer volume of books, poetry and fiction readings, and an extensive travel section on the Pacific Northwest make Powell's a worthy stop. *(1005 W Burnside St. on the edge of Northwest district. Bus #20. ☎ 228-4651 or 800-878-7323; www.powells.com. Open daily 9am-11pm.)* For alternative books and 'zines, nearby **Reading Frenzy** carries literature like "The Zapatista Reader." *(921 Oak St. Open M-Sa 11am-7pm, Su noon-6pm.)* Two shops over is **Counter Media** which leans much further from mainstream, carrying—you have been warned!—a highly unusual collection of erotica, comics, and graphic novels. *(927 Oak St. ☎ 226-8141. 18+ only. Same hours as Reading Frenzy.)*

GALLERIES. *First Thursday* (free at PAM) is a guide to local galleries and goings-on. For a nice selection, walk north on NW 9th Ave., turn left on NW Glisan and right on NW 12th Ave. On the way you'll pass some of the area's most engaging spaces, including the **Mark Woolley Gallery,** 120 NW 9th Ave., and the visiting artists' exhibition space at the **Pacific Northwest College of Art,** 1241 NW Johnson. **Quintana Galleries,** 501 SW Broadway, displays work by contemporary Native American artists working in traditional styles.

NORTH & NORTHEAST PORTLAND

Nicknamed "Munich on the Willamette," Portland is the uncontested **microbrewery** capital of the US, and residents are proud of their beer. The visitors center has a list of 26 metro area breweries, most of which happily give tours if you call ahead.

BREWERIES. Widmer Bros. Brewing Co., half a mile north of the Rose Garden, offers free tours that include a video, a viewing of the facilities, and complimentary samples. *(929 N Russell. ☎ 281-2437. Tours F 3pm, Sa 1pm and 2pm.)* Many beer factories are brew pubs, sometimes offering live music with their beers. Try the **Lucky Labrador Brew Pub,** where dogs rule the loading dock for Miser Monday pints. *(915 SE Hawthorne Blvd. ☎ 236-3555. Pints $3.25. Open M-Sa 11am-midnight, Su noon-10pm.)* Also try the **Bridgeport Brewing Co.** (see **Nightlife**). Visit the **Oregon Brewers Guild** to learn how these alchemists work magic on water and hops grain. *(510 NW 3rd Ave. ☎ 295-1862 or 800-440-2537; www.oregonbeer.org. Open M-F 10am-4pm.)*

THE GROTTO. Minutes from downtown on Sandy Blvd., a 62-acre Catholic sanctuary houses magnificent religious sculptures and shrines, as well as running streams and gardens. At the heart of the grounds is "Our Lady's Grotto," a cave carved into a 110-foot cliff, and a replica of Michelangelo's *Pietà*. An elevator ($3, ages 6-11 and 65+ $2.50) ascends from the Meditation Chapel for a serene view that takes in a life-size bronze of St. Francis of Assisi. *(US 30, at NE 85th. ☎ 254-7371. Open daily May-Oct. 9am-8:30pm, Nov.-Apr. 9am-5pm. Exact closing time can vary.)*

SOUTHEAST PORTLAND

OREGON MUSEUM OF SCIENCE & INDUSTRY (OMSI). Flocks of kids are mesmerized by the Paleontology Lab where staff work on real dinosaur bones. The motion simulator ($3.50) spruces up the immobile exhibits and the Omnimax Theater provides an experience like no other. The Murdock Planetarium presents astronomy matinees and moonlights with rockin' laser shows—the Pink Floyd show is highly recommended. While at OMSI, visit the Navy's last diesel submarine, the U.S.S. Blueback. She never failed a mission, starred in the 1990 film *The Hunt for Red October*, and gets fantastic mileage. *(1945 SE Water Ave., 2 blocks south* *of Hawthorne Blvd. Right next to the river. Bus #63. ☎ 797-4000; www.omsi.edu. Open daily June 15th to Labor Day 9:30am-7pm; otherwise Tu-Sa 9:30am-5:30pm. Museum and Omnimax admission each cost $7, ages 3-13 and seniors $5. Omnimax ☎ 797-4640. Shows start on the hr. Su-Tu 11am-4pm, and W-Sa 11am-7pm. Th 2-for-1 tickets after 7pm. Planetarium ☎ 797-4646. Matinees daily $4; laser shows W-Su evenings $6.50. U.S.S. Blueback ☎ 797-4624. Open Tu-Su 10am-5pm. 40min. tour $4. OMSI offers a package, as well: admission to the museum, an Omnimax film and either the planetarium or the sub, $16, kids and seniors $12.)*

CRYSTAL SPRINGS RHODODENDRON GARDEN. Over 2500 rhododendrons of countless varieties and colors surround a lake and border an 18-hole public golf course. Take a mellow stroll through bloom-strewn paths, past cascading waterfalls and 90-year old rhodies. The flowers are in full bloom from March to May. *(SE 28th Ave., near Woodstock. Just west of Reed College. Bus #63, or take #19 Woodstock to 28th and Woodstock, and walk up 28th. Open daily Mar. 1 to Labor Day dawn-dusk; Oct.-Feb. 8am-7pm. Tu and W free, Th-M $3, under 12 free.)*

WASHINGTON PARK

Ever wonder where Nike's craze for trail running shoes came from? Once you visit Washington Park, with its miles of beautiful trails, lofty trees, and serene gardens, you won't ask again. If possible, schedule in a day to enjoy the park to its fullest. Holding some of Portland's premier (and least expensive) attractions, the park is shaped like a large "V." Take the MAX to "Washington Park," and you will be rocketed via elevator to the base of the V, where the **Zoo** and **World Forestry Center** are found. The Washington Park Shuttle (10am-8pm), free with valid MAX ticket, stops in the Zoo parking lot, at the **Rose Garden** and **Japanese Garden,** runs through a posh neighborhood, then to the **Hoyt Arboretum's** visitors center. From there the bus completes its circuit with another 5min. ride back to the MAX and zoo. Though the tall trees and moss-covered paths seem to beckon camping, it's not allowed, and there are police horse patrols at night.

JAPANESE GARDENS. Just across from the Rose Garden, these grounds complete the 1-2 punch of what is one of Portland's best destinations. Planned and planted in the early 60s, the gardens shift gracefully between various styles of landscape design. The Dry Landscape Garden *(Karsansui)* is an amazing example of Zen simplicity and beauty, and the mossy paths and rushing streams are sure to help you achieve that state. *(611 SW Kingston Ave. ☎ 223-1321. Open Apr.-Sept. Tu-Su 10am-7pm, M noon-7pm; Oct.-Mar. Tu-Su 10am-4pm, M noon-4pm. Tours daily at 10:45am and 2:30pm. $6, seniors 62+ $5, students $3.50, under 6 free.)*

HOYT ARBORETUM. Forming the wooded backdrop for the rest of Washington Park's sights, Hoyt features 183 acres of trees and 12 mi. of trails with tree-themed names, including the charming, wheelchair-accessible **Overlook** and **Bristlecone Pine Trails.** All this in an area that 100 years ago was clear-cut. The 26 mi. **Wildwood Trail** winds through Washington and Forest Parks, connecting the Arboretum to the Zoo and Japanese Garden. *Let's Go* recommends picking up a free map at the World Forestry Center, as trails are sometimes poorly marked. *(4000 SW Fairview Blvd. ☎ 228-8733. Visitors center open daily 9am-4pm.)*

FOREST PARK. Just north of Washington Park stretches a 5000-acre tract of wilderness. Washington Park provides access by car or foot to this sprawling sea of green, the largest park completely enclosed within a US city. A web of trails leads into lush forest, past scenic overlooks, and through idyllic picnic areas. The **Pittock Mansion,** within Forest Park, was built by Henry L. Pittock, founder of the daily *Oregonian.* Enjoy a striking panorama of the city from the lawn of this 85-year-old, 16,000 sq. ft. monument to the French Renaissance.

A ROSE EAT ROSE WORLD An eminent source of Portland pride, during the summer the International Rose Test Garden is a sea of blooms and floral fragrance, arresting the eye and confirming Portland's title as the City of Roses. The garden serves as a botanical version of the pharmaceutical clinical trial. Experimental roses (hybrids usually, but some are genetically engineered) undergo rigorous two-year evaluations here and at 18 other test gardens: those that pass muster at a sufficient number of sites become commercial. At this point they need a name, which you can pick for a mere $50,000. Those that fail their tests, alas, are destroyed (and you thought school exams were stressful). Though these pre-grad roses might lead stressful lives, a walk in the garden is sure to lighten any heart. Peak blooms occur at 5-6 week intervals beginning around Memorial Day and lasting until September. Blooms reach their highest peak in June. *(400 SW Kingston Ave. ☎823-3636. Open daily 5am-10pm. Free, but donations appreciated.)*

OREGON ZOO. The zoo has gained fame for its successful efforts at elephant breeding. Exhibits include a Cascade Mountains-like goat habitat and a marine pool as part of the zoo's "Great Northwest: A Crest to Coast Adventure" program. The zoo also features weekend educational talks and a **children's petting zoo.** For over 22 years, from late June to August, nationally touring artists have performed at the **Rhythm and Zoo Concerts** on the concert lawn. *(☎234-9694. W-Th 7pm; free with zoo admission.)* **Zoobeat Concerts** feature artists in blues, bluegrass, pop, and world beat on selected summer weekend evenings. *(4001 SW Canyon Rd. ☎226-1561. Open 9am-6pm in summer, hours vary by season. $7.50, seniors $6, ages 3-11 $4.50; 2nd Tu of each month free after 1pm.)*

OREGON

ENTERTAINMENT

Prepare for culture. Upon request, the Visitor's Association (see **Practical Information,** p. 74) will fork over a thick packet outlining the month's events. Outdoor festivals are a way of life in Portland; the city's major daily newspaper, the **Oregonian,** lists upcoming events in its Friday edition. The city's favorite free cultural reader, the Wednesday **Willamette Week,** is a reliable guide to local music, plays, and art. Drop boxes are all over town, and the paper's office is right across from the library. **The Rocket** (bimonthly, free) provides comprehensive coverage of alternative and punk music for the whole Northwest. **Mercury** (weekly, free) gives a salty, humorous take on Portland life and lists current events in a section titled "My, what a busy week!" Yuppies find their interests represented weekly in **Ourtown,** which lists downtown goings-on. Also call the *Oregonian's* **Inside Line** (☎225-5555) for up-to-date information on happenings in the area.

MUSIC

Although first-rate traveling shows never miss Portland, and many have bargain tickets available, some of the greatest shows are free and outdoors. Live music venues are listed under **Nightlife,** below.

Oregon Symphony Orchestra, 923 SW Washington St. (☎228-1353 or 800-228-7343). Box office open M-F 9am-5pm; during Symphony Season Sa 9am-5pm, as well. Classical and pop Sept.-June $15-60. Students and seniors can purchase tickets half-price 1hr. before show time. "Symphony Sunday" afternoon concerts ($10-15). "Monday Madness" offers $5 student tickets 1 week before showtime. Call for park performance info. Wheelchair accessible. Infrared listening devices available.

High Noon Tunes (☎223-1613), at Pioneer Courthouse Sq. Jammed concerts mid-July-Aug. W noon-1pm. A potpourri of rock, jazz, folk, and world music.

Sack Lunch Concerts, 1422 SW 11th Ave. (☎222-2031; www.oldchurch.org), at Clay St. and the Old Church. Classical and jazz music W at noon (usually 1hr.).

Chamber Music Northwest, 522 SW 5th Ave. #725 (☎294-6400). Performs late June-July M, Th, and Sa at Reed College Kaul Auditorium; Tu and F at Catlin Gabel School. Call for directions. Shows at 8pm. Additional shows occur periodically throughout the year. $17-33, ages 7-14 and students with ID $5.

THEATER

Theater in Portland meets all tastes, ages, and budgets. The **Portland Center for the Performing Arts (PCPA)** is the fourth-largest arts center in the US. Free **backstage tours** begin in the lobby of the Newmark Theater, at SW Main and Broadway. (☎248-4335; www.pcpa.com. Tours every 30min. W and Sa 11am-1pm. Any bus to the Transit Mall; walk from there.) **Friends of the Performing Arts Center** (☎274-6555) stages the monthly **Brown Bag Lunch Series,** a glimpse of free professional productions on weekdays around noon. The *Oregonian* has details.

Portland Center Stage (☎274-6588), in Newmark Theater of PCPA at SW Broadway and SW Main. Classics, modern adaptations, and world premiers run late Sept.-Apr. Tu-Th and Su $21-38, F-Sa $21-44. $10 youth matinee seats sometimes available (25 and under). Half-price student rush tickets sometimes available 1hr. before curtain.

Oregon Ballet Theater, 1120 SW 10th Ave. (☎227-0977 or 888-922-5538). One of the best companies on the West Coast. Six productions Oct.-June. $5-80; half-price student rush often available 1hr. before curtain; check tourist office for discount tickets.

Artists' Repertory Theater, 1516 SW Alder St. (☎241-1278). Recruits local talent for top-notch, low-budget, and experimental productions. T-Th and Su matinees $24, seniors $18; F-Sa $28. Students always $15.

CINEMA

Portland is a haven for cinema lovers. With the help of the *Oregonian*, a full-price ticket to just about any screen can be scrupulously avoided, and McMenamins' theater-pubs are one of a kind.

Mission Theater and Pub, 1624 NW Glisan (☎288-3286 or 888-249-3983), serves home-brewed ales and sandwiches ($6-7). Watch second-run flicks while lounging on couches or in the old-time balcony. Shows begin 5:30, 8, and 10pm. $2-3. 21+.

Baghdad Theater and Pub, 3702 SE Hawthorne Blvd. (☎288-3286). Bus #14. This cine-pub is housed in a former vaudeville theater, with a separate pub in front. 21+. First show is at 5:30pm, and 2 others follow at approximately 2hr. intervals. Pub open M-Sa 11am-1am, Su noon-midnight. $2-3.

Cinema 21, 616 NW 21st St. (☎223-4515), part of Nob Hill's bustling strip. Mean, clean, and pistachio green. Mostly documentary, independent, and foreign films. $6, students $5, under 12 and seniors $3; Sa-Su first matinee $3.

Northwest Film Center, 1219 SW Park Ave. (☎221-1156; www.NWfilm.org), screens documentary, foreign, classic, experimental, and independent films at the historic **Guild Theatre,** 829 SW 9th Ave., 2 blocks north of PAM, as well as in the museum's auditorium. Every Feb. the center also hosts the **Portland International Film Festival,** with 100 films from 30 nations. Screenings begin sometime between 7pm and 9pm. Box office opens 30min. before each show. $6.50, students and seniors $5.50.

THE LOCAL STORY

A HIRSUTE PURSUIT

Hidden among factories and behind one of the least pretentious facades of any brewery around, ***Hair of the Dog Brewing Company*** *produces what might just be the best beer in a city known for its microbreweries.* Let's Go *took a tour of the small-scale brewery from co-owner Alan Sprints and got the skinny on the brewing process. These brews are superlative, and the experience is an essential notch on the micro-brew belt.* (4509 SE 23rd Ave. ☎232-6585. Tours by appointment weekdays only. 12 oz. bottles $3, 1.5L "magnums" $10.)

Q: Do your beers ferment in bottles?
A: They do ferment in the bottles, but it's a very small refermentation, just enough to get bubbles... if you do any more than that the bottles will explode.

Q: But they mature like wine?
A: Yeah.

Q: And what's the reason for that?
A: Higher alcohol content, more hops, and also the bottle conditioning process... it's more like champagne, where the product is naturally fermented. That's a better environment for the product to age.

Q: Does that prevent contamination?
A: Refermentation scavenges oxygen out of the liquid, and that helps stop failing and off-flavors that might occur in beer if it ages.

SPORTS

When Bill Walton led the **Trailblazers** (☎321-3211, tickets $15-65) to the 1979 NBA Championship, Portland went berserk—landing an NBA team in the first place was a substantial accomplishment for a city of Portland's size. The closest the Blazers have come to a title repeat came in 2000, when they lost to the Los Angeles Lakers in the Western Conference Championships. The Blazers play November to May in the sparkling new **Rose Garden Arena** by the Steel Bridge in Northeast Portland, with its own stop on MAX. Portland is also home to the Portland **Fire** of the WNBA professional women's basketball league. The **Winter Hawks** of the Western Hockey League (☎238-6366; tickets $12-20) play from September to March in the Rose Garden Arena and at the **Coliseum.** Take bus #9 or MAX. **PGE** (Portland General Electric) **Park,** 1844 SW Morrison St., on the other side of town, is home to the **Beavers,** Portland's AAA-league baseball team. The San Diego Padres also have an A-league affiliated team in Portland. (☎223-2837. June-Sept. Gen. admission $3.)

FESTIVALS

Rose Festival, 5603 SW Hood Ave. (☎227-2681). Like Alpacas? Then check out the Alpaca show. Portland's premier summer event offers concerts, celebrities, auto racing, an air show, and the largest children's parade in the world. Larger events require tickets, but smaller ones are free.

Waterfront Blues Festival (☎282-0555 or 973-3378), early July. Outrageously good entertainment featuring blues, folk, and other artists on 3 stages with open air seating. Suggested donation is $3-5 and 2 cans of food to benefit the Oregon Food Bank.

Oregon Brewers Festival (☎778-5917; www.oregonbrewfest.com), on the last full weekend in July. The continent's largest gathering of independent brewers (72 breweries) parties at Waterfront Park. $1 per taste, $3 per mug. Under 21 must be with parent.

Mt. Hood Festival of Jazz (☎219-9833, www.mthoodjazz.com), on the first weekend in Aug. at Mt. Hood Community College in Gresham. Take I-84 to Wood Village-Gresham exit and follow the signs, or ride MAX to the end of the line. The PNW's premier jazz festival. Wynton Marsalis and the late Stan Getz have been regulars. Tickets from $29 per night, more through Ticketmaster. 3-day passes $70-130. Reserve well in advance.

NIGHTLIFE

Once an uncouth and rowdy frontier town, always an uncouth and rowdy frontier town. Portland's nightclubs cater to everyone from the iron pumping college athlete to the nipple-pierced neo-goth aesthete. Bigger, flashier clubs rule **Old Town** and central **Downtown,** where mainstream, punk, jazz and gay joints all come alive on weekends. In the **Pearl District** and **Nob Hill,** yuppies and college kids kick back together in spacious bars. In the **Southeast,** cramped quarters make for instant friends over great music and drinks. Hidden in the Northeastern suburb of **Laurelhurst,** locals gather in intimate clubs to listen to the best of the city's folk and rock. The plentiful neighborhood pubs often have the most character and the best music. Mischievous minors be warned: the drinking age is strictly enforced.

DOWNTOWN & OLD TOWN

Ohm, 31 NW 1st Ave. (☎223-9919; www.clubohm.com), at Couch under the Burnside Bridge. A venue dedicated to electronic music and unclassifiable beats. Achieve oneness dancing in the cool brick interior, or give your ears and feet a break and mingle outside. Tu brings Dhalia, W Breakbeat and Trance, Th Spoken word, and weekends often bring big-name live DJs. 21+. Cover $3-15. Open M-W 9pm-2:30am, Th-F 9pm-3:30am, Sa 9pm-4am, Su 9pm-3am. After-hours for some shows and special events stretch past 6am. Kitchen service until 2am.

Brig, The Nightclub Fez, Red Cap Garage, Panorama and **Boxxes,** 341 SW 10th St. (☎221-7262; www.boxxes.com), form a network of clubs along Stark St. between 10th and 11th. On weekdays the clubs are connected, but on weekends they are often sealed off—check at the door to see what is happening where. The 23-screen video and karaoke bar is where magic happens. On weekends, the crowds are mixed everywhere except Boxxes (which is always gay); on weekdays, all the clubs are predominantly gay. Cover $2-5. Open M-Su 9pm-2:30am; Panorama stays open until 4 or 4:30am F-Sa.

Satyricon, 125 NW 6th Ave. (☎243-2380), on the bus mall. A venue perfectly suited for punk and alternative, this intimate space hosted the Northwest's best long before grunge rock was the new kid on the block. Won't open unless a show is booked, so call ahead. 21+. Nightly cover $4-10, bigger draws $10-15. Open daily 10pm-2:30am.

(Continued from previous page)

Q: Are you more interested in product consistency, or do you prefer experimenting with different brews?

A: I enjoy when people like using our beer for celebrating special events and special occasions... it makes me feel good. If it wasn't for people that enjoyed the beer, brewing it wouldn't be so much fun.

Q: What about the name of the brewery, Hair the Dog?

A: Originally, the term literally referred to using the hair of a dog that bit you to help heal the bite. They'd chase a dog down, cut off some of its hair, [then] wrap it around the wound. And that helped chase away the evil spirit.

Q: And that's also for a hangover...?

A: Yes, the term later became used in reference to curing a hangover—drinking some of the "hair of the dog" you had the night before (more beer).

Q: Do these beers, having a higher alcohol content, give drinkers a stronger hangover the next morning?

A: All I know is we've generated quite a few hangovers.

Q: Oh yeah? [Feels head and eyes the empty glass.]

A: Whether they're worse or not I don't know. It depends on what you're used to drinking. We only use quality ingredients, so you should have a quality hangover.

Kells Irish Pub, 112 SW 2nd Ave. (☎227-4057). With a cigar bar and wood and brass interior, Kells caters to a more upscale crowd, but a great space and live Irish music every night of the week make sure that crowd is always buzzing. 21+. Happy Hour M-F 4-7pm and 11pm-1am. Open Su-W 11:30am-1am, Th-Sa 11:30am-2am.

Embers, 110 NW Broadway (☎222-3082), at Couch St. Follow rainbows to the dance floor, or watch fish swim in the bar counter. Retro and house music. The crowd is mostly gay on weekdays, but predominately straight on weekends. Happy hour until 7pm. Special events on Thurs. Open daily 11:30am-2:30am.

SOUTHEAST & HAWTHORNE

Produce Row Cafe, 204 SE Oak St. (☎232-8355). Bus #6 to SE Oak and SE Grand; walk west along Oak toward the river. A huge deck, hip staff, and enough beers to give a German a headache. 30 beers on tap and over 150 in bottles. Rotating line-up of bands (jazz, rock, bluegrass) and open-mic. Domestic bottles $2, pints $3. Open M-Th 11am-midnight, F-Sa noon-1am, Su noon-11pm.

Dots Cafe, 2521 SE Clinton St. (☎235-0203). Listen to Black Sabbath, electronica, jazz, and everything else in the company of Portland's young hipsters. The usual excellent microbrews, $6 pitchers of Pabst Blue Ribbon, and a regal assemblage of kitsch memorabilia accompany Victorian paintings. Rent a pool table for $0.25 per game. Cheese fries $3.50. Open daily noon-2am.

Sweetwater's Jam House, 3350 SE Morrison St. (☎233-0333). Rasta decor features life-sized swordfish and an authentic ganja sack, mon. Reggae music nightly. Affordable ($5-7) drinks; an extensive rum list includes "Joe vs. the Volcano," which arrives on fire. Food is excellent, but pricey. Open M-Th 5pm-1am, F-Sa 12pm-2am, Su 12pm-11pm.

OREGON

LAURELHURST

The Laurel Thirst Public House, 2958 NE Glisan St. (☎232-1504), at 30th Ave. Bus #19. Local talent makes a name for itself in 2 intimate rooms of groovin', boozin', and schmoozin'. Burgers and sandwiches $5-8. Free pool Su-Th before 7pm. Cover $3-6 after 8pm. Open Su, Tu-Th 9am-1:30am, M noon-1:30AM, F-Sa 9am-2am.

Beulahland, 118 NE 28th Ave. (☎235-2794), at Couch opposite the Coca-Cola bottling plant. Bus #19. A small venue with local art on the walls and huge, inflatable toys hanging from the ceiling. DJs on F, often spinning Ska; live music Sa. No cover. Happy hour 4-7pm. Open Su-Th 7am-midnight, F-Sa 7am-2:30am.

PEARL DISTRICT & NOB HILL

Jimmy Mak's, 300 NW 10th Ave. (☎295-6542), 3 blocks from Powell's Books at Flanders. Jam to Portland's renowned jazz artists. Shows 9:30pm-1am. Cover $3-6. Vegetarian-friendly Greek and Middle Eastern dinners ($8-17). Open Tu-Sa 11am-2am.

Bridgeport Brewing Co., 1313 NW Marshall (☎241-3612; www.bridgeportbrew.com), at 13th St. This old wood-beamed rope factory is the zenith of beer and pizza joints, with tables cut from old bowling alleys and sheltered outdoor eating. The on-site microbrewery produces a range of British-style ales. Open M-Th 11:30am-11pm, F-Sa 11:30am-midnight, Su 1-10pm. Also at 3632 SE Hawthorne (☎233-6540).

DAYTRIP FROM PORTLAND: SAUVIE

From I-405, Vaughn or Yeon Ave., take US 30 W (dir.: "Mount St. Helens"). After about 20min. watch for Sauvie Island signs to the right; one can also take bus #17 (St. Helens Rd.) from SW 6th and Salmon (40-50min.).

Peaceful Sauvie Island, found just northwest of downtown Portland at the confluence of the Columbia and Willamette Rivers, is part farming community and part nature preserve. A bridge connects Sauvie to the mainland at its southern tip, where produce-growing farms dominate, broken up only by pick-your-own berry stands and farmers markets. Most Portlanders head to Sauvie for its **beaches,** located on the northeast side of the island, which, along the rest of the northern half of the island, form the bird-laden **Sauvie Island State Wildlife Preserve.** Parking in the preserve requires a permit, and is efficiently enforced (daily permit $3.50, yearly $11). To get one, stop at **Sam's Cracker Barrel Grocery,** and grab a 10¢ map of the island while you're there. Sam's is located just over the bridge, about 50 yd. north on Sauvie Island Rd. (☎621-3960. Open daily 7am-8pm.) Plan ahead; Sam's is several miles from the beaches and is the most convenient place on the island to buy a permit. To get to the beaches head east and north from Sam's along Gillihan Loop Rd., and after 5 mi. bear right onto Reeder Road. Go another 4 mi. on Reeder and the beaches will be to your right. The local park office should know if there are any current advisories against dipping. The **Fish and Wildlife Office** (☎621-3488) is on the western side of the island, just north of where Reeder Rd. and Sauvie Island Rd. meet; they'll also be able to recommend nice routes for a short hike around the preserve (the preserve is closed to hikers from late Sept. to mid-April). Sauvie is short on roofed accommodations, but camping is available at **Sauvie Cove RV Park,** 31421 NW Reeder Rd., just south of the beaches. (☎621-9881. Sites with water and fire pits $17. RV sites also available for short and long-term stays.)

NEAR PORTLAND

MOUNT HOOD ☎503/541

You can't miss it—a magnet for the eyes, Mt. Hood is by far the most prominent feature on Northwest Oregon's horizon. Fumaroles and steam vents near the top mark this as a (relatively) recently active volcano, but that's no deterrent for thousands of outdoors enthusiasts. Home to many ski resorts—one is the only resort in the lower 48 open year-round—the mountain satisfies Portland's skiing needs. The surrounding ridgelines and mountains are relatively mellow compared to the other mega-volcanoes to the north, Mt. Adams and Rainier, allowing for decent, non-technical hiking, albeit with less spectacular views. The mountain gets its fair share of climbers to a 11,235 ft. summit.

ORIENTATION & PRACTICAL INFORMATION

Mt. Hood stands near the junction of US 26 and Hwy. 35, 1½hr. east of Portland via US 26. For a more scenic drive, take I-84 along the Columbia River Gorge to Exit 64 and approach the mountain from Hood River (see p. 90) on Hwy. 35. **Government Camp,** 50 mi. east of Portland, has food, accommodations, and gear rental.

Greyhound buses (☎800-231-2222) leave from the **Huckleberry Inn** (☎503-272-3325) in Government Camp to Portland (2hr., 1 per day, $8) and Bend (3hr., 1 per day, $17). Call ☎911 in an **emergency;** the nearest **hospitals** are in Portland and Hood River. The **post office** is at 88331 E Govt. Camp Loop Rd., in Government Camp. (☎800-275-8777. Open M-F 8:30am-5pm.) **Postal Code:** 97028. **Area code:** 503 to the west and south of Mt. Hood; 541 for Hood River and the northeast.

Hood River Ranger District Station, 6780 Hwy. 35, is 11 mi. south of Hood River and 25 mi. north of the US 26 and Hwy. 35 junction. It has more specialized info on the three ranger districts in the vicinity, as well as a variety of trail maps ranging from free to $5. (☎541-352-6002. Open Memorial Day-Labor Day daily 8am-4:30pm; Labor Day-Memorial Day closed Sa-Su.) **The Mt. Hood Info Center,** 65000 E US 26, 16 mi. west of the junction of US 26 and Hwy. 35 and 30 mi. east of Gresham at the entrance to the Mt. Hood village, has topo maps and info on ranger districts. The friendly staff will also direct you to the best trails. (☎503-622-7674 or 888-622-4822; www.mthood.org. Open June-Oct. daily 8am-6pm; Nov.-May 8am-4:30pm.)

ACCOMMODATIONS & CAMPING

Most campgrounds in **Mt. Hood National Forest** cluster near the junction of US 26 and Hwy. 35, although they can be found along the length of both highways on the way to Portland or Hood River. To get to a **free camping** spot near the mountain, take the sign towards Trillium Lake (a few miles east of Govt. Camp on Hwy. 26), then take a dirt road to the right ½ mi. from the entrance with sign "2650 13," go 200 yards, and make a left towards "Old Airstrip." Campsites with fire rings line the abandoned runway. For a far more expensive, less outdoorsy experience, stay in a hotel in **Government Camp** or on the mountain itself. (☎877-444-6777. Sites $9.)

Lost Lake Resort (☎541-386-6366; www.lostlakeresort.org). From Hwy. 35, turn east onto Woodworth Dr., right onto Dee Hwy., and then left on Lost Lake Rd. (Forest Service Rd. 13). Offers sites with water and toilets. A 3 mi. hike around the lake provides views of Mt. Hood. Rent a canoe ($8 per hr., $40 per day), or fish in the trout-stocked lake for free. 121 sites, $15; RV sites without electricity, $18; cabins, $45-100. Showers. ❶

Trillium Lake, 2 mi. east of the Timberline turn-off on US 26. Trails surround the crystal-clear lake. Water and toilets, lots of RVs. Paved, secluded sites, $12; lakeside, $14. ❶

Still Creek, 1 mi. west of Trillium Lake off US 26, offers sites that are unpaved and have a quieter, woodsy feel. Potable water, toilets, few RVs. $12-14. ❶

Sherwood, 14 mi. north of US 26 and just off Hwy. 35, beside a rambling creek. Potable water, pit toilets. Sites $10. No showers. ❶

Huckleberry Inn, 88611 Hwy. 26 Business Loop, (☎227-2335). TVs in rooms. Coin-op laundry. In summer 6 people for $85. In winter 4 people for $85. ❸

OREGON

FOOD

Cafeteria food at the ski resorts is extraordinarily overpriced; bring a bag lunch. Food in Government Camp is more reasonable.

Mt. Hood Brewing Co., 87304 E. Government Camp Loop (☎272-3724; www.mthoodbrewing.com). An angler-friendly interior with good burgers ($7-8.50) and plenty of on-site brewed beers. Open Su-W noon-10pm, Th-Sa noon-11pm. ❷

Huckleberry Inn, 88611 Hwy. 26 Business Loop (☎272-3325), Government Camp. A bit overpriced, but the portions are large. Omelettes $7.25. Open 24 hr. ❷

SIGHTS

Six miles up a road just east of Government Camp stands the historic **Timberline Lodge** (☎622-7979), built by hand in 1937 under the New Deal's Works Progress Administration. On the Timberline grounds is the **Wy'East Day Lodge,** which offers complimentary ski storage in the wintertime. Timberline's **Magic Mile** express lift carries passengers above the clouds for spectacular views of the mountains and ridges north, though if it's sunny extra elevation doesn't improve on the view from the Timberline lodge road. ($8, ages 7-12 $6, under 7 free.)

In the summer, Mount Hood Ski Bowl opens its **Action Park,** which features Indy Kart racing ($5 per 5min.), horseback riding ($25 per hr.), mini-golf ($5), batting cages ($1 for 10 pitches), helicopter rides ($20), bungee jumping ($25), and an alpine slide for $5. (☎222-2695. Open M-Th 11am-6pm, F 11am-7pm, Sa-Su 10am-7pm.) The Ski Bowl maintains 40 mi. of bike trails ($5 trail permit), and **Hurricane**

Racing rents mountain bikes from mid-June to October ($10 per hr.; half-day $25, full-day $32; trail permit included). The Mt. Hood Visitors Center also lists hiking trails on which mountain biking is **free.**

HIKING

Hiking trails encircle Mt. Hood; simple maps are posted around **Government Camp.** The free *Day Hikes* booklet describes 34 trails in the area and is available from the Mt. Hood Information Center (see **Orientation and Practical Information,** p. 87). A Northwest Forest parking pass is required at several trailheads. ($5 per day or $30 per year; available at the Mt. Hood Info Center.) Mt. Hood is also a respectable technical alpine climb. **Timberline Mountain Guides,** based out of Timberline Lodge, guides summit climbs for $375. (☎541-312-9242; www.timberlinemtguides.com.) **Mountain Tracks Ski and Snowboard Ski Shop,** in the Huckleberry Inn, has details on more ski trails. (☎503-272-3380. Closed summers.)

Mirror Lake Trail (6 mi. loop, several hours). Trailhead at a parking lot off US 26, 1 mi. west of Government Camp. A very popular dayhike, this trail winds its way to the beautiful Mirror Lake through the forest. Easy to moderate hiking.

Timberline Trail (41 mi., overnight). Trailhead at **Timberline Lodge** (see **Downhill Skiing,** below) was constructed by the New Deal Civilian Conservation Corps in the 1930s and circles the mountain, offering incomparable views of the Cascades. Strenuous.

Old Salmon River Trail (5 mi. round-trip, 2-3hr.). Take Hwy. 26 to Welches. 1 mi. east of the signal, turn onto Salmon River Rd., and go for 2½ mi. Winds up gentle grades through the forests and meadows, and has creek-crossings in spring. Moderate.

Trillium Lake Loop (4½ mi. loop, 1-2hr.). Trailhead in the day-use area of the Trillium Lake campground. A lakeside trail offering wildlife-viewing and alpine wetlands that becomes a challenging cross-country ski course in winter. Easy to moderate.

SKIING

Two resorts on the mountain itself and one on nearby **Tom Dick Peak** rank best among the many ski areas around Mt. Hood. All offer **night skiing** and **terrain parks.** Mt. Hood Meadows is considered the best during the winter for its breadth of terrain and decent snow, but when the temperature drops and the rain changes over to powder, Mt. Hood Ski Bowl has the biggest vertical drops and steepest terrain. Timberline isn't anything special by wintertime standards, but skiers and riders swarm to the slopes in summertime, as do thousands of Monarch butterflies.

Mount Hood Meadows (☎337-2222; snow report 503-227-7669 or 541-386-7547). 9 mi. east of Government Camp on Hwy. 35. The volcanic terrain is a highlight, offering all kinds of interesting features from a natural half-pipe (it's off the Cascade Express lift, below the trail with the huge ridge/cornice) to the stark and steep Heather Canyon. Huge volumes of snow, it's not always the driest, but there's plenty of it. Mt. Hood Meadows has $25 lift tickets through participating hotels, including the **Bingen School Hostel** (see p. 91). Open Nov. to May daily 8am-4pm. Lift tickets $41, ages 7-12 $21. Night skiing Dec.-Mar. W-Su 4-10pm, $17. Ski rental package $22, ages 7-12 $15; snowboard package $28, ages 7-12 $21. Beginner package with lift ticket, lesson, and rental $50.

Mount Hood Ski Bowl, 87000 E US 26 (☎503-222-2695 or 800-754-2695), in Government Camp 2 mi. west of Hwy. 35. Just a little guy, with a vertical drop of 1500 ft. The season is shorter (Nov.-Apr.) because of its lower elevation; however, with 34 lit trails, they offer the most night skiing in America and have a great terrain park. Open M-Tu 3:30-10pm, W-Th 9am-10pm, F 9am-11pm, Sa 8:30am-11pm, Su 8:30am-10pm. Lift tickets $26-30, under 12 $18; $16 per night. Ski rental package $19, $12; snowboard package $27 per day, $21 per night.

Timberline (☎622-0717; snow report ☎503-222-2211). Off US 26 at Government Camp. Timberline becomes a hub for hucking, jibbing and general new-school craziness in the summer—other than Whistler, it's the only resort open. Though a large portion of the resort gets cordoned off to those paying top dollar for summer ski or riding camps, a few lanes of the snowfield stay open. **Beware solar devastation:** you'll wish you were never born if you don't bring goggles or sunglasses and **plenty** of sunscreen. Also, unless you never fall, it's advisable to wear long-sleeved tops and bottoms, since the snow is soft but granule-like and gives a nasty "Palmer burn" if slid on. Slopes are intermediate to advanced. Open winter daily 9am-4pm; spring and fall 8:30am-2:30pm; summer 7am-1:30pm. Night skiing Jan.-Feb. W-F 4-9pm, Sa-Su 4-10pm. Lift tickets $38. Ski rental package $21; snowboard package $33.

COLUMBIA RIVER GORGE ☎541/509

Stretching 75 stunning miles east from Portland, the Columbia River Gorge carries the river to the Pacific Ocean through woodlands, waterfalls, and canyons. Heading inland along the gorge, heavily forested peaks give way to broad, bronze cliffs and golden hills covered with tall pines. Mt. Hood and Mt. Adams loom nearby, and breathtaking waterfalls plunge over steep cliffs into the river. The river widens out and the wind picks up at the town of Hood River, providing some of the world's best windsurfing. Once fast and full of rapids, the Columbia is more placid now, as dams now channel the water's fury for hydroelectric power.

TRANSPORTATION

To follow the gorge, which divides Oregon and Washington, take **I-84** east from Portland to Exit 22. Continue east uphill on the **Historic Columbia River Hwy. (US 30),** which follows the crest of the Gorge and affords unforgettable views. Or stay on I-84, which follows the Columbia River; **Hwy. 14** runs the length of the Washington side of the river. **Hood River,** at the junction of I-84 and **Hwy. 35,** is the hub of activity in the Gorge. It gives access to the larger city of **Dalles** to the east and **Mt. Hood** (see p. 87) to the south. **Bingen, WA** (BIN-jin), across the Hood River Bridge ($0.75 toll), gives access to the forests of **Mt. Adams** (see p. 232). **Maryhill, WA** is 33 mi. west of Bingen on Hwy. 14.

Trains: Amtrak (☎800-872-7245) disgorges passengers at foot of Walnut St. in **Bingen, WA,** across from Monterey Bay Fiberglass in the Burlington-Northern Santa Fe terminal. 1 train leaves per day for **Portland** (2hr., $10-18) and **Spokane** (6hr., $30-63).

Buses: Greyhound, 600 E. Marina Way (☎541-386-1212), in the Hood River DMV building. Off I-84 at Exit 64, take a left at the intersection before the toll bridge and follow the signs to the DMV, the 2nd building on the right. Open M-F 8:30-11:30am and 1:30-4:30pm. To **Portland** (1¼hr., 4 per day, $12).

Public Transportation: Columbia Area Transit (CAT; ☎386-4202) provides door-to-door service within the Hood River area for $1.25; call for pick-up. Also provides weekend shuttle to Meadows during ski season ($3). Open daily 8am-4:30pm.

PRACTICAL INFORMATION

Visitor Information: Hood River County Chamber of Commerce, 405 Portway Ave. (☎541-386-2000 or 800-366-3530; www.hoodriver.org), in the Expo Center north off Exit 63. Helpful information on events in the region complements a plentiful collection of maps. Open Apr.-Oct. M-F 9am-5pm, Sa-Su 10am-5pm; Nov.-Mar. M-F 9am-5pm. Many other visitors centers also line the gorge.

Outdoor Information: Columbia Gorge National Scenic Area Headquarters, Sprint's Waucoma Center Bldg., 902 Wasco St. #200 (☎541-386-2333; www.fs.fed.us/r6/columbia), Hood River. Forest Service camping map ($4). Open M-F 7:30am-4:30pm.

Internet Access: Hood River Library, 601 State St. (☎541-386-2535), Hood River, up the hill near Wy'East Whole Foods. 2 computers with 30min. Internet access for free; sign up well in advance. Open M-Th 8:30am-8:30pm, F-Sa 8:30am-5pm.

Weather: ☎541-386-3300.

Emergency: ☎911.

Hood River Police: 211 2nd St. (non-emergency ☎541-386-3942).

Hospital: Hood River Memorial, 13th and May St. (☎541-386-3911). 24hr. emergency.

Post Office: 408 Cascade Ave. (☎800-275-8777), Hood River. Open M-F 8:30am-5pm. **Postal Code:** 97031.

ACCOMMODATIONS

Hotel rooms in Hood River typically start around $50 and spiral upward from there. Cheaper motels line the west end of Westcliffe Dr., north off Exit 62 of I-84, although they're usually full on the weekends. Camping in state parks along the river is generally affordable. **Ainsworth State Park** is also readily accessible (see **Portland,** p. 75). For a full list of camping facilities, contact the Visitors Center.

Bingen School Inn Hostel/Columbia Gorge Outdoor Center (☎509-493-3363; www.bsi-cgoc.com). 3rd left after the yellow blinking light onto Cedar St.; from there it's 1 block up the hill on Humbolt St. An outdoorsy converted schoolhouse with airy rooms, both dorm-style and private. In the summer, **windsurfing lessons** ($65 per 3hr., beginner to advanced) and **rentals** ($30 per day, $185 per week) are available. Kitchen, laundry, climbing wall, volleyball net, outdoor grill, TV/VCR, school lockers, and linen are available. Winter guests score $20 Hood Meadows lift tickets. Dorms $15; 5 large private rooms $35 for 2 people, $10 per additional person. ❶

Beacon Rock State Park (☎509-427-8265), 7 mi. west of the Bridge of the Gods on Washington's Hwy. 14. Easy access to hiking, mountain biking, fishing, and rock climbing. 28 secluded, woodsy sites $16. Coin showers. ❶

Viento State Park (☎541-374-8811 or 800-452-5678). 8 mi. west of Hood River off I-84. Offers a noisy but pleasant experience, and easy access to river hiking. Showers and toilets. 13 tent sites $14, 61 RV sites $16. Handicap facilities available. ❶

Lone Pine Motel, 2429 Cascade St. (☎541-387-8882), Hood River, just west of Safeway, rents comfortable hostel-style rooms with fridges, microwaves, and TV for almost nothing, but rarely has openings. Rooms $25-60, or $125 for week. ❷

FOOD

Safeway, 2249 W Cascade St., has groceries. (☎541-386-1841. Open daily 6am-1am.) **Wy'East Whole Food Market,** 110 5th St., off Oak St. in Hood River, complements its natural food selection with handmade sandwiches ($4-5) and a java, smoothie, and juice bar. (☎541-386-6181. Open M-F 7:30am-6:30pm, Sa 9am-6pm, Su 10am-5pm.)

River City Saloon, 207 Cascade Ave. (☎541-387-2583), hosts bluegrass and rock musicians. Chicken parm sandwich $9. Happy Hour ($2.50 microbrews) 4:30-6:30pm. **Internet access** $1 per 15min. Open daily 4:30pm-2am. ❷

Full Sail Brewing Company and Pub, 506 Columbia Ave. (☎541-386-2247; www.fullsailbrewing.com). Take 5th St. 2 blocks toward the river from Oak St. Relax on the deck with a view of the river. Grill food $6-12. Open daily noon-9pm. ❷

Sage's Cafe, 202 Cascade Ave. (☎541-386-9404). Cheap, hearty breakfasts ($3-6) and lunchtime options including quiche or a sandwich ($2.50 and $4.50). Open M-F 7am-6pm, Sa 8am-6pm, Su 8am-5pm. ❶

SIGHTS

MARYHILL MUSEUM OF ART. This elegant museum sits high above the river on the Washington side. It was built in the 1920s by Sam Hill, a great benefactor of the area and instigator of the historic preservation of the Columbia Gorge. Hill was a friend of Queen Marie of Romania, whose coronation garb is displayed along with Rodin plasters. *(35 Maryhill Museum Dr. Hwy. 14 from Bingen or I-84 to Biggs, Exit 104; cross Sam Hill Bridge, then turn left onto Hwy. 14 for 3 mi. ☎509-773-3733. Open daily mid-Mar. to mid-Nov. 9am-5pm. $7, seniors $6, ages 6-16 $2.)*

STONEHENGE. Sam Hill built this full-scale replica of the English monument out of concrete as a memorial to the men of Klickitat County killed in WWI. Thinking that the original monument was used in sacrificial rituals before its astronomical properties became known, Hill hoped to express that "humanity still is being sacrificed to the god of war on fields of battle." People gather here for patriotic holidays and pagan celebrations alike. *(3 mi. farther east along Hwy. 14.)*

OREGON

OUTDOOR ACTIVITIES

WATERFALLS

A string of waterfalls adorns the Historic Columbia River Hwy. (US 30) east of Crown Point; pick up a waterfall map at the visitors center in Hood River. A short paved path leads to the base of **Latourell Falls,** 2½ mi. east of Crown Point. East another 5½ mi., **Wahkeena Falls,** beautiful and visible from the road, splashes 242 ft. down a narrow gorge. The base of the falls is less than half a mile farther east on Historic Columbia River Hwy. From I-84 Exit 31, take the underpass to the lodge. On a platform, you can watch the falls crash into a tiny pool. For a more strenuous hike, follow the **Larch Mountain Trail** to the top of the falls. Multnomah Falls visitors center in the lodge has free trail maps. (☎504-695-2372. Open daily July-Aug. 9am-8pm; June and Sept. 9am-7pm; Oct.-May 9am-5pm.)

WINDSURFING

Frequent 30mph winds make Hood River a windsurfing paradise. Considered one of the best sites in the world for freestyle sailboarding (the professional term for the sport), Hood River attracts some of the best windsurfers around, making watching as interesting as participating. The venerated **Rhonda Smith Windsurfing Center,** in the Port Marina Sailpark, Exit 64 of I-84, under the bridge and left after the blinking red light, offers classes. (☎541-386-9463. $140 for 2 3hr. classes. Includes free evening practice.) Lessons are also available from the **Bingen School Inn** (see **Accommodations**). **Big Winds,** 207 Front St., has cheap beginner rentals, plenty of helpful advice, and a wealth of equipment. (☎541-386-6086. $25 per 2hr.) Watch surfers in action at **The Hook,** a shallow, sandy cove off Exit 63 of I-84. Here, beginners learn the basic techniques of starting, handling, and jibing before moving out to the deep water of the river. **Spring Creek Fish Hatchery,** a.k.a. "The Hatch," is on Hwy. 14 west from Bingen. This is where to see the very best in the windsurfing business; there is plenty of parking, and the shore offers a view of the most popular stretch of water.

MOUNTAIN BIKING

The Gorge also has excellent mountain biking, with a wide variety of trails for bikers of all skill levels. **Discover Bicycles,** 205 Oak St., rents mountain bikes ($8-10 per hr., $50-60 per day), suggests routes, and sells maps for $2-5. (☎541-386-4820; www.discoverbicycles.com. Open M-Sa 9am-7pm, Su 9am-5pm.)

Seven Streams Canyon Loop (8 mi. loop, 1-2hr.). To get to the trailhead, take Oak St. from Hood River past where it merges with W. Cascade, and then turn left on Country Club Rd. After 1½ mi., take a right on Post Canyon Rd. and park on the right where the road becomes gravel. The trail offers great views as it winds through canyons. Moderate.

Mosier Twin Tunnels (4½ mi., 1hr.). A segment of the Historic Columbia River Hwy. that is too narrow for cars, between Hood River and Mosier. Parking is available at both the east and west end of the tunnels for $3. Offers mainly an on-road ride, with views of the river and the tunnels. Easy to moderate.

Surveyor's Ridge Trail (22 mi. round-trip, several hours). To get to the trailhead, take Rte. 35 south from Hood River for 11 mi. to Pinemont Dr. (Rd. 17), and go east for 6 mi. Turn right onto the dirt road at the "Surveyors Ridge" sign and park in the area by the power lines. Trail mainly follows the ridgeline and offers spectacular views of the Hood River Valley, Mt. Hood, and Mt. Adams. Open June-Oct. Moderate to strenuous.

HIKING

Mazama Trail (7½ mi., several hours). Take Hwy. 35 for 13 mi. to Woodworth Rd., then go 3 mi. to Dee Hwy. (281). Turn right and go 5 mi. before turning and following the signs to Lost Lake for 7 mi. on Rd. 18, then turn left onto Rd. 1810. Take 1810 to 1811, and drive 3 mi. to the trailhead. This trail begins in the forest, with Mt. Hood acting as a magnificent backdrop, then climbs up a steep ridge and through a dense forest to flowered glades and amazing vistas. Open June-Oct. $3 permit required. Strenuous.

Catherine Creek Trail (1¼ mi. round-trip, less than 1hr.). From Bingen, go east on Hwy. 14 and turn left on County Rd. 1230 at Rowland Lake. After about 1½ mi., park at the Catherine Creek lot. Goes along a paved path on the Washington side through wildflowers with dramatic views of the Columbia River and Mt. Hood. Easy.

Mt. Hamilton Trail (4½ mi. round-trip, several hours). Follow the directions in **Accommodations,** above, to **Beacon Rock State Park,** and park in the lot east of Beacon Rock, the 848 ft. neck of an old volcano. Climbing 2250 ft. up Mt. Hamilton on the Washington side of the river, the trail leads hikers up switchbacks to find the summit bursting with wildflowers in June and July. Moderate to difficult.

THE COAST: US 101

If not for the renowned US 101, Oregon's sandy beaches and dramatic seaside vistas might be only a beautiful rumor to those on the interior. Wherever the windy, bustling two lanes of US 101 part from the coast, a narrower road sticks to the stretches of unspoiled coast. The famous beaches complement the already scenic drive, and a chain of state parks ensures that no outdoors activity is unavailable.

There are 17 major state parks along the coast, many of which offer **campgrounds** with electricity and showers. While most of the traffic seems to be tourists in RVs, some savvy travelers choose to experience the coast by **bicycle**. In summer, prevailing winds blow southward, keeping at the backs of cyclists and easing their journey. Cyclists can contact virtually any Visitors Center or Chamber of Commerce on the coast for a free copy of the *Oregon Coast Bike Route Map*, which provides invaluable info for the ride. **Buses** run up and down the coast, stopping in most sizeable towns. Many local lines are affiliates of Greyhound and make connections to major urban centers like Seattle, Portland, and Eugene. The fastest way to experience the coast, however, is by car.

ASTORIA

☎503

Established in 1811 by John Jacob Astor's trading party, Astoria is the oldest US city west of the Rocky Mountains. Originally built as a fort to guard the mouth of the Columbia River, it quickly became a port city for ships heading to Portland and Longview, WA. A much more pleasant and less expensive destination than the overrun resort cities to the south, Astoria offers the same beautiful views of the Pacific Ocean from nearby **Ft. Stevens State Park.** Its Victorian homes, bustling waterfront, rolling hills, and persistent fog suggest a smaller-scale San Francisco. Differentiating it from that metropolis is a microclimate with wicked winter storms; hurricane-force winds aren't uncommon, and many come to watch storms roll into the Columbia river outlet.

TRANSPORTATION

From Astoria, US 30 runs 96 mi. to Portland. Astoria, a convenient link between Washington and the Oregon coast, can also be reached from Portland on US 26 and US 101 via **Seaside** (see p. 99). Two bridges run from the city: the **Youngs Bay Bridge** leads southwest where Marine Dr. becomes US 101, and the **Astoria Bridge** spans the Columbia River into Washington.

Buses: Pierce Pacific Stages (☎692-4437). A Greyhound affiliate. Pickup at Video City, 95 W Marine Dr., opposite the Chamber of Commerce. To **Portland** (3hr., $22). **Sunset Empire Transit,** 465 NE Skipanon Dr. (☎861-7433 or 800-766-6406), Warrenton. Pickup at Duane and 9th St. To **Seaside** (7 per day; $2.25, seniors, students, and disabled $1.75).

Public Transportation: Astoria Transit System (contact Sunset Empire for info, above). Local bus service M-Sa 7am-7pm. Fare $0.75; seniors, students, and disabled $0.50.

Taxis: Yellow Cab (☎325-3131 or 861-2626). Runs 6am-10pm. Base $2, $1.80 per mi.

ORIENTATION & PRACTICAL INFORMATION

Astoria is a peninsula that extends into the Columbia River, approximately 7 mi. from the ocean beaches in both Fort Stevens and nearby Washington. All streets parallel to the water are named in alphabetical order, except for the first one.

Tourist Information: 111 W Marine Dr. (☎325-6311), just east of Astoria Bridge. Loads of info on Astoria and its surrounding attractions. Open June-Sept. M-F 8am-6pm, Sa 9am-6pm, Su 9am-5pm; Oct.-May M-F 8am-5pm, Sa-Su 11am-4pm.

Equipment Rental: Bikes and Beyond, 1089 Marine Dr. (☎325-2961), rents bikes ($15 per half-day, $25 per day) and boats.

WINE & CHEESE, TOGETHER AT LAST A block up from the Maritime Museum is the Shallon Winery, 1598 Duane St., where owner Paul van der Veldt presides over a kingdom of fantastic wines. A self-proclaimed connoisseur of fine food, he insists that visitors call him at any time of day or night before considering a meal at any restaurant within 50 mi. Samplers taste wines made from local berries and the world's only commercially produced whey wines (from the cheese factories in Tillamook). Approach the cranberry-and-whey wine with caution; the fruity taste belies its high alcohol content. Sampling lemon meringue pie wine is likely to be the highlight, and Paul's chocolate orange wine is quite the decadent liqueur. (☎325-5978; www.shallon.com. Must be 21+ to drink. Open almost every afternoon. Gratuities and purchases appreciated.)

Laundromat: Maytag Self-Service Laundry, 127 W Bond St. (☎325-7815), 1 block away from Marine Dr. Wash $1, dry $0.25 per 10min. or $0.50 per 40min. Detergent $0.75. Open daily 8am-9pm, last wash load at 7:45pm.

Emergency: ☎911.

Crisis Line: ☎800-562-6025.

Police: 555 30th St. (☎325-4411).

Hospital: Columbia Memorial, 2111 Exchange St. (☎325-4321). 24hr.

Internet Access: Astoria Library, 450 10th St. (☎325-7323). For 1hr. of free Internet access sign up a day in advance, or get 15min. walk-up (ID required). Open Tu-Th 10am-7pm, F-Sa 10am-5pm. **Gunderson's Sunnyside Cybercafe,** at the foot of 6th St. (☎325-8642), has 2 computers. Open Tu-F 7:30am-5pm, Sa-Su 8am-5pm.

Post Office: 748 Commercial St. Open M-F 8:30am-5pm. **Postal Code:** 97103.

ACCOMMODATIONS & CAMPING

Motel rooms can be expensive and elusive during summer. US 101, both north and south of Astoria, is littered with clean and scenic campgrounds.

Ft. Stevens State Park (☎861-1671; reservations 800-452-5687), over Youngs Bay Bridge on US 101 S, 10 mi. west of Astoria. Rugged, empty beaches and hiking and bike trails surround the campground. Toilets, water. Reservations ($6) recommended. Wheelchair accessible. 600 sites, $18; full RV sites $21; hiker/biker sites $4.25 per person; yurts $29. Showers included. ❷

Grandview B&B, 1574 Grand Ave. (☎325-0000 or 325-5555). Intimate, cheery, and luxurious rooms. Includes delicious breakfast. Rooms with shared bath from $45, private bath from $71. Off-season 2nd night is $36. ❸

Lamplighter Motel, 131 W. Marine Dr. (☎325-4051 or 800-845-8847), between the Pig 'n' Pancake diner and the Visitors Center. Spotlessly clean, well-lit rooms with cable TV and phones. Large bathrooms, refrigerators. Coffee available in the lobby all day. Rooms $49-55, less in winter. Senior discount in winter. ❸

FOOD

Safeway, 1153 Duane St., provides groceries. (☎325-4662. Open daily 6am-midnight.) A small but growing **farmer's market** convenes each summer Sunday downtown at 12th St.

Columbian Cafe, 1114 Marine Dr. (☎325-2233). Local banter, wines by the glass, and fantastic pasta and seafood ($10-15, lunches $5-8) make it worthwhile. Try "Seafood" or "Vegetarian Mercy"—name the heat your mouth can stand and the chef will design a meal for you ($8-9). Open M-Tu 8am-2pm, W-Sa 8am-9pm, Su 9am-2pm. ❷

Home Spirit Bakery and Cafe, 1585 Exchange St. (☎325-6846). Eat a tasty, inexpensive meal in a restored Victorian home just a block away from the Shallon Winery. Call ahead. Open lunch Tu-Sa 11am-2pm, dinner Th-Sa 5:30-8pm. ❷

Someplace Else, 965 Commercial St. (☎325-3500). Complementing the delicious Italian fare is the nightly special ($5-14), a popular dish from a different country every night. Open W-Su 11:30am-2pm and 4-9pm. ❷

Urban Cafe, 1119 Commercial St. (☎338-5133). No 2 sq. m of the restaurant are alike, as part of a chaotic but endearing decoration scheme. Very satisfying dinner quesadillas $7; lunches around $7. Open M-Th 9am-9pm, F-Sa 9am-10pm. ❶

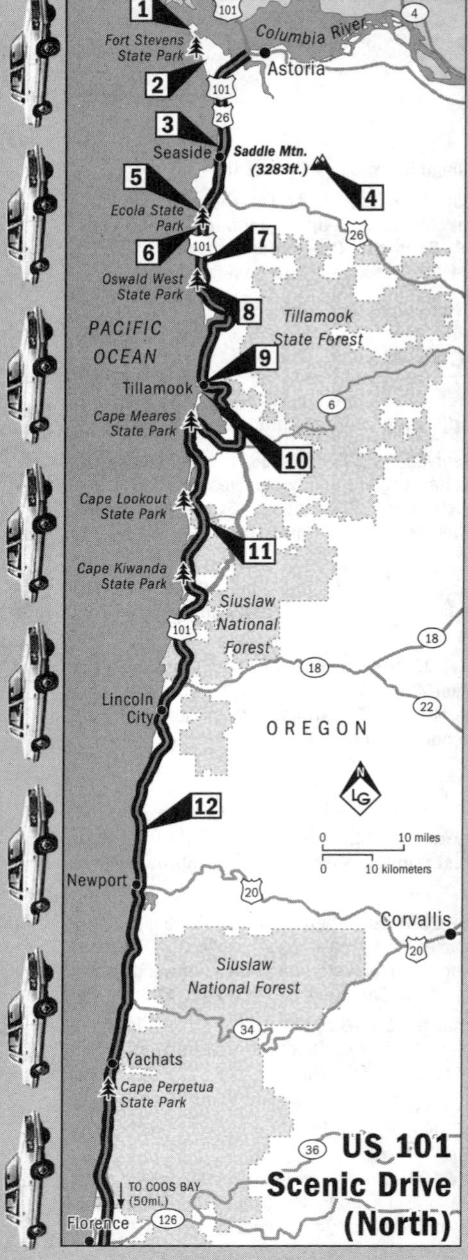

TIME: 7hr. end-to-end

DISTANCE: 320 mi.

SEASON: Year-round

From the Long Beach peninsula and Astoria in the north to Brookings in the south, US 101 hugs the shoreline along the Oregon Coast, linking a string of touristy resorts, small, unspoiled fishing villages, and pristine state parks. Oregon's beaches are some of the largest and most beautiful you will ever see; miles of untouched sand will keep the most picky beach comber content, and those brave enough to face the cold will enjoy the ocean waves. Touristy but gorgeous resort towns like Canon Beach and small communities like Bandon that line the Pacific Ocean make the Oregon Coast a worthy destination.

US 101 NORTH

1 SOUTH JETTY. Located in Ft. Stevens State Park, the jetty has great board- and kayak-surfing opportunities off the coast.

2 WRECK OF THE PETER IREDALE. Surfers flock to this popular Ft. Stevens area. The wreck has a peculiar effect on the waves as they come in.

3 THE COVE. Catch a wave at this spot, a beach near Seaside that few people know about. A great place to avoid the crowds.

4 SADDLE MOUNTAIN. This is the highest peak in the coastal range. From the summit, you can see the Pacific Ocean and the Cascades.

5 ECOLA STATE PARK. Ecola, with its many ascending trails, is the best place to see Cannon Beach's distinctive volcanic coastline.

6 CANNON BEACH. One of most desirable locations on the coast, with white sand and great weather.

7 HUG POINT. Make sure you visit here at low tide; it's the only time you can access the incredible network of tidal caves.

8 OSWALD WEST STATE PARK. Visit this surprising headland rainforest, enjoying the shelter of spruce and cedar trees.

9 TILLAMOOK. There are great hiking and biking routes in the nearby mountains, but Tillamook is known for having some of America's best cheese.

10 SALMON FISHING. This hidden estuary has some of the best salmon runs in the US.

11 THREE CAPES LOOP. This network of three state parks, Cape Meares, Cape Lookout, and Cape Kiwanda, is one of the coast's principal attractions.

12 OTTER CREST LOOP. A detour from US 101, this 4 mi. stretch of road has spectacular views of the ocean.

US 101 SOUTH

1 OREGON DUNES RECREATION AREA. These shifting dunes offer opportunities for multiple outdoors activities, including everything from dune buggy rides to sandboarding.

2 REEDSPORT. A popular stopover by the dunes, Reedsport has excellent camping and is a great place to rest between runs on the sand.

3 WINCHESTER BAY. This coastal city, close to Reedsport, houses an excellent surf spot on the coast. Rent crab traps to try and capture the elusive creatures; even if you can't get one, cheap meal options abound here.

4 UMPQUA DUNES TRAIL. Solitary and beautiful, this several-hour hike places you right in the middle of dunes as far as the eye can see. Free from the noise of ATVers and highway motorists, it's just you and the sand all the way.

5 SHARKS! The ocean around Bandon and Coos Bay is filled with Great Whites. Ask any surfer who looks like a veteran, and odds are someone they know will have had a close encounter. Surf shops will have info on when it's safe to go out, and when it's best to stay away from the beach.

6 HUNTER'S COVE. A beautiful spot on the coast and a major destination for windsurfing. Ask locals for information on how to find it, where to rent windsurfing equipment, and where to get lessons.

7 SAMUEL H. BOARDMAN STATE PARKS. Explore 15 mi. of countless trails, some leading to beaches covered in volcanic rocks. Don't be surprised if an exploratory hike unexpectedly ends at an intimate seaside cove.

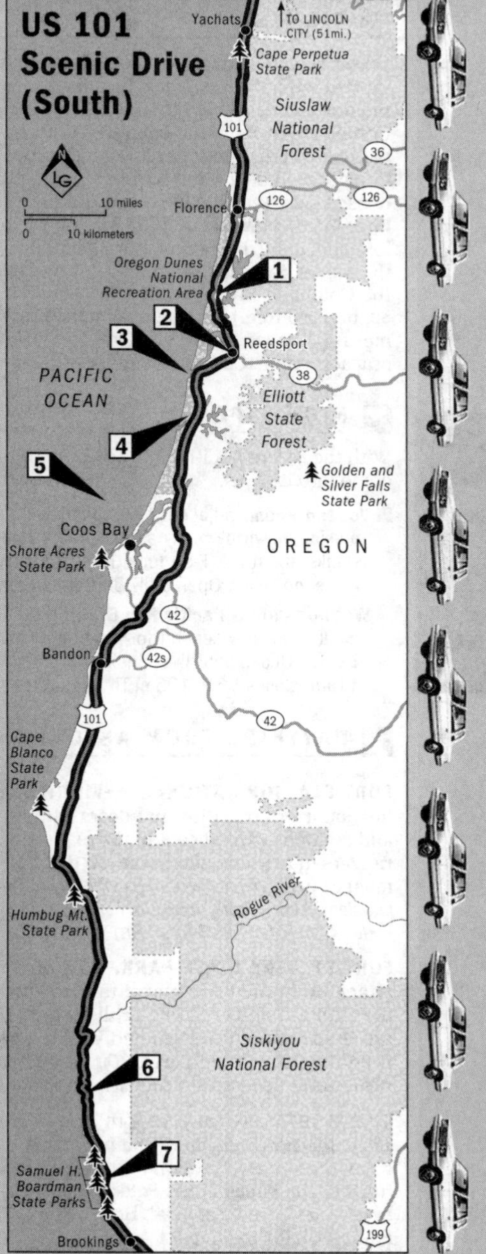

SIGHTS

On the rare clear day, **Astoria Column** grants its climbers a stupendous view of Astoria cradled between **Saddle Mountain** to the south and the **Columbia River Estuary** to the north. You can get there by following signs from 16th Ave. and Commercial St. Completed in 1926, the column on Coxcomb Hill Rd. encloses a dizzying 164 steps past newly repainted friezes depicting local history; picture something like an exceptionally well-decorated barber's pole jutting into the sky, albeit one that (luckily) doesn't spin. (Open dawn-10pm, parking $1.) The cavernous, wave-shaped **Columbia River Maritime Museum,** 1792 Marine Dr. on the waterfront, is packed with marine lore, including displays on the salmon fisheries that once dominated Astoria. Among the model boats is the 1792 vessel that Robert Grey first steered into the mouth of the Columbia River. (☎325-2323. Open daily 9:30am-5pm. $5, seniors $4, ages 6-17 $2, under 6 free.) The annual **Astoria-Warrenton Crab and Seafood Festival** is a misnomer for a large assembly of Oregon winemakers, brewers, and restaurants. ($5 general admission. Call the Chamber of Commerce, ☎800-875-6807, for more info.)

OREGON

NIGHTLIFE

With the recent addition of the Voodoo Room, the nightlife in Astoria has begun to come into its own.

Voodoo Room, adjacent to Columbian Cafe (☎325-2233). The new hot venue for live music, known by many as the artists' hang. Egyptian sarcophagi complete the scene. Drinks about $4. F-Sa funk, jazz, and every other kind of music; cover $3-5. Su bluegrass, no cover. Open daily 5-10pm or later.

Wet Dog Cafe & Pacific Rim Brewing Co., 144 11th St. (☎325-6975). Youthful crowds pack in every weekend for hip-hop and top-40 music. Burgers $5.50-8, microbrews $3.25. Occasional live music. Game room. DJ Th-F. 21+ after 9pm. Opens daily at 11am, closes Su-W 10pm, Th 1am, and F-Sa 1:30am. Dinner until 9pm.

DAYTRIPS FROM ASTORIA

FORT CLATSOP NATIONAL MEMORIAL. Reconstructs Lewis and Clark's winter headquarters from journal descriptions. The fort has been completely restored and contains exhibits about the explorers' quest for the Pacific Ocean. In summer, rangers in feathers and buckskin demonstrate quill writing, moccasin sewing, and musket firing. *(5 mi. southwest of town on US 101, south from Astoria to Alt. Rte. US 101; follow signs 3 mi. to park. ☎861-2471. Open June-Labor Day daily 8am-6pm; winter 8am-5pm. $2, under 17 free, families $4 per car.)*

FORT STEVENS STATE PARK. Fort Stevens was constructed in 1863 to prevent attack by Confederate naval raiders and was significantly upgraded in 1897 with the addition of 8 concrete artillery batteries. Several of these remaining batteries are the focus of a self-guided walking tour (about 2hr.) that begins up the road from the campground area. *(Off US 101 on a narrow peninsula 10 mi. west of Astoria. ☎861-2000. Day-use pass $3. Get a map and pass from the camp registration.)*

SOUTH JETTY. Great places to board- or kayak-surf near Astoria are at the South Jetty, the northern tip of the peninsula in Fort Stevens state park. Waves get big when the wave refraction off the jetty kicks in. Everyone loves catching a wave in front of the **Wreck of the Peter Iredale** that sticks out of the sand, even though the breaks are nothing special. Both beaches are easy to find within Fort Stevens State Park; look for parking lot A or B for the South Jetty; the main road goes straight to the wreck of the Peter Iredale. No shop specializes in surfboards in Astoria, but **Pacific Wave** in Warrenton, immediately across the Youngs Bay Bridge in the mall on the right, embraces the growing kayak-surfing movement and offers lessons. They'll also have the latest wave forecasts and other surf info.

SEASIDE ☎503

In the winter of 1805-1806, explorers Lewis and Clark made their westernmost camp near Seaside. While the amenities were few and far between at the time, after the development of a resort in 1870 the situation improved and visitors began to pour in. The tourism industry, replete with indoor mini-golf and barrels of saltwater taffy, has transformed Seaside from a remote coastal outpost to a bustling beachfront. For those uninterested in video arcades, Seaside still has merit as a base for exploring the beautiful Oregon coast. Seaside is also less expensive than nearby Cannon Beach, and its hostel is one of the best in the Northwest.

ORIENTATION & PRACTICAL INFORMATION

Seaside lies 17 mi. south of Astoria and 8 mi. north of Cannon Beach along **US 101.** The most direct route between Seaside and Portland is **US 26,** which intersects US 101 just south of Seaside near Saddle Mountain State Park. The Necanicum River runs north-south through Seaside, two blocks from the coastline. In town, US 101 becomes **Roosevelt Dr.,** and another major road, **Holladay Dr.,** splits off from it. **Broadway** runs perpendicular to the two, and is the town's main street and a tourist-dollar black hole. Streets north of Broadway are numbered, and those south of Broadway are lettered. The **Promenade** (or "Prom") is a paved foot-path that hugs the beach for the length of town.

Buses: Pierce Pacific Stages (☎692-4437; call Greyhound at 800-231-2222 for schedules and fares), a Greyhound affiliate, departs the hostel at 3pm for **Portland** (3¼hr., $24) and **Seattle, WA** (5½hr., $37, via **Kelso, WA**).

Public Transportation: Sunset Empire Transit (☎861-7433 or 800-776-6406) runs between Astoria and Cannon Beach 7 times per day M-Sa, stopping at the hostel in addition to the bus stops. Tickets available from drivers. Round-trip $4.50; seniors, disabled, students, and ages 6-12 $3.50; under 6 free.

Taxis: Yellow Cab (☎738-5252). $1.75 base, $1.50 per mi.

Tourist Information: Chamber of Commerce, 7 N. Roosevelt Dr. (☎738-6391 or 800-444-6740), on US 101 and Broadway. The **Seaside Visitor Bureau** (☎738-3097 or 888-306-2326; www.seasideor.com) is in the same building. Open June-Aug. daily 8am-5pm; Oct.-May M-F 9am-5pm, Sa-Su 10am-4pm.

Equipment Rental: Prom Bike Shop, 622 12th Ave. (☎738-8251), at 12th and Holladay, rents bikes, in-line skates, beach tricycles, and surreys. Excellent repair work. Must be 18+ to sign for rental. Open daily 10am-6pm. Bikes $6 per hr., $25-30 per day.

Laundry: Clean Services, 1223 S. Roosevelt Dr. (☎738-9513). Open daily 8am-10pm. Wash $1.25, dry $0.25 per 5-8min. Detergent $0.75.

Emergency: ☎911.

Police: 1091 S Holladay Dr. (☎738-6311).

Coast Guard: 2185 SE Airport Rd. (☎861-6140), in Warrenton.

Hospital: Providence Seaside Hospital, 725 S Wahanna Rd. (☎717-7000).

Internet Access: Seaside Library: 60 N Roosevelt Dr. (☎738-6742). Free 20min. of Internet access. Open Tu-Th 9am-8pm, F-Sa 9am-5pm, Su 1-5pm.

Post Office: 300 Ave. A (☎800-275-8777), off Columbia Ave. Open M-F 8:30am-5pm, Sa 8:30-10:30am. **Postal Code:** 97138.

ACCOMMODATIONS & CAMPING

Seaside's expensive motels are hardly an issue for the budget traveler thanks to the large hostel on the south side of town. Motel prices are directly proportional to their proximity to the beach and start at $50 (less during the off-season). The closest state parks are **Fort Stevens** ❶ (☎861-1671; see p. 98), 21 mi. north, and **Saddle Mountain** ❶ (☎800-551-6949), 10 mi. east, off US 26 after it splits with US 101. Drive 8 mi. northeast of Necanicum Junction, then another 7 mi. up a winding road to the base camp. (Drinking water. 10 sites. Oct.-Apr. $7; May-Sept. $10.) Sleeping on the beach in Seaside is illegal, as it is in all of Oregon.

Seaside International Hostel (HI), 930 N Holladay Dr. (☎738-7911). Free nightly movies, a well-equipped kitchen, an espresso bar, and a grassy yard along the river make this lively hostel live up to its reputation. Office open 8am-11pm. Kayak and canoe rental ($9-10 per 2hr.). Call well ahead for weekends. 34 large bunks. $16, nonmembers $19; private rooms with bath and cable TV $36-42, nonmembers $39-65. $2 off for touring cyclists. ❷

Colonial Motor Inn, 1120 N Holladay Dr. (☎738-6295 or 800-221-3804). With colonial furniture, free snacks, and clean, quiet rooms, this little motel is a standout for the price. Free Internet in office. Singles $50; doubles $70. $15-20 less in winter. ❸

Riverside Inn, 430 S Holladay Dr. (☎738-8254 or 800-826-6151). Cozy bedrooms, a deck overlooking the river, and skylights. This B&B is a quiet respite from the Seaside motel madness. Rooms have private bath and TV. Homemade breakfast. Doubles from $70; Oct.-Apr. from $65; singles $5 less. ❸

OREGON

FOOD

Prices on Broadway, especially toward the beach, are outrageous. **Safeway,** 401 S. Roosevelt Dr., stocks the basics. (☎738-7122. Open daily 6am-midnight.)

Morning Star Cafe, 280 S. Roosevelt Dr. (☎717-8188), opposite Safeway. Comfy beat-up couches and aging board games will remind you of your old basement rec room. Breakfast panini $3.50. Enjoy a sandwich ($3-4) or quiche ($3.50) with a mocha ($3). Open daily 7am-7pm. ❶

The Stand, 101 N. Holladay Dr. (☎738-6592), serves the cheapest Mexican meals around to a local crowd. Burritos $2.25-4. Open daily 11am-8pm. ❶

Harrison's Bakery, 608 Broadway (☎738-5331). Seaside's famous beach bread and a font of frosted treats, made every day at low tide. Hosteling discounts and plate-sized donuts. Open W-M 7am-4pm. ❶

SIGHTS & ENTERTAINMENT

Seaside's tourist population (which often outnumbers that of true locals) swarms around **Broadway,** a garish strip of arcades and shops running the half mile from Roosevelt (US 101) to the beach. "The Arcade," as it is called, is the focal point of downtown and attracts a youthful crowd. Bumper cars, basketball games, and other methods of fleecing visitors abound. The turnaround at the end of Broadway signals the end of the **Lewis and Clark Trail.**

The Seaside Aquarium, 200 N Prom, is smaller than its companion in Newport, but makes up for its small size by giving visitors the chance to feed playful harbor seals. (☎738-6211. Open Mar.-June daily 9am-5pm; July-Dec. open Su-Th

9am-6pm, F-Sa 9am-8pm; winter open W-Su 9am-5pm but days open may change, so call ahead. $6, seniors $4.75, ages 6-13 $3, 5 and under free, families as large as 6 $19. Seal feeding $0.75.)

Perhaps the US's premier recreational road race, the **Hood to Coast Relay** is the ultimate team running event. Held annually at the end of August, runners tear up the trails between Mt. Hood and Seaside (195 mi.) to the cheers of 50,000 spectators. About 750 12-person teams run three 5 mi. shifts in this 1-2 day relay race. For info, call ☎292-2626 or 800-444-6749.

OUTDOOR ACTIVITIES

Seaside's beachfront is sometimes crowded despite bone-chilling water and strong undertows that more or less preclude swimming. For a slightly quieter beach, head to **Gearhart,** 2 mi. north of downtown off US 101, where long stretches of dunes await exploration. The local surfers know that one of Northern Oregon's **finest breaks** is south of town in **The Cove,** but don't tell anyone that *Let's Go* told you. To get there, take Ave. U towards the beach of Hwy. 101 and then make a left on Edgewood. **Cleanline Surf,** 719 1st Ave., rents surfing gear. (☎738-7888, or 888-546-6176. Open summer daily 10am-8pm; winter M-Sa 10am-6pm, Su 10am-5pm.)

CANNON BEACH ☎503

Many moons ago, a rusty cannon from a shipwrecked schooner washed ashore at Arch Cape, giving this town its name. Today, home to a veritable army of boutiques, bakeries, and galleries, Cannon Beach is a more refined alternative to Seaside's crass commercialism. Arguably the most desirable location on the entire Oregon Coast because of its amazing ocean views and interesting shops, Cannon Beach is always crowded with Portlanders and other tourists. If you're just driving down US 101, it's well worth the small detour to take an exit down Hemlock St. and take in the view.

ORIENTATION & PRACTICAL INFORMATION

Cannon Beach lies 8 mi. south of Seaside, 42 mi. north of Tillamook on US 101, and 79 mi. from Portland via US 26. Lovely **Ecola and Oswald State Parks** lie just to the north and a few miles south of the town, respectively. The four exits into town from US 101 all lead to Hemlock St., which is lined with galleries and restaurants.

Buses: Sunset Transit System (☎800-776-6406). To **Seaside** ($0.75) and **Astoria** ($2.25). **Cannon Beach Shuttle** traverses downtown; to board, just signal to the driver. Runs daily 9am-6pm. $0.75 donation requested.

Tourist Information: Cannon Beach Chamber of Commerce and Visitor Info, 207 N. Spruce St. (☎436-2623), at 2nd St. Open M-F 9:30am-5pm. Visitor Info open M-Sa 10am-5pm, Su 11am-4pm.

Equipment Rental: Mike's Bike Shop, 248 N. Spruce St. (☎436-1266 or 800-492-1266). Mountain bikes $6-8 per hr., $20-30 per day. Beach tricycles $8 per 1½hr., electric bikes $12 per hr. Open daily 10am-5pm. **Cleanline Surf,** 171 Sunset Blvd. (☎436-9726; www.cleanlinesurf.com). Surfboards and boogieboards $15 per day, wetsuits $20 per day, the complete package $35. Open summer M-F 10am-6pm, Sa 9am-7pm, Su 10am-6pm; winter daily 10am-5pm. **Surf lessons** are given by Tony Gardner (☎738-6448). $55 for 2hr., 2 students for $80.

Emergency: ☎911.

Police: 163 Gower St. (☎436-2811).

Medical Care: Providence North Coast Clinic, 171 Larch St. (☎717-7000), in Sandpiper Sq. Non-emergency care only; nearest emergency care in **Seaside** (see p. 99). Open M-F 8:30am-noon and 1:15-4:30pm.

Internet Access: Cannon Beach Library, 131 N. Hemlock St. (☎436-1391). $6 per hr. Open M-W and F 1-5pm, Th 1-7pm. **Copies and Fax,** 1235 S. Hemlock St. (☎436-2000). $5 for 1st 30min., $5 for each additional hr. Open M-F 10am-6pm.

Post Office: 163 N. Hemlock St., 97110 (☎436-2822). Open M-F 9am-5pm. **Postal Code:** 97110.

ACCOMMODATIONS & CAMPING

During the winter season, inquire about specials; many motels offer two-for-one deals. In the summer, however, it's a seller's market, so most motels have two night minimum stays if you want a reservation. Real budget deals are a short drive away: the **Seaside International Hostel** is 7 mi. north (see p. 100), and **Oswald West State Park** (see p. 103), 10 mi. south of town, has a stunning campground. **Nehalem Bay State Park,** only a few miles farther south than Oswald West outside of Nehalem, has plentiful camping options.

McBee Cottages, 888 S. Hemlock St. (☎436-2569). The office is in the **Sandtrap Inn** at 539 S. Hemlock St. Bright and cheerful rooms a few blocks from the beach. Some kitchen units and cottages available. $60; winter $45. ❸

Wright's for Camping, 334 Reservoir Rd. (☎436-2347), off Hwy. 101. Tree-shaded sites make this family-owned campground a relaxing retreat from RV mini-cities. Showers, toilets. Wheelchair accessible. Reservations advised in summer. 19 sites, $17. ❶

OREGON

FOOD

The deals are down Hemlock St. in mid-town. **Mariner Market,** 139 N. Hemlock St., holds 7439 grocery items on its expansive shelves. (☎436-2442. Open July-Sept. Su-Th 8am-10pm, F-Sa 8am-11pm; Oct.-June Su-Th 8am-9pm, F-Sa 8am-10pm.)

Lazy Susan's Cafe, 126 N. Hemlock St. (☎436-2816), in Coaster Sq. This Cannon Beach favorite has an intimate, woodsy interior. Excellent homemade scones ($1.75). Omelettes $7-8. Open summer daily 7:30am-10pm; winter M and W-Th 8am-2:30pm, F-Sa 8am-8pm, Su 8am-5pm. ❷

Cafe Mango, 1235 S. Hemlock St. (☎436-2393), in Haystack Sq. An up-and-coming new restaurant where Midtown Cafe used to be. Savory crêpes $5-7, omelettes about $9. First-rate service. Open summer Th-M 7:30am-2:30pm. ❸

Bill's Tavern, 188 N. Hemlock St. (☎436-2202.) A local spot for down-to-earth eatin'. Beer on tap is brewed upstairs. Basic pub grub $3-8.25. Pints $3. Open Th-Tu 11:30am-midnight, W 4:30pm-midnight. Kitchen closes around 9:30pm. ❶

ENTERTAINMENT & OUTDOOR ACTIVITIES

Cannon Beach has expensive, sporadically elegant galleries and gift shops. A stroll along the 7 mi. stretch of flat, bluff-framed beach suits many better. **Coaster Theater,** 108 N. Hemlock St., is a small playhouse that stages theater productions, concerts, dance performances, comedy, and musical revues year-round. Schedule varies, so call or check the website. (☎436-1242; www.coastertheater.com. Box office open W-Sa 1-8pm. Tickets $12-15.)

The best place to enjoy the dramatic volcanic coastline of Cannon Beach is at **Ecola State Park,** which attracts picnickers, hikers, and surfers alike. Have a look at Ecola Point's views ($3 entrance fee) of hulking **Haystack Rock,** which is spotted with (and by) seagulls, puffins, barnacles, anemones, and the occasional sea lion.

Follow signs from Hwy. 101. **Indian Beach** is a gorgeous surfing destination; catch waves between volcanic rock walls, with a freshwater stream running down the beach to rinse the salt off after you're done. To surf, rent boards from **Cleanline Surf,** 171 Sunset Blvd. (☎436-9726. Surfboards and boogieboards $15 per day; wetsuits $20 per day. Open M-F 10am-6pm, Sa 9am-7pm, Su 10am-6pm; winter daily 10am-5pm.) There is also good hiking in the area:

Indian Beach Trail (2 mi., about 1hr.) leads to the Indian Beach tide pools, which teem with colorful sea life. Follow signs to "Ecola" to reach trailhead. Easy to moderate.

Tillamook Head Trail (12 mi. round-trip, several hours). Leaves from Indian Beach, and hugs the coast to the mini-cape that separates Seaside Beach from Cannon Beach. The trail passes the top of Tillamook head (2 mi. up the trail), where 5 hiker sites await those willing to make the trek for free camping. Moderate.

Saddle Mountain Trail (5 mi. round-trip, several hours), 14 mi. east of Cannon Beach on US 26, climbs the highest peak in the Coast Range. The trail leads to the mountain's 3283 ft. summit and ends with astounding views of the Pacific Ocean, Nehalem Bay, and the Cascades. Moderate to difficult.

CANNON BEACH TO TILLAMOOK ☎503

The coastal mountains south of Cannon Beach culminate in a scenic section of roadway that cuts into the ocean cliffside of Neahkannie Mountain. Farther south is **Tillamook State Forest,** so named after the infamous Tillamook Burn (a series of fires in 1933) reduced 5 sq. mi. of coastal forest near Tillamook to charcoal. While nature has restored Tillamook State Forest to health, coastal towns to the west are still scarred. The coastline alongside these tiny towns is much less crowded than Seaside and Cannon Beaches. Tourist info for the area is available at the visitors center in Tillamook (see p. 103) or the Rockaway Beach Chamber of Commerce, 103 S. 1st St., off US 101. (☎355-8108. Open M-F 10am-3pm.)

HUG POINT. The tidal caves, Hug Point's main claim to fame, are accessible only at low tide. The beach is framed by tall cliffs, and secluded picnic tables dot the headlands near the parking lot. The point is about 2 mi. south of Cannon Beach.

OSWALD WEST STATE PARK. Ten miles south of Cannon Beach, Oswald West State Park is a tiny headland rainforest of hefty spruce and cedars. Local surfers call the sheltered beach here **Short Sands Beach,** or Shorty's; with a first-rate break and camping so close by, the beach is a premier surf destination. The beach and woodsy campsites are only accessible by a ¼ mi. trail off US 101, but the park provides wheelbarrows for transporting gear from the parking lot to the 29 sites. (Open Mar.-Nov. Sites $15.) The campground fills quickly; call ahead. From the south side of the park, a segment of the Oregon Coast Trail leads over the headland to 1661 ft. Neahkahnie Mountain.

NEHALEM. Eight miles south of Oswald State Park, a cluster of made-in-Oregon-type shops along US 101 make up Nehalem. The **Nehalem Bay Winery,** 34965 Hwy. 53, 3 mi. south of town, has free tastings of local cranberry and blackberry vintages. The backpacker-friendly winery sponsors performances in a small theater and an annual reggae and bluegrass festival, providing a forum for general bacchanalian revelry. (☎368-9463. Open summer daily 9am-6pm; winter 10am-5pm.)

TILLAMOOK ☎503

Although the word Tillamook (TILL-uh-muk) translates to "land of many waters," to the Northwest it is synonymous with cheese. Tourists come by the hundreds to gaze at blocks of cheese being cut into smaller blocks on a conveyor belt at the

Tillamook Cheese Factory. The dairy cows themselves give the town a rather bad odor; still, two good museums, hiking and biking in the nearby coastal mountains, and the Three Capes Loop redeem Tillamook for the adventurous traveler.

ORIENTATION & PRACTICAL INFORMATION. Tillamook lies 49 mi. south of Seaside and 44 mi. north of Lincoln City on **US 101.** It's also 74 mi. west of Portland on **Rte. 6** and **US 26.** Tillamook's main drag, US 101, splits into two one-way streets downtown: **Pacific Ave.** runs north and **Main Ave.** runs south. The cross streets are labeled numerically. **Ride the Wave Bus Lines** (☎800-815-8283) runs locally (M-Sa; $1) as well as to Portland (2½hr., 5 per week, $10). Find a list of campsites and hiking trails in Tillamook County at the **Tillamook Chamber of Commerce,** 3705 US 101 N, in the big red barn near the Tillamook Cheese Factory, 1½ mi. north of town. (☎842-7525. Open summer M-Sa 9am-5pm, Su 10am-4pm; winter M-F 9am-5pm, Sa 10am-3pm.) **Equipment repair** is at **Trask Mt. Cycle,** 2011 3rd St., by Pacific Ave., where they also give good advice and sell maps of mountain biking trails in the area. (Open M-Th 9am-8pm, F-Sa 9am-9pm, Su 11am-7pm.) Call ☎911 in an **emergency,** or notify the **police,** 210 Laurel St. (☎842-2522), in City Hall, or the **Coast Guard** (☎322-3531). **Tillamook County Library,** 210 Ivy Ave., offers 3 computers with 30min. of free **Internet access.** (☎842-4792. Open M-Th 9am-9pm, F-Sa 9am-5:30pm.) The **post office** is at 2200 1st St. (☎800-275-8777. Open M-F 9am-5pm.) **Postal Code:** 97141.

ACCOMMODATIONS & CAMPING. Motel prices in Tillamook are steep (and aren't helped by the 7% city lodging tax), but the camping is some of the area's finest. The only reasonably priced motel in town is the **MacClair Inn ❹,** 11 Main Ave. at the center of town, which rents huge, clean rooms. Enjoy the outdoor pool, hot tub, and sauna. (☎842-7571 or 800-331-6857. Singles $66, doubles $73. 10% AAA discount. Credit card required.) **Kilchis River Park ❶,** 6 mi. northeast of town at the end of Kilchis River Rd., which leaves US 101 1 mi. north of the factory, has 35 sites between a mossy forest and the Kilchis River. The campground itself is mostly geared towards families, with a baseball field, volleyball court, horseshoes, and swimming. Mountain bikers can find excellent trails within short rides of the campground on former logging roads. Hiking options abound in the mountains, and the campground offers access to one of the **best salmon-fishing** rivers in the lower 48. (☎842-6694. Water, toilets. Open May-Oct. Tent sites $10; walk-ins $3.) To sleep on the sand, try the **campgrounds** on the Three Capes Loop.

FOOD. Tillamook may be a cheese-lover's paradise, but other food choices in town are lacking. Pick up some Velveeta at **Safeway,** 955 US 101, on the north side of downtown. (☎842-4831. Open daily 6am-1am.) The **Blue Heron French Cheese Company ❷,** 2001 Blue Heron Dr., north of town and 1 mi. south of the Tillamook Cheese factory, has tasty deli sandwiches. Although the sheer quantity of items for sale is almost overwhelming, sandwiches stand out at $6.25. (☎842-8281. Open summer daily 8am-8pm; winter 9am-5pm. Deli open 11:30am-4pm.)

SIGHTS. Plane buffs and all who celebrate mechanical marvels will appreciate the impressive **Tillamook Naval Air Station Museum,** 2 mi. south of town. This hulking 7 acre former blimp hangar is the largest wooden clear-span structure in the world. The airy cavern is home to over 34 fully functional war planes, including WWII beauties like the P-38 Lightning and a PBY-5A Catalina. It also has some modern fighter jets on loan from the navy. (☎842-1130. Open daily 10am-5pm. $9.50, over 65 $8.50, ages 13-17 $5.50, 12 and under $2.) Downtown, the **Tillamook County Pioneer Museum,** 2106 2nd St., features exceptionally thorough collections of WWII medals, rifles, and collectibles. Also displays the head-turning work of taxidermist and big game hunter Alex Walker. (☎842-4553. Open M-Sa 8am-5pm, Su 11am-5pm. $2, seniors $1.50, ages 12-17 $0.50, under 12 free.)

THREE CAPES LOOP ☎503/541

Between Tillamook and Lincoln City, US 101 wanders east into wooded land, losing contact with the coast. The Three Capes Loop is a 35 mi. circle that connects a trio of spectacular promontories—Cape Meares, Cape Lookout, and Cape Kiwanda State Parks—that will almost certainly make you linger longer than you expect; plan accordingly. The loop leaves US 101 at Tillamook and rejoins it about 10 mi. north of Lincoln City. Unless time is of the utmost importance, taking the loop is a far better choice than driving straight down US 101.

CAPE MEARES STATE PARK. Cape Meares State Park, at the tip of the promontory jutting out from Tillamook, protects one of the few remaining old-growth forests on the Oregon Coast. The mind-blowing **Octopus Tree**, a gnarled Sitka spruce with six candelabra trunks, looks like the imaginative doodlings of an eight-year-old. The **Cape Meares Lighthouse** operates as an illuminating on-site interpretive center. (Open May-Sept. daily 11am-4pm; Oct. and Mar.-Apr. F-Sa 11am-4pm. Free.) If you walk down to the lighthouse, bring binoculars or use the $0.25 viewer to look at the amazing seabird colony on the giant volcanic rock. As you drive south of Cape Meares, a break in the trees reveals a beach between two cliffs; this is a beautiful, quiet place to pull off the road and explore.

Oceanside and Netarts lie a couple miles south of the Cape, and offer overpriced gas, a market, and a few places to stay that tend to fill up fast. **The Terimore ❸,** 5103 Crab Ave., in Netarts, has the least expensive rooms in the two towns, some with ocean views. (☎842-4623 or 800-635-1821. Rooms with views $60-70, without $45-60.) Try the **Whiskey Creek Cafe ❷,** 6060 Whiskey Creek Road in Neharts. Popular for their oysters fresh from the bay; halibut and chips costs $9.25. (☎842-5117. Open Su-Th 11am-9pm, F-Sa 11am-10pm.)

CAPE LOOKOUT STATE PARK. Another 12 mi. southwest of Cape Meares, Cape Lookout State Park offers a small, rocky beach with incredible views of the surrounding sights. It also has some fine camping near the dunes and the forests behind them. (☎842-4981 or 800-551-6949. $16.) From here, the 2½ mi. **Cape Trail** heads past the 1943 crash site of a military plane to the end of the lookout, where a spectacular 360-degree view featuring **Haystack Rock** awaits. The **Cape Lookout campground ❷** offers fine camping near the dunes and the forests behind them, although sites with better privacy tend to go far in advance. 216 sites. Toilets and showers. (☎842-4981, 800-551-6949. Tent sites $16, non-camper showers $2. State park has $3 day use fee.)

CAPE KIWANDA STATE PARK. Cape Kiwanda State Park (☎800-551-6949), 1 mi. north of Pacific City, is the jewel of the Three Capes Loop's triple crown. This sheltered cape draws beachcombers, kite-flyers, volleyball players, surfers, and windsurfers, not to mention the odd snowboarder out to ride a giant sand hill. A walk up the sculptured sandstone on the north side (wear shoes with good grips) reveals a **hypnotic view** of swells rising over the rocks, forming crests, and smashing into the cliffs. If the surf is up, head to **South County Surf,** 33310 Cape Kiwanda Dr., a little ways of the beach, where the walls are lined with shots of wipeouts and the Northwest's biggest surfing days. (☎503-965-7505. Surfboard rental $20 until 5pm; boogieboard $10; wetsuit $15. Open Tu-F, Su 10am-5pm, Sa 9am-5pm.)

PACIFIC CITY. The nearest town to Cape Kiwanda, Pacific City is a hidden gem that most travelers on US 101 never even see. If you plan to stay overnight, the **Anchorage Motel ❸,** 6585 Pacific Ave., offers homey rooms. (☎541-965-6773 or 800-941-6250. Rooms from $45, offseason from $37.) Camping on beaches in Oregon is illegal, but local youth have been known to camp near the beach, or on more secluded beaches north of Cape Kiwanda. The town hides away some surprisingly good restaurants; the **Grateful Bread Bakery ❷**, 34805 Brooten (BRAW-ten) Rd., creates monuments to the art of dining. Get anything from a vegetarian stuffed focaccia ($7) to one of many excellent omelettes. (☎965-7337. Summer Th-Tu 8am-8:30pm; winter Th-M 8am-8:30pm.)

LINCOLN CITY ☎541

Lincoln City is actually five towns wrapped around a 7 mi. strip of ocean-front motels, gas stations, and souvenir shops along US 101. Most budget travelers, and this travel guide, will tell you that the Three Capes area is far superior as a destination. As one of the largest "cities" on the North Coast, Lincoln City can, however, be used as a gateway to better points north and south.

ORIENTATION & PRACTICAL INFORMATION. Lincoln City lies between Devils Lake and the ocean, 42 mi. south of Tillamook, 22 mi. north of Newport, and 88 mi. southwest of Portland. The city proper is divided into quadrants: the D River ("the smallest river in the world") is the north-south divide; US 101 divides east from west. **Greyhound** buses, 3350 NW US 101 (☎800-454-2487) depart from Wendy's at the north end of town to **Newport** (50min., 2 per day, $7) and **Portland** (2½hr., 2 per day, $13). Tickets are available at the **visitors center** (801 US 101 SW #1. M-Sa 9am-4:30pm, Su 10am-3:30pm; see below.) **Robben-Rent-A-Car,** 3244 US 101 NE, rents for $28 per day and $0.15 per mi. after 50 mi. Must be 21+ with credit card. (☎994-2454 or 800-305-5530. Open daily 8am-5pm.) The **Oregon Surf Shop,** 4933 US 101 SW, rents a wetsuit and surfboard for $30 per day, or wetsuit and boogie board for $25; expert instructors offer lessons for $30 per hour. Sit-on-top kayaks are $25 per 4 hours. (☎996-3957 or 877-339-5672. Open M-F 10am-5pm, Sa 9am-5pm, Su 10am-5pm.) **Public showers** ($1.25) are yours at the **Lincoln City Pool,** 2150 NE Oar Pl. (☎994-5208. Open in summer M-F 5:30am-9pm, Sa 11am-9pm, Su noon-4:30pm; call for winter hours.) In an **emergency,** call ☎911 or contact the **police,** at 1503 East Devils Lake Rd. SE (☎994-3636). **Samaritan North Lincoln Hospital** is at 3043 NE 28th St. (☎994-3661). **The Driftwood Library,** 801 US 101 SW, provides 1hr. of free **Internet access.** (☎996-2277. Open M-W 9am-9pm, Th Sa 9am-5pm.) The **post office** is at 1501 East Devils Lake Rd. SE, 97367. (☎800-275-8777. Open M-F 9am-5pm.) **Postal Code:** 97367.

ACCOMMODATIONS & FOOD. Beautiful, small rooms await at the **Captain Cook Inn ❸,** 2626 US 101 NE. (☎994-2522 or 800-994-2522. Singles $48; doubles $52.) **Dory Cove ❸,** 5819 Logan Rd., at the far north of town, is the locals' unanimous choice for affordable seafood. Dinners start at $10 a plate. (☎994-5180. Open summer M-Sa 11:30am-8pm, Su noon-8pm; winter M-Th 11:30am-8pm, F-Sa 11:30am-9pm, Su noon-8pm.) There's a **Safeway,** 4101 NW Logan Rd., at the north end of town. (☎994-8667. Open daily 6am-midnight.)

DEPOE BAY & OTTER CREST LOOP ☎541

Rest stops and beach-access parking lots litter the 30 mi. of US 101 between Lincoln City and Newport. Diminutive Depoe Bay boasts gray whale viewing along the town's low seawall, at the **Depoe Bay State Park Wayside** and the **Observatory Lookout,** 4½ mi. to the south. Go early in the morning on a cloudy day during the annual migration (Dec.-May) for your best chance of spotting the giants. **Tradewinds Charters** (☎765-2345 or 800-445-8730) has 6hr. ($70) fishing and crabbing trips, and 1hr. ($15) and 2hr. ($20) whale watching trips. **Dockside Charters** offers similar trips; turn east at the only traffic light in Depoe Bay. They're next to the Coast Guard. (☎765-2545 or 800-733-8915. 5hr. fishing $55; 1hr. whale watching $15, ages 13-17 $11, ages 4-12 $7.) Just south of Depoe Bay, detour from US 101 on

OREGON

the renowned **Otter Crest Loop,** a twisting 4 mi. excursion high above the shore that affords spectacular vistas at every bend and includes views of **Otter Rock** and the **Marine Gardens.** A lookout over the aptly named **Cape Foulweather** has telescopes ($0.25) for spotting sea lions lazing on the rocks. **The Devil's Punch Bowl,** formed when the roof of a seaside cave collapsed, is also accessible off the loop. It becomes a frothing cauldron during high tide when ocean water crashes through an opening in the side of the bowl. **Otter Rocks** beach is known as a great place to learn to surf; beginners can have a blast in the smaller breaks close to shore.

NEWPORT ☎541

After the miles of malls along US 101, Newport's renovated waterfront area of pleasantly kitschy restaurants and shops is a delight. Newport's claim to fame, however, is the world-class **Oregon Coast Aquarium.** Best known as home to Keiko the Orca of *Free Willy*, the aquarium offers several interesting exhibits. This, in addition to the Mark Hatfield Marine Science Center and loads of inexpensive seafood, make Newport a marine lover's starred attraction.

ORIENTATION & PRACTICAL INFORMATION

Corvallis lies 55 mi. east of Newport on **US 20,** Lincoln City is 22 mi. north of town on **US 101,** and Florence sits 50 mi. south. Newport is bordered on the west by the foggy Pacific Ocean and on the south by Yaquina Bay. US 101, known in town as the **Coast Hwy.,** divides east and west Newport. US 20, known as **Olive St.** in town, bisects the north and south sides of town. Just north of the bridge, **Bay Boulevard** (accessible via Herbert St., on the north side of the bay bridge) circles the bay and runs through the heart of the port. Historic Nye Beach, bustling with tiny shops, is on the northwest side of town in between 3rd and 6th St.

Buses: Greyhound, 956 10th St. SW (☎265-2253 or 800-454-2487), at Bailey St. Open M-F 8-10am and 1-4:15pm, Sa 8am-1pm. To **Portland** (4hr., 2 per day, $18); **San Francisco** (16½-21hr., 3 per day, $76); and **Seattle** (9hr., 2 per day, $45).

Taxis: Yaquina Cab Company (☎265-9552). $2.25 base, $2.25 per mi.

Visitor Information: Chamber of Commerce, 555 Coast Hwy. SW (☎265-8801 or 800-262-7844; www.discovernewport.com). 24hr. info board outside. Open M-F 8:30am-5pm; summer also Sa-Su 10am-4pm.

Laundry: Eileen's Coin Laundry, 1078 Coast Hwy. N (☎265-5474). Wash $1.25, dry $0.25 per 8min. Open daily 6am-11pm.

Emergency: ☎911. **Weather and Sea Conditions:** ☎265-5511.

Police: 169 SW Coast Hwy. (☎265-5331).

Coast Guard: ☎265-5381.

Hospital: Samaritan Pacific Community Hospital, 930 Abbey St. SW (☎265-2244).

Internet Access: Newport Public Library: 35 Nye St. NW (☎265-2153), at Olive St., offers 30min. of free Internet access every day on 6 computers. Open M-Th 10am-9pm, F-Sa 10am-6pm, Su 1-4pm.

Post Office: 310 2nd St. SW (☎800-275-8777). Open M-F 8:30am-5pm, Sa 10:30am-1:30pm. **Postal Code:** 97365.

ACCOMMODATIONS & CAMPING

Motel-studded US 101 provides affordable but sometimes noisy rooms. Nearby monster camping facilities often fill on summer weekends.

Beverly Beach State Park, 198 123rd St. NE (☎265-9278; reservations 800-452-5687), 7 mi. north of Newport and just south of Devil's Punch Bowl. A year-round campground of gargantuan proportions. Non-camper showers $2. 129 tent sites, $17; 76 electrical, $20; 53 full RV sites, $21; 21 yurts, $29; hiker/biker $4.25. ❶

City Center Motel, 538 Coast Hwy. SW (☎265-7381 or 800-627-9099), opposite the visitors center. Spacious but oddly empty rooms. Singles $30, doubles $45. ❷

Money Saver Motel, 861 SW Coast Hwy. (☎265-2277 or 888-461-4033). Basic rooms with friendly management. Singles $42 in summer, $32 in winter; doubles $60 summer, $45 winter. ❷

South Beach State Park, 5580 Coast Hwy. S (☎867-4715), 2 mi. south of town. Near the quiet South Beach, the campground has sparse conifers which offer little shelter and no privacy. Offers 2 hr. kayak tours on nearby Beaver Creek, May-Sept., for $10 per person. 227 electric RV sites, $20; 22 yurts, $29; hiker/biker sites $4.28. Showers $2 for non-campers. ❶

Inn at Yaquina Head, 2633 S Pacific Way. (☎888-867-3100.) Large rooms with views of the bay and marina. Continental breakfast. Jacuzzi, exercise room. Call for rates. ❸

OREGON

FOOD

Food in Newport is surprisingly varied, but seafood is the dining option of choice. **Oceana Natural Foods Coop,** 159 2nd St. SE, has a small selection of reasonably priced health foods and produce. (☎265-8285. Open daily 8am-8pm.) **J.C. Sentry,** 107 Coast Hwy. N, sells standard supermarket stock. (☎265-6641. Open 24hr.)

Mo's Restaurant, 622 Bay Blvd. SW (☎265-2979). Just about always filled to the gills, this is the original location of what is now a regional franchise. Go for the clam chowder ($7) or fish and chips ($9). Open daily 11am-10pm. ❷

April's, 749 3rd St. NW (☎265-6855), down by Nye Beach, is the pinnacle of local dining. The serene ocean view and good food are worth every penny. Tables fill early, especially on weekends. Dinners $12-19; daily specials are pricier. Towering chocolate eclairs $4. Reservations suggested. Open Tu-Su for dinner from 5pm. ❹

Canyon Way Restaurant & Bookstore, 1216 SW Canyon Way (☎265-8319). Browse through the petite bookstore before or after your meal. Deli sandwiches hover around $6. Dinner entrees in the restaurant are pricier ($16-21). Restaurant open Tu-Sa: lunch 11am-3pm, dinner 5pm-9pm. Bookstore open M 10am-5pm, Tu-Sa 10am-9pm. Deli open Tu-Sa 10am-4pm. ❸

Rogue Ale & Public House, 748 Bay Blvd. SW (☎265-3188). They "brew for the rogue in all of us," and bless 'em for it. Plenty of brew on tap–including "extreme ales" for the expert drinker–and garlic ale bread to boot ($2.25). Most lunch items about $10-13. Locals pack it in for F and Sa night trivia. Fish and chips with Rogue Ale batter $10. Open daily 11am-2:30am; food until 11:30pm. ❸

SIGHTS

MARK O. HATFIELD MARINE SCIENCE CENTER. This is the hub of Oregon State University's coastal research. The 300 scientists working here ensure rigorous intellectual standards for the exhibits, which are on fascinating topics that range from chaos—demonstrated by a paddle wheel/waterclock—to climactic change and a behavioral analysis of Wile E. Coyote's causality. While the live octopus can't be played with, a garden of sea anemones, slugs, and bottom-dwelling fish awaits your curiousity in the touch tanks. *(At the south end of the bridge on Marine Science Dr. ☎867-0100. Open daily 10am-5pm; winter Th-M 10am-4pm. Donations accepted.)*

OREGON COAST AQUARIUM. More famous, less serious, and much more expensive than the Science Center is the Oregon Coast Aquarium. This world-class aquarium housed Keiko, the much-loved *Free Willy* Orca during his rehabilitation before he returned to his childhood waters near Iceland. The **Passages of the Deep** exhibit features a 200 ft. undersea tunnel; experience being surrounded by sharks, rays, and fish. *(2820 Ferry Slip Rd. SE, at the south end of the bridge. ☎867-3474; www.aquarium.org. Open June-Sept daily 9am-6pm; Sept.-June 10am-5pm. $10.25, seniors $9.25, ages 4-13 $6.25.)*

ROGUE ALE BREWERY. The Brewery has won more awards than you can shake a pint at. Cross the bay bridge, follow the signs to the aquarium, and you'll see it. 20 brews, including Oregon Golden, Shakespeare Stout, and Dead Guy Ale, are available at the pub in town (see **Food**, above) or upstairs at **Brewers by the Bay,** where taster trays of four beers cost $4.50. *(2320 Oregon State University Dr. SE. Brewers by the Bay ☎867-3664. Brewery ☎867-3660. Open Su-Th 11am-9pm, F-Sa 11am-10pm. Free tours of the brewery leave daily at 4pm, depending on demand.)*

NEWPORT TO REEDSPORT ☎541

OREGON

From Newport to Reedsport, US 101 slides through a string of small towns, beautiful campgrounds, and spectacular stretches of beach. The **Waldport Ranger Station,** 1049 Pacific Hwy. SW, is located 16 mi. south of Newport in Waldport. The office describes hiking in **Siuslaw National Forest,** a patchwork of three wilderness areas along the Oregon Coast. Furnishes detailed maps ($4-6) and advice on the area's campgrounds. (☎563-3211. Open M-F 8am-4pm.)

CAPE PERPETUA. Cape Perpetua, 11 mi. south of Waldport and 40 mi. north of Reedsport, is the highest point on the coast (803 ft.) and arguably its high point for scenic beauty. Even if you're only passing through, drive to the top of the Cape Perpetua **viewpoint** (2 mi.) and walk the quarter-mile loop at the top. Gaze out at the ocean, as well as the headlands to the north and south. Those looking for a more challenging hike can take the difficult 1¼ mi. **St. Perpetua Trail** from the visitors center up to the same viewpoint. The **Cape Perpetua Interpretive Center,** 2400 US 101, just south of the viewpoint turn-off, has informative exhibits about the surrounding area and hilarious rangers. (☎547-3289. Open May-Nov. M-Sa 9am-5pm, Su noon-5pm, and open for whale week, Christmas-New Year's.) At high tide, witness an orgy of thundering spray in the **Devil's Churn** (¼ mi. north of the visitors center down Restless Water Trail) and **Spouting Horn** (¼ mi. south down Captain Cook Trail). The two sites, as well as the **tidal pools,** are connected; the tidal pools can also be reached from the visitors center. The **Cape Perpetua campground ❶** is an excellent place to sleep. Located at the viewpoint turn-off, it has 37 sites alongside a tiny, fern-banked creek. (☎877-444-6777 for reservations. Water, toilets. Firewood $5. Sites $15.) The **Rock Creek Campground ❶,** 8 mi. farther south, has 16 sites under mossy spruces a half-mile from the sea. (Drinking water, toilets. $14.)

ALPHA FARM. A communal alternative to the coast's bourgeois tourism. Members farm and produce giftshop-type items to support the communal purse. Drive 14 mi. east of **Florence,** a long strip of fast-food joints and expensive motels, to the tiny community of **Mapleton;** press on 30min. along Rte. 36 and then 7 mi. up Deadwood Creek Rd. Anyone willing to lend a hand with the chores is welcome to camp out or stay in the beautiful, simple bedrooms. Visitors can stay up to three days; afterward, a long-term commitment to the farm is required. The **Alpha Bit Cafe ❶,** in Mapleton on Rte. 126, is owned and staffed by the very chill and very dreadlocked members of Alpha Farm. (Farm ☎964-5102; cafe 268-4311. Cafe open Sa-Th 10am-6pm and F 10am-9pm.)

OREGON DUNES & REEDSPORT ☎541

Nature's ever-changing sculpture, the **Oregon Dunes National Recreation Area,** presents sand in shapes and sizes unequaled in the Northwest. Formed by millennia of wind and wave action, the dunes shift constantly and the sand sweeps over footprints, tire marks, and—in years past—entire forests. Perhaps the only hotbed of "reverse conservation," the dunes are actually greening rapidly as European beachgrass, planted in the 1920s, spreads its tenacious roots and sparks concerns that the dunes may disappear in as few as 100 years. Get them while they're hot: the dunes have something for everyone, from the hard-partying buggy or ATV rider to the hiker seeking solitude in the endless expanses of windblown sand.

ORIENTATION & PRACTICAL INFORMATION

The dunes stretch from Florence to Coos Bay, broken only where the Umpqua and Smith Rivers empty into Winchester Bay. On the south side of the bay is the town of **Winchester,** to the north is **Reedsport.** At the junction of **Rte. 38** and **US 101,** Reedsport is 185 mi. southwest of Portland, 89 mi. southwest of Eugene, and 71 mi. south of Newport.

OREGON

Tourist Information: Oregon Dunes National Recreation Area Visitor Center, 855 US 101 (☎271-3611; www.fs.fed.us/r6/siuslaw/oregondunes.htm), at Rte. 38 in Reedsport, just south of the Umpqua River Bridge. Has displays, a 10min. video on dune ecology, and essential info on fees, regulations, hiking, and camping. Maps $4-6. Open June-Oct. daily 8am-4:30pm; Nov.-May M-F 8am-4:30pm, Sa 10am-4pm. The **Chamber of Commerce** (☎271-3495 or 800-247-2155), at the same location and open the same hours, has dune buggy rental info and motel listings.

Passes and Permits: Most parking areas in the NRA now require day-use passes, which are $5 per day or $30 per year. The **Northwest Forest Pass** can be purchased at most places where it is required. Those staying at a campground and already paying a $15 fee are exempt from day-use fees.

Laundromat: Coin Laundry, 420 N 14th St. (☎271-3587), next to McDonald's in Reedsport. Wash $1.25, dry $0.25 per 7½min. Open daily 8am-9:30pm.

Emergency: ☎911.

Police: 146 N 4th St. (☎271-2100).

Coast Guard: ☎271-2138.

Internet Access: Reedsport Public Library, 395 Winchester Ave. (☎271-3500). 1hr. of free access. Open M 2-8:30pm, Tu-W and F 10am-6pm, Th 2-6pm, Sa-11am-2pm.

Post office: 301 Fir Ave. (☎800-275-8777), off Rte. 38. Open M-F 8:30am-5pm. **Postal Code:** 97467.

ACCOMMODATIONS & CAMPING

Although they often fill during summer, motels with singles from $40 abound on US 101. Fourteen campgrounds, many of which are very near the dunes, also dot the coast. During the summer, RVs and ATVers dominate local campsites. Permits for dispersed camping (allowed on public lands 200 ft. from any road or trail) are required year-round and available at the **Dunes Information Center.** The campgrounds that allow dune-buggy access are parking-lot style **Driftwood II** ❶

(69 sites, off Siltcoos Rd. about 7 mi. south of Florence), **Spinreel** ❶ (36 sites), **Horsfall** ❶ (69 sites, showers), and **Horsfall Beach** ❶ (34 sites, toilets, water; $15). Limited reservations at ☎800-280-2267; call five days in advance.

Harbor View Motel, 540 Beach Blvd. (☎271-3352), off US 101 in Winchester Bay, is so close to the marina that there are boats in the parking lot. A robotic frog welcomes guests to the office. Rooms are comfortable and clean, with striking color schemes. Queen $39; double occupancy $46. Kitchens $2 more. ❸

William M. Tugman State Park (☎759-3604; reservations 800-452-5687), 8 mi. south of Reedsport on US 101. Close to gorgeous Eel Lake. Slightly less privacy, but still well-sheltered. Wheelchair accessible. Hiker/biker camping is the most private ($4). Water and electricity. 115 sites, $15; yurts $27. Non-camper showers $2. ❶

Carter Lake Campground, 12 mi. north of Reedsport on US 101. Boat access to the lake; some sites are lakeside. The well-screened spots are as quiet as it gets out here. No ATVs. Nice bathrooms. Open May-Sept. 23 sites, $15. ❶

Eel Creek Campground, 10 mi. south of Reedsport. Sandy, spacious sites hidden from the road and each other by tall brush. Trailhead for the 2½ mi. Umpqua Dunes Trail, one of the best dune walks. Toilets, water. No RV sites or ATVs. 53 sites, $15. ❶

FOOD

Cheap, tasty food prevails in Winchester Bay and Reedsport. Grab a shrink-wrapped T-bone and a box of fudgesicles at **Safeway,** right off US 101 in Reedsport. (Open daily 7am-11pm.) The **Bayfront Bar and Bistro** ❸**,** 208 Bayfront Loop in Winchester Bay, is a classy but casual choice on the waterfront. For lunch, a salmon burger is $6.25, and grilled oysters are $9.25. Dinner is pricey ($9-16), but tasty. (☎271-9463. Open Tu-Su 11am-9pm.) **Back to the Best** ❷**,** on US 101 at 10th St., may look dated, but the food is fresh. Sandwiches with such fineries as smoked gouda cost $6.95. (☎271-2619. Open M-F 6am-6pm, Sa 7am-6pm, Su 8am-5pm.)

OUTDOOR ACTIVITIES

Depending on where you see them, the dunes will leave widely varying impressions. Regions that allow off-road vehicles will probably seem like mazes of madcap buggy riders, but other hiker-only areas offer timeless dreamscapes with nothing but sand, shrubs, and footprints vanishing in the wind.

OFF-ROAD RIDING. For an unmuffled and undeniably thrilling dune experience, venture out on wheels. While there are no accurately defined buggy trails through the dunes, simply following other riders can yield the best action in the

PART OF A COMPLETE BREAKFAST Each year, over 22,000 gray whales *(Eschrichtius robustus)* migrate northward from their warm winter calving grounds in Mexico to an Arctic summer smorgasbord nurtured by increased energy from the midnight sun. During the 19th century, these whales were hunted almost to extinction. Whalers would kill a calf, wait for its mother to investigate, and then harpoon her. Today, gray whales have regained their high population levels to the point that native groups like the Makah Nation have renewed ceremonial and subsistence whale hunts with international support. The secret of the whales' success might be in their diet; unlike the slowly rebounding humpbacks, which eat major commercial fish species, the gray whales feed on creatures that would make a human's stomach turn: fish roe, mud shrimp, and crab larvae.

FROM THE ROAD

RIDING THE DUNES

I had just crested the highest point of the "Coliseum" dune, a short walk from Umpqua Beach parking lot #3 in the Oregon Dunes, and the wind was pulling a smoky plume of sand up into my face. I grabbed my sandboard (essentially a snowboard made to ride on sand), slid my bare feet fit into the bindings, and attempted to descend. 20 or 30 ft. down the 33 degree-steep dune, I caught an edge and started cartwheeling down the hill. When I slid to a halt, I spat out the sand in my mouth, attempted (and failed) to pry sand out of my ear, jumped up, and ran to the next hill.

As my day of sandboarding wore on, the experience got better and better. I realized that waxing the board before each run was essential for a smooth ride. Furthermore, I learned that the drier the sand was, the faster the ride was; I sought out the driest terrain possible. Most of all, however, I learned that I needed a pair of goggles to guard my eyes from the relentless sand.

What does sandboarding have over snowboarding? For starters, you have to earn your rides by hiking back up the hill. The dunes are beautiful, and the powerful rays of the summer sun merely heighten the experience. Gliding down the hill and sending up billows of sand with the sun beating down is one of best, and some would say only, ways to truly see the dunes. Riding the dunes is worth a shot

sand. Plenty of shops on Hwy. 101 between Florence and Coos Bay rent and offer tours, and most either transport ATVs to the dunes or are located on them; the **National Recreation Area Visitors Center** also offers a list of places that rent. **Dune Buggy Adventures,** off Hwy. 101 in Winchester Bay, rents Suzuki Scrambler 90s for $35 per hour, and 250 Trailblazer ATVs for $40 per hour. $150 deposit required. (☎271-6972. Open summer 8am-last rider in, call for winter hours.)

ON-FOOT HIKING. Simply put, the dunes are beautiful and require a hiker's slow pace to be fully appreciated. Multiple ecosystems separated by the sands harbor birds, insects, and occasional larger animals such as foxes. The vast stretches of sand south of Winchester Bay and around Eel Creek represent dunes at their most primal. The experience of any dayhike is heightened by solitude: go early or late to avoid other tourists.

Umpqua Dunes Trail. With little to guide you besides an occasional marking pole, the "trail" wanders through unparalleled beauty in the sand slopes, wind cornices and rippled surfaces of the dunes. The area is ATV-free, and you'll probably find yourself wandering along the ridgetops of the dunes while exploring an occasional patch of vegetation and being enraptured by the beauty and solitude of the area. The views are best when the sun is low in the sky and the shadows highlight the precise transitions between slopes and other wind-sculptured features. Walk as long as you like; the trail goes 2 mi. to the ocean over progressively softer sand, requiring several hours of hiking. Access the trailhead off US 101, ¼ mi. south of Eel Creek campground.

Oregon Dunes Overlook (Tahkenitch Creek Trail). Most tourists content themselves with stopping at the Oregon Dunes overlook. Here, they peer out at a smallish stretch of oblique dunes whose lines of shrub stretch to the ocean. 1½-3 hr. walks off the overlook are far more satisfying, though, and feature a wider variety of dunes to explore. Wildlife lovers will enjoy this hike the most—you'll experience a constant barrage of bird calls from the cover of the shrubs.

OTHER ACTIVITIES. Bird-watching is popular around Reedsport; lists of species and their seasons are available at the **visitors center.** Throughout August, the **Crab Bounty Hunt** offers a whopping $10,000 reward for catching a particular tagged crustacean. Traps can be rented in Winchester Bay; rumor has it that the crab is most often caught in Salmon Harbor.

COOS BAY, NORTH BEND, & CHARLESTON ☎541

The largest city on the Oregon Coast, Coos Bay still has the feel of a down-to-earth working town. Nearby North Bend blends in at the border, while tiny Charleston sits peacefully a few miles west on the coast. This is one of the few places on the Pacific where life slows down as you near the shore, with a string of state parks along the coastline and a pristine estuary near Charleston Bay. Coos Bay was also home to Steve Prefontaine, the US Olympian and distance running legend who died in a tragic car accident in his early 20s.

ORIENTATION & PRACTICAL INFORMATION

US 101 jogs inland south of Coos Bay, rejoining the coast at Bandon. From Coos Bay, **Rte. 42** heads east 85 mi. to **I-5,** and US 101 continues north over the bridge into dune territory. **Coos Bay** and **North Bend** are so close together that one town merges seamlessly into the next, but street numbers start over again at the boundary; for instance, there are two Broadways, one for each city. US 101 runs along the east side of town (as Coos Bay's Broadway), and **Cape Arago Hwy.** runs along the west side, connecting Coos Bay to **Charleston** and the coast.

Buses: Greyhound, 275 N Broadway (☎267-4436), Coos Bay. Open M-Th 6:30am-5pm, F-Sa 6:30am-4pm. To **Portland** (6½hr., 3 per day, $30) and **San Francisco, CA** (14hr., 2 per day, $69-74).

Taxis: Yellow Cab (☎267-3111). $5 anywhere within town, and $1 per mi. outside.

Car Rental: Verger, 1400 Ocean Blvd. (☎888-5594), Coos Bay. Must be 23+ with credit card. Open M-F 8am-5:30pm, Sa 9am-5pm. Cars from $28, 150 mi. per day free, $0.25 per mi. thereafter.

Tourist Information: All the following cover the whole area.

Bay Area Chamber of Commerce, 50 E Central Ave. (☎269-0215 or 800-824-8486), off Commercial Ave., Coos Bay. Open M-F 9am-5pm, Sa 10am-4pm; in summer also Su noon-4pm.

North Bend Visitor Center, 1380 Sherman Ave. (☎756-4613), on US 101, south of North Bend bridge. Open in summer M-F 8am-5pm, Sa 10am-5pm, Su 12:30-5pm; winter M-F 8am-5pm.

Charleston Visitor Center (☎888-2311), at Boat Basin Dr. and Cape Arago Hwy., has brochures. Open May-Sept. daily 9am-5pm.

Outdoor Information: Oregon State Parks Information, 89814 Cape Arago Hwy. (☎888-8867), Charleston. Open M-F 8am-noon and 1-4:30pm.

Equipment Rental: High Tide Rental, 8073 Cape Arago Hwy. (☎888-3664). In Charleston, diagonally across from the Charleston Visitor Center. Rents every piece of gear necessary to fully enjoy the land and water of Coos Bay. Kayaks $20 per 2hr., bikes $15 per day, crab pots $8. Open Tu-Th 8am-4pm, F 7am-9pm, Sa 8am-9pm, Su 8am-4pm. **Rocky Point Surf and Sport** (☎266-9020), Coos Bay. Rents surfboards and wetsuits, each for $15 per day. 3½hr. lesson $105. Gives directions to the local spots, Bastendorff Beach and Lighthouse Beach.

Laundromat: Wash-A-Lot, 1921 Virginia Ave. (☎756-5439), North Bend. Wash $1.50; dry $0.25 per 6min. Open 24hr.

Emergency: ☎911. **Police:** 500 Central Ave. (☎269-8911), Coos Bay.

Coast Guard: 63450 Kingfisher Dr. (☎888-3266), Charleston.

Women's Crisis Line: ☎756-7000. 24hr.

Hospital: Bay Area Hospital, 1775 Thompson Rd. (☎269-8111), Coos Bay.

Internet Access: Coos Bay Library, 525 W Anderson Ave. (☎269-1101), Coos Bay. Free 30min. of Internet access. Open M-W 10am-8pm, Th-F 11am-5:30pm, Sa 11am-5pm.

Post Office: 470 Golden Ave. (☎800-275-8777) at 4th St., Coos Bay. Open M-F 8:30am-5pm.

Postal Code: 97420.

ACCOMMODATIONS & CAMPING

Cheap, noisy motels line Hwy. 101 for those just passing through; quieter rooms with a roof lie close to the outdoors attractions in Charleston. Campers, rejoice: the nearby state-run and private sites allow full access to the breathtaking coast.

Captain John's Motel, 63360 Kingfisher Dr. (☎888-4041), in Charleston. Escapes the highway noise and attracts anglers; this is the closest good place to the state parks and the estuary. Crab rings $2.50 per day. Queen from $46; 2 double beds from $55. ❸

Bluebill Campground (☎271-3611), off US 101, 3 mi. north of North Bend. Camping among sandy scrub; some sites with good privacy. Follow the signs to the Horsfall Beach area, then continue down the road to this US Forest Service campground. ½ mi. to the ocean and dunes. Closed in winter. 18 sites, $15. ❶

Sunset Bay State Park, 89814 Cape Arago Hwy. (☎888-4902; reservations 800-452-5687), 12 mi. south of Coos Bay and 3½ mi. west of Charleston. Akin to camping in a well-landscaped parking lot; **loop B** sites have a bit more seclusion. Sunset Beach is worth it. 138 sites, $16; full RV sites $19; yurts $27; hiker/biker sites $4. ❶

OREGON

FOOD

A **Safeway** is at 230 E Johnson Ave. off US 101 north, at the southern end of town. (Open daily 6am-1am.)

Blue Heron Bistro, 100 Commercial Ave. (☎267-3933), at the corner of Broadway in Coos Bay. Eclectic World War II memorabilia decorates this restaurant where diners enjoy delicious sandwiches, both hot and cold ($8), and handmade dinners with international flavors ranging from Italy to Germany ($9-13). Knock back a glass of Liefmaus Framboise ($5), and call it a meal. Open M-Sa 11am-10pm, Su 5-10pm. ❸

Cranberry Sweets, 1005 Newmark St. (☎888-9824), Coos Bay, near junction of Ocean Blvd. and Newmark St. This far-from-average candy factory serves up enough ambitious ventures (think beer squares and cheddar cheese fudge) to make lunch moot. $2-5 per lb. Cheapskates may exploit the free samples. Open M-Sa 9am-6pm, Su 11am-4pm. ❶

SIGHTS & EVENTS

Four miles south of Charleston up Seven Devils Rd., the **South Slough National Estuarine Research Reserve** ("Slough" is pronounced "Slew") is one of the most fascinating and under-appreciated venues on the central coast. Spreading out from a small interpretive visitors center, almost 7 sq. mi. of salt- and freshwater estuaries nurture all kinds of wildlife, from sand shrimp to blue herons to deer. Check the interpretive center first to see if there are any guided hikes or paddles going out (free), or to start on some of the short trails leading from the center. A great way to observe wildlife close-up by canoe or kayak is to start from the Charleston marina (near the Charleston Bridge) at low tide, and paddle into the estuary with the tide and out as it subsides; much of the interior is miserable mud flats at low tide. (☎888-5558; www.southsloughestuary.com. Open June-Aug. daily 8:30am-4:30pm; Sept.-May M-F 8:30am-4:30pm. Trails open year-round dawn-dusk.)

Inland 24½ mi. from Coos Bay, at **Golden and Silver Falls State Park,** three trails lead to the awesome Golden Falls, a 210 ft. drop into the abyss, and the beautiful Silver Falls, thin sheets of water cascading down a rock face. From Coos Bay, take the Eastside-Allegany exit off US 101, and follow it along a narrow, gravel road.

For two weeks in mid-July, Coos Bay plays host to the **Oregon Coast Music Festival,** the most popular summer music event on the coast. A week of jazz, blues, and folk is followed by a week of performances by the renowned festival orchestra. (☎267-0938. Festival concerts $6-10, orchestra concerts $12-17.) Art exhibits and a free classical concert in Mingus Park spice up the festival even for the ticketless.

OUTDOOR ACTIVITIES

Sunset Bay, 11½ mi. from Coos Bay on Cape Arago State Hwy., has been rated one of the top 10 American beaches. Sheltered from the waves by two parallel cliffs, the warm, shallow bay is perfect for **swimming.** The magnificent and manicured **Shore Acres State Park** rests a mile beyond Sunset Bay on the Cape Arago Hwy. (☎503-888-3732. Open summer daily 8am-9pm; winter 8am-dusk. $4 per car. Wheelchair accessible.) Once the estate of local lumber lord Louis J. Simpson, the park contains elaborate botanical gardens that outlasted the mansion and a short trail to peaceful Simpson Beach. Displays rose gardens and several rare trees: should monkeys invade, *Let's Go* suggests you find the Monkey Puzzle Tree (*Araucaria araucana)* to thwart the pestering primates. At the south end of the highway is breezy **Cape Arago,** notable for the rich life of its tide pools. Paved paths lead out toward the tip of the cape and provide an excellent view of Shell Island, a quarter-mile offshore, which is a protected elephant and harbor seal rookery. Fishing enthusiasts can hop on board with **Bob's Sportfishing,** operating out of a small building at the west end of the Charleston Boat Basin, where they can buy one-day fishing licenses for $8. (☎888-4241 or 800-628-9633. 5hr. salmon fishing trip $60 mid-May to Sept.)

OREGON

BANDON ☎541

Despite a steady flow of summer tourists, the fishing town of Bandon-by-the-Sea has refrained from breaking out the pastels and making itself up like an amusement park. A few outdoor activities make Bandon worth a stop on a coastal tour.

PRACTICAL INFORMATION. Bandon is 24 mi. south of Coos Bay and 27 mi. north of Port Orford on US 101. The **visitors center** is at 300 SE 2nd St. in Old Town. (☎347-9616. Open summer daily 10am-5pm; winter 10am-4pm.) The **post office** is at 105 12th St. SE (☎800-275-8777. Open M-F 8:30am-4:30pm.) **Postal Code:** 97411.

ACCOMMODATIONS & FOOD. The beautiful Mediterranean exterior of the **Bandon Wayside Motel ❸**, on Rte. 42 south just off US 101, gives way to good rooms with tile floors, nice beds, and cable TV. (☎347-3421. Summer $45-80. Winter $20-40.) The small **Sea Star Guest House ❷**, 375 2nd St., contains the remains of a once-thriving hostel as well as several elegant guesthouse rooms overlooking the marina. (www.seastarbandon.com. 2-person dorm rooms $15; private hostel rooms $25-45; guesthouse rooms $75-105 summer, $55-75 winter.) Two miles north of town and across the bridge, **Bullard's Beach State Park** houses the **Coquille River Lighthouse ❷**, built in 1896. The 185 sites have little privacy. (☎347-2209. $19; yurts $27; hiker/biker sites $4 per person. Showers $2 for non-campers.)

For a tasty and healthy morsel, step into **Mother's Natural Grocery and Deli ❶**, 975 US 101, south of the junction with Rte. 42 south. Vegetarian and organic foods prevail here over pesticides and other evils. Meals cost about $3.75-4.25. (☎347-4086.

Open M-Sa 9am-6pm.) **A&R World Cafe ❷**, adjoining the Sea Star Guest House, serves excellent gyros and other "world food" in a mellow atmosphere. (☎347-8204. Open Tu-Th 7am-8pm, F-Sa 7am-9pm. Breakfast $4-6, lunch $5-7, dinner $9-15.) The best seafood and a great dining room view is at **Bandon Boatworks ❸**, 275 Lincoln Ave. SW. Lunches ($6-9) are more affordable than dinners ($12-20), when the Boatworks breaks out the wine glasses. (☎347-2111. Open M-Sa 11:30am-9pm, Su 11am-8:30pm; winter closed M.)

SIGHTS & EVENTS. A stroll around **Old Town** is pleasant, as is exploring the beach on a horse from **Bandon Beach Riding Stables.** (☎347-3423. $25 for 1hr.) The well-marked beach loop road that leaves from Old Town and joins US 101 5 mi. south passes **Table Rock, Elephant Rock,** and **Face Rock,** three of the coast's most striking offshore outcroppings.

BANDON TO BROOKINGS

Whether it's because of the general lack of development in this area, or the proliferation of offshore volcanic rocks and vertiginous shorelines, this stretch of the coast is the most beautiful segment of the Oregon Coast. With exceptional beauty, though, comes a small price: economically struggling Curry County has a reputation for crime. However, in daylight hours, there is little to detract from the cliff-lined coves and grassy hills.

Cape Blanco State Park, north of Port Orford, offers a long stretch of empty beach; it is the farthest point west on the Oregon Coast and its **lighthouse** is the Coast's oldest, with miles of views north and south. Take a tour of the lighthouse and its mesmerizing lens, from the end of the road leading into the park. (Open Apr.-Oct. Th-M 10am-3:30pm.) Few stop at the **campground ❶** a few miles back from the lighthouse; it offers exceptional seclusion between hedges, plus access to a beautiful but isolated beach. Toilets. $18 electrical RV sites, $4 hiker/biker sites. Showers. **Humbug Mountain State Park ❶**, 6 mi. south of Port Orford, surrounds the heavily-forested mountain; a 3 mi., moderate trail ascends to the 1700 ft. peak with amazing views on top and lush ferns on the trail up. The trail is accessible from a campground at the foot of the mountain, which has 101 tightly packed sites with toilets. (☎332-6774. Tents $16; hiker/biker sites $4. Showers $2 for non-campers.)

Boardman State Park is the best example of Oregon Coast preservation, enclosing 15 mi. of some of the finest and most rugged coastal terrain in Oregon. The park has overlooks and trailheads at 1- to 5-mile intervals along a trail that runs through the park and beyond. With a little bit of footwork, you could easily obtain an entire pristine cove for yourself: just find an empty trailhead parking area, and see where the trail takes you. The undertouristed park begins about 8 mi. north of Brookings. At the very least, stop at the Arch Rock viewpoint, which grants a look at beautiful coves on two sides plus the unusual Arch Rock itself. A complete list of the different trail segments is available, free, at the ranger station in Brookings.

Thirty miles north of Brookings, in **Gold Beach,** you can ride a jet boat up the **Rogue River. Mail Boat Hydro-Jets,** 94294 Rogue River Rd., offers 64, 80, and 104 mi., 6-7hr. whitewater daytrips. (☎247-7033 or 800-458-3511. May-Oct. $30-75.) Longer trips get more whitewater; all trips offer many wildlife viewing opportunities.

BROOKINGS ☎541

Brookings is the southernmost stop on US 101 before California and one of the few coastal towns that remain relatively tourist-free. Here, hardware stores are easier to find than trinket shops, and the beaches are among Oregon's least spoiled. The city also sits in Oregon's "banana belt" (a.k.a. California's "arctic circle"): warm weather is not rare in January, and some Brookings backyards even boast scraggly palm trees. For exhaustive coverage of all that is hot and cool down south, consult *Let's Go: California 2004*.

PRACTICAL INFORMATION. US 101 is called Chetco Ave. in town. Strictly speaking, there are two towns here, separated by the **Chetco River**—Brookings to the north and **Harbor** to the south—which share everything and are referred to as Brookings Harbor. A relatively inconspicuous strip of commercial activity is on Lower Harbor Road: to get there, take Benham Ln. towards the ocean at the south end of town. The **Greyhound** station is at 601 Railroad Ave., at Tanbark. (☎469-3326. Open M-F 8:45am-noon and 4-6:30pm, Sa 8:45am-noon.) Two buses per day run to **Portland** (9hr., $46) and **San Francisco, CA** (12hr., $53). The **Brookings Welcome Center,** 1650 US 101, welcomes from just north of town. (☎469-4117. Open May-Sept. M-Sa 8am-6pm, Su 9am-5pm; Apr. and Oct. M-Sa 8am-5pm, Su 9am-5pm.) The **Chamber of Commerce,** 16330 Lower Harbor Rd., is across the bridge to the south. (☎469-3181 or 800-535-9469. Open summer M-F 9am-5pm, Sa-Su 10am-2pm; winter open M-F only.) The **Chetco Ranger Station,** 555 5th St., distributes info on the **Siskiyou National Forest.** (☎469-2196. Open M-F 8am-4:30pm.) Clean up at **Econ-o-Wash,** next door to the Westward motel on Chetco Ave. (Wash $1.25, dry $0.25 for 7min. Open daily 7:30am-10pm, last wash 9pm.) Rent a kayak ($20) or bike ($15) at **Escape Hatch,** 642 Railroad Ave. (☎469-2914. Open M-F 10am-5:30pm, Sa 10am-5pm.) Get the lowdown on local surf-spots (South Jetty in town, plus Harrison Sponge beach 1 mi. north of town) at **Sessions Surf Co.,** 800 Chetco Ave. (☎412-0810). Guess what's responsible for that semi-circular set of dents on the board in the shop? Don't ponder too long if you're going into the water soon. Rents body board and wetsuit for $10. Get a free hour of **Internet access** at the **library,** 405 Alder St. (☎469-7738. Open M and F 10am-6pm; Tu and Th 10am-7pm; W 10am-8pm, Sa 10am-5pm.) Also try **Java Java,** 612 Chetco Ave., for $5 per hr. (☎412-7444. Open M-F 7am-4pm, Sa 9am-4pm.) The **post office** is at 711 Spruce St. (☎800-275-8777. Open M-F 9am-4:30pm.) **Postal Code:** 97415.

OREGON

ACCOMMODATIONS & FOOD. The Bonn Motel ❸, 1216 US 101, has a heated indoor pool and cable. (☎469-2161. Singles $40; doubles $45; $10 less in winter.) **Harris Beach State Park Campground ❶,** at the north edge of Brookings, has 63 good tent sites set back in the trees. (☎469-2021 or 800-452-5687. Sites $17; full RV sites $20; yurts $28; hiker/biker sites $4. Free showers.) For campsites off the beaten path, travel 15 mi. east of Brookings on North Bank Rd. to the charming **Little Redwood Campground ❶,** alongside a salamander-filled creek. (Drinking water and pit toilet. 12 sites, $10.) **Redwood Bar ❶,** across the way with drinking water, charges $5. Contact the Chetco Ranger Station for info. (☎469-2196.)

A half-sandwich and a cup of soup or chili goes for $4.50 at the **Homeport Bagel Shop ❶,** 1011 Chetco Ave. (☎469-6611. Open M-F 7am-5pm.) A number of seafood spots can be found near the harbor. The locals' favorite is **Oceanside Diner ❷,** 16403 Lower Harbor Rd. (☎469-7971. Open daily 4am-3pm.)

SIGHTS & OUTDOOR ACTIVITIES. Brookings is known statewide for its flowers. In downtown's **Azalea Park,** azaleas encircle pristine lawns and bloom from April to June, at intervals: don't visit for the blooms without calling ahead to make sure the flowers are out. The pride of Brookings is its **Azalea Festival** (☎469-3181), held in Azalea Park over Memorial Day weekend. South Beach is just north of town and offers haunting vistas of angular volcanic rocks strewn about the sea, plus sand that's soft on bare feet. It is also designated a "marine garden." Harris Beach, a bit farther north, has an equally excellent view of the rock diaspora, and has less developed views.

INLAND VALLEYS

While jagged cliffs and gleaming surf draw tourists to the coast, many Oregonians opt for the inland Willamette and Rogue River Valleys for their vacations. Vast tracts of fertile land support agriculture and a burgeoning wine industry, and for decades the immense forests maintained a healthy timber industry. Since the fortunes of logging are now uncertain, tourism has become the industry of choice in small-town Oregon. With festivals galore, Ashland, Eugene, Corvallis, and Salem all attract their fair share of visitors.

SALEM ☎503

The home of Willamette University and the third-largest urban center in Oregon, Salem gives off the vibes of a much smaller city. Boasting fine museums, several renowned wineries, and attractions like the Oregon State Fair, Salem draws throngs of visitors, though it's hardly a hopping tourist destination.

TRANSPORTATION

Salem is 51 mi. south of **Portland** and 64 mi. north of **Eugene** on **I-5. Willamette University** and the **capitol building** dominate the center of the city, and the nearby shops make up the heart of downtown. To reach downtown, take Exit 253 off I-5. Street addresses are divided into quadrants: the **Willamette River** divides east from west. **State St.** divides SE from NE.

Trains: Amtrak, 500 13th St. SE (☎588-1551 or 800-872-7245), across from the visitors center. Open daily 6:15am-7pm. To **Portland** (1½hr., 2 per day, $8-15); **Seattle** (5-7hr., 2 per day, $27-46); and **San Francisco, CA** (17hr., 1 per day, $76-120).

Buses: Greyhound, 450 Church St. NE (☎362-2428). Open M-F 5:30am-8:30pm, Sa 5:30am-8:30pm. To: **Portland** (1½hr., 9 per day, $8-9); **Eugene** (1½-2hr., 10 per day, $10-11); **Seattle, WA** (6hr., 7per day, $25-28). Lockers $1 per day.

Local Transportation: Cherriots Customer Service Office, 220 High St. NE (☎588-2877; www.cherriots.org), provides bus maps and monthly passes. Routes leave from High St. in front of courthouse every hr. M-F 6am-9:30pm, Sa 7am-10pm. All buses have bike racks. Adults $0.75; over 60 and disabled $0.35; under 19 $0.50.

Taxis: Salem Yellow Cab Co. (☎362-2411). $2.20 base, $1.80 per mi.

AAA: 2909 Ryan Dr. NE (☎861-3118 or 800-962-5855). Open M-F 8am-5pm.

PRACTICAL INFORMATION

Tourist Information: 1313 Mill St. SE (☎581-4325 or 800-874-7012; www.scva.org), in the Mission Mill Museum complex; take I-5 Exit 253 and follow signs. Open M-F 8:30am-5pm, Sa 10am-4pm.

Equipment Rental: South Salem Cycle Works, 4071 S Liberty Rd. (☎399-9848). Rents road bikes and hybrids for $15 per day. No shop rents mountain bikes in Salem. Open M-Sa 10am-6pm.

Laundromat: Suds City Depoe, 1785 Lancaster Dr. NE (☎362-9845). Snack bar and big-screen TV. Wash $1.25, dry $0.25 per 15min. Open daily 7:30am-9pm. **Lancaster Self-Service Laundry,** 2195 Lancaster Dr. NE, next to Bi-Mart. Wash 18 lb. for $1.75, or 50 lb. for $4.25. Dry $0.25 per 10min. Open daily 8am-10pm, last load 9pm.

Emergency: ☎911.

Police: 555 Liberty St. SE (☎588-6123), in City Hall room 130.

24hr. Crisis Line: ☎581-5535.

24hr. Women's Crisis Line: ☎399-7722.

Hospital: Salem Hospital, 665 Winter St. SE (☎561-5200).

Internet Access: Salem Public Library, 585 Liberty St. SE (☎588-6315). Free ½hr. of Internet access. 15 computers. Metered parking in the garage next door. Open June-Aug. M 10-6, Tu-Th 10am-9pm, F-Sa 10am-6pm; Sept.-May also open Su 1-5pm.

Post Office: 1050 25th St. SE (☎800-275-8777). Open M-F 8am-5:30pm.

Postal Code: 97301.

ACCOMMODATIONS & CAMPING

The visitors center has a list of B&Bs, which provide a comfortable and often classy setting (from $45). A number of cheaper hotels line Lancaster Dr. along the length of I-5, and camping options are also available.

Silver Falls State Park, 20024 Silver Falls Hwy. Rte. 214 (☎873-8681; reservations ☎800-452-5687). (See **Sights,** below, for directions.) Toilets, water, wheelchair access. 60 tent sites, $16; 44 RV sites, $20; 14 cabins, $35. Warm showers. ❶

Alden House Bed and Breakfast, 760 NE Church St. (☎363-9574 or 877-363-9573). Choose from 6 themed rooms (romantic, cowboy), all of which have private baths. Breakfast in the elegant dining room at 9am. Reservations advised. Rooms $45-65. ❸

Cozzzy Inn, 1875 Fisher Rd. NE (☎588-5423). From I-5 Exit 256 to Lancaster Dr., take Sunnyview Rd. west to Fisher Rd. and make a left. Comfortable rooms, bargain prices (may be changing to a franchise with increased rates, though). Rooms from $37. ❸

Red Lion Hotel (☎370-7888 or 800-733-5466). Take I-5 Exit 256. This full-service chain hotel has large rooms. Jacuzzi, indoor heated pool, exercise room, restaurant downstairs. Summer queens, $70; kings, $80. Winter rooms from $50. ❹

OREGON

FOOD

Salem is no city for the budget gourmet, and most restaurants are somewhat bland. Groceries await at **Roth's,** 702 Lancaster Dr. NE. (☎585-5770. Open daily 6am-11pm.) Hit the **Farmer's Market,** at the corner of Marion and Summer St., for local produce and crafts. (☎585-8264. Open Sa 9am-3pm.)

Off-Center Cafe, 1741 Center St. NE (☎363-9245). Colorfully named breakfasts such as Green Chile Tortoise ($6.25) are enormously satisfying. Standard dinner fare. Open Tu-W and F 7am-2:30pm, Th 6-9pm for dinner, Sa-Su 8am-2pm for brunch. ❷

Fuji Rice Time, 159 High St. SE (☎364-5512), serves traditional Japanese food to the local lunch crowd, who enjoy watching the chef at work in the sushi bar ($4-6). Open M-F 11am-2:30pm and 5-9pm, Sa 4-9pm. ❶

Arbor Cafe, 380 High St. NE (☎588-2353), serves coffees and teas ($2-3) as well as delicious pastries ($1-2) for breakfast; panini and sandwiches for lunch and dinner ($7-8.50). Open M 7:30am-4pm, Tu-Th 7:30am-9pm, F-Sa 8am-10pm. ❷

SIGHTS & ENTERTAINMENT

STATE CAPITOL. This gigantic marble building, topped by a 23 ft. gilt-gold statue of the "Oregon Pioneer," is located in the heart of Salem. (*900 Court St. NE. Bounded by Court St. to the north, Waverly St. to the east, State St. to the south, and Cottage St. to the* *west. ☎986-1388. Open M-F 7:30am-5:30pm, Sa 9am-4pm, Su noon-4pm. In summer, a free tour to the top of the rotunda leaves every 30min., and tours of the various chambers leave every hour; call for off-season tours.)*

SILVER FALLS STATE PARK. A long (12 mi.) loop trail passes by 10 waterfalls. 106 ft. Middle North Falls is an easy 1 mi. hike away: were the waterfalls any closer to the trail, *Let's Go* would suggest bringing soap and shampoo. *(Take Rte. 22 east for 5 mi., then take the exit for Rte. 214 N and follow it for about 18 mi. $3 day use fee.)*

OREGON STATE FAIR. Salem celebrates the end of summer in the 12 days leading up to Labor Day with the annual Oregon State Fair. With a whirl of livestock shows and baking contests, country-folk invade the city and transform it from a picture of complacent suburbia to a barnyard celebration. *(2330 17th St. NE. At the Expo Center. ☎947-3247 or 800-833-0011; www.fair.state.or.us. Open Su-Th 10am-10pm, F-Sa 10am-11pm. $6-7, seniors $3-5, ages 6-12 $2-4.)*

SALEM ART FAIR & FESTIVAL. During the third weekend of July, the Salem Art Association hosts the free **Salem Art Fair and Festival** in Bush's Pasture Park. While the food booths do brisk business and the local wineries pour from their most recent vintage, the artsy and crafty display their wares as bands strum away the afternoon. The visitors center has info on the fair and on local **wineries.**

SALEM CINEMA. This single-screen theater offers refreshing indie film selections. *(Pringle Plaza, 445 High St. SE ☎378-7676; www.salemcinema.com. $7, students $6, seniors 62 and over and children 12 and under $4; matinees $5.)*

OREGON

CORVALLIS ☎541

Unlike so many Oregon towns, this peaceful residential community in the central Willamette Valley has no historic pretensions. Covered in black and orange, the colors of Oregon State University (OSU), for nine months, Corvallis is at heart a college town. Also boasting a gigantic Hewlett-Packard facility, Corvallis keeps pace with the technological world. Life bustles downtown all year, but Corvallis mellows in the summer, hosting a few choice festivals and offering some outdoor exploration in the nearby Willamette and Deschutes National Forests. Corvallis makes for a nice stop on the way to bigger, better places.

ORIENTATION AND PRACTICAL INFORMATION. Corvallis is laid out in a checkerboard fashion that quickly degenerates outside the downtown area. Numbered streets run north-south; east-west streets are a test of U.S. historical knowledge, as they are named after presidents. More recent presidents are to the north, older to the south. Monroe divides the north half of town from south. **Rte. 99 W** splits in town and becomes two one-way streets: northbound **3rd St.** and southbound **4th St. 2nd St.** becomes US 20 north of town and leads to Albany and I-5.

Greyhound, 153 4th St. NW, runs to: **Portland** (2½hr., 5 per day, $14-15); **Seattle, WA** (7hr., 5 per day, $25-27); **Newport** (7½hr., 3 per day, $12); and **Eugene** (1hr., 5 per day, $8-9). Lockers $1 per day. (☎757-1797 or 800-231-2222. Open M-F 6am-6:15pm, Sa-Su 7am-1:30pm.) **Corvallis Transit System,** 501 SW Madison Ave., runs public transit. (☎766-6998; www.ci.corvallis.or.us/pw/cts. Fare $0.60. Service M-F 6:30am-6:30pm, Sa 9:30am-4:30pm.) The **Chamber of Commerce** (☎757-1505) and **Convention and Visitor Bureau** (☎757-1544 or 800-334-8118; www.visitcorvallis.com), both offer **tourist information** at 420 2nd St. NW, the first right past the bridge if you're coming from the east. The visitor bureau has maps of Corvallis and Albany, and provides an excellent map of the bike trails in the area for free. (Open M-F 8am-5pm, Sa-Su 10am-3pm.) **Oregon State University** has its main entrance and info booth at Jefferson and 14th St. (☎737-0123, events info 737-6445. Open M-F 8am-5pm.) **Peak Sports,** 129 2nd St.

NW, is an incredible outdoors shop covering almost all forms of outdoors recreation in three separate, adjacent locations. Sells trail maps ($2-10) and rents mountain bikes ($25 for first day, $15 each day after) and all kinds of kayaks ($30 per day) with gear included. (☎754-6444; www.proaxis.com/~peak. Open M-Th and Sa 9am-6pm, F 9am-8pm, Su noon-5pm.) **Campbell's Laundry,** 1120 9th St. NW, has wash for $1.25, dry $0.25 per 10min. (☎752-3794. Open daily 6am-1am.) Call ☎911 in an **emergency,** or contact the **police,** located at 180 5th St. NW (☎757-6924). The **Corvallis Clinic,** 3680 Samaritan Dr. NW., has **medical services.** Take 9th St. north from downtown. (☎754-1150; walk-ins ☎754-1282. Open M-F 8am-8pm, Sa-Su 10am-5pm.) **Corvallis Public Library,** 645 Monroe St. NW, offers free Internet access on 15 computers, 1hr. max. (☎766-6927. Open M-F 9am-9pm, Sa 9am-6pm, Su noon-6pm.) The **post office** is at 311 2nd St. SW. (Open M-F 8am-5:30pm, Sa 9am-4pm.) **Postal Code:** 97333.

ACCOMMODATIONS. The few campgrounds in and around Corvallis are not the RV mini-cities of their counterparts up and down Western Oregon. The few motels are reasonably priced, but occasionally fill during conventions or important college weekends. The **Budget Inn Motel ❸,** 1480 SW 3rd St., has decently sized rooms for undersized prices. (☎752-8756. Fridges, A/C, cable TV. Singles $35; doubles $45. Kitchenettes $5 extra.) **Salbasgeon Suites ❹,** 1730 NW 9th St., pampers guests with a pool and private spa. The hotel offers free Internet browsers in every room and free continental breakfast. (☎800-965-8808; www.salbasgeon.com. Singles from $88; doubles from $93.)

FOOD AND NIGHTLIFE. Corvallis has a smattering of collegiate pizza parlors, noodle shops, and Mexican food. OSU students prowl Monroe Ave. for cheap, filling grub. **First Alternative Inc.**, 1007 3rd St. SE, is a co-op stocked with a range of well-priced, natural products. (☎753-3115. Open daily 9am-9pm.) The **Safeway** grocery store and pharmacy is at 450 3rd St. SW. (☎753-5502. Open daily 24 hr.) **Bombs Away Cafe ❶,** 2527 Monroe St. NW, goes the extra *kilometro*. A mainstay of the college crowd, the adobe facade hides great burritos ($6-7) and live music every other week. This spot's thriving bar scene explodes on Tuesday with $2 beers; don't neglect Monday $2 margaritas, either. (☎757-7221. Open M-F 11am-midnight, Sa 5pm-midnight, Su 5-9pm. 21+ after 10pm.) **Nearly Normal's Gonzo Cuisine ❶,** 109 15th St. NW, a purple cottage turned veggie-haven, has masses of flowers and hanging plants. The decor whets the appetite for low-price, large portion vegetarian options ($4-8). Sunburgers are $6. (☎753-0791. Open M-F 8am-9pm, Sa 9am-9pm.) **McMenamins ❶,** 420 3rd St. NW, has by far the best pub fare in town. Have a sandwich ($5-7) or try a taster of six hand-brewed ales. Pints cost $3.25. (☎758-6044. Open M-Sa 11am-1am, Su noon-midnight.) If college beer bashes are your thing, find your way to the University frat houses.

ENTERTAINMENT. Ten miles east in **Albany** (off US 20 before I-5), the **River Rhythms** concert series attracts thousands each Thursday night from mid-July through August for free music in the picturesque Monteith River Park. Musical acts vary from bluegrass to candy-coated pop. There are special shows with local performers each Monday night in July. Call the **Albany Visitor Center** for more info. (☎800-526-2256. Open M-F 9am-5pm, Sa 9am-3pm, Su 10am-2pm.) The musically oriented can always check the **KBBR concert line** (☎737-3737).

MOUNTAIN BIKING. Mountain biking is a way of life in Corvallis, and all roads seem to lead to one bike trail or another. A map of the trails around Corvallis can be found at the visitor bureau (see **Practical Information,** above). Those searching for a hard-core mountain biking experience, however, would be better served in the Willamette or Deschutes National Forests near **Sisters.** In any case, riding is no good in the winter season when rains turn the trails to soup. Maps for biking destinations are available at **Peak Sports** ($5; see **Practical Information,** above). The **Oregon State University's McDonald Forest** has marked trails that are mostly flat (with the exception of Dan's trail, a local favorite); the unmarked trails can get sick though with log drops and steep singletrack. Go west out of town on Harrison Blvd. for 4½ mi., then turn right on Oak Creek Dr. until the pavement dead-ends at OSU's lab. An easy place to get lost; a map is useful.

KAYAKING. The class IV "Concussion Run," on the **Middle Santiam,** is known as a summertime classic. The run is short but sweet, and has three rapids that get successively more difficult, culminating with Concussion itself (which must be scouted). Only runs when there's a dam release: call ☎541-367-5132 to get the schedule; 1300-2000 cfs is optimal. The run begins at **Green Peter Reservoir,** and ends at **Foster Reservoir,** off of Hwy. 20; ask the folks at Peak Sports for directions.

EUGENE ☎541

Epicenter of the organic foods movement and a haven for hippies, Eugene has a well-deserved liberal reputation. Any questions about Eugene's leftward alignment can be resolved during the hippie-rific Oregon Country Fair. As home to the University of Oregon, the city is packed with college students during the school year before mellowing out considerably during the summer. Though a recent wave of drug-related crime has left some parts of Eugene less safe than others, its Saturday market, nearby outdoor activities, and overall sunny disposition make Oregon's second-largest city one of its most attractive.

OREGON

TRANSPORTATION

Eugene is 111 mi. south of Portland on I-5. The main north-south arteries are, from west to east, **Willamette St., Oak St., Pearl St.,** and **High St. Hwy. 99** runs east-west and splits in town—**6th Ave.** runs west, and **7th Ave.** goes east. The **pedestrian mall** is downtown, on Broadway between Charnelton and Oak St. The numbered avenues run east-west and increase toward the south. Eugene's main student drag, **13th Ave.,** leads to the **University of Oregon (U of O)** in the southeast of town. Walking the city is very time-consuming—the most convenient way to get around is by bike. Every street has at least one bike lane, and the city is quite flat. The **Whittaker** area, around Blair Blvd. near 6th Ave., can be unsafe at night.

Trains: Amtrak, 433 Willamette St. (☎687-1383), at 4th Ave. To **Seattle, WA** (6-8hr., 2 per day, $35-60) and **Portland** (2½-3hr., 2 per day, $17-29). Open daily 5:15am-9pm and 11pm-midnight.

Buses: Greyhound, 987 Pearl St. (☎344-6265), at 10th Ave., runs to **Seattle** (6-9hr., 7 per day, $34) and **Portland** (2-4hr., 10 per day, $16). Open daily 6:15am-9:35pm.

Public Transportation: Lane Transit District (LTD; ☎687-5555), handles public transportation. Map and timetables at the LTD Service Center, at 11th Ave. and Willamette St. Fare $1.25, seniors and under 18 $0.50. Runs M-F 6am-11:40pm, Sa 7:30am-11:40pm, Su 8:30am-8:30pm. Wheelchair accessible.

Taxis: Yellow Cab (☎746-1234).

Car Rental: Enterprise Rent-a-Car, 810 W 6th Ave. (☎344-2020). $33 per day; unlimited mileage within OR. Out-of-state $0.25 per mi if over 200 mi. Will beat any competitor's price. 10% county tax. 21+. Credit card required for out-of-town customers. Open M-F 7:30am-6pm, Sa 9am-noon.

AAA: 983 Willagillespie Rd. (☎484-0661), near Valley River Center Mall, 2 mi. north of the U of O campus. Open M-F 8am-5:30pm.

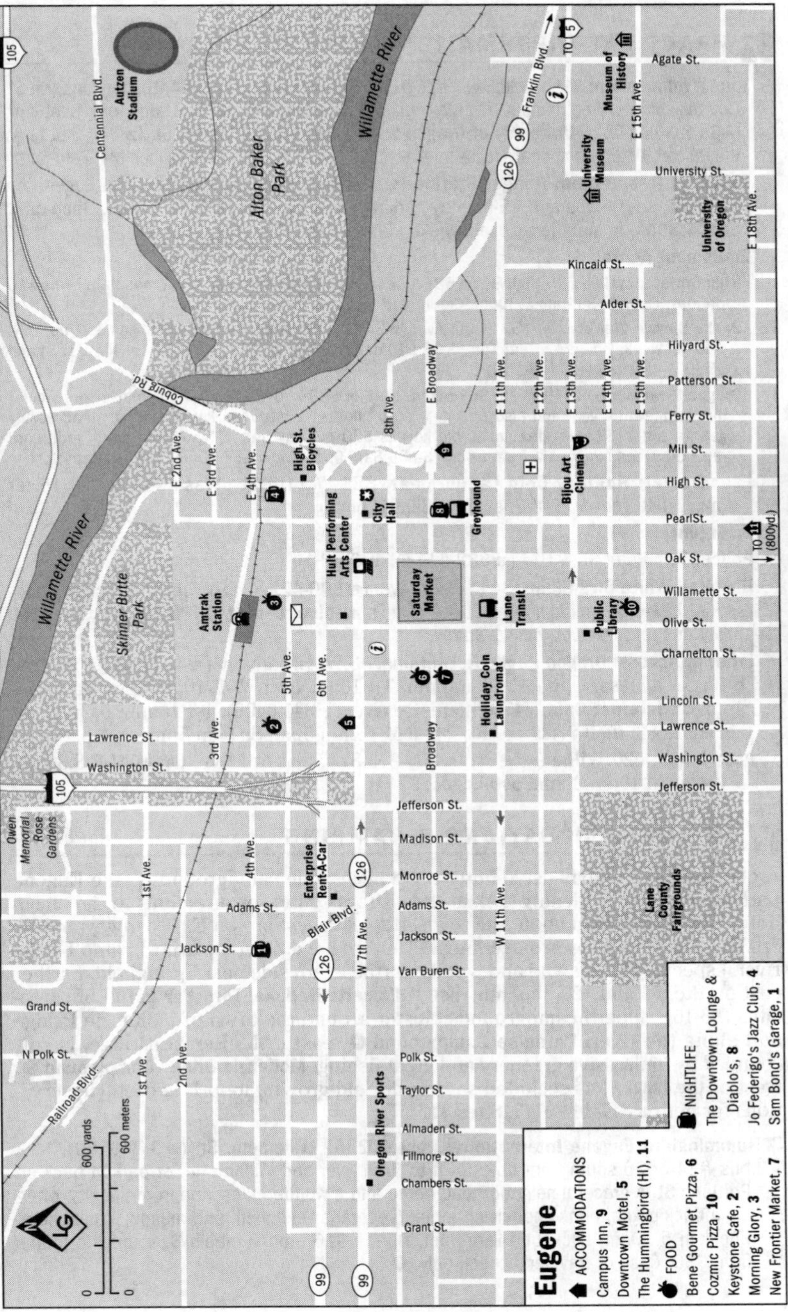

Eugene

ACCOMMODATIONS
- Campus Inn, **9**
- Downtown Motel, **5**
- The Hummingbird (HI), **11**

FOOD
- Bene Gourmet Pizza, **6**
- Cozmic Pizza, **10**
- Keystone Cafe, **2**
- Morning Glory, **3**
- New Frontier Market, **7**

NIGHTLIFE
- The Downtown Lounge & Diablo's, **8**
- Jo Federigo's Jazz Club, **4**
- Sam Bond's Garage, **1**

PRACTICAL INFORMATION

Tourist Information: 115 W. 8th Ave., #190 (☎484-5307 or 800-547-5445), door on Olive St. Courtesy phone. Free maps. Open May-Aug. M-F 8:30am-5pm, Sa-Su 10am-4pm; Sept.-Apr. M-Sa 8:30am-5pm. **University of Oregon Switchboard,** 1244 Walnut St. (☎346-3111), in the Rainier Bldg., is a referral service for everything from rides to housing. Open M-F 7am-6pm.

Outdoors Information: Ranger Station (☎822-3381), about 60mi. east of Eugene on Rte. 126, sells maps and $5-per-day parking passes for the National Forest. Open daily 8am-4:30pm in summer; closed weekends in winter.

Equipment Rental:

High Street Bicycles, 535 High St. (☎687-1775), downtown. Full-suspension mountain bikes $40 per day. Open M-Sa 9am-5:30pm. Credit card required.

Paul's Bicycle Way of Life, 152 W 5th Ave. (☎344-4105). Friendly staff. City bikes $12 per day, $60 per week. Open M-F 9am-7pm, Sa-Su 10am-5pm. Also at 2480 Alder St. (☎342-6155) and 2580 Willakenzie (☎344-4150).

Oregon Riversports, 1640 W 7th St. (☎334-0696 or 888-790-7235; www.oregonriversports.com) rents whitewater gear and also arranges "social floats." Whitewater kayak rentals, all accessory gear included $25 per day, inflatable kayaks $30 per day, rafts $55-75 per day. Credit card required. Open summer M-F 9am-6pm, Sa-Su 8am-6pm; winter M-F 10am-6pm, Sa 9am-6pm.

Laundromat: Holliday Coin Laundromat, 381 W 11th St., Wash $1, dry $0.75 for 10min., detergent $0.50. Open daily 6am-11pm.

Emergency: ☎911.

Police: 777 Pearl St. #107 (☎682-5111), at City Hall.

Hospital: White Bird Clinic, 341 E 12th Ave. (☎800-422-7558). Free 24hr. crisis counseling. Low-cost medical care at the clinic's **medical center,** 1400 Mill St. Open M-F 8:30am-noon, by appt. only 1-3pm.

Internet Access: Oregon Public Networking, 43 W. Broadway (☎484-9637), has free Internet access. Open M 10am-6pm, Tu 10am-4pm, W-F 10am-6pm, Sa noon-4pm. **CS Internet Cafe,** 747 Willamette Ave. (☎345-0408). 1st 15min. of Internet access is $2, then $7.20 per hr. Open M-F 7am-5pm, Sa 9am-5pm.

Post Office: 520 Willamette St. (☎800-275-8777), at 5th Ave. Open M-F 8:30am-5:30pm, Sa 10am-2pm. **Postal code:** 97401.

OREGON

ACCOMMODATIONS & CAMPING

A choice hostel, inexpensive hotels, and accessible campgrounds make Eugene particularly budget-friendly. Ask at the visitors center for directions to the cheap hotel chains scattered about the town—the cheapest are on E. Broadway and W. 7th Ave., and tend toward seediness. Tenters have been known to camp by the river, especially in the wild and woolly northeastern side near Springfield. Farther east on Rte. 58 and 126, the immense **Willamette National Forest ❶** is full of campsites ($6-16). Superb campgrounds cluster around the town of McKenzie Bridge and along the river. **Paradise Campground ❶,** east of McKenzie Bridge, is surrounded by impressive greenery and great fishing. **McKenzie Bridge Campground ❶,** west of the town, has secluded sites under old-growth; loop B is best. (Reservations for both ☎877-444-6777. Sites $12.)

Hummingbird Eugene International Hostel, 2352 Willamette St. (☎349-0589). Take bus #24 or 25 south from downtown to 24th Ave. and Willamette, or park in back on Portland St. A graceful neighborhood home and a wonderful escape from the city, offering a back porch, book-lined living room, (vegetarian) kitchen, and mellow atmosphere. Check-in 5-10pm. Lockout 11am-5pm. Dorms $16, nonmembers $19; private rooms from $30. Cash or traveler's check only. ❶

Pine Meadows (☎942-8657 or 877-444-6777). Take I-5 S. to Exit 172, then head 3½ mi. south, turn left on Cottage Grove Reservoir Rd., and go another 2½ mi. Alongside a reservoir with plenty of RV and jet ski traffic. Open just before Memorial Day-Labor Day. 92 sites, $12. Another 15 sites ¼ mi. down the road, $6. Free showers. ❶

Schwarz Park (☎942-1418 or 877-444-6777), off I-5 S. Exit 174, about 15min. south of Eugene. Go straight down the off-ramp and left at the first traffic light, then go past the village green for about 5½ mi. The camp lies below beautiful and swimmable Dorena Lake. Flat and quiet. Toilets and water. 82 sites, $12. ❶

Downtown Motel, 361 W 7th Ave. (☎345-8739 or 800-648-4366), located near downtown and the highway, but still quiet and peaceful. Fridges and free sweets. Strong coffee in the morning. Singles $35; doubles $40. ❸

Campus Inn, 390 E Broadway (☎343-3376), has plenty of amenities like Starbucks coffee in the spotless rooms, cable TV with HBO, and tea in the lobby. Free continental breakfast. Singles from $56; doubles from $74. AAA and AARP discounts. ❹

FOOD

Eugene's downtown area specializes in gourmet food; the university hangout zone at 13th Ave. and Kincaid St. has more grab-and-go options, and natural food stores are everywhere. *Everything* is organic. The **New Frontier Market,** with the **Broadway Bistro and Wine Bar,** at 200 W Broadway and Charnelton, is an organic store that also features an amazing wine bar and take-out lunch counter. (☎685-0790. Open M-Th 7am-9pm, F 7am-10pm, Sa-Su 8am-8pm.) For groceries, head to **Safeway,** 145 E 18th Ave. at Oak. (☎485-3664. Open daily 6am-2am.)

ORGANIC DINING

Perhaps most noteworthy of Eugene dining is the craze for "organically grown" products. Avoiding antibiotics, hormones, and nasty chemicals like strychnine, these restaurants only serve food that undergoes organic certification. Visit www.tilth.com for more info.

Keystone Cafe, 395 W. 5th St. (☎342-2075), serves creative dinners with entirely organic ingredients and many vegetarian options. Famous pancakes $3.25. Open daily 7am-5pm. ❶

Morning Glory Cafe and Bakery, 450 Willamette Ave. (☎687-0709), is decorated with provocative images of female supermodels in a mockery of mainstream sexual culture, and the waitstaff is pierced to complete the alternative feel. Though the food is a bit pricey, it gets local raves. Even a caffeine habit can be satisfied organically here, since Morning Glory shares space and a counter with **Out of the Fog Organic Coffee House.** Breakfast dishes and sandwiches $6-7.50. Open Tu-Su 7:30am-3:30pm. ❷

Cozmic Pizza, 1430 Willamette Ave. (☎338-9333), has vegetarian, organic pizzas served thin, perfectly crusted and piping hot. Offers occasional live music in the "magic garden," a central courtyard with a trickling fountain. Service can be slow. Small pizzas that serve 1 are $5, $0.25 per extra topping. Open daily 11:30am-11pm. ❶

OTHER RESTAURANTS

The Glenwood, 1340 Alder St. (☎687-0355), on 13th Ave., has delicious, cheaper-than-usual sandwiches and a sunny deck—just expect to compete with crowds of students during the school year. The $6.50 lunch special includes a pizza slice, salad, and drink. Open daily 7am-10pm. ❶

Bene Gourmet Pizza, 225 W. Broadway (☎284-2700), serves just that. Pies $12-19. Open M-F 11am-9pm. ❸

OUTDOOR ACTIVITIES

To escape the city, Eugene residents flock to the **McKenzie River Corridor,** which harbors the clear and continuous rapids of the McKenzie River and a gentle trail along its banks. For rafting, the Upper McKenzie is a wild and scenic stretch, and is much preferred to the sometimes clear-cut lower section.

KAYAKING & RAFTING. Within an 1½hr. drive from Eugene, the McKenzie River has several stretches of class II-III whitewater. It is best enjoyed in June, when warm weather and high water conspire for a thrilling but comfortable ride. The Upper McKenzie is continuous for 14 mi. and can easily be paddled within 2-2½hr. One class III, 9 mi. trip begins at Olallie Campground and ends at Paradise Campground. Both access points are on Rte. 126; Olallie is about 12 mi. east of McKenzie Bridge. A class II+ stretch begins at the Paradise Campground and continues downstream. These are not the only options, as many campgrounds along the river offer access; put-ins upstream of Olallie Campground are feasible except during late-summer low water.

High Country Expeditions, on Belknap Springs Road about 5 mi. east of McKenzie Bridge, is one of the few rafting companies that floats the Upper McKenzie. (☎888-461-7233. Half-day, 14mi. trips $50; full-day, 18-19mi. trips $75. Student and senior discounts.)

HIKING. The 26 mi. **McKenzie River Trail** starts 1½ mi. west of the ranger station (trail map $1) and ends north at Old Santiam Rd. near the Fish Lake Old-growth Grove. Parallel to Rte. 126, the trail winds through mossy forests, and leads to two of Oregon's most spectacular waterfalls—**Koosah Falls** and **Sahalie Falls.** They flank **Clear Lake,** a volcanic crater now filled with crystal clear waters. The entire trail is also open to mountain bikers and considered fairly difficult because of the volcanic rocks. A number of Forest Service campgrounds cluster along this stretch of Rte. 126. More ambitious hikers can sign up for overnight permits at the ranger station and head for the high country, where the hiking opportunities are endless.

DRIVING. To see the country as 19th-century settlers saw it, take Rte. 126 east from Eugene. On a clear day, the mighty and snow-capped **Three Sisters** are visible. Just east of **McKenzie Bridge,** the road splits into a scenic byway loop. Rte. 242 climbs east to the vast lava fields of **McKenzie Pass,** while Rte. 126 turns north over Santiam Pass and meets back with Rte. 242 in Sisters (see p. 142). Rte. 242 is often blocked by snow until the end of June. The exquisite drive winds its narrow way between **Mt. Washington** and the **Three Sisters Wilderness** before rising to the high plateau of McKenzie Pass. Here, lava outcroppings once served as a training site for astronauts preparing for lunar landings. The Civilian Conservation Corps-built **Dee Wright Observatory** has incredible views on clear days. The **McKenzie Ranger Station,** 3 mi. east of McKenzie Bridge on Rte. 126, has more info. (☎822-3381. Open summer daily 8am-4:30pm; winter M-F 8am-4:30pm.) Check with rangers about hiking permits (usually free) before going to the trailheads. The **Willamette National Forest** (see **Practical Information,** p. 124) has information on the McKenzie Pass.

HOT SPRINGS. The large and popular Cougar Lake features the Terwilliger Hot Springs, known by all as **Cougar Hot Springs.** Drive through the town of Blue River, 60 mi. east of Eugene on Rte. 126, and then turn right onto Aufderheide Dr. (Forest Service Rd. 19), and follow the road 7¼ mi. as it winds on the right side of Cougar Reservoir. (Open dawn until dusk. $3 per person. Clothing optional.) The **Blue River Reservoir,** on the way up, is being drained until 2004, so brace yourself for an ugly look into its now-dry depths. To get there, go 4 mi. east of Blue River on Rte. 126, turn right onto Aufderheide Dr. (Forest Service Rd. #19), and follow the road 7 mi. along the side of Cougar Reservoir.

SIGHTS

Every Saturday the area around 8th Ave. and Willamette St. fills up for the **Saturday Market**, featuring live music and stalls hawking everything from hemp shopping bags to tarot readings. The food stalls serve up delicious, and cheap, local fare. Right next to the shopping stalls is the **farmer's market,** where you can buy (you guessed it) organic, locally-grown produce. (Sa 10am-5pm, rain or shine.) Take time to pay homage to the ivy-covered halls that set the scene for *National Lampoon's Animal House* at Eugene's centerpiece, the **University of Oregon.** The visitor parking and info booth is just left of the main entrance on Franklin Blvd. Tours begin from the reception desk at **Oregon Hall.** (At E 13th Ave. and Agate St. ☎346-3014. Tours M-F 10am and 2pm, Sa 10am. Reception desk open M-F 8am-5pm.) A few blocks away, the **Museum of Natural History,** 1680 E. 15th Ave., at Agate St., shows a collection of relics from native cultures, including the world's oldest pair of shoes. (☎346-3024; http://natural-history.uoregon.edu. Open W-Su noon-5pm. Suggested donation $2.)

ENTERTAINMENT

The **Eugene Emeralds** are the local Triple-A minor league baseball team; they play in **Civic Stadium,** at 20th Ave. and Pearl St., throughout the summer. (For tickets call ☎342-5376. The season lasts from mid-June to mid-Sept. Adults $5-8, children $4-7.) The *Eugene Weekly* (www.eugeneweekly.com), a free mag available all over town, has a list of concerts and local events as well as features on the greater Eugene community. The *Sentient Times* (www.sentienttimes.com) is worth a read to see Eugene's liberal side in print. The **Community Center for the Performing Arts** operates the **WOW Hall,** 291 W 8th Ave., a historic dance venue on the National Register of Historic Places. All kinds of public speaking, dance, and theater events, as well as workshops and classes, are hosted here. Tickets are available at the Hall and at local ticket outlets. (☎687-2746. Open M-F 3-6pm. Tickets up to $15.) High-brow culture finds a home at the extravagant **Hult Center for the Performing Arts,** One Eugene Center, at 7th Ave. and Willamette St. The two theater halls host a variety of music from Tool to Tchaikovsky and from blues to Bartók, as well as theater and opera. (Info ☎682-5087, ticket office 682-5000, 24hr. event info 682-5746. Free tours Th and Sa at 1pm. Tickets $8-55; some student and senior discounts. Box office open Tu-F 11am-5pm, Sa 11am-3pm, and 1hr. before curtain.) The **Bijou Art Cinema,** 492 E 13th Ave. at Ferry St., is a local favorite where indie and art films are screened in the sanctuary of an old Spanish church. (☎686-2458. Box office open 20min. before the first screening. Th-Sa $6.50, Su-W $5, seniors $4. Late night shows $3.)

OREGON COUNTRY FAIR. The fair takes place in **Veneta,** 13 mi. west of town on Rte. 126, and is by far the most exciting event of the summer. Started in 1969 as a fundraiser for a local Waldorf school, the fair has become a magical annual gathering of hippies, artists, musicians, misfits, and activists. Every July, 50,000 people, many still living in Haight-Ashbury happiness, flock from across the nation to experience this festival unlike any other. Hundreds of performers crowd onto seven different stages, and 300 booths fill with art, clothing, crafts, herbal remedies, exhibits on alternative energy sources, and food. Lofty tree houses, parades of painted bodies, dancing 12 ft. dolls, and thousands of revelers transport travelers into an enchanted forest of frenzy. Parking is extremely limited ($5) and the fair requires advance tickets. Most people park for free at Civic Stadium, at 19th and Willamette in Eugene. From there, free buses run every 10min. from 10am until the fairgrounds close at 7pm. (☎343-4298; www.oregoncountryfair.org. Every year on the weekend after the Fourth of July. Tickets F and Su $10, Sa $15; not sold on site.) Nearby camping for the weekend is available through Fastixx. (☎800-992-8499. $30-36 per person.)

OREGON BACH FESTIVAL. From June 25 to July 11, 2004, Baroque authority Helmut Rilling conducts performances of Bach's concerti and other works by Bach's contemporaries. (☎346-5666 or 800-457-1486; http://bachfest.uoregon.edu. Concert and lecture series $13; main events $20-45.)

NIGHTLIFE

According to some, Eugene's nightlife is the best in Oregon, outside of Portland. Not surprisingly, the string of establishments by the university along 13th St. are dominated by the college crowd. Come nightfall, bearded hippies mingle with pierced anarchists and muscle-bound fratboys in Eugene's eclectic nightlife scene. In the *Animal House* tradition, the row by the university along 13th Ave. is often dominated by fraternity-style beer bashes. Refugees from this scene will find a diverse selection throughout town. Check out *Eugene Weekly* for club listings.

OREGON

Sam Bond's Garage, 407 Blair Blvd. (☎431-6603). Take bus #50 or 52 or a cab at night. A laid-back gem in the Whittaker neighborhood. Live entertainment every night complements an always-evolving selection of local microbrews ($3 per pint). Open daily 3pm-1am.

The Downtown Lounge/Diablo's, 959 Pearl St. (☎343-2346), offers a casual scene with pool tables upstairs and Eugene's most beautiful people shaking their thangs amid flame-covered walls downstairs. Cover $2-3. Open W-Sa 9pm-2:30am.

John Henry's, 77 W. Broadway (☎342-3358; www.johnhenrysclub.com), is Eugene's prime site for punk, reggae, and virtually any other kind of live music you'd like to hear. Call or check the website for schedule and covers. Open daily 5pm-2:30am. **Jo Federigo's Jazz Club and Restaurant,** 259 E. 5th Ave. (☎343-8488), across from 5th St. Market, swings with jazz nightly. Shows start 9:30pm. Open M-F 11:30am-2pm and 5-10pm, Sa-Su 5-10pm. Jazz club daily 8:30pm-1am.

GRANTS PASS ☎541

Workers building a road through the Oregon mountains in 1863 were so overjoyed by the news of General Ulysses S. Grant's Civil War victory at Vicksburg that they named the town Grants Pass after the burly President-to-be. Today, the city colonizes the hot, flat valley with espresso stands and fast-food joints. A fine place to sleep, but real adventure lies in the Rogue River Valley and Illinois Valley regions.

PRACTICAL INFORMATION. The town lies within the triangle formed by **I-5** in the northeast, **Rte. 99** in the west, and the **Rogue River** to the south. In town, Rte. 99 splits into one-way **6th** and **7th St.,** which run through the heart of downtown and separate east from west. The railroad tracks (between G and F St.) divide north and south addresses. Within the confines of historic downtown, north-south streets are numbered and east-west streets are lettered. **Greyhound,** 460 NE Agness Ave. (☎476-4513; open M-Sa 6am-6:45pm), at the east end of town, runs to **Portland** (5½hr., 5 per day, $30) and **San Francisco, CA** (12hr., 4 per day, $49). **Enterprise,** 1325 NE 7th St., rents cars from $30 plus $0.25 per mi. after 150 mi.; they'll also match any price. (☎471-7800. Must be 21+ with a credit card. Open M-F 7:30am-6pm, Sa 9am-noon.)

The **Chamber of Commerce,** 1995 NW Vine St., off 6th St., provides info beneath an immense plaster caveman. (☎476-7717 or 800-547-5927. Open M-F 8am-5pm, Sa 9am-5pm, Su 10am-4pm; winter closed Sa and Su.) **MayBelle's Washtub** is at 306 SE I St. at 8th St. (☎471-1317. Wash $1.25, dry $0.25 per 8min. Open daily 7am-10pm; last wash 8:30pm.) In an **emergency,** call ☎911 or contact the **police,** 500 NW 6th St. (☎474-6370). The **hospital** is at 500 SW Ramsey Ave. (☎472-7000), just south of town. Get **Internet access** at the **Josephine County Library,** 200 NW C St., where it's free for 1hr. on one of six computers. (☎474-5480. Open M-Th 10am-7pm, F-Sa 10am-5pm.) The **post office** can be found at 132 NW 6th Ave. at F St. (☎800-275-8777. Open M-F 9am-5pm.) **Postal Code:** 97526.

ACCOMMODATIONS & CAMPING. Grants Pass supports one of every franchise motel on earth, from Motel 6 to the Holiday Inn Express. The one-of-a-kind cheapo motels are farther back from the interstate on 6th St. and cost $25-35. The owner of the huge **Fordson Home Hostel (HI) ❶,** 250 Robinson Rd., gives tours of the antique tractors and vortex on his 20 secluded acres. Perks include free bike loans and $2 off the nearby Oregon Caves entrance fee. Located 38 mi. southwest of Grants Pass; follow US 199 to Rte. 46 east, and after 6 mi., turn onto Upper Holland Loop Rd. After 1 mi., you'll hit Robinson Rd. (☎592-3203. Reservations mandatory. $12, nonmembers $15. Bicyclists, backpackers, and students with ID $2 off.) For clean and welcoming, if aging, rooms, the **Parkway Lodge ❸,** 1001 NE 6th St. off Exit 58, fits the bill; they provide cable and fridges upon request. (☎476-4260. Singles from $32, doubles $45; cheaper in winter.) Of the camping options, **Valley of the Rogue State Park ❶** is your best choice. 12 mi. east of town off I-5 Exit 45B. The valley is just wide enough for the river, a row of tents, RVs interspersed with a few trees, and the noise of the interstate. (Tents $15; electric $17; full RV sites $18; yurts $27.)

OREGON

FOOD. For spatulas and spaghetti noodles, try **Safeway,** 115 NE 7th St. (☎479-4276. Open daily 6am-1am.) The **Growers' Market,** held in the parking lot between 4th and F St., is the state's largest open-air market and has arts and crafts, produce, food, and music everywhere. (☎476-5375. Sa mornings at 9am and 1pm.) **Thai BBQ ❶,** 428 SW 6th St. at J St., is decorated like an English teahouse but serves authentic Thai. Fancier than the name suggests but just as cheap: most lunch dishes are $5.25, and many dinner entrees are only a few dollars more. (☎476-4304. Open M-Sa 11am-9pm.) **Matsukaze ❷,** 1675 NE 7th St. at Hillcrest, is the best Japanese food in town. At what has become a youth hangout, traditional entrees run $4-15. (☎479-2961. Open M-Th 11am-2pm and 5-9pm, F 11am-2pm and 5-9:30pm, Sa 5-9:30pm; winter closes 30min. earlier.)

RAFTING & KAYAKING. The **Rogue River** is the greatest draw in the town of Grants Pass. A federally protected "Wild and Scenic River," the Rogue can be enjoyed by raft, jetboat, mail boat, or hiking on foot. Anglers are in good company—Zane Grey and Clark Gable used to roam the Rogue River with tackle and bait. For more information on fishing licenses and the best places to go, head to the ranger station off I-5 at Exit 58. Prime rafting and kayaking can be found on a powerfully scenic 35 mi. stretch of Class III and IV rapids starting just north of Galice. Paddling this restricted area requires a permit ($10) or guide. To get extra permits, try ☎479-3735 exactly 9 days before your trip; see www.or.blm.gov/rand for more info. Although the rest of the river near Grants Pass is very popular, it is not nearly as scenic, and can be downright residential; still, the whitewater gives plenty of thrills, especially for the uninitiated. The river can be found just outside of **Merlin,** where the necessary equipment can be procured as well. To get there, head west off I-5 Exit 61. **White Water Cowboys,** 210 Merlin Rd., rents rafts, and offers shuttle services. (☎479-0132. Discounts possible in May, early June, and late Sept., as well as for multi-day rentals. $65-95 per day.) **Orange Torpedo Trips,** in the same building, runs tours down every section of the Rogue river in orange inflatable kayaks. OTT was the first to use these interesting contraptions all the way back in 1969. (☎479-5061 or 800-635-2925; www.orangetorpedo.com. 2hr. for $30; half-day "dinner trip" for $50; full-day for $70, all on the Rogue.)

SPELUNKING. To reach **Oregon Caves National Monument,** 30 mi. south of Grants Pass via US 199, drive through plush, green wilderness to Cave Junction, and then 20 mi. east along Rte. 46. Here, in the belly of the ancient Siskiyous, enormous pressure and acidic waters created some of the only caves with walls of glistening marble in North America. A typical guided cave tour ($7.50; seniors $6.50) runs 1½hr. and begins every 15min. in the summer and every hour from September to December. The temperature inside is 42°F, and the walk can be rather strenuous. Tours last 1¼hr. An "off-trail" tour for those who like their exploration a bit more extreme leaves every summer morning at 10am and lasts 4hr. (☎592-2100 or 593-3400; www.nps.gov/orca/cavetour.htm. $25; reservations recommended. Open mid-Mar. to Nov. daily 9am-6:30pm.)

OREGON

ASHLAND ☎541

Set near the California border, Ashland mixes hip youth and British literary history, setting an unlikely but intriguing stage for the world-famous **Oregon Shakespeare Festival,** P.O. Box 158, Ashland 97520 (☎482-4331; www.osfashland.org). From mid-February to October, drama devotees can choose among 11 Shakespearean and newer works performed in Ashland's three elegant theaters. But to locals and the outdoorsy, Ashland is far more than a town crazy for an old, dead bard: unexpected in every way, it's a small (pop. about 20,000, not including students) town crammed between mountains to the west and east and culturally smeared somewhere between liberal Portland and new-age Northern California; the dining and partying befit a town ten times its size. To add to the fun, Ashland and the surrounding area are packed with all the biking, boating, hiking, and beautiful people you could ever hope for. Ashland is a great place to linger a few more weeks than planned.

JOURNEY'S END

Ashland is in the foothills of the Siskiyou and Cascade Ranges, 285 mi. south of Portland and 15 mi. north of the California border, near the junction of **I-5** and **Rte. 66. Rte. 99** cuts through the middle of town on a northwest-southeast axis. It becomes **N Main St.** as it enters town from the west, and then splits briefly into **East Main St.** and **Lithia Way** as it runs through the highly walkable downtown. Farther south, Main St. changes name again to **Siskiyou Blvd.,** where Southern Oregon University (SOU) is flanked by affordable motels.

Buses: Greyhound (☎482-8803) runs from Mr. C's Market, where I-5 meets Rte. 99 north of town. 3 buses per day to: **Portland** (8hr., $45); **Eugene** (6hr., $25); **Sacramento** (7hr., $46); **San Francisco** (11hr., $53).

Public Transportation: Rogue Valley Transportation (RVTD; ☎779-2877), in Medford. Bus schedules available at the Ashland Chamber of Commerce. The #10 bus runs between the transfer station at 200 S Front St. in **Medford** and the plaza in Ashland (35min.), then makes several stops on a loop through downtown Ashland. An in-town fare is $0.25. #10 runs through Ashland every 30min. daily 5am-7pm.

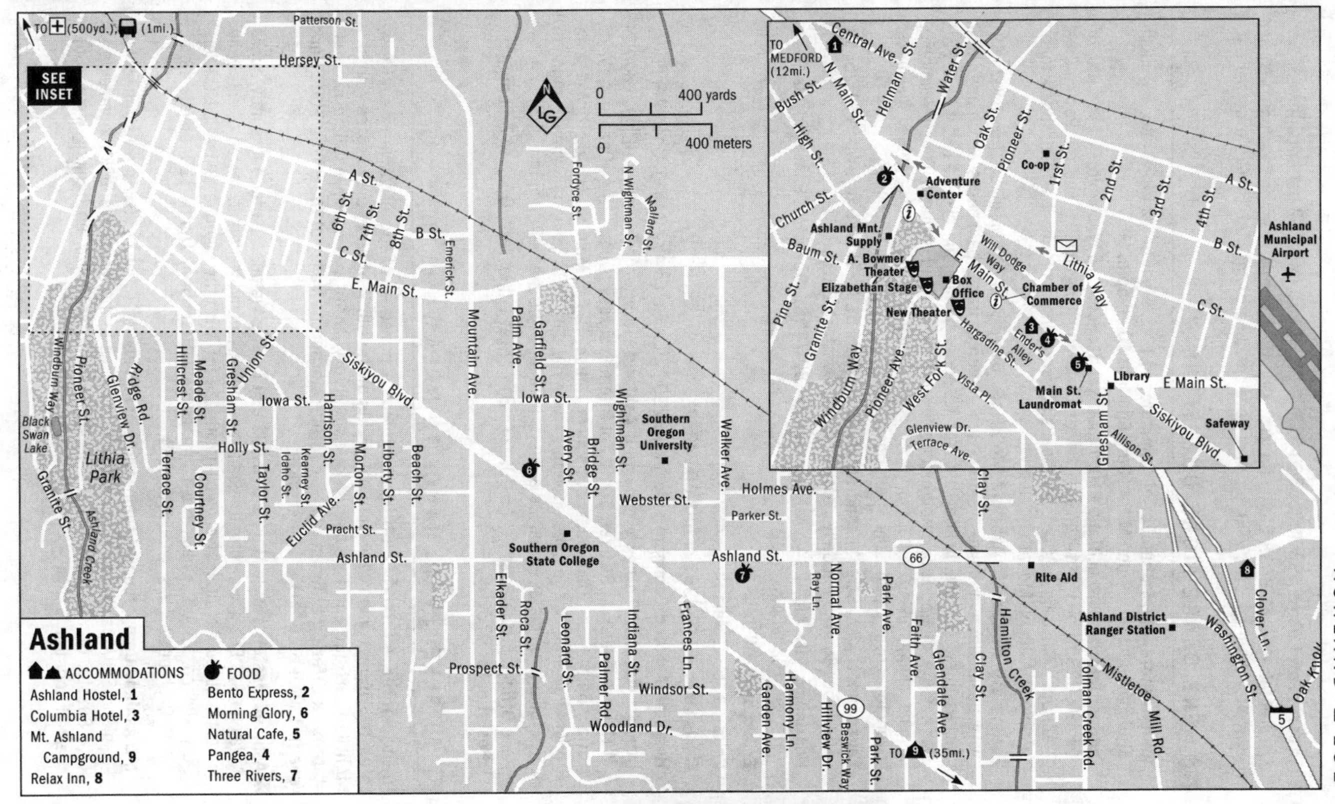
Ashland
ACCOMMODATIONS
Ashland Hostel, 1
Columbia Hotel, 3
Mt. Ashland Campground, 9
Relax Inn, 8
FOOD
Bento Express, 2
Morning Glory, 6
Natural Cafe, 5
Pangea, 4
Three Rivers, 7
SEE INSET
TO (500yd.), (1mi.)
TO MEDFORD (12mi.)
TO (35mi.)
0 400 yards
0 400 meters
Ashland Municipal Airport
Oak Knoll
Clover Ln.
Washington St.
Ashland District Ranger Station
Mill Rd.
Mistletoe
Tolman Creek Rd.
Rite Aid
Hamilton Creek
Clay St.
Glendale Ave.
Faith Ave.
Park Ave.
Park St.
Beswick Way
Normal Ave.
Hillview Dr.
Ray Ln.
Harmony Ln.
Garden Ave.
Ashland St.
Walker Ave.
Parker St.
Holmes Ave.
Frances Ln.
Windsor St.
Woodland Dr.
Southern Oregon University
Webster St.
Indiana St.
Palmer Rd.
Wightman St.
Bridge St.
Avery St.
Leonard St.
Southern Oregon State College
Garfield St.
Iowa St.
Roca St.
Palm Ave.
Elkader St.
Prospect St.
Mountain Ave.
Mallard St.
N Wightman St.
Fordyce St.
Emerick St.
B St.
8th St.
7th St.
6th St.
A St.
C St.
E. Main St.
Siskiyou Blvd.
Beach St.
Liberty St.
Morton St.
Pracht St.
Euclid Ave.
Harrison St.
Kearney St.
Idaho St.
Taylor St.
Union St.
Holly St.
Gresham St.
Meade St.
Courtney St.
Hillcrest St.
Terrace St.
Ridge Rd.
Glenview Dr.
Lithia Park
Pioneer St.
Ashland Creek
Windburn Way
Black Swan Lake
Granite St.
Patterson St.
Hersey St.
Central Ave.
N. Main St.
Helman St.
Water St.
Oak St.
Pioneer St.
1rst St.
2nd St.
3rd St.
4th St.
Co-op
Adventure Center
Ashland Mnt. Supply
A. Bowmer Theater
Elizabethan Stage
New Theater
Box Office
Will Dodge Way
Lithia Way
Chamber of Commerce
Ender's Alley
Hargadine St.
Main St. Laundromat
Library
Gresham St.
Allison St.
Safeway
E Main St.
Vista Pl.
West Fork St.
Glenview Dr.
Terrace Ave.
Pioneer Ave.
Windburn Way
Granite St.
Pine St.
Baum St.
Church St.
High St.
Bush St.
OREGON

Taxis: Yellow Cab (☎482-3065, 800-527-0700), $2.50 base, $2 per mi. 24hr.

Car Rental: Budget, 3038 Biddle Rd. (☎779-0488), at the airport in Medford. $30 per day, $0.20 per mi. after 200 mi. Must have credit card. Ages 21-24 $10 extra per day.

HERE CEASE MORE QUESTIONS

Tourist Information: Chamber of Commerce, 110 E. Main St. (☎482-3486; www.ashlandchamber.com). Open M-Sa 10am-6pm, Su 10am-5pm.

Outdoor Information: Ashland District Ranger Station, 645 Washington St., off Rte. 66 (☎482-3333), by Exit 14 on I-5, provides info on hiking, biking, and the Pacific Crest Trail. Open M-F 8am-4:30pm. For the inside scoop the outdoors, it's better to talk to the people at Ashland Mountain Supply.

Equipment Rental: Ashland Mountain Supply, 31 N Main St. (☎488-2749; www.ashlandmountainsupply.com). Rents internal frame backpacks and many other "accessories" (ice axe, helmet, etc.) for $5 per day. Mountain bikes $13 for 2hr., $30 per day. Cash deposit or credit card required. Copious and multidisciplinary (climbing, fishing, skiing, biking) outdoors advice is free; they can refer fishing guides for almost every local river. Open daily 10am-6pm.

Laundromat: Main Street Laundromat, 370 E Main St. (☎482-8042). Wash $1.25, dry $0.25 per 8min. Open daily 7am-11pm, last wash at 10pm.

Pharmacy: Rite Aid, 2341 Ashland St. (☎482-7406). Open M-F 8am-9pm, Sa 9am-7pm, Su 10am-6pm.

Emergency: ☎911.

Police: 1155 E Main St. (☎482-5211).

Crisis Line: ☎779-4357 or 888-609-4357. 24hr.

Hospital: Ashland Community Hospital, 280 Maple St. (☎482-2441). Open 24hr.

Internet Access: The newly expanded **Ashland Library,** 410 Siskiyou Blvd. (☎482-1151), at Gresham St. Free 30min. of Internet access. Open M-Tu 10am-8pm, W-Th 10am-6pm, F-Sa 10am-5pm. **Evo's Java House,** 376 E Main St. (☎482-2261), also offers free access, and once or twice a week you can check your mail while listening to live folk, punk, metal, or maybe a duet. There might be a cover then, though.

Post Office: 120 N. 1st St. (☎800-275-8777), at Lithia Way. Open M-F 9am-5pm. **Postal code:** 97520.

TO SLEEP, PERCHANCE TO DREAM

In the winter, Ashland is a budget traveler's paradise of motel vacancy and low rates; in summer, every room in town fills in the blink of an eye and rates rise sky high. Only rogues and peasant slaves arrive without reservations. The nearest state park offering a decent-sized campground is the **Valley of the Rogue State Park** (see p. 129), about 30 mi. north on I-5.

Ashland Hostel, 150 N Main St. (☎482-9217). The Victorian parlor and sturdy bunks play host to PCT hikers, theater-goers, and other Ashland visitors in search of entertainment, outdoors or in. It's very well-positioned for living the nightlife to its fullest. Laundry, kitchen. No A/C. Check-in 5-10pm. Lockout 10am-5pm. Dorms $20; private rooms $50. Cash or travelers' checks only. ❷

Mt. Ashland Campground, 20min. south of Ashland off I-5 at Exit 6. Follow signs for Mt. Ashland Ski Area through the parking lot. 7 sites in the forest overlook the valley and Mt. Shasta. Can be snowy in June. Fire pits and pit toilets, no drinking water. Suggested donation $3. ❶

OREGON

Columbia Hotel, 262½ E Main St. (☎482-3726 or 800-718-2530). Oozes with charm; don't expect a full-service chain hotel. A reading alcove and morning tea round out this historic home turned Euro-style hotel. Only 1½ blocks from theaters. June-Oct. rooms $65; private baths begin at $95. Mar.-June $49-89. 10% HI discount in off-season. ❹

Relax Inn, 535 Clover Ln. (☎482-4423 or 888-672-5290), just off I-5 at Exit 14 behind a 76 gas station. The small building conceals recently remodeled rooms with cable TV and A/C. Singles $43; doubles $52. ❸

FOOD OF LOVE

The incredible food selection on N. and E. Main St. has earned the plaza a culinary reputation independent of the festival, though the food tends to be pricey. **The Ashland Food Cooperative,** 237 1st St., stocks cheap and mostly organic groceries in bulk. (M-Sa 8am-9pm, Su 9am-9pm.) Cheaper groceries are available at **Safeway,** 585 Siskiyou Blvd. (☎482-4495. Open daily 6am-midnight.)

Evo's Java House and Revolutionary Cafe, 376 E. Main St. (☎774-6980). If you're hungry and sick of the Man keeping you down, fight back at Evo's, where the politics are as radical as the vegetarian burritos and sandwiches ($3.50-$5) are tasty. Open M-Sa 7am-5pm, Su 7am-2pm. ❶

Morning Glory, 1149 Siskiyou Blvd. (☎488-8636), deserves a medal for "most pleasant dining environment," earned either inside by the fireplace and bookcases or outside by the rose-entwined wooden porticos. Sandwiches around $9. Open daily 7am-2pm. ❸

Three Rivers, 1640 Ashland St. (☎482-0776). If you eat Indian food like a camel drinks water, load up here for the weeks ahead. The tandoori chicken and the rest of the buffet are quite tasty. All-you-can-eat lunch buffet $6.95, dinner buffet $7.95. Open M-Su 11:30am-2:30pm and 5pm-9pm. ❶

Pangea, 272 E Main St. (☎552-1630), offers a menu of creative, filling wraps and grilled panini sandwiches. The Wrap of Khan is a meal by itself ($7). Almost anything on the menu can be made without meat. Open daily 11:00-9pm. ❷

Natural Cafe, 358 E Main St. (☎888-5493). Vegetarian options abound. Good food and an outdoors deck that's unbeatable for people-watching. Sandwiches (about $5) and salads ($6-7) for lunch or dinner. Open Su-Th 7am-9pm, F-Sa 7am-10pm. ❶

Bento Express, at the corner of Granite St. and N Main St., is a tiny restaurant offering large portions of rice and cheap *bento* lunches to go. *Bao* and potstickers are $1.75, *bento* meals are $4.25. Open M-Sa 11am-5pm, Su noon-4pm. ❶

DRINK DEEP ERE YOU DEPART

Ashland's renowned nightlife, concentrated around N. and E. Main St., tends toward either the raucous and collegiate or the mellow and laid-back. Try the excellent microbrews at the supremely relaxed **Siskiyou Brew Pub,** 31 Water St., just off N. Main St. by the hostel. (☎482-7718. Occasional live music. Open daily until around 11pm.)

Ashland remains a cultural center even after the festival ends. Local and touring artists alike play throughout the year to the town's enthused audiences. The **Oregon Cabaret Theater,** at 1st and Hagardine St., stages light musicals in a cozy former church with drinks, dinners, and Sunday brunch. Tickets $15-23, food not included; reservations required 48 hr. in advance. (☎488-2902; www.oregoncabaret.com. Box office open Th-Sa, M 11am-2pm, 3pm-6pm M, W-Sa; Th open 4pm-6pm and Su 4pm-

THE INSIDER'S CITY

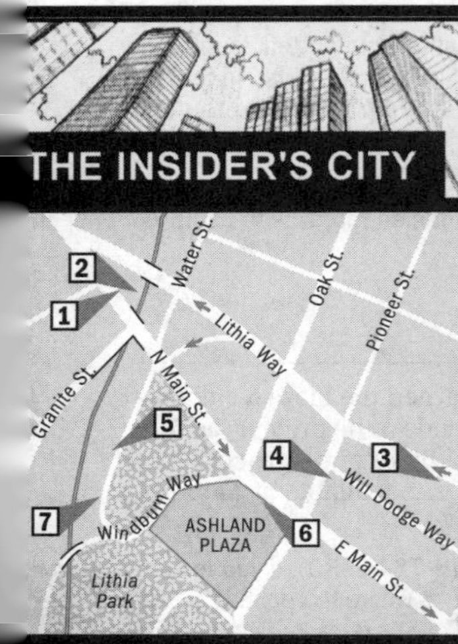

ASHLAND PUB CRAWL

Ashland has a nightlife scene denser than the darkest of micro-brewed stouts—you could easily enjoy a week of hard partying among the clubs and bars on E Main St. between 2nd St. and Water St. Most bars are dominated by students during the school year, and some bars have a reputation for frat brother patrons. Come summertime, everything is less crowded (but still hopping) and far mellower. All bars are 21+ unless otherwise noted.

1. Start your night by mellowing out with a drink on the huge outdoor deck at the **Ashland Creek Bar & Grill,** 92 N Main St. (☎482-4131). W DJ. F-Sa blues, ska and reggae. Cover $1-3. Open M-Th, Su 11am-1am, F 11am-2am, Sa 11am-8pm.

2. When you've taken in all that the Bar & Grill has to offer, head to the **Siskiyou Brew Pub,** 31 Water St. (☎482-7718), the most laid-back bar in town. Live music once or twice a week. Cover $5-10. Call or drop by for business hours.

8:00pm when there is a performance.) Small groups, such as the **Actor's Theater of Ashland** (☎535-5250), **Ashland Community Theatre** (☎482-7532), and **Southern Oregon University**'s theater department (☎552-6346) also sporadically raise the curtains year-round. Ashland also finds space for great music. When in town, the traveling **Rogue Valley Symphony** performs in the Music Recital Hall at SOU and at Lithia Park. (☎552-6398. Tickets run from $31; students $10.) In July and August, the **State Ballet of Oregon** graces the stage in a variety of venues Monday nights. The **Palo Alto Chamber Orchestra** giving hit performances at the Elizabethan Theatre, weather permitting. (☎482-4331. Tickets $10. M nights in late June.)

MIDSUMMER MADNESS

The **Oregon Shakespeare Festival,** P.O. Box 158, Ashland 97520 (☎482-4331; www.osfashland.org) was begun in 1935 by local college teacher Angus Bowmer as a nighttime complement to the daytime boxing matches in the old **Chautauqua Dome.** Today, the site of the dome is the festival's featured theater; instead of local college students, professional actors perform 11 plays in repertory, five or six of which are contemporary and classical works. Performances run on the three Ashland stages from mid-February through October and any boxing now is over scarce tickets. The 1200-seat **Elizabethan Stage,** an outdoor theater modeled after an 18th-century London design, is open from mid-June to mid-October, and hosts three Shakespeare plays per season. The **Angus Bowmer Theater** is a 600-seat indoor stage that shows one Shakespearean play and a variety of dramas. The **New Theater,** awaiting a $7 million donor for a name, seats 250-350 and serves as a modern replacement for the aging **Black Swan** theater. The 2004 schedule includes *King Lear*, *Much Ado About Nothing*, and all three *Henry VI* plays, as well as Suzan-Lori Parks's Pulitzer Prize-winning *Topdog/Underdog*.

In mid-June, the **Feast of Will** celebrates the annual opening of the Elizabethan Theater with dinner and merry madness in Lithia Park. ($12. Call box office for details.) **Festival Noons,** a mix of lectures and concerts held in the courtyard just outside the Elizabethan Theatre, occur almost every day at noon beginning in mid-June. Most are free, but some require tickets ($2-10), available at the box office.

TICKETS. Ticket purchases are recommended six months in advance. The **Box Office,** 15 S. Pioneer St., is next to the Elizabethan and Bowmer Theaters, and across the street from the New Theater. (☎482-4331;

www.osfashland.org. Open Tu-Su 9:30am-8:30pm, M 9:30am-5pm. General mail-order and phone ticket sales begin in January, and many weekend shows sell out within the first week. Tickets cost $22-39 for spring previews and fall shows, summer shows $29-52, plus a $5 handling fee per order for phone, fax, or mail orders. Children under 6 are not admitted. Those under 18 receive 25% discounts in the summer and 50% in the spring and fall. For complete ticket info, visit the web site.)

Last-minute theater-goers should not abandon hope. At 9:30am, the box office releases **unsold tickets** for the day's performances. Prudence demands arriving early; local patrons have been known to leave their shoes in line to hold their places. When no tickets are available, limited priority numbers are given out. These entitle their holders to a designated place in line when the precious few returned tickets are released (1:30pm for matinees, 6pm for evening shows). For those truly desperate for their Shakespeare fix, the box office also sells 20 clear-view **standing room tickets** for sold-out shows on the Elizabethan Stage ($11, available on the day of the show). Half-price **rush tickets** are occasionally available 1hr. before performances not already sold out. Some half-price matinees are offered in the spring and in October, and all three theaters hold full-performance **previews** in the spring and summer at considerable discounts. Unofficial ticket transactions take place all the time just outside the box office, but festival employees advise those "buying on the bricks" to check the date and time on the ticket carefully and pay no more than the face value.

BACKSTAGE TOURS. **Backstage tours** provide a wonderful glimpse of the festival from behind the curtain. Tour guides (usually actors or technicians) divulge all kinds of anecdotes—from the story of the bird songs during an outdoor staging of *Hamlet* to the time when a door on the set used for almost every stage entrance and exit locked itself midway through the show, provoking over 30min. of hilarious improvisation before it was fixed during intermission. (Tours leave from the Black Swan Tu-Sa. Start at 10am and last 2hr. Call box office in case of changes. $10, ages 6-17 $7.50; no children under 6.)

THE GILDED MONUMENTS

LITHIA PARK. Before it imported Shakespeare, Ashland was naturally blessed with **lithia water,** which contains dissolved lithium salts reputed to have miraculous healing powers. It is said that only

(Continued from previous page)

3 If you want to shoot pool, the place to be is **Q's,** 140 Lithia Way (☎488-4880). M Billiards tournaments in this outstanding pool hall with a mostly student patrons. No cover. Open Th-Sa 11am-2:30am, Su-W 11am-1am.

4 Once you've cleaned out your friends playing 9-ball, let the dancing begin at **Tabú,** 76 Will Dodge Way (☎482-3900). Choice acoustics and a great bar area sheltered from the dance floor give this place a trendy, classy feel. Th and Sa salsa, F house/techno. Cover $2-3. Open W-Su 11:30am-3pm, daily 5pm-10pm for dinner. Club open Th-Sa 10pm-2am, and *tapas* served until 2am.

5 After dancing, regain your saucy edge with an ale from **Black Sheep,** 51 N Main St. (☎482-6414). Follow the Union Jack into one of the only authentic English pubs in Oregon. No cover. Open daily 11:30am-1:30am.

6 If drinking ballads aren't your thing, get technological at **Kat Wok,** 62 E Main St. (☎482-0787). A mainstream club scene, with laser lights and a glow-in-the-dark pool table. Cover $3-5. Call or drop by for business hours.

7 Finally, to grab a beer, see the game, and just sample a slice of student life, check out **Louie's,** 41 N Main St. (☎482-9701), a sports bar with cheap beer that is constantly packed during the school year. No cover. Open M-Sa 11am-2:30am, Su 11am-9pm.

one other spring in the world has a higher lithium concentration. To try the water, hold your nose (to avoid sulfur salts) and head for the circle of fountains in plaza center. Besides aquatic phenomena, Lithia Park features free concerts, readings, nature walks around hiking trails, a Japanese garden, and swan ponds. On summer weekends, there is an artisans' market.

EMIGRANT LAKE PARK. Scads of kids and kids-at-heart flock to the 280 ft. **waterslide** at **Emigrant Lake Park,** 6 mi. east of town on Rte. 66. Popular for boating, hiking, swimming, and fishing, the park offers fantastic views of the valley. ($3 entry fee. Ten slides for $5 or unlimited slides for 3hr. $10-12. Park open daily 8am-sunset, waterslide May-Sept. noon-6:30pm.)

MT. ASHLAND. If your muscles demand a little abuse after all this theater-seat lolly-gagging, head out to Mt. Ashland for some serious **hiking** and **biking.** One of the best options for those looking for a long day's worth of downhill is a shuttle to the Mt. Ashland Ski Lodge (elev. 6200 ft.) that allows a 15-25 mi. ride down to Ashland. (elev. 1800 ft.) **Bear Creek Bicycles,** 1988 Hwy. 99 N, offers this service and $3 Jackson County bicycle maps; unfortunately, you'll have to rent your mountain bike elsewhere. (☎488-4270. Shuttle leaves 9:30am Sa and Su, $10.) Both hiking and biking on and around Mt. Ashland require a Northwest forest pass, available at the ranger station for $5 per day. The ranger station can also provide an excellent and comprehensive guide to hiking and biking in the area for free. The folks at the **Adventure Center** (see **Equipment Rental,** p. 132) can give tips on biking trails.

Pacific Crest Trail (3½ mi. one-way, 2hr.). Forest boundary to Grouse Gap. Take Exit 6 off I-5 and follow the signs along the Mt. Ashland Access Rd. for 7¼ mi. to the sign denoting the Rogue River National Forest Boundary. This section of the Pacific Crest Trail begins to climb Mt. Ashland, passing through forests and meadows covered with wildflowers, and ends at the Grouse Gap shelter. Moderate.

Wagner Butte Trail (5¼ mi. one-way, several hours). From Ashland, take Rte. 99 north of town to Rapp Rd. in Talent. Turn left and drive 1 mi. to the junction with Wagner Creek Rd. and then 8 mi. to Forest Rd. #22. Turn left and drive 2 mi. to the trailhead across from a parking area. This trail climbs 3000 ft. through a landslide area and tufts of old-growth fir to the top of Warner Butte. Breathtaking views on sunny days. Strenuous.

Horn Gap Mountain Bike Trail (3 mi. one-way or 9 mi. loop, 1-3hr.). To reach the trailhead from Lithia Park, take Granite St. along Ashland creek 1 mi. to Glenview, and park alongside the road. This is the upper trailhead; the lower trailhead is 4 mi. down the road. This ride offers both incredible views of Mt. Ashland and technical fun in steep slopes and several slalom courses. It can be linked with Rd. 2060 to create the 9 mi. loop. Moderate.

SKIING

At the top of the 9 mi. road leading from I-5 Exit 6 is **Mount Ashland,** a small ski area with 23 runs, a vertical drop of 1150 ft., a new half-pipe, and over 100 mi. of free **cross-country** trails. (☎482-2897, snow report ☎482-2754; www.mtashland.com. Lift tickets $27, ages 9-17 and seniors $22, 8 and under free. Starting at the beginning of Jan., lift tickets on Tu are only $15. Ski rentals $17 per day, snowboards $25. Open from late Nov. to mid-Apr. daily 9am-4pm. Night skiing Th-Sa 4-10pm.)

RAFTING

The wild and scenic Upper Klamath offers hard-core class IV-V action all summer. Depending on water level, the run can be a technical rock-bash or a continuous wave-train ride. In general, rafters prefer the run since the especially sharp rocks have ruined many an upside-down kayaker's day (and dental work). If water color is your only criterion for a river, don't paddle here; it's brown. **The Adventure Center,** 40 N Main St. (☎488-2819 or 800-444-2819; www.raftingtours.com), guides rafting trips. (Half-day $69; full-day $119-139; bike tours around Mt. Ashland $69 for 3hr., $119 per day. A water release schedule is available at ☎800-547-1501, or http://www.pacificorp.com/applications/hydro/waterrelease.cfm.)

CENTRAL & EASTERN OREGON

Central Oregon stretches between the peaks of the Cascades to the west, and Eastern Oregon spans gorges, desert mountain ranges, and alkali flats to the east. Except for Portlanders, most Oregonians live in Central Oregon, west of the Willamette Valley. Tourists come to eastern Oregon for the rodeos and festivals, or to toe the Oregon Trail. Backcountry hikers hit majestic Mt. Hood, Hells Canyon—the deepest gorge in the US—and the isolated volcanic features and wildlife preserves of the southeast. The severe landscape has changed little but never ceased to test the resolve of its inhabitants. The fertility of the land and the harshness of winter have nurtured and taken their toll upon game, hunters, wheat, and farmers.

THE CASCADES

The Cascade range connects California's Mt. Shasta with Washington's Mt. Rainier. Once highly volcanic, the Cascades have settled down enough for wind and water to have their way. Slicing Oregon almost completely from north to south, the Cascades create a natural barrier for moisture and lush vegetation. Central Oregon's towns are dotted throughout the mountains and receive most of the precipitation from the Pacific Ocean; more arid, less populated regions lie to the east.

BEND ☎541

Surrounded by a dramatic landscape, with volcanic features to the south, the Cascades to the west, and the Deschutes River running through its heart, Bend attracts outdoor enthusiasts from all over the Pacific Northwest. Its proximity to wilderness areas makes Bend an unbeatable base for hiking, rafting, and skiing, while the charming downtown is packed with restaurants, pubs, and shops. Settled in the early 1800s as "Farewell Bend," a pioneer trail waystation along the Deschutes, Bend is now a secret that everyone knows. SUVs with bikes, boards, or boats on top have replaced covered wagons, and the Three Sisters to the west are viewed as insurance against boredom, not a daunting obstacle.

ORIENTATION & PRACTICAL INFORMATION

Bend is 160 mi. southeast of Portland, 144 mi. north of Klamath Falls on **US 97,** and 100 mi. southeast of Mt. Hood via **US 26** and **Rte. 97. US 97 (3rd St.)** bisects the town. Downtown lies to the west along the Deschutes River; **Wall St.** and **Bond St.** are the two main arteries. From east to west, Franklin Ave. becomes Riverside

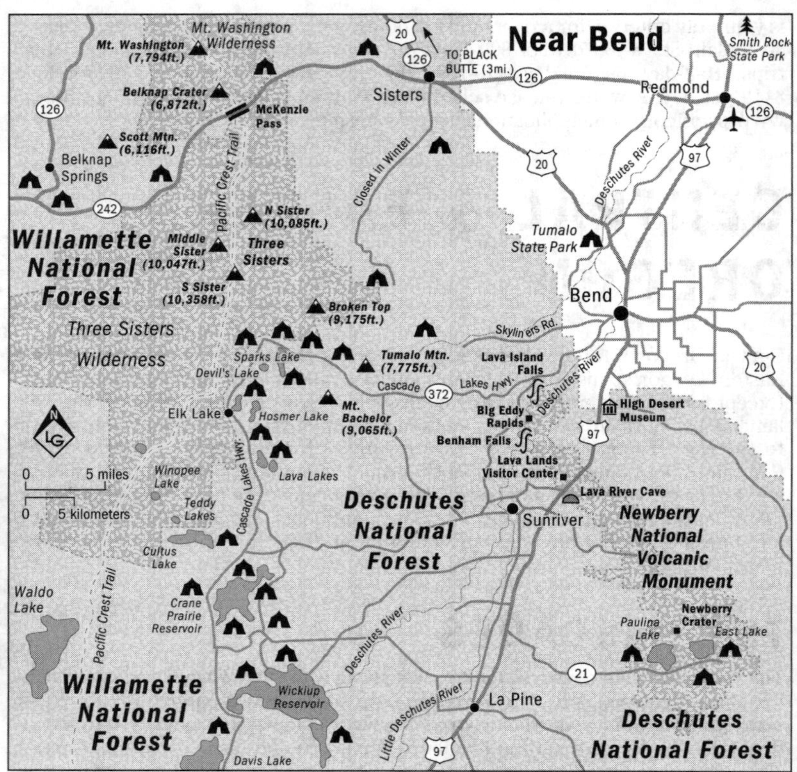

Blvd.; at the edge of Drake Park, Tumalo St. becomes Galveston Ave.; Greenwood Ave. becomes Newport Ave.; 14th St. becomes Century Dr. and is the first leg of the **Cascade Lakes Highway.** Before you explore, get a map at the **visitors center.**

Buses: Greyhound, 63076 US 97N (☎382-2151), in the Highway 97 gas station. Open M-F 8am-1:30pm and 2:30-5pm, Sa 8:30am-3pm, Su 8:30am-2pm. Call for info on other bus and van lines. To **Eugene** (2½hr.; 1 per day; $23) and **Portland** (4½hr.; 1 per day; $25-27).

Taxis: Owl Taxi, 1919 NE 2nd St. (☎382-3311). $2 base, $2 per mi.

Tourist Information: Bend Chamber and Visitors Bureau, 63085 US 97N (☎382-3221; www.visitbend.org). Full-time ranger on duty. Offers a mother lode of brochures in addition to an "Attractions and Activities Guide" and a map of the area. Also has Internet access. Open M-Sa 9am-5pm.

Outdoor Information: The forest headquarters maintains an info desk at the visitors center. A "Recreation Opportunity Guide" covers each of the 4 ranger districts. **Deschutes National Forest Headquarters,** 1645 20E (☎383-5300; open M-F 7:45am-4:30pm) and **Bend/Fort Rock District Ranger Station,** 1230 NE 3rd St. #A262 (☎383-4000; www.fs.fed.us/r6/deschutes), have additional info on Deschutes National Forest. Both open M-F 7:45am-4:30pm. **Oregon Dept. of Fish and Wildlife,** 61374 Parrell Rd., sells fishing licenses for $8 per day; inquire about hunting permits. (☎388-6363. Open M-F 8am-5pm.)

Bike & Ski Rental:

Hutch's Bicycles, 725 NW Columbia Ave. (☎382-9253; www.hutchsbicycles.com). Front suspension bikes $20 per day, $15 per 4hr. Full $45 per day. Open M-F 9am-7pm, Sa-Su 9am-6pm.

Sunnyside Sports, 930 NW Newport Ave. (☎382-8018; www.sunnysidesports.com), has front suspension bikes for $20 per day; each additional day $10. Cross-country skis $10-20 per day; each additional day $5. Open M-Th 9am-7pm, F 9am-8pm, Sa-Su 8am-6pm.

Pine Mountain Sports, 133 SW Century Dr. (☎385-8080; www.pinemountainsports.com), has mountain bikes for $20 per day. Also rents skis and snowshoes ($25 and $10). Open M-Sa 9am-6pm, Su 10am-5pm. Full suspension models at all shops are $45 per day.

Kayak and Canoe Rental: Alder Creek, 805 SW Industrial Way, on the river next to the Colorado Ave. bridge (☎317-9407). An excellent source of river level info and advice on boating in the area. Whitewater kayak rental $30 per day.

Laundromat: Westside Laundry and Dry Cleaners, 738 NW Columbia Ave. (☎382-7087). Wash $1.25, dry $0.25 per 10min. Open daily 6:30am-9:30pm.

Emergency: ☎911.

Police: 711 NW Bond St. (☎388-0170).

Hospital: St. Charles Medical Center, 2500 NE Neff Rd. (☎382-4321).

Internet Access: Try the **Deschutes County Library,** 601 NW Wall (☎388-6679). Free, fast Internet access on the 2nd floor next to the reference desk. Open M-Th 10am-8pm, F 10am-6pm, Sa 10am-5pm, Su 1-5pm. **Cafe Internet,** 141 SW Century Dr. (☎318-8802), offers broadband Internet access and a wide variety of games. $2 for 15 minutes, $10 for an entire Saturday of network gaming. Open M-Sa 10am-6pm.

Post Office: 777 NW Wall St. Open M-F 8:30am-5:30pm, Sa 10am-1pm. **Postal code:** 97701.

OREGON

ACCOMMODATIONS & CAMPING

Most of the cheapest motels line 3rd St. just outside of town, and rates are surprisingly low. **Deschutes National Forest** ❶ maintains a huge number of lakeside campgrounds along the **Cascade Lakes Highway,** west of town; all have toilets. (RVs $15-21; tents $12-18.) Backcountry camping in the national forest area is free. Parking permits may be required. Contact the **Bend/Ft. Rock Ranger District Office** (see above) for more info.

Bend Cascade Hostel, 19 SW Century Dr. (☎389-3813 or 800-299-3813). From 3rd St., take Greenwood west until it becomes Newport, then take a left on 14th St. Pillows, sleepsacks, and blankets are provided. Laundry $1 wash, dry $0.50. Kitchen. Lockout 9:30am-4:30pm. Curfew 11pm. $15; seniors, students, cyclists, and HI $14; under 18 with parents half-price. ❶

Tumalo State Park, 62976 OB Riley Rd. (☎382-3586 or 800-551-6949), 4 mi. north of Bend off US 20W. Riverside campsites go early, despite road noise. Though crowded with people, curious chipmunks vastly outnumber humans. Lots of tubing nearby. Hikers and bikers $4. 65 sites $17; 22 full RV sites $21; 4 yurts $29. Solar showers ($2) available. ❶

Rainbow Motel, 154 NE Franklin Ave. (☎382-1821 or 888-529-2877). Large, clean rooms surround a central mini-park lined with roses. TV, microwave, fridge. Free continental breakfast included. Summer queen $50. Winter single $35; double $45. ❸

FOOD

Bend has a huge number of restaurants. Four mega-markets line south 3rd St. **Devore's Good Food Store and Wine Shop,** 1124 Newport NW, peddles wine, cheese, and all things organic. (☎389-6588. Open M-Sa 8am-7pm, Su 10am-

6pm.) For good coffee and pastries, try **Tuffy's Coffee & Tea ❶,** 961 NW Brooks St., right off the intersection of Wall St. and Greenwood Ave. (☎389-6464. Open daily 7am-7pm.)

Taqueria Los Jalapeños, 601 NE Greenwood Ave. (☎382-1402), fills a simple space with locals hungry for good, cheap food, like $1.75 burritos. Open in summer M-Sa 11am-8pm, in winter 11am-7pm. ❶

Mother's Juice Cafe, 1255 NW Galveston St. (☎318-0989). Friendly staff blends exquisite smoothies ($4). Try the Mt. Everest sandwich ($5.75, $3.75 for half). Open summer M-Sa 7am-8pm; winter M-Sa 7am-7pm; Su 11am-5pm. ❶

Westside Bakery and Cafe, 1005 NW Galveston St. (☎382-3426). You won't be able to peel your eyes away from the tempting case of sugary desserts (under $3) on your way to the table. Burgers and sandwiches ($5.50-7). Open daily 6:30am-2:30pm. ❶

Baja Norte, 801 NW Wall St. in downtown (☎385-0611), serves delicious tacos, burritos, and other wrapped Mexican-style meals. Open daily 11am-9pm. ❶

Kuishinbo Kitchen, 114 NW Minnesota St. (☎385-9191). Grab a Japanese lunch to go. *Bento* ($5.25-6.75) is good, but most people order yakisoba noodles with tofu or meat ($4-6). Open M-F 11am-6:30pm, Sa 11am-4pm. ❶

OREGON

SIGHTS & FESTIVALS

HIGH DESERT MUSEUM. The museum is one of the premier natural and cultural history museums in the Pacific Northwest. Fantastic life-size dioramas recreate rickety cabins, cramped immigrant workshops, and Pauite tipis. An indoor desertarium offers a peek at shy desert creatures. Catch one of the hourly talks on various desert subjects, and don't miss the 7000 sq. ft. wing featuring birds of prey in their natural habitats, including the endangered spotted owl. *(59800 Hwy. 97 S, 3½ mi. south of Bend on US 97. ☎382-4754; www.highdesert.org. Arrive early to beat crowds. Open daily 9am-5pm. $7.75, ages 13-18 and 66+ $6.75, ages 5-12 $4.)*

DRAKE PARK & THE CASCADE FESTIVAL OF MUSIC. Picnic by the river with Canadian geese at beautiful Drake Park. The park hosts many events and festivals, most notably the Cascade Festival of Music, a weeklong series of classical and pop concerts during the week before Labor Day. *(Between Mirror Pond and Franklin St., one block from downtown. ☎382-8381; www.cascademusic.org. Tickets $16-25, rush tickets, students, and under 12 half-price.)*

OUTDOOR ACTIVITIES

The outdoors opportunities near Bend are limitless, and without peer in Oregon. From skiing, snowboarding, and snowshoeing in the winter to hiking, biking, and whitewater in the summer, Bend can be an inexpensive outdoor adventure waiting to happen. The **Three Sisters Wilderness Area,** north and west of the Cascade Lakes Hwy., is one of Oregon's largest and most popular wilderness areas. Pick up a parking permit at a ranger station or the Visitors Center ($5). Within the wilderness, the **South Sister** is the most accessible peak, making for a simple hike in late summer that threads between glaciers. The other Sisters provide more difficult technical climbs, with opportunities for multi-pitch ice or rock climbs.

SKIING. Those who ski the 9065 ft. **Mount Bachelor,** with its 3365 ft. vertical drop, are in good company—Mt. Bachelor has been home to the US Ski Team and the US Cross-Country Ski Team, and hosts many of the largest snowboarding competitions in the country. Many consider this the best ski resort in Oregon, with snow that's unusually dry in comparison to the soppy stuff farther west in the Cascades. The ski season runs September to June. (☎800-829-2442, snow report 382-7888. Alpine day tickets $43, ages 7-12 $22.) A shuttle bus service runs the 22 mi. between the parking lot at the corner of Simpson and Columbia in Bend and the mountain (Nov.-May; $2). Many nearby lodges offer **ski packages** (contact Central Oregon Visitor's Association at ☎800-800-8334 for info). **Chairlifts** are open for sightseers during the summer. (Open daily 10am-4pm. $10, seniors $9, ages 7-12 $6. A parking permit is necessary for all cars on the mountain; $5 per day from the ranger. See **Orientation and Practical Info,** p. 137, for equipment rental info.)

MOUNTAIN BIKING. Mountain biking is forbidden in the wilderness area, Benders have plenty of other places to spin their wheels. Be forewarned: the loose "pummy dust"—ground up pumice—makes riding slow and corners sketchy. The most renowned area for biking is "Phil's Trail," which fills the space between Skyliners Rd. and the Cascade Lakes Highway west of Bend. A $9 map from one of the bike shops (see above) is necessary, as is a compass. Go west on Skyliners Road out of Bend 2½ mi., then make a left (south) on Forest Road 220. Try **Deschutes River Trail** (6 mi.) for a fairly flat, forested trail ending at **Deschutes River.** To reach the trailhead, go 7½ mi. west of Bend on S. Century Dr. (Cascade Lakes Hwy.) until Forest Service Rd. 41, then turn left and follow the signs to Lava Island Falls. For a technical ride, hit **Waldo Lake Loop,** a grueling 22 mi. around the lake (4-4½hr.). Take Cascade Lakes Hwy. to Forest Service Rd. 4290. A guide to mountain bike trails around Bend ($9) and *Mountain Biking in Central Oregon* (free) are available at the **Bend/Ft. Rock District Ranger Station.** You can rent bikes and get outfitted at **Sunnyside Sports**, 930 NW Newport Ave. (☎382-8018. Open Sa-Th 9am-7pm, F 9am-8pm. Mountain bikes $20-40 per day.)

RAFTING & KAYAKING. Bend has an enormous kayaking and rafting community. The powerful Deschutes River has year-round flows thanks to dam releases for irrigation, and its rapids—formed by lava flows—are unusual and range from class II to unrunnable gnar-gnar. Two good playspots satisfy boaters' everyday needs. **First Street Rapids** has a mellow, class II-III wave above a recovery pool, in a non-scenic setting below a dam. To get there, cross over to the west side of the Deschutes River and work north and east via 3rd St. to 1st St, which then dead ends at First Street Rapids Park. **Big Eddy** is the other big playspot, although the recovery pools are brief at summertime high flows, necessitating either a quick roll or a facemask. The class III-IV or IV stretch, depending on flow, is accessed by taking 14th St. south 6½ mi. from Bend, and then making the next left after passing the Inn of the 7th Mountain. Take the road marked by "Big Eddy/Aspen." A common run is to put in at Aspen and take out above Lava Island Falls. Along the same road, several of the Deschutes' falls (really huge rapids, not waterfalls), including Lava Island Falls, have extreme descents.

Rafting companies take half-day trips from Aspen to above Lava Island Falls. These usually last 3hr. and cover the upper Deschutes's fairly tame waters. Full-day trips require a 1hr. drive to Maupin to run the Class III+ rapids of the lower Deschutes. **Sun Country Tours** runs half-day and full-day trips out of the Sun River Resort, 17 mi. south of Bend off US 97, and at 531 SW 13th St. in Bend. (☎800-770-2161. Half-day $40; full-day $95-105, ages 6-12 $80-105.) **River Drifters** offers trips on the Deschutes as well, but also has trips to other rivers close by. (☎800-972-0430; www.riverdrifters.net. Trips on the Deschutes are $65-75 per day for adults, $55-65 for kids. Trips to other rivers such as the Klickitat and the Sandy Gorge cost $75.)

DAYTRIP FROM BEND: NEWBERRY NATL. MONUMENT

The Newberry National Volcanic Monument was established in 1990 to link and preserve the volcanic features in south Bend. Featuring such volcanic wonders as **Lava Butte, Lava River Cave, Newberry Crater,** and **the Paulina Lakes,** the Newberry National Monument offers visitors plenty of sights and a wealth of hiking. Immediately behind the **Lava Lands Visitor Center** is **Lava Butte,** a 500 ft. cinder cone from which lava once flowed. Between Memorial Day and Labor Day, you can drive 2 mi. up the narrow road (no RVs) that leads to the butte. (13 mi. south of Bend on US 97. ☎593-2421. Required parking fee $5, free with a Golden Eagle Passport. Open mid-May-Labor Day daily 9am-5pm; Apr. to mid-May and Labor Day to Oct. W-Su 9:30am-5pm.) The monument's centerpiece is **Newberry Crater,** the remains of what was once the Newberry Volcano, one of three volcanoes in Oregon likely to erupt again "soon." The 500 sq. mi. caldera contains Paulina Lake and East Lake. (13 mi. south of Lava Lands Visitor Center on US 97, then 13 mi. east on Rte. 21. Parking within the national monument requires a $5 permit, available from the ranger or the visitors center; parking free with a Golden Eagle Pass.)

Obsidian Flow Trail (½ mi.). This is the result one of the most recent geological events in the Cascades, the Big Obsidian Flow. Formed only 1300 years ago when the Newberry volcano erupted, 170 million cubic yards of obsidian are crossed by this trail. Easy.

Paulina Lake Trail (7 mi.). Beginning at the visitors center and circumnavigating the gorgeous Paulina Lake, this trail provides views of the wildlife surrounding the lake. Paulina Lake also offers excellent fishing. Easy to moderate.

Crater Rim Trail (21 mi.). Encirling the entire Newberry Caldera, the trail offers vistas of the entire Bend area as well as the surrounding mountains. While hikers share this trail with bikers and horseback riders, there are plenty of sights to go around. Difficult.

SISTERS ☎541

A gateway to the nearby **Deschutes National Forest** and **Cascade Lakes,** Sisters offers those in town and those just passing through the same warm welcome. Unfortunately, it sometimes seems like *everyone* is just passing through. Authentic or not, Sisters features a refined old West look, which is bolstered by the annual Sisters Rodeo. Sisters also provides access to climbing facilities in nearby Smith Rock State Park and the sights of the Warm Springs Indian Reservation.

ORIENTATION & PRACTICAL INFORMATION

From Sisters, **Rte. 126** heads east to **Redmond** (20 mi.) and **Prineville** (39 mi.), and joins **US 20** to cross the Cascades to the west. **Rte. 242** heads southwest over McKenzie Pass to rejoin Rte. 126 and blend into **Cascade St.** The **visitors center,** 164 N Elm St., is one block from Cascade St. (☎549-0251; www.sisterschamber.com. Open M-F 9am-5pm; Sa-Su hours vary, call ahead.) Sisters' **Deschutes National Forest Ranger District Station,** on the corner of Cascade and Pine St., has info on nearby campgrounds, local dayhikes, and biking trails, and sells the required $5 parking permit for the park. (☎549-7700. Open summer M-F 7:45am-4:30pm, Sa 8am-4pm; winter M-F 7:45am-4:30pm.) **Eurosports,** 182 E Hood St., **rents** mountain bikes, snowshoes, snowboards, and cross-country and alpine skis. (☎549-2471. Bikes: front suspension $20 per day, $100 per week; full suspension $25 per day, $125 per week. Snowshoes, shaped skis, and snowboards $12-25 per day. Open summer daily 9am-5:30pm; winter M-F 9am-5:30pm, Sa-Su 8am-5:30pm.)

CAMPING & FOOD

Budget travelers generally pass up expensive Sisters for Bend's cheap lodging (see **Bend Accommodations,** p. 139). Camping, however, is as good as it gets in the Deschutes National Forest. The Ranger District maintains many spectacular **campgrounds** near Sisters; most of them cluster around **Camp Sherman,** a small community on the Metolius River 16 mi. northwest of Sisters. Two noteworthy sites are **Riverside ❶,** 10 mi. west on Rte. 20 and 4 mi. northeast on Rd. 14 (pumped water; 16 sites, $10), and **Allingham ❶,** 1 mi. north of the Camp Sherman store on Rd. 14 (piped water; 10 sites, $12). Both are maintained by **Hoodoo Recreation Services** through the ranger. Contact Hoodoo at ☎822-3799 or www.hoodoo.com for more info. Riverside's walk-in sites provide refuge from motor vehicles, and Allingham's drive-in sites perch right on the river, with ample fishing opportunities (with an $8 license).

Plan on exploring Sisters during the daylight hours; things are slow at 6pm and dead by dark. Overpriced food is available anytime at the faux-western tourist joints, but delis that close by 5, or even 3pm, are better for purse and palette. **Sisters Bakery ❶,** 251 E Cascade St., has all kinds of baked goods, including $2.25 marionberry cobbler, $3 loaves of top-notch bread, and $2.50 tasty chocolate eclairs. (☎549-0361. Open M-Sa 5am-6pm; in summer also open Su 6am-4pm.) **The Harvest Basket ❷,** 110 S Spruce St., features organic groceries and fresh fruit smoothies. (☎549-0598. Open M-F 9am-7pm, Sa 9am-6pm, Su 10am-5pm.)

SIGHTS & FESTIVALS

The Museum at Warm Springs is located off Hwy. 26 north of Sisters and Bend (look for the signs), on the **Warm Springs Indian Reservation.** A stunning piece of architecture, it documents the tribal history of the Wasco, Paiute, and Warm Springs Indians with interactive and informative exhibits. (☎553-3331. Open daily 10am-5pm. $6, seniors $5, ages 5-12 $3.) The annual **Sisters Rodeo,** over the second weekend in June, draws big-time wranglers to this tiny town for 3 days and nights of bronco-riding, calf-roping, and steer-wrestling, all in pursuit of the $100,000 purse. Have a rip-roaring time at the Rodeo Parade and the Buckaroo Breakfast. (☎549-0121 or 800-827-7522. $8-12. Shows often sell out.)

HIKING

A 45 mi. segment of the Pacific Crest Trail runs from Lava Lakes through the Three Sisters Wilderness, with numerous opportunities for side-hikes. A $5 per day permit, available at the trailheads or from the ranger in Sisters, is required for most activities. The ranger station in Sisters also offers free guides to popular hiking and biking trails in the region.

Metolius River Trail (10 mi.). Go west on Rte. 20 from Sisters, then make a right at the sign for Camp Sherman (Rd. 14). Proceed 7 mi. on Rd. 14 past the "Head of the Metolius" and park at the Wizard Falls Fish Hatchery, right on the Metolius River. This trail is also open to mountain biking, and is considered superlative though difficult for that purpose. (☎595-6611. Open daily 8am-5pm.) An easy hike, but a tricky bike.

Black Butte Trail (2 mi. one way, 2hr. up; can be pushed in 45min.). The view on top is the attraction: alongside an active fire lookout, survey 180 degrees of Cascades from Mt. Adams to Broken Top. Bring binoculars if you want to see glaciers. Moderate.

Black Crater (8 mi.). About 11 mi. west of sisters off the left side of Rte. 242. Deeper in the mountains, the strenuous round-trip hike up Black Crater offers unsurpassed views of snow-capped peaks and lava flows on McKenzie Pass, and intimate encounters with volcanic debris. Access is often limited due to snow.

McKenzie Pass (15 mi.). West of Sisters on Rte. 242. The site of a relatively recent lava flow that created barren fields of rough, black **A'A** (AH-ah) lava. The ½ mi. trail from the Dee Wright Observatory winds among basalt boulders, cracks, and crevices.

OTHER OUTDOOR ACTIVITIES

Opportunities for both novice and hard-core **mountain biking** abound near Sisters. No bikes or motor vehicles are allowed in official wilderness areas, but most other trails and little-used dirt roads are open to bikes. The ranger station distributes a packet detailing local trails; the friendly people at Eurosports also have info on the best trails (see p. 142). Half an hour from Sisters, the majestic rock spires of **Smith Rock State Park** are a popular **rock climbing** destination. Pick up a trail guide from the ranger, or at the park. For learning climbers, **First Ascent** has lessons. To get there, take Rte. 126 to Redmond, then go north for 9 mi. on US 97, and follow the signs from the town of Terrebonne.(☎800-325-5462. $175 per day; $95 per person per day for 2 people; $80 per person per day for 3 or more people.)

OREGON

CRATER LAKE & KLAMATH FALLS ☎541

The deepest lake in the US, the seventh deepest in the world, and one of the most beautiful anywhere, Crater Lake is one of Oregon's signature attractions. Formed about 7700 years ago in a cataclysmic eruption of Mt. Mazama, it began as a deep caldera and gradually filled itself with centuries's worth of melted snow. The circular lake plunges from its shores to a depth of 1936 ft. Though it remains iceless in the winter, its banks, which loom as high as 2000 ft. above the 6176 ft. lake surface, are snow-covered until July. Visitors from all over the world circle the 33 mi. Rim Drive, gripping the wheel as the impossibly blue water enchants them. Klamath Falls, one of the nearest cities, makes a convenient stop on the way to the park and contains most of the services, motels, and restaurants listed below.

TRANSPORTATION

Rte. 62 skirts the park's southwestern edge as it arcs 130 mi. between Medford in the southwest and Klamath Falls, 56 mi. southeast of the park. West of the park, Rte. 62 follows the Upper Rogue River. To reach Crater Lake from Portland, take **I-5** to Eugene, and then **Rte. 58** east to **US 97** south. From US 97, **Rte. 138** leads west to the park's north entrance, but Crater Lake averages over 44 ft. of snow per year, and snowbound roads usually keep the northern entrance closed as late as July; the roads to **Rim Village** stay open year-round. Before July, enter the park from the south. **Rte. 62** runs west from US 97 about 40 mi. south of the park, through the small town of **Fort Klamath,** and on to the south access road that leads to the caldera's rim. Another 20 mi. of southward travel from the intersection of Rte. 62 and US 97 brings you to Klamath Falls.

Trains: Amtrak (☎884-2822 or 800-872-7245; www.amtrak.com). Follow Klamath Ave. until you see signs for the station. Open daily 7:30am-11am and 8:30pm-10pm. To **Redding, CA** (4.5hr., $26).

Buses: Greyhound, Mollie's Truck Stop, 3817 US 97N (☎882-4616). Open M-F 8am-1:00am, Sa 6-9am and midnight-12:45am. One bus runs daily to **Portland** ($42-48) via **Eugene** (4.5hr., $19).

Public Transportation: Basin Transit Service (☎883-2877) runs 6 routes. Runs M-F 6am-7:30pm, Sa 10am-5pm. $0.90, seniors and disabled $0.45.

Taxis: Classic Taxi (☎850-8303). $2 base, $2 per mi. 24hr.

Car Rental: Budget (☎885-5421), at Klamath Falls airport. From S 6th St., go south on Washburn Dr. and follow the signs. $30 per day M-F, $0.25 per mi. after 100 mi. $26 per day Sa-Su, 100 free mi. per day. Open M-F 7am-10pm, Sa-Su 8:30am-6pm.

PRACTICAL INFORMATION

Tourist Information: Chamber of Commerce, 507 Main St. (☎884-0666 or 800-445-6728; www.klamath.org). Open M-F 8am-5pm.

Outdoor Information: William G. Steel Center (☎594-2211, ext. 402; www.nps.gov/crla), 1 mi. from the south entrance. Free backcountry camping permits. Open daily 9am-5pm. **Crater Lake National Park Visitors Center** (☎594-3100), on the lake shore at Rim Village. Open daily June-Sept. 8:30am-6pm. Park main phone ☎594-3000; www.nps.gov/crla.

Park Entrance Fee: Cars $10, hikers and bikers $5. Free with Golden Eagle Passport.

Laundromat: Main Street Laundromat, 1711 Main St. (☎883-1784). Wash $1.25, dry $0.25 per 12min. Open M-Sa 8am-8pm; last wash 7pm.

Emergency: ☎911.

Police: 425 Walnut St. (☎883-5336).

Crisis and Rape Crisis Line: ☎800-452-3669. 24hr.

Hospital: Merle West Medical Center, 2865 Daggett Ave. (☎882-6311). From US 97 N, turn right on Campus Dr., then right onto Daggett. 24hr. emergency room.

Internet Access: Klamath County Library, 126 S 3rd St. (☎882-8894). Has 6 slow computers with 1hr. free Internet access. Open M, Tu, and Th 10am-5pm, W 1pm-8pm, F-Sa 10am-5pm, Su 1pm-5pm.

Post Office: Klamath Falls, 317 S. 7th St. (☎800-275-8777). Open M-F 7:30am-5:30pm, Sa 9am-noon. **Crater Lake,** in the Steel Center. Open M-Sa 9am-noon and 1-3pm. **Postal Code:** 97604.

ACCOMMODATIONS & CAMPING

Klamath Falls has plenty of affordable hotels that make easy bases for Crater Lake. If you'd rather live in the trees, **Forest Service campgrounds** ❶ (usually about $5) line **Rte. 62** through Rogue River National Forest to the west of the park. The park itself contains two campgrounds, both of which are closed until roads are passable. **Backcountry camping** is allowed in the park; a backcountry permit, free from the Steel Center, is required.

Townhouse Motel, 5323 S 6th St. (☎882-0924). 3 mi. south of Main, on the edge of Klamath Falls' strip-mall land, offers clean, comfy rooms at good prices. Cable, A/C, no phones. Singles $30; doubles $35. ❷

Williamson River Campground, 30 mi. north of Klamath Falls on 97N, is the best of the many camps in the area, run by the National Forest Service. Situated on the winding river, it offers secluded sites with toilet and water. Tents only $6. ❶

OREGON

Mazama Campground (☎594-2255, ext. 3703), near the park's south entrance off Hwy. 62. Tenters and RVs swarm this monster facility when it opens in mid-June, and some don't leave until it closes in Oct. Mostly tent sites. Few electrical RV sites. **Loop G** is more secluded and spacious, but opens later in the year. Toilets, laundry, telephone. A general store, and gas, open 7am-10pm daily. Wheelchair accessible. No reservations. 213 sites, tents $16, RVs $21. ❶

Lost Creek Campground (☎594-2255), in the southeast corner of the park, 3 mi. on a paved road off Rim Dr. 16 mid-sized sites set amid pines. Water, toilets. No reservations. Usually open mid-July to mid-Sept.; check with Steel Center. Tent sites $10. ❶

Cimarron Motor Inn, 3060 S 6th St. in Klamath Falls (☎882-4601), has clean and comfortable rooms, plus continental breakfast. 1 or 2 people $65; 3 or 4 $75. ❹

Collier Memorial State Park and Campground (☎783-2471), 30 mi. north of Klamath Falls on US 97, offers small tent and RV sites with little privacy just off the Williamson River. The brilliant green lichen hanging off the timber is a highlight, ironically, as a logging museum is just south of the campground. Toilets and laundry. Sites $15; Full RV sites $18. Showers. ❶

FOOD

Eating cheap ain't easy in Crater Lake, with dining limited to a cafeteria, restaurant, and cafe in Rim Village. **Klamath Falls** has some affordable dining and a **Safeway** at Pine and 8th St., one block north of Main St. (☎882-2660. Open daily 6am-11pm.) A lot of eats in Klamath Falls go hand in hand with billiards; if you're a pool shark, Main St. between 5th and 7th St. is the place to go. The **Fort Klamath General Store,** 52608 Hwy. 62, offers canned goods, sells gas, and houses a cafe. (☎381-2263. Open summer daily 7am-10pm; winter 7am-8pm.)

Where's **Waldo's Mongolian Grill and Tavern?** 610 Main St. (☎884-6863). This large restaurant and lounge might play techno or reggae even if most patrons are wearing stetson hats. The food is standard Mongolian BBQ (you choose the ingredients, they cook them); the lounge has just about every equipment-intensive bar game (pool, shuffleboard, etc.) known to man. Youthful bar scene weekends. Medium bowl $8.50, all-you-can-eat $10. Open M-Th 11am-11:30pm, F-Sa 11am-1am. ❷

Plentiful Bakery, 2918 Altima Dr. off S 6th St. (☎273-6622). Basic, homemade goodness hits the spot in this small cafe. Be like the locals and have soup and a sandwich for $5.50 or stick with salad ($3-6). Open daily 6am-9pm. ❶

Cattle Crossing Cafe (☎381-2344) on Hwy. 62 in Fort Klamath. Waffle breakfasts ($3-7), burgers ($5-7), and dinners ($7-14) are capped off by mouth-watering homemade pie ($2.75 a slice). Open Apr.-Oct. daily 9am-6pm. ❷

Beckie's Cafe, in the tiny town of Union Creek just south of the Rogue River Gorge (☎560-3563), is a decent place to fuel up en route to or from the lake on Rte. 62, west of the lake. Specialty burgers $6.25. Open summer 8am-9pm. ❷

OUTDOOR ACTIVITIES

Crater Lake averages over 44 ft. of snow per year, and snowbound roads can keep the northern entrance closed as late as July. Before July, enter the park from the south. The park entrance fee is $10 for cars, $5 for hikers and cyclists. The area around Crater Lake is filled with all sorts of outdoor adventures. With ample options for hiking and biking, as well as easy access to the backcountry regions outside the park, you may feel overwhelmed with options. A good jumping off point is the Steel Center (see **Outdoor Information,** p. 145), or the

Rim Village, where the information center and the Crater Lake Lodge are located. **Crater Lake Lodge** (☎594-2255; 830-8700 for reservations) is a few hundred yards east of Sinnott Memorial Overlook in the Rim Village. Rooms are very expensive, but fun in the lodge can be had for free: make a quick visit to the rustic "great hall," rebuilt from its original materials, and warm yourself by the fire or relax in a rocking chair on the observation deck. The friendly staff will be happy to help you find any info on the Lake that you need. In addition to trails around the lake, the park contains over 140 mi. of wilderness trails for hiking and cross-country skiing. Picnics, fishing (with artificial lures only), and swimming are allowed, but surface temperatures reach a maximum of only 50°F. Park rangers lead free tours daily in the summer and periodically in the winter (on snowshoes).

DRIVING

Rim Dr., usually not open until mid-July, loops 33 mi. around the rim of the caldera, high above the lake. Pull-outs are strategically placed along the road wherever a view of the lake might cause an awe-struck tourist to drive off the cliff. Don't despair when the caldera walls block sight of the lake: the views of Cascade volcanoes as distant as Mt. Shasta, 100 mi. south, will console your eyes.

HIKING

Most visitors never stray far from their vehicles as they tour the lake, so hiking provides a great way to get away from the crowds. Trailheads are scattered along the rim, so just park and hike away from the road. The Steel Center has a trail map and info about which trails are closed due to weather.

Watchman Peak (¾ mi. one-way, 1hr.). Begins on the lake's west side. Short, but yields a great view of Wizard Island. One of the lake's two active cinder cones. Moderate.

Mt. Scott (5 mi. round-trip, 2-3hr.). The trailhead is 17 mi. clockwise from Rim Village. Although steep, the ascent to the top of 9000 ft. Mt. Scott and the historic fire tower on top affords a beautiful panoramic view of the lake. Moderate to strenuous.

Cleetwood Cove Trail (2¼ mi. round-trip, 2hr.), leaves from the north edge of the lake and is the only route down to the water and the park's most traveled trail. It drops 700 ft. in 1 mi. to get to the shore. Moderate to strenuous.

ON THE LAKE

In the summer, park rangers lead hour-long boat tours from the Cleetwood Cove trailhead. Aside from giving a comprehensive history of the lake and its formation, the tours provide breathtaking views of both **Wizard Island,** a cinder cone rising 760 ft. above the lake, and **Phantom Ship Rock,** a spooky rock formation. (Tours run 7 times daily 10am-4:30pm between late June and mid-Sept. $19.25, under 11 $11.50.) The boat tours provide foot access to the island, which can be hiked for a view into its crater. Land-lubbers may prefer picnics and fishing (artificial lures only) at the bottom of the trail. Though the lake (supposedly without outlet, though many contend the Rogue River drains out the bottom) was virtually sterile when modern man found it; it has since been stocked with rainbow trout and kokanee. Those who walk down to the lake at Cleetwood Cove can take a dip, but the water reaches a maximum temperature of only 50°F (10°C).

BACKCOUNTRY EXPLORATION

A hiking trip into the park's vast **backcountry** leaves all the exhaust and tourists behind. Hiking or climbing inside the caldera is prohibited. Other than near water sources, dispersed camping is allowed anywhere in the area but is complicated by the absence of water and the presence of bears. Get info and required backcountry permits for free at either visitors center. The **Pacific Crest Trail** begins from the trailhead ¾ mi. west of the south entrance. The ultimate backcountry trail passes through the park and three backcountry campsites, giving great views of mountain meadows, old-growth timber, and, of course, the lake. Another excellent loop begins at the **Red Cone trailhead** on the north access road, passing the less-traveled **Crater Springs, Oasis Butte,** and **Boundary Springs trails.** However, it is impaired by the snow until July and opens only at the discretion of the ranger. Contact the Steel Center for more information.

UPPER ROGUE RIVER

If you prefer your water more vertical than anything the lake can offer, try the Upper Rogue, easily accessible from Rte. 62 southwest of Crater Lake. Emerging from a spring on the northern slope of Mt. Mazama, the river contends with the area's many lava flows by raging through scenic gorges, passing through huge waterfalls and cataracts, and even going underground for a stretch. Despite all this, the fish are doing alright, especially in places like **Casey State Park,** 46 mi. SW of the park; here, the angling is good but crowded.

Mill Creek Falls drops 173 ft. into a deep canyon downstream of the **Avenue of Giant Boulders,** where a huge jumble of rocks offers navigational puzzles for the feet and sublime **sunning** for your back. The pools formed between cascades also make for equally great **splashing around.** From Rte. 62, easy, short trails to both sites are accessed from a trailhead; follow signs to "Mill Creek Falls/Prospect Access Road," about 32 mi. SW of Crater Lake on Rte. 62.

Things get steamier for the Rogue as it approaches to Mt. Mazama: lava flows are clearly at work in both the **Natural Bridge** and the **Rogue River Gorge.** The river performs a natural, but still frightening, disappearing act under the bridge, where it descends into a lava tube and reappears 200 ft. downstream. In the Gorge, the river is forced through a lava flow and gets angry about it, smashing through in a series of short but raging waterfalls. The gorge has been kayaked, amazingly, and advanced/expert kayakers may put in *below* the Natural Bridge for unusual, lava-formed class IV rapids. Class VI Therapy Falls, after a right jog about 0.5-1.5 mi. into the run, with an absolute must portage before the jog on river left, could very well be lethal for any party that goes without knowing the run, especially at high water in spring. The Gorge and Natural Bridge are about 20 and 23 mi. SW of Crater Lake on Rte. 62, respectively.

HELLS CANYON & WALLOWA MTNS. ☎541

The northeast corner of Oregon is the state's most rugged, remote, and arresting country, with jagged granite peaks, glacier-gouged valleys, and azure lakes. East of La Grande, the Wallowa Mountains (wa-LAH-wah) rise abruptly, looming over the plains from elevations of more than 9000 ft. Thirty miles east, North America's deepest gorge plunges to the Snake River. It may take a four-wheel-drive vehicle to get off the beaten path, but those with the initiative and the horsepower will find stunning vistas and heavenly solitude in the backcountry.

TRANSPORTATION

There are three ways to get to the **Wallowa Valley,** which lies between the **Hells Canyon National Recreation Area** and the **Eagle Cap Wilderness.** From **Baker City,** Rte. 86 heads east through **Halfway** (also known as **Half.com,** the world's first dot-com city) to connect with Forest Rd. 39, which winds north over the southern end of the Wallowas, meeting Rte. 350 (also known as Little Sheep Creek Hwy.) 8 mi. east of

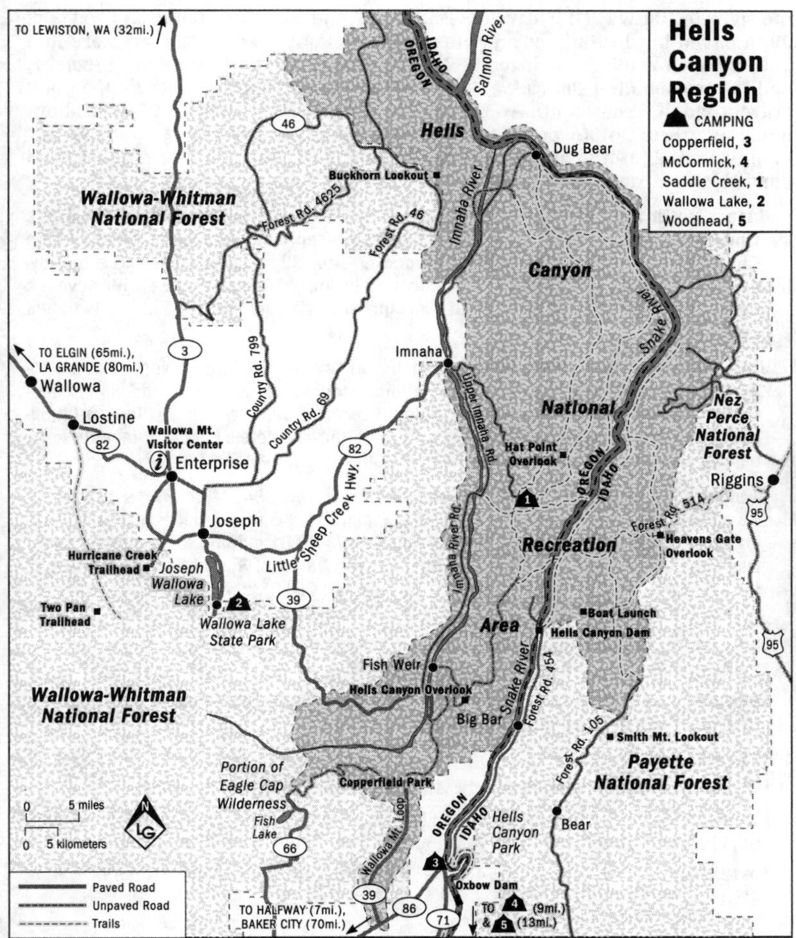

Joseph. From **La Grande,** Rte. 82 arcs around the north end of the Wallowas, through the small towns of Elgin, Minam, Wallowa, and Lostine, continuing through **Enterprise** and **Joseph,** and terminating at **Wallowa Lake.** From **Lewiston, Idaho,** Rte. 129 heads south into Washington, then over Rattlesnake Pass, becoming Rte. 3 in Oregon and joining Rte. 82 in Enterprise.

ORIENTATION & PRACTICAL INFORMATION

Three main towns offer services within the area: Enterprise, Joseph, and Halfway. Joseph lies 6 mi. east of Enterprise on Rte. 82. In **Enterprise,** Rte. 82 is called North St., and in Joseph it goes by Main St. **Halfway** is about 65 mi. south of Joseph. To get there, take E Wallowa Rd., off Main St. in Joseph, and follow the signs to Halfway (the drive takes 2hr., the majority of which is on **Forest Rd. 39,** a paved but brutally curvy route). Other major roads in the area are **Rte. 350,** a paved route from Joseph 30 mi. northeast to the tiny town of **Imnaha,** and the **Imnaha River Rd.** (a.k.a. Country Rd. 727 and Forest Rd. 3955), a good gravel road that runs south from Imnaha to reconnect with Forest Rd. 39 about 50 mi. southeast of Joseph. The invaluable and free Wallowa County Visitor Map is available in visitors centers and ranger stations, as are current road conditions information.

Buses: Moffit Brothers Transportation (☎569-2284) runs the **Wallowa Valley Stage Line,** which makes one round-trip M-Sa between **Joseph** and **La Grande.** Pickup at the **Chevron** on Rte. 82 in Joseph, the **Amoco** on Rte. 82 in Enterprise, and the **Greyhound terminal** in La Grande. Will stop and pickup at Wallowa Lake with advance notice. One-way from **La Grande** to: **Enterprise** ($10); **Joseph** ($11); and **Wallowa Lake** ($15).

Visitor Information: Wallowa County Chamber of Commerce, 936 W North St. (☎426-4622 or 800-585-4121), in Enterprise. General tourist info as well as the comprehensive and free *Wallowa County Visitor Guide.* Open M-F 8am-5pm. **Hells Canyon Chamber of Commerce** (☎742-4222), in the office of Halfway Motels (see **Accommodations,** below), provides info on accommodations, outfitters, and guides.

Outdoor Information: Wallowa Mountains Visitor Center, 88401 Rte. 82 (☎426-5546; www.fs.fed.us/r6/w-w), on the west side of Enterprise. $6 map a necessity for navigating area roads. Open Memorial Day to Labor Day M-Sa 8am-5pm, Su noon-5pm; Labor Day to Memorial Day M-F 8am-5pm. **Hells Canyon National Recreation Area Office,** 2 mi. south of Clarkston, WA on Rte. 129 (☎509-758-0616), carries all sorts of information on Hells Canyon. Open M-F 7:45-11:30am and 12:30-4:30pm.

Laundromat: Joseph Laundromat and Car Wash, on Rte. 82 in Joseph, across from the Indian Lodge Motel. Wash $1, dry $0.25 per 8min. Open daily 6am-10pm.

Emergency: ☎911. **Police:** State police ☎426-3036. In Enterprise, 108 NE 1st St. (☎426-3136), at the corner of North St.

Fire: ☎426-4196.

Hospital: Wallowa Memorial, 401 NE 1st St. (☎426-3111), in Enterprise.

Internet Access: The **Enterprise Public Library,** 101 NE 1st St. (☎426-3906), at Main St., charges $4 for 30min. and $6 per hr. Open M, F noon-6pm, T-Th 10am-6pm.

Post Office: 201 W North St. (☎426-5980), on Rte. 82 in Enterprise. Open M-F 9am-4:30pm. **Postal Code:** 97828.

OREGON

ACCOMMODATIONS & CAMPING

Most of the towns along Rte. 82 have motels with plenty of vacancy during the week. On weekends rooms are more scarce. Campgrounds here are plentiful, inexpensive, and sublime. Pick up the free *Campground Information* pamphlet at the Wallowa Mountains Visitor Center (see p. 150) for a complete listing of sites in the area. Many **free campgrounds** are not fully serviced, and recent improvements to some (water and pit toilets) have resulted in fees ($5-8) for formerly free sites. Insect repellent is a must during summer, when most campgrounds are open.

Indian Lodge Motel, 201 S Main St. (☎432-2651 or 888-286-5484), on Rte. 82 in Joseph. Elegant rooms with dark wood furniture and plush blue carpet. A/C, cable, coffeemakers, fridges. Singles $37; doubles $49. Winter singles $32; doubles $40. ❷

Country Inn Motel, 402 W North St. (☎426-4986 or 877-426-4986), in Enterprise. Reminiscent of a country farmhouse. Rooms stay remarkably cool without A/C. Cable, coffeemakers, fridges. Singles $50, doubles $54. Rates lower in winter. ❸

Wallowa Lake State Park Campground (☎432-4185; reservations 800-452-5687), at the eastern end of Rte. 82. Books 11 months in advance. Full-service camping. Flushing toilets, potable water. Tent sites $17, full RV sites $21. Showers. ❶

Snake River Campgrounds (☎785-3323). Only three are open year-round: **Copperfield,** at the northern end of Hwy. 86; **McCormick,** 12 mi. south of Copperfield off Hwy. 71; and **Woodhead,** 4 mi. south of McCormick on Hwy. 71. Restrooms. No reservations. Tent sites $6, RV sites $10. Hot showers at Woodhead. ❶

Saddle Creek Campground. From Rte. 82, turn on E Wallowa Rd. (a.k.a. Rte. 350) in Joseph. Drive 19 mi. on the unpaved and steep Hat Point Rd. 7 sites perched on the lip of Hells Canyon feature unbelievable views. No water. Wheelchair accessible. Free. ❶

FOOD

If you're heading out onto the roads of Hells Canyon, bring some provisions—a flat or breakdown could require a roadside meal or two. Find groceries at **Safeway,** 601 W North St., on Rte. 82 in Enterprise. (☎426-3722. Open daily 6am-10pm.)

Wildflour Bakery, 600 N Main St. (☎432-7225), in Joseph, offers an amazing selection of scrumptious baked goods, as well as giant sourdough and cornmeal pancakes ($2 per cake). Sit on the patio and enjoy the day with a chicken sausage sandwich or giant burrito ($5). Open M and W-Sa 7am-3pm, Su 7am-noon. Breakfast til 11am. ❶

Embers Brew House, 207 N Main St. (☎432-2739), in Joseph. In the summer, the patio is packed outside this popular dinner spot. Sample 5 of 17 microbrews ($5). Fries $4. Open June-Sept. daily 11am-11pm; winter Su-Th 11am-8pm, F-Sa 11am-11pm. ❶

Old Town Cafe, 8 S Main St. (☎432-9898), in Joseph. Sit in the outdoor grotto and dig into a bottomless bowl of homemade soup ($3) or a giant fresh baked cinnamon roll ($1.75). Breakfast all day. Open F-W 7am-2pm. ❶

Vali's Alpine Delicatessen Restaurant, 59811 Wallowa Lake Hwy. (☎432-5691), in Wallowa Lake. For 28 years in this small, alpine-esque cottage, Mr. Vali has cooked one authentic European dish each night and Mrs. Vali has served it. Hungarian Kettle Goulash $8.50; schnitzel $12. Reservations required for dinner. Breakfast W-Su 9-11am, dinner seatings W-Su at 5 and 8pm. After Labor Day, open Sa and Su only. ❷

OUTDOOR ACTIVITIES

HELLS CANYON

The canyon's endearing name comes from its legendary inaccessibility and hostility to human habitation. The walls of Hells Canyon drop over 8000 ft. to the **Snake River,** which makes it the deepest canyon in North America.

LOOKOUTS. Hells Canyon Overlook, the most accessible of the lookout points, is up Forest Rd. 3965. The road departs Rd. 39 about 5 mi. south of the Imnaha River crossing. The broadest and most eye-popping views are from the **Hat Point Lookout Overlook,** where visitors can climb a 90 ft. wooden fire lookout. To get there, go 24 mi. up a steep but well-maintained gravel road (not recommended for trailers) from Imnaha (Forest Rd. 4240, a.k.a. Hat Point Rd.), and follow the signs. There are pit toilets at the overlook and several picnic sites for day use. The **Buckhorn Lookout** lies far off the beaten path, 42 mi. northeast of Joseph, and offers lofty views of the Imnaha River Valley. Take Rte. 82 north 3 mi. out of Joseph or 3 mi. south out of Enterprise, and look for the green sign for Buckhorn. Turn off and follow Zumwalt Rd. (a.k.a. Country Rd. 697, which turns into Forest Rd. 46) for approximately 40 bumpy miles to Buckhorn—about a half-day round-trip. Also at that end of the canyon, the immense **Hells Canyon Dam** lies 23 mi. north of Oxbow on Rte. 86 (turns into Forest Rd. 454). This drive is one of only three ways to get near the bottom of the canyon by car, and the dam is the only place to cross.

HIKING. There are over 1000 mi. of trails in the canyon, only a fraction of which are maintained. Most are only open in April. The dramatic 56 mi. **Snake River Trail** runs by the river for the length of the canyon. At times, the trail is cut into the side of the rock with just enough clearance for a horse's head. This trail can be followed from **Dug Bar** in the north down to the Hells Canyon Dam or accessed by steep trails along the way. From north to south, **Hat Point, Freezeout,** and **P.O. Saddle** are access points. To reach Dug Bar, get a high-clearance 4WD vehicle and hit the steep, slippery Forest Rd. 4260 for 27 mi. northeast from **Imnaha.** Bring snakebite kits, boots, and water. Rangers patrol the river by boat at least once a day.

WATER. The easiest way to see a large portion of the canyon is on the Snake River by jet boat or raft; both pursuits are guaranteed to drench. Numerous outfitters operate out of Oxbow and the dam area; the Wallowa Mountains Visitors Center (see p. 150) and all local chambers of commerce have a list of the permittees. **Hells Canyon Adventures,** 4200 Hells Canyon Dam Rd., 1½ mi. from the Hells Canyon Dam in Oxbow, runs a wide range of jet boat and raft trips. (☎785-3352 or 800-422-3568. Jet boats 2hr. $30, 3hr. $40, full day $105. Whitewater rafting $140 for a day trip.)

WALLOWA MOUNTAINS

Without a catchy, federally approved name like "Hells Canyon National Recreation Area," the Wallowas often take second place to the canyon. They are equally magnificent, however, as their canyons echo with the rush of rapids and their jagged peaks cover with wildflowers in spring.

HIKING. Over 600 mi. of **hiking trails** cross the **Eagle Cap Wilderness** and are usually free of snow from mid-July to October. Deep glacial valleys and high granite passes make hiking this wilderness difficult. It often takes more than a day to get into the most beautiful areas, so carry adequate supplies and prepare for sudden weather changes. The 5 mi. hike to **Chimney Lake** from the **Bowman** trailhead on the Lostine River Rd. (Forest Rd. 8210) traverses fields of granite boulders sprinkled with a few small meadows. A little farther on lie the serene **Laverty, Hobo,** and **Wood Lakes,** where the road is less traveled. The **Two Pan** trailhead at the end of the Lostine River Rd. is the start of a forested 6 mi. hike to popular **Minam Lake,** which makes a good starting point for those heading to other backcountry spots.

By far the most popular area in the Eagle Cap Wilderness is the **Lakes Basin** (a 7-9 mi. hike from the Two Pan trailhead), where explorers can find unsurpassed scenery, good fishing, and hikes to Eagle Cap Peak. While it is possible to escape the crowds in the basin during the week, the lake is packed on weekends. **Steamboat, Long,** and **Swamp Lakes** (also accessible from the Two Pan trailhead) are as magnificent as the Lakes Basin but receive only half as many visitors. Rangers at the visitors center can also recommend more secluded routes. Many excellent dayhikes to **Lookingglass, Culver, Bear, Eagle, Cached, Arrow,** and **Heart Lakes** start from the Boulder Park trailhead, on Forest Rd. 7755, on the southern side of the Eagle Cap Wilderness (accessible from Baker City and Halfway).

FISHING. Fishing in the alpine lakes of Eagle Cap is incredible, but it's illegal even to catch and release without a permit. Some fish, such as bull trout, are entirely protected. Get permits ($8 per day, $49 per year) and the *Oregon Sport Fishing Regulations* booklet at any local sporting store.

BURNS ☎541

Tiny Burns and its even tinier neighbor Hines serve as traveler waystations and supply centers. Packed with cheap motels and fast food joints, Burns offers sustenance, shelter, and a wealth of information on the surrounding country. And what great outdoor country it is: ideally situated between the Ochoco and Malheur National Forests, Steens Mountain, the Alvord Desert, and the Malheur National Wildlife Refuge, Burns is the center for outdoor activities in the otherwise uninhabited wilderness of southeastern Oregon.

ORIENTATION & PRACTICAL INFORMATION. US 20 from Ontario and **US 395** from John Day converge 2 mi. north of Burns, continue through Burns and Hines as one, and diverge about 30 mi. west of town. US 20 continues west to Bend and the Cascade Range; US 395 runs south to Lakeview, OR and California; Rte. 205 runs south to Frenchglen and Fields (see below). Although buses and vans run to and from some of the nearby towns, you're better off making like Moses and heading for the desert than waiting for public transportation there. **Harney County Chamber of Commerce,** 76 E Washington St., has excellent maps and info on both towns. (☎573-2636. Open M-F 9am-5pm.) Even more useful are the **Burns Ranger District (Malheur National Forest)** and **Snow Mountain Ranger District (Ochoco National Forest),** in Hines. These outdoor resources share an office on the main drag about 4½ mi. south of Burns, and provide information on camping, hiking, and every other wilderness activity imaginable in the surrounding countryside. (☎573-4300. Open M-F 8am-4:30pm.) **Burns Bureau of Land Management (BLM),** on US 20 West, is a few miles west of Hines. The BLM office and the BLM web site provide essential information on the federally controlled areas of southeastern Oregon, including Steens Mountain and the Malheur Wildlife Refuge. The office also has a nifty relief map, and sells recreation maps for $4. (☎573-4400; www.or.blm.gov/burns. Open M-F 7:45am-4:30pm.) Call ☎911 in an **emergency,** or contact the **police,** 242 S Broadway (☎573-6028). The **hospital,** at 557 W Washington St. (☎573-7281), has 24hr. emergency care. The **post office** can be found at 100 S Broadway. (☎800-275-8777. Open M-F 8:30am-5pm.) **Postal Code:** 97720.

ACCOMMODATIONS & FOOD. The **Bontemps Motel ❷**, 74 W Monroe St., provides comfortable rooms with firm beds and some cool jungle-style lampshades. Cable TV and A/C; kitchenettes are about $5 more. (☎573-2037 or 800-229-1394. Singles $30; doubles $35; pets $5.) There's a **Days Inn ❸** at 577 W Monroe St. (☎573-2047. Singles $52, doubles $57.) **Joaquin Miller ❶** campground, just off of US 395 19 mi. north of town, has free camping surrounded by Ponderosa pines. Pit toilets; no water. **Safeway** is at 246 W Monroe St. (☎573-6767. Open daily 6am-11pm.) **Broadway Deli ❶**, 528 N Broadway Ave., sells cheap but good and filling sandwiches ($4.75) and homemade soups ($2 per bowl). It's a great alternative to fast food fare. (Open M-F 8am-4pm. Sa 11am-3pm.) **Elk Horn Cafe/Linda's Thai Room ❷**, 457 N Broadway, juxtaposes Thai cuisine and greasy spoon fare, ornate chandeliers and Thai spiritual figures against elk wallpaper. Decent Thai or Chinese dinners $8-12. (☎573-3201. Open daily 8am-2pm, 5-9pm.)

NEAR BURNS ☎541

MALHEUR NAT'L WILDLIFE REFUGE & DIAMOND CRATERS

About 40 mi. south of Burns, miles of sagebrush give way to the grasslands and marshes of **Harney** and **Malheur Lakes,** where thousands of birds end their migratory flight paths each year at **Malheur National Wildlife Refuge.** Stretching 35 mi. south along Rte. 205, the refuge covers 185,000 acres and is home to 58 mammal species and over 320 species of birds, including grebes, ibis, plovers, shrikes, owls, wigeons, and waxwings. The best time to see the birds is in April; bald eagles are best seen in the coldest months. The refuge takes 2hr. to traverse, and some areas require a 4WD vehicle.

OREGON

The refuge headquarters, 6 mi. east of Rte. 205 on a well-marked turn-off between Burns and Frenchglen, houses a useful **visitors center** that provides trail directions and area info. (☎493-2612. Open M-Th 7am-4:30am, F 7am-3:30pm, Sa-Su 8am-4pm.) No camping is allowed within the refuge, but **accommodations** are available at the **Malheur Field Station ❷,** an old government training camp 5 mi. west of headquarters. Make reservations well in advance, especially for spring, fall, and holiday weekends. Toilets and potable water. Meals are available in high season (April and May) when large groups are eating. Basic housekeeping is expected of the guests. (☎493-2629. Spartan bunks $20; available for large groups. Kitchenette singles $23, $18 if shared. Singles in a trailer $40; doubles $60; RV sites $16.) The Field Station occasionally teaches classes on wildlife in the refuge; these are open for large groups only, but extra space is sometimes available. Call to inquire.

HIKING. Hiking is generally allowed only along roads. Two short trails depart from the visitors center. Also, the largely unmarked and primitive **Loop Trail** (11 mi. loop, several hr.) departs from "P-Ranch" just before Frenchglen. This moderately difficult trail offers great opportunities to see migratory birds.

DIAMOND CRATERS. A well-marked turn-off 30 mi. south of Burns on Hwy. 205 leads to the **Diamond Craters,** located just east of the Malheur Refuge. This outstanding national area has more than meets the eye, and is a geologist's playground of craters, lava flows, and cinder bomb piles. For laypeople, the BLM's self-guided tour (available at any visitors center, ranger station, or at the hotel or mercantile in Frenchglen) and a fair bit of patience are essential to make any sense of the volcanic history here. The **Lava Pit Crater** is most worth a stop. Bring water and watch out for rattlesnakes; the nearest medical facilities are in Burns, 55 mi. to the northwest.

The 100-year-old **Hotel Diamond ❹,** 12 mi. east of Rte. 205 on Diamond Lane, seems young in relation to the craters but proves a sophisticated rest stop for the dedicated explorer. (☎493-1898; www.central-oregon.com/hoteldiamond. Breakfast $1.50-4.75; dinner $10-15, for guests or by reservation only. No children allowed. A small double with shared bath starts at $55; with private bath $90.)

FRENCHGLEN ☎541

An hour south of Burns along Rte. 205, Frenchglen provides access to wildlife refuges and the western side of the Steens Mountain via the Steens Mtn. Loop. **Fields,** 55min. farther south of Frenchglen on Rte. 205, at the southern tip of the mountain, provides access to the eastern face and the Alvord Desert. Both towns are little more than a few buildings along the highway, but they can provide food, shelter, and sound advice. **Frenchglen Mercantile ❶,** on Rte. 205, has gas, some groceries, and, from June through August, big deli sandwiches for $4.50 (☎493-2835). (Open daily 7am-8pm.) The owners also run a bar and a **guesthouse ❹** connected to the main store, with two very comfortable rooms. (☎493-2738. $65.) The **Steens Mountain Resort,** North Steens Mtn. Loop Rd. just 3 mi. outside of town, also has a small general store with canned goods, ice cream, and laundry facilities. (☎493-2415. Wash $0.75, dry $0.50 for 20min. Showers $5. Open daily 8:30am-6pm.)

FIELDS ☎541

About 5 mi. northwest of Fields, Rte. 205 squeezes through a small pass and the scenery rapidly evolves from rugged to lunar, with hulking fault-block mountains all around. Consisting of only a few houses, the rambling **Fields Station** is home to four businesses owned by the same family: they've lived here 30 years. The general store and gas station are the last of each for miles. The **cafe ❶** serves remarkably large burgers ($4.25), scrumptious onion rings ($2), and 6000 milkshakes a year ($3). The **hotel and campground ❸** next door to the cafe rent very nice rooms and sites. (☎495-2275. Singles $40; doubles $55; RV sites $10; tenting areas $2.)

STEENS MOUNTAIN ☎541

Oregon's most unearthly landscape lies in the southeast, where the **Steens Mountain** rises to an elevation of nearly 10,000 ft. and reaches a vertical mile above an uninhabited, bone-dry alkali flat to the east. Although its fault block geology might seem a let-down from the western view—the sloped road ascends very gradually—on the substantially more remote east side, the incredible 30 mi. north-south stretch of mountain presents huge cliffs and deep canyons. Contact the Burns District BLM for road info and get **maps** of the area at the **Frenchglen Hotel** and the **Steens Mountain Resort** (see above). There are four campgrounds on the west side, all with pit toilets and drinking water; they charge $6-8 per night. Each is just off the Steens Mtn. Rd., which leaves from Frenchglen. **Page Springs ❶,** only 5 mi. from Frenchglen, is accessible year-round and has 36 grassy sites surrounded by cliffs; **Fish Lake ❶,** 19 mi. in and 1½ mi. up toward the mountain, has 23 sites and a boat ramp to access the best fishing in the area; **Jackman Park ❶,** 3 mi. farther in, has 6 mountainside sites; and **South Steens ❶,** a few miles farther, features 21 sites and 15 equestrian sites. The campgrounds on the east side are free and offer plenty of solitude; as a major plus, the stargazing doesn't get any better. **Pike Creek ❶** has a pit toilet and a creek nearby. It's 1½ mi. north of the Alvord Hot Springs (see below). Make a left after the second creek north of the desert (marked by a line of trees), and drive up the *very* rough road. Keep your eyes peeled; it's easy to miss.

DRIVING. Don't think that driving is a cop-out—the 66 mi. dirty track **Steens Mountain Loop Rd.** (open July-Oct.) is rutted, washboardy, and bound to be a full-on adventure for any 2WD vehicle. It climbs the west slope of the mountain from Rte. 205 near Frenchglen, and rejoins the highway only 8 mi. farther south.

OTHER EXPLORATION. Though hot, dusty, and chock full of rattlesnakes, the canyons of the mountain, gouged deep into the rock by glacial activity, are beautiful and difficult hikes. **Pike Creek** trail (see above for directions; the trail and road are unmarked) begins as an old mining road, goes past an abandoned mining shack and under towering rock spires, and then gradually fades about 1½ mi. in as it switchbacks and continues to the mouth of Pike Creek's canyon. To find the trail, just walk up the creek. Follow the cairns in the canyon. The trail ends at the mouth, but the summit arête can be attained by a very difficult scree scramble—there's no trail—to the top. (Hiking to the mouth is moderate to strenuous. To the summit is very strenuous and takes 1-1½ days.)

Another trip, lasting four days, ascends the **Big Indian Creek Gorge** on the west side to the summit, and then descends via the **Little Blitzen River Gorge,** also on the west side. Filterable water is usually available. The canyons are also good for shorter dayhikdayhikes, returning via the ascent route. A popular and moderately difficult hike is along the **Blitzen River trail** (4 mi. one-way, several hours) which follows along the river, crossing in certain places to avoid steep cliffs, to some great places to **fish.** The river passes through the Steens Mtn. Resort.

OREGON

ALVORD DESERT

The utterly flat and barren Alvord Desert supports no terrestrial life. On the other hand, if a giant metal craft lands while bearing beings from outer space, don't worry: the Alvord Desert is reportedly the US space shuttle's 4th-choice landing spot. It's also a favored place for sand yachting, where the wheeled sailcraft can achieve speeds up to 100 mph. Regattas are held occasionally. For those piloting more mundane craft, roads lead out onto the desert plain, allowing car access to the desert. Regardless of your recreational intentions, a gaze over this *bona fide* wasteland is worth the long trip—although enjoying the desert requires a sense of humor. Drive 25 mi. north on the East Steens Rd., a dirt road just west of Fields. Continue north past the Alvord Desert about 1½hr. to Rte. 78, which can be taken west back to Burns. Make sure to bring lots of water and plenty of gas.

The borate-rich **Alvord Hot Springs** emerges next to the desert; a couple of enterprising, and probably reclusive, miners once extracted the cleaning agent borax up a dirt road opposite the springs. A tin shack houses a small pool for bathing, kept much cooler than the 174°F of the spring. It's on the right side of the road, about 200 ft. north of a cattleguard. About 20 mi. farther north, **Mann Lake** is open to excellent fishing and **free camping ❶** with pit toilets but no piped water. For those in search of a burly, multi-day desert adventure well beyond anything a car could give, the Desert Trail runs through the area. **Trail guides** and info are available from the Desert Trail Association (☎475-2960) in Burns.

JOHN DAY FOSSIL BEDS ☎541

The John Day Fossil Beds National Monument is one of Eastern Oregon's most precious gems. A place where paleontological reputations are made, the beds hold the bones of ancient monsters from saber-tooths to ever-elusive gomphotheres. Though no original fossils are on display outdoors in the Monument, the beds lack nothing in topographical exuberance. The **Sheep Rock, Painted Hills,** and **Clarno** units each depict one facet of a 40-million-year geological history. The nearby town John Day is at best a stopover.

ACCOMMODATIONS. Magone Lake ❶ (mah-GOON) is a popular campground with fishing, hiking, and swimming. To get there from John Day, take US 26 east 9 mi. to Keeney Forks Rd. N and follow the signs for 15 mi. to the campground. (Potable water. 23 sites, $5.) **Clyde Holiday State Park ❶**, 7 mi. west of town on US 26, has grassy sites and a less-than-primitive aura. It offers electricity, carpeting, and foam mattresses. (☎932-4453, reservations 800-452-5687. Hiker and bicyclist sites $4; 30 sites with RV sites, $16; 2 tepees, $28. Showers for non-campers $2.)

For those preferring a bed and a roof, **Dreamer's Lodge ❸**, 144 N Canyon Blvd., has large rooms with A/C, fridges, microwaves, and cable TV. (☎575-0526. Singles $52; doubles $56; $7-9 more for a kitchenette. AAA and AARP discounts.) **Little Pine Inn ❸**, 250 E Main St., is less expensive and has free breakfast deals at a local restaurant. (☎575-2100. Singles $41; doubles $46.)

FOOD. Pick up groceries at **Chester's Thriftway**, 631 W Main St., in John Day Plaza. (☎575-1899. Open daily 7am-9pm.) Sit down and have a burger or a steak at the **Grubsteak Mining Co. ❶**, 149 E Main St. Pool and beer ($2 bottles) are available at the saloon in the back. (☎575-1970. Open daily 7am-10pm.) Enjoy a sit-down meal at **Dayville Cafe ❷**, 212 W Franklin St. (Rte. 26) in Dayville. Big breakfasts, grilled sandwiches ($5-6) and country dinners ($10-15) are served in a calico country atmosphere. Everything is fresh and homemade by mom and pop. (☎987-2132. Open Tu-Sa 7am-8pm, Su 8am-5pm. No credit cards.)

OUTDOOR ACTIVITIES. The **Sheep Rock Unit** has some of the best hiking in the area, with trails that show off prehistoric fossils. It also contains the **visitors center** on Rte. 19, 2 mi. north of US 26. The center has displays, exhibits, and an award-winning video produced by high school students that explains the history of the fossil beds. (☎987-2333. Open daily 9am-5pm.) The **Blue Basin** area (3 mi. up the road from the visitors center) provides two distinct hiking opportunities: the **Island in Time Trail**, an easy 1 mi., 1 hr. round-trip into the canyon that passes by a blue-green rock formation, and the **Blue Basin Overlook Trail**, a more challenging 3 mi., 2½hr. loop up to the basin's rim and a view of the John Day River Valley. The former's fossil replicas of sea turtles and saber-toothed carnivores are intriguing, but are surpassed by the latter's views of brightly colored badland spires.

Five miles north of US 26 from the turn-off, 3 mi. west of Mitchell, the **Painted Hills Unit** offers several short hikes that present a better way to examine the beautifully colored mounds, once tropical rainforests. It focuses on an epoch 30 million years ago, when the land was in geologic transition. Smooth mounds of brilliant red, yellow, and black sediment are most vivid at sunset and dawn, or after rain when the whole gorge glistens with brilliantly colored layers of claystone.

The **Clarno Unit**, the monument's oldest section, on Rte. 218, is accessible by US 97 to the west or Rte. 19 to the east. Its trails wind through ancient ash-laden mudflows from volcanic eruptions. While all of the hikes are short, and many of them more scenic than strenuous, all offer up ample opportunities to witness the stark beauty of this national monument.

STRAWBERRY MOUNTAIN WILDERNESS

Tall, rocky peaks make the Strawberry Mountains a great cure for any case of desert blues. Needle-sharp summit ridges, snow-lined cliffs, and forested lakes make it a justly popular destination for Oregon city-folk. Though it can get slightly crowded (by wilderness standards) with vacationers and their angry dogs, a weekday trip will offer refreshing views and clean (but thin) air. To squeeze in the best views in the least time, try dayhikes and overnight camping in the **lakes basin**, around **Strawberry Lake.** Backpackers enjoy more solitude in the west side of the wilderness, accessible from forest roads south of John Day. Ask at the ranger station for details; in any case, wilderness maps are essential as trail signs are perplexing. Get one at the Prairie City **ranger station** (☎820-3311), located on the right as you come into from John Day, for $3. In case of emergency, **Blue Mtn. Hospital** is in John Day, 170 Ford Rd. (☎575-1311).

To get to **Strawberry Campground** and the trailhead for the lakes basin, make a right on Main St. in Prairie City, 13 mi. east of John Day. Take the next left, and then drive straight at the mountains on Road 60, which becomes Road 6001; follow it until the end. The **campground ❶** itself is a decent campsite with potable water (sites $8). A better, cheaper option is to hike up into the high country. **Free camping ❶** is allowed anywhere in the wilderness; many people camp around Strawberry Lake, fewer at the more rugged **Little Strawberry Lake** and its surrounding streams.

Strawberry Lake, a moderate 1½ mi. hike from Strawberry Campground, is the base of most of the popular trails. A strenuous 6 mi. (4hr. up) trail through the lake to the top of Strawberry Mountain passes through ghostly-white burns and subalpine meadows peppered with wildflowers. The windy and razor-sharp 9000 ft. summit ridge has a view across the rest of the Strawberry wilderness and the Monument Rock wilderness. To get there, head up the trail to Little Strawberry Lake from the south side of Strawberry Lake.

WASHINGTON

WASHINGTON FACTS & FIGURES

Capital: Olympia. **Area:** 66,582 sq. mi. **Population:** 5,685,300.
Motto: *"Alki"* ("by and by" in Salish). **Nickname:** Evergreen State.
State Bird: Goldfinch. **State Fruit:** Apple. **State Employer:** Microsoft.
State Gem: Petrified wood. **State Fossil:** Columbian Mammoth.

What is now Washington was home to only some 400 settlers when Oregonians rallied for territorial recognition in the 1840s. The indigenous nations of the coast and plains still outnumbered the newcomers when Washington was made a territory in 1853 (encompassing much of present-day Idaho and Montana). By 1863, 4000 settlers had journeyed along the Oregon Trail and the state had attained roughly its present shape. Over the 20th century, the development of the state's towns depended on the course of railroads linking the west with the east. During World War II, Seattle's resource-driven economy was transformed by the nation's need for ships and aircrafts.

On Washington's western shore, concert halls and art galleries offer cosmopolitan entertainment within easy reach of Puget Sound, its gorgeous islands, and the temperate rainforests of the Olympic Peninsula. Seattle is the home of coffee, grunge, Microsoft, scattered hilly neighborhoods, fantastic parks, and miles of waterfront. The lush San Juan Islands boast puffins, sea otters, and sea lions. Pods of orcas circle the islands, followed by pods of tourists in yachts and kayaks. East of Puget Sound, the North Cascades rise up with fury and the Columbia River flows from the Canadian border to the Pacific Ocean, interrupted by numerous dams providing the state with water and electricity.

Buses cover most of Washington, although navigating the Olympic Peninsula requires some dexterity with a patchwork of county schedules. The train from Los Angeles to Vancouver makes many stops in western Washington; another line extends from Seattle to Spokane and on to Chicago.

HIGHLIGHTS OF WASHINGTON

ROCK out at the Experience Music Project in Seattle (p. 173).

EXPLORE The micro-environments of ONP, on the Olympic Peninsula (p. 205).

BURN with envy at the North Cascades Smokejumpers Base (p. 225).

CONQUER spectacular Mt. Rainier (p. 235).

ADMIRE the work of Tacoman glass artists at the Tacoma Museum of Glass (p. 183).

SCALE the dramatic peaks of North Cascades National Park (p. 205).

SEATTLE ☎206

Seattle's serendipitous mix of mountain views, clean streets, espresso stands, and rainy weather proved to be the magic formula of the 1990s. Although a slowdown in the tech sector has turned some computer magnates' smiles into frowns, the setting and culture continue on in Seattle without missing a beat. The city is one of the youngest and most vibrant in the nation, and Seattle has the country's highest

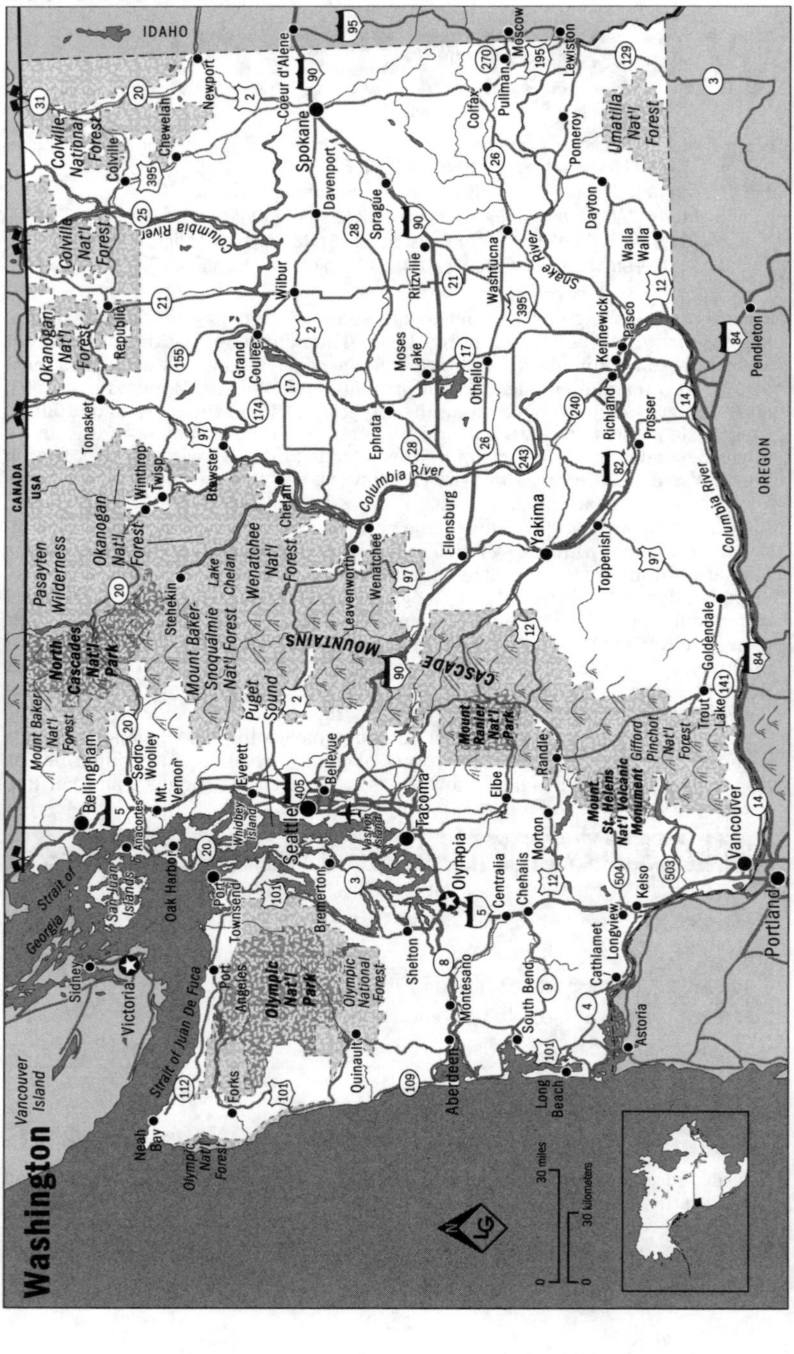
Washington
CANADA
USA
IDAHO
OREGON
Vancouver Island
Strait of Georgia
Strait of Juan De Fuca
San Juan Islands
Whidbey Island
Vashon Island
Puget Sound
Lake Chelan
Columbia River
Snake River
CASCADE MOUNTAINS
Olympic Nat'l Park
Olympic National Forest
Olympic Nat'l Forest
Mount Baker Nat'l Forest
North Cascades Nat'l Park
Pasayten Wilderness
Okanogan Nat'l Forest
Colville National Forest
Colville Nat'l Forest
Mount Baker-Snoqualmie Nat'l Forest
Wenatchee Nat'l Forest
Mount Ranier Nat'l Park
Mount St. Helens Nat'l Volcanic Monument
Gifford Pinchot Nat'l Forest
Umatilla Nat'l Forest
Victoria
Sidney
Neah Bay
Forks
Port Angeles
Port Townsend
Oak Harbor
Anacortes
Bellingham
Mt. Vernon
Sedro-Woolley
Everett
Seattle
Bellevue
Bremerton
Tacoma
Olympia
Shelton
Quinault
Aberdeen
Montesano
Centralia
Chehalis
South Bend
Long Beach
Cathlamet
Longview
Kelso
Astoria
Vancouver
Portland
Elbe
Morton
Randle
Trout Lake
Goldendale
Stehekin
Leavenworth
Wenatchee
Chelan
Ellensburg
Yakima
Toppenish
Prosser
Richland
Kennewick
Pasco
Pendleton
Walla Walla
Dayton
Pomeroy
Lewiston
Moscow
Pullman
Colfax
Washtucna
Ritzville
Othello
Moses Lake
Ephrata
Sprague
Davenport
Spokane
Coeur d'Alene
Newport
Chewelah
Colville
Republic
Tonasket
Winthrop
Twisp
Brewster
Grand Coulee
Wilbur
30 miles
30 kilometers

percentage of residents with a college degree. A nearly epidemic fixation on coffee has also made it one of the most caffeinated. The droves of newcomers provide an interesting contrast to the older residents who remember Seattle as a city-town, not a thriving metropolis bubbling over with young millionaires. Computer and coffee money have helped drive rents sky high in some areas, but the grungy, punk-loving street culture still prevails in others. In the end, there is a nook or cranny for almost anyone in Seattle.

The Emerald City sits on an isthmus, with mountain ranges to the east and west. Every hilltop in Seattle offers an impressive view of Mt. Olympus, Mt. Baker, and Mt. Rainier. To the west, the waters of Puget Sound glint against downtown skyscrapers and nearly spotless streets. The city's artistic landscape is as varied and exciting as its physical terrain. Opera always sells out, and the *New York Times* has complained that there is more good theater in Seattle than on Broadway. When Nirvana introduced the world to their discordant sensibility, the term

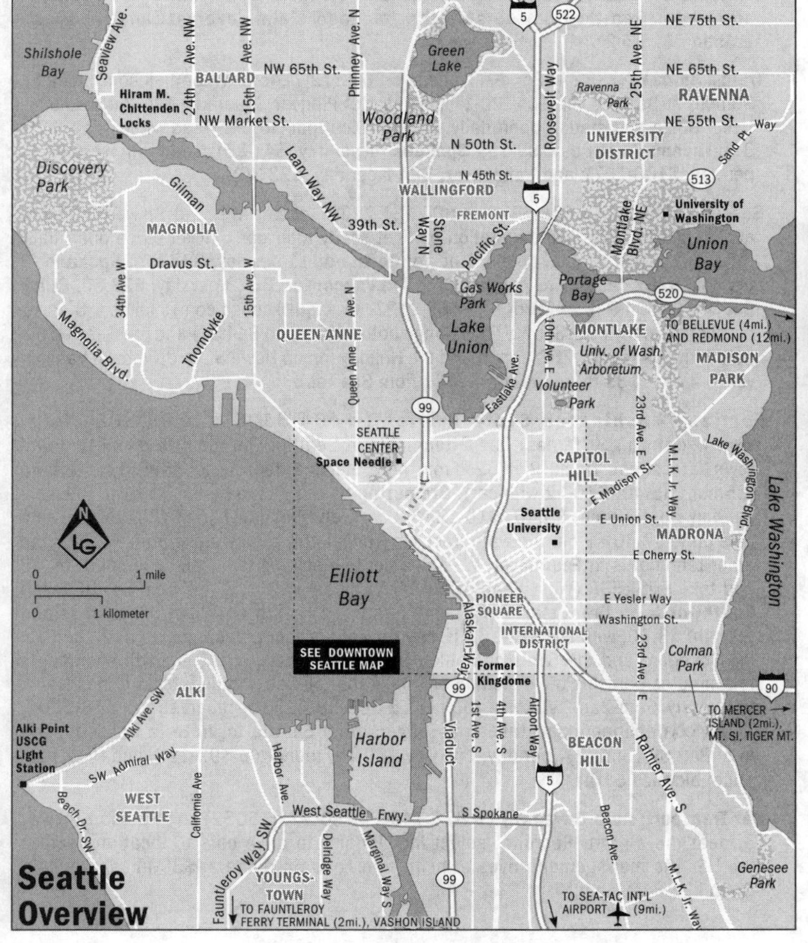

"grunge" and Seattle became temporarily inseparable, and the city that produced Jimi Hendrix again revitalized rock 'n' roll. Good bands thrive in grunge's wake, keeping the Seattle scene a mecca for edgy entertainment. Bill Gates of Microsoft and Howard Shultz of Starbucks have built vast and perhaps only marginally evil empires on the backs of software and coffee beans, but Seattle's residents go about their lives in a state of caffeinated bliss.

INTERCITY TRANSPORTATION

Flights: Seattle-Tacoma International (Sea-Tac; ☎431-4444; www.portseattle.org), on Federal Way, 15 mi. south of Seattle, right off **I-5** (signs are clear). Bus #194 departs the underground tunnel at University St. and 3rd Ave. (30min., every 30 min. 5:25am-8:45pm, $1.25-2, children $0.50) and #174 departs Union & 2nd Ave. (45min., every 30min. 5:25am-3:30am, $1.25-2) for the airport. These routes leave from the airport for Seattle from outside the baggage claim (every 15min. 4:45am-2:45am, $1.25-2).

Trains: Amtrak (☎382-4125, reservations ☎800-872-7245; www.amtrak.com), King St. Station, at 3rd and Jackson St., 1 block east of Pioneer Square next to the stadiums. Ticket office and station open daily 6:15am-10:30pm. To: **Portland** (4 per day, $26-37); **Tacoma** (4 per day, $9-15); **Spokane** (4 per day, $41-85); **San Francisco, CA** (1 per day, $100-167); and **Vancouver, BC** (1 per day, $23-36).

Buses: Greyhound (☎628-5526 or 800-231-2222), at 8th Ave. and Stewart St. Try to avoid night buses, since the station can get seedy after dark. Ticket office open daily 6:30am-2:30am, station open 24 hr. To: **Portland** (11 per day, $22.50); **Spokane** (3 per day, $28); **Tacoma** (8 per day, $5); and **Vancouver, BC** (8 per day, $23.50. **Quick Shuttle** (☎604-940-4428 or 800-665-2122; www.quickcoach.com) makes 5-8 cross-border trips daily from Seattle (Travelodge hotel at 8th and Bell St.) and the Sea-Tac airport to the **Vancouver, BC** airport and the Holiday Inn on Howe St. in downtown Vancouver (4-4½hr.; $33 from downtown, $41 from Sea-Tac).

Ferries: Washington State Ferries (☎464-6400 or 888-808-7977; www.wsdot.wa.gov/ferries) has 2 terminals in Seattle. The main terminal is downtown, at Colman Dock, Pier 52. From here, service departs to **Bainbridge Island** (35min.; $5.40, $10-12 with car), **Bremerton** on the Kitsap Peninsula (1hr.; passenger-only boat 40min; $5.40, $10-12 with car), and **Vashon Island** (25min., passengers only, $7.40). From the waterfront, passenger-only ferries leave from Pier 50. The other terminal is in **Fauntleroy,** West Seattle; to reach the terminal, drive south on I-5 and take Exit 163A (West Seattle) down Fauntleroy Way. Sailings from Fauntleroy to **Southworth** on the Kitsap Peninsula (35min.; $4, with car $10); **Vashon Island** (15min; $3.50, with car $12-16.) If ferry travel is in your plans, pick up both the *Sailing Schedule* and the *Fares* pamphlet. Services are tricky, so it is worth spending a few minutes perusing the schedule or calling the toll-free info line. Most ferries leave, frequently 6am-2am. **Victoria Clipper** (☎800-888-2535, reservations 448-5000; www.victoriaclipper.com) takes passengers from Seattle to **Victoria** only. Departs from Pier 69 (3hr.; 2-4 per day; one-way $60-75, round-trip $99-125, under 12 half-price; bicycles $10.)

Car Transport: Auto Driveaway (☎878-7400 or 800-235-5052), on Pacific Highway S, near the airport. Recruits "select individuals" to drive cars to locations across the US. The management loves to hear from *Let's Go* readers. $300 cash deposit. Open M-F 8am-5pm.

ORIENTATION

Seattle stretches from north to south on an isthmus between **Puget Sound** to the west and **Lake Washington** to the east. The city is easily accessible by car via **I-5,** which runs north-south through the city, and by **I-90** from the east, which ends at I-5 southeast of downtown. Get to **downtown** (including **Pioneer Square, Pike Place Market,** and the **waterfront**) from I-5 by taking any of the exits from James St. to Stewart St. Take the Mercer St./Fairview Ave. exit to the **Seattle Center;** follow signs from there. The Denny Way exit leads to **Capitol Hill,** and, farther north, the 45th St. exit heads toward the **University District.** The less crowded **Rte. 99,** also called **Aurora Ave.** or the Aurora Hwy., runs parallel to I-5 and skirts the western side of downtown, with great views from the Alaskan Way Viaduct. Rte. 99 is often the better choice when driving downtown or to **Queen Anne, Fremont, Green Lake,** and the northwestern part of the city. For more detailed directions to these and other districts, see the individualized neighborhood listings under **Food** (p. 167), **Nightlife** (p. 178), and **Sights** (p. 172).

LOCAL TRANSPORTATION

Even the most road-weary drivers can learn their way around the Emerald City. Street parking creates many blind pull-outs in Seattle, so be extra careful when turning onto cross roads. Downtown, **avenues** run northwest to southeast and **streets** run southwest to northeast. Outside downtown, everything is simplified: with few exceptions, avenues run north-south and streets east-west. The city is in **quadrants:** 1000 1st Ave. NW is a far walk from 1000 1st Ave. SE.

When driving in Seattle, **yield to pedestrians.** They will not look, so make sure you do. Locals drive slowly, calmly, and politely; police ticket frequently. Downtown driving can be nightmarish: parking is expensive, hills are steep, and one-way streets are ubiquitous. Read the street signs carefully, as many areas have time and hour restrictions; ticketers know them by heart. **Parking** is reasonable, plentiful, and well lit at **Pacific Place Parking** between 6th and 7th Ave. and Olive and Pine St., with hourly rates comparable to the meters and at **Seattle Center,** near the Space Needle. (☎652-0416. 24hr. $2 per hr.; $19 per day.) Park at the Needle and take the monorail to the convenient **Westlake Center** downtown. If you are driving in Seattle, prepare yourself for heavy traffic, especially on I-5, at almost any hour of the day. Public transportation on the whole in Seattle is not stellar. Inhabitants and visitors alike must settle for above-ground transportation. Although buses are large and schedules are flexible, the transit is slow and infrequent.

The **Metro ride free zone** includes most of downtown Seattle (see **Public Transportation,** below). The **Metro** buses cover King County east to North Bend and Carnation, south to Enumclaw, and north to Snohomish County, where bus #6 hooks up with **Community Transit.** This line runs to Everett, Stanwood, and into the Cascades. Bus #174 connects to Tacoma's Pierce County System at Federal Way.

Seattle is a **bicycle-friendly** city. All buses have free, easy-to-use bike racks (bike shops have sample racks on which to practice). Between 6am and 7pm, bikes may only be loaded or unloaded at stops outside the ride free zone. Check out Metro's *Bike & Ride*, available at the visitors center. For a bike map of Seattle, call **City of Seattle Bicycle Program** (☎684-7583).

Public Transportation: Metro Transit, Pass Sales and Information Office, 201 S Jackson St. (☎553-3000 or 24hr. 800-542-7876). Open M-F 9am-5pm. The bus tunnel under Pine St. and 3rd Ave. is the heart of the downtown bus system. Fares are based on a 2-zone system. **Zone 1** includes everything within the city limits (peak hours $1.50, off-peak $1.25). **Zone 2** includes everything else (peak $2, off-peak $1.25).

Ages 5-17 always $0.50. **Peak hours** in both zones are M-F 6-9am and 3-6pm. Exact fare required. Weekend day passes $2.50. Ride free daily 6am-7pm in the downtown **ride free area,** bordered by S Jackson on the south, 6th and I-5 on the east, Blanchard on the north, and the waterfront on the west. Free **transfers** can be used on any bus, including a return trip on the same bus within 2hr. Most buses are **wheelchair accessible** (info ☎684-2046). The **Monorail** runs from the Space Needle to Westlake Center every 10min. 7:30am-11pm. ($1.50, seniors $0.75, ages 5-12 $0.50.)

Taxi: Farwest Taxi (☎622-1717), $1.80 base, $1.80 per mi.; **Orange Cab Co.** (☎522-8800), $1.80 base, $1.80 per mi.

Car Rental: U Save Auto Rental, 16223 Pacific Hwy. S (☎242-9778). $34 per day for compacts, plus $0.22 per mi. over 100 mi. Unlimited mileage in BC and WA. Must be 21 with a major credit card. **Enterprise,** 11342 Lake City Way NE (☎364-3127). $36 per day for compacts, plus $0.20 per mi. over 150 mi. Their **airport location,** 15667 Pacific Hwy. S (☎246-1953), charges an additional 10%.

PRACTICAL INFORMATION

TOURIST & FINANCIAL SERVICES

Tourist Information: Seattle's Convention and Visitors Bureau (☎461-5840; www.seeseattle.org), at 7th and Pike St., on the 1st floor of the convention center. Helpful staff doles out maps, brochures, newspapers, and Metro and ferry schedules. Open M-F 9am-4pm.

Outdoor Information: Seattle Parks and Recreation Department, 100 Dexter Ave. N (☎684-4075). Open M-F 8am-5pm for info and pamphlets on city parks. **Outdoor Recreation Information Center,** 222 Yale Ave. (☎470-4060), in REI (see **Equipment Rental,** below). A joint operation between the Park and Forest services. Able to answer any questions that might arise as you browse REI's huge collection of maps and guides. Unfortunately, the desk is not set up to sell permits. Free brochures on hiking trails. Open Su-F 10:30am-7pm, Sa 10am-7pm. Closed M late Sept. to late spring.

Equipment Rental:

REI, 222 Yale Ave. (☎223-1944 or 888-873-1938), near Capitol Hill. The mothership of camping supply stores rents everything from camping gear to technical mountaineering equipment (see **Outdoor Activities,** p. 180). Open M-F 10am-9pm, Sa-Su 10am-7pm.

The Bicycle Center, 4529 Sand Point Way (☎523-8300), near the Children's Hospital, rents mountain and hybrid bikes ($3 per hr., $25 per day; 2hr. min.). Credit card deposit required. Open M-Th 10am-8pm, F 10am-7pm, Sa 10am-6pm, Su 10am-5pm.

Gregg's Greenlake Cycle, 7007 Woodlawn Ave. NE (☎523-1822). Wide range of bikes conveniently close to Green Lake and Burke-Gilman bike trails ($7 per hr., $25-30 per day, $30-35 per 24hr., $120 per week). Photo ID and cash or credit card deposit required. Also rents in-line skates ($7 per hr., $20 per day, $25 per 24hr.). Overnight rentals require deposit. Open M-F 10am-9pm, Sa-Su 10am-6pm.

Currency Exchange: Thomas Cook Foreign Exchange, 400 Pine St. (☎682-4525), on the 3rd floor of the Westlake Shopping Center. Open M-Sa 9:30am-6pm, Su 11am-5pm. Also behind the Delta Airlines ticket counter and at other airport locations.

Travel Agencies: Council Travel, 4311 University Way (☎632-2448). Open M-F 10am-6pm, Sa 10am-5pm. Also at 424 Broadway Ave. E (☎329-4567), in Capitol Hill. Open M-F 10am-6pm, Sa 10am-5pm. **STA Travel,** 4341 University Way (☎633-5000; www.statravel.com), at NE 45th. Open M-F 10am-6pm, Sa 10am-5pm.

Short-term Work Opportunities: City of Seattle Personnel Department, 710 2nd Ave., 12th fl. (job hotline ☎684-7999, www.cityofseattle.net/jobs/).

LOCAL SERVICES

Bookstores: Elliott Bay Books, 101 S Main St. (☎624-6600), in Pioneer Sq. Vast collection with 150,000 titles. Sponsors a reading and lecture series almost every day, all year long. Most readings are weekdays at 7:30pm or weekend afternoons. Coffeehouse in the basement. Open M-F 9:30am-10pm, Sa-Su 10am-10pm.

Ticket Agencies: Ticketmaster (☎628-0888) in Westlake Center and every Tower Records store. **Ticket/Ticket,** 401 Broadway E (☎324-2744), on the 2nd floor of the Broadway Market, sells half-price day-of-show tickets for theatres, music, clubs, cruises, tours, and more. Cash only. Sales only done in person. Open Tu-Sa noon-7pm, Su noon-6pm. Also in **Pike Place Market information booth** at 1st Ave. and Pike St. 30min. free parking in garage under Harrison St. with ticket purchase. Open Tu-Su noon-6pm.

Laundromat: Sit and Spin, 2219 4th St. (☎441-9484). A laundromat local hot spot (see **Nightlife,** p. 178). Wash $1.25, dry $0.25 per 10min. Open Su-Th 11am-midnight, F-Sa 11am-2am.

EMERGENCY & COMMUNICATIONS

Emergency: ☎911.

Police: 810 Virginia St. (☎625-5011).

Crisis Line: ☎461-3222.

Rape Crisis: King County Sexual Assault Center (☎800-825-7273). Crisis counseling and advocacy. **Harborview Medical** (☎731-3000), **Harborview Center for Sexual and Traumatic Stress** (☎521-1800). All 24hr.

Medical Services: International District Emergency Center, 720 8th Ave. S, Ste. 100 (☎461-3235). Medics with multilingual assistance available. Clinic M-F 9am-6pm, Sa 9am-5pm; phone 24hr. **U.S. Health Works,** 1151 Denny Way (☎682-7418). Walk-in. 7am-6pm. **Swedish Medical Center, Providence Campus,** 500 17th Ave. (☎320-2111), for urgent care and cardiac. 24hr.

Internet Access: The **Seattle Public Library,** 800 Pike St. (☎386-4636), is stashed away in a temporary building near the convention center until spring 2004. After renovations are complete, the library will return to its original site at 1000 4th Ave. (at Madison). A visitor's library card (must have local address) lasts 3 months ($10). One-time visitors can use Internet for free with photo ID. Open M-W 10am-8pm, Th-Sa 10am-6pm, Su 1-5pm. **Capitol Hill Net,** 216 Broadway Ave E (☎860-6858), charges $6 per hr. 15min. free with food purchase of $1.50. *Let's Go* readers and all hostelers get 15min. free. Open M-Su 8am-midnight.

Post Office: 301 Union St. (☎748-5417 or 800-275-8777) at 3rd Ave. downtown. Open M-F 8am-5:30pm, Sa 8am-noon. General delivery window open M-F 9am-11:20am and noon-3pm. **Postal Code:** 98101.

PUBLICATIONS

The city's major daily, the *Seattle Times* (☎464-2111; www.seattletimes.com), lists upcoming events in its Thursday "Datebook" section. Its major "competitor" (actually its partner), the *Seattle Post-Intelligencer*, has an award-winning sports section and great news coverage, but does not publish on Sunday. The Thursday listings of the *Seattle Weekly* (www.seattleweekly.com) are free and left-of-center. Even farther over is *The Stranger* (free), which covers music and culture, materializing Thursdays at music, coffee, and thrift shops. *The Rocket*, a bimonthly publication, relays music and entertainment info from all over the Northwest. *Arts Focus*, free at most bookstores, covers performing arts. *Seattle Arts*, published by the Seattle Arts Commission, is especially good on visual arts. Both are monthlies. The weekly *Seattle Gay News* sells on Fridays at newsstands.

ACCOMMODATIONS

Seattle's hostel scene is not amazing, but there are plenty of choices and establishments to fit all types of personalities. The **Vashon Island Hostel** is probably the best bedding in the area and most certainly the most relaxing (see **Accommodations,** p. 190). **Pacific Reservation Service** arranges B&B singles in the $50-65 range. (☎800-684-2932; www.seattlebedandbreakfast.com. Open M-F 8am-5pm.)

DOWNTOWN

Seattle International Hostel (HI), 84 Union St. (☎622-5443 or 888-622-5443), at Western Ave., right by the waterfront. Take Union St. from downtown; follow signs down the stairs under the "Pike Pub & Brewery." Great location overlooking the water, but the space itself can feel like a cramped dorm on full nights. Coin laundry. Internet access $0.15 per min. 7-night max. stay in summer. Reception 24hr. Check-out 11am. No curfew. Reservations recommended. 199 beds; $22, nonmembers $25. $2 extra for bathroom in dorm room. Private rooms sleep 2-4; $54, nonmembers $60. ❶

Green Tortoise Backpacker's Hostel, 1525 2nd Ave. (☎340-1222; fax 623-3207), between Pike and Pine St. on the #174 or 194 bus route. A young party hostel downtown; lots of people, lots of activities. Free beer on F, free dinner on M, free breakfast daily (7am-9:30am), and free Internet access. Kitchen, library, patio, and laundry. Bring your own bedding; blanket $1. $20 cash key deposit required. Reception 24hr. Dorm beds $22 with credit card, $21 with cash; private rooms $50. ❶

Moore Hotel, 1926 2nd Ave. (☎448-4851 or 800-421-5508; www.moorehotel.com), at Virginia, 1 block east from Pike Place Market, next to historic Moore Theater. Built in 1905, the Moore Hotel beckons visitors with an open lobby, cavernous halls, and attentive service. Singles $39, with bath $59; doubles (1 bed) $49, with bath $68. Big room with 2 beds and bath $86. Large suites, some with kitchen, $150. ❸

Commodore Hotel, 2013 2nd Ave. (☎448-8868), at Virginia. Pleasant decor and only a few blocks from the waterfront. Front desk open 24hr., but no visitors past 8pm. Singles $59, with bath $69; 2 beds and bath $79. ❸

West Coast Vance Hotel, 620 Steward St. (☎441-4200). Built in 1926, the West Coast Vance offers charming rooms starting at $95. The hotel is located within walking distance from Pike Place Market as well as the 5th Ave. shopping district. ❺

OUTSIDE DOWNTOWN

For inexpensive motels farther from downtown, drive north on Hwy. 99 (Aurora Ave.) or take bus #26 to the neighborhood of Fremont. Budget chain motels like the **Nites Inn ❸,** 11746 Aurora Ave. N, line the highway north of the Aurora bridge. (☎365-3216. Singles from $42; doubles $46.) Look for AAA approval ratings.

Corona Apartments, 715 2nd Ave. N (☎856-8630), on the south slope of Queen Anne Hill, 3 blocks east from the Space Needle and the Seattle Center. Long-term accommodations for travelers. Backyard, kitchen, garden, and laundry. Applications available at the Green Tortoise Hostel (allow a few days for processing). Single studios from $495 per month (3-month min. stay).

The College Inn, 4000 University Way NE (☎633-4441; www.collegeinnseattle.com), at 40th St. NE. Quiet place near UW campus and its youthful environs. This European-style inn offers charming rooms with classy brass fixtures. All rooms share bathrooms. Free continental breakfast. Singles from $45; doubles $50-80. Credit card required. ❸

FOOD

Although Seattleites appear to subsist solely on espresso and steamed milk, they do occasionally eat. The finest fish, produce, and baked goods are at **Pike Place Market.** The **University District** supports inexpensive and international cuisine. The **Chinatown/International District** offers tons of rice, pounds of fresh fish, and enough veggies to keep your mother happy, all at ridiculously low prices. **Puget Sound Consumer Coops (PCCs)** are local health food markets at 7504 Aurora Ave. N (☎525-3586), in Green Lake, and at 6514 40th NE (☎526-7661), in the Ravenna District north of the university. Capitol Hill, the U District, and Fremont close main thoroughfares on summer Saturdays for **farmers markets.**

PIKE PLACE MARKET & DOWNTOWN

In 1907, angry citizens demanded the elimination of the middle-man and local farmers began selling produce by the waterfront, creating the Pike Place Market. Business thrived until an enormous fire burned the building in 1941. The early 1980s heralded a Pike Place renaissance, and today thousands of tourists mob the market daily. (Open M-Sa 9am-6pm, Su 11am-5pm. Produce and fish open earlier; restaurants and lounges close later.) In the **Main Arcade,** on the west side of Pike St., fishmongers compete for audiences as they hurl fish from shelves to scales. The market's restaurants boast stellar views of the sound.

An **information booth** faces the bike rack by the Main Arcade, at 1st Ave. and Pike St. (☎461-5800. Open Tu-Su 10am-noon.) Restaurants south of Pike Place cater mostly to suits on lunch breaks and tourists, but there are many sandwich and pastry shops covering downtown.

Piroshki, Piroshki, 1908 Pike St. (☎441-6068), across the street from the front entrance of the market building. The *Russian Piroshki* is a croissant-like dough baked around sausages, mushrooms, cheeses, salmon, or apples doused in cinnamon. Watch the *piroshki* process in progress while awaiting your order. Open daily 8am-7pm. ❶

Soundview Cafe (☎623-5700), on the mezzanine in the Pike Place Main Arcade. The sandwich-and-salad bar is a good place to enjoy a view of Puget Sound. Breakfast and lunch $3-6. Open M-F 8am-5pm, Sa 8am-5:30pm, Su 8am-5pm. ❶

THE LOCAL STORY

FISHY BUSINESS

Part of the quintessential Seattle experience is a trip to the historic Pike Place Market. Let's Go *spoke to the* **Bear,** *one of the famous Pike Place fish-throwers, in July of 2002.*

Q: Do you throw fish?
A: Yes, all day long.

Q: How long have you been working at the Pike Place Market?
A: 16 years.

Q: How many fish are thrown per day?
A: Lots.

Q: Ever hit someone with a fish?
A: Yes. There was the Amish woman one day. I hit her right in the forehead.

Q: What did she do?
A: Nothin', what could she do? She was Amish.

Q: Has anyone had a serious injury from a hit?
A: Nobody has died yet.

Q: What do you throw the most?
A: Fish.

Q: What kind?
A: Dead ones for the most part.

Q: What's a popular fish?
A: The monk fish, with its mouth open. Everybody gotta look at that one when they come in....all you gotta do is hang out and you'll have a fun experience.

Garlic Tree, 94 Stewart St. (☎441-5681), 1 block up from Pike Place Market. The smell will drag you in. Loads of fabulous veggie, chicken, and seafood stir-fry ($7-9). Try the tofu chapche ($6.95). Open M-Sa 11am-8pm. ❷

Emmett Watson's Oyster Bar, 1916 Pike Place (☎448-7721). Oyster Bar Special–2 oysters, 3 shrimp, bread, and chowder–is $6.25. Shelves of bottles show off the selection of brews. Open M-Th 11:30am-8pm. F-Sa 11:30am-9pm. Su 11:30am-6pm. ❷

WATERFRONT

Budget eaters, steer clear of Pioneer Square: instead, take a picnic to **Waterfall Garden,** on the corner of S Main St. and 2nd Ave. S. The garden sports tables and chairs and a man-made waterfall that masks traffic outside. (Open daily 8am-6pm.)

Mae Phim Thai Restaurant, 94 Columbia St. (☎624-2979), a few blocks north of Pioneer Sq. between 1st Ave. and Alaskan Way. Slews of pad thai junkies crowd in for cheap, delicious Thai cuisine. All dishes $6. Open M-Sa 11am-7pm. ❷

Ivar's Fish Bar, Pier 54 (☎467-8063), north of the square. A fast-food window that serves the definitive Seattle clam chowder ($2). Clam and chips ($4.99). Open M-Th and Su 10am-midnight, F-Sa 10am-2am. ❶ For a slightly more upscale seafood meal, check out **Ivar's Restaurant** next door (same hours). ❸

INTERNATIONAL DISTRICT

Along King and Jackson St., between 5th and 8th Ave. east of the Kingdome, Seattle's International District is packed with great eateries. Competition keeps prices low and quality high, and unassuming facades front fabulous food. Lunch specials are particularly appealing, and the long lines move quickly.

Uwajimaya, 600 5th Ave. S (☎624-6248). The Uwajimaya Center is a full city block of groceries, gifts, videos, and CDs; it's the largest Japanese department store in the Northwest! There is even a food court, plying Korean BBQ and Taiwanese-style baked goods. Open M-Sa 9am-11pm, Su 9am-10pm. ❷

Tai Tung, 655 S King St. (☎622-7372). Select authentic Chinese and Mandarin cuisine from one of the largest menus around. Grab a bite at the bar, where menus are plastered on the wall. Entrees $5-12. Open Su-Th 10am-11pm, F-Sa 10am-1:30am. ❷

Ho Ho Seafood Restaurant, 653 S Weller St. (☎382-9671). Generous portions of tank-fresh seafood. Stuffed fish hang from the ceilings. Lunch $5-7 (until 4pm), dinner $7-12. Open Su-Th 11am-1am, F-Sa 11am-3am. ❷

CAPITOL HILL

With bronze dance-steps on the sidewalks and neon storefronts, **Broadway** is a land of espresso houses, imaginative shops, elegant clubs, and plenty of eats. Although not the cheapest place to eat, it has a great variety of cuisine options catering to most budgets and taste buds. Bus #7 runs along Broadway; bus #10 runs through Capitol Hill along more sedate **15th St.** Free parking is behind the reservoir at Broadway Field, on 11th Ave.

Bimbo's Bitchin' Burrito Kitchen, 506 E Pine (☎329-9978). The name explains it, and the decorations (fake palm trees and lots of plastic) prove it. Walk right on through the door to the **Cha Cha,** a similarly-decorated bar (tequila shots $3.50). Spicy Bimbo's burrito $4.25. Open M-Th noon-10pm, F-Sa noon-1am, Su 2-9pm. ❶

Ristorante Machiavelli, 1215 Pine St. (☎621-7941), right across the street from Bauhaus (see **Cafes,** below). A small Italian place that locals fiercely love. Pasta $8-10. Open M-Sa 5-11pm. ❷

HaNa, 219 Broadway Ave. E (☎328-1187). Packed quarters testify to the popularity of the sushi here. Lunch sushi combo platter with rice and soup $7.25. Dinner $9-10. Open M-Sa 11am-10pm, Su 4-10pm. ❷

Honey Hole Sandwiches, 703 E Pike (☎709-1399). The primary colors and veggie-filled sandwiches make you feel healthy and happy. The hummus-loaded "Daytripper" is a treat ($5.50). Open daily 10am-2am. ❶

UNIVERSITY DISTRICT

The neighborhood around the immense University of Washington ("U-Dub"), north of downtown between Union Bay and Portage Bay, supports funky shops, international restaurants, and yes, coffeehouses. The best of each lies within a few blocks of University Way, known as "Th' Ave." Restaurants run rampant here. The Ave. supports everything from Denny's to bubble tea. Think student budget: this is probably the cheapest place to eat in the city. On Saturdays (June-Oct.) a **farmers market** at 50th and University Way NE sells fresh fruit and veggies to eager students. To get there, take Exit 169 off I-5 N, or take one of buses #70-74 from downtown, or #7 or 9 from Capitol Hill. (Open 9am-2pm).

Flowers, 4247 University Way NE (☎633-1903). This 20s landmark was a flower shop; now, the mirrored ceiling tastefully reflects an all-you-can-eat vegetarian buffet ($7.50). Great daily drink specials: $2 tequila shots W, $3 well sours Th, $3 margaritas Sa. Open M-Sa 11am-2am, Su 11am-midnight. ❶

Neelam's, 4735 University Way NE (☎523-5275), serves up the best authentic Indian cuisine in the University District, and the price is right. Open daily for lunch (buffet $5.95) 11:30am-3pm, dinner 5-10pm. ❷

Araya's Vegan Thai Cuisine, 4732 University Way NE (524-4332). Consistently rated among the top vegan restaurants in Seattle, Araya's will satisfy any vegetarian or vegan desire. Lunch buffet ($6.50) 11:30am-3:30pm. Open M-Th 11:30am-9pm, F-Sa 11:30am-9:30pm, Su 5pm-9pm. ❷

CAFES

The coffee bean is Seattle's first love. One cannot walk a single block without passing a Starbuck's or Tully's. But if you're looking for a more unique experience, check out the funky cafes on Capitol Hill or in the University District.

CAPITOL HILL

Bauhaus, 301 E Pine St. (☎625-1600). The Reading Goddess looks from above the towering bookshelves, protects patrons, and oversees service of drip coffee ($1) or Kool-Aid ($1). Open M-F 7am-1am, Sa 7am-1am, Su 8am-1am.

The Globe Cafe, 1531 14th Ave. (☎324-8815). Seattle's next literary renaissance is brewing here. Quotes overheard at the Globe are plastered on the tables. Fabulous all-vegan menu. Stir-fry tofu $4-6. Open Tu-Su 7am-3pm.

UNIVERSITY DISTRICT

Espresso Roma, 4201 University Way NE (☎632-6001). A pleasant patio, and quasi-former-warehouse interior result in spacious tables with an open air feel. The Ave.'s cheapest coffee. Mocha $2. Internet access $0.15 per min. After 7pm, get a grande for the price of a tall. Open M-F 7am-10pm, Sa-Su 8am-10pm.

Ugly Mug, 1309 43rd St. (☎547-3219), off University Way. Off-beat in a 10,000 Maniacs-thrift store sort of way. Eclectic chair collection is quite comfortable. Wide sandwich selection (turkey foccaccia $4). Open daily 7:30am-6pm.

Gingko Tea, 4343 University Way NE (☎632-7298). If you dig tea over coffee, you'll find a niche at Gingko's. Classical music supplies the background; wood furniture and floral cushions provide the foreground. 5 types of chai ($2.55). Bubble tea $2.45. Open M-Th 10:30am-11pm, F-Sa 10:30am-12pm, Su 11am-10pm.

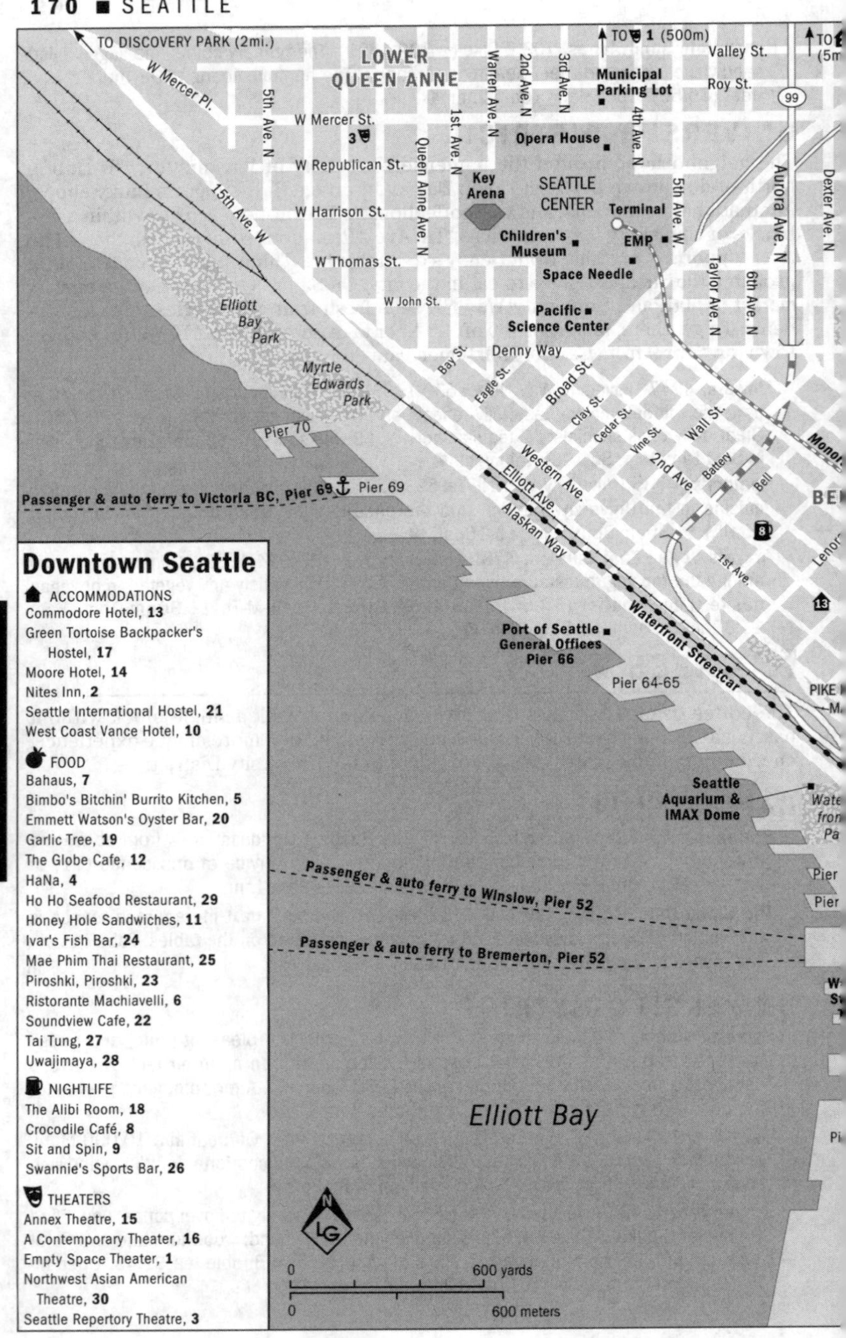
Downtown Seattle
ACCOMMODATIONS
Commodore Hotel, 13
Green Tortoise Backpacker's Hostel, 17
Moore Hotel, 14
Nites Inn, 2
Seattle International Hostel, 21
West Coast Vance Hotel, 10
FOOD
Bahaus, 7
Bimbo's Bitchin' Burrito Kitchen, 5
Emmett Watson's Oyster Bar, 20
Garlic Tree, 19
The Globe Cafe, 12
HaNa, 4
Ho Ho Seafood Restaurant, 29
Honey Hole Sandwiches, 11
Ivar's Fish Bar, 24
Mae Phim Thai Restaurant, 25
Piroshki, Piroshki, 23
Ristorante Machiavelli, 6
Soundview Cafe, 22
Tai Tung, 27
Uwajimaya, 28
NIGHTLIFE
The Alibi Room, 18
Crocodile Café, 8
Sit and Spin, 9
Swannie's Sports Bar, 26
THEATERS
Annex Theatre, 15
A Contemporary Theater, 16
Empty Space Theater, 1
Northwest Asian American Theatre, 30
Seattle Repertory Theatre, 3
TO DISCOVERY PARK (2mi.)
TO 1 (500m)
LOWER QUEEN ANNE
W Mercer Pl.
W Mercer St.
W Republican St.
W Harrison St.
W Thomas St.
W John St.
5th. Ave. N
Queen Anne Ave. N
1st. Ave. N
Warren Ave. N
2nd Ave. N
3rd Ave. N
4th Ave. N
5th Ave. W.
Taylor Ave. N
6th Ave. N
Aurora Ave. N
Dexter Ave. N
Valley St.
Roy St.
99
Municipal Parking Lot
Opera House
Key Arena
SEATTLE CENTER
Terminal
Children's Museum
EMP
Space Needle
Pacific Science Center
Denny Way
15th Ave. W
Elliott Bay Park
Myrtle Edwards Park
Pier 70
Pier 69
Passenger & auto ferry to Victoria BC, Pier 69
Bay St.
Eagle St.
Broad St.
Clay St.
Cedar St.
Vine St.
Wall St.
Battery
Bell
2nd Ave.
1st Ave.
Western Ave.
Elliott Ave.
Alaskan Way
Waterfront Streetcar
Port of Seattle General Offices Pier 66
Pier 64-65
Seattle Aquarium & IMAX Dome
Passenger & auto ferry to Winslow, Pier 52
Passenger & auto ferry to Bremerton, Pier 52
Elliott Bay
N
LG
0
600 yards
600 meters

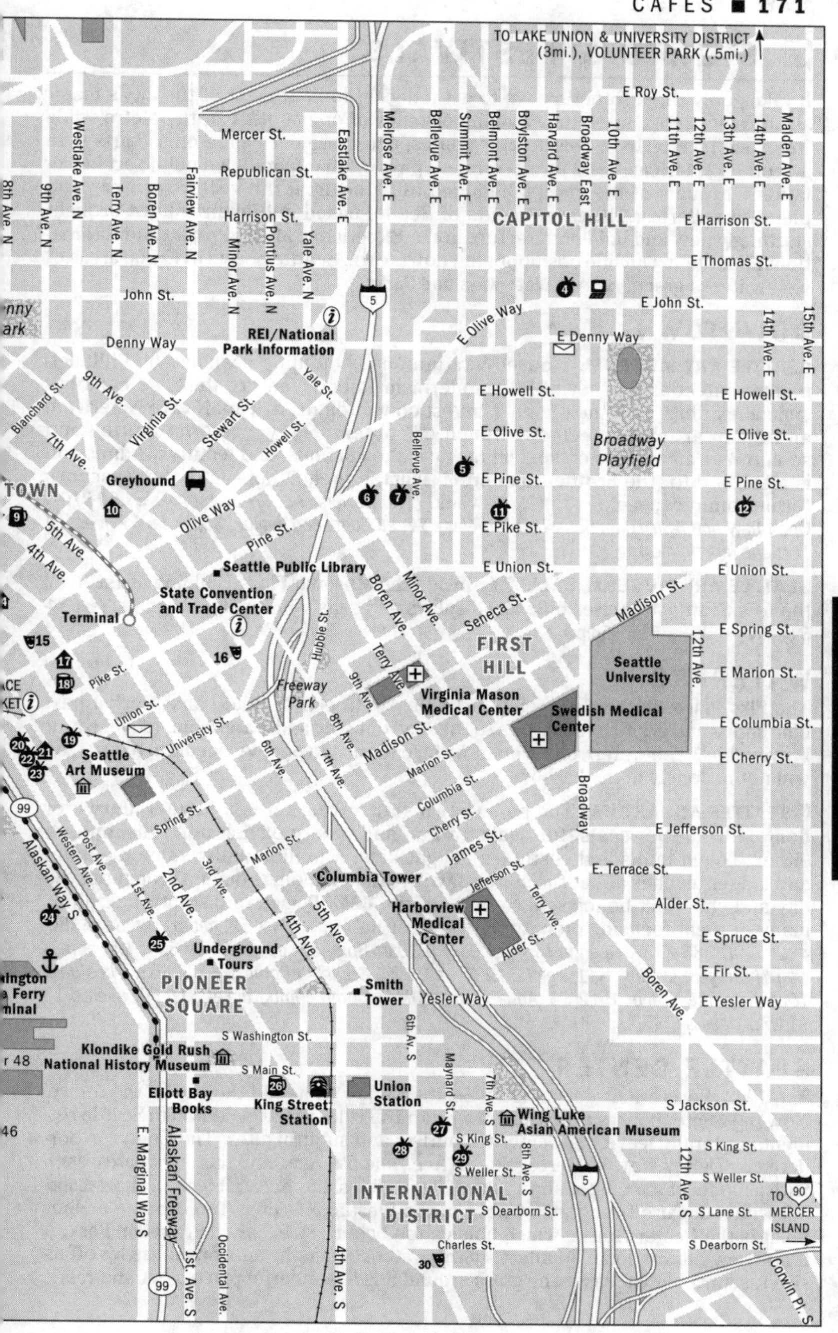
TO LAKE UNION & UNIVERSITY DISTRICT (3mi.), VOLUNTEER PARK (.5mi.)
CAPITOL HILL
FIRST HILL
PIONEER SQUARE
INTERNATIONAL DISTRICT
REI/National Park Information
Greyhound
Seattle Public Library
State Convention and Trade Center
Terminal
Seattle Art Museum
Broadway Playfield
Seattle University
Virginia Mason Medical Center
Swedish Medical Center
Harborview Medical Center
Columbia Tower
Freeway Park
Underground Tours
Smith Tower
Klondike Gold Rush National History Museum
Elliott Bay Books
King Street Station
Union Station
Wing Luke Asian American Museum
TO MERCER ISLAND
Yesler Way
Denny Way
E Olive Way
Madison St.
Broadway
Alaskan Way S
Alaskan Freeway
E. Marginal Way S

SIGHTS & FESTIVALS

It takes only three frenetic days to get a decent look at most of the city's major sights, since most are within walking distance of one another or the Metro's ride free zone (see p. 163). Seattle taxpayers spend more per capita on the arts than any other Americans, and the investment pays off in unparalleled public art installations throughout the city (self-guided tours begin at the visitors center), and plentiful galleries. The investments of Seattle-based millionaires have brought startlingly new and bold architecture in the Experience Music Project and International Fountain. Outside cosmopolitan downtown, Seattle boasts over 300 areas of well-watered greenery (see **Waterways and Parks,** p. 179).

DOWNTOWN

SEATTLE ART MUSEUM. Housed in a grandiose building designed by Philadelphia architect and father of Postmodernism Robert Venturi, the SAM balances special exhibits with the region's largest collection of African, Native American, and Asian art and an eclectic bunch of contemporary western painting and sculpture. Call for info on special musical shows, films, and lectures. Admission is also good for the **Seattle Asian Art Museum** (a branch housed in the museum's former building; see p. 174) for a week. *(100 University St., near 1st Ave. ☎654-3100. Open Tu-W and F-Su 10am-5pm, Th 10am-9pm. $7, students and seniors $5, under 12 free; first Th of the month free.)*

SEATTLE ART MUSEUM GALLERY. Inside the Museum Plaza Building at 1st Ave., the free **Seattle Art Museum Gallery** displays and sells work by local artists. *(☎654-3176. Open M-Sa 11am-5pm.)*

WASHINGTON

WATERFRONT

The **Pike Place Hillclimb** descends from the south end of Pike Place Market past chic shops and ethnic restaurants to the Alaskan Way and waterfront. (An elevator is available.) The waterfront is lined with vendors and people; needless to say, you will not be lonely in the harbor.

SEATTLE AQUARIUM. The aquarium's star attraction is a huge underwater dome, but harbor seals, fur seals, otters, and plenty of fish don't disappoint, either. Touch tanks and costumes delight kids. A million-dollar salmon exhibit and ladder teaches about the state's favorite fish. Feedings occur throughout the day and shouldn't be missed. Next door, the **IMAX Dome** cranks out Imax films, many of them focusing on natural events or habitats. *(Pier 59, near Union St. ☎386-4320, TDD 386-4322. Open in summer daily 9:30am-8pm; off-season 10am-6pm; last admission 1hr. before closing. $11, ages 6-12 $7, ages 3-5 $5. IMAX Dome ☎622-1868. Films daily 10am-10pm. $7, ages 6-12 $6. Aquarium and IMAX Dome combo ticket $16.50, ages 6-12 $11.75, ages 3-5 $5.)*

SEATTLE CENTER

The 1962 World's Fair demanded a Seattle Center to herald the city of the future. Now the Center houses everything from carnival rides to ballet, although Seattle residents generally leave the Center to tourists and suburbanites. The Center is bordered by Denny Way, W Mercer St., 1st Ave., and 5th Ave., and has eight gates, each with a model of the Center and a map of its facilities. It is accessible via a short **monorail** which departs from the 3rd floor of the Westlake Center. The center's anchor point is the Center House, which holds a food court, stage, and **Information Desk.** A brand-new International Fountain squirts water 20 ft. in the air from all angles off its silver, semispherical base. The grass around it is a wonderful place to sit and relax.

(Monorail: every 15min. M-F 7:30am-11pm, Sa-Su 9am-11pm. $1.50, seniors $0.75, ages 5-12 $0.50. Info Desk: open daily 11am-6pm. For info about special events and permanent attractions, call ☎684-8582 (recorded info) or 684-7200 for a real live person.)

EXPERIENCE MUSIC PROJECT (EMP). Undoubtedly the biggest and best attraction at the Seattle Center is the new, futuristic, abstract, and technologically brilliant Experience Music Project. The museum is the brainchild of Seattle billionaire Paul Allen, who originally wanted to create a shrine to worship his music idol Jimi Hendrix. But nothing this man does is small. Splash together the technological sophistication and foresight of Microsoft, dozens of ethnomusicologists and multimedia specialists, a collection of musical artifacts topping 80,000, the world-renowned architect Frank Gehry, and enough money to make the national debt appear small (fine, it was only $350 million), and you guessed it, you have the rock 'n' roll museum of the future. The building alone—consisting of sheet metal molded into abstract curves and then acid-dyed gold, silver, purple, light-blue, and red—is enough to make the average person gasp for breath. Walk in and strap on your personal computer guide (MEG) that allows you to interact with the exhibits. Hear clips from Hendrix's famous "Star Spangled Banner" as you look at the remnants of the guitar he smashed on a London stage. Move into the Sound Lab and test your own skills on guitars, drums, and keyboards linked to computer teaching devices and cushioned in state-of-the art sound rooms. When you are ready, step over to On Stage, a first-class karaoke-gone-haywire, and blast your tunes in front of a virtual audience. Expect to spend several hours testing your creativity, jamming to punk/hip-hop/blues/folk, and much, much more—in fact, locals tend to make a day out of it, using readmission to go in and out several times. Unfortunately this much to do does come with a hefty price tag. *(325 Fifth St. at Seattle Center. From I-5, take Exit 167 and follow signs to Seattle Center. Bus #3, 4, or 15. ☎367-5483 or 877-367-5483; TDD 770-2771; www.emplive.com. Open in summer Su-Th 9am-6pm, F-Sa 9am-9pm; off-season Su-Th 10am-5pm, F-Sa 10am-9pm. $20; seniors, military, and ages 13-17 $16; ages 7-12 $15. Free live music Tu-Sa in the lounge; national acts perform for a price almost every F and Sa in the Sky Church.)*

WASHINGTON

SPACE NEEDLE. The Space Needle was built in 1962 for the Seattle World's Fair. When this 607 ft. rotating building was constructed it was hailed as futuristic and daring. Today, the EMP has stolen part of the Needle's glory, but the Space Needle is still recognized internationally as a symbol of Seattle. The Needle provides a great view (on a clear day) and an invaluable landmark for the disoriented. The elevator ride itself is a show—operators are hired for their unique talents. The needle houses an observation tower and a high-end 360° rotating restaurant. *(☎905-2100. $12.50, seniors $11, ages 4-10 $5.)*

PACIFIC SCIENCE CENTER. The get-down-and-dirty approach of this museum ropes kids into loving to learn. Ride a high-rail bike, tread water in a giant hamster wheel, or play virtual basketball. The tropical butterfly garden is fantastic and the Center also houses a **laserium** that quakes to rock as well as two **IMAX theaters.** *(200 2nd Ave. N. Monorail or bus #1, 2, 3, 4, 6, 8, 19, 24. ☎443-2001; www.pacsci.org. Exhibits open in summer daily 10am-6pm; winter Tu-F 10am-5pm, Sa-Su 10am-6pm. $9, seniors and ages 3-13 $6.50, under 3 free. Laserium ☎443-2850. Laser shows nights Th $5, F-Su $7.50, matinee $2.50. IMAX ☎443-4629. Shows daily from 10am-7pm. $7.50, seniors or ages 3-13 $6.50. Various combo tickets are sold, ranging from $12.50-24.50 for adults.)*

PIONEER SQUARE & ENVIRONS

From the waterfront or downtown, it's just a few blocks south to historic **Pioneer Square,** centered around Yesler Way and 2nd Ave., home of the first Seattleites. The 19th-century buildings, restored in the 1970s and now home to chic shops and trendy pubs, retain their historical intrigue. Pioneer Square is extra busy on game day as baseball moms and dads walk their children to Safeco Field Baseball Park to see the Mariners in action.

UNDERGROUND TOUR. Originally, downtown stood 12 ft. lower than it does today. The tour guides visitors through the subterranean city of old. Be prepared for lots of company, comedy, and toilet jokes. Tours depart from Doc Maynard's Pub, 610 1st Ave. "Doc" Maynard, a charismatic and colorful early resident, gave a plot of land here to one Henry Yesler to build a steam-powered lumber mill. The logs dragged to the mill's front door earned the street its nickname, **Skid Row,** and the smell of the oil used to lubricate the slide was so overwhelming that the self-respecting Seattleites of the day left the neighborhood to gamblers and prostitutes. *(☎682-4646 or 888-608-6337; www.undergroundtour.com. 1½hr. tours daily, roughly hourly 10am-6pm. $9, seniors and students ages 13-17 $7, children $5. Cash only, AAA and HI 10% discount. No reservations—arrive early on weekends.)*

INTERNATIONAL DISTRICT/CHINATOWN

Seattle's **International District/Chinatown** is three blocks east of Pioneer Square, up Jackson on King St.

WING LUKE MEMORIAL MUSEUM. This hole-in-the-wall gives a thorough description of life in an Asian-American community, investigates different Asian nationalities in Seattle, and shows work by local Asian artists. Special exhibits add even more to the tight space. The museum also hands out the helpful *Walking Tour of the International District. (407 7th Ave. S ☎623-5124. Open Tu-F 11am-4:30pm, Sa-Su noon-4pm. $4, seniors and students $3, ages 5-12 $2. Free 1st Th of the month.)*

SEATTLE ASIAN ART MUSEUM. What do you do when you have too much good art to exhibit all at once? Open a second museum; which is just what SAM did, creating a wonderful stand-on-its-own attraction. The collection is particularly strong in Chinese art, but most of East Asia is admirably represented. *(In Volunteer Park, just beyond the water tower. ☎654-3100. Open Tu-Su 10am-5pm, Th 10am-9pm. Suggested donation $3, under 12 free; free with SAM ticket from the previous 7 days; SAAM ticket good for $3 discount at SAM.)*

UNIVERSITY OF WASHINGTON ARBORETUM. The Arboretum nurtures over 4000 species of trees, shrubs, and flowers, and maintains superb trails. Tours depart the **Graham Visitor Center,** at the southern end of the arboretum on Lake Washington Blvd. *(10 blocks east of Volunteer Park. Bus #11, 43, or 48 from downtown. ☎543-8800. Open daily sunrise to sunset, visitors center 10am-4pm. Free tours 1st Su of the month.)*

PUBLIC ART. Landmarks of the International District include the abstract Tsutakawa sculpture (corner of Maynard and Jackson), and the gigantic dragon mural and red-and-green pagoda in Hing Hay Park (S King and Maynard St.). Although you will not find many trees in the park, the pagoda provides a nice respite from the sun (or rain).

VOLUNTEER PARK. Although it is unsafe (and closed) at night, the park is a popular afternoon destination. The **outdoor stage** often hosts free performances on summer Sundays. Scale the **water tower** at the 14th Ave. entrance for a stunning 360° panorama of the city and the Olympic Range. The **glass conservatory** houses dazzling orchids. *(Between 11th and 15th Ave. at E Ward St., north of Broadway. Open daily in summer 10am-7pm; winter 10am-4pm; Free.)*

UNIVERSITY DISTRICT, FREMONT, & BALLARD

The northern districts of Seattle include neighborhoods that seem to be entirely at odds with each other, and yet somehow eek out a peaceful co-existence. The University district is a young and multi-cultural scene revolving around the main drag "The Ave." Fremont is a small community, busy with plans of secession from the nation. Scandinavians have concentrated in Ballard.

HENRY ART GALLERY. Specializing in modern and contemporary, the Henry reflects its curators' enthusiasm with unconventional installations and rarely-seen artists. In 2003, check out contemporary art from Mexico's past decade, including Frida Kahlo and Diego Rivera (Oct.-Jan.), and "Out of Site: Fictional Architectural Spaces" (Nov.-Feb.). *(Located at the intersection of 41st NE and 15th NE Ave. ☎616-9894; www.henryart.org. Open Tu-Su 11am-5pm, Th 11am-8pm. $6, seniors $4.50, all students free. Free Th after 5pm.)*

THOMAS BURKE MUSEUM OF NATURAL HISTORY & CULTURE. Savor the chance to see the only dinosaur bones on display in Washington and a superb collection on Pacific Rim cultures. You will enjoy kid-friendly explanations of the natural history of Washington's formation. Across the street, the astronomy department's old stone **observatory** is open to the public. *(45th St. NE and 17th Ave. NE. In the northwest corner of the U Washington campus. ☎543-5590; observatory ☎543-0126. www.washington.edu/burkemuseum. Open daily 10am-5pm and until 8pm on Th. $6.50, seniors and students $3, under 5 free. Special exhibits occasionally more.)*

FREMONT. This area is home to residents who pride themselves on their love of art and antiques, and the liberal atmosphere of their self-declared "center of the world" under Rte. 99. Twice in the past 10 years Fremont has applied to secede from the United States. A statue entitled **"Waiting for the Inner-City Urban"** laments the loss of the neighborhood's public transportation to downtown. The **immense troll** beneath the Aurora Bridge on 35th St. grasps a Volkswagen Bug with a confounded expression. Some say kicking the bug's tire brings good luck; others say it hurts the foot. A flamin' **Vladimir Lenin** resides at the corner of N 36th and N Fremont Pl.; this work from the former Soviet Union will be around until it's bought by a permanent collection, presumably of Soviet artwork.

NORDIC HERITAGE MUSEUM. Just east of the U District, the primarily Scandinavian neighborhood of **Ballard** offers a wide variety of Scandinavian eateries and shops along Market St. The museum presents realistic exhibits on the history of Nordic immigration and influence in the US. Stumble over cobblestones in old Copenhagen, or visit the slums of New York City that turned photographer and Danish immigrant Jacob Riis into an important social reformer. The museum hosts a **Viking festival** (☎789-5708) the weekend after the 4th of July and a series of **Nordic concerts** by national and international musicians throughout the year. *(3014 NW 67th St. Bus #17 from downtown or bus #44 from the U District, transferring to #17 at 24th and Market. ☎789-5707. Open Tu-Sa 10am-4pm, Su noon-4pm. $4, seniors and students $3, ages 6-18 $2.)*

ANNUAL EVENTS

Pick up a copy of the visitors center's *Calendar of Events*, published every season, for event coupons and an exact listing of innumerable area happenings. The first Thursday evening of each month, the art community sponsors **First Thursday,** a free and well-attended gallery walk. Watch for **street fairs** in the University District during mid- to late May, at Pike Place Market over Memorial Day weekend, and in Fremont in mid-June. The International District holds its annual two-day bash in mid-July, featuring arts and crafts booths, East Asian and Pacific food booths, and presentations by a range of groups from the Radical Women/Freedom Socialist Party to the Girl Scouts. For more info, call **Chinatown Discovery** (☎382-1197), or write P.O. Box 3406, Seattle 98114.

Puget Sound's yachting season begins in May. **Maritime Week,** during the third week of May, and the **Shilshole Boats Afloat Show** (☎634-0911), in August, give area boaters a chance to show off their crafts. Over the 4th of July weekend, the Center for Wooden Boats sponsors the free **Wooden Boat Show** (☎382-2628) on Lake Union. Blue blazers and deck shoes are *de rigeur*. Size up the entrants (over 100 wooden boats), then watch a demonstration of boat-building skills. The year-end blow-out is the **Quick and Daring Boatbuilding Contest,** when hopefuls try to build and sail wooden boats of their own design, using a limited kit of tools and materials. Plenty of music, food, and alcohol make the sailing smooth.

Opening Day (☎325-1000), 1st Sa in May. A celebration of spring, water, and boats. Highlight is the Montlake Cut parade of yachts and the Windermere Cup crew races. Free.

Northwest Folklife Festival (☎684-7300), on Memorial Day weekend. One of Seattle's most notable events, held at the Seattle Center. Dozens of booths, artists, musicians, and dancers celebrate the area's heritage. $5 suggested donation.

Bite of Seattle (☎232-2982), in mid-July. Bite size to full meals from free to $8. Decide for yourself what is the best of Seattle. Free.

Seattle Seafair (☎728-0123; www.seafair.com), spread over 4 weeks beginning in early July. The biggest, baddest festival of them all. Each neighborhood contributes with street fairs, parades large and small, balloon races, musical entertainment, and a seafood orgy. Major city wide torch run culminates the event.

Bumbershoot (☎281-7788; www.bumbershoot.org), over Labor Day weekend. A massive 4-day arts festival that caps off the summer, held in the Seattle Center. Attracts big-name rock bands, street musicians, and a young, exuberant crowd. 4 days $48-52; 2 days $28-34; 1 day $15-20. Tickets are cheaper if you buy them in advance. Additional tickets needed for certain big-name concerts or events. Prices subject to change.

ENTERTAINMENT

Seattle has one of the world's most famous underground music scenes and the third-largest theater community in the US (second to New York and Chicago), and supports performance in all sorts of venues, from bars to bakeries. The big performance houses regularly sell half-price tickets and alternative theaters offer high-quality drama at downright low prices. The free **Out to Lunch** series (☎623-0340) brings everything from reggae to folk dancing to downtown parks, squares, and office buildings during summer (June-Sept., M-F). The **Seattle Public Library** screens free films as part of the program and hosts daily poetry readings.

MUSIC & DANCE

The **Seattle Opera** performs favorites from August to May. In October 2003, the Opera House will re-open after renovations (until then all Opera House performances will be in the **Mercer Arts Arena**). Buffs should reserve well in advance, although rush tickets are sometimes available. (☎389-7676; www.seattleopera.com. Students and seniors can get half-price tickets 1½hr. before the performance. Open M-F 9am-5pm; tickets from $35.) The **Pacific Northwest Ballet** performs at the Opera House (Sept.-June). In 2003, look for the *Merry Widow* (Sept.-Oct.), *Russian Nights* (Jan.-Feb.), and *Sleeping Beauty* (May). (☎441-2424. Half-price rush tickets available to students and seniors 30min. before showtime. Tickets from $15.) The **Seattle Symphony** performs in the new Benaroya Hall, 200 University St. at 3rd Ave., from September to June. (☎212-4700, tickets 215-4747; www.seattlesymphony.org. Ticket office open M-F 10am-6pm, Sa 1-6pm. Tickets from $15, most from $25-39; seniors half-price; students (day of show) $10.) Even if you won't be hearing the symphony, drop by the new concert hall to take in Chihuly glass chandeliers and a Rauchenberg mural. (☎215-4895. Tours M-F noon and 1pm.) Free organ concerts bring out large crowds on the 1st Monday of the month at 12:30pm as well. The **University of Washington** offers its own program of student recitals and concerts by visiting artists. The **World Series** showcases dance, theater and chamber music (tickets $25-40). Some lectures and dances are much cheaper ($5-10). Contact the Meany Hall box office, 4001 University Way. Half-price student rush tickets are available half an hour before show at the box office. (☎543-4880. Open Oct.-May M-F 10am-6pm; summer M-F 10:30am-4:30pm.)

THEATER

The city hosts an exciting array of first-run plays and alternative works, particularly by talented amateur groups. Rush tickets are often available at nearly half price on the day of the show (cash only) from **Ticket/Ticket** (see p. 165).

The Empty Space Theatre, 3509 Fremont Ave. N (☎547-7500; www.emptyspace.org), 1½ blocks north of the Fremont Bridge. Comedies in the small space attract droves. Season runs Oct. to early July. Tickets $20-30. Under 25 $10 and previews (first 4 shows of a run) $22. Half-price tickets 30min. before curtain. Box office open on show days Tu-Su noon-5pm, Tu-F 12am-5pm non-show days.

Seattle Repertory Theater, 155 Mercer St. (☎443-2222; www.seattlerep.org), at the wonderful Bagley Wright Theater in the Seattle Center. Contemporary and classic winter productions (and Shakespeare). Tickets $15-45 (cheaper on weekdays), seniors $32, under 25 $10. Rush tickets 30min. before curtain $20. Box office open daily noon-8pm during season (Sept.-June).

A Contemporary Theater (ACT), 700 Union St. (☎292-7676). Summer season (April-Nov.) of off-beat premieres. $28-45. Under 25 $10. Office open Tu-Su noon-7pm.

Annex Theatre (☎728-0933). A rogue theater group without a regular space—call their number to find out where they are performing. Refreshing emphasis on company-generated material and unconventional theater. Pay-what-you-can previews. Tickets $10-12. Shows usually Th-Sa at 8pm and Su at 7pm.

Northwest Asian American Theater, 409 7th Ave. S (☎340-1445), in the International District next to the Wing Luke Asian Museum. Excellent new theater with pieces by Asian Americans. Year-long season. Tickets $15, students $12. Open M-F 10am-6pm.

CINEMA

Seattle is a cinematic paradise. Most of the theaters that screen non-Hollywood films are on Capitol Hill and in the University District. Large, first-run theaters are everywhere, including the 16-screen **Loews Cineplex Meridian** (☎223-9600) at 7th Ave. and Pike. **Seven Gables,** a local company, has recently bought up the Egyptian, the Metro, the Neptune, and 25 other theaters. $28 buys admission to any five films at any of their theaters. Call ☎443-4567 (movie phone) for local movie times and locations. On summer Saturdays, **outdoor cinema** in Fremont begins at dusk at 670 N 34th St., in the U-Park lot by the bridge, behind the Red Door Alehouse. Enter as early as 7pm to catch live music that starts at 8pm. **TCI Outdoor Cinema** shows everything from classics to cartoons for free at the Gasworks Park. (☎694-7000. Live music 7pm-dusk.) Aspiring independent filmmakers or actors/actresses should check out the Alibi Room for readings (see **Nightlife,** below).

The Egyptian, 801 E Pine St. (☎323-4978), at Harvard Ave. on Capitol Hill. This Art Deco art-house is best known for hosting the **Seattle International Film Festival** in the last week of May and 1st week of June. The festival's director retrospective features a personal appearance by said director. Festival series tickets available at a discount. $8.25, seniors $5.25.

The Harvard Exit, 807 E Roy St. (☎323-8986), on Capitol Hill, near the north end of the Broadway business district. Quality classic and foreign films. Converted women's club that has its own ghost and an enormous antique projector. $8.25, students and seniors $5.25. Cash only.

Seven Gables Theater, 911 NE 50th St. (☎632-8820), in the U District just off Roosevelt, a short walk west from University Way. Another art-house cinema in an old house showing art, independent, and international films. Entrance is shaded by trees. $8.25, 1st show of the day $5.25, seniors $5.25. Cash only.

Grand Illusion Cinema, 1403 NE 50th St. (☎523-3935), in the U District at University Way. Plays world cinema flicks and exciting international films. Frequently revives old classics and hard-to-find films. One of the last independent theaters in Seattle. $7, seniors and children $5, matinees $4.50.

Little Theatre, 608 19th Ave. (☎675-2055), at Mercer St. on Capitol Hill. A non-profit theater showing documentaries and independent films. $7, seniors and children $5, matinees $4.50.

SPORTS

Seattleites cheered recently when the home team, the **Mariners,** moved out of the Kingdome, where in 1995 sections of the roof fell into the stands. The "M's" are now playing baseball in the half-billion dollar, hangar-like **Safeco Field,** at 1st Ave. S and Royal Brougham Way S, under an enormous retractable roof. Saving the game from frequent rain-outs is simply a matter of pushing a single button labelled "Go" and costs a mere $1.50 in electricity. (Tickets ☎622-4487; www.ticketmaster.com. From $10.) Seattle's football team, the **Seahawks**, are perennial NFC Western Division contenders whose new stadium is one of the most modern in the world. (Tickets ☎628-0888. From $10.)

On the other side of town and at the other end of the aesthetic spectrum, the sleek **Key Arena** in the Seattle Center hosts Seattle's NBA basketball team, the **Supersonics** (☎628-0888). The men now share their turf with their female counterparts: the WNBA expansion team, the **Seattle Storm** (☎628-0888; www.storm.wnba.com). The **University of Washington Huskies** football team has contended in the PAC-10 for years and doesn't plan to let up. Call the Athletic Ticket Office (☎543-2200) for Huskies schedules and prices.

WASHINGTON

NIGHTLIFE

Seattle has moved beyond beer to a new nightlife frontier: the cafe-bar. The popularity of espresso bars in Seattle might lead one to conclude that caffeine is more intoxicating than alcohol, but often an establishment that poses as a diner by day brings on a band, breaks out the disco ball, and pumps out the microbrews by night. Many locals tell tourists that the best spot to go for guaranteed good beer, live music, and big crowds is Pioneer Square, where UW students from frat row dominate the bar stools. You may prefer to go to Capitol Hill, or up Rte. 99 to Fremont, where the atmosphere is usually more laid-back than in the Square. Wherever you go, but especially downtown, do stay alert—Seattle is big city, and has the homelessness, crime, and dark alleys that come with size.

DOWNTOWN

The Alibi Room, 85 Pike St. (☎623-3180), across from the Market Cinema, in the Post Alley in Pike Place. A remarkably friendly local indie filmmaker hangout. Bar with music open 7 nights. A downstairs dance floor open F and Sa. Brunch Sa and Su. No cover. Open daily 11am-3pm and 5pm-2am.

Crocodile Cafe, 2200 2nd Ave. (☎448-2114; www.thecrocodile.com), at Blanchard in Belltown. Cooks from scratch by day, and features live music by night (Tu-Sa). Shows usually start 9pm; some require advance ticket purchase. 21+ after 9pm. Cover $6-22. Open Tu-F 11am-11pm, Sa 8am-11pm, Su 9am-3pm.

PIONEER SQUARE

Pioneer Square provides a happening scene, dominated by twentysomethings, frat kids, and cover bands. Most of the area bars participate in a joint cover (F-Sa $10, Su-Th $5) that will let you wander from bar to bar to sample the bands. The larger venues are listed below. Two smaller venues, **Larry's,** 209 1st Ave. S (☎624-7665) and **New Orleans,** 114 1st Ave. S (☎622-2563) feature great blues and jazz nightly (no cover weekdays). Not part of the Pioneer Square joint cover because it's often free, **J and M Cafe and Cardroom,** 201 1st Ave. (☎292-0663) is in the center of Pioneer Square, often blasting rock and blues (Th, no cover) or disco and top 40 (W, $6).

Bohemian Cafe, 111 Yesler Way (☎447-1514), pumps reggae every night. 3 sections—a cafe, a bar, and a stage—are all adorned with art from Jamaica. Live shows 6 nights per week, often national acts on weekends. Happy Hour 4-7pm. Occasional cover. Open M-Th and Sa 4pm-2am, F 3pm-2am.

Central Tavern, 207 1st Ave. S. (☎622-0209), One of the early venues for grunge has now become a favorite for bikers. Live rock 6 nights a week at 9:30pm. Tu open mic. Part of the joint cover. Open daily 11:30am-2am, kitchen closes 8ish.

Last Supper Club, 124 S. Washington St. (☎748-9975), at Occidental. 2 dance floors, DJed with everything from 70s disco (F) to funky house, drum & bass, and trance (Su). Cover varies. Open W-Su 5pm-2am.

Swannie's Sports Bar, 222 S Main St. (☎622-9353). Share drink specials with pro ballplayers who stop by post-game. Any Seattle sports junkie will swear this is the place to be. Drink specials change daily. Open M-Su 11:30am-2am.

CAPITOL HILL

East off of Broadway, Pine St. is cool lounge after cool lounge. Find your atmosphere and acclimatize. West off of Broadway, Pike St. has the clubs that push the limits (gay, punk, industrial, fetish, dance) and break the sound barrier.

Linda's Tavern, 707 Pine St. E (☎325-1220). A very chill post-gig scene for Seattle rockers. On Tu night a live DJ plays jazz and old rock. W is movie night. Expanded menu, liquor, and breakfast on weekends. No cover. Open daily 4pm-2am.

Neighbors, 1509 Broadway (☎324-5358; www.neighboursonline.com). Enter from the alley on Pike. A gay dance club for 20 years, Neighbors prides itself on techno slickness. Open 7 nights a week; frequent drag nights and special events.

Elysian Brewing Co., 1211 E Pike St. (860-1920), serves microbrews to a young crowd. "The Immortal" Indian Pale Ale and Dragon's Tooth Oatmeal Stout are two favorites. Try the gourmet bar food (Ahi taco $8.95). Open M-Sa 11am-2am, Su noon-midnight.

WATERWAYS & PARKS

Thanks to the foresight of Seattle's early community and the architectural genius of the Olmsted family, Seattle enjoys a string of parks and waterways.

LAKE UNION. Sailboats fill Lake Union, situated between Capitol Hill and the University District, and the **Center for Wooden Boats** can supply boats, with a moored flotilla of new and restored craft for rent. (*1010 Valley St. ☎382-2628; www.cwb.org. Open daily 11am-7pm. Rowboats from $23, sailboats from $16.*) **Gasworks Park,** at the north end of Lake Union, fills the grounds of a retired oil-refining facility, necessitating frequent EPA checks. Fittingly, the park hosts a **4th of July Fireworks show,** and is a celebrated kite-flying spot. *(Take bus #26 from downtown to N 35th St. and Wallingford Ave. N.)* **Gasworks Kite Shop** provides the high-flying vehicles. *(3420 Stone Way ☎633-4780. Open M-F 10am-6pm, Sa 10am-5pm, Su 11am-5pm.)* **Urban Surf** rents surfboards, in-line skates, snowboards and kiteboards. *(2100 N Northlake Way, opposite park entrance. ☎545-9463. Boards $15 per day. Skates $5 per hr., $16 per day. Open M-F 10am-7pm, Sa 10am-5pm, Su 11am-5pm.)*

WOODLAND PARK & WOODLAND ZOO. Woodland Park is mediocre, but the zoo has won a bevy of AZA awards (the zoo Oscars, if you will) for best new exhibits. The African Savanna and the Northern Trail exhibits are both full of zoo favorites: grizzlies, wolves, lions, sasquatch, giraffes, and zebras. *(5500 Phinney Ave. N I-5 50th St. exit or N 50th St. Bus #5 from downtown. ☎684-4800. Park open daily 4:30am-11:30pm. Zoo open May to mid-Sept. daily 9:30am-6pm; mid-March to April and mid-Sept. to mid-Oct. 9:30am-5pm; winter 9:30am-4pm. $9.50, seniors $8.75, ages 6-17 $6.50.)*

DISCOVERY PARK. Across the canals and west of the locks lie the 534 bucolic acres of Discovery Park, at 36th Ave. W and W Government Way, on a lonely point west of the Magnolia District and south of Golden Gardens Park. Grassy fields and steep, eroding bluffs, while dangerous for hikers, provide a haven for birds forced over Puget Sound by bad weather around the Olympic Mountains. A **visitors center** is right by the entrance. A popular beach and lighthouse are also open for exploration, but only via free **shuttle.** The **Daybreak Star Indian Cultural Center** at the park's north end is operated by the United Indians of All Tribes Foundation as a social, cultural, and educational center. *(Discovery Park: ☎386-4236. Open daily 6am-11pm. Visitor Center: 3801 W Government Way. Bus #24 or 33. Open Tu-Su 8:30am-5pm. Beach: open June-Sept. Sa-Su 11:45-4:30pm. Donation requested. Cultural Center: ☎285-4425. Open M-F 9am-5pm, Sa 10am-noon, Su noon-5pm. Free.)*

WASHINGTON

OUTDOOR ACTIVITIES

BIKING. Seattle has more bike-commuters than any other American city. The city prides itself on 30 mi. of bike-pedestrian trails, 90 mi. of signed bike routes, and 16 mi. of bike lanes on city streets. Over 1000 **cyclists** compete in the 190 mi. **Seattle to Portland Race** in mid-July. Call the **bike hotline** (☎522-2453) for info. On five **Bicycle Sundays** from May to September, Lake Washington Blvd. is open exclusively to cyclists from 10am to 6pm. Call the **Citywide Sports Office** (☎684-7092) for info. The **Burke-Gilman Trail** makes for a longer ride. It runs from the University District along Montlake Blvd., then along Lake Union and all the way west to Chittenden Locks and Discovery Park. Runners also enjoy the Burke-Gilman.

HIKING. 4167 ft. **Mt. Si** is the most climbed mountain in the state of Washington, and with good reason. Just an hour from downtown Seattle, hikers can reach a **lookout** that showcases Mt. Rainier, the Olympic Mountains, and Seattle in just a few hours (1 mi. one-way). A 4hr. hike (4 mi. one-way) brings you to **Haystack Basin,** the false summit. Don't try climbing higher unless you have rock-climbing gear, though. To get to Mt. Si, take I-90 East to SE Mt. Si Rd. (2 mi. from Middle Fork). Cross the Snoqualmie River Bridge to the trailhead parking lot. **Tiger Mountain** is another great day-hike near Seattle. A 4hr. hike (5½ mi. round-trip) leads to the summit of West Tiger Mountain (2522 ft.). Take I-90 to Tiger Mountain State Forest. From the Tradition Plateau trailhead, walk to Bus Road-Trail and then to West Tiger Trail. If you parked outside the gated lot, stay for sunset! For additional information, check out *55 Hikes around Snoqualmie Pass*, by Harvey Manning.

DROP THE PACK. After a few months backpacking it's no surprise that your shoulders start bruising like unrefrigerated steaks. Fortunately, there is a cure: sea kayaks. Kayaking is the perfect way to explore the nooks of Washington's labyrinthine Puget Sound, and rental boats are readily available. A truly unique resource is the Cascadia Marine Trail, a network of seaside campsites and launching spots maintained specifically for paddlers and sailors. The trail stretches from the San Juans south to Olympia, has over 40 places to pitch a tent along the way, and has been recognized as one of 16 Millennium Trails in the country. Routes in the south of the Sound tend to be shorter and more protected, perfect for beginner and intermediate boaters. Paddling in the north sound can be dangerous due to ship traffic and fast tides, so be sure you know your stuff before biting this off. Companies that rent often offer moderately-priced guided trips for anywhere from half-day to multi-day excursions. Fees for camping vary site to site (free-$10). For information and help planning a trip contact the Washington Water Trails Association, 4649 Sunnyside Ave. N, Room 305 Seattle, WA 98103 (☎545-9161; www.wwta.org).

WHITEWATER RAFTING. Although the rapids are hours away by car, over 50 **whitewater rafting** outfitters are based in Seattle and are often willing to undercut one another with merciless abandon. **Washington State Outfitters and Guides Association** (☎877-275-4964) provides advice; although their office is closed in summer, they do return phone calls and send out info. The **Northwest Outdoor Center,** 2100 Westlake Ave., on Lake Union, gives $50-70 instructional programs in whitewater and sea kayaking. (☎281-9694. Kayak rentals $10-15 per hr. Weekdays 3rd and 4th hours are free. Make reservations. Open M-F 10am-8pm, Sa-Su 9am-6pm.)

DAYTRIPS

EAST SOUND. Seattleites leave the city en masse to play in this bikers', picnickers', and suburbanites' paradise rolled into one. Entirely unnecessary Range Rovers and outdoor shopping plazas litter the landscape. Companies buy up expanses of East Sound land, smother them in sod and office complexes, and call them "campuses"—witness **Microsoft,** which has nearly subsumed the suburb of Redmond. Rapid growth has had its benefits, though. The wealthy and beautiful suburb of **Bellevue** is home to Bill Gates, among others. The small but interesting **Bellevue Art Museum** stands strong in a new building surrounded by malls and parking lots. The museum focuses mainly on contemporary art, and makes a good destination for a rainy day. *(510 Bellevue Way NE. In central Bellevue just south of NE 8th St., west of I-405. ☎425-519-0770. Open Tu, W, F, Sa 10am-5pm, Th 10am-8pm, Su noon-5pm. $6, students and seniors $4; free first Th and last Sa of every month.)* The July **Bellevue Jazz Festival** attracts both local cats and national acts. *(Cross Lake Washington on one of 2 floating bridges to arrive in East Sound.)*

JIMI HENDRIX'S GRAVE. Rock pilgrims trek out to the grave of Seattle's first rock legend, **Jimi Hendrix,** to pay homage to the greatest guitarist who ever lived. Jimi's grave is in Greenwood Cemetery, in the town of Renton. Plan on spending some time driving down labyrinthine streets. Once you find the cemetery, look for the grave toward the back, just in front of the sun dial. *(Bus #101 from downtown to the Renton Park 'n' Ride, then switch to #105 to Greenwood Cemetery. Drivers take the Sunset Blvd. exit from Rte. 405—follow Sunset Blvd., not Park—turn right onto Branson, and right again on NE 4th. The Cemetery is on a hill, just next to a McDonalds.)*

LAKE SAMMAMISH STATE PARK & FURTHER EAST. The exits along I-90 east of the city contain several hidden treats. Swim, water-ski, and play volleyball to your heart's content within **Lake Sammamish State Park,** a weekend hot spot on the eastern shores of the lake. *(Take I-90 east to Exit 15, and follow the very large brown signs.)*

Just outside of **Snoqualmie,** 29 mi. east of Seattle, is the astounding **Snoqualmie Falls.** Formerly a sacred place for the Salish, the 270 ft. wall of water has generated electricity for Puget Power since 1898. Five generators buried under the falls work hard to provide energy for 1600 homes. It is particularly spectacular in spring, when the falls are swollen with melt-off. *(Take the Snoqualmie Parkway exit from I-90.)*

As I-90 leaves the sound, the road rises into mountains that offer some fantastic **dayhikes.** You can really take your pick—for information, contact the **Issaquah Chamber of Commerce** (☎425-392-7024), at 155 NW Gilman in downtown Issaquah, just past the State Park. They sell maps ($5-6) and can help set you up with a route.

BOEING. The Seattle area is surrounded by the vast factories of **Boeing,** the city's most prominent employer and site of the largest covered structure in North America. Boeing offers **public tours** of the facilities in Everett, about 15min. north of the city, where 747s, 767s, and 777s are made. Just seeing how such large pieces are moved and assembled makes the tour worth it. Arrive early because the limited tickets often run out in the summer. The tour includes a theater show and a short walk through the facilities. *(Take I-5 north to exit 189 and then go west on 526. Signs are clear. ☎800-464-1476; www.boeing.com. Tours 9, 10, 11am, 1, 2, and 3pm. $5, seniors or under 16 $3. Tours M-F 9am-3pm. Ticket reservations $10, cash only.)*

WASHINGTON

MUSEUM OF FLIGHT. South of Seattle at Boeing Field is the **Museum of Flight.** The huge structure enshrines flying machines, from canvas biplanes to chic fighter jets, under a 3-story roof. Tour Eisenhower's old Air Force One, or fly in a nauseatingly realistic flight simulator and explore the red barn where William E. Boeing founded the company in 1916. Photographs and artifacts trace the history of flight from its beginnings through the 30s. *(9404 E Marginal Way S. Take I-5 south to Exit 158 and turn north onto E Marginal Way S and follow for ½ mi. Bus #174. ☎206-764-5700. Open M-Su 10am-5pm, 1st Th of month, 10am-9pm. Free tours of the museum every 30min., 10am-3:30pm. $9.50, seniors $8.50, ages 5-17 $5, under 5 free. Free after 5pm on 1st Th of the month.)*

BREMERTON. Nosing into Puget Sound between the Olympic Peninsula and Seattle, the Kitsap Peninsula's deep inlets seemed a natural spot in which to park a fleet of nuclear-powered submarines. The instant you set foot in **Bremerton,** the hub of the peninsula, you see that is exactly what happened. *(Washington State Ferries ☎206-464-6400 or 800-843-3779; www.wsdot.wa.gov/ferries. 2 boats run between downtown Seattle and Bremerton. A regular ferry runs daily (1hr.; $5.10, car and driver $11.25). Passenger only ferry runs M-F (40min.; $6.10; departs Pier 50). Bremerton Area Chamber of Commerce, 301 Pacific Ave. ☎360-479-3579; www.bremertonchamber.org. Open M-F 9am-4pm; booth at ferry dock open on weekends.)*

BREMERTON NAVAL MUSEUM & USS TURNER JOY. The museum, replete with WWII photos, 10 ft. models of ships, and a 14th-century wicker basket from Korea believed to be the world's oldest existing cannon, is sure to please any Navy buff. *(☎360-479-7447. Open M-Sa 10am-5pm, Su 1-5pm. Donations appreciated.)*

Behind the museum, explore the destroyer **USS Turner Joy,** the ship that fired the first American shots of the Vietnam War. It is managed by the Bremerton Historic Ships Association. For a closer view of the retired ships that fill Bremerton harbor, join the **Navy Ship Tour** at the *Turner Joy* and scoot along mothballed submarines and aircraft carriers. Tours leave from the Ship's Store in Port Orchard, across the harbor, but stop in Bremerton before heading to the boats. *(USS Turner Joy: ☎360-792-2457. Self-guided tours $7, seniors $6, children $5, military in uniform free; buy tickets at Turner Joy gift shop. Navy Ship Tour: ☎360-792-2457. Open June-Aug. daily; May and Sept. Sa and Su only. Tours last 45min. $9, seniors $8, children $6.)*

DAYTRIP FROM SEATTLE: TACOMA

Tacoma, founded as a sawmill town in the 1860s, was called "The City of Destiny" when it was designated the western terminus of the first railroad to reach the Northwest. In the 20th century, however, Seattle became the industrial and cultural hub of the region. Recently, however, Tacoma has emerged from Seattle's shadow. In July 2002, Tacoma opened the Museum of Glass to showcase the city's native and internationally renowned glassblower, Dale Chihuly. The Museum of Glass is linked to the Washington State History Museum and the Tacoma Art Museum by the awesome Chihuly Bridge of Glass across I-705.

Tacoma is Washington's third largest city and lies on **I-5,** 32 mi. (30min.) south of Seattle and 28 mi. (30min.) northeast of Olympia. Take Exit 132 from I-5 and follow the signs to the city center. There are several public transportation options for getting to Tacoma; **SoundTransit** runs two of these. The **Sounder** is a commuter train that runs from Tacoma in the morning, and from Seattle in the evening (1hr.; $4). Pick up a schedule booklet from Union Station in Seattle. Both SoundTransit options arrive at the Puyallup Ave. Station in Tacoma, which is shared with **Greyhound.** (510 Puyallup Ave. ☎383-4621. Open daily 8am-9pm.) They also run buses to **Portland** (8 per day, $21.25) and **Seattle** (8 per day, $5). Point Defiance is Tacoma's ferry terminal. Get the skinny on Tacoma at the **Visitor Information Center,** 1119 Pacific Ave., 5th floor (☎253-627-2846 or 800-272-2662; open M-F 9am-5pm), or from the desk in the back of the Washington State Museum gift shop (see **Sights,** below; open M-Sa 10am-4pm, Su noon-5pm). The superb *Pierce County Bicycle Guide Map* shows bike routes and lists trails near Mt. Rainier. Tacomans are bicycle enthusiasts.

MUSEUM OF GLASS. In 2002, the much anticipated, $63-million Museum of Glass and International Center for Contemporary Art opened its doors to visitors. The highlight inside is the "hot shop," an amphitheater and glassblowing studio where visitors can watch art-in-action. The outdoor draw is the 500 ft. long Chihuly Bridge of Glass. The bridge displays 1700 works by renowned glass artist Dale Chihuly. *(1801 E. Dock St. ☎866-468-7386, www.museumofglass.org. Open Tu-W and F-Sa 10am-5pm, Th 10am-8pm, and Su noon-5pm. $8, seniors and students $6, children $3. Free every 3rd Th 5pm-8pm.)*

WASHINGTON STATE HISTORY MUSEUM. The shiny $40-million museum houses interactive, stereophonic exhibits on Washington's history through the 1800s. A sprawling model train on the 5th floor is a highlight for children, railroad buffs, and child railroad buffs. *(1911 Pacific Ave. ☎888-238-4373; www.wshs.org. Open Tu, W, F 10am-4pm, Th 10am-8pm (free 4-8pm), Sa 10am-5pm, Su noon-5pm. $7, seniors $6.50, students $5, children under 5 free.)*

POINT DEFIANCE PARK. The 698-acre park is a wonderful place to pass time on a warm day, but it's a secret everyone knows about. Besides being a spot to relax, the park is excellent for other more active and visual pursuits. A 5 mi. driving and walking loop passes all the park's attractions, offering postcard views of Puget Sound and access to miles of woodland trails. In spring, the park is bejeweled with flowers; a rhododendron garden lies nestled in the woods along the loop.

Owen Beach looks across at Vashon Island and is a good starting place for a ramble down the shore. The park's prize possession is the **Point Defiance Zoo and Aquarium.** The zoo boasts more than 5000 animals, including penguins, puffins, polar bears, beluga whales, and sharks. The meticulously restored **Fort Nisqually** was built by the British Hudson Bay Company in 1832 as they expanded their trade in beaver pelts. The series of 19th-century cabins contains museum-like exhibits of the lives of children, laborers, and natives. *(Park: take Rte. 16 to 6th Ave., go east on 6th Ave., then head north on Pearl St. ☎305-1000. Open daily from dawn until 30min. after dusk. Zoo: 5400 N Pearl St. ☎404-3678 or 591-5337; www.pdza.org. Open Jan.-Mar. 9:30am-4pm, Apr. 9:30am-5pm, May-Sept. 9:30am-7pm, Oct.-Dec. 9:30am-4pm. $7.75, seniors $7, youth $6, students $4. Fort: ☎591-5339. Open daily June-Aug. 11am-6pm; Sept.-Apr. W-Su 11am-4pm. $3, seniors $2, ages 5-12 $1.)*

PUGET SOUND

Stretching from Admiralty Inlet to Whidbey Island, this unusually deep body of water runs a full 100 mi. up to the Straits of Juan de Fuca and Georgia. The Sound was originally discovered by George Vancouver, who generously decided that an island was good enough for him and granted the naming rights to his second lieutenant Peter Puget. Sharing the seas with the shipping trade and frequenting the harbors of Seattle, Tacoma, Everett, and Port Townsend, modern US Navy submarines and battleships are now based in Bremerton. The Alaska Marine Highway also ends its voyage here in the Sound.

OLYMPIA ☎360

Inside Olympia's seemingly interminable network of suburbs, there lies a festive downtown area known for its art, antiques, liberalism, and of course, irresistible microbrews. Evergreen State College lies a few miles from the city center, and its highly-pierced, tree-hugging student body spills into the mix in a kind of chemistry experiment that gets progressively weirder when politicians join in. Named Olympia because of its superb view of the Olympic mountains, the city is also a logical launching pad into Olympic National Park.

TRANSPORTATION

Settled at the junction of **I-5** and **US 101** between **Tumwater** (to the south, I-5 Exit 102) and **Lacey** (to the east, I-5 Exit 108), Olympia makes a convenient stop on any north-south journey. I-5 Exit 105 leads to the **Capitol Campus** and **downtown** Olympia. **Capitol Way** divides the city's East and West downtown streets. The west side of downtown borders freshwater **Capitol Lake** and salty **West Bay,** also known as **Budd Bay.** The **4th Ave.** bridge divides the two bodies of water and leads to the city's fast-food-chain-infested section. Navigating Olympia's one-way streets on **bike** or **foot** is easy, and all public buses have bike racks.

Trains: Amtrak, 6600 Yelm Hwy. (☎923-4602 or 800-872-7245). In neighboring Lacey (I-5 Exit 108), but bus #64 runs between downtown and the station. Open daily 8:15am-noon, 1:45-3:30pm, 5:30-8:30pm. To **Portland** (2½hr., 4 per day, $22-27) and **Seattle** (1¾hr., 4 per day, $13-18).

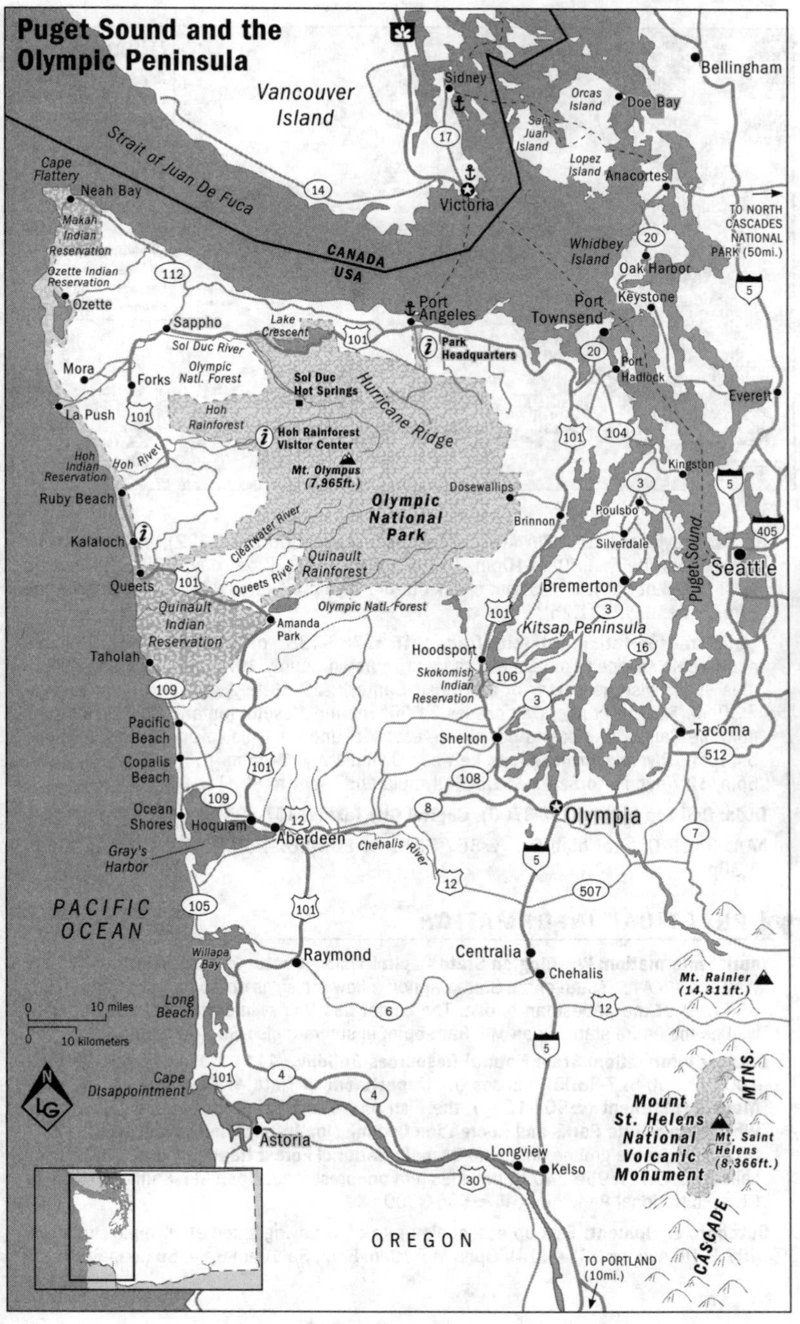
Puget Sound and the Olympic Peninsula
Vancouver Island
Strait of Juan De Fuca
Cape Flattery
Neah Bay
Makah Indian Reservation
Ozette Indian Reservation
Ozette
Sappho
Lake Crescent
Port Angeles
Park Headquarters
Sol Duc River
Olympic Natl. Forest
Mora
Forks
La Push
Hoh Rainforest
Sol Duc Hot Springs
Hurricane Ridge
Hoh Rainforest Visitor Center
Mt. Olympus (7,965ft.)
Hoh Indian Reservation
Hoh River
Ruby Beach
Kalaloch
Queets
Clearwater River
Olympic National Park
Quinault Rainforest
Queets River
Olympic Natl. Forest
Quinault Indian Reservation
Amanda Park
Taholah
Pacific Beach
Copalis Beach
Ocean Shores
Hoquiam
Aberdeen
Gray's Harbor
Chehalis River
PACIFIC OCEAN
Willapa Bay
Raymond
Long Beach
Cape Disappointment
Astoria
OREGON
Sidney
Victoria
CANADA
USA
Orcas Island
Doe Bay
San Juan Island
Lopez Island
Anacortes
Bellingham
TO NORTH CASCADES NATIONAL PARK (50mi.)
Whidbey Island
Oak Harbor
Keystone
Port Townsend
Port Hadlock
Everett
Kingston
Dosewallips
Brinnon
Poulsbo
Silverdale
Puget Sound
Seattle
Bremerton
Kitsap Peninsula
Hoodsport
Skokomish Indian Reservation
Shelton
Tacoma
Olympia
Centralia
Chehalis
Mt. Rainier (14,311ft.)
Longview
Kelso
Mount St. Helens National Volcanic Monument
Mt. Saint Helens (8,366ft.)
CASCADE MTNS.
TO PORTLAND (10mi.)
0 10 miles
0 10 kilometers
LG

WASHINGTON

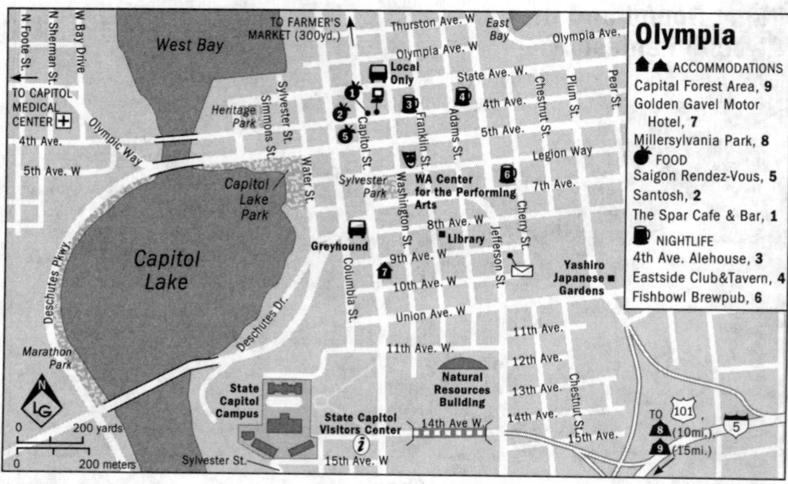

Buses: Greyhound, 107 7th Ave. SE (☎357-5541 or 800-231-2222), at Capitol Way. Office open daily 8:30am-10pm. To **Portland** (2¾hr., 7 per day, $22.50); **Seattle** (1¾hr., 4-6 per day, $7.25; but check out the **Olympia Express,** below); and **Spokane** (9hr., 3 per day, $31.25).

Public Transportation: Intercity Transit (IT; ☎786-1881 or 800-287-6348). Reliable and flexible service to almost anywhere in Thurston County, even with a bicycle. Schedules at the visitors center or at Transit Center, 222 State Ave. Open M-F 7:30am-5:30pm. $0.75 per ride. Day passes $1.50. The most useful route is #42, which runs from the Capitol Campus to downtown, eastside, and westside (every 15min., 6:45am-5:45pm). **Olympia Express** runs between Olympia and **Tacoma** (55min., M-F 5:50am-6pm, $2; Tacoma to Seattle $1.50; Olympia and Lacey to Sea-Tac $2).

Taxis: Red Top Taxi (☎357-3700). **Capitol City Taxi** (☎357-4949).

AAA: 2415 Capitol Mall Dr. (☎357-5561 or 800-562-2582). Open M-F 8:30am-5:30pm.

PRACTICAL INFORMATION

Tourist Information: Washington State Capitol Visitor Center (☎586-3460), on Capitol Way at 14th Ave., south of the State Capitol; follow the signs on I-5, or from Capitol Way turn west at the pedestrian bridge. The center has tourist information for Olympia as well as the entire state. Open M-F 8am-5pm; in summer also Sa-Su 10am-3pm.

Outdoor Information: State Natural Resources Building, 1111 Washington St. (☎902-1000 or 800-527-3305), houses the **Department of Natural Resources (DNR)**. The **Maps Department** (☎902-1234), the **Fish and Game Office** (☎902-2200), and the **Washington State Parks and Recreation Commission Information Center** (☎800-233-0321) are on the ground floor. **The Olympic National Forest Headquarters,** 1835 Black Lake Blvd. SW (☎956-2400), provides info on forest land. Open M-F 8am-4:30pm. For Olympic National Park info, call ☎565-3000.

Outdoors Equipment: Pick up essentials or go on a buying spree at Olympic Outfitters, 407 E 4th Ave. (☎943-1114). Open M-F 10am-8pm, Sa 10am-6pm, Su noon-5pm.

WASHINGTON

Laundromat: Westside Laundry, 2103 Harrison Ave. NW (☎943-3857), in a strip mall on the west side of town. Wash $1.75, dry $0.25 per 7min. Open daily 9am-10pm.

Emergency: ☎911.

Police: 900 Plum St. SE (8am-5pm ☎753-8300; 5pm-8am ☎704-2740), at 8th Ave.

Crisis Line: ☎586-2800. 24hr.

Women's Services: Safeplace ☎754-6300 or 800-364-1776.

Hospital: Providence St. Peter Hospital, 413 Lilly Rd. NE (☎491-9480). Follow signs northbound on I-5, Exit 107; southbound Exit 109. Emergency 24hr.

Internet Access: Olympia Timberland Library, 313 8th Ave. SE (☎352-0595), at Franklin St. Up to 1hr. free Internet access. Open M-Tu 10am-9pm, W-Th 11am-9pm, F-Sa 10am-5pm, Su 1pm-5pm. **Olympia World News**, 116 E 4th Ave. (☎570-9536), off Washington St. $3 per hr. Open M-Sa 11am-11pm, Su 11am-9pm.

Post Office: 900 Jefferson SE (☎357-2289). Open M-F 7:30am-6pm, Sa 9am-4pm. **Postal Code:** 98501

ACCOMMODATIONS & CAMPING

Olympia motels cater to policy-makers ($60-80), but options in Tumwater are more affordable. Try **Motel 6 ❸,** 400 W Lee St. (☎754-7320. Singles $40; doubles $45.) For free camping, head to the **Capital Forest Multiple Use Area**.

The Golden Gavel Motor Hotel, 909 Capitol Way (☎352-8533). A few blocks north of the Capitol building. Clean, spacious, 70s-style rooms are a siren call for travelers not on the corporate account. Singles $46; doubles $54. AAA/senior discount $2. ❸

Millersylvania State Park, 12245 Tilly Rd. S (☎753-1519; reservations 888-226-7688), 10 mi. south of Olympia. Take Exit 95 off I-5 N or S, turn onto Rte. 121 N, then take a left at the stop sign. A few secluded sites, most in the back of the park. Some kitchens available. 20-day max. stay. Wheelchair accessible. 168 sites. $15; RV sites $21; sites for bicyclists $6. Showers $0.25 per 3min. ❶

Capital Forest Multiple Use Area, 15 mi. southwest of Olympia. Take Exit 95 off I-5. Grab a forest map at the state DNR office (see **Practical Information,** above). 90 campsites spread among 7 campgrounds, administered by the DNR. All sites have bathrooms and water. Free. No showers. ❶

FOOD

Diners, veggie eateries, and Asian quick-stops line bohemian 4th Ave. east of Columbia. Get slightly upscale groceries at the 24hr. **Safeway,** 520 Cleveland Ave. (☎943-1830), off Capital Blvd. in Tumwater, a quarter-mile south of the Capitol building. The **Olympia Farmer's Market,** 700 N Capitol Way, is a great place to stroll, people-watch, and grab cheap eats from small vendors. (☎352-9096. Open Apr.-Oct. Th-Su 10am-3pm; Nov.-Dec. Sa-Su 10am-3pm.)

The Spar Cafe & Bar, 114 E 4th Ave. (☎357-6444), has been a hot spot for beer, burgers ($7), and cigars for decades. A national historic monument and still operating to the tunes of live jazz every Sa night (8pm-midnight). Cafe open M-Th 6am-9pm, F-Sa 6am-11pm, Su 6am-8pm. Bar open M-Th 11am-midnight, F-Sa 11am-2am. ❷

Saigon Rendez-Vous, 117 W 5th Ave. (☎352-1989). The queen of Olympia's many Vietnamese restaurants with a huge vegetarian menu (but meat eaters will be able to find a tasty meal here, too). Entrees $5-8. Open M-Sa 10:30am-10:30pm, Su noon-9pm. ❶

Santosh, 116 W 4th Ave. (☎943-3442), west of Capitol Way. All-you-can-eat Indian lunch buffet $6.95. Regular dishes $8-12. Open Su-F 11.30am-2:30pm, 5-9:30pm, Sa 11am-2:30pm and 5-10pm. ❷

NIGHTLIFE

Olympia's nightlife seems to have outgrown its daylife. Labels like K Records and Kill Rock Stars, with their flagship band Bikini Kill, have made Olympia a crucial pitstop on the indie rock circuit. *The Rocket* and the city's daily *Olympian* list shows.

Fishbowl Brewpub & Cafe, 515 Jefferson St. SE (☎943-3650), 2 blocks south off 4th. With fish painted on outside walls and an indoor aquarium, this brewpub captures Olympia's love for the sea, art, and beer. The British ales ($3.25) are named after fish. Kitchen, open daily until 11pm, offers sandwiches and pasta ($3.50-7). Occasional live music. Open M-Sa 11am-midnight, Su noon-10pm.

Eastside Club and Tavern, 410 E 4th Ave. (☎357-9985). Old and young come to play pool and sip pints of microbrews. Pints $2.50. Frequent drink specials. M pints $1.75, Th $2. Happy hour daily 4-7pm, pints $1.75. Open M-F noon-2am, Sa-Su 3pm-2am.

4th Ave. Alehouse & Eatery, 210 E 4th Ave. (☎786-1444). Townfolk gather for "slabs" of pizza ($3.75), seafood baskets ($5-6), and one of the 30 regional draft microbrews. Pints $3, $2 during happy hour (5pm-7pm). Live tunes, from blues to rock to reggae (Th-Sa 9pm). Cover $3-10. Open M-F 11:30am-2am, F-Sa noon-2am.

SIGHTS & EVENTS

Olympia's main draw is definitely its political scene, so don't miss the chance to see WA state tax dollars in action.

STATE CAPITOL. Olympia's crowning glory is the State Capitol, a complex of state government buildings, carefully sculpted gardens, veterans' monuments, and fabulous fountains, including a remarkable replica of Copenhagen's Tivoli fountain. Get a free tour of the **Legislative Building,** constructed in 1927 and styled after Rome's St. Peter's Basilica. The newly renovated interior enshrines a six-ton Tiffany chandelier and six bronze doors depicting the state's history. *(I-5 to Exit 103. Visitors Center ☎586-3460. Call 586-8687 for more info and options for the disabled. Free tours depart from front entrance daily on the hr. 10am-3pm; 11am tour is most in-depth. Open for tourists to explore M-F 8am-5pm, Sa-Su 10am-4pm.)*

WOLF HAVEN INTERNATIONAL. This sanctuary provides a permanent home for captive-born gray wolves (reclaimed from zoos or illegal owners). During the summer weekly **Howl-ins** are a sort of vaudeville-inspired wolf-and-human romp. *(3111 Offut Lake Rd. 10 mi. south of the capitol, near Millersvania Park. Take Exit 99 off I-5, turn east, and follow the brown signs. ☎264-4695 or 800-448-9653; www.wolfhaven.org. Open May-Sept. W-M 10am-5pm; Oct. and Apr. 10am-4pm. Nov.-Jan. and Mar. Sa-Su 10am-4pm. 45min. tours on the hr.; last tour leaves 1hr. before closing. $6, seniors $5, ages 3-12 $4. Howl-ins summer Sa evenings, reservations required; $10, children $8.)*

NISQUALLY NATIONAL WILDLIFE REFUGE. **Nisqually National Wildlife Refuge** shelters 500 species of plants and animals and miles of open trails. People come to walk and above all, bird-watch. Bald eagles, shorebirds, and northern spotted owls nest here. The trails are open daily from dawn to dusk and are closed to cyclists, joggers, and pets. The visitors center offers free binocular loans and info packets—just leave behind an ID. *(Off I-5 between Olympia and Tacoma at Exit 114. ☎753-9467. Visitors centers office open W-Su 9am-4pm. Park office open 7:30am-4pm. Park open dawn to dusk. $3 per person or family.)*

ZOUNDS! MOUNDS! Baffling scientists since the mid-1800s, Mima (my-mah) Mounds have spawned wild speculation about their origins. An evenly spaced network of small, perfectly rounded hills covers the prairies just outside the Capital Forest, 12 mi. southwest of Olympia. Anthropology fanciers attribute the mounds' existence to the arcane labors of a nation of yesteryear, biology buffs cite giant gophers, and delusional paranoids cry government conspiracy. The scientific community is torn among hypotheses ranging from glacial action to seismic shock waves; by 1999, no fewer than 159 Mima-related papers had been published. Today, the Mounds inhabit some of the last remaining prairie in the Pacific Northwest, providing visitors with an opportunity to learn about the region's natural history and mystery. To reach the Mounds, take Exit 95 off I-5 and follow the signs to Littlerock. From Littlerock, follow more signs to the Capital Forest and watch for the marked dirt road to the parking lot and trailhead. (Open daily 8am-dusk. For info, call the DNR ☎748-2383.)

VASHON ISLAND ☎206

Although it's only a 25min. ferry ride from Seattle and an even shorter hop from Tacoma, Vashon (VASH-in) Island remains inexplicably invisible to most Seattle tourists. This artists' colony feels like the San Juan Islands without the tourists or an economy to cater to them. Vashon is the perfect place for a one-day trip, a multi-day exploration, or a base from which to explore Seattle.

TRANSPORTATION. Vashon Island stretches between **Seattle** and **Tacoma** on its east side and between **Southworth** and **Gig Harbor** on its west side. The town of **Vashon** lies at the island's northern tip; ferries stop at both the south and north ends of the island. **Washington State Ferries** (☎464-6400 or 888-808-7977; www.wsdot.wa.gov/ferries) runs ferries to Vashon Island from 4 different locations. A passenger ferry departs downtown **Seattle** (25min., 8 per day M-F, $5.50), while ferries from **Fauntleroy** in West Seattle and **Southworth** in the Kitsap Peninsula take cars and walk-on passengers. (Fauntleroy ferries 15min., Southworth ferries 10min.; both $3, car and driver $10-13.) A fourth ferry departs from **Point Defiance** in Tacoma and arrives in Tahlequah (15min.; $3, car and driver $10-13). To get to the Fauntleroy terminal on the mainland from Seattle, drive south on I-5 and take Exit 163A (West Seattle/Spokane St.) down Fauntleroy Way. To get to Point Defiance in Tacoma, take Exit 132 off I-5 (Bremerton/Gig Harbor) to Rte. 16. Get on 6th Ave. and turn right onto Pearl St.; follow signs to Point Defiance Park and the ferry. Seattle's **King County Metro** services the downtown ferry terminal, Fauntleroy ferry terminal, and Vashon Island. Buses #54, 116, 118, and 119 run between Seattle and Fauntleroy. Bus #54 picks up at 2nd and Pike St. Save your transfer for the connection on Vashon. Buses #118 and 119 service the island's east side from the north ferry landing through Vashon to the south landing. Bus #117 services the west side of the island. The island is in a different fare zone than Seattle. (☎553-3000 or 800-542-7876. 30min., buses every 30min. 5:15am-1:40am. One zone $1.25. Between zones $1.75.)

PRACTICAL INFORMATION. The **Thriftway** (see **Food,** below) provides maps, as does the Vashon-Maury **Chamber of Commerce,** 17637 SW Vashon Hwy. (☎463-6217). **Joy's,** 17318 Vashon Hwy., has laundry facilities. (☎463-9933. Wash $1.50, dry $0.25 per 10min. Open M-F 7am-8:30pm, Sa-Su 8am-8pm.) Other services include: **Vashon Pharmacy,** 17617 Vashon Hwy. (☎463-9118. Open M-F 9am-7pm, Sa 9am-6pm, Su 11am-1pm.); **emergency,** ☎911; **police,** ☎463-3783. The **library,** 17210 Vashon Hwy., has free **Internet access.** (☎463-2069. Open M-Th 11am-8:30pm, F 11am-6pm, Sa 10am-5pm, Su 1-5pm.) The **Post office** is at 1005 SW 178th St. (☎800-275-8777. Open M-F 8:30am-5pm, Sa 10am-1pm.) **Postal Code:** 98070.

ACCOMMODATIONS & FOOD. The **Vashon Island AYH Ranch Hostel (HI) ❶,** 12119 SW Cove Rd., 1½ mi. west of Vashon Hwy., is an oasis just 30min. away from Seattle. Though this frontierland packed with teepees and log-cabin bunkhouses is a destination in its own right, the hostel is also a perfect place to dump a car so you can ferry downtown Seattle. 100 acres call for hiking and biking. (☎463-2592. Free pancake breakfast. Free 1-gear bikes, mountain bikes $6 per day. Sleeping bag $2. 24hr. check-in. Open May-Oct. Bicyclists $11, members $13, nonmembers $16. Teepee and covered wagons also $13/$16. Private double $45; nonmembers $55; $10 per extra person.) A shuttle to the morning ferry is $1.25. The hostel's new B&B, **The Lavender Duck ❸,** 16503 Vashon Hwy., just north on Vashon Hwy., has pleasant, themed rooms and a beautiful living room and kitchen. (☎567-5646. Check in at the hostel. $70.) The meadows are the island's only legal place to **camp ❶,** and campers can use the hostel's kitchens, showers, and common space. ($9 per person, children half-price.) Get creative in the hostel's kitchens with supplies from the large and offbeat **Thriftway,** downtown at 9740 SW Bank Rd. The bulk food section is a camper's dream come true. All buses from the ferry terminal stop there, and a free phone connects to the hostel. (☎463-2100. Open daily 8am-9pm.) The **Stray Dog Cafe ❷,** 17530 Vashon Hwy., has tasty vegetarian and vegan options. (☎463-7833. Open M-Tu 7am-3pm, W-F 7am-3pm and 6-9pm, Sa 8am-3pm, Su 8am-4pm.) **Bishop's Cafe and Lounge ❷,** 17618 Vashon Hwy., has plenty of meals for meat-lovers (burger mania on Monday is $4.25) and many options for the night owl in all of us, as well: video games, pool, big screen TVs, and pints of beer. (☎463-5959. Restaurant open daily 10am-10pm. Bar 11am-2am.) **Fred's Homegrown Restaurant,** 17614 Vashon Hwy SW., serves Vashon locals fresh and healthy meals daily. Breakfast $3-5, lunch $6-7, dinner $7-10. (☎463-6302. Open M-F 8am-3pm, Tu-Sa 5pm-9pm, Sa-Su 8am-2pm.)

SIGHTS & OUTDOOR ACTIVITIES. Vashon Island provides wonderful but strenuous biking, a sometimes-unbalanced relationship celebrated at the **Bicycle Tree,** off the Vashon Hwy. past Sound Food, where a misbehaving little two-wheeler is lodged in the woods. To get to **Point Robinson Park,** a gorgeous spot for a picnic, take Ellisburg Rd. off the Vashon Hwy. to Dockton Rd. to Pt. Robinson Rd. **Free tours** of the 1885 **Coast Guard lighthouse** are available (☎217-6123. Summer weekends noon-3:30pm.) **Vashon Island Kayak Co.,** at Burton Acres Park, Jensen Point Boat Launch, runs guided tours ($65) and rents sea kayaks. (☎463-9257. Open F-Su 10am-5pm. Call and leave a message for weekday rentals. Singles $15 per hr., $55 per day; doubles $25, $80.) More than 500 acres of woods in the middle of the island are interlaced with mildly difficult **hiking trails.** The **Vashon Park District,** 17130 Vashon Hwy., can tell you more. (☎463-9602. Open daily 8am-4pm.) Count on some culture no matter when you visit—one in 10 residents of Vashon is an artist.

WASHINGTON

WHIDBEY ISLAND ☎360

Clouds wrung dry by the mountains west of Seattle release a scant 20 in. of rain each year over Whidbey Island, a beach-ringed strip of land that offers peaceful relaxation in the San Juan islands. The town of **Coupeville,** in Whidbey's middle, is a great place to start exploring the four state parks and historic reserve, where rocky beaches meet bluffs crowded with wild roses and blackberries. **Oak Harbor,** northeast of Coupeville, is a much larger town offering chain stores and a Thursday farmers' market. MacGregor's free *Whidbey Island* is full of maps and info on coastal towns.

TRANSPORTATION. **Washington State Ferries** (☎206-464-6400 or 800-843-3779; www.wsdot.wa.gov/ferries) provides frequent service from the mainland to the island. One ferry connects mainland **Mukilteo,** 10 mi. south of Everett and 19 mi. north of Seattle, with **Clinton,** on the south end of the island (20min.; every 30min.; $2.70, car and driver $5-6.25, bike $0.90). The other connects **Port Townsend** on the Olympic Peninsula with the **Keystone terminal** near Ft. Casey State Park (see **Accommodations,** below), at the "waist" of the island (30min.; every 45min.; $2, car and driver $7-8.75, bike $0.35). You can drive onto the island along Rte. 20, which heads west from **I-5,** 12 mi. south of Bellingham, at Exit 230. **Rte. 20** and **Rte. 525** meet near Keystone and form the transportation backbone of the island, linking significant towns and points of interest. **Island Transit** (☎678-7771 or 321-6688) provides free, hourly public transportation all over the island and has info on connections to and from **Seattle,** but no service Sundays. All buses have bike racks that hold up to two bikes. Flag a bus down anywhere that is safe for it to stop. The **Visitor Info Center,** 207 Main St., is a self-serve station filled with maps and brochures. Just look for the tiny building with a giant American flag. For **Traveler Info,** tune to 1610AM. The **Coupeville Public Library,** 788 NW Alexander, provides free **Internet access.** (☎678-4911. M, W 10am-8pm; Tu, Th-Sa 10am-5pm.)

ACCOMMODATIONS. Ebey's Landing National Historic Reserve, a Department of the Interior protected beach, covers much of the peninsula and has great views of the islands, the surrounding Olympic Mountains, and Port Townsend. Two State Parks lie near Ebey's Landing. **Fort Ebey State Park ❶** lies just north and east off Rte. 20 (☎678-4636. Open daily 6:30am-dusk, booth hours Su-Th 6am-7pm, F-Sa 9am-10am, 2pm-3pm, 6pm-8pm. 50 sites. $16, RV $22, hiker/biker $6.) **Fort Casey State Park ❶,** just south of Fort Ebey, is home to old bunkers and military paraphernalia on a peninsula with unsheltered, slightly crowded sites with views of the straits. (☎800-452-5687. $16; no RV sites. Showers $0.25 per 3min.) An interpretive center lies at the **Admiralty Point lighthouse.** (Open Apr.-Oct. Th-Su 11am-5pm.) To avoid the busier state parks, try **Rhododendron campground ❶,** 1½ mi. before Coupeville; look for the small tent sign on eastbound Rte. 20/525; if you see the recycling plant you've just passed it. (☎679-7373; ballfields, picnic sites, restrooms. 6 primitive sites. $8.) The beautiful **South Whidbey State Park ❶,** amid old-growth forest by the beach, was once a favorite camp of the Skagit and Snohomish tribes. Numerous trails cut through the woods and beach. (☎206-321-4559, reservations 888-226-7688. 46 sites; $16, RV sites $22, hiker/biker $8.) If you prefer a B&B to a tent, the **Anchorage Inn ❹,** 807 North Main Street in Coupeville, offers comfortable Victorian rooms. (☎678-5581. $80.)

FOOD. **La Paz ❷,** 8898 Hwy. 525 right off of the ferry dock, is a Baja-style Mexican restaurant in Clinton, replete with loud colors and beans. A tasty seafood taco with rice is $7. (☎341-4787. Open daily noon-3pm for lunch and 5-8pm for dinner; open F-Sa until 9pm for dinner.) Seaside **Coupeville,** Washington's 2nd-oldest town, makes for a nice stroll. At the bakery, **Knead and Feed ❷,** 4 Front St., you can eat a fabulous lunch ($3-8). (☎678-5431. Open M-F 10am-3pm, Sa-Su 9am-4pm.) For coffee, a pizza ($4), and a great patio view, walk down the stairs to **Great Times Espresso ❶,** 12 Front St. (☎678-5358. Open M-F 7am-7pm, Sa-Su 8am-7pm.)

SIGHTS & OUTDOOR ACTIVITIES. At the north tip of the island, on Rte. 20, the crowded **Deception Pass Bridge,** the nation's first suspension bridge, connects Whidbey Island to Fidalgo Island. A secret cave at one end held 17th-century prisoners who were forced to make wicker furniture. Deception Pass itself is a thin sliver of water that can be brought to the boil by tides; white-water kayakers come here to test their mettle against the salt-water rapids. **Deception Pass State Park,** 41229 SR (☎675-2417), surrounds the pass itself, and is the most heavily used of Whidbey's four state parks (especially on weekends). There are camping facilities, a saltwater boat launch, and a freshwater lake good for swimming, fishing, and boating. The **campground** ❶ is subjected to jet noise from EA6B Navy attack aircraft from nearby Whidbey Island Naval Air Station, in Oak Harbor. (☎888-226-7688. Reservations suggested. 250 sites; $16, RV sites $22, hiker/biker $5.)

BELLINGHAM ☎360

Situated between Seattle and Vancouver, Bellingham (pop. 67,000) is a dream city for the outdoor adventurer—Mt. Baker and the North Cascades are just a stone's throw to the east, and Bellingham Bay offers an array of ocean adventures, from kayaking to whale watching. Historic Bellingham was an industrial port city reliant upon rich mineral and timber resources. Today, Bellingham's port still thrives, but is home to a large fishing fleet and ferry boats, while the town also accommodates **Western Washington University** (14,000 students).

ORIENTATION & TRANSPORTATION. Bellingham lies along **I-5,** 90 mi. north of **Seattle** and 57 mi. south of **Vancouver, BC.** Downtown centers on **Holly St.** and **Cornwall Ave.,** next to the Georgia Pacific pulp mill (Exits 252 and 253 off I-5). **Western Washington University (WWU)** sits atop a hill to the south. The hip town of **Fairhaven,** where ferries, buses, and trains stop, is south of Bellingham and serviced by public transit. Catch a train at **Amtrak,** 401 Harris Ave., in the bus and train station next to the ferry terminal. (☎734-8851 or 800-872-7245. Counter open daily 8:45am-12:30pm and 1-4:30pm.) Two per day to **Seattle** (2½hr., $20) and **Vancouver, BC** (1½hr., $14.) **Greyhound** is in the same station next to the ferry terminal. (☎733-5251 or 800-231-2222. Open M-F 8am-6pm, Sa-Su 8am-5pm.) Buses run to **Seattle** (2hr.; 5 per day, 7 on F, $14-15); **Mt. Vernon** (30min.; 5 per day, $6-8); and **Vancouver, BC** (2hr.; 4 per day, $12.) Private shuttles run ferries to the nearby San Juan Islands (see p. 196). **Public Transportation** routes all start at the Railroad Avenue Mall terminal, between Holly and Magnolia St. (☎676-7433. M-F 5:50am-6:30pm. $0.50, under 6 or over 84 free. No transfers. Buses run every 30 or 60min.) **City Cab** (☎773-8294 or 800-281-5430) and **Yellow Cab** (☎734-8294) service the town.

WASHINGTON

PRACTICAL INFORMATION. Services include a friendly, well-organized **Visitors Info Center,** 904 Potter St. Take exit 253 (Lakeway) from I-5. (☎671-3990. Open daily 8:30am-5:30pm.) **Equipment Rental: Fairhaven Bikes,** 1103 11th St., rents bikes ($20-30 per day) and in-line skates. (☎733-4433. Open M-Th 9:30am-7pm, F 9:30am-8pm, Sa 10am-6pm, Su 11am-5pm.) **Bellingham Cleaning Center,** 1010 Lakeway Dr., offers washing for $1.50 and drying for $0.25 per 8min. (☎734-3755. Open daily 6am-10pm). Other services include: **emergency,** ☎911; **police,** 505 Grand Ave. (☎676-6913. Open M-F 8am-5:30pm.); **crisis Line,** ☎800-584-3578; **St. Joseph's General Hospital,** 2901 Squalicum Pkwy. (☎734-5400. Open 24hr.) Access the **Internet** at the **library,** 210 Central Ave., at Commercial St. opposite City Hall. (☎676-6860. Open M-Th 10am-9pm, F-Sa 10am-6pm; also Sept.-May Su 1-5pm.) The **Post Office** is at 315 Prospect St. (☎800-275-8777. Open M-F 8am-5:30pm, Sa 9:30am-3pm.) **Postal Code:** 98225.

ACCOMMODATIONS. Bellingham does not have a hostel, but Blaine, 17 miles north, offers the **Hostelling International-Birch Bay** ❶, 7467 Gemini Street, which is within walking distance of Birch Bay. (☎371-2180. Office open 7:30am-9:30am and 5pm-10pm. 49 beds. $14 HI members, $17 nonmembers.) In Bellingham proper you can pick from a strip of budget motels on N. Samish Way (2min.

off exit 252). The **Bay City Motor Inn ❸** is at 116 N. Samish Way. (Singles from $40; doubles $50.) If you prefer to stay in the heart of the downtown area, the **Bellingham Inn ❸,** 202 E Holly St. off I-5 Exit 253, has queen beds, clean rooms, and cable TV. (☎734-1900. Singles $42; doubles $50.) If you want to camp close to the city, head to **Larrabee State Park ❶,** on Chuckanut Dr., 7 mi. south of town. Larrabee offers 14 mi. of trails with views of the San Juan Islands, bouldering, a boat launch, restrooms and showers, and even clamming. (☎902-8844; reservations 1-888-226-7688. 85 sites, $14; RV sites $20. Reservations suggested. Park open daily 6:30am-dusk.)

FOOD. The **Community Food Co-op,** 1220 N Forest St., at Maple St., has all the essentials for the healthy eater, plus a tasty cafe in the back. (☎734-8158. Open daily 8am-9pm, cafe closes at 8pm.) The Saturday **Bellingham Farmer's Market,** at Chestnut St. and Railroad Ave., has 115 vendors selling fruit, vegetables, seafood, and homemade doughnuts. (☎647-2060. Apr.-Oct. Sa 10am-3pm.) Locals feast on huge burritos starting at $3 at **Casa Que Pasa ❶,** 1415 Railroad Ave. Gallery space for local artists. (☎738-8226. Open daily 11am-11pm, tequila bar open until 1am.) For a taste of local brew, check out the **Boundary Bay Brewery & Bistro ❷,** 1107 Railroad Ave. (☎647-5593.) Pints are $3.25, while burgers and nachos cost $7. Bang out a few songs on the piano at **The Old Town Cafe ❶,** 316 West Holly St., which makes

delectable breakfasts. Buttermilk pancakes are $3.75; breakfast specials start at $5 and are served all day. (☎671-4431. Open M-Sa 6:30am-3pm, Su 8am-2pm.) **Tony's ❷,** 1101 Harris Ave., is in Fairhaven Village, just blocks from the ferry. This garden and cafe serves ice cream, bagels, and the infamous $4.50 Toxic Milkshake, made with espresso grounds. (☎738-4710. Open M-F 7am-9pm, Sa-Su 7:30am-9pm.)

SIGHTS & ENTERTAINMENT. The **Whatcom Museum of History and Art,** 121 Prospect St., occupies four buildings along Prospect St., most notably the bright red former city hall. Photographs of turn-of-the-century Pacific Northwest logging scenes by Darius Kinsey are a highlight. (☎676-6981. Open Tu-Su noon-5pm. Wheelchair accessible. Free.) The ARCO Exhibits Building and Whatcom Children's Museum are also worth a visit. **Big Rock Garden Park,** 2900 Sylvan St., is a 3-acre Japanese-style sculpture garden, featuring mostly contemporary work. Take Alabama St. east and then go left on Sylvan for several blocks. Call ahead for a schedule. (☎676-6985. Park open in summer 7am-9pm, winter 8am-6pm.)

In the second week of June, lumberjacks from across the land gather for axe-throwing and log-rolling at the **Deming Logging Show.** To reach the show grounds, take Rte. 542 (Mt. Baker Hwy.) 12 mi. east to Cedarville Rd. and then turn left and follow signs. (☎592-3051. $5, ages 3-12 $3.) The **Bellingham Festival of Music** brings symphony, chamber, folk, and jazz musicians from around the world during the first two weeks of August. All concerts are in Western Washington University Auditorium at 8pm. (☎676-5997. Tickets $18-23; students half-price.) Also in August is the **Mount Baker Blues Festival** (☎671-6817) at Rivers Edge Tree Farm in Deming. Memorial Day weekend sees the mother of all relays, the **Ski to Sea Race** (☎734-1330.) Participants sand-ski, run, canoe, bike, and sea kayak 85 miles from Mt. Baker to the finish line at Bellingham Bay. Families, friends, and spectators join the participants in a grand parade and festival at the race's conclusion.

OUTDOOR ACTIVITIES. The 2½ mi. hike up **Chuckanut Mountain** leads through a quiet forest to a view of the islands that fill the bay. On clear days, Mt. Rainier is visible from the top. The trail leaves from the North Chuckanut Mountain Trailhead off Old Samish Hwy., about 3 mi. south of city limits. Alternatively, from Clayton Beach, you can hike a mile to an excellent vista of the San Juan Islands. From the viewpoint, hike the **Fragrance Lake Trail** if you're interested in an afternoon swim (1 mi. from viewpoint to lake). The beach at **Lake Padden Park,** 4882 Samish Way, has the warmest water in the Puget Sound; take bus #44 1 mi. south of downtown. The park also has tennis courts, playing fields, hiking trails, a boat launch (no motors allowed), and fishing off the pier. (☎676-6985. Open daily 6am-10pm.) The popular **Rotary Interurban Trail** (great for biking and running) travels 7 mi. from **Fairhaven Park** to **Larrabee State Park** along the relatively flat route of the old Interurban Electric Railway. Breaks in the trees permit a glimpse of the San Juan Islands. Several trails branch off the main line and lead into the Chuckanut Mountains or down to the coast; get a map from the visitors center at Larrabee.

NEAR BELLINGHAM: BLAINE & BIRCH BAY

A small border town 20 mi. north of Bellingham, Blaine is home to the west's busiest border station between Canada and the US. Directly on the US border, Blaine's main attraction is the **Peace Arch State Park.** To reach the park, take I-5 Exit 276, then turn north onto 2nd St. The Peace Arch contains relics of early US and Canadian ships of discovery and commemorates the Treaty of Ghent, which ended the War of 1812 and inaugurated the long era of peace between Canada and the US. (☎332-8221. Open daily 8am-dusk.) The **Harbor Cafe ❸,** 295 Marine Dr., halfway down Blaine's main pier, serves the best seafood in town. (☎332-5176. Open M-F 7am-9pm, Sa-Su 7am-10pm.)

MOUNT BAKER ☎360

Rising 10,778 ft. above sea level, Mt. Baker is the crown of the 1.7 million-acre Mt. Baker-Snowqualmie National Forest. Mt. Baker hasn't erupted for 10,000 years, but occasional steam rises from this active volcano. A yearly average of 615 in. (51¼ ft.) of snowfall makes for excellent snowboarding and skiing. No high speed lifts here; just great bowls, chutes, glades, and cheap lift tickets. During the summer, hikers and mountaineers challenge themselves on its trails.

TRANSPORTATION & PRACTICAL INFORMATION. To get to this hotbed of outdoor activity, take I-5 Exit 255, just north of Bellingham, to Rte. 542, known as the Mt. Baker Hwy.; 58 mi. of roads through the foothills afford views of Baker and other peaks in the range. The highway ends at Artist Point (5140 ft.), with spectacular wilderness vistas. The road closes at Mt. Baker Ski Area in winter. For trail maps, backcountry permits, or further info about both the National Forest and National Park, stop by the Glacier Ranger Station, located on 542 just before the National Forest. (☎599-2714. Open daily May-Oct. 8am-4:30pm.)

CAMPING. **Silver Lake Park ❶,** 9006 Silver Lake Rd., is 3 mi. north of the highway at Maple Falls. The park has 73 sites, 4 mi. of hiking trails, swimming, and fishing. Buy a 2-day license in Maple Falls for $7, and catch a few of the 17,000 trout stocked yearly in Silver Lake. (☎599-2776. Sites $17; RV sites $19.) More primitive and closer to the mountain is **Douglas Fir Campground ❶,** past Glacier at Mile 36 off Rte. 542 (30 sites, $12), and **Silver Fir Campground ❶,** at Mile 46 off Rte. 542. (Water. 21 sites, $12.) **Glacier Creek Lodge ❸,** 10036 Mt. Baker Hwy. is a fine option for the night. Free breakfast and a steamy hot-tub are pluses. 2 night min. stay on weekends during ski season. (☎599-2991. Reservations essential during peak winter and summer seasons. Singles or doubles $44, cabins $115-165.)

WASHINGTON

WINTER SPORTS. Baker is arguably the birthplace of the snowboard, and boards are wildly popular here. The volcano packs soft powder for longer than any other nearby ski area, staying open from early November through May. The ski area has seven diesel-powered lifts and the lowest lift ticket rates in the Northwest. There is no snow-making or shaping on the mountain's 1500 vertical feet of runs. Contact the **Mt. Baker Ski Area Office** in Bellingham for more info. (☎734-6771; www.mtbakerskiarea.com. Lift tickets Sa-Su and holidays $35, Th-F $27, M-W $25; under 16 and seniors $27, $22, $21.) In the winter many trails become impromptu cross-country ski trails and snowshoe tracks.

HIKING. Many roads and trails are covered in snow well into the summer so call ahead to check which trails are accessible. In June, you can access the Glacier Overlook along **Heliotrope Ridge** (Road 39 off Hwy. 542). This 3 mi. trail is the starting point for mountaineers heading up Baker, and offers hikers an excellent view of the mountain. The **Lake Ann Trail** (5 mi., multi-day) is one of the favorites in the area. This steep trail leads 5 mi. to the lake of the same name, then continues to the Lower Curtis Glacier. **Skyline Divide,** on Road 37 off Hwy. 542, is also a great day-hike that provides stunning views of the North Cascade range (3½ mi. one way.) Hikers can make the inevitable Robert Frost references along the **Fire and Ice Trail,** a picturesque half-mile loop beginning on Rte. 542. The first part of the trail is wheelchair accessible. For a hike up to a beautiful, remote lake, head up to **Tomyhoi Lake Trail** (4 mi. one-way, full day). Take forest service road 3065 north from the highway as far as it will go.

MOUNTAINEERING. If you're looking to summit a peak in the North Cascades, considerable experience in mountaineering and glacier travel is necessary. Check out Fred Beckey's *Cascade Alpine Guide: Climbing and High Routes* or contact the **American Alpine Institute,** 1515 12th St. (☎671-1505; www.aai.cc.) Both provide information on routes, and the American Alpine Institute provides guides.

SAN JUAN ISLANDS

With hundreds of tiny islands and endless parks and coastline, the San Juan Islands are an explorer's dream. The islands enjoy nothing less than perfect weather: between May and September the average daily high temperature is in the upper 60s to low 70s, the sun shines almost every day, and only 1 in. of rain falls each summer month in this "rain-shadow" of the Olympic Mountains. The scattered small towns showcase each islands' uniqueness. Tourists storm the islands in July and August, so plan a visit in late spring or early fall. The *San Juanderer* has tide charts and ferry schedules, and is free on ferries or at visitors centers. A trip to the San Juan Islands requires thinking ahead as the info you need may be available only in Seattle; be sure to book early if you are planning a summertime visit to the San Juan Islands.

INTER-ISLAND TRANSPORTATION

WASHINGTON

Washington State Ferries (☎206-464-6400 or 888-808-7977; www.wsdot.wa.gov/ferries) has frequent daily service to **Lopez** (40min.), **Orcas** (1½hr.), **San Juan Island** (1hr.), and **Shaw** (1hr.) from **Anacortes;** check the schedule available at visitors centers in Puget Sound. Travel time to the islands depends on the number of stops. To save on fares, travel directly to the westernmost island on your itinerary, then return: eastbound traffic travels for free. The ferries are packed in summer, so call ahead to ask when to arrive. Generally, you should get there at least 1hr. (2hr. on weekends) prior to departure. (Passengers $9-11 from Anacortes to Friday Harbor, vehicles $26-35 from Anacortes to Friday Harbor. Eastbound inter-island: passengers free, vehicles $13. Cash and credit cards accepted in Anacortes, inter-island ferries cash only.) To reach the terminal from Seattle, take **I-5** north to Mt. Vernon, then **Rte. 20** west to Anacortes, and then follow signs. The **Bellingham Airporter** (☎866-235-5247) runs shuttles between **Sea-Tac** (see p. 162) and **Anacortes** (10 per day; $31, round-trip $56).

Victoria Clipper (☎1-800-888-2535; www.victoriaclipper.com), departs **Seattle**'s Pier 69 daily for San Juan Island, arriving at Spring St. Landing, one block north of the state ferry dock in **Friday Harbor** (2½hr.; $38, round-trip $59), or at **Rosario Resort,** on Orcas Island (3¼hr.; mid-May to mid-Sept.; $58, round-trip $89; 1 week advance discount; children half-price). **Island Commuter** (☎734-8180 or 888-734-8180) departs **Bellingham** for **Rosario Resort** (1¼hr.), **Friday Harbor** (2¼hr.), and islands on the way ($25, round-trip $35, ages 6-12 half-price, under 6 free; bicycles $5). **Kenmore Air** (☎800-543-9595) flies to San Juan from Seattle (4-5 times per day; one-way $96-105, round-trip $159-169).

SAN JUAN ISLAND ☎360

San Juan Island is the longest trek from Anacortes, yet it is the most popular tourist destination. Ferries drop off passengers in Friday Harbor, the largest town in the archipelago. San Juan Island is the easiest island to explore on a budget since the ferry docks right in town, the roads are good for cyclists, and a shuttle bus services the island. San Juan is home to a National Historic Park and **Lime Kiln State Park,** the only designated whale watching park in the world.

LOCAL TRANSPORTATION

With bicycle, car, and boat rentals within blocks of the ferry terminal, **Friday Harbor** is a convenient base for exploring San Juan. Miles of poorly marked roads access all corners of the island. It's wise to carefully plot a course on the free **map** available at the visitors centers, real estate offices, and gas stations.

Buses: San Juan Transit (☎378-8887 or 800-887-8387; www.san-juan.net/transit.com). Travels from Friday Harbor to Roche Harbor on the hr. and will stop upon request ($4, return trip $7; from Friday Harbor to Westside $4, return trip $7; day pass $10, 2 day pass $17. Tours $17, depart Friday Harbor at 11am and 1pm. Call ahead for reservations.)

Ferries: Washington State Ferries; see **Transportation**, above.

Taxis: San Juan Taxi (☎378-3550). $4 base, $1 per person, $1 per mi. after the 1st mi.

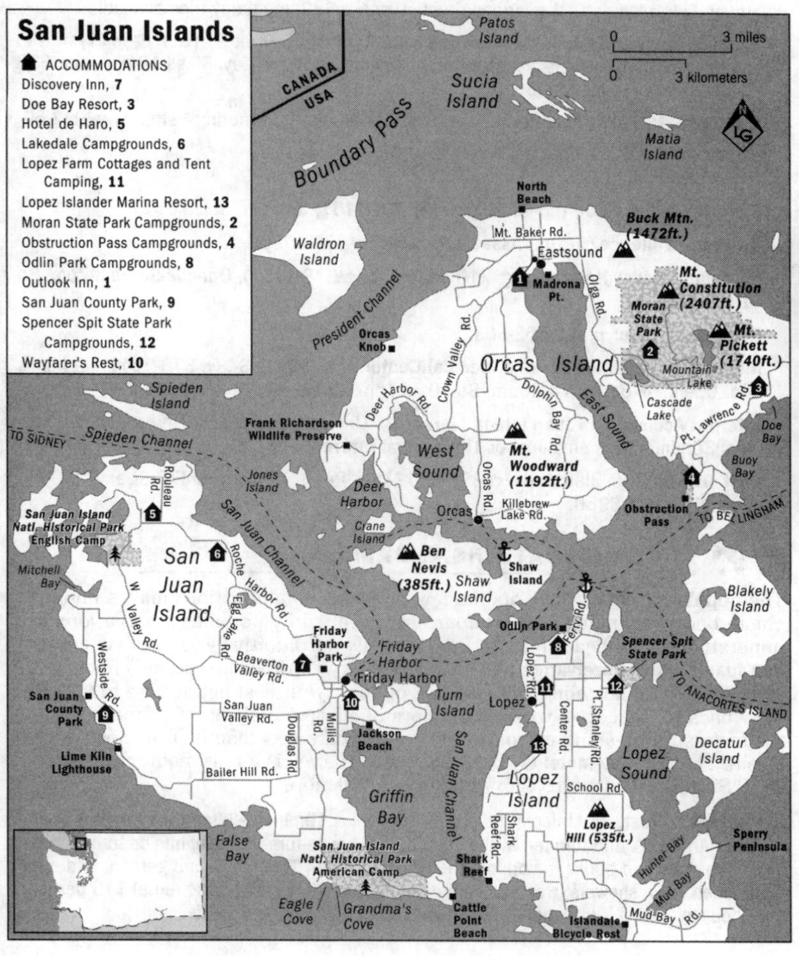

PRACTICAL INFORMATION

Visitor Information: Chamber of Commerce, 1 Front St. 2a (☎378-5240; www.sanjuanisland.org or www.guidetosanjuans.com), is upstairs on the corner of Front St. and Spring St. Stop in for a map and information on tours.

Outdoor Information: San Juan National Historic Park Information Center (☎378-2240; www.nps.gov/sajh), on the corner of First St. and Spring St. Open daily in summer 8:30am-4:30pm; winter 8:30am-4pm.

Tours: A host of companies offer tours; shopping around (especially looking at fliers at the tourist office) pays dividends. **San Juan Boat Tours** (☎800-232-6722), at Spring St., docks a block right from ferry, has a 66-passenger boat with speakers to pick up the Orcas' chat. (3hr., departs daily at 12pm; $39, children $29). **Sea Quest Expeditions** (☎378-5767), a non-profit education, research, and conservation group, runs kayaking tours daily all year. Call to arrange trips. Day-trip $59; multi-day trips available.

Equipment Rental: Island Scooter and Bike Rental, 85 Front St. (☎378-8811) next to Friday's Crabhouse, rents scooters for $17 per hr., $51 per day. Bikes $6 per hour, $30 per day. Open daily 9am-6pm.

Laundromat: Sail-In Laundromat, on East St. behind the waterfront strip. Wash $2.50, dry $2.50. Open daily 7am-8pm.

Emergency: ☎911.

Police: 135 Rhone St. (non-emergency ☎378-4151), at Reed St.

Domestic Violence/Sexual Assault Services: ☎378-8680.

Pharmacy: Friday Harbor Drug, 210 Spring St. (☎378-4421). Open M-Sa 9am-7pm, Su 10am-4pm.

Red Tide Hotline: ☎800-562-5632.

Medical Services: Inter-Island Medical Center, 550 Spring St. (☎378-2141), at Mullis Rd. Open M-F 8:30am-4:30pm, Sa 10am-1pm. **Crisis:** ☎378-2345. 24hr.

Internet Access: San Juan Island Library, 1010 Guard St. (☎378-2798), provides visitors 30min. of free emailing, or 1hr. general **Internet** use.

Post Office: 220 Blair Ave. (☎378-4511), at Reed St. Open M-F 8:30am-4:30pm. **Postal Code:** 98250.

WASHINGTON

ACCOMMODATIONS & CAMPING

The popularity of San Juan and its few budget accommodations makes finding a cheap bed challenging. The campgrounds are wildly popular; reservations are imperative. While beautiful, the B&Bs are also prohibitively expensive; contact **San Juan Central Reservation** (☎888-999-8773; www.fridayharbor.com) for help. If you miss out on hosteling and camping options, your best bet may be to take the ferry back to Anacortes where a plethora of cheap motels line Commercial Ave., the main street leading up to the ferry. Prices are less than half of those on the island. The **Gateway Motel ❸,** 2019 Commercial Ave., is a reasonable deal. (☎293-2655. Singles $49; doubles $55; with kitchen $10 more.)

Wayfarer's Rest, 35 Malcolm St. (☎378-6428), a 10min. walk from the ferry up Spring onto Argyle St. and turn left at the church. This house-turned-hostel has beautiful homemade driftwood bunks, a comfortable living area with TV, a patio and garden, and a full kitchen. Coin showers, washers, and dryers ($2 wash, $2 dry). Bike rental $15 per day. Check-in 2-9pm. Bunk room $22; private room and cabins $55. ❷

San Juan County Park, 380 Westside Rd. (☎378-1842), 10 mi. west of Friday Harbor, along the bay. 20 sites are perched on a bluff with a fantastic sunset view. Water, toilets. Open daily 7am-10pm. Make reservations 7-90 days ahead. Vehicle sites $23; walk-ins $6. ❶

Lakedale Campgrounds, 4313 Roche Harbor Rd. (☎378-2350 or 800-617-2267), 4 mi. from Friday Harbor, just west of Egg Lake Rd. Some sites near lakes. Office hours 8am-10pm. Reservations suggested, but campers can almost always find spots. Fishing permits $4 per day, non-campers $8 per day. Boat rental. Open Mar. 15-Oct. 15; cabins year-round. Vehicle sites $24, plus $5.75 per person after 2; hiker/biker sites $8 per person; 4-person tent-cabins from $45. Cheaper rates in off-season. ❶

Hotel de Haro, Roche Harbor, 248 Reuben Memorial Drive (☎378-2155 or 800-451-8910). This hotel was built in 1886 and overlooks a busy harbor and beautiful formal garden. Classic hotel rooms with shared bath $69 (Oct.-May), $79 (May-Sept.). ❹

Discovery Inn, 1016 Guard St. (☎378-2000 or 1-800-822-4753), located about a mile from the buzz of Friday Harbor. Offers an outdoor jacuzzi, sauna, sun decks, and gardens. Singles and doubles in off season $79, summertime $105. ❺

FOOD

Both the quality and quantity of food at **King's Market,** 160 Spring St., will trick you into thinking you're on the mainland; once you see the bill, however, reality will strike. (☎378-4505. Open in summer M-Sa 7:30am-10pm, Su 7:30am-9pm.) Plan ahead to avoid missing a meal; many cafes and restaurants close early.

Thai Kitchen, 42 1st St. (☎378-1917), next to the Whale Museum. A popular dinner spot with a beautiful patio for flower-sniffing or star-gazing. Try the fresh lime juice with the popular Pad Thai. Lunch dishes around $7, dinners $8-12. Open for lunch Tu-Sa 11:30am-2:30pm, dinner daily 5-9pm. ❸

San Juan Donut Shop, 209 Spring St. (☎378-2271). Stop in for bottomless coffee ($1.25) and fresh donuts ($0.75) while you wait for the ferry. Open daily 6am-3pm. ❶

Hungry Clam Fish and Chips, 130 1st St. (☎378-3474), serves up excellent fresh beer-battered Alaskan Cod (fish and chips $5.50-8.50). Open daily 11am-7pm. ❷

Blue Dolphin Cafe, 185 1st St. (☎378-6116), is a local favorite for a hearty breakfast or lunch. Tall stack of pancakes $3.50, hot sandwiches from $6. Daily specials are a good bet if you've got a few extra bucks. Open daily 5am-2pm. ❷

Vic's Drive Inn, 25 2nd St. (☎378-8427), serves up the cheapest burger in Friday Harbor ($2). You'll also find a quarter pizza pie or apple pie for $2.50. Open M-F 7am-7pm, Sa 7am-2pm. ❶

Front Street Ale House, 1 Front St. (☎378-2337), serves cold brews from the San Juan Brewing Co. located just next door. San Juan local micro-brews taste fantastic after a long day of biking or paddling. Pints $4, Open daily 11am-11pm. ❷

SIGHTS

Driving around the 35 mi. perimeter of the island takes about 2hr.; on bike, it makes for the perfect day-long tour. The **West Side Rd.** traverses gorgeous scenery and provides the best chance for sighting **orcas** from three resident pods. To begin a tour of the island, head south and west out of Friday Harbor on Mullis Rd. (Bikers may want to do this route in the opposite direction, as climbs heading counterclockwise around the island are much more gradual.)

WHALE MUSEUM. The museum has a collection of artifacts and whale skeletons as well as modern tools used for whale research. Step into a phone booth and listen to the sound of orcas, dolphins or walruses. Local whale art adds a colorful backdrop to the experience. Call their whale hotline at ☎800-562-8832 to report sightings and strandings. *(62 First St. N. ☎378-4710 or 800-946-7227. Open June-Sept. daily 10am-5pm; call for winter hours. $5, seniors $4, students and ages 5-18 $2, under 5 free.)*

SAN JUAN ISLAND NATIONAL HISTORICAL PARK. Two national historic parks preserve a living memory of tensions between the British and American camps co-occupying San Juan Island in the mid-19th century. The American army built its barracks on Cattle Point, located on southeastern San Juan Island. Today, **American Camp** is the more elaborate of the park's two halves. The **visitors center** explains the history of the curious conflict, while a self-guided trail leads from the shelter to an excellent view of Mt. Baker at the Redoubt. For a slightly longer hike, head to the top of Mt. Finlayson. You'll see Mt. Rainier to the southeast, the Olympic Mountains to the south, and BC to the west (Mt. Finlayson trail). **English Camp,** on the island's north end, exhibits a greater number of historic buildings, and contains one of Washington's largest Big Leaf Maple trees. The Bell Point trail is a pleasant 2 mi. loop. During the summer on Saturday afternoons, the two camps alternate re-enacting Pig War-era life. *(To get to American Camp, follow Cattle Point Rd. south from Friday Harbor. British Camp can be reached by Roche Harbor Rd. ☎378-2240. Camp open daily June-Aug. dawn-11pm; Sept.-May Th-Su. Visitors center open daily 8:30am-5pm. Guided walks June-Sept. Sa 11:30am. Re-enactments June-July 12:30-3:30pm. Free.)*

OUTDOOR ACTIVITIES

Tourism on San Juan Island are centered around Orca whales. The San Juan Islands are home to three pods of Orcas, creatively dubbed pods J, K, and L. San Juan Island receives the majority of whale watching attention due to the whales' travel patterns north and south through the Haro Strait. In the summer, whales are seen daily from **Lime Kiln Point State Park,** along West Side Rd. This location is renowned as the best **whale watching** spot on the island. Take the short hike to the whale watching balconies, where cliffside crowds watch as killer whales prowl for salmon between occasional acrobatics. More determined whale watchers might prefer a **cruise;** see **San Juan Boat Tours,** p. 198. Keep in mind, San Juan has almost as many whale watching boats as it does whales, and whale watching can sometimes feel like whale boat-watching. When choosing a company, ask about boat size; smaller boats can usually get closer to the whales. Kayak tours will also seek out Orcas; see **SeaQuest Expeditions** and **Crystal Seas Kayaking,** p. 198.

The island provides several laid-back hiking trails as well as picturesque beaches, both relaxing options for the afternoon. If the sky is clear, make the half-mile jaunt down the road to **Cattle Point** for views of the distant Olympic Mountains, or stop by **South Beach,** a stretch of dazzling shoreline. Also in the south, **Eagle Beach** and **Grandma's Cove** are considered two of the finest beaches on the island. Heading east from West Side Rd., Mitchell Bay Rd. leads to a steep half-mile trail to **"Mount" Young,** a good tall hill within viewing range of Victoria and the Olympic Range. The gravel False Bay Rd., heading west from Cattle Point Rd., runs to **False Bay,** where **bald eagles** nest. During spring and summer, nesting eagles are visible at low tide along the northwestern shore.

ORCAS ISLAND ☎360

Mount Constitution overlooks much of Puget Sound from its 2407 ft. summit atop Orcas Island—this high point is touted as the best 360 degree marine viewpoint in North America. A small population of retirees, artists, and farmers dwell here in understated homes surrounded by green shrubs and the bronze bark of madrona trees. With a commune-like campground and resort, and the largest state park in Washington, Orcas Island has the best budget tourist facilities in the San Juans.

Unfortunately, much of the beach is occupied by private resorts and closed to the public. Moran State Park offers a relaxing wilderness experience while Eastsound provides a movie theater, several restaurants, a museum, and shopping.

ORIENTATION & PRACTICAL INFORMATION

Orcas is shaped like a horseshoe, lending a commonsensical name to the main thoroughfare, **Horseshoe Hwy.** The ferry lands on the southwest tip at **Orcas Village. Eastsound,** the main town, is at the top of the horseshoe, 9 mi. northeast. **Olga** and **Doe Bay** are another 8 and 11 mi. down the eastern side of the horseshoe, respectively. Pick up a map in one of the four shops at the ferry landing.

Ferries: Washington State Ferries, see p. 196.

Taxis: Orcas Island Taxi (☎376-8294). $3.50 flat rate, $1.50 per mi.

Visitor Information: San Juan Island houses the more official tourist facilities. **Pyewacket Books** (☎376-2043), in Templin Center, in Eastsound at N Beach Rd., has good island books.

Equipment Rental: Wildlife Cycles 350 North Beach Rd., (☎376-4708), at A St. in Eastsound. Bikes $7.50 per hr., $30 per day. Open M-Sa 9am-6pm, Su noon-3pm. **Dolphin Bay Bicycles** (☎376-4157), near the ferry. $25 per day, $55 for 3 days.

Sporting Goods: Eastsound Sporting Goods, 1 Main Street (☎376-5588), Templin Center #4. Caters to all your outdoor equipment needs and rents fishing rods for $10 per day. Open in summer daily 9:30am-9pm.

Emergency: ☎911.

Domestic Violence/Sexual Assault Services: ☎376-1234.

Pharmacy: Ray's (☎376-2230, after-hours emergencies 376-3693), Templin Center #3, in Eastsound at N Beach Rd. Open M-Sa 9am-6pm.

Internet Access: Library (☎376-4985), at Rose and Pine in Eastsound. Walk up the path from Prune Alley. Open M-Th 10am-7pm, F-Sa 10am-5pm. **Orcas Online,** 254 N Beach Rd. (☎376-4124), in Eastsound. $5 per 30min. Open M-Sa 9am-5:30pm.

Post Office: 221 A St. (☎376-4121), in Eastsound. Open M-F 9am-4:30pm. **Postal Code:** 98245.

WASHINGTON

ACCOMMODATIONS & CAMPING

B&Bs on Orcas charge upwards of $85 per night; call ☎376-8888 for advice. Camping is the cheapest option on Orcas. Reservations are important during summer.

Doe Bay Resort (☎376-2291), off Horseshoe Hwy. on Pt. Lawrence Rd., 5 mi. east of Moran State Park. A former commune and then Human Potential Center, this retreat keeps the old feel in its guise as vacation spot. Cafe (open daily 8:30am-12pm, 6pm-9pm), treehouse, and a co-ed clothing-optional hot tub and steam sauna. Sauna $4 per day. Office open 11am-9pm. Kayak rentals through Shearwater Adventures (see **Outdoors Information,** below). Private rooms start at $55; yurts $75; camping $25. ❸

Moran State Park, State Rte. 22 (ranger ☎376-2326, reservations 1-888-226-7688 or www.parks.wa.gov). Follow Horseshoe Hwy. straight into the park, 14 mi. from the ferry on the east side of the island. The most popular camping in the islands, but sites are often reserved months in advance (you can reserve as early as 9 months prior to your stay). At Cascade Lake, you can rent rowboats and paddleboats ($12-13 per hr., $35-45 full day). 4 campgrounds throughout the park contain 151 sites. About 12 sites are open year-round. Car sites $16, hiker/biker sites $6. ❶

Obstruction Pass. Accessible by boat or foot. Turn off the Hwy. just past Olga, and head south (right) on Obstruction Pass Rd. Follow the gravel road marked Obstruction Pass Trailhead to the trailhead and parking lot. Some of the only free camping in the San Juan Islands. Pit toilets, no water. Access to nice pebble beaches on Puget Sound. 11 sites. ❶

Outlook Inn (☎376-2200), on Horseshoe Hwy. in Eastsound, just West of N. Beach Rd. (☎376-2200), offers rooms with shared baths from $64-84. A good budget option if you want a room in town. ❹

FOOD

Essentials can be found in Eastsound at **Island Market,** 469 Market St. (☎376-6000. Open M-Sa 8am-9pm, Su 10am-7pm.) For a large selection of groceries, medicines, and vegan cheeses, make a bee-line for **Orcas Homegrown Market,** on N Beach Rd. Try their deli and seafood specials for lunch; most specials are $5-6 and there are always vegetarian options. (☎376-2009. Open daily 8am-9pm.) For loads of fresh local produce, visit the **Farmer's Market** in front of the museum. (Sa 10am-3pm.)

Cafe Jama (☎376-4949), in Eastsound Sq. on N Beach Rd. Perhaps the only place you'll find a Sunday *New York Times* on Orcas Island, Cafe Jama serves up a Northwest breakfast (specialty coffees and homemade muffins) as well as a variety of tasty lunch options: soups, salads and sandwiches $6-8. ❷

Chimayo (☎376-6394), in Our House Building on N Beach Rd. Portions are large, the salsa is fresh, and prices are lower than across the street. Design your own burritos and tacos ($5-9), or get 2 tacos for $3.75. Vegetarian options abound. Open M-F 11am-7pm, Sa 11am-3pm. ❷

Lower Tavern (☎378-4848), at the corner of Horseshoe Hwy. and Prune Alley. One of the few cheap spots open after 5pm. Dig into burgers and fries from $7. Seven beers on tap, pints $2.50-$3.75. Happy hour M-F 4:30-6:30pm. Bar open M-Th 11am-midnight, F-Sa 11am-1am, Su 12pm-7pm. Kitchen open M-Sa 11am-9pm, Su noon-5pm.

Roses Bread and Specialties (☎376-5805) in Eastsound Sq. Those who visit this gem will be rewarded with a huge selection of cheeses, fresh bread, and sweet baked goods. If you aim to make a gourmet picnic lunch for Moran State Park, Roses will provide all you need. Open M-Sa 10am-5pm.

SIGHTS

The **Orcas Island Historical Museum,** 181 N. Beach Rd., is composed of six clustered homesteads constructed between the 1870s and the 1890s. View Lummi and Samish Native American artifacts and explore early colonial life on the islands. Check out the fruit picking exhibit. (☎376-4849. Open Tu-Su 1pm-4pm, F 1pm-7pm. $2, students $1.) The **Rosario Resort,** 1400 Rosario Rd., is home to the mansion of Robert Moran, an industrialist and politician who donated the land that is now Moran State Park. The mansion totals 35,000 sq. feet and cost $2.5 million when it was built in 1905. The fine Honduran Mahogany woodwork is worth a look, as is the largest pipe organ built in a private home in 1905. (☎376-2222. Free.)

OUTDOOR ACTIVITIES

Travelers on Orcas Island don't need to roam with a destination in mind; half the fun lies in rambling around, although those who stray too far from designated trails will often find themselves on private property. The trail to **Obstruction Pass Beach** is the best way to clamber down to the rocky shores. Taking up the majority of Orcas' eastern half, **Moran State Park** is the last large undeveloped area on the San Juans, making it a star outdoor attraction. This is a must-see during even a brief sojourn on the island. Ample trails, steep mountains, and several lakes create a landscape with diverse options for outdoor activity.

HIKING & BIKING

With 5252 acres, Moran offers over 30 mi. of hiking and biking trails. Find a good map and detailed trail descriptions in the free *Treasure in the San Juans: Your Guide to Moran State Park,* available at the registration station. (☎376-2326. Open daily 10am-9:30pm.) Biking in Moran State Park is restricted in the summer months, so be sure to check with the ranger or contact Wildlife Cycles for information (☎376-4708). Roads on Orcas are also a pleasant way to explore the island.

Cold Springs Trail (4¼ mi. one-way, 1 day), goes from the North End Campground up to the summit of Mt. Constitution. Since a road also runs to the summit, those with a little less spunk can catch a ride back down to the camping areas. 2000 ft. gain. Difficult.

Mountain Lake Trail (4 mi. loop, 2-3hr.) starts from the cabin near Mountain Lake campground and loops around Mountain Lake, the larger and more secluded of the parks 2 big lakes. A more mellow trail, great for an easy hike or trail run.

WATER SPORTS

Within the park, two freshwater lakes are accessible from the road, and rowboats and paddleboats can be rented at **Cascade Lake.** ($12-14 per hr.) Anglers also hit Moran's water with glee; Mouton and Cascade Lakes are both stocked with silver cutthroat, rainbow trout, and eastern brook trout. Outside of the park and on salt water, Orcas is probably the best place to kayak in the San Juans, with a wide variety of conditions and far fewer crowds than San Juan Island. **Shearwater Adventures** runs fascinating **sea kayak tours** and classes, and their store in Eastsound is a great information source for more experienced paddlers. (☎376-4699. 3hr. tour with 30min. of dry land training $45. Full-day and multi-day trips available.) **Crescent Beach Kayak,** on the highway 1 mi. east of Eastsound, rents kayaks for paddling the mellow waters of the East Sound. (☎376-2464. $10 per hr., $25 per half-day. Open daily 9am-5pm. Owner will not rent when there are white caps in the water.)

LOPEZ ISLAND ☎360

Smaller than either Orcas or San Juan, "Slow-pez" lacks some of the tourist facilities of the larger islands; still, what it lacks in size it more than makes up for in lethargy. This island is a blessing for those looking for solitary beaches, bicycling without car traffic, rolling farmland, and a small-town atmosphere.

ORIENTATION & PRACTICAL INFORMATION. **Lopez Village,** the largest town, is 4½ mi. from the ferry dock off Fisherman Bay Rd. To get there, follow Ferry Rd. and then take a right onto the first street after Lopez Center (before the Chevron station). It's best to bring a bicycle, unless you're up for the hike. To rent a bike or kayak, head to **Lopez Bicycle Works** and **Lopez Kayak,** both south of the village next to the island's Marine Center. Get an excellent map here or at the **visitors center.** (☎468-2847, 2845 Fisherman Bay Rd. Bikes open July-Aug. daily 9am-9pm Apr.-June and Sept.-Oct. 10am-5pm. Kayaks open daily 10am-5pm. Bikes $5 per hr., $25 per day. Single kayaks $12-25 per hr., $40-60 per day; doubles $20-35 per hr., $60-80 per day. 2hr., 3hr., and day-long trips available.) **Lopez Island Pharmacy** is at 157 Village Rd. (☎468-2616. open M-F 9am-6pm, Sa 10am-

5pm.) The **Lopez Island Library**, 2225 Fisherman Bay Rd., has free **Internet** access. (☎468-2265. Open M and Sa 10am-5pm, W 10am-9pm, and Tu, Th-F 10am-6pm.) For a taxi, call **Angie's Cab** (☎468-2227). Keep it so at **Keep It Clean,** south of the winery. (Wash $2, dry $0.25 per 5min. Open M-F 8:30am-7pm, Sa-Su until 5pm.) Other services include: **domestic violence/sexual assault services,** ☎468-4567; **emergency,** ☎911; **clinic,** ☎468-2245; **post office,** on Weeks Rd. (☎468-2282. Open M-F 8:30am-4:30pm.) **Postal Code:** 98261.

ACCOMMODATIONS AND FOOD. When spending the night on Lopez, camping is the only bargain. Luckily, there are many great sites to pitch a tent. **Spencer Spit State Park ❶,** on the northeast corner of the island about 3½ mi. from the ferry terminal, has seven sites on the beach, 30 nicely secluded wooded sites up the hill, two group sites, and a bunkhouse. Spencer Spit offers good **clamming** in the late spring, unless there is red tide (☎800-562-5632; permit required). The park is closed Nov. 1-Feb. 2. (☎468-2251; reservations 888-226-7688. Toilets, no showers or RV sites. Reservations necessary for summer weekends. Open until 10pm. Sites $15, biker/hiker sites $6, bunkhouse $22.) Voted one of the 10 best places to woo by MSNBC, **Lopez Farm Cottages and Tent Camping ❶,** just north of town on Fisherman Bay Rd., is an agrarian dreamland. Each campsite has a hammock and chairs. Min. age 14. Free morning coffee. Showers that open to the sky. (☎800-440-3556. Sites $28 for double occupancy, "Northwest Scandinavian" cottages $99-150 depending on time of year). **Odlin Park ❶** is close to the ferry terminal, 1 mi. south along Ferry Rd., and offers running water, a boat launch, volleyball net, and baseball diamond as well as nice beaches and pleasant walks. (☎468-2496; reservations 378-1842. 30 sites: beach sites $19, forest sites $16, hiker/biker sites $11.) If you're looking for a roof, **Lopez Islander Marina Resort ❹,** on Fisherman Bay Road, offers rooms with mini-refrigerators and color TV. (☎468-2233. Rooms from $89.50.)

Although Lopez doesn't boast the selection of restaurants that the other two islands do, a good meal is easy to find. Play *boules* while brown-bagging in the grassy park adjacent to the **Village Market,** which has a complete meat and produce department. (☎468-2266. Open daily 8am-8pm.) Across the street, sample fresh pastries, bread, and pizza at **Holly B's ❷.** Try the french bread baked with caramelized onions and brie cheese. Bargain breads go for $2, pastries for $0.80. (☎468-2133. Open W-M 7am-5pm.) For a delicious vegetarian meal, head straight to **Vortex Juice Bar & Good Food ❶,** located in the Old Homestead with Blossom Natural Foods in Lopez Village. You'll smell the wraps, burritos, and homemade soups and salads ($4-8) from across the street. (☎468-4740. Open M-Sa 10am-7pm.) The **Farmer's Market** showcases Lopez island arts and crafts, as well as jams, baked goods, and potted plants. (Open Sa 10am-2pm.)

SIGHTS & OUTDOOR ACTIVITIES. Lopez is attractive to many for the total lack of things to do—the opportunity to spend the day exploring at a snail's pace is a large part of the island's appeal. The small **Shark Reef** and **Agate Beach County Parks,** on the southwest end of the island, have tranquil and well-maintained hiking trails. Watch in wonder at the waves crashing against the rocky beaches at Shark Reef Park, or stroll down Agate's calm and deserted shores. The 2 mi. round-trip hike to **Iceberg Point** promises dramatic ocean scenery. For an agrarian adventure, get a copy of the *Guide to Farm Products on Lopez Island* and visit sheep, cattle, and fruit and vegetable farms. **Lopez Island Vineyards,** 724 Fisherman Bay Rd., San Juan's oldest vineyards, permits visitors to sample all of their wines for $2 per person. (☎468-3644. Open in summer W-Sa noon-5pm, year-round by appointment.)

Lopez Island is ideal for **biking.** The car traffic is minimal and the scenery is top notch. Pick up a copy of the *Bicyclists' Touring Companion for the San Juan Islands* to plan out your route. Circling the island in a day is definitely an attainable goal. Pick up a 2-day **clamming/crabbing** permit at the **Lopez Island Marine Center** on Fisherman Bay Rd. for $8. Then head to Odlin Park or Spencer Spit State Park for some of the best clamming and crabbing in all of Washington.

OLYMPIC PENINSULA

Due west of Seattle and its busy Puget Sound neighbors, the Olympic Peninsula is a remote backpacking paradise. Olympic National Park dominates much of the peninsula, and it prevents the area's ferocious timber industry from threatening the glacier-capped mountains and temperate rainforests. With the pick of three ecosystems—rainforest, beach, or mountain—outdoors enthusiasts have a full plate. Outside of the park, a smattering of Indian reservations and logging and fishing communities lace the peninsula's coastline along US 101. To the west, the Pacific Ocean stretches to a distant horizon; to the north, the Strait of Juan de Fuca separates the Olympic Peninsula from Vancouver Island; and to the east, Hood Canal and the Kitsap Peninsula isolate this sparsely inhabited wilderness from the sprawl of Seattle.

OLYMPIC NATIONAL PARK

AT A GLANCE

AREA: 1400 sq. mi. **CLIMATE:** Fair summers (65-75°F), mild winters (30-40°F). Heavy precipitation. **FEATURES:** Olympic National Forest, Hoh Rainforest, Olympic Mountain Range.	**GATEWAYS:** Forks, Port Angeles, Port Townsend. **CAMPING:** 14-day camping limit. **FEES AND RESERVATIONS:** Permit Registration Fee $5, Individual Nightly Fee $2.

Olympic National Park (ONP) is certainly the centerpiece of the Olympic Peninsula, sheltering one of the most diverse landscapes of any region in the world. With glacier-encrusted peaks, river valley rainforests, and jagged shores along the Pacific Coast, the park has something to offer to everyone. Roads lead to many corners of Olympic National Park, but they only hint at the depths of its wilderness. A dive into the backcountry leaves summer tourists behind and reveals the richness and diversity of the park's many faces. Many try to make this trip in a day or two, but beware: the breadth and distances in the park make it difficult to enjoy in under three or four days.

ORIENTATION

The entire **Olympic Mountain Range** is packed into the peninsula's center, where conical peaks ring huge quantities of moisture from heavy Pacific air. Average precipitation in the park varies, but an annual 12 ft. of rain and snow is common. At altitudes above 3500 ft. it is not rare to encounter snow in late June. The mountains steal so much water that some areas are among the driest in Washington.

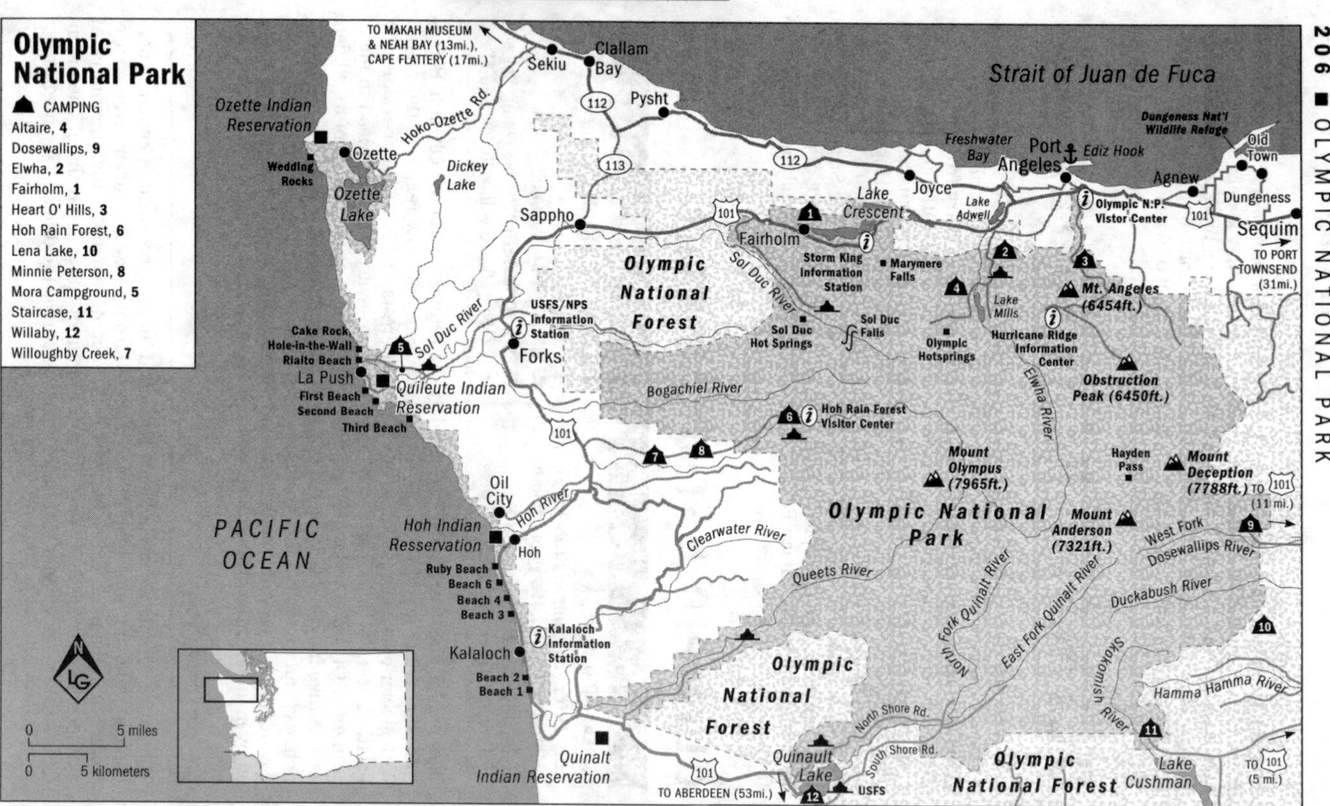

Olympic National Park
CAMPING
Altaire, 4
Dosewallips, 9
Elwha, 2
Fairholm, 1
Heart O' Hills, 3
Hoh Rain Forest, 6
Lena Lake, 10
Minnie Peterson, 8
Mora Campground, 5
Staircase, 11
Willaby, 12
Willoughby Creek, 7
0 5 miles
0 5 kilometers
TO MAKAH MUSEUM & NEAH BAY (13mi.), CAPE FLATTERY (17mi.)
Strait of Juan de Fuca
PACIFIC OCEAN
Ozette Indian Reservation
Wedding Rocks
Ozette
Ozette Lake
Hoko-Ozette Rd.
Dickey Lake
Sekiu
Clallam Bay
Pysht
Sappho
Forks
USFS/NPS Information Station
Sol Duc River
Cake Rock
Hole-in-the-Wall
Rialto Beach
La Push
First Beach
Second Beach
Third Beach
Quileute Indian Reservation
Oil City
Hoh River
Hoh Indian Resservation
Hoh
Ruby Beach
Beach 6
Beach 4
Beach 3
Kalaloch
Kalaloch Information Station
Beach 2
Beach 1
Quinalt Indian Reservation
TO ABERDEEN (53mi.)
Olympic National Forest
Bogachiel River
Clearwater River
Queets River
Fairholm
Lake Crescent
Storm King Information Station
Marymere Falls
Sol Duc Falls
Sol Duc Hot Springs
Hoh Rain Forest Visitor Center
Joyce
Freshwater Bay
Lake Adwell
Olympic Hotsprings
Lake Mills
Port Angeles
Ediz Hook
Olympic N.P. Vistor Center
Hurricane Ridge Information Center
Mt. Angeles (6454ft.)
Obstruction Peak (6450ft.)
Elwha River
Mount Olympus (7965ft.)
Olympic National Park
Hayden Pass
Mount Anderson (7321ft.)
Mount Deception (7788ft.)
North Fork Quinalt River
East Fork Quinalt River
North Shore Rd.
South Shore Rd.
Quinault Lake
USFS
Skokomish River
Lake Cushman
Duckabush River
West Fork
Dosewallips River
Hamma Hamma River
TO 101 (11 mi.)
TO 101 (5 mi.)
Dungeness Nat'l Wildlife Refuge
Old Town
Agnew
Dungeness
Sequim
TO PORT TOWNSEND (31mi.)
101
112
113

Temperate rainforests lie on the west side of ONP, along the coast, and in the **Hoh, Queets,** and **Quinault River valleys.** Moderate temperatures, loads of rain, and summer fog support an emerald tangle dominated by Sitka spruce and Western Red cedar. The rest of the park is populated by lowland forests of Douglas fir and hemlock, with silver fir at higher elevations. Ancient Native American **petroglyphs** and boxy offshore bluffs called **sea stacks** lend a sacred quality to the beaches along the coastline. Swaths of **Olympic National Forest** and private land separate these seaside expanses from the rest of the park. The park's perimeters are well-defined but are surrounded by **Forest Service** land, **Washington Department of Natural Resources (DNR)** land, and other public areas. It's important to remember that the ONP and ONF are maintained by separate organizations. Their usage, purposes, facilities, rules, and regulations differ accordingly.

Each side of the park has one major settlement—**Port Townsend** in the east, **Port Angeles** to the north, and **Forks** in the west. The size of the towns and the services they offer decline as you go west, as does the traffic. The park's vista-filled eastern rim runs up to Port Townsend, from where the much-visited northern rim extends westward. Along a winding detour on Rte. 112, off US 101 westward, the tiny town of **Neah Bay** and stunning **Cape Flattery** perch at the northwest tip of the peninsula; farther south on US 101, the slightly larger town of Forks is a gateway to the park's rainforested western rim. Separate from the rest of the park, much of the peninsula's Pacific coastline is gorgeous.

July, August, and September are the best months for visiting Olympic National Park. Much of the backcountry remains snowed-in until late June, and only summers are relatively rain-free. The Park Service runs free interpretive programs such as guided forest hikes, tidepool walks, and campfire programs out of its ranger stations. For a schedule of events, pick up a copy of the *Bugler* from ranger stations or the visitors center (see below). Erik Molvar's *Hiking Olympic National Park* ($15) is a great resource for hikers, with maps and step-by-step trail logs for over 585 mi. of trails. Although it lacks coverage of coastal areas and can be slightly outdated, Robert Wood's comprehensive *Olympic Mountains Trail Guide* ($15) is the classic book for those planning to tackle the backcountry. *Custom Correct* maps provide detailed topographic information on various popular hiking areas. However, because of the density of helpful ranger stations and adequate signs, most visitors who are sticking to park campgrounds will have little need to purchase additional literature.

TRANSPORTATION

The peninsula provides quite a few transportation options for a place so remote. Highway 101 forms an upside-down "U", passing through almost every place listed. A combination of roads also heads straight west from Olympia, allowing one to bypass the park and then head north on 101, skipping the crowds and going straight to the rainforest. Local buses link Port Townsend, Port Angeles, Forks, and Neah Bay, cost $0.50-$1, and accommodate bicycles. From there rides can be cobbled together to get farther into the park. Vans lines, ride-sharing, and taxis are all options. When combined with bus travel, bicycling can move a traveler around quickly. Be aware, though: the stretch of 101 that runs along Lake Crescent is poor for bikers. Roads into the park are accessible from US 101 and serve as trailheads for over 600 mi. of hiking.

Actually getting to the peninsula to begin the trip requires a bit of planning, but can be rewarding: the trip from Seattle to the farthest end of Olympic National Park can cost as little as $7 (7hr. via Pierce, Grays Harbor, and West Jefferson Transits). A ferry is probably the fastest bet and can work well for those driving too. For more info, contact **Washington State Ferries** (☎888-808-

7977 or 206-464-6400); **Greyhound** (☎800-231-2222); **King** in Seattle (☎800-542-7876); **Pierce** in Tacoma (☎206-581-8000); **Intercity** in Olympia (☎800-287-6348); or **Kitsap** in Kitsap and Bainbridge (☎360-373-2877). For service on the peninsula, contact **Jefferson** in Port Townsend (☎360-385-4777); **Clallam** in Port Angeles (☎800-858-3747); **Grays Harbor** in Aberdeen (☎800-562-9730); **West Jefferson** in the southwest (☎800-436-3950); or **Mason** in the southeast (☎800-374-3747). The hostels around the peninsula know the terrain and will help anyone navigate transit routes around the park.

PRACTICAL INFORMATION

Emergency: ☎911. **Park Headquarters** (☎565-3000). Staffed daily 7am-midnight; winter 7am-5:30pm. Or call the nearest ranger station and report your exact location.

Tourist Information: Olympic National Park Visitor Center, 3002 Mt. Angeles Rd. (☎565-3130; www.nps.gov/olym/home.htm), off Race St. in Port Angeles (see p. 214). ONP's main info center. Contains a children's natural history room, extensive exhibits, and plays a 12min. movie that gives an overview of the park. The info center also distributes an invaluable **park map.** Open in summer daily 9am-5:30pm; winter 9am-4pm. **Park Headquarters,** 600 E Park Ave. (☎565-3000), in Port Angeles, is an administrative office but can answer questions by phone. Open M-F 8am-4:30pm. For the many local **ranger stations,** see specific regions below.

Backcountry Information: Olympic National Park Wilderness Information Center (☎565-3100; www.nps.gov/olym/wic), behind the visitors center, provides trip-planning help and info on food storage and leave-no-trace techniques. Call here for backcountry reservations. Pay the ONP wilderness user fee here or at any ranger station. Quota area permits must be purchased at Ranger Stations. Open Apr.-June 8am-4:30pm; June-Sept. Th-Sa 7:30am-8pm, Su-W 7:30am-6pm; Oct.-Mar. hours vary.

Fees and Reservations: $10 per car; $5 per hiker or biker. Charged at Hoh, Heart o' the Hills, Sol Duc, Staircase, and Elwha entrances. Covers 7 days access to the park; keep that receipt! Backcountry users must pay a $5 permit fee as well as $2 extra per person per night to ranger offices. The National Forest requires a Northwest Forest Pass at most parking areas ($1 per day). **Fishing:** Fishing within park boundaries requires a license except when along the Pacific Ocean. A booklet with all of the park's regulations is available at stations upon request.

Park Weather: ☎565-3131. 24hr.

Park Radio: 530 AM for road closures and general weather conditions. 610 AM for general park rules and information, 1610 AM in Lake Crescent and Quinault areas.

CAMPING

Competition for sites on the peninsula can get fierce, but there would be sufficient space for the entire population of Washington to camp there at once if it so chose. It just takes a little driving to uncover all the treasures of hidden sites. In addition to numerous national park sites, there is a network of state and county sites and several hostels well spaced across the peninsula.

STANDARD CAMPING. Ask at the Olympic National Forest Headquarters in Olympia (see p. 186) about **ONP** campgrounds within its boundaries (sites $8-12). **ONF** maintains six free campgrounds in the Hood Canal Ranger District and other campgrounds within its boundaries; sites at **Seal Rock, Falls View,** and **Klahowga** can be reserved. (☎800-280-2267; www.reserveusa.com. Open daily 8am-midnight. Sites $8-12.) In addition to **Ft. Worden** and **Ft. Flagler**, there are four **state**

parks on the peninsula. (Reservations ☎800-452-5687. Sites $14; RV sites $20; hiker or biker $6.) **Dosewallips** (☎796-4415) and **Lake Cushman** (see **Eastern Rim,** below) are to the east. **Sequim Bay** is northeast of Sequim. (☎683-4235. Table and stove at each site. Restrooms.) Most **drive-up camping** is first come, first served.

BACKCOUNTRY CAMPING. Whether in rainforest, high country, or along the coast, backcountry camping in the park requires a **backcountry permit.** Park offices maintain **quota limits** on backcountry permits for popular spots, including **Lake Constance** and **Flapjack Lakes** in the eastern rim (see below); **Grand Valley, Badger Valley,** and **Sol Duc** in the northern rim (see p. 214); **Hoh** in the western rim (see p. 218); and the coastal **Ozette Loop.** Make **reservations** in advance, especially for the Ozette area, where reservations are required. Contact the Wilderness Info Center to secure a spot. Backpackers should prepare for varied weather conditions. Even in the summer, parts of the park get very wet. Pack appropriately for the weather. **Giardia,** a nasty diarrhea-inducing bacterium, lives in the water here. Water purification tablets are available at the visitors center and most outfitters. **Black bears** and **raccoons** pose another backcountry hazard; when issuing backcountry permits, ranger stations instruct hikers on hanging food out of animals' reach. Cougars have also become a concern, and ranger officials will give you extensive advice on how to maximize your safety. For more on wilderness safety, see p. 34. Above 3500 ft., **open fires** are prohibited; below 3500 ft., maps and signposts indicate if they are allowed. Before any trip, inquire about **trail closures;** winter weather often destroys popular trails.

EASTERN OLYMPIC PENINSULA

The area of the peninsula most accessible from Puget Sound City, the Olympic's eastern edge suffers from a heavy traffic of weekend cabin-renters and daytrippers. Still, the eastern edge of the park, generously padded with a thick strip of National Forest, houses some fun (and generally dry) trails. The big draw, though, is the town that serves as the peninsula's social capitol, Port Townsend. PT is the one settlement west of Olympia that doesn't qualify as "sleepy," making it a welcome change of pace for travelers who have been taking advantage of the park's solitude for a little too long.

PORT TOWNSEND ☎360

Set apart from the rest of the Olympic Peninsula on a small peninsula of its own, Port Townsend is the local cultural hot spot. During the late 1800s, the city's predominance in the entire state of Washington seemed secure. Every ship en route to Puget Sound stopped here for customs inspection, and speculation held that the bustling port would become the capital of the new state. When rumors circulated that rail would connect the town to the east, wealthy families flocked to the bluffs overlooking the port, constructing elaborate Victorian homes and stately public buildings. When rail passed the town by, "the inevitable New York" was left a ghost town, perched on the isolated northeast tip of the Olympic Peninsula and made to subsist by paper-milling and logging. In the 1970s, Port Townsend's neglected Victorian homes were discovered by artists and idealists who turned the town into a vibrant, creative community. Now the business district stands restored, recently declared a national landmark, and the town takes advantage of its 19th-century feel to entice those heading to the park onto Rte. 20 and into town. It is a turn that few who make it regret.

ORIENTATION & PRACTICAL INFORMATION

Port Townsend sits at the terminus of **Rte. 20** on the northeastern corner of the Olympic Peninsula. It can be reached by **US 101** on the peninsula, or from the Kitsap Peninsula across the Hood Canal Bridge. **Kitsap County Transit** meets every ferry and runs to Poulsbo. From Poulsbo, **Jefferson County Transit** runs to PT. The ferry also crosses frequently to and from Keystone on Whidbey Island (see p. 190). Ferries dock at **Water St.**, west of touristy downtown, along **Water** and **Washington St.**, where restaurants, hotels, and motels are located. Laid-back uptown, with a small business district of its own, is four steep blocks up, on **Lawrence St.**

Local Transportation: Jefferson County Transit (**JCT;** ☎385-4777; www.jeffersontransit.com). Peninsula towns are serviced by JCT and neighboring transit systems. Buses run between Ft. Worden and downtown, and also connect to Port Angeles and Seattle. $0.50; seniors, disabled travelers, and ages 6-18 $0.25; extra-zone fare $0.25. Day passes $1.50. A **shuttle** runs between downtown and the Park 'n' Ride lot, right next to the Safeway. There is usually ample parking in town, although usually limited to 2hr.

Taxis: Peninsula Taxi, ☎385-1872. $2 base plus $1.75 per mi.

Visitor Information: Chamber of Commerce, 2437 E Sims Way (☎385-2722 or 888-365-6978; www.ptguide.com), lies 10 blocks southwest of town on Rte. 20. Open M-F 9am-5pm, Sa 10am-4pm, Su 11am-4pm.

Equipment Rental: P.T. Cyclery, 100 Tyler St. (☎385-6470), rents mountain bikes for $7 per hr., $25 per day. Maps $1.75. Ages 100+ free. Open M-Sa 9am-6pm. **Kayak Port Townsend,** 435 Water St. (☎385-6240 or 531-1670; www.kayakpt.com), is part of PT's burgeoning sea-kayaking scene. Rents singles $25 per 4hr.; doubles $40 per 4hr. Windrider sailing craft $25 per hr., $60 per day; ages 84+ free. Open M-F 10am-6pm, Sa 9am-7pm, Su 9am-5pm.

Emergency: ☎911.

Police: 607 Water St. (☎385-2322), at Madison. 24hr.

Crisis Line: ☎385-0321 or 800-659-0321. 24hr. **Sexual Assault Line:** ☎385-5291.

Pharmacy: Safeway Pharmacy, 442 Sims Way (☎385-2860). Open M-F 8:30am-7:30pm, Sa 8:30am-6pm, Su 10am-6pm.

Hospital: 834 Sheridan (☎385-2200 or 800-244-8917), off Rte. 20 at 7th St.

Internet Access: Library, 1220 Lawrence (☎385-3181). Free Internet access, 15min. drop in, up to 1¼hr. by appointment. Open M-W 11am-8pm, Th-Sa 11am-6pm. **Cyber Bean,** 2021 E Sims Way (☎385-9773). 2min. free with latte, $6 per 15min. Open M-F 8:30am-6pm, Sa-Su 8:30am-2:30pm.

Post Office: 1322 Washington St. (☎385-1600). Open M-F 9am-5pm, Sa 10am-2pm. **Postal Code:** 98368.

ACCOMMODATIONS & CAMPING

Port Townsend is a B&B mecca; many of the historic Victorian homes now offer rest to weary travelers. If you're looking to splurge, the striking **Ann Starrett Mansion ❺**, built in 1889, offers rooms starting at $105 (see **Sights,** below).

Olympic Hostel (**HI;** ☎385-0655; www.hiayh.org), in Fort Worden State Park, 1½ mi. from town. Follow the signs to the park at "W" and Cherry St. A converted WWII barracks, the Olympic offers nice clean beds, but the biggest attractions are the surrounding park (over 400 acres!) and beaches. Laundry, tennis courts, frequent concerts, trails, and free pancake breakfast. Private rooms available. Check-in 5-10pm, check-out 9:30am. Book ahead, especially in summer. Beds $14; nonmembers $17. ❶

WASHINGTON

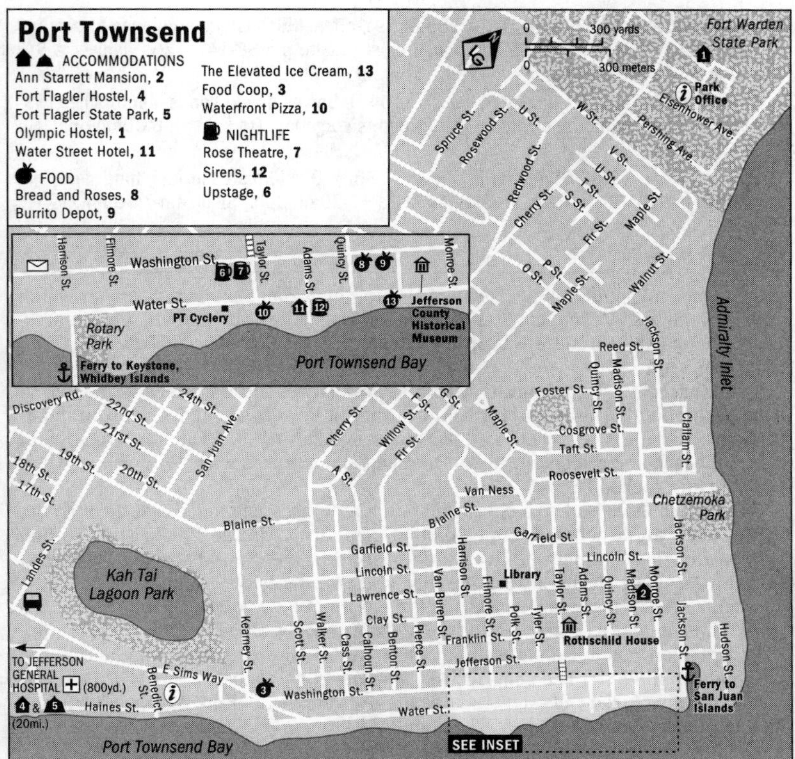

Fort Flagler Hostel (**HI;** ☎385-1288), in Fort Flagler State Park, on gorgeous **Marrowstone Island,** 20 mi. from Port Townsend. Take State Rte. 20 to State Rte. 19 South, go 3 mi., and turn left on State Rte. 116 for 9 mi. into Fort Flagler State Park. The hostel is an old military building just a short hop from the beach. Check-in 5-10pm, lockout 10am-5pm. Call if arriving late. Book ahead for weekends. Open Mar.-Sept. Beds $14, nonmembers $17, hikers/bikers $2 off. ❶

Fort Flagler State Park (☎385-1259). Camping in same place as the hostel. Some sites on the beach. 115 sites. Tents $16; RVs $22; hikers/bikers $6. Book ahead. ❶

Water St. Hotel, 635 Water St. (☎385-5467 or 800-735-9810), is a newly renovated Victorian building with fabulous views of the water and Port Townsend streets. $45-100 in winter, $50-135 in summer. ❸

FOOD

The **Food Coop,** 414 Kearney St., is in a converted bowling alley. Every Wednesday from 3:30-6pm there is a market in their parking lot. (☎385-2883. Open M-Sa 8am-9pm, Su 9am-7pm.) **Safeway,** 442 Sims Way (☎385-2860), is open 24hr.

The Elevated Ice Cream Co., 627 Water St. (☎385-1156), ironically on the ground floor. Serves homemade ice cream that receives rave reviews. Single scoop $2. If you don't want frozen treats, try the sweet shop next door. Open daily 10am-10pm. ❶

Waterfront Pizza, 953 Water St. (☎385-6629), offers little historic ambiance but churns out a damn good pizza on a sourdough crust (12 in. pie $8-14). 12 in. Focaccia $4. Open Su-Th 11am-10pm, F-Sa 11am-11pm. ❷

Bread and Roses, 230 Quincy St. (☎385-1044). Serves baked goods, sandwiches ($3-7), and muffins in cozy environs; the garden is gorgeous. Open M-Sa 6:30am-5pm, Su 6:30am-4pm. ❶

Burrito Depot, 609 Washington St. (☎385-5856). Quick, tasty Mexican food, and Thai thrown in, too. Big burritos $4-6. Open M-Sa 10:30am-8pm, Su 11am-7:30pm. ❶

SIGHTS

Port Townsend is full of huge Queen Anne and Victorian mansions, many of which now serve as B&Bs. The **Ann Starret Mansion,** 744 Clay St., is renowned for its frescoed ceilings and three-tiered spiral staircase. (☎385-3205 or 800-321-0644. Tours daily noon-3pm. $2.)

Point Hudson, where Admiralty Inlet and Port Townsend Bay meet, is the hub of a small shipbuilding area and forms the corner of Port Townsend. Check out boat-builders crafting sea kayaks and sailboats. North of Point Hudson are several miles of **beach** and the beautiful **Chetzemoka Park,** a (guess what) Victorian park at Garfield and Jackson St.

Fort Worden State Park is a sprawling complex most easily accessed through the gates at "W" and Cherry St. (Open daily 6:30am-dusk.) In the 1900s, Fort Worden was part of the "Triangle of Fire," a defense for Puget Sound formed by **Worden** (☎344-4400), **Fort Flagler** across the bay, and **Fort Casey** on Whidbey Island. Fort Worden re-entered service in 1981 as the set for *An Officer and a Gentleman.* Three museums are on the grounds. The **Commanding Officer's Quarters** is stuffed with Victorian furniture. (Open daily June-Aug. 10am-5pm; Mar.-May and Sept.-Oct. Sa-Su 1-4pm. $1.) The **Coast Artillery Museum** is clean-cut. (☎385-0373. Open M-Su 10am-4pm; closed Oct.-Mar. $2.) Sea life lives above the Fort Worden pier at the **Marine Science Center.** (☎385-5582. Open W-M 11am-5pm. $3, children $2.)

ENTERTAINMENT

Port Townsend's music scene is surprisingly lively. *This Week* has the scoop on the nightlife. Steep-side **Sirens,** 823 Water St., hosts live folk and blues (F-Sa) on the deck, which has a great view. (☎379-1100. Happy hour 4-6pm. Occasional cover. Open M-Th 4pm-2am, F-Sa noon-2am.) **Upstage,** 923 Washington St., sup-

THE GIFT THAT JUST WON'T STOP GIVING

In the early part of this century, elk were shipped from Washington to Alaska in an effort to provide more game for hunting, and mountain goats were sent from Alaska to Washington in return. The goats proliferated in Olympic National Park long after hunting was prohibited, damaging endangered native plants by grazing, trampling, wallowing, and loitering. Park Service authorities tried many ways of removing the goats, including live capture and sterilization darts, but nothing really worked. In 1995, they resolved to eliminate the goats once and for all by shooting them from helicopters. Washington Congressman Norm Dicks got this measure postponed, and has since proposed reintroducing the native gray wolf to the park. Wolves were banished in the early part of this century in an effort to provide more game for hunting. To add to the mess, a 2000 study concluded that the goats neither belong in, nor do they substantially damage, the environment. For now, the goats are left hiding deep in the interior of the park.

ports music from classical to country from Thursday to Saturday. (☎385-2216. Cover $3-14. Open daily 4pm-midnight.) The **Rose Theatre,** 235 Taylor St., is one fine art house theater that claims to make the best popcorn in the Northwest. (☎385-1089. $6, seniors $5, children $4; matinees $5.)

Every summer, **Centrum Foundation** (☎385-5320 or 800-733-3608; www.centrum.org) sponsors festivals in Fort Worden Park, including the **Port Townsend Blues Festival** (tickets $20) at the beginning of August, the **Festival of American Fiddle Tunes** (tickets $14) in early July, and **Jazz Port Townsend** (tickets $19-24) the third week of July. The **Port Townsend Writer's Conference** in mid-July is one of the finest in the Northwest. Well-attended guest-readings and lectures cost $5-6. Port Townsend's biggest gathering is the **Wooden Boat Festival** (☎385-3629), held the first weekend after Labor Day. It is organized by **The Wooden Boat Foundation,** 380 Jefferson St. (☎385-3628), an institute that supports lessons and races.

ELSEWHERE ON THE EASTERN PENINSULA

NEAR HOODSPORT. The first info area one passes on US 101 coming in from Olympia is the Hood Canal Ranger Station, just off of the highway in Hoodsport. (☎877-5254. Open in summer daily 8am-4:30pm; winter M-F 8am-4:30pm.) This station is run jointly between the Forest and Park services, so it can answer questions about almost any destination on the peninsula. The station's turnoff also leads to two of the whole peninsula's most popular destinations. The first is a camping and hiking area on Lake Cushman known as Staircase. **Staircase Campground ❶** is a major hub 16 mi. northwest of Hoodsport; take a left after 9 mi. on Rte. 119 and follow the signs. (☎877-5491. RV accessible. 56 sites. $10.) The other much sought-out place is the summit of **Mt. Ellinor,** also past the station. Follow Rte. 119 for 9 mi. to Forest Rd. 24, turn right, and continue to Forest Rd. 2419, following signs to Upper/Lower Trailhead. Look for signs to the Upper Trailhead along Forest Rd. 2419-144. Once on the mountain, hikers can choose either the three-mile path or an equally steep but shorter journey to the summit. Those hiking on the mountain before late July should bring snow clothes.

HAMMA HAMMA RECREATION AREA. Fourteen mi. north of Hoodsport, 8 mi. west off FS Road #25, lies the Hamma Hamma Recreation Area. A 3 mi. hike leads to **Lena Lake,** one of the most popular backcountry lakes on the Olympic Peninsula. From Lena Lake, trails lead to Upper Lena Lake and The Brothers Wilderness. The **Hamma Hamma Campground ❶,** at the Lena Lake Trail-head, has 15 sites. ($10.) For backcountry camping, try **Lena Lake Campground ❶,** located on the west shore of Lena Lake, which offers 29 free sites with compost toilets but no water.

North of the Hamma Hamma, hike 6 mi. to **Royal Lake** for a breathtaking waterfall, summertime wildflowers, and views of the second-highest peak in the Olympics, Mt. Deception. Permits are required for backcountry camping.

QUILCENE. Thirty miles north of Hoodsport, the **Quilcene Ranger Station** (☎765-2200) is available to answer any questions about the National Forest. (Open daily 8am-4:30pm. Closed on weekends in winter.) Nearby, the **Mt. Walker Viewpoint,** 5 mi. south of Quilcene on US 101, is a very popular destination. A one-lane gravel road leads 4 mi. to the lookout, the highest viewpoint in the forest accessible by car. The road is steep, has sheer drop-offs, and should not be attempted in foul weather or with a temperamental car. Picnic tables perch on the east side; feast there while gazing at the north face of 7743 ft. **Mt. Constance.**

NORTHERN OLYMPIC PENINSULA

On the north side of the peninsula, the mountains creep towards the shore, leaving only a thin strip of land that people have settled. Along this stretch of US 101, spur roads regularly reach south into the park, delivering travelers to hot springs, trailheads, and mountain passes. The north strikes a good balance between the isolation of the west and the traffic of the east—solitude can be found, yet transportation is still easy to figure out, especially when using Port Angeles as a base. It is the right balance for someone with only a day or two to see the park, or who is looking to recover from a stint in the isolation of the western park.

PORT ANGELES ☎360

Port Angeles is the "gateway" to the Olympic National Park. The administrative headquarters and main info center are both located here. As US 101 turns west on the peninsula, the traffic thins as only those headed to ONP remain. Port Angeles (PA) is the final stop, the point where the weekend traffic drops off and those here to explore remain. With the park headquarters, transportation connections, and a small, walkable downtown, it has always been a logical stop, but with the addition of a new hostel and several good places to eat, PA is now at least as much a place to recharge batteries and rest aching muscles as it is a place to pass through.

TRANSPORTATION

Buses: Olympic Bus Lines, 221 N Lincoln (☎417-0700), in the Doubletree Hotel parking lot. To **Seattle** (2½hr., 4 per day, $49 round-trip) and **Sea-Tac Airport** (3hr., 3-5 per day, $58 round-trip). **Olympic Van Tours (OVT;** ☎452-3858) runs from the Olympics to **Hoh Rainforest** ($32) and **Hurricane Ridge** ($20). OVT also shuttles to trailheads.

Ferries: 2 different vessels (1 passengers-only) shuttle across the straits to **Victoria, BC. M.V. Coho,** 101 E Railroad Ave. (☎457-4491; www.northolympic.com/coho), runs Mar.-Jan. The Coho does NOT take reservations, so call ahead to find out how early to arrive. (1¾hr.; 4 per day; $8, with bicycle $11.50, with car $31; children $4). **Victoria Express,** 115 E Railroad Ave. (☎800-633-1589; www.victoriaexpress.com), has passenger-only service and does take reservations. (1hr., $12.50, ages 5-11 $7.50, under 5 free). US and Canadian citizens crossing into Canada, children included, need valid proof of citizenship. Other internationals should check their own visa requirements. Day parking lots line Railroad Ave. near the docks ($7-10 per day).

Public Transportation: Clallam Transit System, 830 W Lauridsen Blvd. (☎800-858-3747 or 452-4511; www.clallamtransit.com), serves **Port Angeles** and **Clallam County,** as far as **Neah Bay** and **Forks,** from the transport center on Railroad Ave. at Oak St., a block west of the ferry. Operates M-F 4:20am-9pm, Sa 10am-7pm. Downtown $0.75, ages 6-19 $0.50, seniors $0.25; day pass $2; $0.25 per zone passed.

Taxis: Peninsula Taxi, ☎385-1872. $2 base plus $1.75 per mi.

Car Rental: Evergreen Auto Rental, 808 E Front St. (☎452-8001). From $33 per day plus $0.20 per mi. after 100 mi. Must be 21+ with proof of insurance.

PRACTICAL INFORMATION

Tourist Information: Chamber of Commerce, 121 E Railroad Ave. (☎452-2363 or 877-465-8372; www.portangeles.org), near the ferry. Ask for a guide to the town's art for a fun walking route. Open daily 10am-4pm, longer depending on staff size; winter M-F.

Outdoor Information: The **Olympic National Park (ONP) Visitor Center,** 3002 Mt. Angeles Rd. (☎565-3130), is just outside of town. Open 8:30am-5:30pm; see p. 205 for details. **Port Brook and News,** 104 E 1st St. (☎452-6367), has maps and advice on the region. Open M-Sa 9am-9pm, Su 10am-5pm.

Equipment Rental: Olympic Mountaineering, 140 W Front St. (☎452-0240; www.olymtn.com), rents sturdy gear (external frame pack $15 per day) with lower weekly rates. Offers guided hiking and climbing trips in the ONP (from $150 for 2 people). The shop also features an indoor climbing wall. Open M-Sa 9am-6pm, Su 10am-5pm. **Brown's Outdoor Store,** 112 W Front St. (☎457-4150), rents at low daily rates. Packs $10 per day, tents $10 per day. Call ahead. Open M-Sa 9:30am-6pm, Su noon-4pm. **Sound Bikes and Kayaks,** 120 E Front St. (☎457-1240), rents bikes for $9 per hr.; $30 per day. Leads half-day kayak trips for $40, kayak rentals alone $12 per hr. Open M-Sa 9am-5:30pm.

Laundromat: Peabody St. Coin Laundry, 212 Peabody St. at 2nd St. Wash $1.75, dry $0.25 per 10min. 24hr.

Emergency: ☎911.

Police: ☎452-4545. 24 hr.

Sexual Assault: Safehome, 1914 W 18th St. (☎452-4357).

Pharmacy: Safeway (☎457-0599; see **Food,** below).

Medical: Olympic Memorial Hospital, 939 Caroline St. (☎417-7000) at Washington St. on the waterfront. Open 24hr.

Post Office: 424 E 1st St. (☎452-9275). Open M-F 8:30am-5pm, Sa 9am-noon. **Postal Code:** 98362.

WASHINGTON

ACCOMMODATIONS & CAMPING

Countless motels are found in PA, and, keeping in mind that cleanliness is proportional to price, you can pay what you will. The least expensive motels line US 101 west of town, so cruise First St. to price-shop. Winter rates drop $5-15. West on US 101, halfway between Port Angeles and Lake Crescent, a 6 mi. spur road leads south to two **campgrounds** along the waterfall-rich Elwha River: **Elwha Valley** (40 sites) ❶ and the nearby **Altaire** (30 sites) ❶. Both have drinking water, toilets, and fishing. (☎452-9191. Sites $10.)

Thor Town Hostel, 316 N Race St. (☎452-0931), a friendly refuge 7 blocks east of the city center and 1 mi. north of ranger station. This "work-in-progress" hostel is located in a renovated 100-year old house. Linens and towels provided, laundry $1. Features bike rentals ($8 per day), trailhead shuttles, and bus info. $12, private room $28. ❶

Ruffles Motel, 812 E 1st St. (☎457-7788), is slightly ahead in terms of the price-grime curve. Nice rooms and cable, but no A/C. Singles $47; doubles $55. ❸

Heart o' the Hills Campground, just after the park entrance, overflows with vacationers poised to take Hurricane Ridge by storm. The campground has no RV sites or showers but offers plenty of giant trees, fairly private sites, drinking water, and wheelchair access. (105 sites. $10.) ❶

FOOD

Cheap buffets are ubiquitous in Port Angeles. For a breakfast buffet, try the **Best Western Olympic Lodge ❶,** 140 Del Guzzia (☎452-4995), a $6 all-you-can-eat joint. There is plenty of seafood in town—finding a cheap place to eat is the trick. Picnickers can shop at **Safeway,** 110 E 3rd St., at Lincoln St. (☎457-0788. Open 24hr.)

Thai Peppers, 222 N Lincoln. A new restaurant in town, this place keeps PA natives happy; the seafood is excellent. Lunch specials $6, dinners $8-10. Open M-Sa 11am-2:30pm and 4:30-9pm. ❶

India Oven, 222 N Lincoln (☎452-5170). Before (or after) catching the ferry to Victoria, fill up at the $7 lunch buffet. Regular dishes $8-11. Open daily 11am-10pm. ❷

La Casita, 203 E Front St. (☎452-2289). Regular burritos $5, or spice it up with crab, shrimp, and fish ($9.95). Free, all-you-can-eat tortilla chips to snarf between margaritas ($2). Open M-Th 11am-10pm, F-Sa 11am-11pm, Su noon-10pm. ❶

Bella Italia, 118 E 1st St. (☎457-5442). Hungry vegetarians can sit down to lasagna ($10) or a plate of spaghetti ($7). Open M-Sa 11am-10pm, Su 10:30am-10pm. ❷

SIGHTS & OUTDOOR ACTIVITIES

The main draw of Port Angeles is the National Park, which looms behind the town in the form of Mt. Angeles. Nevertheless, there are several places to enjoy outside of the park if a change of pace is what you are looking for.

The **Fine Arts Center and Sculpture Park,** 1203 E Lauridsen Blvd., near the national park visitors center, has exhibits by Northwest artists in a small space. The surrounding five acres show sculpture in a very entertaining art park. (☎457-3532; www.olympus.net/community/pafac. Gallery open Tu-Su 11am-5pm, art outside open daylight hours year-round. Both free.) Take US 101 east about 4 mi. and turn left. A 5 mi. (2hr.) trail out on the 7 mi. **Dungeness Spit** is the world's longest natural sand spit, extending 6 mi. into the Strait of Juan de Fuca. Over 200 species of birds inhabit this area, as well as loads of indigenous crabs and clams. (Open from 9am until 2hr. before sunset.) The Dungeness Spit also houses a small **campground ❶.** Nearby, the **Olympic Game Farm,** 1423 Ward Rd. off Woodcock St., is a retirement home for animal movie stars. Drive by zebras, llamas, rhinos, and bears, or take a guided walking tour. (☎683-4295 or 800-778-4295; www.olygamefarm.com. Open daily 9am-5pm for driving (until 6pm on Sa); 10am-3pm for walking. Driving tour 4 mi.; $9, children $7. Walking tour 1hr.; $10, $8. Both driving and walking $15, $12.)

While most come to the ridge just to gawk, getting out on your feet is the best way to take in the views without the chatter of families and rangers. Before July, walking on the ridge usually involves snow-stepping. On weekends from late December to late March the Park Service organizes free guided **snowshoe walks** atop the ridge. **High Ridge** (½ mi. loop, 30min.) is a paved trail just off of the Hurricane Ridge parking lot, with access to a view north from **Sunset Point. Klahhane Ridge** (3¾ mi., 5hr.) is a more strenuous hike, leading 2¾ mi. on flat ground, and then turning for 1 mi. of tough switchbacking to actually get to Klahhane.

Accessible by road directly from Port Angeles, **Hurricane Ridge** boasts the best drive-up views of the park's mountainous interior. Clear days promise splendid views of Mt. Olympus and Vancouver Island against a foreground of snow and indigo lupine. RVs and tourists crowd the ridge by day, but seclusion can be found at dawn. To get into the park, take Race Rd. south from US 101 and turn right shortly after the **ONP Visitors Center** (☎565-3132).

LAKE CRESCENT. A massive body of water located in the north-central region of the peninsula, just off US 101, Lake Crescent is often ignored by travelers. The lake offers brisk swimming, blissful picnicking, and frequent sunshine. Storm King Ranger Station is on a small peninsula in the center of the lake and offers all of the regular services. (☎928-3380. Open in summer daily 10am-5pm.)

At the west end of the lake, just past the Fairholm General Store, there is a small road that heads to **Fairholm Campground ❶**, which has wheelchair access, beautiful moss-covered trees, picnic areas, and some sites right on the lakeshore. (☎928-3380. 87 sites, $10.) Several strenuous hikes head out from the lake up the steep slopes. The **Lake Crescent Lodge,** next to the Storm King Station, rents rowboats to help in summertime seduction. (☎928-3211. Rentals 7am-8pm. $8.50 per hr., $20 half-day, $30 full day.) Swimming and trout **fishing** are both popular on the water—but only catch-and-release is allowed (no permit required).

SOL DUC HOT SPRINGS. Just west of the tip of Lake Crescent, a road turns south and follows the Sol Duc river south for 12½ mi. into a large green valley. At the end lies a beacon for tired travelers—hot baths in the **Sol Duc Hotsprings Resort.** The hot springs are in the National Park (so be prepared to fork up a $10 park entrance fee), but operated by the Resort. Hiking is also good in the area; to get information and permits, stop at the **Eagle Ranger Station,** just before the springs. (☎327-3534. Open in summer daily 8am-4:30pm). With its location, it is no surprise that the **Sol Duc Hot Springs Campground ❶** often fills by 3pm. (☎327-3534. Picnic sites. 78 sites, $12.)

With trails leaving the resort, ranger station, and **Sol Duc Trailhead** (at the end of the road, 1 mi. from the campground), Sol Duc is a good leaping-off point, or better yet given the hot baths, return point. **Lover's Lane Trail** (6 mi. loop, 2½hr.) departs the resort and leads to Sol Duc falls before looping back. The lazy or busy just go from the Sol Duc trailhead and make it there in 1½ mi. (1hr.). **Mink Lake** (2½ mi., 5hr.) climbs through a dense forest to a small mountain lake. After this there will be no guilt about pampering oneself in a hot spring. (1500 ft. gain. Strenuous.)

The **Resort ❺** is not inexpensive, but still affordable, with special-end-of-day rates and all-day admission. (Cabins $123; RV sites $22.) Natural spring water is filtered into three man-made mineral pools. To avoid the hot water and sulfur smell, you can also jump in the large chlorinated swimming pool. (☎327-3583; www.northolympic.com/solduc. Open late May-Sept. daily 9am-9pm; spring and fall 9am-7pm. $10; ages 4-12 $7.50; last 2hr. twilight rate $7. Suit, locker, and towel rental available.)

WASHINGTON

NEAH BAY AND CAPE FLATTERY

At the westernmost point on the Juan de Fuca Strait and well away from the National Park is **Neah Bay,** the only town in the **Makah Reservation.** The community has recently become famous for its revival of its gray-whale hunt and is renowned for the "Pompeii of the Pacific," a remarkably-preserved 500-year-old Makah village buried in a landslide. Gorgeous **Cape Flattery** is the most northwesterly point in the contiguous US. James Cook gave the Cape its name in 1778, because it "flattered us with the hopes of finding a harbor." Flattery got them nowhere; the nearest port is Port Angeles, 50 mi. away.

You can reach Neah Bay and Cape Flattery by an hour-long detour from **US 101.** From Port Angeles, **Rte. 112,** a National Scenic Byway, leads west 72 mi. to Neah Bay. From the south, **Rte. 113** runs north from Sappho to **Rte. 112. Clallam Transit System** runs from Port Angeles; take bus #14 from Oak St. to Sappho (1¼hr.), then #16 to Neah Bay. (☎452-4511 or 800-858-3747. 4-5 times per day. $1; seniors $0.50; ages 6-19 $0.85. All-day pass $2)

ACCOMMODATIONS & FOOD. If you're eager to spend a night on a Native American reservation, try the few motels and campgrounds here. The **Cape Motel ❸,** on Rte. 112, offers small but clean rooms, or sack out in a rustic shanty or tentsite. (☎645-2250. Office open 7:30am-10pm. Rooms $50-75; shanty singles $18, $25 as doubles; sites $12.) **Hobuck Beach Campground ❶** is 3 mi. northwest of Neah Bay—follow signs to Ocean Beaches. (20 sites, $10.)

Neah Bay doesn't offer many dining options. A few mediocre cafes line Front St. Pick up picnic materials at **Washburn's General Store,** also on Front St. (☎645-2211. Open M-Sa 8am-9pm, Su 8am-7pm.)

SIGHTS. The **Makah Cultural and Research Center,** in Neah Bay on Rte. 112, is just inside the reservation, opposite the Coast Guard station. The center presents beautiful artifacts from the archaeological site at Cape Alava. The Makah Nation, whose recorded history is 2000 years old, lives, fishes, and produces artwork on this land. (☎645-2711. Open June-Aug. daily 10am-5pm; Sept.-May W-Su 10am-5pm. $5, seniors and students $4, under 5 free. Free tours W-Su at 11am.) During Makah Days, in the last weekend in August, Native Americans from around the region come for canoe races, dances, and bone games (a form of gambling). Visitors are welcome and the salmon is delightful. Call the center for details.

Cape Flattery can be reached through Neah Bay, 8 mi. further northwest. Pick up directions at the Makah Center, or just take the road through town until it turns to dirt. Follow the "Marine Viewing Area" sign once you hit gravel, and continue for another 4 mi. to a small circular parking area, where a trailhead leads half a mile to Cape Flattery. At 3pm, a free, short guided hike leaves from the trailhead. You'll know you're close to the amazing views of **Tatoosh** and **Vancouver Island** when you hear the sound of Tatoosh's bullhorn. The road is excruciatingly bumpy, but the hike reveals some of the more beautiful stretches of ocean around. To the south, the Makah Reservation's **beaches** are solitary and peaceful; respectful visitors are welcome to wander.

Outside the reservation, to the south, dayhikers and backpackers adore the 9 mi. boardwalk loop that begins at Ozette Lake, an ONP area 21 miles off Hwy. 112. The boardwalks alone are a marvel; cedar shakes cut from old-growth red cedar form the attractive walk-ways. One heads toward sea stacks at **Cape Alava,** the other to a sublime beach at **Sand Point.** A 3 mi. hike down the coast links the two legs, passing ancient native petroglyphs. The entire area is mostly prairie and coastal forest, but presents plenty of sand to slog through. Overnighters must make permit reservations in advance; spaces fill quickly in summer. The **Ozette Ranger Station** has further info. (☎963-2725. Open intermittently.) Call the visitors center outside of PA at ☎565-3100 for permit reservations.

WESTERN OLYMPIC PENINSULA

Swinging wildly between rainforest, clear cuts, and dramatic coastline, US 101 traces a manic path through what is a truly stunning landscape. Travelers who drive the extra distance to this side of the peninsula will be rewarded with seclusion and almost unimaginable natural beauty.

FORKS ☎360

Between ONP's northern and western rims lies the logging town of Forks. Once the king timber town in the region, Forks both embraces and mourns its historic legacy. If you're passing through town or grabbing a bite to eat, take time to visit the **Forks Logging Museum.** (☎374-2531. Open M-Su 10am-4pm, logging and mill tours M, W, and F at 9am.) Check out forestry research in action at the **Olympic Natural Resources Center,** just south of the Logging Museum. Students and faculty from the University of Washington (and beyond) use this research facility to experiment with forest management techniques. Forks lies two hours west of Port Angeles and offers the widest selection of services in the western peninsula. Visit during the dry season (summer) if possible; Forks gets more rain than any other city or town in Washington.

ORIENTATION & PRACTICAL INFORMATION. **Clallam Transit** (☎452-4511 or 800-858-374) Rte. #14 serves Forks from **Port Angeles** (M-F; 7 per day; $1.25, disabled, seniors, and ages 6-19 $1). The **Forks Chamber of Commerce,** south of town, offers advice and maps, as well as tours through a real saw mill. (☎374-2531 or 800-443-6757. Open M-F 9am-5pm, Sa 10am-2pm.) The **Department of Natural Resources Main Office,** just off US 101 on the north side of Forks, right next to Tillicum Park, hands out maps of state land on the peninsula. Since tourists who actually stop here are a rarity, the DNR is happy to help. (☎374-6131. Open M-F 8am-4:30pm.) Check your email at the **Library** on 224 S Forks Ave. (☎374-6402. Free. Open M, Tu, W noon-8pm, Th-Sa 10am-5pm.) The **police** are in the City Hall on E Division. (☎374-2223. Open daily 6am-6pm.) The **hospital** (☎374-6271) is just west of 101 on Bogachiel Way. The **post office** is at Spartan Ave. and A St., east of US 101. Open M-F 9am-5pm, Sa 10am-noon. **Postal Code:** 98331.

ACCOMMODATIONS & FOOD. In Forks you'll find a row of motels offering budget prices. The **Town Motel ❸,** 1080 S Forks Ave., has a beautiful garden and comfortable rooms. (☎374-6231. Singles $37-45; doubles $47-55.) Twenty mi. south of Forks on US 101, between Hoh Rain Forest and Kalaloch, you'll find the **Rainforest Hostel ❶,** 169312 US 101. To get there, follow hostel signs off US 101. Family rooms and dorms are available, as are outside trailers for couples or people allergic to the resident dog and cat. The Hostel is a true resource for travelers, with laundry ($2), snacks, ride-sharing, info on buses, and parking. (☎374-2270. Morning **chore** required. Beds $12; family rooms $1 plus $12 per adult, $6 per child. Camping available for bikers, hikers, and busers for $6 per person.)

Off the highway, grab groceries and coffee at **Forks Thriftway,** 950 S Forks Ave. (☎374-6161. Open M-Su 8am-10pm.) The **Raindrop Cafe ❷,** 111 E A St. at S Forks Ave., serves breakfast until 11am, names its burgers after clouds ($3.75-7.50), and serves seriously delicious $7 salads. (☎374-6612. Open in summer M-Sa 6am-9pm, Su 6am-8pm; winter daily 6am-8pm.)

MORA

A quiet beach and campsite that doubles as a trailhead for long beach-following hikes is just 10 mi. west of Forks. In the morning, a haze hangs over the beach, making this area a perfect place to camp. This area is reached by taking US 110 west from just north of Forks.

Mora Campground ❶ is a sprawling 95-site campground that sees quite a bit of traffic from beach-goers. It offers evening programs on weekend nights, as well as toilets and water. (☎374-5460. Sites $10.) **Beach camping** is permitted both north and south of the **Mora Ranger Station.** To camp south of Mora a permit is required, in addition to a short drive to just before **La Push** (permit $5, plus $2 per person). From there, a trail leads down the beach—camping is permitted south of Third Beach and north of Oil City. Before hiking or camping on the coast, pick up a

THE CITY OF (NO) LIGHT. You may notice dim lights in state buildings and supermarkets across the Northwest. An altruistic move by an environmentally-conscious state? Alas, young idealist, we fear the world is not so selfless; the motivation is less about altruism and more about blackmail. Because the western United States is connected by an electrical network, the northwest quickly felt the spring 2001 power shortage in California. Utilities demanded 10% reductions in usage or threatened to raise prices up to 300%. Folks responded with a lot of grumbling, especially about their (least) favorite state down south, but they have made changes, stalling drastic price raises.

required overnight permit, a park map, a tide table, and the useful *Olympic Coastal Strip Info* brochure at a ranger station. Set up camp well above the highest line of tidal debris. North from Mora's **Rialto Beach,** 17 mi. of secluded beach snakes up to **Shi-Shi Beach.** Camping is allowed anywhere north of Ellen Creek with an overnight backcountry permit. Overnight options are numerous, and day-hikers often choose to take an abbreviated version of the same route, stopping at **Hole-in-the-Wall** (1½ mi. round-trip, 2hr.). Rialto Beach is a sight in itself. To get there, head 1½ mi. west from Mora Campground.

HOH RAINFOREST

The place to go to see the western rain forests, Hoh Rainforest sees plenty of guests. The average yearly rainfall in the Hoh Valley is 142 in. (Seattle gets 34 in. annually). The sights are spectacular, the growth is amazing, and the 18 mi. drive into the park from US 101 is an enjoyable patchwork of old-growth, wildflowers, and riverbeds. Turn off from 101 onto the Hoh Valley Rd., and drive about 12 mi. to the park entrance booth. Check out the **Hoh Rainforest Visitors Center** for backcountry permits and assistance in designing a backcountry route. (☎374-6925; www.nps.gov/olym. Open daily mid-June to Labor Day 9am-5pm.) The park maintains 88 **campsites** ❶ near the visitors center ($10) with drinking water and toilets, but has limited facilities for the handicapped. 70 backcountry **campsites** ❶ lie along the 17 mi. Hoh River Trail, which stretches between the Visitors Center and the Blue Glacier at Mt. Olympus (permit required, $5 plus $2 per person). Two free DNR campsites closer to 101, **Minnie Peterson** (7 sites) and **Willoughby Creek** (3 sites), are primitive and without treated water. No reservations are taken, so they are worth checking out to see what is open.

Hikers regularly file into the Hoh parking lot, returning from several popular routes that thread into the park's interior from the rainforest. The Hoh River Trail parallels the Hoh River for 17 mi., a three-day trip that traces through old-growth forests and lowlands to **Blue Glacier** on the shoulder of **Mount Olympus.** Shy Roosevelt elk, the ever-contested northern spotted owl, and the gods of ancient Greece inhabit this area. Closer by, the three-quarter-mile wheelchair-accessible **Hall of Mosses Trail** offers a whirlwind tour of rainforest vegetation. The slightly longer **Spruce Nature Trail** leads 1¼ mi. through old-growth forest, passing more varied vegetation along the banks of the Hoh River.

LAKE QUINAULT

Less visited than the Hoh Rain Forest, Lake Quinault offers its own rain forest and a large, beautiful lake. This lake, at the southwestern corner of ONP, sustains a small enclave of weekend getawayers, anglers, and hikers, many of them bypassing the rest of the peninsula and coming straight north to the lake via Aberdeen. On the southern, more populated side of the lake, the Forest Service operates an info center at the **Quinault Ranger Station,** 353 S Shore Rd. (☎288-2525. Open in summer M-F 8am-4:30pm, Sa-Su 9am-4pm; winter M-F 9am-4:30pm.) On the northern side of the lake, the **Quinault River Ranger Station** performs similar services, but from within the national park, 6 mi. from the highway. (☎288-2444. Open in summer daily 8:30am-5pm.) Campers can drop their gear lakeside in **Willaby Campgrounds** ❶, a quarter-mile before the Forest Service Ranger Station along the south shore of the lake. (☎288-2213. Sites $14.) Be aware—like those in the rest of the area, this campsite fills quickly. The **Lake Quinault Lodge** (☎288-2900 or 800-562-6672), next to the southern ranger station, rents canoes ($13 per hr.), seacycles ($18), rowboats ($11), and kayaks ($16) from their posh establishment.

Lake Quinault is surrounded by a great trail network. Stop at either ranger station for a detailed photocopy of trails in the area. **The North Fork trailhead** is 20 mi. up North Shore Rd. and starts one of the park's most popular multi-day hikes. It stretches 44 mi. north across the park, finishing at **Whiskey Bend** on the north rim near Elwha campgrounds. The week-long trip is one of the easier ones into the heart of the Olympics and has 17 campsites along the way (backcountry permit required). The **Skyline Ridge Trail** (6½ mi. one-way), just south of the North Fork trailhead, leads to the Park's largest yellow cedar. **Three Lakes Point** is an exquisite summit that often remains covered with snow into July. The 7 mi. hike (one-way) from North Fork runs through yellow cedar and prime amphibian habitat. Give the trip several days. **Dayhikes** depart the Quinault Ranger Station, including the 4 mi. **Quinault Lake Loop** and the half-mile **Maple Glade Trail.** Many more are found on the north of the lake, including the new 1 mi. **Kestner Homestead Trail.**

PACIFIC COAST

Approaching its northern terminus, US 101 travels along beautiful coastal shores. Small towns, phenomenal shellfish, and sparkling beaches beckon. Unfortunately, red tide plagues the shellfish population with a bacteria that can be fatal to humans. Check with the visitors centers or www.doh.wa.gov/ehp/sf/biotoxin.htm to see which beaches are open.

WASHINGTON

WILLAPA BAY ☎360

Willapa Bay stretches between the Long Beach Peninsula and the Washington mainland just north of the Washington-Oregon border and the mouth of the Columbia River. Home to the last unpolluted estuary in the nation, this is an excellent place to watch birdlife, especially in late spring and early fall. **US 101** passes the bay as it winds along the Pacific Coast toward Oregon. From Olympic National Park to the north, the highway passes Grays Harbor and the industrial cities of Aberdeen and Hoquiam at the mouth of the Chehalis River. As US 101 passes through Willapa Bay's sparkling sloughs, the quiet forests of Long Island lure seekers of solitude and lovers of wildlife. From the north, stop at the headquarters of the **Willapa National Wildlife Refuge,** just off US 101 on the left, 12 mi. north of the junction between US 101 and Rte. 103 by Chinook. The headquarters offers info on Canada geese, loons, grebes, cormorants, and trumpeter swans. (☎484-3482. Open M-F 7:30am-4pm.) Rangers can give directions and maps to several accessible hiking trails in the region, including Leadbetter Point at the tip of the Long Beach Peninsula. Long Island is home to five limited-use campgrounds, all inaccessible by car. Reaching the island, although it is only a stone's throw away from the mainland, requires finding a boat or bumming a ride on one (boats launch from the headquarters). Because of the difficulty of access, the bulk of tourist traffic is left stranded on the mainland. After reaching the island, hike 2½ mi. along the island's fern-lined main road to pay your respects to the **Ancient Cedars.**

LONG BEACH PENINSULA ☎360

The 28 mi. of unbroken sand that is Long Beach Peninsula is a frenzy of kitsch and souvenir shops sporadically broken up by calm forests and beautiful ocean views. Just don't let the looks deceive you into taking a dip—the water is very cold and carries lethal riptide currents. Accessible by US 101 and Rte. 103, every town has a clearly marked beach access road (unmarked roads end in private property). Fishing, boating, and kite-flying are how residents recuperate from pounding winter storms. Clamming season lasts from October to mid-March (but beware red tide). **Short Stop,** in the Shell Station across from the visitors center, sells non-resident licenses (annual license $23, two-day license $8) along with tips and tide tables.

Like most other towns along the bay, **Ilwaco** was nearly devastated when depleted salmon stocks required a shutdown of the fishery for several years. Salmon steaks are plentiful along the waterfront, where the industry is beginning to recover (barring a ban on fishing). **Pacific Salmon Charters** leads 8hr. fishing tours. (☎642-3466 or 800-831-2695. From $70. Open daily at 5:30am.) The **Long Beach Peninsula Visitors Bureau** is 5min. south of Long Beach on US 101. (☎642-2400 or 800-451-2542; www.funbeach.com. Open M-Sa 9am-5pm, Su 9am-4pm. Call for winter hours.) **Pacific Transit** sends buses from Long Beach as far north as Aberdeen. (☎642-9418. 85¢; exact change required.) Local buses run up and down the peninsula all day. Schedules are available in post offices and visitors centers on the peninsula (local service Sa-Su only). During the last week in August, flyers from Thailand, China, Japan, and Australia compete in the spectacular **International Kite Festival.**

Among the cheap places to hit the hay on the Peninsula is the **Sand-Lo-Motel ❸,** 1910 N Pacific Hwy. (☎642-2600. Rooms from $50; rates drop in winter.) **My Mom's Pie Kitchen ❷,** 1113 S Pacific Hwy., is a delicious respite from steak houses and greasy spoons. (☎642-2342; open W-Sa 11am-6pm.) **Mary's Traditional Dinners ❷** has tasty entrees for $10-14. (Open M-W 4:30-8pm, W-Su 8am-2pm.) For the best meal around, head down Hwy. 103 in Ocean Park to historic **Oysterville.** The star draw of this tiny, whitewashed town is **Oysterville Sea Farms ❸,** at 1st and Clark, which raises and dishes out its namesake mollusk. (☎665-6585. Open daily 10am-5pm.) For some entertainment, head to **Marsh's Free Museum,** 409 S Pacific Way, home to a mechanical fortune teller, Jake the petrified alligator-man, and honky-tonk souvenirs. (☎642-2188; open, ironically, whenever tourists bring money.)

COLUMBIA RIVER ESTUARY ☎360

Several miles south of Long Beach on Washington's southern border, Cape Disappointment guards the Columbia River Estuary. Over the last 300 years, almost 2000 vessels have been wrecked, stranded, or sunk at Cape Disappointment, and even today the Coast Guard is kept busy during the frequent squalls in the area. Fort Columbia State Park lies on US 101 northwest of the Astoria Megler Bridge, 1 mi. east of Chinook on the west side of the highway. The park interpretive center recreates life at the fort and showcases numerous artifacts on the indigenous Chinook people as well as on the white soldiers. (☎777-8221. Open Memorial Day to Oct. 1 daily 10am-5pm; call for winter hours.)

Three miles southwest of Ilwaco, at the southern tip of the Peninsula, **Fort Canby State Park ❶** offers camping and a megadose of Lewis and Clark. The park was the dynamic duo's final destination, and now boasts two lighthouses and a well-pruned campground packed with RVs. The sites fill up quickly in summer. (☎642-3078 or 800-452-5687. Open daily dawn-dusk. 240 sites, $12; RV sites $17; hiker/biker sites $6; cabins and yurts sleep 4 for $35. Reservation fee $6.) At the end of the main road, the spaceship-shaped **Lewis and Clark Interpretive Center** hovers above the ruins of the fort. Inside, a winding display documents their expedition from Missouri to their arrival at the mouth of the

***WILLKOMMEN IN* LEAVENWORTH!** A true experiment in tourism. After the town's logging industry collapsed and the railroad switching station moved to nearby Wenatchee, Leavenworth needed a new *Weltanschauung*. Desperate officials launched "Project Alpine," a gimmick to transform the town into a German village: zoning and building codes necessitated Bavarian-style buildings, waiters learned about bratwurst, polka blasted over the loudspeakers, and German beer flowed. It worked: more than 1.5 million Americans came in 2000, with influxes peaking during the city's three annual festivals. Tasty pretzels and *Schnitzel*, oddly enough, complement the nearby world-class rock climbing and camping. On the eastern slope of the Cascades, Leavenworth is near Washington's geographic center. To get there from Seattle, follow I-5 North to Everett (Exit 194), then US 2 East (126 mi., 2½hr.). From Spokane, follow US 2 West (184 mi., 4hr.). The Chamber of Commerce/Visitor Information Center, 220 9th St. at Commercial St., provides a plethora of pamphlets and brochures. (☎548-5807. Open M-Th 8am-5pm, F-Sa 8am-6pm, Su 10am-4pm; winter M-Sa 8am-5pm.) Indulge in the fabulous location of Bindlestiff's Riverside Cabins, 1600 Hwy. 2. Eight private cabins rest just feet from the beautiful Wenatchee River where you can watch the rafters drift by, borrow the BBQ, and grill on your own private porch. (☎548-5015. Fridge. TV. No phones. 1- and 2-room cabins $63-83.) Camping is also available 8 mi. out of town on Icicle Creek Rd. at a National Forest Campground ($10). Predictably, Leavenworth's food mimics German cuisine; surprisingly, it often succeeds. German *Wurst* booths are tucked between buildings everywhere. When you've had your fill of tourist-watching and sausage-scarfing, embark on an adventure into Leavenworth's extensive hiking, biking, and climbing opportunities in the Wenatchee National Forest.

Columbia. (Open daily 10am-5pm.) **The North Head Lighthouse,** built in 1898, is accessible by a gravel path in the northwest corner of the park, off Hwy. 103; the path has great views down the breakers. The **Cape Disappointment Lighthouse,** built in 1856, is the oldest lighthouse in the Pacific Northwest. In the southeast corner of the park, its distinctive red light can be reached by walking up a steep hill from the Coast Guard station parking lot, or by following a narrow, fairly steep trail from the interpretive center. For a magnificent beach-level view of both lighthouses, drive through the campground area past Waikiki Beach on the North Jetty. Waikiki is the only beach safe for swimming and is a solitary spot for winter beachcombing and ship watching.

CASCADE REGION

Sprawling in the rain shadow of the Cascades, the hills and valleys of the Columbia River Basin foster little more than sagebrush, tumbleweed, and tiny wildflowers among unirrigated dunes. Where the watershed has been tapped, however, a patchwork of farmland yields bumper crops of fruit and wine. Seeking the best of the region, travelers take high alpine routes through the Cascades, where dry hills give way to uncommonly green beauty in the mountains. The Cascades are most accessible in July, August, and September. Many high mountain passes are snowed in during the rest of the year, making access difficult and anything beside skiing and snowshoeing just about impossible.

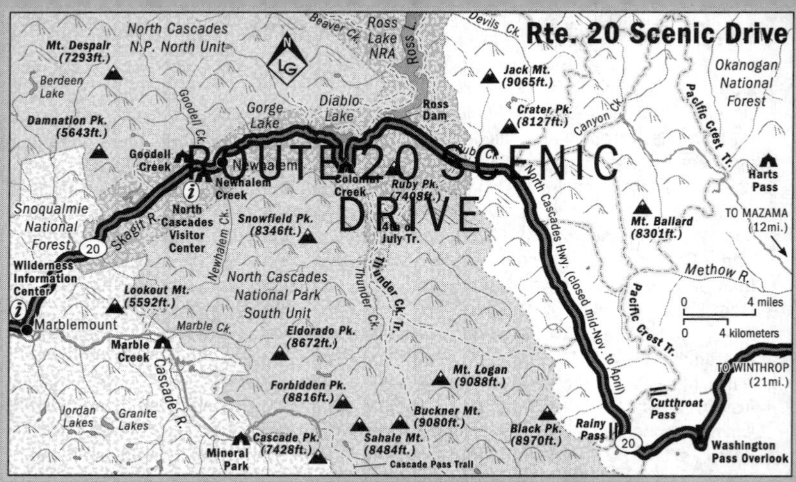

Weaving its way through the craggy peaks and lush valleys of Washington's North Cascades Range, Rte. 20 is nothing short of a blissful driving experience—the road seems to have been designed to afford drivers unadulterated pleasure. Spectacular vistas await at every turn, and a string of small towns scattered along the road provide services. Rte. 20 runs east-west through Northern Washington, traveling through the spectacular scenery of Mt. Baker Snoqualmie National Forest, North Cascades National Park, and Okanogan National Forest.

TIME: 2hr. driving time

DISTANCE: 70 mi.

SEASON: Apr.-Nov.

WEST OF NORTH CASCADES NATIONAL PARK

The westernmost town of note on Rte. 20 is **Sedro Woolley,** a logging town nestled in the rich farmland of the lower Skagit Valley. Sedro Woolley is home to the **North Cascades National Park** and **Mt. Baker-Snoqualmie National Forest Headquarters,** at 810 State Rte. 20, near the intersection with Rte. 9. The helpful rangers and info on activities in the park can help you move out of Sedro, which should be done as quickly as possible, considering the spectacular landscape farther west. (☎856-5700. Open daily 8am-4:30pm; closed in winter Sa-Su.)

Forty miles west of Sedro Woolley is the town of **Marblemount,** whose major attraction is the **Marblemount Wilderness Information Center,** 1 mi. north of West Marblemount on a well-marked road. This is the best resource for backcountry trip-planning in the North Cascades. It is best to explore the park on a multi-day hiking trip. The Information Center is the only place to pick up backcountry **permits,** and they have updates on trails and weather. Permits must be picked up in person no earlier than the day before trip date. (☎873-4500, ext. 39. Open July-Aug. Su-Th 7am-6pm, F-Sa 7am-8pm; in winter call ahead.) Once you leave Marblemount, there are **no major service stations** for more than 69 mi. west—you are entering the wild land of the National Park.

NORTH CASCADES NATIONAL PARK

East from Marblemount and across the Skagit River, Rte. 20 enters the wildest, most rugged park in Washington. The North Cascades National Park is unlike any other—as amazing as the views seem from the car, you can't experience this park's flavor from a vehicle, so make sure to hop out and explore; the area is rife with hiking trails.

The dramatic rocky pinnacles rising abruptly from the park's deep glacial valleys make for the most complex and challenging moutaineering in the continental United States—the region is commonly referred to as "the Alps of North America." Those determined to penetrate the park should allot a stout pair of boots and several days toward that goal. As with every national park in Washington, North Cascades is surrounded by ample national forest. Know which forest you are headed into, as different agencies, permits, and rules apply. The **Marblemount Wilderness Information Center,** 4 mi. west of the park, provides backcountry permits (required for any overnight travel in the park) and info on hikes. Another source for hiking info is the **North Cascades Visitors Center and Ranger Station.** (☎386-4495. Open in summer daily 8:30am-6pm; winter Sa-Su 9am-4:30pm.) The National Park is divided into four sections. The **North Unit** reaches up to the Canadian border, and is the most remote area of the park. The few trails that do cross it begin mainly near **Mt. Baker** or **Hozemon,** a small camp accessible from British Columbia. The **Ross Lake National Recreation Area** runs along Rte. 20 and north along Ross Lake. This is the most highly used area of the park, and the one to which most confine their stay. **South Unit** is pocked by glaciers and is accessible from trails leaving Rte. 20 along its north and east sides, making it an inviting wilderness to explore. Finally, at the park's southernmost tip, the **Lake Chelan National Recreation Area** protects the beautiful wilderness around Stehekin and the northern tip of Lake Chelan.

The park's **Goodell Creek Campground ❶,** at Mile 119 just west of Newhalem, is a beautiful, small area, with leafy sites suitable for tents and small trailers, and a launch site for white-water rafting on the Skagit River. (Pit toilets. 21 sites, $10. Water shut off after Oct., when sites are free.) **Newhalem Creek Campground ❶,** at Mile 120, shares a turn-off with the visitors center. It is a larger facility geared toward RV folk (111 sites, $12).

The amazing **Cascade Pass Trail** begins 22 mi. from the bridge, and continues to Stehekin Valley Rd. The 3hr. hike gains 1700 ft. of elevation in 3½ mi. (Moderate to difficult.) **Thunder Creek Trail** is among the most popular hikes in the area. The 1½ mi. meander through old-growth cedar and fir begins at Colonial Creek Campground at Mile 130 of Rte. 20. (Easy.) A more challenging variation is the 3¼ mi. **Fourth of July Pass Trail.** It begins 2 mi. into the Thunder Creek trail and climbs 3500 ft. toward stupendous views of glacier-draped Colonial and Snowfield peaks. (Moderate to difficult.)

EAST OF NORTH CASCADES NATIONAL PARK

The stretch of road from **Ross Lake,** near the Eastern border of North Cascades National Park, to **Winthrop,** in the Okanogan National Forest, is the most beautiful section of Rte. 20. The frozen creases of a mountain face stand before you. Snow and granite rise on one side of the road, sheer cliffs plummet on the other. Leaving the basin of Ross Lake, the road begins to climb, revealing the craggy peaks of the North Cascades.

The **Pacific Crest Trail** crosses Rte. 20 at **Rainy Pass** (Mile 157) on one of the most scenic and difficult legs of its 2500 mi. course from Mexico to Canada. Near Rainy Pass, scenic trails of 1-3 mi. can be hiked in sneakers, provided the snow has melted (about mid-July). Just off Rte. 20, an overlook at **Washington Pass** (Mile 162) rewards visitors with one of the state's most dramatic panoramas, an astonishing view of the red rocks exposed by **Early Winters Creek** in **Copper Basin.** The area has many well-marked trailheads off Rte. 20 that lead into the desolate wilderness. The popular 2½ mi. walk to **Blue Lake** begins half a mile east of Washington Pass—it's usually snow-free by July and provides a gentle ascent through meadows. An easier 2 mi. hike to Cutthroat Lake departs from an access road 4½ mi. east of Washington Pass. From the lake, the trail continues 4 mi. farther and almost 2000 ft. higher to **Cutthroat Pass** (6820 ft.), treating determined hikers to a breathtaking view of towering, rugged peaks.

About 5 mi. east of Winthrop, the **North Cascades Smoke Jumper Base** is staffed by courageously insane smoke jumpers who give thorough and personal tours of the base, explaining the procedures and equipment they use to help them parachute into forest fires and put them out. To get there, drive east through Winthrop. At the bridge, instead of turning right to follow Hwy. 20, go straight and follow all the curves of the main road. After about 5 mi., the base will be on your right. (☎997-2031. Open in summer and early fall; daily tours 10am-5pm.)

Mounts Baker, Vernon, Glacier, Rainier, Adams, and St. Helens are accessible by four major roads. The North Cascades Hwy. (Rte. 20) is the most breathtaking and provides access to North Cascades National Park. Scenic US 2 leaves Everett for Stevens Pass and descends along the Wenatchee River. Rte. 20 and US 2 are often traveled in sequence as the Cascade Loop. US 12 approaches Mt. Rainier National Park through White Pass and provides access to Mt. St. Helens from the north. I-90 sends four lanes from Seattle to the ski resorts of Snoqualmie Pass and eastward. From the west the state is accessible by bus on I-90 and US 2, and the train parallels I-90. Rainstorms and evening traffic can slow hitching; locals warn against thumbing Rte.20

MOUNT ST. HELENS ☎360

After two months of mounting volcanic activity, Mount St. Helens erupted with a cataclysmic blast on May 18, 1980, transforming what had been a perfect mountain cone into a crater one mile wide and two miles long. The force of the ash-filled blast crumbled 1300 ft. of rock and razed forests, strewing trees like charred matchsticks. Ash from the crater rocketed 17 mi. upward, circling the globe and blackening the region's sky for days. Debris from the volcano flooded Spirit Lake and choked the region's watersheds. Today, Mt. St. Helens is made up of the middle third of the Gifford Pinchot National Forest, as well as the Mount St. Helens National Volcanic Monument. The monument is part national park, part laboratory, and encompasses most of the area around the volcano affected by the explosion. Parts of the monument are off-limits to the public due to experiments, and hikers are obliged to keep to the handful of trails through such areas. Due to federal budget cuts many of the services currently offered on the mountain are slated to be cut back or cancelled. Call ahead to be sure, especially regarding early morning and winter hours.

ORIENTATION

To make the **western approach** (the most popular and worthwhile of the approaches, see p. 228), take Exit 49 off **I-5** and use **Rte. 504,** otherwise known as the **Spirit Lake Memorial Hwy.** The brand-new 52 mi. road has wide shoulders and astounding views of the crater. For most, this is the quickest and easiest daytrip to the mountain, and includes the Mount St. Helens Visitor Center, the Coldwater Ridge Visitor Center, and the Johnston Ridge Observatory. A **southern approach** (see p. 229) on **Rte. 503** skirts the side of the volcano until it connects with **Forest Service Rd. 90.** From there, **Forest Service Rd. 83** leads to lava caves and the Climber's Bivouac, a launch pad for forays up the mountain. Views from the south side don't show the recent destruction, but the green glens and remnants of age-old lava and mud flows make up for it with great hiking and camping. To make a **northern approach** (see p. 231), take **US 12** east from I-5 (Exit 68). The towns of Mossyrock, Morton, and Randle along US 12 offer the **closest major services** to the monument. From US 12, **Forest Service Rd. 25** heads south to Forest Service Rd. 99, which leads 16 mi. into the most devastated parts of the monument. Travelers can stop by the famous and majestic Spirit Lake, and marvel at the huge expanses of blown down forest. Although the monument itself contains no established **campgrounds,** a number are scattered throughout the surrounding national forest. See individual approaches for listings of campgrounds. Talking to a ranger is always your best option.

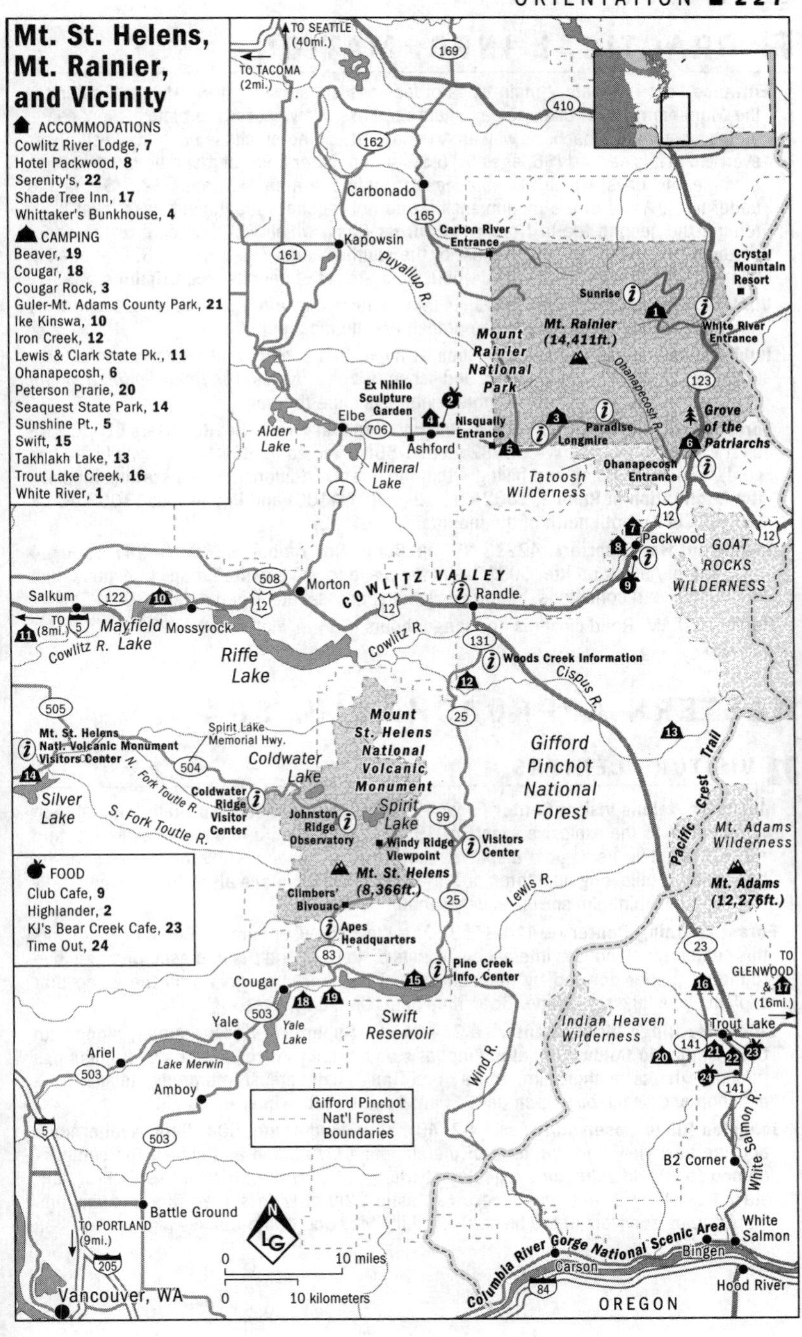
Mt. St. Helens, Mt. Rainier, and Vicinity
ACCOMMODATIONS
Cowlitz River Lodge, 7
Hotel Packwood, 8
Serenity's, 22
Shade Tree Inn, 17
Whittaker's Bunkhouse, 4
CAMPING
Beaver, 19
Cougar, 18
Cougar Rock, 3
Guler-Mt. Adams County Park, 21
Ike Kinswa, 10
Iron Creek, 12
Lewis & Clark State Pk., 11
Ohanapecosh, 6
Peterson Prarie, 20
Seaquest State Park, 14
Sunshine Pt., 5
Swift, 15
Takhlakh Lake, 13
Trout Lake Creek, 16
White River, 1
FOOD
Club Cafe, 9
Highlander, 2
KJ's Bear Creek Cafe, 23
Time Out, 24
TO SEATTLE (40mi.)
TO TACOMA (2mi.)
Carbonado
Kapowsin
Puyallup R.
Carbon River Entrance
Crystal Mountain Resort
Sunrise
Mt. Rainier (14,411ft.)
White River Entrance
Mount Rainier National Park
Ohanapecosh R.
Grove of the Patriarchs
Ex Nihilo Sculpture Garden
Nisqually Entrance
Paradise
Longmire
Ohanapecosh Entrance
Alder Lake
Elbe
Ashford
Mineral Lake
Tatoosh Wilderness
Packwood
GOAT ROCKS WILDERNESS
COWLITZ VALLEY
Salkum
Morton
Randle
Mayfield Lake
Mossyrock
TO (8mi.)
Cowlitz R.
Riffe Lake
Woods Creek Information
Cispus R.
Mt. St. Helens Natl. Volcanic Monument Visitors Center
Spirit Lake Memorial Hwy.
Coldwater Lake
Mount St. Helens National Volcanic Monument
Gifford Pinchot National Forest
N. Fork Toutle R.
Silver Lake
Coldwater Ridge Visitor Center
S. Fork Toutle R.
Johnston Ridge Observatory
Spirit Lake
Windy Ridge Viewpoint
Visitors Center
Pacific Crest Trail
Mt. Adams Wilderness
Mt. St. Helens (8,366ft.)
Mt. Adams (12,276ft.)
Lewis R.
Climbers' Bivouac
Apes Headquarters
Pine Creek Info. Center
TO GLENWOOD & 17 (16mi.)
Cougar
Swift Reservoir
Yale
Yale Lake
Indian Heaven Wilderness
Trout Lake
Ariel
Lake Merwin
Wind R.
Amboy
Gifford Pinchot Nat'l Forest Boundaries
B2 Corner
White Salmon R.
Battle Ground
TO PORTLAND (9mi.)
Columbia River Gorge National Scenic Area
White Salmon
Bingen
Carson
Hood River
0 10 miles
0 10 kilometers
Vancouver, WA
OREGON
WASHINGTON

PRACTICAL INFORMATION

Entrance Fee: There are 2 main types of fees associated with Mt. St. Helens. The first is the **Monument Pass**—this one-day, multi-site pass allows access to almost every center on the western approach, as well as Ape Cave. It can be purchased as a multi-site pass everywhere it is needed ($6, ages 5-15 $2, 4 and under free), or it can be purchased as a single site pass, which allows access to only one area ($3, ages 5-15 $1, 4 and under free). Areas of the monument that do not require a Monument Pass most likely require the second fee, a **Northwest Forest Pass,** which will take care of the entire northern approach, as well as most of the southern area ($5 per day, $30 annually). Climbing the mountain requires a whole separate set of permits (see **Climbing** p. 230).

Visitors Information: There are 9 visitors centers and info stations, listed below by approach. Those on the western approach are the most popular.

Publications: *The Volcano Review,* free at all visitors centers and ranger stations, contains a map, copious information, and schedules of activities. The *Road Guide to Mount St. Helens* ($6), available at visitors centers, is more thorough.

Forest Service Information: Gifford Pinchot National Forest Headquarters, 10600 NE 51st Circle, Vancouver, WA 98682 (☎891-5000, recording 891-5009; www.fs.fed.us/gpnf). Info on camping and hiking within the forest. Additional **ranger stations** and **visitor information** at **Randle,** 10024 US 12 (☎497-1100) and **Packwood,** 13068 US 12 (☎497-1172), both north of the mountain on US 12.

Monument Headquarters, 42218 NE Yale Bridge Rd., Amboy, 98601 (☎247-3900), 4 mi. north of Amboy on Rte. 503. This is *the* place to call or write for any questions prior to the trip: road conditions, permit availability, access, etc. Open daily 7:30am-5pm.

Radio: 530 AM. Road closures and ranger hours. Only in winter.

Emergency: ☎911.

WASHINGTON

WESTERN APPROACH: RTE. 504

VISITORS CENTERS

Mount St. Helens Visitor Center (☎274-2100), opposite Seaquest State Park. A great introduction to the explosive events of 1980. See the film, a manmade lava cave, and other interactive geological displays. Learn how a volcano works before you see its aftermath. A mile-long hike through 2500-year-old wetlands is also offered. Open daily 9am-6pm. 16min. film shown twice per hour.

Forest Learning Center (☎414-3439). The Weyerhaeuser Lumber Company sponsors this center, which houses interesting exhibits on logging and the reforestation of the surrounding timber downed by the explosion. Take the time and watch the video that explains how logging is done. Open May-Oct. 10am-6pm. Free.

Coldwater Ridge Visitor Center (☎274-2131). Superb view of the crater, along with trails leading to **Coldwater Lake.** Emphasis on the area's recolonization by living things through exhibits, a short film, and a ¼ mi. trail. Picnic areas, interpretive talks, and a gift shop and snack bar. Open daily 10am-6pm. Call for winter hours.

Johnston Ridge Observatory (☎274-2140), at the end of Rte. 504. Geological exhibits and the best view from the road of the steaming lava dome and crater. The center is named for David Johnston, a geologist who predicted the May 18, 1980 eruption, stayed to study it, and was killed. Fantastic 22min. wide screen film and exhibits emphasizing survivors of the blast. Open daily May-Oct. 10am-6pm.

ACCOMMODATIONS & FOOD

The only non-camping options close to the park are a few expensive motels that cluster around I-5, Exit 49, near the intersection of Rte. 504. Despite high prices, they book solid in the summer. Try the **Mt. St. Helens Motel ❸,** 1340 Mt. St. Helens Way NE in Castle Rock, 5 mi. from the Mt. St. Helens Visitor Center on Rte. 504. Enjoy free local calls, fridge, TVs, morning coffee, and laundry facilities. (☎274-7721. Singles $55; doubles $75.) **Seaquest State Park ❶,** opposite the Mt. St. Helens Visitor Center, is easy to reach off I-5, and the closest campground with facilities to the park. (☎274-8633, reservations 888-226-7688. Reservations essential. Wheelchair accessible. 92 sites, $14; 16 full RV sites, $20; 4 primitive walk-in sites, $5. Pay showers.) If your coolers and stomachs are empty, Castle Rock is the best place to refuel. Supermarkets and convenience stores lie on the west side of Hwy. 5, while fast food joints and a few restaurants sit on the east. Papa Pete throws a mean and inexpensive pizza at **Papa Pete's Pizza ❷,** 1163 Mt. St. Helens Way NE. A large cheese is $17. (☎274-4271. Open daily 10am-11pm.)

HIKING

The 1hr. drive from the Mt. St. Helens Visitor Center to Johnston Ridge offers spectacular views of the crater and rebounding ecosystem, with plenty of opportunities to park the car and walk along short, well-marked trails. The **Boundary Trail** (3 mi. to the Lake) leads from the Johnston Ridge Observatory to Spirit Lake, and continues 52 mi. to Mt. Adams through sensitive terrain. Moderate to difficult.

WASHINGTON

SOUTHERN APPROACH: RTE. 503

VISITORS CENTERS

Pine Creek Information Station, 17 mi. east of Cougar on Rd. 90, shows a short interpretive film of the eruption. Also the only place in the south of the park with free water to fill up bottles. Open June-Sept. daily 9am-6pm.

Apes' Headquarters, at Ape Cave on Rd. 8303, 3 mi. north of the Rd. 83-Rd. 90 junction (15min. from Cougar). Rangers dish out rental lanterns and guide 45min. lantern walks into the 1900-year-old lava tube daily from 10:30am-4:30pm, every hour on the half hour. On the weekends arrive early to snag a spot. Dress warmly—cave is 42°F. Open late-May to Sept. daily 10am-5:30pm.

CAMPING

Swift Campground (☎503-813-6666), 30min. east of Cougar on Rd. 90 and just west of the Pine Creek Information Station, has spacious sites on Swift Reservoir. It is one of the most popular campgrounds in the area. 93 sites, $12. ❶

Cougar Campground and **Beaver Bay,** 2 and 4 mi. east of Cougar respectively, along Yale Lake; Cougar Lake has 60 sites that are more spread out and private than Beaver Bay's 78 sites ($12-26). ❶

OUTDOOR ACTIVITIES

SPELUNKING

The **Ape Cave** lies 5 mi. east of Cougar, just off of Road 83. The cave is a broken 2½ mi. lava tube formed by an eruption over 1900 years ago. When exploring the cave, wear a jacket and sturdy shoes, and take at least two flashlights or lanterns. The Lower Cave's easy travel attracts most visitors, but the Upper Cave offers a more challenging scramble over rock rubble and lava breakdown. Budget 1¼hr. for the Lower Cave, 3hr. for the Upper Cave. A Monument Pass is required. Rangers lead guided cave explorations every day (see **Apes' Headquarters,** above), as well as rent lanterns. (Rentals $2 each, and stop at 4pm.) No free water is available at Apes.

HIKING

A quarter-mile before Ape Cave on Rd. 83 is the **Trail of Two Forests,** a lava-strewn and wheelchair-accessible boardwalk path above the forest floor. A beautiful forest has emerged, engulfed in lava from thousands of years ago. (Easy.) Rd. 83 continues 9 mi. farther north, ending at **Lahar Viewpoint,** the site of terrible mudflows that followed the eruption. On Rd. 83, 11 mi. northeast of its junction with Rd. 90, the **Lava Canyon Trail #184** hosts a range of challenges: an easy, wheelchair-accessible 40min. stroll yields spectacular views of the **Muddy River Gorge** and **Waterfall;** a more difficult route leads 3 mi. to the site of a now-defunct footbridge over Lava Canyon. Only the brave should venture farther; the trail then continues along a cliff and down a 25 ft. ladder to reach the canyon floor.

CLIMBING

WASHINGTON

The recently reshaped Mt. St. Helens draws hordes of people eager to gaze into the crater to see the source of so much power. It is now the most climbed mountain in the Northwest. The biggest challenge to climbing an otherwise very easy route is getting a permit. Between May 15 and Oct. 31, the Forest Service allows 100 people per day to hike to the crater rim. $15 permits are required to climb anywhere above 4800 ft. ($30 for an annual pass; reservations still required). Reserve in person or write to the Monument Headquarters (see **Practical Information**). Fifty permits per day may be reserved in advance after Feb. 1. Write early; weekends are usually booked by March, and weekdays often fill up as well. The reservation-less can enter a 6pm lottery for the next day's remaining permits at **Jack's Restaurant and Country Store,** 13411 Louis River Rd., on Rte. 503, 5 mi. west of Cougar. (☎231-4276. I-5 Exit 21. Open daily 6am-8:30pm.)

Although not a technical climb, the route up the mountain is a steep pathway of ash strewn with boulders. Often, the scree on the steep grade is so thick that each step forward involves a half-step back (5hr. up; 3hr. down). The view from the lip of the crater, encompassing Mt. Rainier, Mt. Adams, Mt. Hood, Spirit Lake, and the lava dome directly below, is magnificent. Bring sunglasses, sunscreen, sturdy climbing boots, foul-weather clothing, plenty of water, and gaiters to keep boots from filling with ash. Snow covers parts of the trail as late as early summer, making an ice axe a welcome companion. Free camping (no water) is available at the **Climber's Bivouac ❶,** the trailhead area for the **Ptarmigan Trail #216A,** which starts the route up the mountain. The trail is located about 4 mi. up Rd. 83. Note: entry into the crater is strictly prohibited.

WINTER ACTIVITIES

The southern area of Mt. St. Helens has several **SnoParks** along Rte. 90 and Rte. 83, connected by semi-groomed trails. They are popular with cross-country skiers, snowshoers, and snowmobilers. Pick up a pass before going out; they are available in Cougar and Randle during the winter. Another SnoPark is found along Rd. 25, accessible only from Randle.

NORTHERN APPROACH: US 12

VISITORS CENTERS

Woods Creek Information Station, 6 mi. south of Randle on Rd. 25, from US 12. A small station that is designed mainly for drive-through-style quick questions. It is, however, the north's best option past the Randle station (see p. 231). Open June-Aug. daily 9am-4pm.

Windy Ridge Interpretive Site, at the end of Rd. 99 off Rd. 25, 1¼hr. from Randle. Rangers give 30min. talks about the eruption in the outdoor amphitheater before the stunning backdrop of the volcano. Talks every hour on the half-hour between 11:30am-4:30pm. The route to Windy Ridge is lined with several viewpoints, all of them looking onto the area most damaged by the eruption. Stopping is well worth the extra time.

CAMPING

Iron Creek Campground ❶, just south of the Woods Creek Information Station, is the closest campsite to Mt. St. Helens, and has good hiking and beautiful forest along with a good location. All 98 sites can fill up on busy weekends. (Reservations ☎877-444-6777, strongly recommended in summer. Water. Sites $14-28.) The first stop for visitors traveling south on Rd. 25 from Randle and US 12 should be the **Woods Creek Information Station.**

HIKING

Independence Pass Trail #227, a 3½ mi. hike with overlooks of Spirit Lake and superb views of the crater and dome. (Moderate.) A serious hike continues past the intersection with **Norway Pass Trail,** running through the blast zone to the newly reopened **Mt. Margaret peak.** Considered the best hike in the park, the trail is 8 mi. (7hr.) to the peak and back. (Difficult.) Farther west, **Harmony Trail #224** provides a steep hike (2 mi. round-trip) to Spirit Lake. (Moderate to difficult.) Spectacular **Windy Ridge** is the exclamation point of Rd. 99. From here, a steep ash hill grants a magnificent view of the crater 3½ mi. away. The **Truman Trail** (7 mi.) meanders through the Pumice Plain, where hot flows sterilized the land. The area is under constant scrutiny by biologists, so stay on the trail at all times. (Easy to moderate.)

COWLITZ VALLEY/US 12 ☎360

The Cowlitz Valley is a broad, flat area that stretches from the south of Rainier west to Interstate 5. The Valley's location between Rainier, St. Helens, and Adams guarantees that anyone touring the southern Cascades will end up there at some point. Several lakes, services, plenty of inexpensive accommodations, and roads leading to all of the major peaks make the Valley a good stop on almost any itinerary. Exploring tiny back roads is not recommended, as a large population of marijuana farmers in Lewis County might not take kindly to being discovered.

The main road running through the valley is US 12. To figure out the next stop on your tour of the area, drop in at the **Cowlitz Valley Ranger Station,** 10024 US 12, located in Randle, near the center of the valley. The ranger station has lots of information on trails and other outdoor activities. (☎497-1100. Open June-Aug. daily 8am-4:30pm; Sept.-May, closed Sa-Su.) Info is also available 16 mi. to the east, at the Packwood Visitor Information Center, 13068 US 12.

THE LOCAL STORY

OUT OF THE FLYING PLANE, INTO THE FIRE

Smoke jumpers are firefighters who parachute from planes to combat blazes. Let's Go *spoke with* ***Scott Wicklund,*** *a smoke jumper based out of Winthrop, WA, in August of 2002.*

Q: A lot of people would say this is an insane job. How would you respond?

A: People would say this is an insane job because they don't realize all the safety precautions that go into it. It seems crazy because you're jumping out of a perfectly good airplane... into a forest fire! But the reality is that you've got a perfectly good parachute and you know fire behavior. So you land in a place where you're safe from any sort of fire activity, and take the proper measures to control the fire.

Q: How did you decide to do this?

A: I guess growing up my mom said, "Don't get dirty; don't play with fire." I found a job that paid me to do both.

Q: Any memorable stories?

A: The weirdest thing that ever happened to me? One time I landed in an 80 ft. tree, but the parachute didn't catch on the branches. I slid down the side of the tree, picking up speed until I basically knew I was going to break my leg in half a second. All of a sudden, the parachute catches on a branch and I was just hanging there a foot away from the ground. Hanging there perfectly fine. Which was a great feeling.

(☎497-1172. Open summer daily 7:45-11:30am and 12:30-4:30pm; winter closed Sa-Su.) **Packwood** has groceries and other essentials. **Mossyrock** and **Morton** are settlements with services nearer I-5; Morton has a laundromat and grocery near the intersection of Rtes. 7 and 12.

There are several options for camping, including Northwest Forest Pass sites— ask at a station for info. **Ike Kinswa State Park ❶,** on Mayfield Lake's Rte. 122, a 30min. drive west of Randle, about 18 mi. off US 12 from the west, offers camping, swimming (to non-campers, too), and trout fishing year-round. It boasts 101 private sites with full access to a lake that attracts bald eagles and ospreys. (☎983-3402. Reservations are strongly recommended in summer; call 888-226-7688. Sites $16, full RV sites $22, extra vehicle $6. Showers $0.50 per 3min.) Thirteen miles to the west of Ike Kinswa along Rte. 12 on Jackson Hwy., the **Lewis and Clark State Campground ❶** has sites amid old-growth forests, plus BBQs and kitchens. (☎864-2643, reservations 800-452-5687. Group sites available. 25 sites, $13.)

There is excellent **fishing** in the Cowlitz area. Spots downstream of the **Barrier Dam** are crowded for good reason. To get there, travel to Salkum off Rte. 12, go south down Fuller Rd., and follow signs to the Barrier Dam boat launch. There is a tackle shop on the road down. Locals claim that **Mineral Lake** is the best place around to catch fish and that **Riffe Lake** is also worth a cast.

MOUNT ADAMS ☎509

At 12,276 ft., Mt. Adams is the second highest peak in Washington but still one of the least visited. Overlooked throughout its history, it was named after the 2nd U.S. President by Lewis and Clark only because other volcanic heavy-hitters Hood, Rainier, and Baker had already been claimed for British admirals. Still, Mt. Adams's lack of fame works to the advantage of those seeking solitude on its rugged volcanic terrain. Unfortunately, part of the reason Adams lacks recognition is that it's hard to access: it is connected by pavement only to the south, and the gravel roads traveling to the north are closed much of the year due to snow.

ORIENTATION & PRACTICAL INFORMATION. The Mt. Adams District is formed by the southern third of the Gifford Pinchot National Forest, as well as the Mt. Adams Wilderness. The entire area is most accessible from the south, by following Hwy. 141 north from Hood River via

White Salmon. One can also approach from the north, along Forest Rd. 23 (this road is largely unpaved, and usually blocked with snow until June or July). **Amtrak** (☎800-872-7245) is also an option, stopping 20 mi. away in Bingen at the foot of Walnut St., with routes from **Portland** (2hr., $10-17) and **Spokane** (5½hr., $34-60).

If you're coming from the south, your last stop before heading into the great unknown should be Trout Lake, found on Highway 141. Trout Lake's main draw is the **Mt. Adams District Ranger Station,** 2455 Hwy. 141, whose rangers dispense advice, the proper permits, detailed topographic maps of the area for $4, and guides to hiking trails for $6. (☎395-3400; station open M-F 8am-4:30pm, additional weekend hours during summer.) Trout Lake also has a gas station and **General Store,** 2383 Hwy. 141, which sells a small supply of food and essentials at a price that will make you regret not getting them elsewhere. (☎395-2777. Open summer daily 8am-8pm, winter 8am-7pm.) Another option is to pick up provisions on your way up Hwy. 141, at a grocery store in **BZ Corner** or any of the other towns.

Information about the area is available in White Salmon, at the **Mt. Adams Chamber of Commerce Information Center,** just west of the toll bridge from Hood River on Rte. 14. (☎493-3630; Open summer daily 9am-5pm, Oct.-May M-F 9am-5pm.) Equipment rental is best taken care of in Hood River (see **Columbia River Gorge,** p. 90). For road conditions, call ☎360-905-2958. **Emergency:** ☎911. **Police:** 180 W Lincoln, White Salmon (non-emergency ☎493-2660). **Post office:** 2393 Hwy. 141, in Trout Lake. (☎395-2108; open M-F 8:30am-12:30pm, 1-5pm.) **Postal Code:** 98650.

ACCOMMODATIONS & FOOD. The Mt. Adams area is crawling with places to pitch a tent, many of them requiring only a Northwest Forest Pass. The best plan is to stop at the ranger station and tell them what you want to do; they will tell you the best site to use as a base. The closest to Trout Lake is the **Guler-Mt. Adams County Park ❶,** one of the few areas with showers. To get there, take a left at the post office and follow the signs. (Sites with water $10, water and electricity $14.) The biggest pay area near Trout Lake is **Peterson Prairie ❶;** head about 5 mi. past Trout Lake on 141 and another 3 mi. into the National Forest, and look for signs to your right. (30 sites, $11.) On the way, check to see if there is room at **Trout Lake Creek,** a forest-pass-only site just off 141; take a right on Forest Rd. 88 and follow the signs. Both sites put you near the Natural Bridges and Ice Caves, which are off Hwy. 141 on the left and worth a

(Continued from previous page)

Q: Describe the feeling of crashing.

A: You jump out of the airplane, you see the meadow below that you're supposed to be going for, and you're aiming for that; then the wind picks up, and you know you're not going to make it. At that point you start looking for some shorter trees to land in, so you're not hung up too high off the ground. Then you try and cap that tree with your canopy so you're hung up well; they train you to do that. But there's still a bit of chaos. At that point you don't know exactly what's going to happen. A lot of times it's a soft landing, because you go in there and the canopy catches the tree perfectly. Other times, your feet get kicked out from underneath you, you're upside-down and falling, you're not sure that your canopy hung up, your heart's racing a million miles per hour, and then *jerk*, you're hanging.

Q: What's the injury rate like?

A: I have never been injured jumping. We might get two or three sprained ankles, maybe a blown ACL, maybe a broken femur, maybe a broken wrist every year.

Q: Is this a team effort?

A: It is every day. The first thing you do after you land is check with your partner and make sure he's okay. We always jump two at a time.

Q: Would you recommend this job?

A: Yeah, I'd recommend it to anyone who likes having adventures but doesn't want to make a whole lot of money.

quick stop. Perhaps the best camping is 1hr. north of Trout Lake, in the Takhlakh Lake area. There are several different spots, but the best is **Takhlakh Lake Campsite ❶,** which offers amazing views of Mt. Adams presiding over the lake. ($11 per site, $13 for prime sites.) To get there, take the Mt. Adams Rec. Hwy. out of Trout Lake, and then take Forest Road 23 for 1hr. until you see signs—call the ranger station to ask about road openings.

The one budget option that will put a hard roof overhead is found in Glenwood, a 16 mi. drive from Trout Lake. To get there, take the Mt. Adams Rec. Hwy. out of Trout Lake, and then take the first right—a small sign will say Glenwood. Look for the small but friendly **Shade Tree Inn ❷,** 105 E Main St. A motel with attached restaurant, convenience store, and laundromat, it also has excellent views of the mountain from a back balcony. Satellite TV, A/C. (☎364-3471. Reception and store open daily 7am-9:30pm, restaurant 7am-7pm. Singles $45; doubles $55.)

A broader range of luxuries can be found at **Serenity's ❸,** 2291 Hwy. 141, just south of town and across from Trout Lake School. The four spacious cabins with full bath (jacuzzis in 3 cabins), kitchenettes, gas log fireplaces, TV and VCR are geared toward romantic couples, though as many as 6-8 can fit comfortably in the large, lofted bedroom. (Minimum 2 night stay on weekends. Chalets $90-150.)

Get basic foods at **BZ Corner Grocery,** on the left when going north on Hwy. 141 in BZ Corner, about 10 mi. south of Trout Lake. (☎493-2441; open M-Sa 6am-9pm, Su 7am-8pm.) In Trout Lake, **KJ's Bear Creek Cafe ❶,** 2376 Hwy. 141 at the fork of Hwy. 141 and the Mt. Adams Recreational Hwy., has greasy but reasonably priced food. Breakfast meals $4-5, burger $3.60. (☎395-2525; open summer 6am-8pm daily.) Just south of the Trout Lake school is **Time Out ❶,** 2295 Hwy. 141, which serves pizza (small $7) and burgers. (☎395-2767; open M-F 11am-7pm, Sa-Su noon-8pm.)

WASHINGTON

HIKING & MOUNTAIN BIKING. The absolute best resources in the Mt. Adams area for hiking are available at the ranger station: supplement the rangers' advice with the **Forest Services Trail Guide** ($6). Hiking is generally very rewarding—most trails meander in and out of broken-up lava flows and occasionally open up onto good views. If you're driving, many trailheads require a **Northwest Forest Pass** ($5 per day, $30 annually; available at the ranger station). The area can get very dry in the summer, so be sure to bring adequate water; also note that **compasses don't work in lava beds** due to the abundance of underground mineral deposits. A long thaw leaves many trails closed through spring, and bugs can make early summer very uncomfortable.

The half-mile trail to **Sleeping Beauty Peak** starts off at a small trailhead on the left side of Rd. 8810-040, about a quarter-mile from the Rd. 8810 junction (see directions to Trout Lake campground, above). The **Indian Heaven Wilderness Trail** is a mild 10 mi. loop through forest and meadow. Other dayhiking options abound in the Adams area. For multi-day hikes, the most popular is the **Round-the-Mountain Trail.** It does not go around the mountain at all, but rather stretches 8 mi. to the south of Mt. Adams, eventually ending at the border of the Yakama Indian Reservation. This area is closed to hikers lacking tribal permission, so most parties turn around at this point, yielding a 2-3 day 16 mi. journey (although permits to use Yakama land are available from rangers at Bird Lake, off the trail). Mountain biking is permitted on many of the trails in the National Forest. Bikeable trails are clearly marked and are listed in the trail guide available at the ranger station.

CLIMBING. Mt. Adams is laced with at least a dozen mountaineering routes, including the very popular (and relatively easy) **South Spur** and **Mt. Adams Summit Route.** All routes require crampons and an ice axe year-round, and usually do not even open up until June. In addition, climbers should stop at the ranger station to register and purchase a **Cascade Volcano Pass** ($10 for trips on M-Th, $15 for a trip that touches either F, Sa, or Su), required for all parties going higher than 7000 ft. up the mountain. Get climbing info at ☎891-5015.

RAFTING & KAYAKING. Three rivers pour off the flanks of Mt. Adams, through volcanic rock and down to the Columbia River. The **White Salmon River** has several classic runs. The class III-IV section, from BZ Corner to Husum, dives into a craggy gorge with lichen-draped old-growth trees and crumbling lava cliffs. The **Farmlands Run** courses through a beautiful, dark, and vertical-walled canyon, whose flat rim belies the raging class IVs (two V+) below. First-timers should go with a veteran. Immediately downstream of the Farmland's last rapid lurks the class V-VI **Green Truss** section, where the Gorge Games' races are held on its sometimes-lethal waterfalls. A class II+ section from Husum down to Northwestern lake is a popular after-work run.

Other nearby boating options include the **Klickitat River,** famed for its columnar basalt formations and isolated, roadless sections, as well as the **Wind River.** For extreme kayakers, the **Little White Salmon River** has the best paddling in the Northwest. But it's no cakewalk: veterans estimate that only 10% of runs finish without mishap. For rafters, guiding companies line Hwy. 141 around BZ Corner, taking patrons to most rivers in the area. **River Drifters** (☎800-972-0430; www.riverdrifters.net) has lots of options. Two companies operate out of White Salmon—**Zoller's Outdoor Odysseys** (☎800-366-2004) and **All Adventures** (☎877-641-7238). **River Riders,** in Hood River, also has competitive prices (☎800-448-7238). A day of rafting can cost anywhere between $45 and $70.

RUMBLE IN THE MOUNTAINS A long time ago, when wishing still mattered and mountains fought for love, three rumples in the Earth's crust were caught in a love triangle. Legend holds that Pah-toe (Mt. Adams) fought and defeated his brother Wy'East (Mt. Hood) for the love of Squaw Mountain. Dismayed, the broken-hearted Squaw Mountain laid at the feet of Pah-toe and fell asleep, becoming Sleeping Beauty Mountain. Pah-toe, once proud and tall, bowed his head in shame—thus taking his current shape.

BIRD-WATCHING, HUNTING, & FISHING. Though the prolific elk population in the area around Glenwood is conducive to hunting, marksmen beware: the beasts are protected in the nearby Conboy Lake Wildlife Refuge. The elk are familiar with its boundaries and are known to gloat from inside at frustrated hunters. Duck and other fowl can be hunted from within the refuge, however, and many of the streams in the area are fishable for trout and bullheads. Pick up the "Sport Fishing Rules" and "Big Game Hunting Seasons and Rules" guides at local stores for info on all the complex details and seasons. For those who prefer to merely observe wildlife, the refuge is home to nesting sites of rare Sandhill cranes, and guided bird-watching trips leave the ranger station every Friday morning. Bird-watching is reputed to be best right around the first spring break-up.

MOUNT RAINIER NATIONAL PARK ☎360

At 14,411 ft., Mt. Rainier (ray-NEER) presides over the Cascade Range. The Klickitat native people called it Tahoma, "Mountain of God," but Rainier is simply "the Mountain" to most Washington residents. Perpetually snow-capped, this dormant volcano draws thousands of visitors from all around the globe. Clouds mask the mountain for at least 200 days per year, frustrating those who come solely to see

WASHINGTON

its distinctive summit. Rainier is so big it creates its own weather by jutting into the warm, wet air and pulling down vast amounts of rain and snow. Its sharp ridges, steep gullies, and 76 glaciers combine to make Rainier an inhospitable host for the thousands of determined climbers who attempt its summit each year. The non-alpinists among us can explore the old-growth forests and alpine meadows of **Mt. Rainier National Park.** With over 305 mi. of trails through wildflowers, rivers, and hot springs, Mt. Rainier has options for nature lovers.

AT A GLANCE	
AREA: 235,625 acres **CLIMATE:** Characterized by random stormy weather. **FEATURES:** Mount Rainier, large backcountry. **HIGHLIGHTS:** Climbing Rainier, Silver Falls during snowmelt.	**GATEWAYS:** Ashford, Packwood. **CAMPING:** Extensive backcountry options, see p. 238. **FEES:** $10 per car, $5 per hiker. Permits good for 7 days. Backcountry permits free.

TRANSPORTATION

To reach Mt. Rainier from the northwest, take I-5 to Tacoma, then go east on Rte. 512, south on Rte. 7, and east on Rte. 706. This road meanders through the town of **Ashford** and into the park by the Nisqually entrance, which leads to the visitors centers of **Longmire** and **Paradise.** Rte. 706 is the only access road open year-round; snow usually closes all other park roads from November through May. Mt. Rainier is 65 mi. from Tacoma and 90 mi. from Seattle.

Gray Line Bus Service, 4500 W Marginal Way, Seattle (☎206-624-5208 or 800-426-7532; www.graylineofseattle.com), has buses that run from **Seattle** to Mt. Rainier daily May to mid-Sept. (1-day round-trip $54, under 12 $27). Buses leave from the Convention Center at 8th and Pike in Seattle at 8am and return at 6pm. The trip up takes 3½-4hr. (with a few stops at picturesque viewpoints) and allows 2½hr. at Paradise. Rainier Shuttle (☎569-2331) runs daily between **Sea-Tac Airport** and **Ashford** (2hr., 2 per day, $37), or **Paradise** (3hr., 1 per day, $46).

All major roads offer scenic views of the mountain, with numerous roadside lookouts. The roads to Paradise and Sunrise are especially picturesque. Stevens Canyon Rd. connects the southeast corner of the national park with Paradise, Longmire, and the Nisqually entrance, revealing superb vistas of Rainier and the Tatoosh Range. The summer draws hordes of visitors, making parking very difficult at many of the visitors centers and trailheads throughout the afternoon hours.

Rainier weather changes quickly, so pack warm clothes and cold-rated equipment. Before setting out, ask rangers for mountain-climbing, hiking, and equipment recommendations. Group size is limited in many areas, and campers must carry all waste out of the backcountry. Potable water is not available at most backcountry campsites. **All stream and lake water should be treated** for giardia with tablets, filters, or by boiling it before drinking. For more information on preparing for the outdoors, see **Camping and Hiking Equipment,** p. 38.

PRACTICAL INFORMATION

The section of the Mt. Baker-Snoqualmie National Forest that surrounds Mt. Rainier on all but its southern side is administered by **Wenatchee National Forest,** 301 Yakima St., Wenatchee, WA 98807 (☎509-662-4314). The **Gifford Pinchot National Forest** (☎425-750-5000), to the south, has headquarters at 6926 E Fourth Plain

WASHINGTON

Blvd., P.O. Box 8944, Vancouver, WA, 98668. The Packwood ranger station is nearest, at 13068 US 12. (☎494-0600. Open 10am-5pm.) The main web site for the park is www.nps.gov/mora.

Visitor Information:

Longmire Wilderness Information Center (☎569-4453, backcountry reservations only), 6 mi. east of the Nisqually entrance in the southwest corner of the park, is the best place to plan a backcountry trip. Open May 23-Oct. 5 daily 7:30am-4pm.

The Jackson Memorial Visitors Center, at Paradise, has 360 degrees of windows, an information desk, exhibits on the mountain's mischievous ways, and a predictably expensive and not-so-good cafeteria. Open 10am-6pm daily, permits available.

White River Wilderness Information Center (☎663-2273), off Rte. 410 on the park's east side, on the way to Sunrise, is also very good for information. Open May 23-Sept. W 7:30am-4:30pm, Th 7:30am-7pm, F 7am-7pm, and Sa 7am-5pm.

The Wilkeson "Red Caboose" Ranger Station (☎829-5127) is at Carbon River. Open M-Th 8am-4:30pm, F 8am-7pm, Sa 7am-7pm, Su 8am-6pm. These stations all distribute backcountry permits.

The Park Headquarters, Tahoma Woods, Star Rte., Ashford, OR 98304 (☎569-2211; www.nps.gov/mora) is the best place to call with phone inquiries. Open M-F 8am-4:30pm. Free map. *Tahoma News,* distributed at park entrances and ranger stations, is a useful source of maps, hiking recommendations, and safety precautions.

Equipment Rental: Rainier Mountaineering, Inc. (☎627-6242, www.rmiguides.com), in Paradise across from the Paradise Inn and in Ashford next to Whittaker's Bunkhouse. Expert RMI guides lead summit climbs, seminars, and special programs (for dear prices). Open May-Sept. daily 7am-8pm; Oct.-Apr. M-F 9am-5pm. Rents ice axes ($13), crampons ($13), boots ($24), packs ($24), and helmets ($10) by the day.

Climbing: Glacier climbers and mountain climbers intending to scale above 10,000 ft. must register in person at Paradise, White River, or Wilkeson Ranger Stations to be granted permits. Cost-recovery fee $15 per person. Annual pass $25.

Emergency: ☎911.

Hospital: The nearest medical facilities are in **Morton** (40 mi. from Longmire) and **Enumclaw** (5 mi. from Sunrise). **Tacoma General Hospital,** 315 Martin Luther King Way (☎253-552-1000), has 24hr. emergency facilities.

Internet access: See **Whittaker's Bunkhouse,** below. $3 per 30min.; $5 per hr.

Post Office: In the **National Park Inn,** Longmire. Open M-F 8:30am-noon and 1-5pm. Located in the **Paradise Inn** (see below). Open M-F 9am-noon and 12:30-5pm, Sa 8:30am-noon.

Postal Code: Longmire 98397, Paradise 98398.

ACCOMMODATIONS

Longmire, Paradise, and Sunrise offer expensive accommodations. For a bed, stay in Ashford or Packwood. Alternatively, camp and convince yourself that your tent has a roof and heating, and is a hostel.

Hotel Packwood, 104 Main St. (☎494-5431), in Packwood 20min. south of Ohanapecosh or 1hr. south of Nisqually. Charming since 1912. A sprawled-out grizzly graces the parlor. Grr. Singles and doubles $39-49. Private bath extra. ❸

Whittaker's Bunkhouse (☎569-2439), 6 mi. west of the Nisqually entrance. Owned by Lou Whittaker, a long-time RMI guide. View his accomplishments (he was in the first party to climb the North Face of Everest) in the photos hanging from nearly every wall. Espresso bar, but no kitchen or bedding. Book ahead. Spacious co-ed dorms with 2 baths. Dorms $30; private rooms $75-100. ❸

FROM THE ROAD

RAINIER AREA KAYAKING

Creeks and rivers in the Rainier area suck in all lovers of "adventure" and "fun," which can be translated out of the Northwest kayaker's vernacular as "self-punishment" and "pain." When I descended two rivers in the shadow of Rainier and Adams, I had all the "fun" I could handle, and more.

First came McCoy Creek. Everything went more or less okay (not counting when I slipped off a rock and nearly got swept into an undercut slot) until we got to an unportageable (read: no way out but down the river), virtually unscoutable, two-tiered 25 ft. beast of a waterfall. I plopped off okay, but the paddler behind me, Chad, blew a crucial move to cross the current and got recirculated in a vicious monster of a hole. Forced out of his boat but still trapped in the hole, he was underwater so long I started to remind myself how many pumps per minute to do in CPR. After an hour or so of recovery, Chad revealed the Northwest boater's attitude towards thrashings: "Whatever, I'll be back here next year."

I could only convince one of the four guys who had paddled with me on McCoy to come back out to Rainier the next day. Perhaps a bit reluctant, my friend Dan showed up an hour and a half late, and we put on Johnson Creek at 4:30 in the afternoon. The scenery was beautiful, mossy, and wooded. After the first portage (an hour-long mission to traverse 150 ft. of logs and thorns),

Paradise Inn (☎569-2413; reservations ☎569-2275), in Paradise. Built in 1917 from Alaskan cedar at 5400 ft. Large dining facility with exquisite-looking, and expensive, food. Open late May-Oct. Book ahead. Very popular during the summer. Small singles and doubles from $75, each extra person $12. ❹

The Cowlitz River Lodge, 13069 US 12 (☎494-7378), on the east end of Packwood right across from the Packwood Information Center. The Lodge offers very nice rooms for a decent price. Singles $50; doubles $67. ❸

CAMPING

Backcountry camping requires a **permit,** free from ranger stations and visitors centers. (☎569-4453. Reserve ahead.) Inquire about trail closures before setting off. Hikers with a valid permit can camp at well-established trailside, alpine, and snowfield sites (most with toilets and water source). Fires are prohibited except in backcountry campgrounds.

Camping in national forests outside the park is free. Avoid eroded lakesides and riverbanks; flash floods and debris flows are frequent. Campfires are prohibited, except during the rainy season. Check with ranger stations for details. There are six campgrounds within the park. For reservations, apply in person at the visitors centers; after February, call ☎800-365-2267 (international ☎301-722-1257) or visit http://reservations.nps.gov. National Park campgrounds are handicapped-accessible, but have no RV sites or showers. Coin-op showers are available at **Jackson Memorial Visitors Center,** in Paradise. Alternatively, the **Packwood RV Park** has pay showers for $3 at the corner of Main St. and US 12 in Packwood. **Sunshine Point** ❶, a quarter-mile beyond the Nisqually entrance, is a quiet site to the south. (Open year-round. Quiet hours 10pm-6am. 18 sites, $10.) **Cougar Rock** ❶, 2¼ mi. north of Longmire in the southwest, is near a glacial river. (Quiet hours 10pm-6am. Open June-Sept. Reservations required June 28 to Labor Day. 173 individual sites, $15. Winter season $12. 5 group sites, $3 per person.) **Ohanapecosh** ❶, 11 mi. north of Packwood on Rte. 123, in the southeast, provides secluded sites with great scenery. (Open May-Sept. Reservations required, often booked solid. 205 sites, $15; winter $12.) About 150 ft. outside of the Ohanapecosh entrance, a dirt road descends from the highway and turns into a T. Either fork takes you to free camping spots under tall trees. **White River** ❶ is 5 mi. west of White River on the way to Sunrise in the northeast. (Open late June-Sept. 112 sites, $10.)

FOOD

The general stores in the park sell only last-minute trifles like bug repellent (well worth it). An extra state-park tax is charged, so stock up before you arrive. **Blanton's Market,** 13040 US 12 in Packwood, is the closest decent supermarket to the park and has an ATM in front. (☎494-6101. Open summer daily 7am-9pm, winter 7am-8pm.) **Highlander ❷,** in Ashford, serves standard pub fare in a single dimly-lit room with a pool table. Burgers $6-7. (☎569-2953; open daily 7am to anytime between 10pm and 2am. Restaurant closes at 9pm.) **Club Cafe ❷,** 13016 Hwy. 12, is in Packwood. A small, down-home diner. Their omelettes always elicit oohs and ahhs. (☎494-5977; open daily 7am-7pm.)

OUTDOOR ACTIVITIES

Rainier's moody weather makes it a tricky destination. Clouds and freezing rain can sweep in at any time, making the fireplace at **Paradise Inn** the mountain's most attractive destination. In the winter, huge volumes of snow close most of the park (almost 70 ft. fell at Paradise in 2002), and trails often remain snow-covered well into summer. But hit Rainier on a good day, and the rewards are huge. Hiking is probably the best bet, as ample views and fascinating terrain are ubiquitous.

HIKING. The hiking trails are far too numerous to list—Rainier is easily Washington's most versatile area. One option is a **ranger-led interpretive hike,** which can delve into anything from area history to local wildflowers. Each visitors center conducts hikes and most of the campgrounds have evening talks and campfire programs. **Camp Muir** (9 mi. round-trip), the most popular staging ground for a summit attempt, is also a challenging dayhike. It begins on Skyline trail (which is itself a popular dayhiking option), and then heads north on Pebble Creek Trail. The latter half of the hike is covered in snow for most of the year.

A beautiful, and easier, half-day hike wanders along the Ohanapecosh River by **Silver Falls** (a sight to behold during spring snowmelt), then up to the **Grove of the Patriarchs,** whose stately cedars have patiently awaited your arrival since the days of feudalism and the Magna Carta. A trail leads to the falls from Ohanapecosh campground, and a shorter route begins at a pulloff on the west side of Rte. 123, just south of the intersection with 706. The Grove can be accessed just inside the Ohanapecosh entrance.

(Continued from previous page)

though, we knew we might get more than we bargained for. Actually, we hadn't bargained for anything, since all we knew to expect was a runnable 20 ft. waterfall in the middle of a deep canyon. Our certainty turned to shock, though, when we realized the falls was blocked by logs and was clearly unrunnable—hitting any of them would mean certain death. One glance at the imposing rock walls around us led to a quick, inescapable conclusion. "Dude, we're screwed," I explained to Dan.

With no other choice, we began tackling the walls inch by inch, hauling our boats by rope over mud, rocks, and brush. Two and a half hours later and well past dark, I wedged my 40 lb. boat into a tree, curled up in the fetal position, and mumbled something incoherent. In addition to the steepness of the canyon walls (if I had pushed hard enough against the wall, I would have tumbled backwards off the face), the arrangement of fallen logs was so devilish that it slowed our pace to a few feet per minute and produced a combination of rage, frustration, and resignation. As it turned out, when I had lost all hope we were only 100 ft. below a forest road on the canyon rim—my friend, in a burst of superhuman endurance, had pressed on and discovered it. So, after a mild 1½ hr. stumble down the road, we reached Dan's car and some oh-so-tasty Peanut Butter and Jelly sandwiches.

—Carleton Goold

CLIMBING. A trip to the summit of Rainier requires substantial preparation and expense. The ascent involves a vertical rise of more than 9000 ft. over 9 mi., and usually takes two days with an overnight stay at **Camp Muir** on the south side (10,000 ft.) or **Camp Schurman** on the east side (9500 ft.). Each camp has a ranger station, rescue cache, and toilet. Permits cost $30 per person. Only experienced climbers should attempt the summit, and no one should try going solo; novices can be guided to the summit with the help of **Rainier Mountaineering, Inc.** after a day-long basic climbing course. For details, contact Park Headquarters or RMI (see **Practical Information,** p. 237).

CHELAN ☎509

The serpentine body of Lake Chelan (sha-LAN) undulates some 55 mi. southeast through the Wenatchee National Forest and the Lake Chelan National Recreation Area toward the Columbia River and US 97. Here, the green mountains of North Cascades National Park transform into the bone-dry brown hills and apple orchards that surround the town of Chelan. Unfortunately, the town itself is disappointingly touristy—the economy is structured around family tourism that usually involves renting a house for an extended stay. There is little the in town to draw the budget traveler. The real attraction of Chelan is at the docks, where several ferries leave for the beautiful wilderness farther up the lake.

ORIENTATION & PRACTICAL INFORMATION. The town of Chelan rests on the southeast end of Lake Chelan, along Hwy. 97, 190 mi. (4hr.) east of and west of Spokane. **US 97** cuts through the town along the lake and becomes its main street, **Woodin Ave.** Look out for speed traps near the lake.

WASHINGTON

Link, the local bus service, runs Rte. 21 and 31 hourly between the Chamber of Commerce and Wenatchee. (☎662-1155; www.linktransit.com. 1¼hr., M-F 6am-6pm, $0.50-1.) **Northwest Trailways** (☎800-366-3830, or through Greyhound 800-231-2222) departs Wenatchee for **Seattle** (3½hr., 2 per day, $23) and **Spokane** (3½hr., 1 per day, $23). For **ferry** service, see **Stehekin,** p. 242. The **Chamber of Commerce,** 102 E Johnson, off Manson Hwy., has info on the town. (☎682-3503 or 800-424-3526; www.lakechelan.com. Open summer M-F 9am-5pm, Sa-Su 10am-3pm; winter M-F 9am-5pm.) The **Chelan Ranger Station,** 428 W Woodin Ave. on the lake, is the place to buy maps ($4) or Northwest Forest Passes ($5) for parking. (☎682-2549. Open June-Sept. daily 7:45am-4:30pm; Oct.-May M-F 7:45am-4:30pm.) **Chelan Boat Rentals,** 1210 W Woodin, is one of the shops on the lake that rents small fishing boats ($15 per hr.), jet skis (from $30 per hr., $100 per day), and bikes ($15 per hr.). (☎682-4444. Open daily 9am-8pm.) **Town Tub Laundry** is by the Pennzoil station on the east end of Woodin Ave. (Wash $1.75, dry $0.25 per 10min. Open daily 8am-9pm.) **Electrik Dreams,** 246 W Manson Rd., Suite 1, provides **Internet access** for $9 per hour. (☎682-8889. Open M-Th 11am-10pm, F-Sa 11am-9pm.) Call ☎911 in an **emergency,** or contact the **police,** located at 207 N Emerson St. (☎682-2588). A 24hr. **crisis line** can be reached at ☎662-7105, and there's a 24hr. **pharmacy** at **Safeway** (☎682-4087. Open M-F 9am-7pm, Sa 8am-6pm, Su 10am-6pm.) A **hospital** is at 503 E Highland St. (☎682-3300. Open 24hr.) The **post office** is at 144 E Johnson St. (☎682-2625. Open M-F 8:30am-5pm.) **Postal Code:** 98816.

ACCOMMODATIONS & CAMPING. Most Chelan motels and resorts are rather pricey. The **Apple Inn ❸,** 1002 E Woodin, boasts a hot tub, pool, and shuttle service. (☎682-4044. Singles $49; doubles $59. Winter $35, $39.) **Mom's Montlake Motel ❸,** 823 Wapato, south off Woodin Ave. on Clifford, is a summertime mom-and-pop operation with clean, microwave- or kitchen-equipped rooms. (☎682-5715. Singles $49; doubles $59.) Most campers head for **Lake Chelan State Park ❶**, a pleasantly grassy, but crowded, campground 9 mi. up the south shore of the lake with a beach, swimming area, small store, picnic sites, a boat launch, playing fields, and jet ski rentals. (☎687-3710 or reservations 800-452-5687. Bus #21. Sites $14; full RV sites $20.) **Twenty-Five Mile Creek State Park ❶** is a smaller, but no less crowded, site; it boasts a beach, a boat launch, and small store. (☎687-3610 or 800-452-5687. Reservations recommended Apr.-Sept. 63 sites, $14; 23 RV sites, $20.) Campers are also free to pitch tents anywhere in the national forest, but may only light fires in established fire rings.

FOOD. The cheapest food in Chelan is at local fruit stands, although a few good places can be found slightly outside of town on E Woodin. **Safeway,** 106 W Manson Rd., has groceries. (☎682-2615. Open daily 6am-11pm.) **Bear Foods** (a.k.a. Golden Florin's General Store), 125 E Woodin Ave., provides health food. (☎682-5535. Open M-Sa 9am-7pm, Su noon-5pm.) Behind the unassuming facade of **Local Myth ❶**, 122 Emerson St., Art and the gang create mind-blowing pizzas from whole-wheat dough and fresh ingredients. The pizzas ($7 and up), calzones ($6-9), and conversations are unbeatable. (☎682-2914. Open Tu-Sa 11:30am-9pm.) Pick up baked goods and throw down shots of wheatgrass ($2.50) or espresso ($1) over at **The Rising Sun Bakery ❶**, 514 E. Woodin Ave. (☎682-8938. Open M-F 9am-5pm.) **Flying Saucers ❶**, 116 S Emerson, has mocha, chai tea, cinnamon rolls (all $2), and aura galore in a converted 50s diner with flying saucers hanging from the ceiling. (☎682-5129. Open summer M-Sa 7am-8pm; winter M-F 7am-4pm.)

DAYTRIP FROM CHELAN: GRAND COULEE DAM

As the climate warmed 18,000 years ago, a small glacier blocking a lake in Montana gave way, releasing floodwaters that swept across eastern Washington, gouging out layers of soil and exposing the layers of granite and basalt below. The washout carved massive canyons, called coulees, into a region now known as the Channeled Scab Lands, which composes most of the striking, mesa-filled country south of the dam across its largest canyon, the Grand Coulee.

From 1934 to 1942, 7000 workers toiled on the construction of the **Grand Coulee Dam,** a local remedy for the agricultural woes of the drought and the Great Depression, but a travesty for conservationists and Native Americans. Nearly a mile long, this behemoth is the world's largest solid concrete structure and irrigates the previously parched Columbia River Basin, all while generating more power than any other hydroelectric plant in the United States. The amount of concrete used to construct Grand Coulee would be enough to construct a standard 6 ft. wide sidewalk around the globe at the equator. The Columbia River, raised 350 ft. by the dam, forms both **Franklin D. Roosevelt Lake** and **Banks Lake,** where "wet-siders" from western Washington flock for swimming, boating, and fishing.

The dam hulks at the junction of Rte. 174 and Rte. 155, about 75 mi. east of Chelan and 90 mi. west of Spokane. The rotund **Visitor Arrival Center,** on Rte. 155 just north of Grand Coulee, is filled with disconnected exhibits on the construction, operation, and legacy of the dam. A guided tour of the third and newest powerplant begins every 30min. between 10am and 5pm (contact the visitors center for more info). On summer nights, a spectacularly cheesy yet technically amazing 36min. laser show chronicles the structure's history on the spillway of the dam. Watch from the visitors center for guaranteed sound (and arrive at least an hour early to beat the crowds), or park at Crown Point Vista off Rte. 174 and tune in to 89.9 FM. (☎509-633-9265. Open June-July daily 8:30am-11pm; Aug. 8:30am-10:30pm; Sept. 8:30am-9:30pm; Oct.-May 9am-5pm. Show late May-July daily 10pm; Aug. 9:30pm; Sept. 8:30pm. Free.) If you plan to spend the night after the light show, head to the only federal campground in the area, **Spring Canyon Campground ❶**, 5 mi. east of the damn. Tent sites $10.

STEHEKIN ☎509

Stehekin (steh-HEE-kin) counts among the most magical places in Washington. An isolated village at the wetter, quieter, more welcoming northern end of Lake Chelan, its main connection to the rest of the world is a 50 mi. ferry route; the only other option is hiking in on the extensive Pacific Crest Trail or float-planing in. This isolation has preserved a wild, beautiful place. With McGregor Mountain looming and total silence just a 5min. walk out of the small settlement, Stehekin is a destination that entertains the outdoorsy for days on end.

INTERCITY TRANSPORTATION. Three **ferries** ply the lake in summer. The ferries proceed along a shoreline where mountain goats and brown bears roam: this alone makes the ride worthwhile. All are operated by the **Lake Chelan Boat Company,** 1418 W Woodin, about 1 mi. west of downtown Chelan. (☎682-2224 or reservations 682-4584; www.ladyofthelake.com. Open May-Oct.) The *Lady of the Lake II*, a 350-person ferry, makes one round-trip to Stehekin per day. (4hr. with a 1½hr. layover, 8:30am, $25). This ferry also picks up from Fields Point, 16 mi. up South Shore Rd. near **Twenty-Five Mile Creek State Park** (9:45am; parking $3 per day, $17 per week). You can request that the ferry stop at Prince Creek or Moore Point campgrounds along the Lakeshore Trail (see **Outdoor Activities,** below). Arrange in advance to be picked up, then flag them down with a bright article of clothing. The smaller *Lady Express* makes an express trip to Stehekin (2¼hr. with a 1hr. layover, $44). A combination ticket for the *Lady Express* or *Lady of the Lake II* to Stehekin and back also runs $41, and allows just over 3hr. in Stehekin. A new high-speed catamaran, the *Lady Cat,* makes two round-trips per day (1¼hr. with a 1½hr. layover, 7:45am and 1:30pm, $89). Book ferry tickets in advance on summer weekends; they will not accept credit cards on the day of travel.

LOCAL TRANSPORTATION. Stehekin itself is small enough that two legs and two minutes are all one needs to cross it—transport isn't a problem. Getting further up the road to trailheads and campsites can be an issue, though. **Discovery Bikes** rents two-wheelers. (☎884-4844. $3.50 per hr., $10 per half-day, $15 per day.) From mid-May to mid-October, a shuttle leaves from the ferry and runs up Stehekin Valley Rd. to High Bridge campground (45min., 4 per day). The $6 NPS shuttles continue on to Bridge Creek campground (30min.) and Glory Mountain (1hr.) from July to mid-October. From mid-May to mid-June, the NPS shuttle runs to High Bridge upon request. (☎856-5700, ext. 340. Reservations recommended.)

CAMPING & FOOD. The Park Service maintains 12 **campgrounds** along the Stehekin River off Stehekin Valley Rd. All except the area closest to Stehekin are geared toward the hiker. **Purple Point ❶**, right next to the ferry landing, is unique in its amenities: it has water, bathrooms, and free showers. All need reservations, so stop at the ranger station and have them help you figure out how to get there. **Per-**

mits are free, and required for backcountry camping and hiking. (Permits available at the **visitors center;** call ☎856-5700, ext. 340.) The **Stehekin Valley Ranch** ❸ offers more expensive lodging than the camping alternative. (☎800-536-0745. Cabins $60 for stays of 5 days or more; price includes meals and transportation.) A delicious **dinner** ❸ at the Ranch costs about $14. (☎682-4677. Reserve ahead. Open M-F 9am-5pm.) The **Lodge Restaurant** ❸, at the landing, serves dinner that runs $6-17. (☎682-4494. Open 7:30am-8pm.) Two miles up the road, the **Stehekin Pastry Company** ❶ lures hikers out of the hills for sticky buns. (Open June 1-Sept. 23 daily 8am-5pm; May 26-June 15 and Sept. 24-Oct. 8 Sa-Su 8am-5pm.)

OUTDOOR ACTIVITIES. Some short, scenic dayhikes surround the landing. The simple ¾ mi. **Imus Creek Trail** is an interpretive hike that offers great views of the lake, starting behind the Golden West Visitor Center. (Easy.) The moderately steep **Rainbow Loop Trail** offers stellar valley views. The 4½ mi. trail begins 2½ mi. from Stehekin; shuttles run to the trailhead five times a day, but it's close enough to walk. (Moderate.) From Purple Creek, take a right turn to reach the switchbacks of the steep 15 mi. (round-trip) **Purple Creek Trail.** The 5700 ft. climb is tough, but the rewards include glimpses of nearby glaciers. (Difficult.) The 17½ mi., 2- to 3-day **Lakeshore Trail** begins by the Visitor Center and follows the north shore of Lake Chelan to Prince Creek, never rising more than 500 ft. above the lake but offering splendid views of the surrounding peaks. (Easy.)

An unpaved road and many trails probe north from Stehekin into **North Cascades National Park.** Two hikes begin at High Bridge. The mellow **Agnes Gorge Trail** is the second trailhead on the left, 200 yards beyond the bridge, and travels a level 2½ mi. through forests and meadows with views of 8115 ft. Agnes Mountain. (Easy.) Behind the ranger cabin, the **McGregor Mountain Trail** is a strenuous straight shot up the side of the mountain, climbing 6525 vertical feet over 8 mi. and ending with unsurpassed views of the high North Cascades peaks. (Difficult.) The last half-mile is a scramble up ledges. This extremely challenging trail is often blocked by snow well into July; check at the visitors center before starting out. The shuttle to Bridge Creek provides access to the **Pacific Crest Trail,** which runs from Mexico to Canada. The North Cascades portion of this trail has been called its most scenic by many who have completed the colossal journey. (Moderate to difficult.)

The **Rainbow Falls Tour,** in Stehekin, is a guided bus tour that coincides with ferry arrival times. It zooms through the valley and its major sights: the Stehekin School, the last one-room schoolhouse in Washington; the Stehekin Pastry Company; and Rainbow Falls, a misty 312 ft. cataract. ($7, ages 6-11 $4, under 6 free. Tickets available on ferries.)

EASTERN WASHINGTON

Lying in the Cascade's rain shadow, the hills and valleys of the Columbia River Basin foster little more than browning grass, sagebrush, and tumbleweed. Where the construction of dams and canals has made irrigation possible, the desert has bloomed into a land of bountiful fruit crops and their dazzling by-product: tasty, high-quality wines. Sunshine fills the days and attracts the moody and depressed "wetsiders" from rainy Western Washington. The calm beauty and dry, hot air of the region invite a pleasant and lazy vacation of wine-tasting and apple-munching.

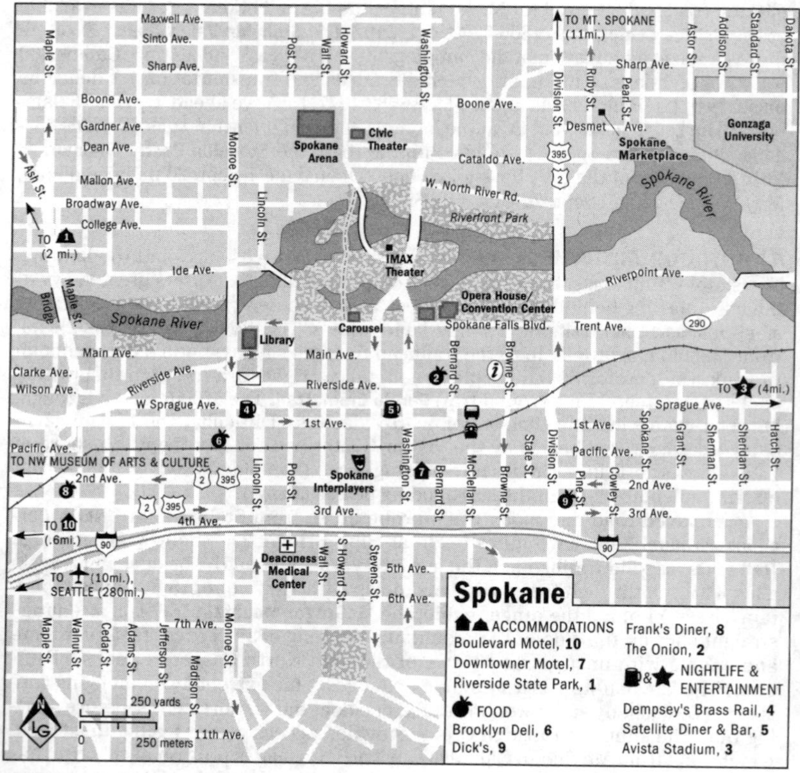

SPOKANE

☎509

Ah, 1974: Gerald Ford in the White House, Elvis in the white suit, and Spokane (spoe-KAN) in the world's spotlight. Built on silver mining and made prosperous as an agricultural rail link, Spokane found fame when the World's Fair came to town in 1974. Parks, department stores, and skyways sprang up in preparation for the city's promising future. Today, cafes catering to a college crowd and 50s-style burger joints make for a suburban atmosphere, and the melancholy remains of Spokane '74 slumber in Riverfront Park. A small-town America feel, pleasant outdoor parks, and the culture of a larger city make Spokane '03 worthy of a stopover.

TRANSPORTATION

Spokane is 280 mi. east of Seattle on I-90, between Exits 279 and 282. Avenues run east-west parallel to the **Spokane River,** streets run north-south, and both alternate directions one-way. The city is divided north-south by **Sprague Ave.** and east-west by **Division St.** Downtown is the quadrant north of Sprague Ave. and west of Division St., wedged between I-90 and the river.

Airplanes: Spokane International Airport (☎624-3218), off I-90 8 mi. southwest of town. Most major carriers service **Seattle, Portland,** and beyond.

Trains: Amtrak, 221 W 1st Ave. (☎624-5144; 800-USA-RAIL), at Bernard St. Counter open daily 10pm-6am. All trains depart 1-3am. 1 train per day to **Portland, OR** ($35-75, depending on season and availability) and **Seattle.**

Buses: Greyhound, 221 W 1st Ave. (☎624-5251), at Bernard St., in the same building as Amtrak. Ticket office open daily 7:30am-6:20pm and 12:15-2:20am. One-way to: **Portland, OR** (8-10hr., 3 per day, $40) and **Seattle** (6hr., 5 per day, $30.25). **Northwestern Trailways** (☎838-5262 or 800-366-3830) shares the same terminal, serving other parts of WA and large cities. Ticket office open daily 8am-6:45pm. Senior discounts.

Taxis: Checker Cab (☎624-4171). **Yellow Cab** (☎624-4321). Both run 24hr.

Car Rental: U-Save Auto Rental, 918 W 3rd St. (☎455-8018), at Monroe St. Cars from $39 per day, $195 per week. Unlimited mileage within WA for more than 3 days; otherwise $0.20 per mi. after 200 mi. Must be 21+ with major credit card; $5 per day if under 25. Open M-Su 7am-7pm.

PRACTICAL INFORMATION

Tourist Office: Spokane Area Convention and Visitors Bureau, 201 W Main St. (☎800-248-3230). Exit 281 off I-90. Offers free Internet access and local phone calls. Open May-Sept. M-F 8:30am-5pm, Sa 9am-5pm, Su 10am-3pm; Oct.-Apr. M-F 8:30am-5pm.

Equipment Rental: Mountain Gear, 2002 N Division St. (☎325-9000 or 800-829-2009; www.mgear.com) rents canoes ($45 per day), kayaks ($25-$45 per day), and snowboards ($24). Open M-F 9:30am-8pm, Sa 9:30am-6pm, Su 11am-5pm.

Laundromat: Otis Hotel Coin-Op, 110 S Madison St. (☎624-3111), at 1st Ave. $1 wash, dry $0.25 per 20min. Open daily 7am-7pm.

Washington Road Conditions: ☎800-695-7623.

Emergency: ☎911.

Police: ☎456-2233. 24hr. crime-report line.

Crisis Line: ☎838-4428. 24hr.

Medical Services: Rockwood Clinic, 400 E 5th Ave. (☎838-2531 or 459-1577), at Sherman St. Open daily for walk-ins 8am-8pm.

Internet Access: Spokane **Library,** 906 W Main St. (☎444-5333). 15min. free. Open M and Tu noon-8pm, W-F 10am-6pm. Also see the **Visitors Bureau,** above.

Post Office: 904 W Riverside. Ave. (☎800-275-8777). Open M-F 6am-5pm. **Postal Code:** 99210

ACCOMMODATIONS & CAMPING

Cheaper motels are sprinkled among the chains along Rte. 2 toward the airport, and others can be found on the north end of town along Division Ave.

Boulevard Motel, 2905 W Sunset Blvd. (☎747-1060). Take 4th Ave. southwest from downtown to the I-90 Business Loop, which becomes Sunset Blvd. The recently-renovated rooms are so clean you could eat off the floor. Singles $35; doubles $46. ❷

Downtowner Motel, 165 S Washington St. (☎838-4411), at 2nd Ave. Aging exterior and a mint-green ivy motif. This motel's prices and convenient downtown location can't be beat. Continental breakfast and cable included. Singles $33; doubles $37. ❷

Riverside State Park (☎800-233-0321; reservations ☎800-452-5687), 6 mi. northwest of downtown. Take the Maple St. Bridge north and turn left at the brown park sign; follow signs to Rte. 291 (Nine Mile Rd.), turn left onto Rifle Club Rd. and follow to the park. 101 newly rebuilt sites in a sparse ponderosa forest near the river. Sites $14; RV sites $20; hiker/biker sites $6. Showers $0.25 per 3min. ❶

FOOD

The **Spokane Marketplace,** 1100 N Ruby St., at DeSmet St., sells fresh fruit, baked goods, and crafts. (☎456-0100. Open Apr. Sa 9am-4pm; May-Dec. W and Sa 9am-4pm.) Groceries are at **Safeway,** 1617 W 3rd St. (☎624-8852. Open 24hr.)

The Onion, 302 W Riverside Ave. (☎624-9965), at Bernard St., serves amazing burgers ($6-8) and huckleberry shakes ($3) amid throngs of locals and visitors who've been coming here since 1978. Open daily 11am-about 11pm. ❷

Frank's Diner, 1516 W 2nd Ave. (☎747-8798), at Walnut St., operates out of a 1906 observation railroad car. Breakfast all day long. More elegant than most pricier restaurants. Breakfast $4-8. Open Th-Sa 6am-9pm, Su-W 6am-7pm. ❶

Dick's, 10 E 3rd Ave. (☎747-2481), at Division St. Look for the huge panda sign near I-90 and find burgers by the bagful. A time warp—customers eat in their parked cars and pay 1950s prices (burgers $0.63; fries $0.63; shakes $0.93). Open M-Th 8am-midnight, F-Sa 8am-1am, Su 9am-midnight; mid-June to Aug. open 1hr. later. ❶

Brooklyn Deli, 122 S. Monroe (☎835-4177). This small, friendly joint serves turkey avocado and tasty vegetarian sandwiches (don't forget to ask for a pickle!). Half-sandwich $4.25, whole $6.50. Open M-F 10am-7pm, Sa 10am-5pm. ❶

NIGHTLIFE & ENTERTAINMENT

For local happenings, pick up the *Spokesman-Review* Friday "Weekend" section, or look for the *Inlander* or the *Wrap*, both available at the library.

Dempsey's Brass Rail, 909 W 1st Ave., has a hot dance floor, flashy decor, and free Internet access by the bar. Drag Diva shows (F-Sa) and rainbow-striped beer taps make Dempsey's "the place to be gay." Happy hour 3-7pm daily. (☎747-5362. Kitchen serves dinner daily 3-8pm. Open Su-Th 3pm-2am, F-Sa 3pm-4am.) **Satellite Diner and Bar,** 425 W Sprague Ave., is a great place to people-watch until 4am over biscuits and gravy ($3.25). Microbrews $3. Happy hour daily 4pm-7pm. (☎624-3952. Open M-F 7am-4am, Sa-Su 6pm-4am; bar closes at 2am.)

The **Spokane Indians** play single-A baseball in the Northwest League of Professional Baseball from June to August in **Avista Stadium,** at the Spokane Fairgrounds, 602 N Havana St. (☎535-2922; www.ticketswest.com. Great seats only $4, seniors $3.) The minor league **Spokane Chiefs** play hockey in the Canadian Hockey League September through March in **Spokane Memorial Arena,** 720 W Mallon Ave. To get there, follow signs from the Maple St. exit off I-5. (☎535-7825. Box office open M-F 10am-6pm. Seats $7-15.)

SIGHTS

MANITO PARK. One of the most beautiful spots in Spokane, this park boasts five sections of lovingly-maintained flowerbeds. Commune with the carp in the **Nishinomiya Japanese Garden,** sniff the blooming roses on **Rosehill** in late June, relax in the elegant **Duncan Garden,** or sniff around in the **David Graiser Conservatory** and the **Joel Farris Perennial Garden.** *(4 W 21st Ave. From downtown, go south on Bernard St. and turn left on 21st Ave. ☎ 625-6622. Open 24hr.; buildings locked from dusk-8am. Free.)*

RIVERFRONT PARK. The centerpiece of downtown, the park is Spokane's civic center and the place for a pleasant stroll. Developed for the 1974 World's Fair, the park's 100 acres are divided down the middle by the rapids that culminate in Spokane Falls. In the park, the **IMAX Theater** houses your basic five-story movie screen and a projector the size of a Volkswagen Bug. **Serendipity Cycles,** in the park, rents surrey cycles. The park hosts **ice-skating** in the winter. *(Park: 507 N Howard St., just north of downtown. ☎ 456-4386; www.SpokaneRiverfrontPark.com. Theater: ☎ 625-6686. Shows June-Sept. on the hour; call for winter schedule. Open daily 11am-9pm. $7, under 12 $5, over 62 $6. Carousel: Open Su-Th 11am-8pm, F-Sa 11am-10pm. $1.75 per whirl, under 12 or over 62 $1. A 1-day pass, $15, covers both, plus a ferris wheel, park train, sky ride, and more. Cycling: Open daily June-Aug. 10am-9pm. $12 per hr., $20 per hr. with trailer. Ice skating: $4.50, under 12 and over 62 $3.50; skate rental $2.)*

MUSIC. Spokane Symphony Orchestra calls the **Opera House** home. The opera house also hosts traveling **Broadway shows** and special performances. *(Opera House: 334 W Spokane Falls Blvd. Ticket Office: 601 Riverside in the Mezzanine of the Bank of America building. ☎ 326-3136. Open M-F 9:30am-5:30pm. Box office at the Opera House: open M-F 10am-5pm. Orchestra: www.spokanesymphony.com. Symphony tickets $11-13.)* Known for locally produced shows, the **Civic Theater** has a downstairs space for experimental productions. *(1020 N Howard St., opposite the Spokane Veteran's Memorial Arena. ☎ 325-2507 or 800-446-9576. Musicals $18, plays $15.)* The **Spokane Interplayers Ensemble** is a resident professional theater troupe. *(174 S Howard St. ☎ 455-7529. Season runs Sept.-June Tu-Sa. $20, students $10, seniors 20% off.)*

BRITISH COLUMBIA

BC FACTS & FIGURES

Capital: Victoria. **Area:** 947,796 sq. km. **Population:** 4,067,200.
Motto: *Splendor Sine Occasu* (Splendor Without Diminishment).
Bird: Steller's Jay. **Flower:** Pacific dogwood. **Tree:** Western Red Cedar.
Holiday: BC Day (Aug. 1) **Sales Tax:** 7% PST plus 7% GST. **Drinking Age:** 19.

Before Europeans plunked themselves down for frontier lives in the huge territory now known as British Columbia, tribal nations (including the Kwakwaka'wakw, Nuu-cha-nulth, and Coast Salish, had already developed complex societies all across the land. Eventually, gold was discovered north and east of Vancouver in 1858, bringing in a flood of prospectors. Vancouver blossomed into the metropolis it is today on account of the Canadian Pacific Railroad, which made the town its western terminus in 1886.

Today, residents swear backwards and forwards that BC is the most beautiful place on earth, and most visitors share the opinion upon their departure. It's easy to see why. Small, developed communities surround the metropolitan areas, and breathtaking wilderness is never more than a short drive away. Vancouver's relaxed populace enjoys the most diverse nightlife in western Canada, and gets two full months of summer to enjoy Burrard Inlet's sweeping beaches and snow-capped horizons. Vancouver's location on the mainland side of the Strait of Georgia affords immediate access to the Gulf Islands and Vancouver Island. Sechelt Peninsula, north along the mainland, is less developed than its surroundings and boasts amazing diving, kayaking, and hiking amid the largest trees in Canada.

HIGHLIGHTS OF BRITISH COLUMBIA

EDUCATE yourself in Vancouver's famous **Museum of Anthropology** (see p. 261).

SKI to your heart's content at **Whistler/Blackcomb** (see p. 267).

PICNIC by the beach at **Lighthouse Park** (see p. 264).

SOAK away your sorrows in **Radium Hot Springs** (see p. 325).

LEAP off a bridge in **Nanaimo** (see p. 286).

CHILL with the Haida on **Moresby Island** (see p. 350).

SCUBA DIVE off the **Sechelt Peninsula** (p. 265).

VANCOUVER ☎604/778

Like any self-respecting city on the west coast of North America, Vancouver boasts a thriving multicultural populace; the Cantonese influence is so strong that it is often referred to by its nickname, "Hongcouver." With Vancouver supporting North America's third largest Chinatown and plenty of the world's other major cultures and ethnicities, visitors are never hard-pressed to find delicious representa-

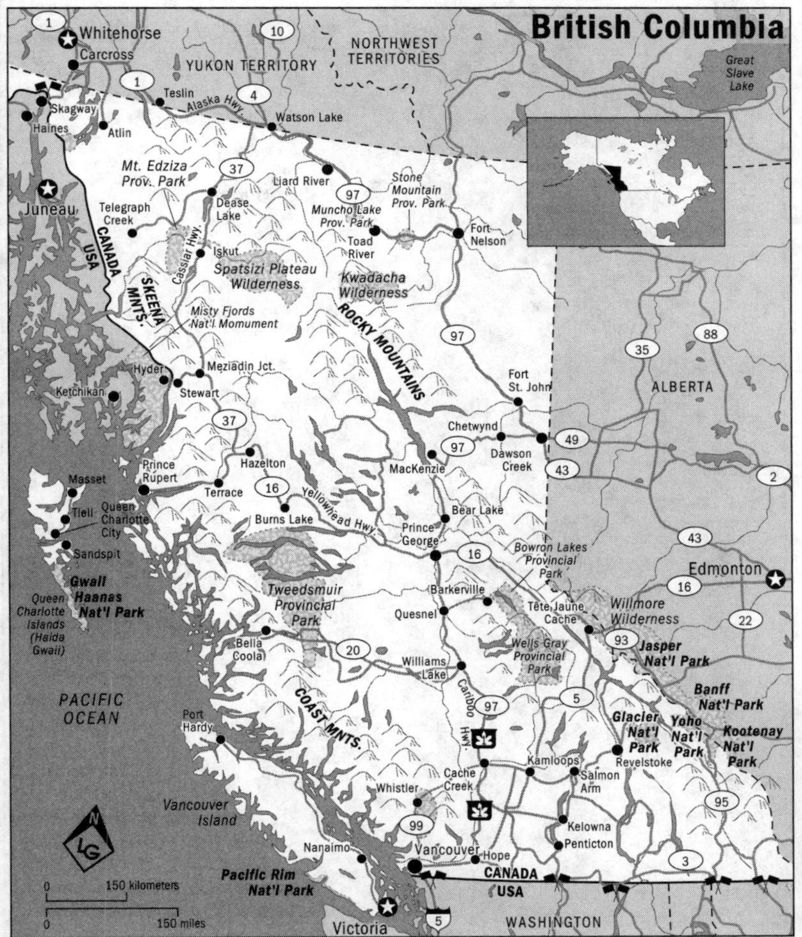

tions of foreign culinary traditions. As a bonus for adventurous visitors, Vancouver's diversity and urban excitement are so closely hemmed by mountains, forest, and ocean that the city almost feels like a wilderness town; for better or worse, it is hard to avoid the outdoors.

When the city incorporated in 1886, logging was its economic mainstay. Since then, Vancouver has been routinely reshaped by waves of immigration. Thousands of Chinese immigrants (whose work at the turn of the century made the completion of the trans-Canada railroad possible) settled at the line's western terminus, founding the city's Chinatown.

More recent developments on the cultural landscape include a trend among young Canadians from all points east to migrate to this western city. This ongoing influx of immigrants has ensured that the city's landscape remains peppered with new folks and their cultural contributions. And while there is some degree

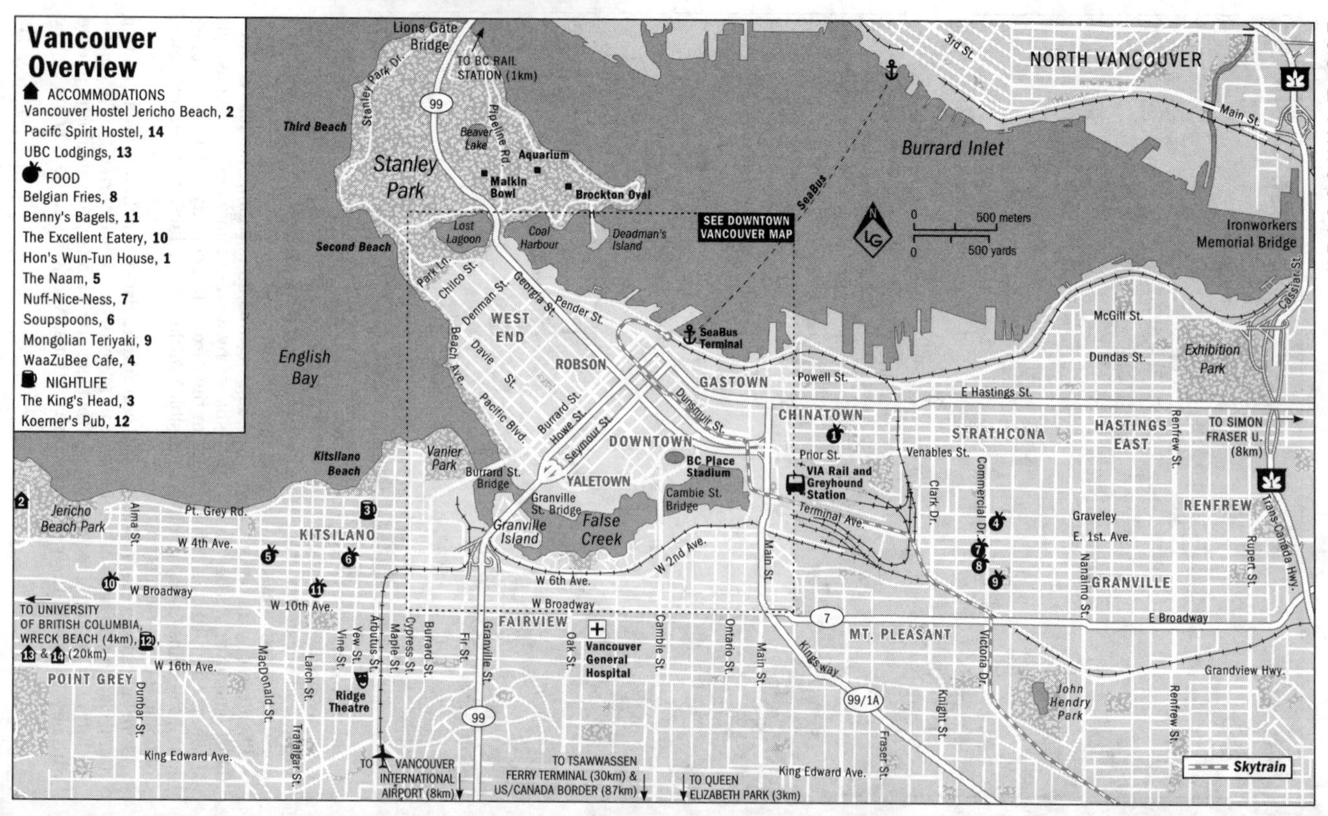

Vancouver Overview
ACCOMMODATIONS
Vancouver Hostel Jericho Beach, 2
Pacifc Spirit Hostel, 14
UBC Lodgings, 13
FOOD
Belgian Fries, 8
Benny's Bagels, 11
The Excellent Eatery, 10
Hon's Wun-Tun House, 1
The Naam, 5
Nuff-Nice-Ness, 7
Soupspoons, 6
Mongolian Teriyaki, 9
WaaZuBee Cafe, 4
NIGHTLIFE
The King's Head, 3
Koerner's Pub, 12
Lions Gate Bridge
TO BC RAIL STATION (1km)
NORTH VANCOUVER
3rd St.
Main St.
Burrard Inlet
SeaBus
Ironworkers Memorial Bridge
Cassiar St.
Third Beach
Stanley Park Dr.
Stanley Park
Beaver Lake
Pipeline Rd.
Aquarium
Malkin Bowl
Brockton Oval
SEE DOWNTOWN VANCOUVER MAP
0 500 meters
0 500 yards
Second Beach
Lost Lagoon
Coal Harbour
Deadman's Island
Park Ln.
Chilco St.
Denman St.
Georgia St.
Pender St.
WEST END
SeaBus Terminal
McGill St.
Dundas St.
Exhibition Park
English Bay
Beach Ave.
Davie St.
ROBSON
GASTOWN
Powell St.
E Hastings St.
Pacific Blvd.
Burrard St.
Howe St.
Seymour St.
Dunsmuir St.
CHINATOWN
STRATHCONA
HASTINGS EAST
Renfrew St.
TO SIMON FRASER U. (8km)
Kitsilano Beach
Vanier Park
Burrard St. Bridge
DOWNTOWN
BC Place Stadium
Prior St.
Venables St.
VIA Rail and Greyhound Station
YALETOWN
Cambie St. Bridge
Clark Dr.
Commercial Dr.
Jericho Beach Park
Alma St.
Pt. Grey Rd.
KITSILANO
Granville St. Bridge
Granville Island
False Creek
Terminal Ave.
Graveley
E. 1st. Ave.
RENFREW
Rupert St.
Trans-Canada Hwy.
W 4th Ave.
W 2nd Ave.
W 6th Ave.
GRANVILLE
Nanaimo St.
W Broadway
W 10th Ave.
TO UNIVERSITY OF BRITISH COLUMBIA, WRECK BEACH (4km), 12, 13 & 14 (20km)
FAIRVIEW
Vancouver General Hospital
Main St.
E Broadway
MT. PLEASANT
Arbutus St.
Yew St.
Vine St.
Cypress St.
Maple St.
Burrard St.
Fir St.
Granville St.
Oak St.
Cambie St.
Ontario St.
Kingsway
Victoria Dr.
W 16th Ave.
POINT GREY
MacDonald St.
Larch St.
Ridge Theatre
Grandview Hwy.
John Hendry Park
Dunbar St.
Trafalgar St.
Knight St.
Fraser St.
Renfrew St.
King Edward Ave.
TO VANCOUVER INTERNATIONAL AIRPORT (8km)
TO TSAWWASSEN FERRY TERMINAL (30km) & US/CANADA BORDER (87km)
TO QUEEN ELIZABETH PARK (3km)
King Edward Ave.
Skytrain

of self-segregation among the city's neighborhoods, Vancouverites largely appreciate the diversity. Perhaps the best evidence of (and maybe even the reason for) this is the abundance of fine ethnic restaurants of every imaginable cuisine and budget level.

PHONE CODES In 2001, Vancouver switched to 10-digit dialing. All the old numbers will remain 604, but new numbers will have the area code 778. Should you encounter problems, confirm the area code of the number you are trying to reach at www.addthecode.com.

INTERCITY TRANSPORTATION

Flights: Vancouver International Airport (☎604-207-7077; www.vancouverairport.com), on Sea Island, 23km south of the city center. A **Visitors Center** (☎604-303-3601) is on level 2. Open daily 8am-11:30pm. To reach downtown, take bus #100 "New Westminster Station" to the intersection of Granville and 70th Ave. Transfer there to bus #20 "Fraser." An **Airporter** (☎604-946-8866 or 800-668-3141) bus leaves from airport level 2 for downtown hotels and the bus station. (4 per hr.; 6:30am-midnight; $12, seniors $9, ages 5-12 $5.)

Ferries: BC Ferries (☎888-BC-FERRY; www.bcferries.com) connects Vancouver to the **Gulf Islands,** the **Sechelt Peninsula,** and **Vancouver Island.** Fares are lowest in the winter off-season. Ferries to the **Gulf Islands, Nanaimo** (2hr.; 4-8 per day; $10, $8.25 in winter; cars $25-34) and **Victoria** (1½hr.; 8-16 per day; $8/$25; bikes $2.50, car $25-34) leave from the **Tsawwassen Terminal,** 25km south of the city center (take Hwy. 99 to Hwy. 17). To reach downtown from Tsawwassen by bus (1hr.), take #640 "Scott Rd. Station," or take #404 "Airport" to the Ladner Exchange, then transfer to bus #601. More ferries to **Nanaimo** (1½hr.; 8 times per day; $9.50, $8 in winter; car $24-33.50) and the **Sechelt Peninsula** (fare charged only from Horseshoe Bay to Langdale; 40min.; 8-10 per day; $8-9.50, ages 5-11 less, car $24-33.50; off-season slightly cheaper) depart the **Horseshoe Bay Terminal** at the end of the Trans-Canada Hwy. in West Vancouver. Take "Blue Bus" #250 or 257 on Georgia St. to get there from downtown. (40min.)

Trains: VIA Rail, 1150 Station St. (☎888-842-7245; US ☎800-561-3949; www.viarail.com) runs eastbound trains. Open M, W, Th, and Sa 9:30am-6pm; Tu, F, and Su 9am-7pm. 3 trains per week to eastern Canada via **Edmonton, AB** (23hr., $263) and **Jasper, AB** (17hr., $196). **BC Rail,** 1311 W 1st St. (☎800-663-8238; www.bcrail.com), in North Vancouver just over the Lions Gate Bridge at the foot of Pemberton St., runs to **Whistler** and northern BC. Take the **BC Rail Special Bus** on Georgia St. (June-Sept.) or the **SeaBus** to North Vancouver, then bus #239 west. Open daily 8am-8pm. Trains to **Prince George** (14½hr.; Su, W, F at 7am; $247); **Whistler** (2¾hr., daily, $49); and **Williams Lake** (10hr.; W, F, Sa at 7am; $165).

Buses: Greyhound Canada, 1150 Station St. (☎604-683-8133 or 800-661-8747; www.greyhound.ca), in the VIA Rail station. Open daily 7:15am-11:45pm. To **Banff, AB** (14hr., 5 per day, $112); **Calgary, AB** (15hr., 5 per day, $125); and **Jasper, AB** (2 per day, $129). **Pacific Coach Lines,** 1150 Station St. (☎604-662-8074; www.pacificcoach.com), runs to **Victoria** every time a ferry sails (3½hr., $29 includes ferry). **Quick Shuttle** (☎940-4428 or 800-665-2122; www.quickcoach.com) makes 8 trips per day from the Holiday Inn on Howe St. via the airport to: **Bellingham, WA** (2½hr.; $22, $17 with student ID), **Seattle, WA** (4hr.; $33/$22 with student ID), and the **Sea-Tac airport** (4½hr.; $33/$22 with student ID). **Greyhound USA** (☎800-229-9424 or 402-330-8552; www.greyhound.com) goes to **Seattle** (3-4½hr., $23.50).

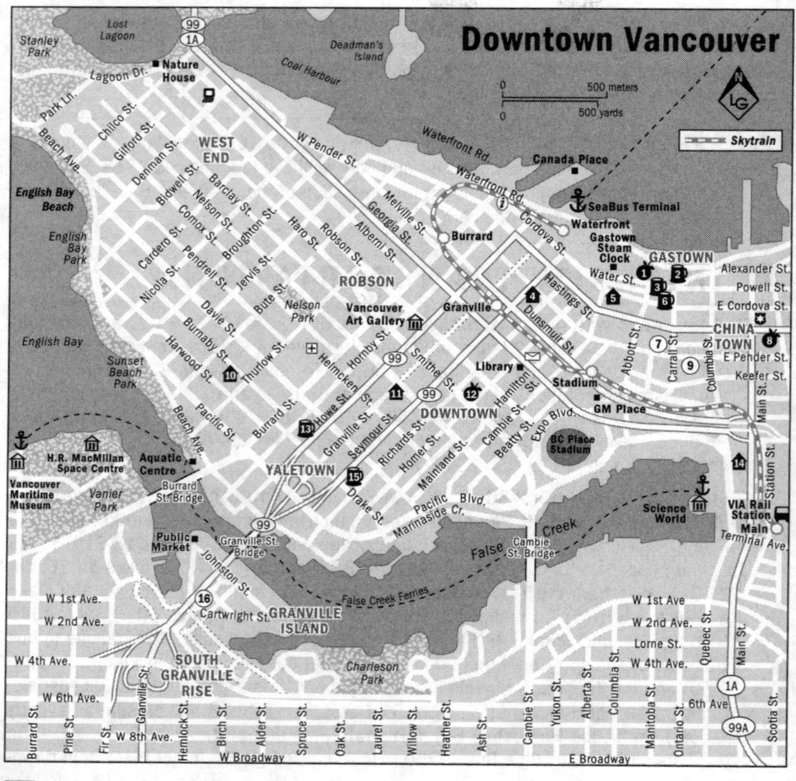

ORIENTATION

Vancouver lies in the southwestern corner of mainland British Columbia. It is divided into distinct regions, mostly by waterways. South of the city flows the **Fraser River** and to the west lies the **Georgia Strait,** which separates the mainland from Vancouver Island. **Downtown** juts north into the Burrard Inlet from the main mass of the city and **Stanley Park** goes even further north. The **Lions Gate** suspension bridge over Burrard Inlet links Stanley Park with North and West Vancouver **(West Van),** known collectively as the **North Shore;** the bridges over False Creek south of downtown link downtown with **Kitsilano ("Kits")** and the rest of the city. West of Burrard St. is the **West End. Gastown** and **Chinatown** are just east of downtown. The **University of British Columbia (UBC)** lies to the west of Kitsilano on Point Grey, while the **airport** is on Sea Island in the Fraser River delta tucked between S. Vancouver and **Richmond** to the south. **Hwy. 99** runs north-south from the US-Canada border through the city along **Oak St.,** through downtown, then over the Lions Gate bridge. It joins temporarily with the **Trans-Canada Hwy. (Hwy. 1)** before splitting off again and continuing north to Whistler (see p. 267). The Trans-Canada enters from the east, cuts north across the **Second Narrows Bridge** to the North Shore, and ends at the Horseshoe Bay ferry terminal. Most of the city's attractions are grouped on the peninsula and farther west.

Downtown Vancouver

ACCOMMODATIONS
Cambie Int'l Hostel, **5**
C&N Backpackers Hostel, **14**
Global Village Backpackers, **11**
Seymour Cambie Hostel, **4**
Vancouver Hostel Downtown, **10**

FOOD
Kam's Garden Restaurant, **8**
La Luna Cafe, **1**
Subeez Cafe, **12**

NIGHTLIFE
The Irish Heather, **6**
Odyssey, **13**
The Purple Onion, **2**
Sonar, **3**
Sugar Refinery, **15**

OTHER
Dr. Sun Yat-Sen Classical Chinese Garden, **9**
Granville Island Brewing Co., **16**
World's Skinniest Building, **7**

Vancouver is a major point of entry for heroin, with an active street trade in this drug and marijuana; there is a high addict population. While incidences of armed assaults, armed robbery, and murder are low by US standards, the rates for crimes are higher than in most other Canadian cities. Walking around by day is safe most anywhere and downtown is relatively safe at night on main streets. The area east of Gastown, especially around **Hastings** and **Main St.,** is home to many of Vancouver's down, out, and addicted, and should be avoided late at night if possible.

LOCAL TRANSPORTATION

If you're on the outskirts of Vancouver with a car, consider using the **Park 'n' Rides.** These are cheap or free parking lots at major transit hubs where you can leave your car for the day and take public transit into town. From the southeast, exit Hwy. 1 at New Westminster and follow signs for the Pattullo Bridge. The lot is over the bridge and to the right, on the corner of Scott Rd. and King George Hwy. Park for $1 per day and take the **SkyTrain** downtown.

Public Transit: Transit timetables are available at public libraries, city hall, community centers, and **Vancouver Travel Infocentre** (see **Practical Information,** p. 253). The pamphlet *Discover Vancouver on Transit* lists bus numbers for every major site in the city. **Coast Mountain Buslink** (☎604-953-3333; www.translink.bc.ca) is the bus system that covers most of the city and suburbs, with direct transport or easy connections to airport and the ferry terminals (see **Intercity Transportation,** above). The city is divided into 3 concentric zones for fare purposes. Riding in the **central zone,** which encompasses most of Vancouver, costs $2. During peak hours (M-F before 6:30pm), it costs $3 to travel between 2 zones and $4 for 3 zones. During off-peak hours, all zones are $2. Ask for a **free transfer** (good for 1½hr.) when you board buses. **Day passes** $8; sold at all 7-11 and Safeway stores, SkyTrain stations, and HI hostels. Seniors and ages 5-13 for 1 zone or off-peak $1.50; 2 zones $2; 3 zones $3; day pass $6. Bikes can travel on the rack-equipped #404/#601 combination to the Tsawassen ferry terminal. **SeaBus** and **SkyTrain:** Same contact information as the buses, above. Included in the normal bus fare. The SeaBus shuttles passengers across the busy waters of Burrard Inlet from the foot of Granville St. downtown (Waterfront SkyTrain station) to **Lonsdale Quay** at the foot of Lonsdale Ave. in North Vancouver. The SkyTrain is a light rapid transit system, with a 28km track from Vancouver to **Burnaby, New Westminster,** and **Surrey** in 40min. 20 stations with service every 5min. **Bikes** may be brought on board the SeaBus, but not on the SkyTrain.

Car Rental: Most car rental services, located at the airport, require that you be 21+ to rent a vehicle. **EZ Car Rentals** (☎604-240-5383) has no such requirement.

Taxis: Yellow Cab, ☎604-681-1111 or 800-898-8294. **Vancouver Taxi,** ☎604-871-1111. **Black Top and Checker Cab,** ☎604-731-1111.

PRACTICAL INFORMATION

LOCAL SERVICES

Tourist Information: 200 Burrard St., plaza level (☎604-683-2000), near Canada Place. BC-wide info on accommodations, tours, and activities. Courtesy reservation phones. Open daily 8:30am-6pm.

Travel Outfitter: The Travel Bug, 2667 W Broadway (☎604-737-1122). Everything you need to get around, from maps to bags to guides. 10% HI discount on accessories. Open M-Tu 10am-6pm, W-F 10am-7:30pm, Sa noon-5pm, Su 10am-6pm.

Tours: The Gray Line, 255 E 1st Ave. (☎879-3363 or 800-667-0882). Narrated bus tours. The Double Decker Bus stops at over 20 sights. Unlimited use for 2 days $26; seniors $25, ages 5-12 $14. Buses run 8:30am-4:30pm. Hostels run sporadic tours.

Consulates: Canadian Consulate General, 412 Plaza 600 (☎604-443-1777). **British Consulate General,** 900 4th Ave., Ste. 3001 (☎604-622-9255). **U.S. Consulate General**, 1095 W. Pender (☎604-685-4311).

Equipment Rental: Stanley Park Cycle, 766 Denman (☎604-688-0087), near Stanley Park. Mountain bikes or 21-speed from $3.50 per hr., $10.50 per 5hr. Open daily 8am-8pm. The immensely popular and knowledgably staffed **Mountain Equipment Co-op (MEC),** 130 W Broadway (☎604-872-7858; www.mec.ca), rents tents, sleeping bags, and kayaks. Open M-W 10am-7pm, Th-F 10am-9pm, Sa 9am-6pm, Su 11am-5pm.

Laundry: Davie Laundromat, 1061 Davie St. (☎604-682-2717), $2.50 per load. Open daily 8am-8pm.

Gay and Lesbian Information: The Centre, 1170 Bute St. (☎684-5307), offers counseling and info. *Xtra West* is the city's gay and lesbian biweekly, available here and around Davie St. in the West End. Open M-F 9:30am-7pm. Try www.gayvancouver.bc.ca for events.

Weather: ☎604-664-9010; www.weatheroffice.com.

Road Conditions: Talking Yellow Pages ☎604-299-9000. Select #7623.

EMERGENCY AND COMMUNICATIONS

Emergency: ☎911.

Police: 312 Main St. (☎604-665-3321), at Powell.

Crisis Center: ☎604-872-3311. 24hr. **Rape Crisis Center:** ☎604-255-6344. 24hr.

24hr. Pharmacy: Shoppers Drug Mart, 2979 W Broadway (☎604-733-9128), and 1125 Davie St. (☎604-669-2424). Open 24hr.

Hospital: Vancouver General Hospital, 895 W 12th Ave. (☎604-875-4111). **UBC Hospital,** 2211 Westbrook Mall (☎604-822-7121), on the UBC campus.

Internet Access: Library: 350 W Georgia St. (☎604-331-3600). Free Internet. Open M-Th 10am-8pm, F-Sa 10am-5pm, Su 1-5pm. Free email at 20 other branches; check White Pages.

Post Office: 349 W Georgia St. (☎604-662-5725). Open M-F 8am-5:30pm. **Postal Code:** V6B 3P7. **Area Code:** 604.

ACCOMMODATIONS

Greater Vancouver B&Bs are a viable option for couples or small groups (singles from $45, doubles from $55). Agencies like **Town and Country Bed and Breakfast** (☎604-731-5942) or **Best Canadian** (☎604-738-7207) list options. **HI hostels** are a good bet for clean and quiet rooms; some non-HI options can be seedy or rowdy.

DOWNTOWN AND WEST END

Vancouver Hostel Downtown (HI), 1114 Burnaby St. (☎604-684-4565 or 888-203-4302), in the West End. Sleek and clean 225-bed facility between downtown, the beach, and Stanley Park. Library, kitchen, rooftop patio. Pub crawls W, F; frequent tours of Granville Island. Travel agency in the lobby. Reception open 24hr. Reservations recommended in summer, when prices may increase slightly. $20, nonmembers $24; private doubles $55, nonmembers $64. ❷

Global Village Backpackers, 1018 Granville St. (☎604-682-8226 or 888-844-7875; www.globalbackpackers.com), on the corner of Nelson, next to Ramada Inn. Ask the hostel for a refund of your taxi fare. Funky technicolor hangout in an area with great nightlife. Internet, pool, laundry. Dorms for HI, ISIC, other hosteling members $21.50, nonmembers $25; doubles $57/$60, with bath $62/$65. ❷

Seymour Cambie Hostel, 515 Seymour St. (☎604-684-7757). The quieter of 2 downtown Cambie hostels. Pub crawls, movie nights (Su-M), soccer games during summer season (Sa), free tours of Granville Island Brewery (Tu at noon, 2pm, and 4pm). Laundry, kitchen, and Internet access. No lockers, storage available for $2 per day. July-Sept. dorm $22.50. Oct.-June dorms $20; singles $40; weekly rates $130. ❷

C&N Backpackers Hostel, 927 Main St. (☎ 604-682-2441 or 888-434-6060), 300m north on Main St. from the train station. Cheap meal deals with the **Ivanhoe Pub** ($2.50 breakfast all day) make this recently renovated hostel a bargain. Kitchen, laundry ($1 per wash or dry), bikes ($10 per day). May-Sept. dorms $16; doubles $40. Weekly rates available, monthly rates available in winter. ❶

GASTOWN

Cambie International Hostel, 300 Cambie St. (☎604-684-6466 or 877-395-5335). Free airport pickup 10am-8pm. The Cambie offers easy access to the busy sights and sounds of Gastown. Common room, laundry. No kitchen, but free hot breakfast. Pool tables in the pub. 24hr. reception. June-Sept. dorms $20, singles $45. Oct.-May dorms $17.50, singles $40. ❷

KITSILANO & ELSEWHERE

Vancouver Hostel Jericho Beach (HI), 1515 Discovery St. (☎604-224-3208 or 888-203-4303), in Jericho Beach Park. Follow 4th Ave. west past Alma, bear right at the fork, or take bus #4 from Granville St. downtown. Peaceful location with a great view across English Bay. 280 beds in 14-person dorm rooms. 10 family rooms. Free linen, kitchen, TV room, laundry, cafe (breakfasts around $6, dinner $7-8), parking $3 per day. Bike storage free for guests. Open May-Sept. Reservations imperative in summer. $18.50, nonmembers $22.50; family rooms $50-60. ❷

Pacific Spirit Hostel/UBC Lodgings, 1935 Lower Mall (☎604-822-1000), at Place Vanier on the University of British Columbia campus. Bus #4 or #10 from city center. Continue down University Blvd. from bus loop until you turn right on Lower Mall. Standard dorm singles for a hostel price. Free linen, laundry, TV lounges, shared microwave and fridge; pubs and food on campus. Free Internet. Open May-Aug. Singles $24-84. 10% HI or ISIC discount at hostel. ❸

CAMPING

Capilano RV Park, 295 Tomahawk Ave. (☎604-987-4722), at foot of Lions Gate Bridge in North Van. Pool, laundry. Reception open daily 8am-11pm. 2-person sites $28-38, extra person $3.50; full RV sites $38 and up with auto club membership, $46 and up without. Showers. ❸

Richmond RV Park, 6200 River Rd. (☎604-270-7878 or 800-755-4905), near Holly Bridge in Richmond, a 30min. drive from Vancouver. Follow the Westminster Hwy. west into Richmond from Hwy. 99, turn right on No. 2 Rd., then right on River Rd. Limited privacy. Open Apr.-Oct. 2-person sites $17.50; RV sites $24 and up. Showers. 10% AAA/CAA discount. ❷

Hazelmere RV Park and Campground, 18843 8th Ave. (☎604-538-1167, fax 604-538-1080), in Surrey, a 45min. drive from downtown. Close to the US/Canada border. Off Hwy. 99A, head east on 8th Ave. Quiet sites on the Campbell River, 10min. from the beach. Full RV sites $26; 2-person sites $23; additional person $3; under 7 free. Showers $0.25 per 5min. ❷

ParkCanada, 4799 Hwy. 17 (☎604-943-5811), in Delta 30km south of downtown, near Tsawwassen ferry terminal. Take Hwy. 99 south to Hwy. 17, then go east for 2.5km. The campground, located next to a waterslide park, has a pool. 2-person sites $18.50; RV sites $21 and up; additional person $2. Free showers. ❷

FOOD

The diversity and excellence of Vancouver's international cuisine makes the rest of BC seem positively provincial. Vancouver's **Chinatown** and the **Punjabi Village** along Main and Fraser, around 49th St., both serve cheap, authentic food. Every type of world cuisine, from Vietnamese noodle shops to Italian cafes to succulent yet-cheap-sushi, seems represented along **Commercial Drive,** east of Chinatown.

Restaurants in **downtown** compete for the highest prices in the city. The **West End** caters to diners seeking a variety of ethnic cuisines (check out the globe-spanning lineup on Denman Street), while **Gastown** lures tourists fresh off the cruise ships. Many cheap and grubby establishments along Davie and Denman St. stay open around the clock. Dollar-a-slice, all-night **pizza places** pepper downtown. In Kits, **Buy-Low Foods,** at 4th and Alma St., keeps it real. (☎604-222-8353. Open daily 9am-9pm.) Downtown, **SuperValu** is at 1255 Davie St. (☎604-688-0911. Open 24hr.)

WEST END, DOWNTOWN, AND GASTOWN

Subeez Cafe, 891 Homer (☎604-687-6107), at Smithe, downtown. Serves hipster kids in a cavernous setting. Eclectic menu, from vegetarian gyoza ($7) to organic beef burgers ($9), complements a lengthy wine list and home-spun beats (DJs W, F, and Sa from 9pm to midnight). Weekly specials. Entrees $7-15. Open M-F 11:30am-1am, Sa 11am-1am, Su 11am-midnight. ❸

Ukrainian Village, 815 Denman St. (☎604-687-7440). Three kinds of fresh borscht ($4.75 each) complement traditional dishes like schnitzel or Kiev cutlet (each $10.50). $5.95 combo lunch specials bring you back to the Dnieper in savory style. Open daily for lunch 11:30am-5pm, dinner 5pm-10pm. F and Sa dinner runs until 11pm. ❷

La Luna Cafe, 117 Water St. (☎604-687-5862), in Gastown. Loyal patrons swear by the coffee, which is roasted on-site. Cheap, satisfying sandwiches ($3.95-4.95), homemade soups ($3). Internet $1 per 12min. Open M-F 7:30am-5pm, Sa 10am-5pm. ❶

BRITISH COLUMBIA

COMMERCIAL DRIVE & EAST VANCOUVER

Mongolian Teriyaki, 1918 Commercial Dr. (☎604-253-5607). Diners fill a bowl with meats, veggies, sauces, and noodles, and the chefs fry everything up and serve it with miso soup, rice, and salad for only $5 (large bowl $5.95). Take-out menu. Open daily 11am-9:30pm. ❶

WaaZuBee Cafe, 1622 Commercial Dr. (☎604-253-5299), at E 1st St. Sleek, metallic decoration, ambient music, and artwork accompany the inventive food. New brunch menu boasts Belgian waffles and other classics ($5-8). Veggie spinach and ricotta agnoilotti pasta $13, Thai prawns $8, veggie burger $7. Open M-F 11:30am-1am, Sa 11am-1am, Su 11am-midnight. ❸

CANNABUSINESS British Columbia's buds fare well at Amsterdam's Cannabis Cup (the World Cup of pot smoking), and at an estimated $1.1 billion, generate half as much annual revenue as the province's logging industry. Most ganja dollars come from exports, and most exports go straight to the US. In 1998, Canada legalized hemp plants containing very low levels of the psychoactive compound THC, giving visitors and locals full legal freedom to enjoy fibrous rope. At some Vancouver cafes, however, public marijuana smoking is commonplace. What's the source of such seeming herbal impunity? Vancouver police don't seem to treat small-time pot smoking behind closed doors as a criminal offense, despite federal law. The police do tend to have moments of forgetfulness, though, at which point they raid the shops. For a connoisseur's perspective and news on further legalization efforts, tune in to the mind-altering www.cannabisculture.com or www.pot-tv.net. Educate yourself on the issues by visiting the BC Marijuana Party Bookshop and HQ at 307 W. Hastings St., which has literature, clothing, and other party paraphernalia. (☎604-682-1172. Open M-Th 10:30am-6pm, F-Sa 10:30am-7pm, Su 11am-6pm.)

Nuff-Nice-Ness, 1861 Commercial Dr. (☎604-255-4211), at 3rd. Nice price and no fuss in this small Jamaican deli. Large jerk chicken with salad and rice $7.50; beef, chicken, or veggie patty $2; oxtail $7.72. Open M-Sa noon-9pm, Su noon-8pm. ❷

Belgian Fries, 1885 Commercial Dr. (☎604-253-4220). If you've never had it, try what CBC Montreal calls the "Best Poutine in BC," a concoction of fries, curds, and gravy. Huge portions serve two ($5). Open M-F 11:30am-10pm, Su 11:30am-9pm. ❶

KITSILANO

The Naam, 2724 W 4th Ave. (☎604-738-7151), at MacDonald St. Bus #4 or 7 from Granville Mall. One of the most diverse vegetarian menus around, with great prices to boot. Crying Tiger Thai stir fry $9; several kinds of veggie burgers under $7; tofulati ice cream $3.50. Live music nightly 7-10pm. Birthday discounts equal your new age (e.g., 25 years old means 25% off!). Open 24hr. ❷

Benny's Bagels, 2505 W Broadway (☎604-731-9730). Every college student's dream. Serves the requisite beer ($3 per glass), bagels ($0.75, $2.25 with cream cheese), and sandwiches and melts ($5.50-7.50). Open Su-Th 7am-1am, F-Sa 24hr. ❶

The Excellent Eatery, 3431 W Broadway (☎604-738-5298). Candlelight, sushi, and pop art. Reserve 1 of 2 canopied booths. Sushi $3.50-6. Mango-tuna-avocado sushi $4.25. Open M-Th 5pm-12:30am, F-Sa 5pm-1am, Su 5-11:30pm. ❶

Soupspoons, 2278 W. 4th Ave. (☎604-328-7687). This Parisian bistro offers panini and sandwiches ($6), salads ($3), and 10 ever-changing soups. The Beachpack gets you a chilled soup, baguette sandwich, and drink for $6.50. Open daily 10am-9pm. ❶

CHINATOWN

The prettiest are usually the priciest in Chinatown and adjacent **Japantown.** For guaranteed good food, stop in restaurants that are crowded with locals. Lively afternoons make this a better place for lunch than dinner.

Hon's Wun-Tun House, 268 Keefer St. (☎604-688-0871). This award-winning Cantonese noodle-house is the place to go (bowls $3.50-6). Over 300 options make reading the menu take almost as long as eating from it. Attentive service. Open daily 8:30am-10pm; in summer F-Su until 11pm. Cash only. ❷

Kam's Garden Restaurant, 509 Main St. (☎604-669-5488). Authentic, no-frills Chinese food and plenty of it. Huge noodle platters $5-9. Open daily 10:30am-8pm. ❶

ENTERTAINMENT

MUSIC, THEATER, & FILM

The renowned **Vancouver Symphony Orchestra** (☎604-876-3434) plays September to May in the refurbished **Orpheum Theatre** (☎604-665-3050), at the corner of Smithe and Seymour. In summer, tours of the theater are given ($5). The VSO often joins forces with other groups such as the **Vancouver Bach Choir** (☎604-921-8012).

Vancouver has a lively theater scene. The **Vancouver Playhouse Theatre Co.** (☎604-873-3311), on Dunsmuir and Georgia St., and the **Arts Club Theatre** (☎604-687-1644), on Granville Island, stage low-key shows, often including local work. **Theatre Under the Stars** (☎604-687-0174), in Stanley Park's Malkin Bowl, puts on outdoor musicals in the summer. Have some laughs at the **Theatresports League** at the Arts Club New Revue Stage on Granville Island. The world-famous improvisational theater company performs competitive improv, comedies, and improv jam sessions W-Sa at 8pm and F-Sa at 10pm. (Box office ☎687-1644. Open M-Sa 9am-showtime. Tickets $15, students $12.)

The **Ridge Theatre,** 3131 Arbutus, shows arthouse, European, and vintage film double features. (☎604-738-6311. $5, seniors and children $4.) The **Hollywood Theatre,** 3123 W Broadway, shows a mix of arthouse and second-run mainstream double features for cheaper than the other theaters around downtown. (☎515-5864. $5, on M $3.50, seniors and children $3.50.) The **Blinding Light!! Cinema,** 36 Powell St., shows indie films and hosts special events such as the monthly Multiplex experimental music and film series. (☎604-878-3366; www.blindinglight.com. $5.) The **Paradise,** 919 Granville (☎604-681-1732), at Smithe, shows triple features of second-run movies for $4.

SPORTS

One block south of Chinatown on Main St. is **BC Place Stadium,** at 777 S Pacific Blvd., home to the Canadian Football League's BC Lions and the world's largest air supported dome (tickets from $15). The NHL's **Vancouver Canucks** call the nearby **GM Place** home. Tickets for both are often available as late as game day (from $40). The **Vancouver Canadians** play AAA baseball in Nat Bailey Stadium, at 33rd. Ave. and Ontario, opposite Queen Elizabeth Park, offering some of the cheapest sports tickets going (tickets from $8). For tickets and info call **Ticketmaster** at ☎604-280-4400 or visit www.ticketmaster.ca.

FESTIVALS & ANNUAL EVENTS

As with almost everything else, buying tickets in advance for these festivals often results in drastically reduced prices.

Chinese New Year will fall on Feb. 23, 2003. Fireworks, music, and dragons in the streets of Chinatown and beyond.

Alcan Dragon Boat Festival. End of June each year. (☎604-696-1888; www.canadadragonboat.com). Traditional food and dance from around the world, and dragon boat racing on False Creek. $9, seniors and youth $5, family $20.

Du Maurier International Jazz Festival Vancouver, June 21-July 1, 2003 (☎604-872-5200 or 888-438-5200; www.jazzvancouver.com). Draws over 500 performers and bands for 10 days of jazz, from acid to swing. Free concerts in Gastown, at the Roundhouse on Davie St., and around Granville Island. Other events range from $10-60.

Vancouver Folk Music Festival, July 18-20, 2003 (☎604-602-9798 or 800-985-8363; www.thefestival.bc.ca). Performers from around the world give concerts and workshops in July. Very kid-friendly. $35-50 per day, $110 for the weekend. Ages 13-18 $22-25, $55; ages 3-12 $12 for the weekend or $7 per day. Under 2 and over 65 free.

HSBC-Power Smart Celebration of Light, late July-early Aug. (☎604-738-4304; www.celebration-of-light.com). Pyrotechnicians light up the sky over English Bay on Sa and W nights. Hundreds of thousands gather to watch, closing off downtown streets.

Holy Pride! Late July to early Aug. (www.vanpride.bc.ca). This is Vancouver's gay and lesbian festival. Events include dances, parties, games, music, and a parade. Tickets and info from Ticketmaster or Little Sisters (see above).

Vancouver International Film Festival, late Sept.-early Oct. (☎604-685-0260; www.viff.org). This event showcases 275 movies from over 50 countries, with particular emphasis on Canadian films, East Asian films, and documentaries. $6-8.

Vancouver International Comedy Festival Late July-early Aug. (☎604-683-0883; www.comedyfest.com). Comics from all over the world converge on Granville Island in late July for 11 days of chortles and antics. Expect to pay big for the big acts, and much less for the unknowns. $10 and up.

NIGHTLIFE

Vancouver's nightlife centers around dance clubs playing beats and DJs spinning every night. Local pubs inundate communities with relaxed options for a post-work drink. The free weekly **Georgia Straight** publishes comprehensive club and event listings, restaurant reviews, and coupons. **Discorder** is the unpredictable monthly publication of the UBC radio station CITR. Both are available in local cafes, and *Georgia Straight* can be found around town in newspaper bins.

GASTOWN

Sonar, 66 Water St. (☎604-683-6695). A popular beat factory. Sa House, W hip-hop and reggae, and F turntablist. Pints $3.75-5. Open daily 8pm-2am, Su 9pm-midnight.

The Irish Heather, 217 Carrall St. (☎604-688-9779). The 2nd-highest seller of Guinness in BC, this true Irish pub and bistro serves up memories of the Emerald Isle. Full 20oz. draughts ($5.20 before tax), mixed beer drinks ($5.60 before tax), and a helping of bangers and mash ($14) will keep those eyes smiling. Lots of veggie dishes, too. Live music in the evening, Tu-Th. Open daily noon-midnight.

The Blarney Stone, 216 Carrall St. (☎604-687-4322). For a more raucous Irish experience, join the mostly university crowd for live music by a band called Killarney, a fixture for 18 years. Cover $5-7, Th $5 cover goes to charity. Open W-Sa 7pm-2am.

Purple Onion, 15 Water St. (☎604-602-9442). Sucks in the crowd with an eclectic music selection and inviting lounge chairs. DJs spin acid jazz, disco, soul, and funk in the back room. The lounge features live blues, R&B, jazz, and funk acts W-Sa. Don't miss the frenetic "Platinum Saturdays," followed by the more relaxed "Sanctuary Sundays." M and W-Sa $3-8 cover; Tu no cover, Su $1. Open M-Th 9pm-2am, F-Sa 8pm-2am, Su 9pm-midnight.

DOWNTOWN

Sugar Refinery, 1115 Granville St. (☎604-331-1184). Where those involved in film, art, and music go to relax. An ever-changing program of events, music, and spoken word entertains while the tasty vegetarian meals please the stomach. Entrees $7.50-9, big sandwiches $5-7.50, tap beers served in mason jars $4.25-5.75. Open M-F 5pm-12pm, Sa-Su 5pm-2am, kitchen open throughout.

Atlantis, 1320 Richards St. (☎604-662-7707). Candlelit dining booths and a weekend dress code. Wields one of the most advanced stereo and light systems in Vancouver. F Hip-hop, Sa top 40, W house. Open M 9pm-2am, F-Sa 9am-4pm.

Odyssey, 1251 Howe St. (☎604-689-5256). Embark on a high-energy journey. F-Sa cranks out beats to a mainly gay crowd. Male go-go dancers spice it up F. Su and W Drag Night. $3-6. Open daily 9pm-2am.

The Drink, 398 Richards St. (☎604-687-1307). Nightclub with a diverse repertoire including alternative Tu, "Noche Havana" latin W, House Party Th with $2.50 drinks, and hip-hop and reggae Sa. Open W 8pm-2am, Th-Sa 9pm-2am, Su noon-2am.

KITSILANO

The King's Head, 1618 Yew St. (☎604-738-6966), at 1st St., in Kitsilano. Cheap drinks, cheap food, relaxing atmosphere, and a great location near the beach. Bands play acoustic sets on a tiny stage. Daily drink specials. $3 pints. Open daily 8am-midnight.

Koerner's Pub, 6371 Crescent Rd. (☎604-822-0983), on UBC campus. Owned and operated by the Graduate Student Society, this is the place to meet a smart special someone. Mellow M's with live music and open jam, W techno night. Open late Aug. to mid-Apr. M-F noon-1am, Sa 4pm-1am; summer M-Sa 4pm-midnight.

SIGHTS

DOWNTOWN

VANCOUVER ART GALLERY. This gallery is host to fantastic temporary exhibitions and home to a varied collection of contemporary art. *(750 Hornby St. in Robson Square. ☎604-662-4700. Open M-Su 10am-5:30pm, Th 10am-9pm; call for winter hours. $12.50, seniors $9, students $7, under 12 free; Th 5-9pm pay-what-you-can; 2-for-1 HI discount.)*

CHINATOWN

The neighborhood bustles with restaurants, shops, bakeries, and **the world's narrowest building** at 8 W Pender St. In 1912, the city expropriated all but a 1.8m (6 ft.) strip of Chang Toy's property in order to expand the street; he built on the land anyhow. The serene **Dr. Sun Yat-Sen Classical Chinese Garden** maintains imported Chinese plantings, carvings, and rock formations in the first full-size authentic garden of its kind outside China. *(578 Carrall St. ☎604-689-7133. Open May to mid-June daily 9:30am-5:30pm; mid-June to Aug. 9:30am-6:30pm; Sept. 9:30am-5:30pm; Oct.-Apr. 9:30am-4pm. Admission to part of the garden is free, while another section is $7.50, students $5, seniors $6, children free, families $18. Tours every hr. 10am-6pm.)* Don't miss the sights, sounds, smells, and tastes of the weekend **night market** along Pender and Keefer St., the first in North America. *(Open F-Su 6:30-11am.)* Chinatown itself is relatively safe, but its surroundings make up some of Vancouver's more unsavory sections. *(Chinatown is southeast of Gastown. Bus #22 north on Burrard St. leads to Pender and Carrall St., in the heart of Chinatown.)*

GARDENS

The city's temperate climate, which also includes ample rain most months of the year, allows floral growth to flourish. Locals take great pride in their private gardens, and public parks and green spaces also showcase displays of plant life.

VANDUSEN BOTANICAL GARDEN. Some 55 acres (22 hectares) of former golf course have been converted into an immense garden showcasing 7500 taxa from six continents. An international **sculpture** collection is interspersed with the plants, while more than 60 species of **birds** can be seen in areas such as the Fragrance Garden, Children's Garden, Bonsai House, Chinese Medicinal Garden, or the Elizabethan Maze, which is planted with 3000 pyramidal cedars. Daily tours given at 2pm;

alternatively, follow a self-guided tour tailored to show the best of the season. The Flower & Garden Show is the first weekend of June. *(5251 Oak St. at W 37th. From downtown take #17 Oak bus and get off at West 37th and Oak. ☎604-878-9274; www.vandusengarden.org. Free parking. Mostly wheelchair-accessible. Apr.-Sept. Open daily June-Aug. 10am-9pm; mid-Aug.-Sept. 10am-8pm; Oct.-Mar. 10am-4pm; Apr. 10am-4pm; May 10am-8pm. $5 in winter, $7 in summer: for seniors and ages 13-18 $3.50/5.50; ages 6-12 $2/3.75)*

BLOEDEL FLORAL & BIRD CONSERVATORY. Journey from tropics to desert in 100 paces inside this 43m diameter triodetic geodesic dome, constructed of plexiglass bubbles and aluminum tubing. The conservatory, maintained at a constant 18°C (65°F), is home to 500 varieties of exotic plants and 150 birds. Its elevation also affords great views of downtown Vancouver. *(Center of Queen Elizabeth Park on Cambie and 37th Ave., a few blocks east of VanDusen. ☎604-257-8584. Open Apr.-Sept. M-F 9am-8pm, Sa-Su 10am-9pm; Oct.-Mar. daily 10am-5pm. $4, over 65 $2.80, ages 13-18 $3, ages 6-12 $2, under 5 free.)*

UNIVERSITY OF BRITISH COLUMBIA (UBC)

The high point of a visit to UBC is the breathtaking **Museum of Anthropology.** The high-ceilinged glass and concrete building houses totems and other massive carvings, highlighted by Bill Reid's depiction of Raven discovering the first human beings in a giant clam shell. The actual site of the discovery is in the Queen Charlotte Islands (see p. 340). *(6393 NW Marine Dr., bus #4 or 10 from Granville St. Museum. ☎604-822-5087 or 604-822-5087; www.moa.ubc.ca. Open May-Sept. Tu 10am-9pm, M and W-Su 11am-5pm. $9, students and seniors $7, under 6 free; Tu after 5pm free.)* Across the street caretakers tend to **Nitobe Memorial Garden,** the finest classical Shinto garden outside of Japan. *(☎604-822-6038. Open daily mid-Mar. to mid-May 10am-5pm; mid-May through Aug. 10am-6pm; Sept.-Oct. 10am-5pm. $3, seniors $2, students $1.50, under 6 free.)* The **Botanical Gardens** are a collegiate Eden encompassing eight gardens in the central campus, including the largest collection of rhododendrons in North America. *(6804 SW Marine Dr. ☎604-822-9666. Same hours as Nitobe Garden. $5, seniors $3, students $2, under 6 free. Discounted admission for both Nitobe and the Botanical Gardens.)*

STANLEY PARK

Established in 1889 at the tip of the downtown peninsula, the 1000-acre **Stanley Park** is a testament to the foresight of Vancouver's urban planners. The thickly wooded park is laced with cycling and hiking trails

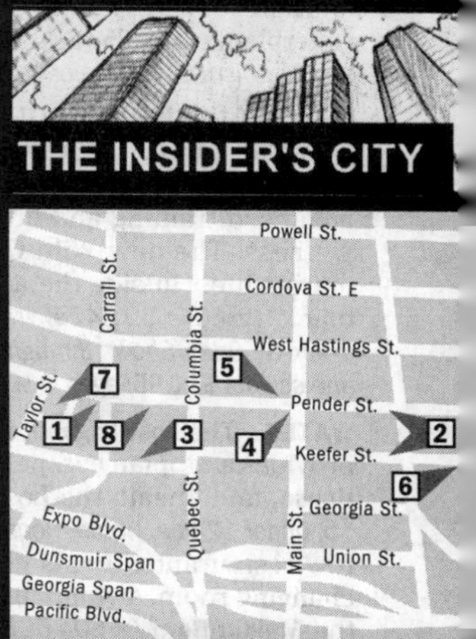

VANCOUVER CHINATOWN

Savvy tourists should take a break from downtown's slick hot spots and experience Chinatown, Vancouver at its most raw and energized.

1. Gawk at the impossibly narrow **Sam Kee Building,** said to be the narrowest in the world.
2. Barter, bicker, and haggle at the **Chinatown Night Market.** Open June-Sept. F-Su 6:30-11:30pm.
3. Let the tranquil **Dr. Sun Yat-Sen Classical Chinese Garden** (☎604-689-7133) ease your stress.
4. Enjoy great Chinese food on the cheap at **Kam's Garden Restaurant** (☎604-689-7133).
5. Recognize the trials and successes of Chinese Canadians at the **Winds of Change Mural.**
6. Choose your meal from hundreds at **Hon's Wun-Tun House** (☎604-688-0871).
7. Visit the huge **Western Han Dynasty Bell.**
8. Explore the permanent and changing exhibitions at the **Chinese Cultural Center** (☎604-658-8865).

and surrounded by an 10km **seawall** promenade popular with cyclists, runners, and rollerbladers. *(☎257-8400. To get to the park, take #23, #123, #35, or #135 bus. A free shuttle runs between major destinations throughout the park June-Sept. 10am-6pm.)*

VANCOUVER AQUARIUM. The aquarium, on the park's eastern side not far from the entrance, features exotic aquatic animals. BC, Amazonian, and other ecosystems are skillfully replicated. Dolphin and beluga whales demonstrate their advanced training and intelligence by drenching gleeful visitors in educational wetness. The new Wild Coast exhibit allows visitors to get a close-up view of marine life. Outside the aquarium, an **orca fountain** by sculptor Bill Reid glistens black. *(☎604-659-3474; www.vanaqua.org. Open daily July-Aug. 9:30am-7pm; Sept.-June 10am-5:30pm. Shows throughout the day from 10am-5:30pm. $15.75, students, ages 13-18 and seniors $11.95; ages 4-12 $8.95; 3 and under free.)*

WATER. The **Lost Lagoon,** brimming with fish, birds, and the odd trumpeter swan, provides a utopian escape from the skyscrapers. **Nature walks** start from the **Nature House,** underneath the Lost Lagoon bus loop. *(Walks ☎604-257-8544. 2hr. Su 1-3pm. $5, under 12 free. Nature House open June-Aug. F-Su 11am-7pm.)* The park's edges boast a few restaurants, tennis courts, a cinder running track with hot showers and a changing room, swimming beaches staffed by lifeguards, and an outdoor theater, the **Malkin Bowl** *(☎604-687-0174).* For warm, chlorinated water, take a dip in the **Second Beach Pool.** *(Next to Georgia St. park entrance. Pool ☎604-257-8370. $4, ages 13-18 $3, ages 65+ $2.40, ages 6-12 $2. Towels $2, lockers $0.25. Open May 19-June 10 M-F noon-8:45pm; June 11-Sept. 3 M-F 10am-8:45pm; May 19-Sept. 3 Sa-Su 10am-8:45pm.)*

FALSE CREEK & GRANVILLE ISLAND

GRANVILLE ISLAND BREWING COMPANY. Canada's first micro-brewery offers daily tours of the facility, including free samples. *(Under the bridge at the southern tip of the island. ☎604-687-2739. Tours daily noon, 2, and 4pm. $9.75, students and seniors $7.75, includes samples of 4 brews and a souvenir glass. Call for store hours.)*

H.R. MACMILLAN SPACE CENTRE. Housed in the same circular building as the **Vancouver Museum,** the space center runs a motion-simulator ride, planetarium, and exhibit gallery, as well as frequent laser-light rock shows. *(1100 Chestnut St. Bus #22 south on Burrard St. from downtown. ☎604-738-7827. Open July-Aug. daily 10am-5pm, Sept.-June closed M. $13.50, students and seniors $10.50; laser-light show $9.35. Vancouver Museum ☎604-736-4431. Open daily 10am-5pm; winter closed M. $10, seniors $8, under 19 $6. Combined admission to both museums $17, youth $11.)*

BEACHES

Vancouver has kept its many beaches relatively clean (for an urban area). Follow the western side of the Stanley Park seawall south to **Sunset Beach Park,** a strip of grass and beach extending all the way along **English Bay** to the Burrard Bridge. The **Aquatic Centre,** 1050 Beach Ave., at the southeast end of the beach, is a public facility with a sauna, gym, and 50m indoor pool. (☎604-665-3424. Call for public swim hours, generally M-Th 9am-4:20pm and 8pm-9:55pm, F 9am-4:20pm and 8:20-8:55pm, Sa 10am-9pm, Su 1-9pm. $4, ages 13-18 $3, ages 6-12 $2, ages 65+ $2.40.)

Kitsilano Beach ("Kits"), across Arbutus St. from Vanier Park, is another local favorite for tanning and beach volleyball. For fewer crowds, more young 'uns, and free showers, visit **Jericho Beach** (head west along 4th Ave. and follow signs). A cycling path at the side of the road leads to the westernmost end of the UBC campus. West of Jericho Beach is the quieter **Spanish Banks;** at low tide the ocean retreats almost a kilometer, allowing for long walks on the flats.

Most of Vancouver's 31km of beaches are patrolled daily by lifeguards from late May to Labour Day between 11:30am and 9pm.

OUTDOOR ACTIVITIES

Three local mountains loom above the city on the North Shore, bringing the locals out year-round. In winter, all three offer night skiing and heavier snow than mountains farther from the ocean. Their size and impact on your wallet are much smaller than Whistler, which is a 2hr. drive north on Hwy. 99 (see p. 267). In summer, all offer challenging hiking and beautiful views of the city from the top.

GROUSE MOUNTAIN. The ski hill closest to downtown Vancouver has the crowds to prove it. Take bus #236 from the North Vancouver SeaBus terminal, which drops passengers off at the Super Skyride, an aerial tramway open daily from 9am-10pm. The slopes are lit for skiing until 10:30pm from mid-November to mid-April. (☎604-984-0661; snow report 986-6262; www.grousemountain.com; . Lift tickets $35, youths $25, seniors $19, children $15; night passes at a reduced rate. Tramway $21.95, seniors $19.95, ages 13-18 $12.95.) The steep 2.9km **Grouse Grind Trail** is popular among Vancouverites in the summer; it climbs 853m to the top of the mountain and takes a good 2hr. The Skyride back down costs $5.

CYPRESS BOWL. Cypress Bowl in West Vancouver provides a less crowded ski alternative. It boasts the most advanced terrain of the local mountains on its 23 runs. Head west on Hwy. 1, and take Exit 8 (Cypress Bowl Rd.). A few minutes before the downhill area, the 16km of groomed trails at Hollyburn **cross-country ski area** are open to the public. In summer, the cross-country trails are excellent for **hiking** and **berry-picking.** (☎604-922-0825; snow report 604-419-7669; www.cypressbowl.com. Discount tickets available at Costco supermarkets.)

MOUNT SEYMOUR. Take bus #211 from the Phibbs Exchange at the north end of the Second Narrows Bridge to **Mt. Seymour Provincial Park.** Trails leave from Mt. Seymour Rd., and a paved road winds 11km to the top. The Mt. Seymour ski area is the cheapest skiing around. Its marked terrain is also the least challenging, although the spectacular backcountry is the preferred terrain of many top pro snowboarders. (www.mountseymour.com. Midweek lift tickets $19, seniors $15, ages 6-12 $9; weekends and holidays $29, ages 6-12 $12, seniors $19.)

IN RECENT NEWS

CRIME & (NO) PUNISHMENT

Any nighttime walk through the streets east of Gastown reveals Vancouver's entanglement in illicit drugs. Aside from the trade in BC marijuana, parts of Vancouver are awash in harder substances, especially heroin.

Since 1990, Vancouver police have logged over 50 homicides related to gangland battles and turf wars beween Indian-led gangs, including the brazen 1998 nightclub assassination of reputed gangster kingpin Bindy Johal. Despite Johal being shot dead in the middle of a crowd of more than 300, no suspects have been named in his murder—and many of the killings go unsolved.

This is due in large part to a not unjustifiable fear of violent reprisals against those who choose to cooperate with law enforcement authorities. The dismal conviction rate against those suspects who are actually tried in court also dampens potential witness cooperation—four years before his assassination, Johal and several associates were acquitted for the murder of another suspected drug cartel leader.

The continued violence has distressed community activists and has led the Vancouver Police Department to create a special task force. But with four more murders in the opening months of 2002, and with the fierce demand for drugs in the Vancouver area, these efforts must overcome substantial obstacles.

WILDLIFE ADVENTURES

The Lower Mainland of British Columbia hosts a huge variety of wild critters, including mule deer, black bear, wolves, cougars, and more than a few bird species. The **Guide-Outiftters Association of British Columbia,** 7580 River Rd., Suite 250, Richmond, BC (☎604-278-2688) is a BC-wide information and contact clearinghouse for those interested in hunting game. Those interested in importing firearms into Canada should consult the Canadian government's **Firearms Centre** (☎800-731-4000). If you'd rather seek a communion with the water, contact the **Deep Cove Canoe and Kayak Center**, 2156 Banbury Rd., North Vancouver, which offers 2hr. canoe and kayak rentals for $28 or 2hr. twin rentals for $40. 3hr. introductory lessons for novices are $60, and overnight kayak trips up to campsites on Indian Arm are also available. (☎604-929-2268; www.deepcovekayak.com. Reservations suggested in summer. Apr.-Oct. 9am-9pm)

DAYTRIPS FROM VANCOUVER

EAST OF NORTH VAN. East of the city center, the town of **Deep Cove** in North Vancouver luxuriates in saltiness, and sea otters and seals ply pleasant **Indian Arm. Cates Park,** at the end of Dollarton Hwy. on the way to Deep Cove, has popular swimming and scuba waters and makes a good bike trip out of Vancouver. Trails leave from Mt. Seymour Rd., and a paved road winds 11km to the top for access to hiking and biking. See also **Local Mountains,** p. 263. *(Bus #210 from Pender St. to the Phibbs Exchange on the north side of Second Narrows Bridge. From there, take bus #211 or 212 to Deep Cove. Bus #211 also leads to Mount Seymour Provincial Park.)*

LIGHTHOUSE PARK. If you only get out of Vancouver once, go to gorgeous **Lighthouse Park.** Numerous trails, including an easy 3km loop that covers most of the park (plan to spend a couple hours walking it), criss-cross the 185-acre park. To reach one of the best picnic spots in the world, walk down the path toward the lighthouse, hang a left at the buildings, keep right at the fork in the trail, and walk to a large flat rock. Some **rock climbing,** consisting of sea cliff top-roping and bouldering, can be found at Juniper Point on the west side of the park. *(Head across Lions Gate Bridge from Stanley Park and west along Marine Dr. for about 10km through West Van. 50km round-trip from downtown; blue bus #250 goes right to the park's entrance. For a park map stop by the West Van. Parks & Community Services Office at 750 17th St., 2nd floor. ☎604-925-7200. Open M-F 8:30am-4:30pm.)*

REIFEL BIRD SANCTUARY. Reifel Bird Sanctuary is on 850-acre Westham Island. The marshland supports 265 bird species, and spotting towers are set up for extended bird-watching. April, May, October, and November are the best months to visit. *(Westham Island lies northwest of the Tsawwassen ferry terminal and 16km south of the city. ☎604-946-6980. Open daily 9am-4pm. $4, seniors and children $2.)*

LYNN CANYON. An idyllic setting that provides easy hiking for city escapists. Unlike the more famous Capilano (below), the suspension bridge here is free, uncrowded, and hangs 50m above the canyon. The park offers more trails than Capilano; several are 10-20min., but longer hiking trails are also plentiful. Swimming is not recommended; many have died over the years from the treacherous currents and falls. *(SeaBus to Lynn Canyon Park, in North Vancouver. Take bus #229 from the North Vancouver SeaBus terminal to the last stop (Peters Rd.) and walk 500m to the bridge. ☎604-981-3103. Open summer 7am-9pm; spring and fall 7am-8pm; winter 7am-6pm.)*

CAPILANO SUSPENSION BRIDGE. You and every other Vancouver tourist will enjoy crossing the precarious Capilano Bridge. Although the bridge was built in 1889, it remains awe-inspiring, spanning 137m and swaying 70m above the river. A few short trails meander through the surrounding old-growth forest. Guided tours every 15min. in summer. *(3735 Capilano Rd. North Van. 10min. from town. Drive through Stanley Park, over the Lions Gate Bridge, north 1km. on Capilano Rd. From Hwy. #1 take Exit 14 and go north.5km. Or take bus #246 from downtown to Ridgewood stop and walk 1 block north to park. ☎985-7474; www.capbridge.com. Open in summer daily 8:30-dusk; winter 9am-5pm. $13.95, seniors $10.75, students $7.95, child 6-12 $3.75, under 6 free. CAA, AAA 20% discount; HI members get student rate.)*

SECHELT PENINSULA ☎604

Tucked between the Strait of Georgia and Porpoise Bay, Sechelt (SEE-shelt) is one of BC's greatest secrets. Only 1½hr. by road and ferry from downtown Vancouver, this quiet seaside paradise remains miles away in attitude, lifestyle, and even climate. The region offers a rich array of outdoor activities: world-class kayaking, hiking, scuba diving, biking, and even skiing are close-by.

ORIENTATION & PRACTICAL INFORMATION. Sechelt is the largest community on the Sunshine Coast, 27km west of the **BC Ferries,** Langdale Ferry Terminal (☎886-2242 or 888-223-3779). The fare on the ferry between Langdale and Horseshoe Bay is only charged on the way from the mainland to Sechelt (40min.; 8-10 per day; $8, under 12 $4, car $30; off-season slightly cheaper). **Malaspina Coach Lines** (☎885-3666) runs to **Vancouver** (2 per day, $10.75 plus ferry fare). **Sunshine Coast Transit System** (☎885-3234) buses run from Sechelt to the ferry terminal (adult $1.50, students and seniors $1). **National Tilden,** 5623 Wharf St., rents cars. (☎885-9120. From $50 per day; $0.25 per km over 100km; winter rates start at $44.) Hail a **Sunshine Coast Taxi** at ☎885-3666. The **visitors center** is located in the Trail Bay Centre at Trail Ave. and Teredo St. next to Home Hardware. (☎885-0662 or 877-633-2963. Open year-round M-Sa 9:30am-5:30pm, Su 10am-4pm; off season closed on Su.) **Trail Bay Sports,** at Cowrie St. and Trail Ave., rents mountain bikes and sells fishing gear and permits as well as other useful outdoor gear. (☎885-2512. Bikes $10 per hr., $45 per 8hr. Open in summer M-Th and Sa 9am-6pm, F 9am-9pm, Su 10am-4pm; winter M-Sa 9:30am-5:30pm.) **Sechelt Coin Laundry** is on Dolphin St. at Inlet Ave. (☎885-3393. Open daily 9am-9pm. Wash $1.75, dry $0.25 per 5min.) **Call** ☎911 in an **emergency,** or get to **St. Mary's Hospital** (☎885-2224), on the highway at the east end of town. The **Sechelt Public Library,** 5797 Cowrie St., has **Internet access** for $1 per 30min. (☎885-3260. Open Tu 10am-5pm, W-Th 11am-8pm, F and Su 1pm-5pm, and Sa 10am-4pm.) The **post office** is on Inlet Ave. at Dolphin St. (☎885-2411. Open M-F 8:30am-5pm, Sa 8:30am-12:30pm.) **Postal Code:** V0N 3A0.

ACCOMMODATIONS & CAMPING. Most of Sechelt's accommodations are pricey, but deals can be found. The comfortable **Moon Cradle Backpacker's Retreat** ❶, 3125 Hwy. 101 across from the golf course, 10km east of Sechelt, is situated on 10 acres of woodland property with a firepit, sauna, laundry, Internet, and bike rentals ($6 per hr.). It can turn into a hangout for the locals, so idyllic silence isn't always the norm. (☎885-2070. $25, students and seniors $22; singles $40, $37; doubles $55, $49.) **Eagle View B&B** ❸, 4839 Eagle View Rd., 5min. east of Sechelt, has rooms with private bath, sitting room with TV/VCR and video collection, an ocean view, complimentary tea and biscuits, and delightful hosts. (☎885-7225. Singles $45-50, doubles $70.)

The provincial parks in the area are dreamy. The family-oriented **Porpoise Bay Provincial Park** ❶, 4km north of Sechelt along Sechelt Inlet Rd./E Porpoise Bay Rd., offers a forested campground with toilets, showers, firewood, playground, and a lovely beach and swimming area. (Reservations ☎800-689-9025. Wheelchair accessible. 84 regular sites, $18; cyclist campsites by the water $9. Gate closed 11pm-7am.) For more seclusion, **Roberts Creek Provincial Park ❶,** 11km east of Sechelt, has private sites amid old-growth Douglas Firs. (Pit toilets, firewood, water. 24 sites, $12.) **Smuggler Cove Provincial Park ❶** has five primitive, free walk-in sites (pit toilets, no water). The sites are accessible by boat, and the cove is an excellent base for kayaking. Head west out of town towards Halfmoon Bay and turn left on Brooks Rd., which leads 3.5km to a parking area. The campsite is 1km along a trail.

FOOD. **Claytons,** in the Trail Bay Centre, is the place to go for groceries. (☎885-2025. Open M-Th 9am-7pm, F 9am-9pm, Sa-Su 10am-6pm.) **The Gumboot Garden Cafe ❶,** 1059 Roberts Creek Rd., 10km east of Sechelt in Roberts Creek, serves delicious meals with organic ingredients. Lunch and breakfast favorites include fries and miso gravy ($3.50) and Thai salad with chicken, salmon, or tofu ($6-7). A variable dinner menu is uniformly excellent and always includes vegan options. (☎885-4216. Open M-W 8am-8pm, Th-Sa 7:30am-10pm, Su 7:30am-6pm.) In Sechelt, the **Old Boot Eatery ❸,** 5520 Wharf St., serves up generous portions of Italian food and local hospitality; pasta entrees are $9-15. (☎885-2727. Open in summer M-Sa 11am-9:30pm; winter 11am-9pm.) **Wakefield Inn ❷,** on the highway (number 6529) 5min. west of Sechelt, dishes out pub fare and live music with a great view of the ocean. Pints are $4-5. (☎885-7666. Music F-Sa 9pm-1am.)

SIGHTS & OUTDOOR ACTIVITIES. The eight wilderness marine parks in the protected waters of **Sechelt Inlet** make for fantastic sea kayaking and canoeing and offer free camping along the shore. **Pedals & Paddles,** at Tillicum Bay Marina, 7km north of town, rents vessels. (☎885-6440. Single kayaks $23 per 4hr., doubles $46; canoes $27. Full-day single kayaks $40, doubles $75; canoes $45.) The intersection of Sechelt and Salmon Inlets is home to the **S.S. Chaudiere artificial reef,** one of the largest wreck dives in North America. **Suncoast Dive Center** rents equipment, teaches lessons, and charters boats (☎740-8006; www.suncoastdiving.com. Regular rental $45 per day; full rental $75 per day; 1 day charter $85). On the other side of the peninsula, **Pender Harbor** offers equally impressive diving; Jacques Cousteau considered this site second only to the Red Sea. **Skookumchuck Narrows** is a popular destination by water or by land to view tidal rapids that bring waves standing 1.5m at peak tides. Tidal schedules are available at the Info Centre or at the trailhead. To get there, drive 54km west to **Earl's Cove** and then 4km towards **Egmont** (about 1hr.). From the parking area, it's a 4km walk to four viewing sites (allow 1hr.). The route to the first site is wheelchair-accessible.

Dakota Bowl and Wilson Creek 4km east of Sechelt have hiking and free cross-country skiing trails. From Sechelt, turn left on Field Rd. and drive 8km to the trailhead. Sechelt's lumber legacy has left it with an extensive system of former logging roads suitable for hiking and mountain biking. The intermediate **Chapman Creek Trail** passes huge Douglas firs en route to **Chapman Falls.** The trailhead is at the top of Havies Rd., 1km north of the Davis Bay Store on Hwy. 101, or access at Brookman Park on the highway. The **Suncoaster Trail** extends over 40km from **Homesite Creek,** near Halfmoon Bay northwest of Sechelt, through the foothills of the **Caren Range,** home of Canada's oldest trees (some as old as 1835 years).

Indoors, the **Sunshine Coast Arts Centre,** on Trail Ave. at Medusa St., showcases local talent in a log building. (☎885-5412. Open July-Aug. Tu-Sa 10am-4pm, Su 1-4pm; Sept.-June W-Sa 11am-4pm, Su 1-4pm. Admission by donation.) They also organize the Hackett Park Crafts Fair, held during the Sechelt's big event, the **Sunshine Coast Festival of the Written Arts,** which attracts talented Canadian and international authors to give **readings** (August 8-11, 2002). Panels are held in the **botanical gardens** of the historic Rockwood Centre, and tickets go early. (☎885-9631 or 800-565-9631. Grounds open daily 8am-10pm.) The **Roberts Creek Community Hall** (☎886-3868 or

740-9616), on the corner of the highway and Roberts Creek Rd., attracts excellent musicians on weekends, from reggae to Latin funk. Tickets ($10-20) can be purchased at the **Roberts Creek General Store** (☎885-3400).

ALONG HWY. 99: SEA TO SKY HWY.

Winding around the steep cliffs on the shore of Howe Sound from Horseshoe Bay to Squamish and then continuing inland to Whistler, the Sea to Sky Hwy. (Hwy. 99) is one of the loveliest, most dangerous, and best loved drives in British Columbia. Sinuous curves combine with brilliant vistas of the Sound and Tantalus Range.

VANCOUVER TO WHISTLER

Numerous provincial parks line the rocky drive to Whistler, providing excellent hiking and climbing opportunities. One worth stopping for is **Shannon Falls,** just off the highway, 3km past the museum. The park affords a 2min. walk (350m) to a spectacular view of a 335m waterfall, the third highest in BC. Steep but well-maintained trails from the falls make for difficult **dayhiking** up to the three peaks of the **Stawamus Chief** (11km round-trip), the second largest granite monolith in the world, which bares a 671m wall of solid granite. The face of the Chief is a popular climb for expert hikers. **Squamish Hostel ❶,** 38490 Buckley Rd., in downtown Squamish, is a common stopover for those tackling the local geography. In summer, the hostel is packed with wandering climbers, as the region between Squamish and Whistler boasts over 1300 excellent routes. (☎892-9240 or 800-449-8614 in BC. Shower, kitchen, linen. $15; private rooms $25.) At **Eagle Run,** a viewing site 4km north of the hostel along the Squamish River, thousands of bald eagles make their winter home along the rivers and estuaries of Squamish Valley. BC Parks runs a spotless **campground ❶** 13km north of Squamish at **Alice Lake.** (Reservations ☎800-689-9025; www.discovercamping.ca. Hot water, firewood. $18.50. Showers.) Nearby **Garibaldi Park** contains a vast number of stunning hikes, including an 18km (round-trip) trail up to **Garibaldi Lake.** The backcountry campgrounds at the lake provide further access to Black Tusk and Cheakamus Lake (trailhead at Rubble Creek parking lot, 25km north of Squamish). The **BC Parks District Office** in Alice Lake Park has trail maps. (☎898-3678. Open M-F 8:30am-4:30pm.) The **BC Forest Service office,** 42000 Loggers Ln., has maps of local logging roads and primitive campgrounds and sells the $10 permits needed to camp at them. (☎898-2100; www.for.gov.bc.ca/Vancouver/district/squamish. Open M-F 8:30am-4:30pm.)

WHISTLER ☎604

This skiers' and snowboarders' utopia is among the top ski destinations in the world, and for good reason: over 7000 acres of ski-able terrain make it the largest ski area on the continent. The mountains are part of Garibaldi Provincial Park, and it takes little effort to get off the beaten path. When the snow melts, bikes (the primary recreation on the summer slopes), boots, horses, and rafts usually fill in for skis, and bundled up ski junkies are replaced by people in baggy shorts who look like they want to be skiing. The town itself is pretty enough, but its shops and restaurants earn it a deserved reputation as an overpriced, outdoor mall.

ORIENTATION & PRACTICAL INFORMATION

Whistler is located 125km north of Vancouver on the beautiful, if dangerously twisty, Hwy. 99. Services are located in **Whistler Village,** most of which is **pedestrian-only. Whistler Creek,** 5km south on Hwy. 99, offers a smaller collection of accommodations and restaurants. The first thing to do upon arriving in town is obtain a map. Otherwise, all is lost.

Greyhound Bus Lines: (☎932-5031 or 800-661-8747; www.whistlerbus.com.) To **Vancouver** from the **Village Bus Loop** (2½hr., 7 per day, $22.50). The Activity Centre sells tickets.

BC Rail: (☎984-5246). **Cariboo Prospector** departs North Vancouver at 7am for Whistler Creek and returns at 6:40pm daily. ($39 one-way. The train station is on Lake Placid Rd. in Creekside; free connecting bus service to the Village.)

Taxi: Whistler Taxi (☎932-3333).

Tourist Office: Activity Centre (☎932-3928), in the Conference Centre, provides maps and booking services. Open daily 8:30am-5pm. The **Chamber of Commerce** and **Info Centre** (☎932-5528. Open daily summer 9am-6pm; winter 9am-5pm) are in a log cabin at the corner of Hwy. 99 and Lake Placid Rd. in Creekside. Alternatively, call **Whistler/Blackcomb** (☎932-3434 or 800-766-0449; www.whistlerblackcomb.com).

Laundry: Laundry at Nester's, 7009 Nester's Rd. (☎932-2960). $2.25 wash, $0.25 per 4min. of drying. Open 8:30am-8:30pm.

Weather Conditions: ☎664-9033.

Emergency: ☎911.

Police: 4315 Blackcomb Way (☎932-3044), in the Village.

Telecare Crisis Line: ☎932-2673.

Medical Services: Whistler Health Care Center, 4380 Lorimer Rd. (☎932-4911).

Internet Access: Whistler Public Library (932-5564), located between Main St. and Northlands Blvd. Free, but long waits. Open M-Tu and Th 10am-8pm, F-Su 10am-5pm.

Post Office: (☎932-5012), in the Market Place Mall. Open M-F 8:30am-5:30pm, Sa 8:30am-12:30pm. **Postal Code:** V0N 1B4. **Area Code:** 604.

ACCOMMODATIONS & CAMPING

Whistler offers great hostels and campgrounds. The Forest Service office in Squamish (see p. 267) has maps for other camping options.

Whistler Hostel (HI), 5678 Alta Lake Rd. (☎932-5492). BC Rail from Vancouver stops right in front on request. 5km south of Whistler Village off Hwy. 99. The Rainbow Park bus runs to the Village ($1.50). The lakeside timber building has a kitchen, fireplace, ski lockers, pool table, Internet, and sauna. Bikes $18 per day. Canoes free on Alta Lake. Check in 8am-11am and 4pm-10pm. Reserve ahead. Bunks $19.50; nonmembers $23.50; under 13 half-price; under 6 free. Private rooms $10 surcharge. ❷

The Fireside Lodge, 2117 Nordic Dr. (☎932-4545), 3km south of the Village. Caters to a quiet, easygoing crowd. The spacious and spotless cabin, filled with funky, angular bedrooms, comes with mammoth kitchen, lounge, sauna, coin laundry, extensive and lively game room, storage (bring your own lock), and parking. Check-in 3:30-8:30pm. 24 bunks: $20; private rooms from $30. ❸

Shoestring Lodge, 7124 Nancy Greene Dr. (☎932-3338), 1km north of the Village. Cable, private bath, laundry, and Internet. Small fee for kitchen use. In-house pub can lead to late-night ruckus outside. Free shuttle to slopes Dec.-Apr. Check-in 4pm, check-out 11am. 4-person dorm $17-30; doubles $90-140; more expensive in winter. ❸

FOOD

Cheap food is hard-won in the Village with the exception of the popular **IGA** supermarket in the Village North. (Open daily 9am-9pm.) Pub food is the most affordable way to find sustenance (meals usually around $10, with a pint $15). Pubs are in almost every other building throughout the Village.

South Side Deli, 2102 Lake Placid Rd. (☎932-3368), on Hwy. 99 by the Husky station 4km south of the Village. Heaping breakfasts, mammoth lunches, and deliciously greasy dinners. Be sure to try the B.E.L.T.C.H. (bacon, egg, lettuce, tomato, cheese, and ham). Open Th-Su 6am-10pm, M-W 6am-3pm. ❷

Uli's Flipside Restaurant, 4433 Sundial Plaza (935-1107). Right next to the main Village Square. Getting closer to the upscale side of things, Uli's offers hearty and worthy Mediterranean-Canadian fare, with almost all dishes falling between $10-15. Worth the splurge after a long day's workout. M-Sa 5pm-1am. ❸

Moguls Coffee Beans, 4208 Village Square (☎932-4845). Right on the Village Square, a tasty and thrifty option. Delectable home-baked goods ($2.25 or less) and sandwiches ($4.50). Open daily 6:30am-9pm. ❶

OUTDOOR ACTIVITIES

WINTER SPORTS. Thirty-three lifts (15 of them high-speed), three glaciers, over 200 marked trails, a mile (1609m) of vertical drop, and unreal scenery makes **Whistler/Blackcomb** a top destination for snow enthusiasts. Parking and lift access for this behemoth are available at six points, but Whistler Creekside offers the shortest lines and the closest access for those coming from Vancouver. A **lift ticket** is good for both mountains and, depending on the timing, costs between $112-141 for three days, with better deals for longer trips. (☎932-3434 or 800-766-0449.) A **Fresh Tracks** upgrade ($15), available every morning at 7am, provides a basic breakfast in the mountaintop lodge on Blackcomb along with the chance to begin skiing as soon as the ski patrol has finished avalanche control. **Cheap tickets** are often available at convenience stores in Vancouver, and rates are sometimes cheaper midweek and early or late in the season. While Whistler offers amazing alpine terrain and gorgeous bowls, most **snowboarders** prefer the younger Blackcomb for its windlips, natural quarter-pipes, and 16-acre terrain park. Endless **backcountry skiing** is accessible from resort lifts and in Garibaldi Park's **Diamond Head** area. Equipment rentals are available through Whistler-Blackcom and through Affinity Sports, located next to Moguls Coffee on the Village Square (☎932-6611).

The BC Parks office in Alice Lake Park (see p. 267) has avalanche info. Avalanches kill people every year, and there are no patrols outside resort boundaries. Always file trip plans and stay within the limits of your experience.

SUMMER ACTIVITIES. While skiing is God in Whistler and lasts until August on the glaciers, life goes on in the summer as the **Whistler Gondola** continues to whisk sightseers to the top of the mountain, providing access to the resort's extensive **hiking trails** and **mountain bike park.** ($22 for hiking only, $32 for mountain bike park.) Hiking trails tend to be short dayhikes, with lengths ranging from 20min. to 5-6hr. and most trails taking less than an hour to complete. For more info on trails and the multitude of other options—such as rafting, fishing, kayaking, off-road tours, mountain climbing, and horseback riding—that make Whistler/Blackcomb famous in the summer, check their web site at www.whistlerblackcomb.com or call the tourist info line (see **Tourist Office,** p. 268).

NORTH OF WHISTLER

JOFFRE LAKES. For a fantastic **dayhike** 65km north of Whistler, climb to the **Joffre Lakes** along a popular 11km path round-trip that passes three glacially-fed lakes and affords spectacular views of **Joffre Peak** and **Slalok Mountain** (accessible in the summer months only, look for the entrance 32km north of Pemberton).

LILLOOET. Little traffic continues north along Hwy. 99 and the drive is eerily remote. **Lillooet** ("B.C's Little Nugget"), 135km north of Whistler, was originally Mile 0 of the historic **Cariboo Gold Rush Wagon Trail,** which led 100,000 gold-crazed miners north to Barkerville between 1862 and 1870. The town itself is small, but oozes with history. The **Chamber of Commerce** (☎256-4364; fax 256-4315) will help you find a place to crash. In the second weekend in June, the town celebrates its heritage during **Lillooet Days** with a host of events including a staged train robbery, mock trial, and execution.

FARTHER NORTH. From Lillooet, Hwy. 99 meanders north another 50km, snaking with the Fraser River until it meets Hwy. 97 11km north of **Cache Creek.** The weary can break half-way for trout fishing and swimming in **Crown Lake** beneath the red limestone cliffs of **Marble Canyon Provincial Park** ❶ (camping $12).

VANCOUVER ISLAND

Vancouver Island stretches almost 500km along continental Canada's southwest coast and is one of only two points in Canada extending south of the 49th parallel. The Kwagiulth, Nootka, and Coastal Salish shared the island for thousands of years until Captain Cook's discovery of Nootka Sound in 1778 triggered European exploration and infiltration. The current culture of Vancouver Island bespeaks its hybrid heritage, presenting a curious blend of totems and afternoon teas. The cultural and administrative center is Victoria, BC's capital, on its southernmost tip.

The Trans-Canada (Hwy. 1) leads north from Victoria to Nanaimo, the transportation hub of the island's central region. Once you get out of Victoria and Nanaimo, wilderness takes over and towns shrink in size, creating a haven for hikers, kayakers, and mountaineers. Pacific Rim National Park, on the island's west coast, offers some of the most rugged and outstanding hiking in North America. On the northern third of the island, crumpets give way to clamburgers, and 4x4 pickups and logging caravans prowl dirt roads.

VICTORIA ☎250

Although many tourist operations would have you believe that Victoria fell off Great Britain in a neat little chunk, its high tea tradition actually began in the 1950s to draw American tourists. Before the invasion of tea, Fort Victoria, founded in 1843, was a fur trading post and supply center for the Hudson Bay Company. But the discovery of gold in the Fraser River Canyon pushed it into the fast lane in 1858, bringing international trade and the requisite frontier bars and brothels. The government soon followed. Victoria became the capital in 1868.

Clean, polite, and tourist-friendly, Victoria is a homier alternative to cosmopolitan Vancouver. Its namesake British monarch and her era of morals and furniture aside, Victoria is a city of diverse origins and interests. Galleries selling native arts operate alongside new-age bookstores, tourist traps, and pawn shops. Double-decker bus tours motor by English pubs while bike-taxis pedal past the markets, museums, and stores that make up the rest of downtown. Victoria also lies within easy striking distance of the rest of Vancouver Island's "outdoor paradise."

TRANSPORTATION

The **Trans-Canada Hwy. (Hwy. 1)** runs north to Nanaimo, where it becomes **Hwy. 19,** stretching north to the rest of Vancouver Island. **The West Coast Hwy. (Hwy. 14)** heads west to **Port Renfrew** and the West Coast Trail unit of the **Pacific Rim National Park.** The

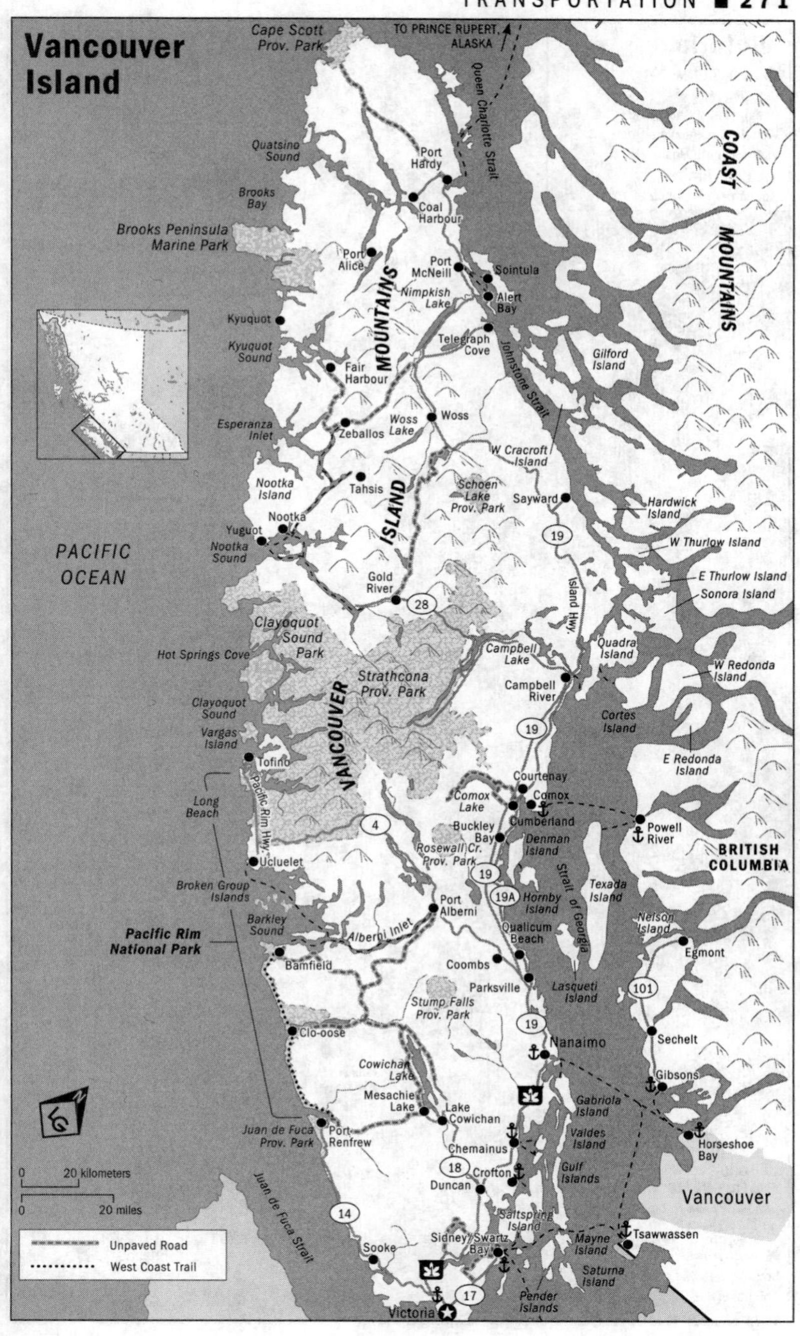
Vancouver Island
Cape Scott Prov. Park
TO PRINCE RUPERT, ALASKA
Queen Charlotte Strait
Quatsino Sound
Port Hardy
Brooks Bay
Coal Harbour
Brooks Peninsula Marine Park
Port Alice
Port McNeill
Sointula
Nimpkish Lake
Alert Bay
Kyuquot
Kyuquot Sound
Telegraph Cove
Fair Harbour
MOUNTAINS
COAST MOUNTAINS
Johnstone Strait
Gilford Island
Esperanza Inlet
Zeballos
Woss Lake
Woss
W Cracroft Island
Nootka Island
Tahsis
ISLAND
Schoen Lake Prov. Park
Sayward
Hardwick Island
Nootka
Yuguot
Nootka Sound
19
W Thurlow Island
PACIFIC OCEAN
Island Hwy.
E Thurlow Island
Sonora Island
Gold River
28
Clayoquot Sound Park
Hot Springs Cove
Campbell Lake
Quadra Island
Strathcona Prov. Park
Campbell River
W Redonda Island
Clayoquot Sound
VANCOUVER
Cortes Island
Vargas Island
Tofino
E Redonda Island
Pacific Rim Hwy.
Courtenay
Long Beach
Comox Lake
Comox
Cumberland
Powell River
4
Buckley Bay
Denman Island
BRITISH COLUMBIA
Ucluelet
Rosewall Cr. Prov. Park
Strait of Georgia
Broken Group Islands
19A
Hornby Island
Texada Island
Port Alberni
Nelson Island
Barkley Sound
Alberni Inlet
Qualicum Beach
Pacific Rim National Park
Egmont
Coombs
Bamfield
Parksville
Lasqueti Island
101
Stump Falls Prov. Park
Clo-oose
Nanaimo
Sechelt
Cowichan Lake
Gibsons
Gabriola Island
Mesachie Lake
Lake Cowichan
Juan de Fuca Prov. Park
Port Renfrew
Valdes Island
Horseshoe Bay
Chemainus
Gulf Islands
0 20 kilometers
0 20 miles
18
Crofton
Duncan
Vancouver
Juan de Fuca Strait
14
Saltspring Island
Tsawwassen
Unpaved Road
Sidney/Swartz Bay
Mayne Island
West Coast Trail
Sooke
Saturna Island
17
Pender Islands
Victoria

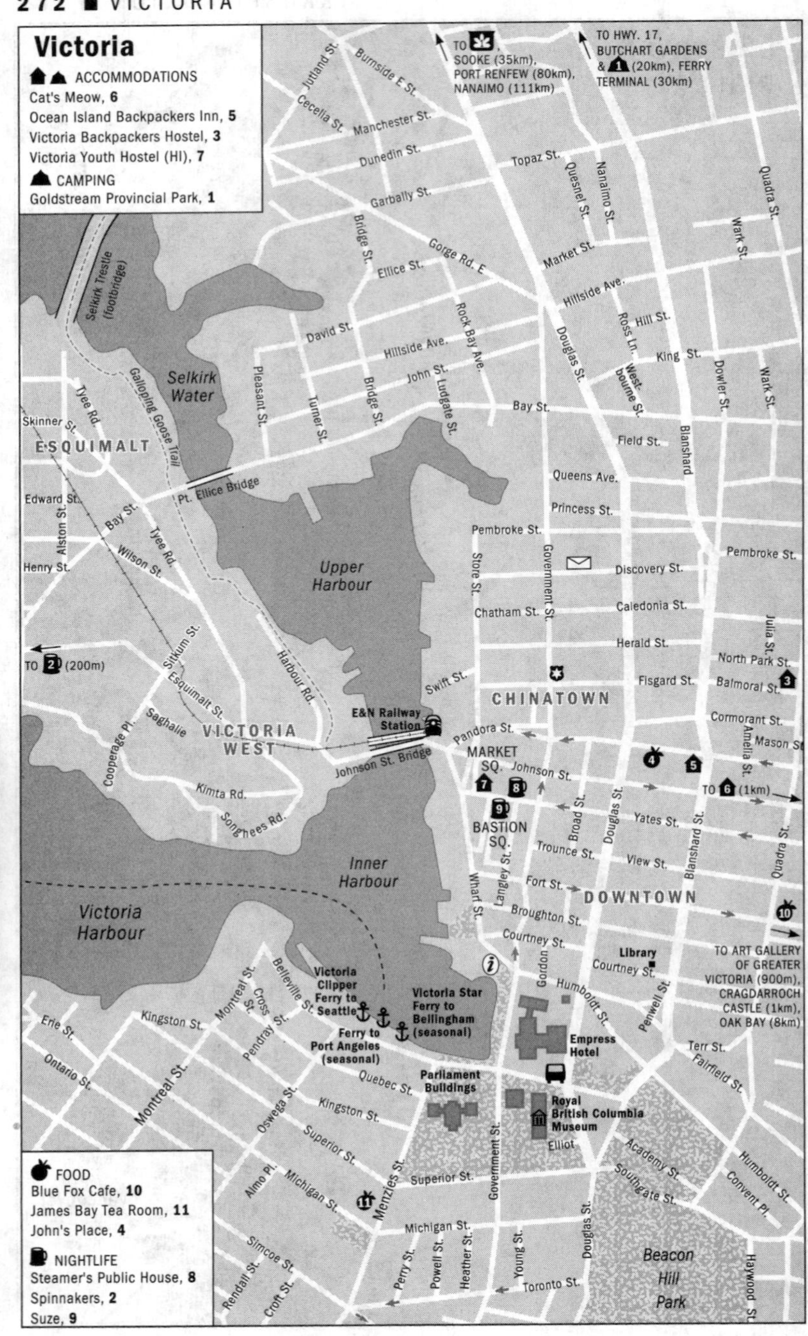

Victoria
ACCOMMODATIONS
Cat's Meow, 6
Ocean Island Backpackers Inn, 5
Victoria Backpackers Hostel, 3
Victoria Youth Hostel (HI), 7
CAMPING
Goldstream Provincial Park, 1
FOOD
Blue Fox Cafe, 10
James Bay Tea Room, 11
John's Place, 4
NIGHTLIFE
Steamer's Public House, 8
Spinnakers, 2
Suze, 9
TO SOOKE (35km), PORT RENFEW (80km), NANAIMO (111km)
TO HWY. 17, BUTCHART GARDENS & 1 (20km), FERRY TERMINAL (30km)
TO 2 (200m)
TO 6 (1km)
TO ART GALLERY OF GREATER VICTORIA (900m), CRAGDARROCH CASTLE (1km), OAK BAY (8km)
Selkirk Water
Upper Harbour
Inner Harbour
Victoria Harbour
ESQUIMALT
VICTORIA WEST
CHINATOWN
DOWNTOWN
MARKET SQ.
BASTION SQ.
E&N Railway Station
Victoria Clipper Ferry to Seattle
Victoria Star Ferry to Bellingham (seasonal)
Ferry to Port Angeles (seasonal)
Empress Hotel
Parliament Buildings
Royal British Columbia Museum
Library
Beacon Hill Park
Selkirk Trestle (footbridge)
Galloping Goose Trail
Pt. Ellice Bridge
Johnson St. Bridge

BRITISH COLUMBIA

Pat Bay Hwy. (Hwy. 17) runs north from Victoria to Swartz Bay ferry terminal and the airport, 30min. from downtown. Driving in Victoria is relatively easy, but **parking** downtown is difficult and expensive. Victoria surrounds the **Inner Harbour;** the main north-south thoroughfares downtown are **Government St.** and **Douglas St.** To the north, Douglas St. becomes Hwy. 1. **Blanshard St.,** one block to the east, becomes Hwy. 17.

Trains: E&N Railway, 450 Pandora St. (schedule ☎383-4324, general info and tickets 800-561-8630), near the Inner Harbour at the Johnson St. Bridge. 10% senior discount. 25% off when booked 7 days in advance. Daily service to **Courtenay** (4½hr.; $44, students with ISIC $29) and **Nanaimo** (2½hr.; $23, students with ISIC $15).

Buses: Gray Line of Victoria, 700 Douglas St. (☎385-4411 or 800-318-0818), at Belleville St., and its affiliates, **Pacific Coach Lines** and **Island Coach Lines,** connect most points on the island. To: **Nanaimo** (2½hr., 6 per day, $17.50), **Port Hardy** (9hr., 1-2 per day, $93), and **Vancouver** (3½hr., 8-14 per day, $29).

Ferries: Bus #70 runs between downtown and the Swartz Bay and Sidney ferry terminals ($2.50). **BC Ferries** (☎888-223-3779; www.bcferries.com. Call 7am-10pm). Service to all **Gulf Islands** (see p. 278). Ferries depart **Swartz Bay** to Vancouver's **Tsawwassen** ferry terminal (1½hr.; 8-16 per day; $8.25-10, bikes $2.50, car and driver $25-35). **Washington State Ferries** (☎656-1831; in the US 206-464-6400 or 800-843-3779; www.wsdot.wa.gov/ferries) depart from **Sidney** to **Anacortes, WA.** A ticket to Anacortes allows free stopovers along the eastward route, including the **San Juan Islands** (2 per day in summer, 1 per day in winter; US$9, car with driver US$41). **Victoria Clipper,** 254 Belleville St. (☎800-888-2535; www.victoriaclipper.com), runs passenger ferries direct to **Seattle** (2-3hr.; 2-4 per day May-Sept., 1 per day Oct.-Apr.; US$62-77, seniors US$90-103, ages 1-11 $50-56). **Black Ball Transport,** 430 Belleville St. (☎386-2202; www.northolympic.com/coho), runs to **Port Angeles, WA** (1½hr.; 4 per day mid-May to mid-Oct., 2 per day Oct.-Dec. and mid-Mar. to mid-May; US$7.75, car and driver US$30, ages 5-11 US$4, bicycle US$3.50).

Public Transportation: BC Transit (☎382-6161; www.bctransit.com). City bus service with connections at the corner of Douglas and Yates St. Single-zone travel $1.75; multi-zone (north to Swartz Bay, Sidney, and the Butchart Gardens) $2.50; seniors $1.10 and $1.75; under 5 free. Get day passes ($5.50, seniors $4) and a free *Rider's Guide* at the library, from any driver, or with maps at **Tourism Victoria. Disability Services** for local transit (☎727-7811) is open M-Th and Su 7am-10pm, F-Sa 7am-midnight.

Car Rental: Island Auto Rentals, 1030 Yates St. (☎384-4881). Starting at $20 per day, plus $0.12 per km after 100km. Insurance $13. 21+. The big companies with comparable rates are located at the bottom of Douglas St. near the Museum.

Taxis: Victoria Taxi (☎383-7111; www.victoria-taxi.com).

PRACTICAL INFORMATION

Tourist Information: 812 Wharf St. (☎953-2033), at Government St. Also a Ticketmaster outlet. Open July-Aug. daily 8:30am-6:30pm; winter 9am-5pm.

Tours: Grayline, 700 Douglas St. (☎388-5248 or 800-663-8390; www.victoriatours.com). Runs several tours in double-decker buses through different parts of the city ($18-87).

Equipment Rental:

Cycle BC Rentals, 747 Douglas St. (☎885-2453; www.cyclebc.ca), guarantees the best prices in town. Bikes from $6 per hr., $19 per day; scooters $12, $45. Motorcycles available. Look for coupons at hostels and hotels. Open summer daily 9am-6:30pm, winter 9am-5pm.

Harbour Rental, 811 Wharf St. (☎995-1211), opposite the visitors center. Rowboats and single kayaks $15 per hr., $49 per day; doubles $25, $69; canoes $19, $49. Open summer daily 10am-8pm; winter 9am-5pm.

Sports Rent, 1950 Government St. (☎385-7368), rents camping equipment. Sleeping bags from $9, tents from $15, packs from $12. Open Tu-Sa 9am-6pm, Su 10am-5pm, M 9:30am-5pm.

Laundromat and Showers: Oceanside Gifts, 102-812 Wharf St. (☎380-1777). Wash $1.25, dry $1. Showers $1 per 5min. Open daily 7am-10pm.

Emergency: ☎911.

Police: 850 Caledonia (☎995-7654), at Quadra St.

Crisis Line: ☎386-6323. 24hr.

Rape Crisis: ☎383-3232. 24hr.

Pharmacy: Shoppers Drug Mart, 1222 Douglas St. (☎381-4321). Open M-F 7am-8pm, Sa 9am-7pm, Su 9am-6pm.

Hospital: Royal Jubilee, 1900 Fort St. (☎370-8000).

Internet Access: $3 per hr. at the **library,** 735 Broughton St. (☎382-7241) at Courtney St. Open M, W, and F-Sa 9am-6pm, Tu and Th 9am-9pm.

Post Office: 621 Discovery St. (☎963-1350). Open M-F 8am-6pm. **Postal Code:** V8W 2L9. **Area Code:** 250.

ACCOMMODATIONS & CAMPING

Victoria has a plethora of budget accommodations. A number of flavorful hostels and B&B-hostel hybrids make a night in Victoria an altogether pleasant experience. More than a dozen campgrounds and RV parks lie in the greater Victoria area. It's wise to make reservations ahead of time in the summer.

Ocean Island Backpackers Inn, 791 Pandora St. (☎385-1788 or 888-888-4180), downtown. This colorful hostel boasts a better lounge than many clubs, tastier food than many restaurants, a fantastic staff, and accommodations comparable to many hotels. Undoubtedly one of the finest urban hostels in Canada. Laundry and e-mail. Limited parking, $5. Depending on the time of year, dorms, $18-23, students and HI members $18-20; doubles $22-55. ❶

The Cat's Meow, 1316 Grant St. (☎595-8878). Take bus #22 to Victoria High School at Fernwood and Grant St. 3 blocks from downtown. This mini-hostel earns its name with 12 quiet beds, friendly conversation, and 2 welcoming cats. Breakfast included. Coin-op laundry, free street parking, discounts on kayaking and whale watching. Dorms $18.50; private rooms $40-45. ❶

Victoria Backpackers Hostel, 1608 Quadra St. (☎386-4471), close to downtown. A funky old house with a small yard, lounge, and kitchen. Newly renovated dorms, lounge, and kitchen. Free linens, towels, and soap. Laundry $2. Dorms $15 or $40 for 3 nights; private rooms $45. ❶

Victoria Youth Hostel (HI), 516 Yates St. (☎385-4511), at Wharf St. downtown. Big and spotless barracks-style dorms. Foosball, pool, video games, TV room, and info desk. Kitchen, free linen. Storage $3 per week. Laundry $2, towel $0.50. Reception 24hr. Dorms July-Sept. $17.25, nonmembers $21.25; private rooms $39-45. ❶

Goldstream Provincial Park, 2930 Trans-Canada Hwy. (☎391-2300; reservations ☎800-689-9025), 20km northwest of Victoria. Riverside area with dayhikes and swimming. Toilets, firewood. Follow the trail on the other side of the highway to a railway trestle in the woods. Gates closed 11pm-7am. 167 gorgeous, gravelly sites, $19. ❶

FOOD

A diverse array of food awaits in Victoria, if you know where to go. Many **Government St.** and **Wharf St.** restaurants raise their prices for summer tourists. **Chinatown** extends from Fisgard and Government St. to the northwest. Coffee shops can be found on every corner. Cook St. Village, between McKenzie and Park Sts., offers an eclectic mix of creative restaurants. **Fisherman's Wharf,** at the end of Erie St., has the day's catch. For groceries, try **Thrifty Foods,** 475 Simcoe St., six blocks south of the Parliament Buildings. (☎544-1234. Open daily 8am-10pm.)

John's Place, 723 Pandora St. (☎389-0711), between Douglas and Blanshard St. Dishing up Canadian fare with a little Mediterranean flair and a Thai twist. Try your hand at an appallingly large breakfast in the presence of greatness (the walls of John's are adorned with the images and autographs of some of North America's finest athletes). Extra selections on Thai night (M) and pierogi night (W). Open M-F 7am-9pm, Sa-Su 8am-9pm and 5-10pm, Su 8am-4pm and 5-9pm. ❷

Blue Fox Cafe, 101-919 Fort St. (☎380-1683). Walk 3 blocks up Fort. St. from Douglas St. A local favorite. Breakfast all day, every day; specials until 11am for under $6. Try the "Bubble & Squeak," sautéed veggies and panfries drowned in cheese and baked ($7). Open M-F 7:30am-4pm, Sa 9am-4pm, Su 9am-3pm. ❶

James Bay Tea Room & Restaurant, 332 Menzies St. (☎382-8282) behind the Parliament Buildings. At James Bay, the sun never sets on the British Empire; a trip to Victoria is improper without a spot of tea. The sandwiches and pastries that accompany tea service ($7.25) or high tea on Sunday ($10.25) are a lower-key version of the archaic High Tea served at the Empress Hotel. Open M-Sa 7am-5pm, Su 8am-5pm. ❷

SIGHTS

If you don't mind becoming one with the flocks of tourists heading to the shores of Victoria, wander along the **Inner Harbour.** You'll see boats come in and admire street performers on the Causeway as the sun sets behind neighboring islands.

ROYAL BRITISH COLUMBIA MUSEUM. This museum houses thorough exhibits on the biological, geological, and cultural history of the province. The First Nation exhibit features a totem room and an immense collection of traditional native art. The museum's **National Geographic IMAX Theater** runs the latest action documentaries on a six-story screen. **Thunderbird Park** and its many totems loom behind the museum and can be perused for free. *(675 Belleville St. ☎356-7226. Open daily 9am-5pm; IMAX 9am-9pm. $13; students, youths, and seniors $10; under 6 free. IMAX double features $15, seniors and youth $12.75, children $7. Combo prices available.)*

BUTCHART GARDENS. The elaborate and world-famous Butchart Gardens, founded by Robert P.'s cement-pouring fortune, sprawl across 50 acres 21km north of Victoria off Hwy. 17. Immaculate landscaping includes the magnificent **Sunken Garden** (a former limestone quarry), the Rose Garden, Japanese and Italian gardens, and fountains. The gardens sparkle with live entertainment and lights at night. Outstanding fireworks on Saturday evenings in July and August draw out the locals. *(Bus #75 Central Saanich runs from downtown at Douglas and Pandora. ($2.50, 1hr.) The Gray Line, ☎800-440-3885, runs a round-trip, direct package including admission ($42, youth $32, child $13; 35min. each way). ☎652-4422. Open daily mid-July to Aug. 9am-10:30pm. $20, ages 13-17 $10, ages 5-12 $2, under 5 free.)*

BUTTERFLY GARDENS. Close to the Butchart Gardens, this enclosure devoted to winged insects is maintained at 20-28°C (80-85°F) and 80% relative humidity. Hundreds of specimens of over 35 species float around visitors' heads alongside (non-butterfly-eating) canaries, finches, and cockatiels, while caterpillars munch on the profusion of tropical plants thriving in the moist environment. The gardens successfully breed giant Atlas Moths, which, with a wingspan of up to 30cm (1 ft.), are the largest species of moth in the world. Perhaps most appealing to the eye, however, are the iridescent hues of the famous morpho butterflies that live the good life in the gardens. *(1461 Benvenuto Ave. Open Mar.-Oct. daily 9am-5pm. $8, seniors and students $7, ages 5-12 $4.50. 10% AAA or family discount.)*

VANCOUVER ISLAND BREWERY. After a few days of hiking, biking, and museum-visiting, unwind with a tour of the **Vancouver Island Brewery.** The 1hr. tour has 20min. of touring and 40min. of drinking. *(2330 Government St. ☎361-0007. 19+. 1hr. tours F-Sa 3pm. $6 for four 4 oz. samples and souvenir pint glass. 19+ to sample.)*

ENTERTAINMENT

The **Victoria Symphony Society,** 846 Broughton St. (☎385-6515), performs regularly under conductor Kaees Bakels. The highlight of the season is the **Symphony Splash,** which is played on a barge in Inner Harbour. The performance concludes with fireworks and usually draws 50,000 listeners (first Su in Aug.; free). For the last 10 days of June, Victoria bops to **JazzFest.** (☎388-4423. $35 per day, or 5-day pass $90.) **Folkfest** hosts multicultural entertainment with food and dancing at Market Square and Ship's Point. (☎388-4728. Late June to early July. $2-12.)

Cineplex Odeon, 780 Yates St. (☎383-0513), rolls out the reels of blockbuster hits every night with all tickets under $8. Around the corner is the **Famous Players** theater, which complements its list of current hits (☎381-9300). To experience the cheapest movies available, visit **The Roxy,** 2657 Quadra St., an old airplane hangar turned movie theatre. (☎382-3370. $5, seniors $2.50; Tu $2.50.) For off-beat and foreign films, head to the **University of Victoria's Cinecenta** in the Student Union. (☎721-8365. Bus #4, 26, 11, or 14. $6.75, seniors and students $4.75, Sa-Su matinees $3.75.) July and August bring **free outdoor screenings** of classic movies to the **Boardwalk Restaurant** at the Ocean Pointe Resort on Wednesday and Thursday at dusk. Those who wish can reserve at the restaurant and get a table at the front, a good meal (expensive), and free blankets (☎360-5889). The Ocean Pointe Resort is the first right after crossing the blue Johnson St. bridge. Parking and screen are around the back to the right. In June, **Phoenix Theaters** (☎721-8000) at UVIC, puts on term-time live theater performances. Victoria goes Elizabethan when the **Annual Shakespeare Festival** lands in the Inner Harbour. (☎360-0234. Mid-July to mid-Aug.)

NIGHTLIFE

English pubs and watering holes abound throughout town. The free weekly *Monday Magazine*, out on Wednesdays, lists who's playing where and is available at hostels, hotels, and most restaurants.

Steamers Public House, 570 Yates St. (☎381-4340). Locals and visitors alike dance nightly to live music, from world-beat Celtic to funk. The best Su entertainment in town. Open stage M, jazz night Tu. Cover $3-5 at night, free M-Tu. Open M-Tu 11:30am-1am, W-Su 11:30am-2am.

Suze, 515 Yates St. (☎383-2829). Trendy lounge and restaurant serves creative pizzas ($11.50-13.50) and Asian-inspired items such as the popular pad thai ($9). Nightly martini specials. Open Su-W 5pm-midnight, Th-Sa 5pm-1am.

Spinnakers Brew Pub, 308 Catherine St. (☎384-6613, office 384-0332). Take the Johnson St. bridge from downtown and walk 10min. down Esquimalt Rd., or stick to the waterfront and you'll walk right by it. The oldest brew pub in Canada is a great place to shoot pool and boasts the best view of the Inner Harbor. Open daily 11am-11pm.

OUTDOOR ACTIVITIES

The flowering oasis of **Beacon Hill Park,** off Douglas St. south of the Inner Harbour, pleases walkers, bikers, and the picnic-inclined; it borders the gorgeous Dallas Rd. scenic drive. The **Galloping Goose,** a 100km trail beginning in downtown Victoria and continuing to the west coast of Vancouver Island, is open to cyclists, pedestrians, and horses. Ask for a map, which includes Transit access info, at the Info Centre. The trail is a part of the **Trans-Canada Trail** (still in progress), which will be the longest recreational trail in the world. When it is finished, it will cover 16,000km and stretch from Coast to Coast.

The **beach** stretches along the southern edge of the city by Dallas St. **Willows Beach** at Oak Bay has particularly white sand—take Fort St. east, turn right on Oak Bay St., and follow to the end. Victoria is a hub for sailing, kayaking, and whale watching tours. The folks at **Westcoast Activities Unlimited,** 1140 Government St., will help you find somewhere or someone to help you do anything, free of charge. (☎412-0993. Open daily 8am-7:30pm.) **Ocean River Sports,** 1437 Store St., offers kayak rentals, tours, and lessons. (☎381-4233 or 800-909-4233. Open M-Th and Sa 9am-5:30pm, F 9:30am-8pm, Su 11am-5pm. Singles $42 per day, doubles $50. Multi-day discounts available.) Most whale watching companies give discounts for hostel guests. **Ocean Explorations,** 532 Broughton St., runs tours in very fast, very fun, very wet Zodiac raft-boats that visit resident pods of orcas in the area. (☎383-6722. Runs Apr.-Oct. 3hr. tours $70, hostelers and students $60, children $49, less in low season. Reservations recommended. Free pickup at hostels.)

DAYTRIP FROM VICTORIA: SOOKE

About 35km west of Victoria on Hwy. 14. To find Hwy. 14, take Hwy. 1 north to the junction. To get to Phillips Rd. from the city, take bus #50 to the Western Exchange and transfer to #61. The potholes are located 5km north of Hwy. 14 on Sooke River Rd.

The Sooke Region Museum, 2070 Phillips Rd., just off the highway, houses a **visitors center** and delivers an excellent history of the area. (☎642-6351. Open daily July-Aug. 9am-6pm; Sept.-June Tu-Su 9am-5pm. Admission by donation.) The **Sooke Potholes** are a chain of deep swimming holes naturally carved out of the rock in the narrow Sooke River gorge. These popular and sun-warmed waters reputedly host some of the best cliff jumping in the area and draw people from all over. Access is through private property owned by **Deertrail Campground and Adventure Gateway** ❶ and costs $10 per vehicle; bikes and hikers free. (☎382-3337. 63 sites, $15-20. Includes entrance fee.) North of Sooke, Hwy. 14 continues along the coast, stringing together two provincial parks and their rugged, beautiful beaches. **Juan de Fuca Provincial Park** is home to China Beach and Loss Creek. **China Beach campground** ❶ has 78 drive-in sites. (☎800-689-9025. $12.) **French Beach Provincial Park** ❶ has tent sites. (☎391-2300. $12.) The **Juan de Fuca Marine Trail** starts at China Beach and heads 47km north to Botanical Beach at Port Renfrew. Trails connect beaches with the road, which is still far enough away to keep the seaside wild. Camping in wide open sites is free at the popular **Jordan River Recreation Area** ❶, 10min. past French Beach. The **Galloping Goose** bike and horse trail (see **Outdoor Activities,** above) passes a day-use area and trails heading east and west across the island's southern tip. The **Sooke River Flats Campsite** ❶, on Phillips Rd. past the museum, has open sites with a large picnic area, showers, toilets, and running water. On **All Sooke Day,** the third Saturday in July, the campsite hosts competitions centered around logging and family fun. (☎642-6076. Gates locked 11pm-7am. Sites $15; sani-dump $5 for non-guests.) Those in search of a roof over their heads will find their needs met within easy striking distance of the village at the **Pacific Trails Hostel ❶**, 8959 W Coast Rd., local name of Highway 14 (642-7007; www.pacifictrailshostel.com. $19.). Blend in with the locals at **Mom's Cafe ❷**, 2036 Shields Rd., in town. Driving from Victoria, turn right after the stoplight. (☎642-3314. Open summer daily 8am-9pm; winter Su-Th 8am-8pm, F-Sa 8am-9pm.)

NEAR VICTORIA: GULF ISLANDS

Midway between Vancouver and Victoria, the Gulf Islands are a peaceful retreat from urban hustle, and much less overrun by summer tourists than the nearby San Juan Islands. While the beaches are uniformly rocky with little sand, the islands are known for a contagiously relaxing lifestyle, as well as excellent kayaking and sailing opportunities. The chain's five main islands, **Galiano, Mayne, Pender, Salt Spring,** and **Saturna,** are visited by BC Ferries at least twice a day.

SALT SPRING ISLAND ☎250

Named for a dozen brine springs discovered on its northern end, **Salt Spring** is the largest (185 sq. km) and most populous of the islands, with the widest range of activities and accommodations. Today, the island is a haven for artists whose medium of choice varies from clay to paint to metal to wood. Visitors will enjoy the vibrant downtown of Ganges, as well as peaceful natural areas in the southern regions of the island.

ORIENTATION & PRACTICAL INFORMATION. Life on Salt Spring Island is centered around the small village of **Ganges;** all of the listings below are in Ganges unless otherwise specified. **BC Ferries** (☎386-3431 or in BC 888-223-3779; www.bcferries.bc.ca), based on **Vancouver Island,** runs two ferries to Salt Spring. One departs **Crofton** and arrives in **Vesuvius** (12-15 times per day; $6 per person, cars $20 round-trip.) The other ferry leaves from **Swartz Bay** and arrives in **Fulford Harbour,** 14.5km south of Ganges (8 per day; $6 per person, cars $20 round-trip). Ferries from **Vancouver** and the other Gulf Islands dock at the **Long Harbor** wharf, 6km northeast of town. In summer, the **Gulf Island Water Taxi** connects Salt Spring Island to both Mayne and Galiano Islands. W and Sa. (☎537-2510. Runs June-Aug. Departs W and Sa 9am, returns 4:40pm. $15 round-trip, bikes free.) The **Info Centre,** 121 Lower Ganges Rd., will help travelers find a place to stay. (☎537-5252. Open July-Aug. daily 9am-6pm; call for winter hours.) **Silver Shadow Taxi** (☎537-3030) tends to the carless. **Marine Drive Car Rentals**, 124 Upper Ganges (☎537-6409), next to **Moby's** (see **Food,** below), rents vehicles starting at $50 per day. The **Bicycle Shop,** 131 McPhillips Ave., rents bikes. (☎537-1544. $5 per hr., $20 per 24hr. Open Tu-F 9am-5pm, Sa 10am-4pm.) **New Wave Laundry,** 124 Upper Ganges Rd., is next to Moby's Marine Pub. (☎537-2500. Wash $2.50, dry $0.25 per 8min. Open M and Th 8am-8pm, Tu-W 8am-6pm, F 10am-6pm, Sa and Su 9am-6pm. Other services include: **public showers,** beneath Moby's ($1 per 5min.); **Pharmasave,** 104 Lower Ganges Rd. (☎537-5534; open M-Sa 9am-6pm, Su 11am-5pm); **emergency,** ☎911; **Internet access** at **CorInternet Cafe,** 134 McPhillips Ave. (☎537-9932; $1 per 15min., youths and seniors $0.50 per 15min.; open Tu-Th 1-8pm, F-Su noon-5pm) or **Salt Spring Books,** 104 McPhillips Ave. (☎537-2812; $0.10 per min.; open M-Sa 8:30am-6pm, Su 9:30am-6pm in summer, and M-Sa 8:30am-5:30pm, Su 9:30am-5pm in winter); **police**

(☎537-5555), on Lower Granges Rd., on the outskirts of town; and the **post office,** 109 Purvis Ln., in the plaza downtown (☎537-2321. Open M-F 8:30am-5:30pm, Sa 8am-noon.) **Postal Code:** V8K 2P1.

ACCOMMODATIONS & FOOD. Salt Spring offers a wealth of both food and B&Bs (from $70) despite its small size. The least expensive beds on the island are 8km south of Ganges in the **Salt Spring Island Hostel (HI) ❶,** 640 Cusheon Lake Rd.—look for the tree-shaped sign that says "Forest Retreat." In addition to three standard dorms in the lodge, the hostel's 10 acres also hide 3 tepees that sleep 3 and 2 hand-crafted **treehouses** that sleep 2-4. Treehouses are wildly popular and reservations are essential. The sparkling clean outdoor composting toilet is brand new. (☎537-4149. Rent bikes from $15 per day, scooters from $20 per 2hr. Linens $2. Open Mar. 15-Oct 15. Tepees $17; dorms $17, nonmembers $20; doubles $40-60; treehouse double $60, nonmembers $70. MC only.) Island bikers will love the overwhelming breakfast at the **Wisteria Guest House ❸,** 268 Park Dr., a short walk from the village. (☎537-5899. Singles $60, doubles $75.)

Ruckle Provincial Park ❶, 23.5km southeast of Ganges, offers some of the best oceanside campsites in British Columbia. Its 78 walk-in sites on the unsheltered Beaver Point overlook the ocean. 8 RV sites are also available. Gate closed 11pm-7am. (☎391-2300 or 877-559-2115. Dry toilets, free firewood. Sites $12.)

If you want to cook up your own fresh halibut, red snapper, rock cod, or king salmon, check out **The Fishery,** 151 Lower Ganges Rd. (☎537-2457). For all other food needs, head to **Thrifty Foods,** 114 Purvis Ln. (☎537-1522. Open June-Sept. daily 8am-9pm; Oct.-May daily 8am-8pm.) **Barb's Buns ❶,** 1-121 McPhillips, sells all kinds of baked goods, including spelt bread and delicious chocolate-hazelnut sticky buns ($2.75). Vegetarians will dig the $5 sandwiches. (☎537-4491. Open in summer M-Sa 6:30am-6pm; winter M-Sa 7am-5:30pm.) The **Tree House Cafe ❶,** 106 Purvis Ln., delivers interesting and tasty sandwiches ($5-7) in the shade of an old plum tree and has open-mic Thursdays (7pm) in addition to live music every night in summer. (☎537-5379. Kitchen open daily 8am-9:30pm. 10% HI discount.)

SIGHTS. Salt Spring Island is perhaps best known for its resident artists. A self-guided **studio tour** introduces visitors to the residences of 36 artisans around the island; pick up a brochure at the visitors center (see **Tourist Information,** p. 278). The century-old **Fall Fair** (☎537-8840), held the 2nd weekend of September, draws farmers from all over the islands to display their produce, animals, and crafts with pride. The **Saturday Market** is a smaller version of the fall fair held in downtown's **Centennial Park** from Easter to Thanksgiving, and is a big deal on the island.

OUTDOOR ACTIVITIES. **Wallace Island** and **Prevost Island** are two excellent kayaking daytrips from Salt Spring. **Sea Otter Kayaking,** on Ganges Harbor at the end of Rainbow Rd., rents boats to experienced paddlers only. They also run 2hr. introductory certification courses ($40), tours including 3hr. sunset ($35) and full-moon trips ($40), and multi-day excursions. (☎537-5678 or 877-537-5678. Singles $25 per 2hr., $55 per day; doubles $40, $80. 15% discount for hostel guests. Open in summer daily 9am-6pm; reservations preferred in winter.) Five of Salt Spring's 10 freshwater lakes are open for swimming. **Blackburn Lake,** 5km south of Ganges on Fulford-Ganges Rd., is one of the less crowded spots, and is clothing-optional. **Hiking** and **biking** options are limited on Salt Spring due to the small and residential nature of the islands. **Ruckle Provincial Park** offers 200 acres of partially settled land and an 11km waterfront trail. **Mt. Maxwell,** 11km southwest of Ganges on Cranberry Rd., offers a stunning vista, and you can drive to the top!

PACIFIC RIM NATIONAL PARK ☎250

AT A GLANCE

AREA: 193 sq. mi.

CLIMATE: Cool foggy summers, mild wet winters; heavy precipitation.

FEATURES: The West Coast Trail, Long Beach, the Broken Group Islands, Juan de Fuca Provincial Park.

HIGHLIGHTS: Kayaking in the Broken Group, hiking the West Coast Trail.

FEES AND RESERVATIONS: $10-$20 camping fee; $95 West Coast Trail fee.

GATEWAYS: Port Renfrew (p. 280), Bamfield (p. 282), and Tofino (p. 283).

The Pacific Rim National Park stretches along a 150km sliver of Vancouver Island's remote Pacific coast. The region's frequent downpours create a lush landscape rich in both marine and terrestrial life. Hard-core hikers trek through enormous old-growth red cedar trees and along rugged beach trails. Long beaches on the open ocean draw beachcombers, bathers, kayakers, and surfers year-round. Each spring, around 22,000 gray whales stream past the park. Orcas, sea lions, bald eagles, and black bears also frequent the area. From October to April, the Pacific Rim area receives 22 rain days per month. In the summer, however, only 10 in. fall each month (the average annual rainfall in the park is 122 in.). The park is comprised of three distinct geographic regions. The southern portion is home to the **West Coast Trail,** which connects the towns of Bamfield and Port Renfrew. The park's middle section—known as the **Broken Group Islands**—is comprised of roughly 100 islands in Barkley Sound. Finally, the northern region of the Park, known as **Long Beach,** is northwest of Barkley Sound. The villages of Ucluelet and Tofino are on the boundaries of this region. The park's administrative office is in Ucluelet, 2185 Ocean Terrace Rd. (☎726-7721).

WEST COAST TRAIL

A winding, 1½hr. drive up Hwy. 14 from Hwy. 1 near Victoria lands you in Port Renfrew. Spread out in the trees along a peaceful ocean inlet, this isolated coastal community of 400 people is the southern gateway to the world-famous

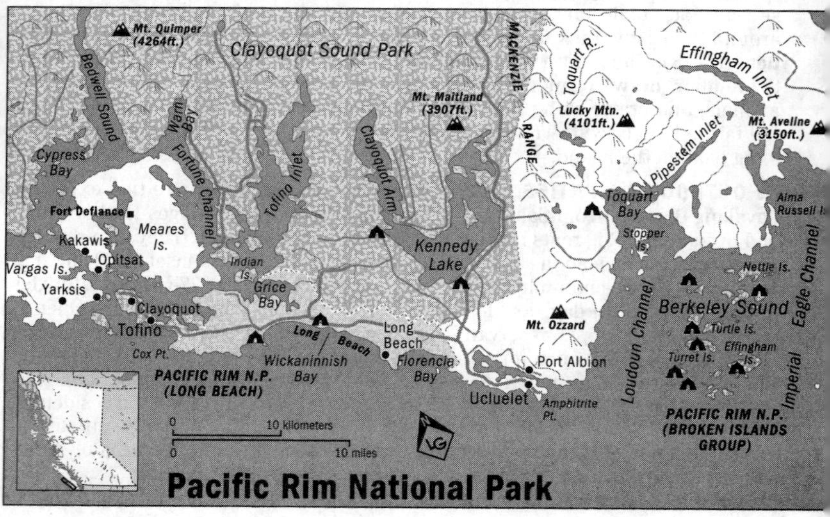

BRITISH COLUMBIA

West Coast Trail. The other end of the trail lies 75km north, in Bamfield. Most hikers take 7 days to travel the entire length of the trail, but it can be done in less. The route weaves through primeval forests of giant red cedars and spruce, waterfalls, rocky slopes, and rugged beach. The uniqueness of the trail lies not only in its spectacular terrain, but also in the man-made scenery. Exciting challenges lie at every bend, but the combination of wet weather and slippery terrain over a long distance means that challenges can also be dangerous. Each year dozens of hikers are evacuated or rescued by park rangers. Most injuries are ankle or knee related, caused by rough and muddy forest trails; on the beach, hikers must be wary of surge channels. Only experienced backpackers should attempt the trail, and never alone. The trail is regulated by a strict and unforgiving quota system; reservations are necessary to hike it and can be made as early as two months prior to departure date. Campsites at the southern end tend to be crowded since they are fewer than in the northern section of the trail. Each day between May 1 and September 30, 52 hikers are allowed to begin the journey from the two trailheads, Pachena Bay in the north and Gordon River in the south (26 from each trailhead; 20 reserved and 6 wait-listed). The maximum group size is 10 people. For more info on the illustrious trek, call **Tourism** (☎800-435-5622) or **Parks Canada** (☎726-7721), or write to Box 280, Ucluelet, BC, V0R 3A0. Hikers pay about $120 per person for access to the trail (reservation fee $25, backcountry camping $90 in summer, ferry-crossing $14). Seek out maps, information on the area, and registration info at one of the two **Trail Information Centres:** in **Port Renfrew** (☎647-5434), at the first right off Parkinson Rd. (Hwy. 14) once in "town"; or in **Pachena Bay** (☎728-3234), 5km south of Bamfield. (Both open daily May-Sept. 9am-5pm.) David Foster Wayne's *Blisters and Bliss* is an excellent guide to the trail ($11).

TRANSPORTATION. **West Coast Trail Express** runs daily from **Victoria** to **Port Renfrew** via the **Juan de Fuca** trailhead. (☎888-999-2288; www.trailbus.com. Runs May-Sept.; 2¼hr., $35.) Buses also run from **Nanaimo** to **Bamfield** (3½hr., $55), **Bamfield** to **Port Renfrew** (3½hr., $50), and **Port Renfrew** or **Bamfield** to **Nitinat** (2hr., $35). Reservations are recommended, and they can be made for

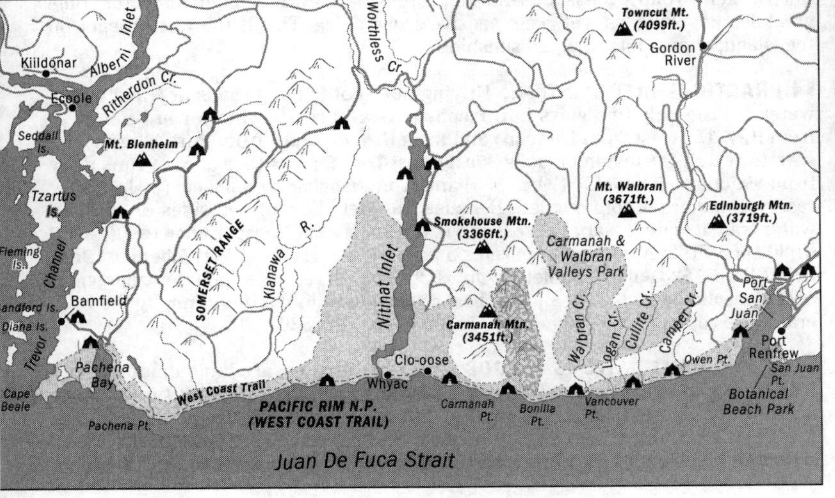

beaches and trailheads along the route from Victoria to Port Renfrew. The **Juan de Fuca Express** operates a water taxi between Port Renfrew and Bamfield. (☎888-755-6578 or 755-6578. 3½hr., $85.)

CAMPING & FOOD. Accommodations are limited outside the park campgrounds, but you can drive to Sooke, near Victoria on Hwy. 14, for numerous B&Bs. Near Port Renfrew and adjacent to the West Coast Trail registration office lies the **Pacheedaht Campground ❶.** (☎647-0090. Sites are first come, first served: tents $10; RV sites $15.) Laundry ($2) can be done at the **Port Renfrew Hotel ❷.** (☎647-0116. Singles from $39. Showers for non-guests $2 for 10min.) A new motel in town, the **West Coast Trail Motel ❸** on Parkinson Rd., provides hikers with a hot tub to soothe aching muscles. (☎647-5565. Singles $65; doubles $74.) On the other end of the West Coast Trail, in Bamfield, camp at the **Pachena Bay Campground ❶,** adjacent to the registration office. (☎728-1287. Sites $18; RV sites $20-25.) The **General Store** on the main road into town has basic groceries. (☎647-5587. Open daily 10am-8pm, winter 11am-5pm.) Almost all of the restaurants in Port Renfrew are inexpensive and offer the usual fare. The **Lighthouse Pub & Restaurant ❸** (☎647-5505), on Parkinson Rd., serves up tasty fish and chips.

OUTDOOR ACTIVITIES. If you only want to spend an afternoon roughing it, visit the gorgeous **Botanical Beach Provincial Park.** Visit at low tide or don't expect to see much (info centers will have tide charts). **Botanical Beach** forms one end of the 47km **Juan De Fuca Marine Trail,** connecting Port Renfrew with **Juan de Fuca Provincial Park** to the east. The trail can be traveled in 4-6 days. Compared to the West Coast Trail, the Juan de Fuca has more forest hiking and fewer opportunities for beach walks. The Juan de Fuca Trail is also cheaper than the West Coast Trail, with no user fee or registration fee. There are a number of **campsites ❶** along the way; overnight permits are required ($5 for a party of 4; self-register at trailheads). For more info on the trail and day-use information, look at the **map** in the Botanical Beach or China Beach parking lots for directions, or call ☎391-2300.

BROKEN GROUP

The Broken Group's 100 islands stretch across Barkley Sound and make for some great sea kayaking, as well as expensive **scuba diving.** This is the wettest spot on the island; expect lots of liquid sunshine.

PRACTICAL INFORMATION. Driving hours of logging roads or traveling by water are the only two ways into **Bamfield.** Gravel roads wind toward Bamfield from **Hwy. 18** (west from Duncan) and from **Hwy. 4** (south from Port Alberni). Be sure to watch for logging trucks. **West Coast Trail Express** (see above) runs daily from **Victoria** to **Bamfield** (4½hr., $55) and from **Nanaimo** to **Bamfield** (3½hr., $55); reservations are recommended. Because Bamfield lies on two sides of an inlet, water transit is necessary to cross town. **Alberni Marine Transportation** (☎723-8313 or 800-663-7192; Apr.-Sept.) operates a passenger ferry from **Port Alberni** to **Bamfield** (4½hr., $23) and **Ucluelet** (4½hr., $25). Other services include: **emergency,** ☎911; **hospital,** ☎728-3312; and the **post office,** near the Bamfield Inn, by the General Store (open M-F 8:30am-5pm). **Postal Code:** V0R 1B0.

ACCOMMODATIONS & FOOD. Accommodations are limited; motels and B&Bs are expensive (singles $50-180; doubles $70-180; the majority are at the higher end). **Marie's B&B ❸** is at 468 Pachena Rd. (☎728-3091. Singles $50; doubles $80. On the mainland, camping is the cheapest option; head to **Pachena Bay Campground ❶** (see above) for tree-rich sites just a short walk from the beach. (☎728-

1287. Sites $24; sani-dump only $26; full RV sites $31.) Eight islands in the archipelago contain primitive campsites ($5 per person.) The **Tides and Trail Market,** 242 Frigate Rd. in Bamfield near the public dock, offers groceries, supplies, and an amazing selection of candy. (☎728-2000. Open daily 8am-8pm.)

OUTDOOR ACTIVITIES. While the Nuu-cha-nulth have navigated these waters for centuries, the Sound can be dangerous to those with less experience. A maze of reefs and rocky islands, combined with large swells, tidal currents, and frigid waters, makes ocean travel in small craft hazardous (but adventuresome). **Alberni Marine Transport** (see **Practical Information,** above) and other operators transport from Ucluelet and Port Alberni to the Broken Group. (3 hr.; one per day M, W, F; $20.) For guided trips, contact **Broken Island Adventures** (☎888-728-6200). For kayak rentals, check with the **Bamfield Kayak Centre** (☎877-728-3535). Several short hiking trails pass through shore and forest at **Pachena Bay, Keeha Beach,** and the **Pachena Lighthouse.**

LONG BEACH

The northern third of Pacific Rim National Park begins where Hwy. 4 hits the west coast after a 1½hr. drive from Port Alberni. Ucluelet (yew-KLOO-let) remains a quiet fishing village until it floods with travelers every July and August. Tofino, with its predominantly surfer-dude populace, is an increasingly popular resort destination, attracting backpackers and wealthy weekend-warriors alike.

ORIENTATION & PRACTICAL INFORMATION

The two towns of Ucluelet and Tofino lie 40km apart at opposite ends of the **Pacific Rim Hwy.,** separated by the lovely and trail-laden Long Beach. **Chinook Charters** (☎725-3431) connects **Victoria** and **Nanaimo** with Tofino and Ucluelet through Port Alberni. Two buses leave daily in summer from **Victoria** to **Tofino** (7hr., $55) via **Ucluelet** (6½hr., $53). The **Long Beach Link** (☎726-7790) connects Tofino with **Long Beach** and Ucluelet in the summer (6 per day; $10 round-trip from either town to Long Beach, $12 round-trip between the two towns). **Lady Rose Marine Services** operates a passenger freighter in summer from Port Alberni to Ucluelet (☎723-8313 or 800-663-7192; 1 per day M, W, and F; leaves at 8am from Port Alberni and 2pm from Ucluelet; 5hr., $25). **Ucluelet Taxi** (☎726-4415) services both towns and everything in between. A trio of **Info Centres** guides visitors. The first is located where Hwy. 4 splits into a road to each town. (☎726-7289. Open Victoria Day to Labor Day daily 11am-7pm.) The Tofino **Info Centre** is at 351 Campbell St. (☎725-3414. Open July-Aug. daily 9am-5pm; winter hours sporadic.) Ucluelet's **Info Centre** is at 227 Main St. (☎726-4641. Generally open daily 10am-5pm; call for hours. Off-season weekends closed.) **Parks Canada Visitor Info** has two branches, one off the Pacific Rim Hwy. inside the park (☎726-4212; open mid-June to mid-Sept. daily 9:30am-5pm), and the other farther in at Wickaninnish Beach. (☎726-7721. Open year-round daily 10:30am-6pm.) The **CIBC Bank** is on 301 Campbell St. (**24hr. ATM**; no currency exchange. Open M-Th 10am-3pm, F 10am-4:30pm.) **Storm Light Marine Station,** 316 Main St., rents sleeping bags for $12 per day and tents for $15 per day. (☎725-3342. Open June-Oct. daily 9am-9pm, Nov.-May 10am-6pm). **Fiber Options,** at the corner of 4th and Campbell, rents bikes for $6 per hr. or $25 per day, credit card required. (☎725-2192. Open June-Sept. daily 9:30am-10pm, Oct.-May 10am-6pm.) For the **weather,** call ☎726-3415. Other services include: **police,** 400 Campbell St. (☎725-3242); **People's Drug Mart,** 460 Campbell St. (☎725-3101; open M-Sa 9.30am-5pm, Su 11am-5pm); and a **hospital,** 261 Neill St. (☎725-3212). Get **Internet access** at the

Blue Raven Coffee House and Cyber Cafe, 1627 A Peninsula Rd., in Ucluelet. (☎726-7110. $2.50 per 20min. or $7 per hr. Open daily 7am-10pm.) In Tofino, head to **Caffe Vincente,** 441 Campbell St. (☎725-2599. $3.72 for 20 min. Open in summer 7am-6pm.) The **post office** is at 161 1st St., at Campbell. (☎725-3734. Open M-F 8:30am-5:30pm, Sa 9am-1pm.) **Postal Code:** V0R 2Z0.

ACCOMMODATIONS & FOOD

Tofino is the place to be, but there are options in Ucluelet and outside the park. In general, there is no free camping, and in the summer both campsites and cheap motels fill up quickly. Reservations are a must after mid-March.

IN UCLUELET. Prices are steep, especially in the summer. Travelers without reservations might get shut out of reasonably priced accommodations and forced into a motel room (singles from $75). The Info Centre gives out a pamphlet listing the many **B&Bs** in town. **Radfords ❷,** 1983 Athlone St. (☎726-2662), off Norah St., is close to town. The owners rent two quaint singles ($40) and a double ($80, $15 per additional guest), and offer fresh muffins, fruit, and a view of the harbor. **Matterson House Restaurant ❹,** 1682 Peninsula Rd., has homemade Canadian fare. Locals love the $14 Matterson Chicken with raspberry cream sauce. (☎726-2200. Open daily 7:30am-9pm.) Taste the northwest in the $9 salmon burgers at **Blueberries Restaurant ❸,** 1627D Peninsula Rd. (☎726-7707. Open daily 7:30am-9:30pm.) For cheaper eats, head to **Roman's Restaurant ❶,** 6-1636 Peninsula Rd., in Davison Plaza. Deli-style subs ($6) and yummy pizza (from $12) are the main draws. (☎726-2888. Open M-F 11am-noon, Sa-Su 4pm-midnight.)

IN & AROUND THE PARK. While there are a number of private **campgrounds** between the park and the towns, they average at least $22 to camp and $30 for RV sites. The ones on the Ucluelet side tend to be cheaper. The **Park Superintendent** (☎726-7721) can be contacted year-round for advance information. **Greenpoint Campground ❶,** 10 km north of the park info center, is the only campground in the park itself and is often full. Greenpoint has 94 regular sites and 20 walk-ins and is equipped with toilets and fire rings. Despite swarms of campers in the summer, it offers hedge-buffered privacy and great beach access. (Reservations essential; call ☎800-689-9025. Walk-in sites are un-reserveable, so arrive at 11am to nab a spot. Walk-in sites $14; drive-in sites $20.) **Ucluelet Campground ❶,** off Pacific Rim Hwy. in Ucluelet, offers sites in the open (better for sun than for privacy) with showers and toilets. (☎726-4355. Open Mar.-Oct. $23; full RV sites $29. Showers $2.) The **golf course** in the park often has private, showerless gravel sites ($15).

IN TOFINO. **Whalers on the Point Guesthouse (HI) ❶,** 81 West St., voted the best hostel in Canada by HI, has room for 64. To get there, turn right on 1st St. from Campbell St. and then left on Main St. (follow to West St.). They offer free sauna, billiards, linen, and harborside views. Check inside for HI discounts around town. Internet $1 for 10min. (☎725-3443. Check-in 7am-2pm and 4-11pm. $22, nonmembers $24.) **Wind Rider Guesthouse ❶,** 231 Main St., is all female (except for kids under 12) and drug and alcohol free. A gleaming kitchen, jacuzzi, and TV room make this a welcoming haven. (☎725-3240. Check-in 3-6pm. Free linen. Dorms $25; private rooms from $60.) Shop for groceries at the **Co-op,** 140 1st St. (☎725-3226. Open M-Sa 9am-8pm, Su 10am-6pm.) **Salals Co-op ❶,** near 4th St. on Campbell, sells organic groceries and has an all-vegetarian menu that includes all-day breakfast ($4.50-10) and lunches for $6-8. (☎725-2728. Open M-Sa 10am-6pm, Su 1pm-6pm.) The **Common Loaf Bake Shop ❶,** 180 1st St., is the best place in Tofino to get a cup of coffee. Thai and Indian dinners are $7-9. (☎725-3915. Open in summer daily

8am-8:30pm; winter 8am-6pm.) The adjacent **Alleyway Cafe ❷,** 305 Campbell, has outdoor seating on driftwood benches. Breakfast is dished up all day until the place reopens as the festive **Costa Azul** with Mexican dinners for under $10. (☎725-3105. Open daily 9am-3pm and 5:30pm-9:30pm.)

OFF ISLAND. On Vargas Island, 20min. off Tofino, the **Vargas Island Inn ❷** rents guest rooms in a classy lodge and two beach cabins. (☎725-3309. Tent sites $15; hostel beds $30; private rooms from $40; cabins from $30.) The boat shuttle is free for guests, but hikers can pay $25 and hike to **free camping** at Ahous Bay (no facilities). For some out of the way R&R, try **Nielson Island Inn ❷,** the only establishment on 20-acre Nielson Island, a 5min. boat ride from Crab Dock. Enjoy the benefits of a small kitchen (the owner will cook dinner with your ingredients), a lush yard, and a trail around the island. (☎726-7968. Free pickup. Singles $35; doubles $50.)

OUTDOOR ACTIVITIES

HIKING. Hiking is a highlight of the trip to the west side of the Island. The trails grow even more beautiful in the frequent rain and fog. The **Rainforest Centre,** 451 Main St. (☎725-2560), in Tofino, has assembled an excellent trail guide for Clayoquot Sound, Tofino, Ucluelet, the Pacific Rim, and Kennedy Lake (available by donation). Park passes cost $3 per 2hr. or $8 per day (available in all parking lots); seasonal passes are also available ($45). Long Beach is, fittingly, the longest beach on the island's west coast, and is the starting point for numerous hikes. The Parks **Canada Visitor Centre** and **Info Centres** (see **Orientation and Practical Information,** p. 283) provide free maps of nine hikes ranging from 100m to 5km in length. On the **Rainforest Trail** (two 1km loops), boardwalks off the Pacific Rim Hwy. lead through gigantic trees and fallen logs of old-growth rainforest. **Bog Trail** (1km) illuminates little-known details of one of the wettest, most intricate ecosystems in the park. You can even view tiny carnivorous plants. (Wheelchair accessible.)

SURFING & KAYAKING. Exceptional **surf** breaks invitingly off **Long Beach** and **Cox Bay** (5km south of Tofino). These two coves funnel large and occasionally dangerous waves toward hordes of young diehards; just don't forget your wetsuit. **Storm Surf Shop** has locations in both Tofino and Ucluelet and rents everything you'll need. (In Tofino: 171 4th St., ☎725-3344. Full wetsuits $13 half-day, $20 full day; surfboard $15, $25.) It is possible to kayak to Meares Island and throughout the sound, although the trailhead is difficult to find. **Pacific Kayak,** at Jamie's Whale Station (see above), provides a map, has the best rates in town, and rents to experienced paddlers. (☎725-3232. Singles $40 per day, doubles $65; 4hr. guided tour $52; multi-day discounts.)

WHALE WATCHING. Every March and April, gray whales migrate past Clayoquot Sound north of Tofino. Six or seven stay at these feeding grounds during the summer. There are more tour companies than resident whales. **Jamie's Whale Station,** 606 Campbell St., just east of 4th St. in Tofino, runs smooth rides in large boats, but rough-riders choose Zodiacs to ride the swells at 30 knots. (☎725-3919 or 800-667-9913. Whale watching $80 per 3hr., students and seniors $70, youths $50; Zodiacs $59 per 2hr., students $53; bear watching $59, students and seniors $53, youths $45.) They also have an outlet in Ucluelet at the bottom of Main St.

HOT SPRINGS. Hot Springs Cove, 1hr. north of Tofino by boat, is one of the least crowded hot springs in all of British Columbia. The Matlahaw Water Taxi, operated by the Hesquiaht First Nation, makes a run or two each day to the cove. (☎670-1106. $35 per person one-way.) The springs are near an exceptionally quiet and lush **campground ❶**, and a footpath to more secluded beaches in the Maquinna

FROM THE ROAD

A WHALE'S TALE

I had heard that the waters around Vancouver Island had amazing wildlife, but until I got on a ship headed to Bamfield, I didn't realize just what a treat the area can be. Ryan, the captain of the ship, was known as a whale expert, so I was hoping for some long-distance sightings.

Ryan said he would try to pick a few whales out of the fog for me. Within ten minutes he was successful—but at much closer range than I had anticipated. As we approached a whale surfacing in the fog, Ryan recognized the animal as a particularly friendly whale named Cookie-Cutter. Like an old friend, the whale approached the boat, completely unafraid. Cookie-Cutter rubbed up against the port side of the boat. The whale was simply overwhelming. Barnacles spotted her smooth gray skin. "Lean over and pet her," Ryan instructed. I was shocked by the suggestion, but who was I to argue? I reached out and stroked the whale's skin. I was overwhelmed to be in such close contact with such a magnificent animal. Cookie-Cutter was smooth to the touch (but surprisingly smelly!) She continued to play with the boat for almost half an hour, as all the passengers came out and enjoyed the whale's company. Ryan eventually had to tear us away from the fun to keep on schedule.

We spotted plenty more animals during the trip. No encounter could match the thrill, however, of my up-close and personal meeting with Cookie-Cutter, truly a friendly giant.

—Posy Busby

Marine Park. (15 private sites, $20.) Seaside Adventures, at 300 Main St. in Tofino, makes two 6hr. trips leaving in the morning and whale watches on the way. All the whale watching companies have trips as well. (☎725-2292 or 888-332-4252. $90, students and seniors $80, children $60.)

UP ISLAND

To a Victorian, anything north of town constitutes being "up Island." 'Nuff said.

NANAIMO ☎250

Primarily a ferry terminal stopover for travelers en route to the rainforests of northern and western Vancouver Island, Nanaimo (na-NYE-moe) appears along the highway as a strip of motels, gas stations, and chain stores. While the city contains several beaches and parks, the semi-urban setting lacks the natural splendor of Vancouver Island's more secluded locations. The silver lining of city life is Nanaimo's ridiculous annual bathtub boat race and legalized bungee jumping.

ORIENTATION & PRACTICAL INFORMATION

Nanaimo lies on the east coast of Vancouver Island, 111km north of Victoria on the **Trans-Canada Hwy. (Hwy. 1),** and 391km south of **Port Hardy** via the **Island Hwy. (Hwy. 19).** Hwy. 1 turns into **Nicol St.** and **Terminal Ave.** in Nanaimo before becoming Hwy. 19A. **Nanaimo Parkway** (Hwy. 19) circumvents the town.

Trains: VIA Rail, 321 Selby St. (☎800-561-8630). To **Victoria** (1 per day, $20).

Buses: Laidlaw (☎753-4371), at Comox Rd. and Terminal Ave., behind Howard Johnson Inn. To: **Port Hardy** (7½hr., 1-2 per day, $82.50); **Tofino** and **Ucluelet** (4hr., 2 per day, $33); and **Victoria** (2¼hr., 6 per day, $20).

Ferries: BC Ferries (☎753-1261 or 888-223-3779), at the northern end of Stewart Ave., 2km north of downtown. To Vancouver's **Horseshoe Bay** (1½hr.; 8 times per day; $8-9.50, car $24-34) and **Tsawwassen** terminals (2hr.; 4-8 per day; $9, car $30-32). The **Scenic Ferry** (☎753-5141) runs from the Maffeo-Sutton Park in downtown to Newcastle Island just offshore (on the hr. 10am-6pm; $5). No vehicles are permitted on the island and the passenger ferry runs only in summer months.

Car Rental: Rent-A-Wreck, 227 Terminal Ave. S (☎753-6461). From $33 per day plus $0.16 per km after 150km. Must be 21+ with major credit card. Free pickup. Open M-F 8am-6pm, Sa 9am-4pm, Su 10am-4pm.

Visitor Info: 2290 Bowen Rd. (☎756-0106), west of downtown. Head south from Terminal Ave. on Comox Rd., which becomes Bowen Rd., or go north from Hwy. 19 on Northfield Rd. Open in summer daily 8am-7pm, winter 9am-5pm.

Laundromat: 702 Nicol St. (☎753-9922), at Robins Rd. in Payless Gas Station. $2.50 per load. Open 24hr.

Equipment Rental: Chain Reaction, in The Realm at 2 Commercial St. (☎754-3309), rents bikes and in-line skates. Bikes $20 per day, $10 for Nicol St. Hostel Guests; $35 per week. In-line skates $15 per day. Open M-Sa 9:30am-6pm.)

Emergency: ☎911.

Police: 303 Prideaux St. (☎754-2345), at Fitzwilliam St.

Crisis Line: ☎754-4447. 24hr.

Pharmacy: London Drugs, 650 Terminal Ave. S (☎753-5566), in Harbour Park Mall. Open M-Sa 9am-10pm, Su 10am-8pm.

Hospital: Nanaimo Regional General Hospital, 1200 Dufferin Crescent (☎754-2141). Open 24hr.

Internet: Free at **Literacy Nanaimo**, 19 Commercial St. (754-8988). Open M-F 9am-4pm, Sa 10am-4pm. A visitor's Internet pass is $5 at the **library,** 90 Commercial St. (☎753-1154.) Open M-F 10am-8pm, Sa 10am-5pm, Su noon-4pm.

Post Office: 650 Terminal Ave. S (☎741-1829), in Harbour Park Mall. Open M-F 8:30am-5pm. **Postal Code:** V9R 5J9

ACCOMMODATIONS & CAMPING

Travelers should never be at a loss for a room in Nanaimo. Cheap motels are packed in like sardines along the main drag.

Nicol St. Hostel, 65 Nicol St. (☎753-1188). A quick walk from the ferry, bus station, or downtown. Lots of freebies: parking, linens, and Internet are just a few. Living room, small tidy kitchen, and laundry facilities. 25 beds; tent sites and ocean views in backyard. Reservations recommended. Dorms $17; doubles $34; sites $10 per person. ❶

Cosmic Cow Guesthouse, 1922 Wilkinson Rd. (754-7150), is a hop, skip, and a jump from the Nanaimo River, 10km south of Nanaimo. From downtown Nanaimo, head south on Hwy. 1 & Nanaimo Pkwy. (#19). Take a left (east) on Cedar Rd. and make a right turn onto Wilkinson Rd. before the bridge. This quiet farmhouse retreat offers solitude, nature trails, bonfires, and free breakfast. Dorms $18, cabins $20. ❶

Living Forest Oceanside Campground, 6 Maki Rd. (☎755-1755), 3km southwest of downtown. 193 large, spacious sites; several amid cedars overlooking the ocean. Clean bathrooms. Sites $17-19; full RV sites $20-23. Showers $1 per 5min. ❶

BRITISH COLUMBIA

FOOD

The highway attracts dives and fast-food joints, many open late or 24hr. Get groceries from **Thrifty Foods** in the Harbour Park Mall. (☎754-6273. Open daily 8am-10pm.) The **Farmer's Market** runs on F (10am-2pm) and W (3pm-7pm) at the Pioneer Waterfront Plaza on Front St. in downtown Nanaimo.

The Dar, 347 Wesley St. (☎755-6524). Up Franklyn from City Hall, take a right on Wesley. A quiet respite from downtown, with tasty Greek and Indian cuisine. Open M-Sa 10am-midnight, Su 4pm-midnight. 15% discount for Nicol St. Hostel guests. ❷

THE LOCAL STORY

ON THE MENU: NANAIMO BARS

These gooey, artery-cloggingly rich layered treats were once sent in care packages from the United Kingdom to hard-working sons in Nanaimo coal mines. They have since become synonymous with this little Canadian town, and are quite a way to finish off a meal (they're sort of a meal in and of themselves, in fact). Heart attack in a baking pan—a worthy claim to fame for a small town.

Layer 1: *½ cup butter, ¼ cup white sugar, 1 egg, 1 tsp. vanilla, 1 tbsp. cocoa, 2 cups graham cracker crumbs, 1 cup unsweetend coconut, ½ cup walnut pieces.* Combine butter, sugar, egg, vanilla, and cocoa in the top of a double boiler, over medium heat, and stir until slightly thickened. Combine crumbs and coconut in a bowl, then pour the hot mixture over top. Stir, and then press into the bottom of a shallow 6x9 in. rectangular pan. Refrigerate.

Layer 2: *2 tbsp. custard powder, 2 cups icing sugar, ¼ cup soft butter, 3 tbsp. milk.* Blend the butter, sugar, milk, and powder until smooth. Spread over first layer.

Layer 3: *5oz. semi sweet chocolate, 1 tbsp. butter.* Melt chocolate and butter in double boiler. Spread the chocolate over layer 2. Chill.

Gina's Mexican Cafe, 47 Skinner St. (☎753-5411). A bright pink landmark on Nanaimo's skyline, Gina's offers unique Mexican fare at a great price with stellar service. Experiment with creative items like the Don Juan, a veggie and cheese omelet in a grilled tortilla ($8). Vegetarian options are plentiful, and the margaritas are stellar. Open M-Th 11am-9pm, F 11am-10pm, Sa noon-10pm, Su noon-8pm. ❷

SIGHTS & EVENTS

SIGHTS. The **Nanaimo District Museum,** 100 Cameron Rd., pays tribute to Nanaimo's First Nation communities with an interactive exhibit on the Snuneymuxw (SNOO-ne-moo) and a section on the coal mining origins of the town. (☎753-1821. Open in summer daily 9am-5pm, in winter Tu-Sa 9am-5pm. $2, students and seniors $1.75, under 12 $0.75.) The **Bastion** up the street was a Hudson's Bay Company fur-trading fort, and it fires a cannon every weekday at noon. (Open July-Sept. W-M 10am-4:30pm. Free.)

EVENTS. The multi-day **Marine Festival** is held the last weekend in July, with many events leading up to the actual festival. Highlights include the **Bathtub Race,** in which contestants race tiny boats built around porcelain tubs with monster outboards from Nanaimo harbor, around Entrance and Winchelsea Islands, and finish at Departure Bay. Officials hand out prizes to everyone who makes it, and they present the "Silver Plunger" to the first tub to sink. The organizer of this bizarre and beloved event is the **Royal Nanaimo Bathtub Society** (☎753-7223).

OUTDOOR ACTIVITIES

BUNGEE JUMPING. Adrenaline-junkies from all over the continent make a pilgrimage to the **Bungy Zone,** 35 Nanaimo River Rd., the only legal bungee bridge in North America. To reach the Zone, take Hwy. 1 south to Nanaimo River Rd. and follow the signs, or take the free shuttle to and from Nanaimo. Plummet 42m (140 ft.) into a narrow gorge (water touches available); variations include a zipline, high-speed rappel, and the Swing. (☎716-7874 or 888-668-7874; nanaimo.ark.com/~bungy. $95, same-day jumps $35. 20% HI discount. **Campsites** ❶ $10 per person.)

HIKING. The serene **Newcastle Island Provincial Park,** accessible only by boat, has 756 automobile-free acres filled with hiking trails, picnic spots, and campsites. (☎754-7893. **Scenic Ferries** run only in summmer, on the hr. 10am-6pm; $5.) The **Shoreline**

Trail that traces the island's perimeter offers great vantage points of Departure Bay. **Petroglyph Provincial Park,** 3km south of town on Hwy. 1, protects carvings inscribed by Salish shamans. A menagerie of animals and mythical creatures decorates the soft sandstone.

WATER. The waters of **Departure Bay** wash onto a pleasant, pebbly beach in the north end of town on Departure Bay Rd., off Island Hwy. Jacques Cousteau called the waters around Nanaimo "The Emerald Sea," and they offer top diving opportunities. The **Nanaimo Dive Association** (☎729-2675) helps visitors find charters, lessons, or equipment. **The Kayak Shack,** 1840 Stewart Ave., near the ferry terminal, rents kayaks, canoes, and camping equipment. (☎753-3234. Singles and canoes $10 per hr., $40 overnight; doubles $15, $60.)

HORNBY ISLAND ☎250

In the 1960s, large numbers of draft-dodgers fled the US to settle peacefully on Hornby Island, halfway between Nanaimo and Campbell River. Today, hippie holdovers of all manners and origins and a similarly long-haired and laid-back younger generation mingle on the island with descendants of 19th-century pioneers. Low tide on Hornby uncovers over 300m of the finest sand in the strait of Georgia. **Tribune Bay,** at the end of Shields Rd., is the more crowded of the two beaches (**Li'l Tribune Bay,** next door, is clothing-optional). The alternative, **Whaling Station Bay,** has the same gentle sands and is about 5km farther north, off St. John's Point Rd. On the way there from Tribune Bay, Helliwell Rd. passes stunning **Helliwell Provincial Park,** where well-groomed trails lead through old-growth forest to bluffs overlooking the ocean.

ORIENTATION & PRACTICAL INFORMATION. There are two main roads on Hornby: the coastal **Shingle Spit Rd.** (try saying *that* 10 times fast) and **Central Rd.,** which crosses the island from the end of Shingle Spit. The island has no public transit and is hard to cover without a bike or car. On-foot travelers have been known to ask friendly faces for a lift at Denman or on the ferry (*Let's Go* does not recommend hitchhiking). The **Laidlaw** (☎753-4371) bus has a flag stop at **Buckley Bay** on Hwy. 19, where the ferry docks. **BC Ferries** has sailings all day from **Buckley Bay** to **Denman** and from Denman to **Hornby**. To reach the Hornby ferry, follow Denman Rd. all the way to end, on the other side of the island. (☎335-0323; www.bcferries.com. $4.50-4.75 per adult; $15-17 with car.) The **visitors center** (☎335-0313; open daily 10am-3pm) and the **Hornby Island Off-Road Bike Shop** (☎335-0444; $8 per hr., $30 per day; children $5, $20; open daily 10am-5pm) are located in the island's **Ringside Market. Hornby Ocean Kayaks** transports kayaks to the calmest of seven beaches and provides guided tours, lessons, and rentals. (☎335-2726. Tours starting at $30; full-day $65. Rentals $24 for 4hr.; $40 per day.) The island's only **24hr. ATM** is at the **Hornby Island Resort** (See **Accommodations and Food,** below). The **post office** is also at the Ringside Market in the Co-op. (Open M-Sa 9:30am-4:30pm; closed 1-1:30pm.) **Postal Code:** V0R 1Z0.

ACCOMMODATIONS & FOOD. At the earthy heart of Hornby sits the grocery-bearing **Co-op** in the Ringside Market. (☎335-1121. Open daily 9am-6pm.) The colorful market, at the end of Central Rd. by Tribune Bay, is also home to artisan **gift shops,** a beach-gear store, and two budget- and vegetarian-friendly restaurants. Most **B&Bs** ❹ cluster around the **Whaling Station, Galleon Beach, and Sandpiper Beach** areas and cost $65-175 per night, with the majority in the $80-90 range. The **Hornby Island Resort** ❶, right at the ferry docks, is a pub/restaurant/laundromat/hotel/campground. The fare at the resort's **Thatch Pub** is standard, but the view from the outdoor deck is not. The **Wheelhouse Restaurant** ❷, with ocean views from a shared deck, has breakfasts from $9 and burgers for $7-8.50. (☎335-0136. Pub open daily 11:30am-midnight; live jazz every F night at 7pm. Restaurant open daily 9:30am-9pm. Sites $20; RV sites $19. Jan.-Mar. sites $14. Private rooms from $75.) **Tribune Bay Campsite ❷**, on Shields Rd., offers 118 sites a quick walk from the island's popular beach. Showers, toilets, and playground. Reservations are necessary July-Aug. (☎335-2359. Sites $24, power $27, cyclists with tent $19.)

FESTIVALS. For one day in the first week of July, the **Hornby Festival** celebrates classical music with a small touch of the popular variety. In addition, island residents offer a $15 walking tour of many local studios, homes, and galleries to raise money for the festival. Call the festival office for info. (☎335-2734; www.mars.ark.com/~festival. Performances $5-15, full pass $165.)

DENMAN ISLAND ☎250

The Denman village center, perched above the Buckley Bay ferry terminal, offers crucial amenities. **Denman Island General Merchants** houses the **visitors center** and the **post office** (postal code V0R 1T0; open 8:30am-4:30pm M-Sa), and sells basic groceries. (☎335-2293. Open summer M-Th 7am-9pm, F-Sa 7am-11pm, Su 9am-9pm; winter hours shorter.) Next door, the **Cafe on the Rock ❶** serves delicious food at delicious prices. Full vegetarian breakfast $6, homemade pie $4, sandwiches $4. (☎335-2999. Open same hours as general store.) The **Denman Island Guest House/Hostel ❶**, 3806 Denman Rd., has a super-relaxed family feel. Check out the gargantuan and amazingly sweet-smelling composting toilet. Features a kitchen, home-baked treats, and a hot tub. (☎335-2688; www.earthclubfactory.com. $17. Bikes $10 per day.) You can pitch a tent at beach-side **Fillongley Provincial Park ❶**, just off Denman Rd., halfway to the Hornby Ferry. (☎335-2325. Reservations recommended; call 800-689-9025. Pit toilets, water. $15.) You can camp for free at **Sandy ❶** or **Tree Island ❶** at the north end of the island. To get there, take a short hike along NW Rd. from the village center, make a left onto Gladstone Way, and head north toward the island with all the trees. (No campfires; access at low tide only.) The island's two lakes, **Graham Lake** and **Chickadee Lake,** offer fine freshwater swimming.

COMOX VALLEY ☎250

With fine hiking, fishing, and skiing, and the southern regions of Strathcona Provincial Park just a hike away, the tourist season never ends in this self-proclaimed "Recreation Capital of Canada." The area's beaches, trails, extensive cave network, and forested swimming holes would take weeks to explore. Sheltering the towns of Courtenay, Comox, and Cumberland, the Comox Valley boasts the highest concentration of artists in Canada and offers many free museums and galleries. In addition, the 1989 discovery of the 80 million-year-old "Courtenay Elasmosaur," which swam in the valley back when the valley was a lake, has transformed the region into a minor mecca of paleontology.

ORIENTATION & PRACTICAL INFORMATION. Courtenay, the largest town in the Valley, lies 108km (1hr.) north of Nanaimo on the **Island Hwy.** (Hwy. 19). In Courtenay, the Island Hwy. heading north joins **Cliffe Ave.** before crossing the river at 5th St., intersecting with **Comox Rd.,** and then once again heading north. **Laidlaw** (☎334-2475) buses run from Courtenay at 2663 Kilpatrick and 27th St. by the Driftwood Mall to **Nanaimo** (2hr., $20), **Port Hardy** (5hr., $64), and **Victoria** (5hr., $40). The **Comox Valley Transit System** connects the valley's three towns. (☎339-5453. Buses run 6:40am-10:20pm. $1.25; seniors $1.) **BC Ferries** links Comox with **Powell River.** (☎888-223-3779; www.bcferries.com. 1¼hr.; 4 per day; $8, car $22-25.)

The **visitors center,** 2040 Cliffe Ave., is in Courtenay. (☎334-3234. Open summer M-F 9am-6pm, Sa-Su 9am-5pm; shorter hours in winter.) **Comox Valley Kayaks,** 2020 Cliffe Ave. beside the visitors center, rents, transports, and leads workshops and full-moon paddles. (☎334-2628 or 888-545-5595; www.comoxvalley.com. Singles $35 per day, doubles $50-63. Open summer daily 10am-6pm; by appointment in winter.) Do **laundry** at **The Pink Elephant,** 339 6th St. (☎897-0167. Wash $1.75; dry $0.25 for 5min. Open M-F 8:30am-7pm, Sa-Su 9am-7pm.) In an **emergency,** call ☎911 or the **police** at ☎338-1321. The **hospital** can be reached at ☎339-2242. For **weather,** call ☎339-5044. Get free **Internet access** at the **library,** on 6th St. next to Thrifty's. (☎338-1700. Open M-F 10am-8pm, Sa 10am-5pm.) The **post office** is at 333 Hunt Place. (☎334-4341. Open M-F 8:30am-5pm.) **Postal Code:** V9N 1G0.

ACCOMMODATIONS & FOOD. The **Comox Lake Hostel ❶,** 4787 Lake Trail Rd., about 8km from town, is within hiking distance of Strathcona Provincial Park. To get there, take 5th St. toward the mountains to Lake Trail Rd., turn west, and just keep going. Free linen, plus kitchen and laundry. Great local swimming. (☎338-1914. Beds $16; tent sites $10 per person.) The new **Courtenay Riverside Hostel ❶,** 1380 Cliffe Ave., provides beds right in town by the river. Private rooms are available. (☎334-1938. Linen, towels, laundry. Dorms $16. Winter ski-and-stay package $50.) The **Mt. Washington Guest House and Hostel ❷** offers rooming right by the ski resort. (898-8141. Hot tub, laundry, free linen. $17-20. Doubles $45-55.) Campers hit **Kin Beach ❶** campground, on Astra Rd. past the Air Force base in Comox. To get there, turn left at the four-way stop in front of the base, take your first right and follow it for 5min. (☎339-6365. Tennis, pit toilets, water. 18 wooded sites, $8.) Despite the trek 25km north from Courtenay, family-oriented **Miracle Beach ❶** on Miracle Beach Dr. is often full. (☎337-5720, reservations 800-689-9025. Sites $19. Showers.) **Comox Valley Farmers' Market** occurs three times per week at different locations: W at 4th St. and Duncan St., F at the Comox Marina, and Sa at the fairground on Headquarters Rd. (May-Sept. 9am-noon). Thaw a TV dinner from **Safeway** on 8th St. in Courtenay. (Open M-Sa 8am-9pm, Su 9am-9pm.) The surprisingly hip **Atlas Cafe ❶,** 250 6th St., serves delicious quesadillas ($5.75-7) and light entrees. (☎338-9838. Open Tu-Th and Sa-Su 8:45am-10pm, F 8:45am-11pm.) **Bar None Cafe,** 244 4th St. off Cliffe Ave. in Courtenay, stocks exceptional vegetarian fare. Open mic on Tu-F, 6-9pm. (☎334-3112. Open M-Sa 8am-7pm.)

SIGHTS. The area's largest draw is the **Mt. Washington** ski area, on the edge of Strathcona Provincial Park (see p. 293). It's only a 30min. drive to the base of the lifts from Courtenay, so staying in a cheap motel is a viable way to avoid the mountain's stratospheric prices. The **Queneesh Gallery,** 3310 Comox Rd., displays the work of some of the finest traditional Salish and Kwakwaka'wakw carvers on northern Vancouver Island. (☎339-7702. Open daily 10am-5pm; Jan.-Feb. closed Su-M.) Inquire at the visitors center about other galleries. The **Cumberland Museum,** 2680 Dunsmuir Ave., displays exhibits on the coal-mining town that in 1920 was home to large Chinese and Japanese communities. (☎336-2445. Open daily 9am-5pm; Oct. to mid-May closed Su. Admission by donation.)

OUTDOOR ACTIVITIES. The snowmelt-fed **Puntledge River** at **Stotan Falls,** a long stretch of shallow waters racing over flat rocks, is a great place for **swimming;** test the current and depths before wading or jumping. Coming from Courtenay on Lake Trail Rd., turn right at the stop sign onto the unmarked road at the first "hostel" sign. Take the next left at the logging road Duncan Bay Main, cross the pipeline, and then park on either side of the one-lane bridge. Comox Lake Hostel (see **Accommodations,** above) can provide a map. For longer trails through the woods, try breath-taking **Nymph Falls,** upriver. From Duncan Bay Main, go left on Forbidden Plateau Rd. to the "Nymph" sign. **Horne Lake Caves Provincial Park,** 55km south of Courtenay off the Island Hwy. on Horne Lake Rd., offers superb caving tours—a genuinely other-worldly experience—for beginners (1½hr., $15; 3hr., $39), and 5 and 7hr. tours involving crawlways, rappelling and the ethics of spelunking. (☎757-8687; reservations www.hornelake.com. $79-109. 15+, bring heavy, non-cotton clothing.) Hikers can explore two short, highly damaged caves for free. **Tiderunner Charters** (☎337-2253 or 334-7116) rents boat and rods.

CAMPBELL RIVER ☎250

A big rock covered with graffiti welcomes visitors to Campbell River, another of BC's many "Salmon Capitals of the World." Jacques Cousteau called Campbell River's incredible fishing and scuba diving "second only to the Red Sea." The number of gas stations and motels along the old Island Hwy. (Hwy. 19A) confirms Campbell River's role as the transportation hub of the island's north. It provides easy access to Strathcona Provincial Park, Port Hardy, and the Discovery Islands.

ORIENTATION & PRACTICAL INFORMATION. Campbell River lies 45km north of Courtenay on the **Island Hwy.** (Hwy. 19). **Laidlaw** (☎287-7151), at 13th and Cedar, sends buses to **Nanaimo** (4 per day, $24.75) and **Port Hardy** (1-2 per day, $58), as well as **Victoria** (4 per day, $44). **BC Ferries** (☎888-223-3779) runs to Quadra Island (all day; $4.50-4.75, cars $10.50-12, ages 5-11 $2.25-2.50). The **visitors center** is off the Island Hwy. near the Tyee Mall, adjacent to the Marina. (☎287-4636. Open summer daily 8am-6pm; winter M-F 9am-5pm.) Call ☎287-4463 for **weather,** and ☎911 in an **emergency.** The **police** can be reached at ☎286-6221, and a **crisis line** at ☎287-7743. The **hospital** is at 375 2nd Ave. (☎287-7111).

ACCOMMODATIONS & FOOD. B&Bs ❹ in Campbell River tend to be a bit expensive (singles $45-70; doubles $60-90), but the Info Centre can help you find a bed to sleep in. The best camping near town is at **Quinsam Campground ❶,** in Elk Falls Provincial Park on Hwy. 28, with space among firs. (Pit toilets. 122 sites, $12.) The **Beehive Cafe ❷,** 921 Island Hwy., has a deck overlooking the water. Breakfast and lunch run $6 and up. For an amazing local treat, try the smoked salmon bagel sandwich. (☎286-6812. Open summer daily 6:30am-10pm; winter 7am-8pm.) Shop for honey at **Super Valu** in the Tyee Mall. (☎287-4410. Open daily 8:30am-9:30pm.) **Spice Island ❷,** 2269 Island Hwy., offers customized meat, seafood, or tofu dishes at 5 levels of spiciness. (☎923-0011. Open Tu-Sa 4:30pm-closing.) Sockeye, coho, pink, chum, and chinook **salmon** are hauled in by the boatload from the waters of the Campbell River. The savvy can reap the fruits of the sea from **Discovery Pier** in Campbell Harbour, and the unskilled can at least buy rich ice cream and frozen yogurt on the pier, which has an artificial reef built to attract fish. (Fishing $2; rod rentals $2.50 per hr., $6 per half-day.) Get a **fishing license** ($6-8 per day, salmon $6.50 extra) at the visitors center or any sports outfitter in town.

SIGHTS & OUTDOOR ACTIVITIES. Tour the **Quinsam River Salmon Hatchery,** 4217 Argonaut Rd., and see a wealth of "natural" resources. The hatchery nurtures little fish to adolescence. (☎287-9564. Open daily 8am-4pm.) **Scuba** gear rentals can be pricey and require proper certification, but **Beaver Aquatics,** 760 Island Hwy., offers a nifty $25 **snorkeling** package that includes suit, mask, snorkel, and fins; they also have a $50 full dive package. (☎287-7652. Open M-Sa 9am-5pm, Su 10am-12pm.) Beaver only supplies equipment, so if you have charter needs, give a call during business hours to **Abyssal Charters** (☎285-2420) for some guided, bubble-blowing, spear-gunning good times.

QUADRA ISLAND

Quadra boasts pleasing landscapes that rival her southern Gulf Island cousins, a European history that is older than that of most settlements on Vancouver Island, and a thriving First Nation community around Cape Mudge. It is one of the world's more relaxing places. The **Kwagiulth Museum and Cultural Centre,** at 37 Weeway Rd., in the village of Cape Mudge just south of Quathiaski Cove, houses a spectacular collection of potlatch regalia confiscated by the government early this century and not returned until as late as 1988. (☎285-3733; www.island.net/~kmccchin. Open M-Sa 10am-4:30pm; in summer also Su noon-4:30pm. $3, seniors $2, children $1. Tours $1 extra.) Quadra is a 10min. ferry ride from Campbell River (see p. 292). **BC Ferries** sail to Quadra every hour on the half hour from Campbell River (see **Orientation,** above). **Quadra Credit Union** (☎285-3327; **24hr. ATM**) and a **visitors center** with maps of island trails and rental info await at the first corner of Harper Rd, across from **Quadra Foods,** which will satisfy your grocery needs and sell you a **fishing license.** (☎285-3391. Open daily 9am-8pm. Licenses $6-8 per day, $6.50 extra for salmon.) Call ☎911 or the **police** (☎285-3631) in an **emergency.** Travel- and world-weary sojourners will find a welcome place to relax at the **Travellers' Rural Retreat ❶,** where remarkable hosts welcome you into their home for as long as you need. Ask for a tour of Jim's driftwood sculptures. (☎285-2477. Call for directions; pick-up available. $16.) Several minutes down Heriot Bay Rd. from the beauty of **Rebecca Spit Provincial Park** and **Heriot Bay,** the **We Wai Kai Campsite ❶** lies on the water. (☎285-3111. Toilets, water, laundry. Sites $15-17. Coin showers.) **Spirit of the West** rents kayaks and runs guided trips that explore Quadra Island's wildlife-rich shores and beyond. (☎800-307-3982; www.kayakingtours.com. Singles $40 per 8hr. day; doubles $55. Full-day tour $89, including a huge lunch; sunset tour $59 with snack; 4-day kayaking with killer whales $857.)

STRATHCONA PROVINCIAL PARK ☎250

Elk, deer, marmots, and wolves all inhabit Strathcona's over 2000 sq. km; it's one of the best-preserved wilderness areas on Vancouver Island and the oldest provincial park in BC. The park spans the land just west of the Comox Valley, reaching north to connect with Campbell River via Hwy. 28. It stretches from sea-level to the highest point on Vancouver Island, 2200m **Golden Hinde.**

ORIENTATION & PRACTICAL INFORMATION. The park is accessible from Courtenay or Campbell River. The two **BC Parks** offices are on **Buttle Lake** (open summer only F-Su 9am-4pm), on Hwy. 28 between Gold River and Campbell River, and **Mt. Washington/Forbidden Plateau,** outside Courtenay off Hwy. 19. For park info, contact the BC Parks District Manager (☎954-4600).

ACCOMMODATIONS & CAMPING. The two frontcountry **campgrounds,** with 161 sites between them, are Buttle Lake and Ralph River. Both are on the shores of Buttle Lake and accessible by **Hwy. 28** and secondary roads (follow the highway signs). **Buttle Lake ❶,** 50km from Campbell River (about 45min. of scenic, but winding driving), has comfortable sites, a playground, and sandy beaches on the lake (pit toilets, water; $15). Less crowded **Ralph River ❶,** 75km (1½hr. drive) west of Campbell River, provides convenient access to the park's best hiking trails ($12). Five smaller marine campsites are accessible only by trails (pick up a map at the park entrance). The **Ark Resort ❶,** 11000 Great Central Lake Rd., just west of Port Alberni off Hwy. 4, rents canoes for the 35km water journey to the Della Falls trailhead (see **Hiking,** below) or provides a water taxi for $85 per person round-trip. (☎723-2657. Sites $19; rooms $45.) For outfitting and outdoor guidance on the doorstep of the park, **Strathcona Park Lodge ❷,** 30km from Campbell River on Hwy.

28, offers equipment rental and experienced guides. The lodge has roomy lakefront houses and a dining hall that serves three meals a day. (☎286-3122. Single kayaks $9 per hr., $37 per day; doubles $14, $53; 17 ft. sailboats $20, $70. Dining hall 7am-9am, noon-2pm $10; 5:30-7pm $17; summer 6-9pm a la carte.)

HIKING. The park offers a great variety of trails of all lengths and difficulties. Visitors who wish to explore Strathcona's **backcountry areas** must camp 1km from main roads and at least 30m away from water sources; campfires are discouraged. Those entering the undeveloped areas of the park should notify park officials of their intended departure and return times and should be well equipped (maps and rain gear are essential). Be sure to check back in with wardens upon your return.

Karst Creek Trail (2km, 45min.). Leaves from the Karst Creek day-use area and passes limestone sinkholes and waterfalls. Easy.

Myra Falls Trail (1km, 20-40min.) starts 1km past Thelwood bridge at the south end of Buttle Lake at a signed parking area. The trail features a walk through old-growth forest and a steep hill with loose rock on the way to the immense, pounding falls. Moderate.

Phillips Ridge (12km round-trip, 7-8hr.). Trailhead at the parking lot just south of the campsite along the highway. The trail leads to Arnica Lake and wildflower-strewn alpine meadows, passing 2 waterfalls and ascending 700m along the way. Difficult.

Elk River Trail (11km one-way, 4-6hr.). This popular trail starts just before Drum Lakes along Hwy. 28; follow signs to trailhead on the left. A campsite at 9km has bear food caches. The trail gains 600m in elevation as it follows an old elk trail to Landslide Lake, where part of Mt. Colonel Foster fell into the water. Moderate.

Della Falls (16km one-way, 7hr.). Splendid in its scenery and remoteness, this trail is accessible only by boat from the west end of Great Central Lake and follows Drinkwater Creek to the base of big, beautiful Della Falls. Moderate.

OUTDOOR ACTIVITIES. Skiers and snowboarders hit the slopes just outside the park boundaries at **Mt. Washington** to take advantage of 10m of annual snowfall. The mountain is accessible from Courtenay; follow Cliffe St. to the end, take a right on 1st St., a left at the end of 1st, and follow signs. A few years ago, one of the nearby lodges actually caved in from too much snow, and lifts have been known to close on occasion because of excess precipitation. (☎338-1386, reservations 888-231-1499; www.mtwashington.ca. $44, over 65 and ages 13-18 $36, ages 7-12 $23, 6 and under free. Night skiing F-Sa 4:30-9pm. $6, 6 and under free.) A lift is open in the summer to satiate the appetites of vista-hungry bikers. ($10, youth and senior $8, under 6 free; with bike $15.) The mountain also offers 40km of cross-country and snowshoe trails; the lodge has rentals. (Alpine ski package $22; cross country $16; over 65 and ages 13-18 $12. Snowboards $36; snowshoes $9.)

PORT McNEILL AREA ☎250

The protected waters and plentiful fish of Johnstone Strait provide a fine summer home for orca pods. Mainland and island settlements near Port McNeill provide fine quiet waterside trips. Sighting charters run $60 for 3-4hr., but lucky visitors can glimpse orcas from the ferry between Port McNeill, Sointula, and Alert Bay, or even from the shoreline. For good whale watching, head 25km south of Port McNeill to the boardwalk town of **Telegraph Cove.** Turn left south of town on the Island Hwy.; over the last 5km, it becomes an unpaved road. **North Island Kayaks,** in Port Hardy (see below), will drop off and pick up kayaks in the cove. (☎949-7707 or 877-949-7707. Kayaks $50 per day; doubles $70; daytrips $125.)

Tiny Cormorant Island and the town of **Alert Bay** is home to a fabulously rich repository of native culture. The cultural legacy of several groups of the **Kwakwaka'wakw** peoples (ka-kwak-QUEW-wak; formerly known as the Kwakiutl or Kwagiulth) sets the fishing village apart from its aquatourist siblings. By the Big House stands a 173 ft. totem pole, the largest in the world. Two kilometers north of the ferry terminal, the pole towers over the **U'mista Cultural Centre,** which houses an astonishing array of Kwakwaka'wakw artifacts repatriated decades after Canadian police pillaged a potlatch. *U'mista* means "the return of a loved one taken captive by raiding parties." (☎974-5403. Open daily 9am-5pm; winter M-F 9am-5pm.) **Sointula,** on the coast of Malcolm Island, is a modern artist and fishing community with Finnish roots known for its December Christmas bazaar.

PRACTICAL INFORMATION. **Laidlaw** (☎956-3556) runs one bus per day to **Port McNeill** from **Victoria** (8hr., $84.75). **BC Ferries** (☎956-4533 or 888-223-3779; www.bcferries.com) runs from Port McNeill to **Sointula** on Malcolm Island (25min.) and **Alert Bay** (45min.; 6 per day; round-trip $5.50-6, car $15). **Visitors centers** are stationed at 351 Shelley Crescent in Port McNeill (☎956-3131; open in summer daily 9am-5pm) and 118 Fir St. in Alert Bay (☎974-5024; open June-Sept. daily 9am-6pm). In an **emergency,** call ☎911. The **hospital** is at 2750 Kingcome Pl. (☎956-4461) in Port McNeill.

ACCOMMODATIONS & FOOD. The **Sun Spirit Hostel and Guesthouse ❶,** 549 Fir St. in Alert Bay, is a welcome spot to play piano and whale watch from the living room. (☎974-2026. $17, cash or traveler's checks only.) Beautiful camping, with a view of the mainland coastal range, is available across the island at **Bere Point Regional Park ❶** near Sointula. (Pit toilets, no water. 12 sites, by donation.) The budget-mindful eschew island restaurants for the hardtack at **ShopRite Grocery,** 99 Fir St. (☎974-2777. Open M-Sa 9am-6pm, Su 10am-5pm.) The **Killer Whale Cafe ❸** in Telegraph Cove is all yellow cedar and stained glass. High prices and erratic service. (☎928-3155. Dinner from $11. Open daily 8am-2:30pm and 4-10pm.)

PORT HARDY ☎250

Port Hardy, an idyllic logging and fishing community, is the southern terminus for the BC Ferries route up the Inside Passage. The northernmost major town on the island, it has a vested interest in tourism. You will be welcomed by a chainsaw-carved sign, erected for the 1500 passengers who sleepily disembark the ferry every other night. These transients join a surge of fishermen preparing for unpredictable fall fisheries on the west coast of BC and a growing indigenous population drawn from more remote towns for schooling and employment.

TRANSPORTATION. Port Hardy, on Vancouver Island, is perched 36km north of Port McNeill and 238km (2½hr.) north of Campbell River on **Hwy. 19. Market St.** is the main drag, running through the shopping district and along a scenic seaside path. **Laidlaw** (☎949-7532), opposite the visitors center on Market St., runs to **Victoria** (8¾hr., $94.15) via **Nanaimo** (6hr., $83) each day at 9am and when the ferry arrives. **BC Ferries** (☎949-6722 or 888-223-3779; www.bcferries.com) depart 3km south of town at **Bear Cove,** for **Prince Rupert** (every other day June-Sept.; winter every Sa and 2nd W $53-106, car $124-218). The Discovery Coast Passage route between Port Hardy and **Bella Coola** runs from mid-June to mid-Sept. ($70-110, car $140-220). Book months ahead for cars. **North Island Taxi** (☎949-8800) services the ferry from all over town for $5.25 per person, $6.50 to the airport.

ORIENTATION & PRACTICAL INFORMATION. To reach the **visitors center,** 7250 Market St., follow Hwy. 19 until the end and take a right on Market St. (☎949-7622. Open M-F 8:30am-6pm, Sa-Su 10am-5pm; winter M-F 8:30am-5pm.) The **Port Hardy Museum** (see **Sights and Outdoor Activities,** below) also has in-depth info on the region. The **CIBC bank,** 7085 Market St., has a **24hr. ATM.** (☎949-6333. Open M-Th 10am-4pm, F 10am-6pm.) **North Star Cycle and Sports,** at Market and Granville St., rents road bikes. (☎949-7221. $20 per day. Open daily 9:30am-6pm.) For all else, there's **Jim's Hardy Sports,** in the Thunderbird Mall on Granville St. (☎949-8382. Open M-Sa 9am-6pm.) Diving rentals can be found at **North Island Diving and Water Sports,** at Market and Hastings St. (☎949-2664. Open Tu-Sa 10am-6pm; full setup $89.) Wash up at the **Shell Gas Station,** on Granville St. (☎949-2366. Wash $1.75; dry $0.25 per 7min. Open 24hr.) **Internet access** is $5 at the **library,** 7110 Market St. (☎949-6661. Open M, W, F noon-5pm and 7-9pm; Tu and Th noon-5pm). Other services include: **Police,** 7355 Columbia St. (☎949-6335); **crisis line,** ☎949-6033; and **hospital,** 9120 Granville St. (☎949-6161). The **postal code** is V0N 2P0.

FOOD. Stock up on groceries before the long ferry ride or trip down the island at **Glenway Foods,** 8645 Granville St. (☎949-5758; open M-Sa 9am-9pm). The burger is this town's budget meal. One of the best is $6 at **I.V.'s Quarterdeck Pub ❶,** 6555 Hardy Bay Rd., on the fishing dock. Their great vegetarian fare is balanced by F prime rib night ($15 with all the trimmings) and $0.25 wings on W and Su. (☎949-6922. Open daily 11am-12:30pm.) The **Oceanside Restaurant & Pub ❶,** 6435 Hardy Bay Rd., just down from I.V.'s at the Glen Lyon Inn, has a terrific view and serves $0.25 wings on W and F. (☎949-7115. Open daily 6:30am-9pm.) Your best breakfast bet is at **Snuggles Restaurant ❶,** 4965 Byng Rd., by the Quatze River Campground. (☎949-7494. Full breakfast starting at $5. Open daily 7:30am-9:30pm.)

ACCOMMODATIONS & CAMPING. The visitors center will reserve B&B rooms for free. (☎949-7622. Call ahead on ferry nights.) The **Dolphin House B&B ❸,** 297 Harbor Rd. in Coal Harbor, is a short excursion (20min.) from Port Hardy. This hidden gem offers incredible ocean views, an array of outdoor activities, and proximity to native villages. Take Island Hwy. 19 to Coal Harbor Rd., turn right at the coffee shop in town, and head past the whale bones. (☎949-7576. Free pickup from ferry, bus station, airport. Singles $50; doubles $60.) **This Old House ❶,** 8735 Hastings, is downtown by the bus station. They rent cozy rooms with balconies upstairs. Free linen, laundry. Backyard BBQ, shared bath. (☎949-8372. 5 hostel beds $20; singles $40; doubles $70.) The proprietors of **The Hudson's Home B&B ❸,** 9605 Scott St., provide all the TLC and custom breakfasts you can handle. Hot tub, Internet, and pickup and drop-off from the bus station. (☎949-5110. Singles $60; doubles $75; mention *Let's Go* and get 10% off.) **Bonita B&B ❸,** relatively new on the scene, offers guests privacy and their own sparkling kitchen to use. (☎949-6787. Singles $50; double $65-70.) Quiet, wooded sites at **Quatse River Campground ❶,** 8400 Byng Rd. (☎949-2395. toilets, laundry; $14, full RV sites $18. Free showers) are a 25min. walk from town but just minutes from **Snuggles Restaurant** (see **Food,** below). Internet access $1.50 per 15min. The camp shares space with a fish hatchery. (☎949-9022. Tours are best Sept.-Nov.) Sites amid an overgrown garden at **Wildwoods Campsite ❶** lie off the road to the ferry, a walk to the terminal, but a hike from town. (☎949-6753. Tent sites $7, RV sites $18.)

SIGHTS & OUTDOOR ACTIVITIES. The **Port Hardy Museum and Archives** is at 7110 Market St., beneath the library. The museum's sea-creature remnants, 19th-century Cape Scott pioneers' personal effects, 8000-year-old tools from Hardy Bay, and erudite curator merit a visit. (☎949-8143. Open M-Sa 10:30am-4:30pm; shortened hours in winter. Donation requested.) A 15min. drive from town brings picnickers to the hard sand of **Storey's Beach,** a good place to put in a kayak or stroll along the rocky shore. Turn left off the Island Hwy. when driving out of town onto Byng Rd. and then take a left on Beaver Harbour Rd. to the water. Nearby, the **Copper Maker,** 114 Copper Way, commissions some of the finest Kwakiutl carvers in the region. From Byng Rd., turn left onto Beaver Harbour Rd., right on Tsak'is Way, and right again. (☎949-8491. Call for hours.) Farther down Tsak'is Way, a ceremonial and community **bighouse** overlooks the sea from the heart of Fort Rupert village, a site inhabited by the Kwakiutl for thousands of years. **Petroglyphs** adorn rocks near **Fort Rupert;** ask at the museum for advice in locating them at low tide. At the north end of the village stands the decaying stone chimney of Fort Rupert, an outpost built in 1849 by the Hudson's Bay Company.

A map of logging roads from the visitors center will allow you to explore the **geological curiosities** of the region's limestone bedrock or just get out into the woods: Devil's Bath sinkhole, the Vanishing and Reappearing Rivers, and several spelunkable caves are all located toward **Port Alice** (40min. from town). **Odyssey Kayaking** can equip and transport you. (☎902-0565. Singles $35 per day; doubles $55. Must have one experienced paddler in your group.) They also offer guided day trips for $95, including a delicious lunch. The Port Hardy area is known for some of the world's best **cold-water diving. Sun Fun Divers** (☎956-2243; www.sunfundivers.com) rents gear ($60 first day, $25 second day), and runs half-day ($45) and full-day ($90) trips out of Port Hardy and Port McNeill.

INTERIOR BRITISH COLUMBIA

From the jagged snow-capped Rocky Mountains, the Fraser River courses and hurdles its way through 1300km of canyons and plateaus on its journey toward a land more arid than the Pacific. The sweeping agricultural basin in the middle of BC between the Rockies and the Coast Range mountains sees much more sun than the coast and is a vacation hot spot for city-slickers and backcountry adventurers alike. The Rockies form the boundary that was finally breached by rail lines to unite Canada, and the mountains still constitute a large part of western Canada's identity. Today they are home to hugely popular national parks and thousands of square kilometers of hiking, climbing, and camping. Bus and train routes cross the interior and pass by various means through the mountains.

FRASER RIVER CANYON

In 1808, Simon Fraser enlisted the help of native guides to make the perilous expedition down the river from Mt. Robson to Vancouver. Today's route from Cache Creek to Hope on the Trans-Canada Hwy. (Hwy. 1) makes his trailblazing seem like a distant dream. Up close, the canyon is a good place to feel small, with 200km of pounding rapids below and pine sprouting out of near-vertical rock walls above.

In quiet **Hope,** travelers will find a tranquil town despite its fame as the Chainsaw Carving Capital. Hope's location at the intersection of several highways ensures easy arrival and departure. The **Trans-Canada Hwy. (Hwy. 1)** originates in Vancouver,

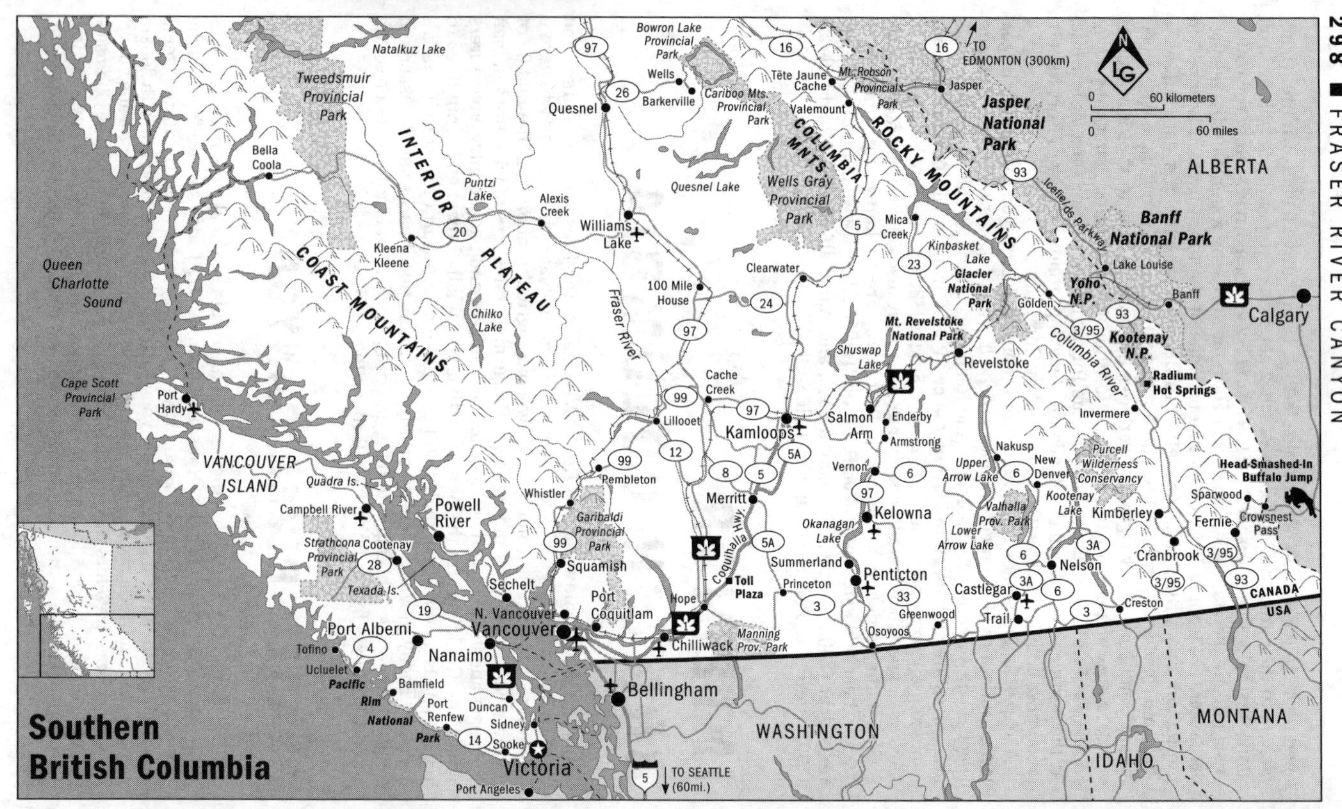
Southern
British Columbia
ALBERTA
MONTANA
IDAHO
WASHINGTON
CANADA
USA
0 60 kilometers
0 60 miles
TO EDMONTON (300km)
TO SEATTLE (60mi.)
ROCKY MOUNTAINS
COLUMBIA MNTS
INTERIOR PLATEAU
COAST MOUNTAINS
VANCOUVER ISLAND
Queen Charlotte Sound
Cape Scott Provincial Park
Port Hardy
Bella Coola
Tweedsmuir Provincial Park
Natalkuz Lake
Kleena Kleene
Puntzi Lake
Chilko Lake
Alexis Creek
Williams Lake
Quesnel
Wells
Barkerville
Bowron Lake Provincial Park
Cariboo Mts. Provincial Park
Quesnel Lake
100 Mile House
Fraser River
Clearwater
Wells Gray Provincial Park
Tête Jaune Cache
Valemount
Mt. Robson Provincial Park
Jasper
Jasper National Park
Icefields Parkway
Lake Louise
Banff
Banff National Park
Calgary
Yoho N.P.
Kootenay N.P.
Radium Hot Springs
Golden
Glacier National Park
Kinbasket Lake
Mica Creek
Revelstoke
Mt. Revelstoke National Park
Columbia River
Invermere
Purcell Wilderness Conservancy
Kimberley
Cranbrook
Fernie
Sparwood
Crowsnest Pass
Head-Smashed-In Buffalo Jump
Creston
Kootenay Lake
Nelson
New Denver
Nakusp
Upper Arrow Lake
Lower Arrow Lake
Valhalla Prov. Park
Castlegar
Trail
Greenwood
Osoyoos
Penticton
Summerland
Okanagan Lake
Kelowna
Vernon
Armstrong
Enderby
Salmon Arm
Shuswap Lake
Kamloops
Cache Creek
Merritt
Coquihalla Hwy.
Toll Plaza
Princeton
Manning Prov. Park
Hope
Chilliwack
Lillooet
Pembleton
Garibaldi Provincial Park
Whistler
Squamish
Port Coquitlam
Bellingham
Vancouver
N. Vancouver
Sechelt
Powell River
Texada Is.
Cootenay
Strathcona Provincial Park
Quadra Is.
Campbell River
Port Alberni
Nanaimo
Duncan
Sidney
Victoria
Sooke
Port Angeles
Port Renfew
Bamfield
Pacific Rim National Park
Ucluelet
Tofino

passes through Hope, and then bends north to Yale and eventually Cache Creek, where it meets the **Cariboo Hwy. (Hwy. 97**; see p. 328). **Hwy. 7** runs west along the north bank of the Fraser River to Vancouver's suburbs. **The Crowsnest Hwy. (Hwy. 3)** winds east through breathtaking country including Manning Provincial Park, through Kootenay Country to Nelson, and over Crowsnest Pass into Alberta. The **Coquihalla Hwy. (Hwy. 5)** is a new toll road ($10) running north to Kamloops, and preferred by most heading to the Rockies in a hurry—it's faster as long as the miles of grueling 8% grade don't get the best of the cars.

HOPE ☎604

Buses arrive in Hope at the **Greyhound** station, 677 Old Hope-Princeton Way, a hub for bus travel throughout the region. (☎869-5522. Open 7:30am-1pm, 2:10pm-2:40pm, and 4pm-9pm.) Buses run north on the Coquihalla to **Kamloops** (2½hr., 3 per day, $32), then east to **Banff** (10½hr., 3 per day, $94), **Calgary** (12hr., 3 per day, $112), and **Jasper** (8½hr., 2 per day, $87); north on Hwy. 1 along the Fraser Canyon to **Cache Creek** (2¾hr., 2 per day, $30); east on Hwy. 3 to **Penticton** (3½hr.; 2 per day, 1 on Sa; $37) and points east; and west to **Vancouver** (2½hr., 8 per day, $21). Many try and hitch north on Hwy. 1, where rides are reputedly easy to find (*Let's Go*, however, does not recommend hitchhiking). **Gardner Chev-Olds,** 945 Water Ave., rents cars. (☎869-9511. $40 per day, 7th day free. $0.13 per km after 100km. Must be 25+ with credit card. Open M-Sa 8am-6pm.) For biking, hiking, fishing, and hunting needs, stop by **Cheyenne Sporting Goods,** 267 Wallace St. (☎869-5062). The **Visitors Centre,** 919 Water Ave., provides the riveting, self-guided **Rambo Walking Tour** (*First Blood* was filmed here) in addition to sharing info on Fraser River Canyon and Manning Park. (☎869-2021 or 800-435-5622. Open M-F 9am-5pm.) Ask about the **Carving Walking Tour** through downtown, and make sure to take a break from the tour in Memorial Park, the city's pleasant green spot. The **police** are located at 690 Old Hope-Princeton Way (☎869-7750), and the **post office** at 777 Fraser St. **Postal Code:** V0X 1L0.

There's a motel on every corner downtown in Hope (singles $45-55). On the outskirts of town, **Holiday Motel ❸,** 63950 Old Yale Rd., offers an outdoor swimming pool, playground, volleyball court and fire-pit. (☎869-5352. Rooms with cable TV start at $40. Tent sites $15; RV sites $22; both include showers.) Campers can head for the big trees at the spacious **Coquihalla Campsite ❶,** 800 Kawkawa Lake Rd., off 6th Ave., on the east side of town along the banks of the Coquihalla River. (☎869-7119 or 888-869-7118. Open Apr.-Oct. 122 sites, $17; river sites $20; RV sites $23.) Shop for groceries at **Buy and Save Foods,** 489 Wallace St. (☎869-5318. Open July-Aug. daily 8am-10pm; Sept.-June 8am-9pm.) Locals love the generous portions and homemade cherry pie ($3.50 per slice) at the **Home Too Restaurant ❷,** 665 Hope Princeton Hwy. (☎869-5558.)

AROUND HOPE ☎604

A number of excellent hikes begin in or near Hope. Find the lush **Rotary Trail** (20min.) on Wardle St. at the confluence of the Fraser and Coquihalla Rivers. **Mt. Hope Loop** (45min.) offers an impressive view of the town and surrounding area (hike begins at intersection of Hwy. #1 and Old Hope Princeton Way, across from Rainbow Junction). To reach **Lookout Trail** (3½-4hr. round-trip), turn right under the Hwy. 1 overpass at Old Hope-Princeton Way. (Challenging.) Pause for a pleasant diversion at **Kawkawa (a.k.a. Suckers) Creek,** off Union Bar Rd., enhanced in 1984 to aid the late summer and mid-fall salmon spawning. The boardwalk along the creek leads to a swimming hole and popular picnicking spot. **Manning Provincial**

Park (☎840-8836), 15min. east of Hope on Hwy. 3, has more extensive hiking options with over 70,000 hectares of cedar rainforest and flowering alpine meadows. Set up your tent at one of four **campgrounds** ❶ throughout the park (Lightning Lake Campground, Coldspring, Mule Deer and Hampton; 350 sites total, $12-18.50). **Paintbrush Nature Trail,** at Blackwall Peak, provides a rare opportunity to enjoy subalpine meadows (bloom late July to early August). The path is wheelchair-accessible. (1km, 20 min.) For a more difficult hike, the **Pacific Crest Trail** passes through Manning beginning at Windy Joe. Parking lot on the Gibson Pass Road. (13km one way.)

OTHELLO-QUINTETTE TUNNELS. The **Coquihalla Canyon Recreation Area** is a 5-10min. drive out of Hope along Kawkawa Lake Rd. Here the **Othello Quintette Tunnels,** blasted through solid granite, provide mute evidence of the daring engineering that led to the opening of the **Kettle Valley Railway** in 1916. The dark tunnels lead to narrow bridges over whitewater that shoots through the gorge. These tunnels set the backdrop to many Hollywood adventure-classics: *First Blood (Rambo), Shoot to Kill,* and *Far from Home: Adventures of Yellowdog.* To get there, turn right on Othello Rd. off Kawkawa Lake Rd. and right again on Tunnel Rd.; allow 30min. to walk through the tunnels.

LADY FRANKLIN ROCK AND RAFTING. For an even closer view of the Fraser River, head 36km north on Hwy. 1 to the town of **Yale.** Take the first right after the stop light, then follow the gravel road for about 1km to a view of the majestic **Lady Franklin Rock,** which splits the river into two sets of heavy rapids. **Fraser River Raft Expeditions,** south of town, runs full-day whitewater trips almost daily on the Fraser and its tributaries. Travelers can stay the night in their oversized teepee or in the B&B. (☎863-2336 or 800-363-7238 for reservations. Class III-IV rapids; $110 includes lunch. **Camping** $5 per person; teepee $10 per night; B&B double $70.)

HELL'S GATE AIRTRAM. When Simon Fraser made his pioneering trek down the river, he likened one tumultuous stretch of rapids, 25km north of Yale on Hwy. 1, to the Gates of Hell—where "no human beings should venture." The Hell's Gate Airtram, 43111 Hwy. 1, carries the vertigo-immune 500 ft. down into the canyon in four minutes, although acrophobes and budgeteers may prefer the nearby 1km trail down to the river. (☎867-9277. $11, seniors $9.50, ages 6-18 $7, families $29.)

KAMLOOPS ☎250

T'Kumlups, a Shuswap word meaning "where the waters meet," fits the town well, as it surrounds the convergence of the North and South Thompson rivers, and the heavily traveled Hwys. 5 and 1. The landscape looks something like California (complete with wineries!); in addition, over 200 lakes lie within an hour's drive of town. That, combined with a fine hostel, outdoor live music in the summer, and numerous outdoor adventure opportunities, makes the town a great base for day-tripping in the area, or a good waystation on long highway voyages.

ORIENTATION & PRACTICAL INFORMATION. Kamloops lies 356km east of Vancouver and 492km west of Banff, anchoring the junction of the heavily traveled Yellowhead (Hwy. 5) and Trans-Canada (Hwy. 1). **VIA Rail** (☎800-561-8630) trains stop at North Station, 11km north of the city center off Hwy. 5, making three runs per week to **Edmonton, AB** (15hr., $20) and **Vancouver** (8½hr., $92). **Greyhound,** 725 Notre Dame Ave. (☎374-1212), departs Kamloops for **Vancouver** (4½hr., 5 per day, $49); **Jasper, AB** (6hr., 3 per day, $60); and **Calgary, AB** (9hr., 4 per day, $82). **Kamloops Transit System** (☎376-1216) buses cost $1.50. **Cycle Logical,** 194 Victoria St. (☎828-2810), rents bikes for $25 per day. Kamloops claims to be the largest (think: area) city in North America; a free transit map from the visitors center is handy. The **Visitors Centre** is just off the Trans-Canada Hwy at Exit #368. (☎374-3377 or 800-662-1994. Open mid-May to Aug. daily 9am-6pm; Sept.-May M-F 9am-5pm.) **McCleaners,** 437 Seymour St. (☎372-9655), is a McLaundry. The **police** are at 560 Battle St. (☎828-3000 or ☎911) in the city center. Free **Internet access** is at the **public library,** 466 Victoria St. (☎372-5145. Open Tu-Th 10am-9pm, M and F-Sa 10am-5pm, Su noon-4pm.) The **post office** is at 217 Seymour St. (☎374-2444. Open M-F 8:30am-5pm.) **Postal Code:** V2C 5K2.

ACCOMMODATIONS & FOOD. The excellent **Kamloops Old Courthouse Hostel (HI) ❶**, 7 W Seymour St., is in fact a turn-of-the-century courthouse. The giant common room still sports a jury box, judge's bench, and witness stand, compensating for the tightly-packed dorm rooms. (☎828-7991. Check-in 8am-noon and 5-10pm. 75 beds. $16, nonmembers $20; private rooms $5 surcharge.) Campers can stay the night 8km east of the city center at **Kamloops View Tent & Trailer Park ❶**, 1-4395 Trans-Canada Hwy. E. Features forty sites, flush toilets, and laundry. (☎573-3255. Sites $16; full RV sites $25. Free showers.) A huge variety of foods lines Victoria St., the main strip downtown. For the best breakfast in Kamloops, try **Amsterdam Pancake House ❶**, 369 Victoria St., which serves Dutch-style *pannenkoeken* ($5-9) and $5-6 grilled sandwiches. (☎377-8885. Open daily 8am-3pm.)

SIGHTS. Every night in July and August at 7:30pm there is "Music in the Park," as bands perform in **Riverside Park** on the banks of the Thompson River. The **Wanda Sue Paddle Boat,** 2472 Thompson Dr., gets you up close and personal with the river on a 2hr. cruise. (☎374-7447. 1-3 cruises per day. $12, seniors $11, ages 6-12 $7.) **Secwepemc Museum and Heritage Park,** 355 Yellowhead Hwy., is devoted to preserving the culture and heritage of the Shuswap people. It contains the reconstructed remains of a 2000-year-old Shuswap village. Located near the site of a school from which the Canadian government removed native children as late as the 1970s, the museum is a testament to the historical endurance of the First Nations. (☎828-9801, www.secwepemc.org. Open Memorial Day to Labor Day M-F 8:30am-8pm, Sa-Su 10am-6pm; Labor Day to Memorial Day M-F 8:30am-4:30pm. Summer $5, youths and seniors $4; off-season $1 less.) The annual **Cattle Drive** (☎800-288-5850) gives you the opportunity to live an expensive Western dream from Nicola Ranch to Kamloops. Would-be ranchers lacking mounts have to pay a hefty ransom ($745-1315, "posse" rates available) for rentals. The cattle drive runs once a year in mid-July. Booking early is essential.

OUTDOOR ACTIVITIES. Sun Peaks, 1280 Alpine Rd., a 45min. drive north of Kamloops, is a powdery magnet for snowboarders and skiers. The mountain's large vertical drop (881m) and annual snowfall (559cm), as well as the six glades, justify the somewhat pricey tickets. In summer, the lift carries hikers and bikers up to trails and wildflower meadows. (☎800-807-3257; www.sunpeaksresort.com. Hiking $12, seniors and ages 13-18 $11, ages 6-12 $9; mountain biking $26, $22, $12; winter $48, $34, $28.) To get to Sun Peaks, take Hwy. 5 north from Kamloops, turn right at Heffley Creek and continue 31km. The resort also hosts the annual **Ice Wine Festival** (☎861-6654; www.owfs.com) in late January. The **Stake Lake Trails** form a network of cross-country skiing terrain, with a good selection of beginner and intermediate options. Take Exit 366 from Hwy. 1 south of Kamloops, and follow Lac Le Jeune Rd. for 20min. Ask for a map at the visitors center or get one at the hut in winter. (Snow report ☎372-5514. $7 per day, $30 per 5 days. Summer usage for biking or hiking is free.)

For an up-close look at the creatures inhabiting the area surrounding the rails, check the **Wildlife Park,** 15min. east of Kamloops along Hwy. 1, a non-profit organization devoted to rehabilitating local wildlife. (☎573-3242. $8, ages 65+ and 13-16 $6, ages 3-12 $5.) Local climbers head out to **rock climb** at a crag about 25km west of Kamloops on Hwy. 1. Always in the shade, these 35 easy to moderate sport climbs offer a scenic view of Kamloops Lake. **Ropes End** climbing gym, 975 B Laval Cres. (☎372-0645), has more details. Cheap fly-fishing trips start at $20 through **Ark Park Trout Fishing.** Call for transportation info (☎573-3878; www.arkpark.com). In winter, call **Alaskan Husky Adventures** in nearby Clearwater to get your mushing on with frighteningly efficient blue-eyed dogs. Multiple tours available. (☎866-587-0037; www.dogsleddingadventures.com.)

SHUSWAP LAKE REGION ☎250

From the dugout canoes of the Shuswap to the RVs of today's vacationers, the warm waters and productive fisheries of the sublime Shuswap Lake have attracted people for centuries. The area is a peaceful place to stay for the night or to stop and enjoy the scenery. Salmon Arm, a metropolis compared to the nearby villages, is still unexceptional but for its lakefront situation and its poster-perfect backdrop of rolling, forested mountains. Beware: if you are going to try and find your way through Salmon Arm off the highway, have a good map—the streets are confusing. The area is rich in camping and fishing opportunities, making it a popular destination for British Colombians looking for a relaxing weekend getaway.

ORIENTATION & PRACTICAL INFORMATION. Shuswap Lake is shaped like a sideways 'H.' Hwy. 1 hugs the northern arm of the lake before dipping south and following the southern arm east from Salmon Arm. The **Salmon Arm Transit System** (☎832-0191) has scheduled ($1.25, M-Sa) and door-to-door service ($1.50, M-F). The **visitors center** is at 751 Marine Park Dr. (☎832-6247 or 877-725-6667; fax 832-8382. Open May-Sept. M-Su 9am-7pm; Oct.-Apr. M-F 9am-5pm.) **Greyhound** is located at 50 10th St. SW (☎832-3962). Wash clothes at **Shuswap Laundry,** 330 Ross St. (☎832-7300. Open daily 7am-10pm.) In an **emergency,** call ☎911. Free **Internet** is at the **library,** in Picadilly Pl. Mall on 10th Ave. SW. (☎832-6161. Open M, W-Th, and Sa 10am-5pm; Tu and F 10am-8pm.) The **post office** is at 370 Hudson St. NE. (☎832-3093. Open M-F 8:30am-5pm.) **Postal Code:** V1E 4M6.

ACCOMMODATIONS & CAMPING. **Squilax General Store and Caboose Hostel (HI) ❶,** 10km east of Chase, 8km west of Sorrento on Hwy. 1, sleeps travelers on board three Canadian National Railway cabooses. All three were specially outfitted for hosteling with kitchenettes and restrooms. Ample lounge space, a "sweat lodge," and laundry facilities are also part of the package. (☎675-2977. 24 beds, $14; nonmembers $18. Tent sites by the river $8. Showers.) **B&Bs ❹** are the way of Salmon Arm; for help finding a cheap one (prices range $45-100), visit or call the visitors center or Chamber of Commerce (see above). Campgrounds in Salmon Arm, especially those on Shuswap Lake, are often crowded and cramped. There are a handful of them on the lake side of Hwy. 1, about 10km west of Salmon Arm. For a much more peaceful stay, take the extra 30min. to drive to **Herald Provincial Park ❶,** 27km northwest of Salmon Arm by following signs off Hwy. 1. The park maintains 119 campsites with a large swimming area and access to dayhiking along Margaret Falls. (Reservations ☎800-689-9025. $18.50 includes firewood, hot showers, and toilets. See **Entertainment and Outdoor Activities,** below.)

FOOD. The best food deal for miles around awaits at the **Real Canadian Wholesale Club,** 360 Hwy. 1. Even the non-bulk items cost less than at a supermarket. (☎804-0258. Open M-F 9am-9pm, Sa 9am-6pm, Su 10am-5pm.) Farther west on Hwy. 1, **De Mille Fruits and Vegetables,** 3710 10th Ave. SW, markets local produce and, in August and September, incredible sweet corn. (☎832-7550. Open June-Sept. daily 8am-8pm; Oct.-May 8am-6:30pm.) To try bannock, a type of bread eaten by natives, stop at the **B&B Bannock Booth ❶.** It is located across the bridge on Squilax-Anglemont Rd., north of the hostel. The Smoked Salmon Bannock ($3) is sure to convert you. Satisfy your sweet tooth at **Wee Willie's Deli ❶,** 160 Lakeshore Dr. They also have freshly baked bread. (☎832-3888. Open M-Sa 7:30am-5:30pm.)

ENTERTAINMENT & OUTDOOR ACTIVITIES. **Caravan Farm Theatre,** 8km northwest of Armstrong and 45min. from Salmon Arm, presents top-notch performances during summer. Tickets are available from the Squilax General Store and Hostel. (☎546-8533. Call for show times. $6-12.) The Farm overflows with remnant hippie charm, and organic produce, and musical instruments dangle from the trees. For an outstanding Native Dance Competition, see the Powwow in July; the visitors center has show times. The mystery of curds is solved in a tour at **Gort's Gouda Cheese Factory,** 1470 50th St. SW. The tour is short and filled with tasty samples. Skip the tour, stock up on bargain cheeses, and watch the cheese-making process through viewing windows, from cow to wax package. (☎832-4274. Tours mid-June to Aug. M-W and F 10am, store M-Sa 9am-5pm.)

The area's outdoors attractions revolve around the waterways that surround town, and range from fishing for kokanee and rainbow trout in Lake Shuswap to taking a 10min. walk through **Herald Park** (see **Accommodations,** above) and viewing the lovely **Margaret Falls.** When doing the latter, be careful to stay on the path; the habitat is recovering from excessive trampling. Closer to town, many trails meander along the nature preserve on the banks of Lake Shuswap, where you can catch a glimpse of the rare Western grebe. Call Shuswap Lakes Tourism Assoc. (☎800-661-4800) for the date of this year's spring **Grebe Festival. Interior Whitewater Expeditions,** in Scotch Creek, leads 2hr. trips on the reasonably gentle (Class II-IV) **Adams River.** (☎800-661-7238. $44, under 16 $34; 15% HI discount.) The paths along the river can be hiked or mountain-biked on an 18km round-trip trail. Take Squilax-Anglemont Rd. north across the bridge, just west of the Squilax General Store, and the trail heads upriver across the first narrow bridge on the road.

OKANAGAN VALLEY

Known throughout Canada for its bountiful fruit harvests, the Okanagan (oh-kuh-NAH-gan) Valley lures visitors with summer blossoms, ample sun, plentiful wineries, and tranquil lakes. The **Okanagan Connector** (Hwy. 97C) links Vancouver to the valley in a 4hr. drive, making the valley a popular vacation destination among sun-starved coastal British Columbians. In the winter, **Big White Ski Resort** and **Apex Mountain** resort attract skiers looking to avoid long lines and pricey lift tickets at Whistler. Travelers looking to earn cash can sign on to pick fruit at one of the many orchards stretching south from Penticton to the US border along Hwy. 97.

KELOWNA ☎250

In the heart of the Okanagan Valley, Kelowna (kuh-LOW-nuh) is one of Canada's richest agricultural regions and a popular tourist destination. Kelowna (pop. 105,000) lies on the east shore of 170km long Okanagan Lake, halfway between Penticton in the south and Vernon in the north. The town's fruit stands, acclaimed wineries, unique blend of chains and independent shops, and sunshine draw thousands of vacationing Vancouverites every summer. And in the winter, those not skiing in Whistler find the slopes of Big White Ski Resort equally rewarding.

TRANSPORTATION

Kelowna lies 400km east of Vancouver, 602km west of Calgary, and 86km north of Penticton on **Hwy. 97** at the eastern shore of Okanagan Lake. Hwy. 97, **Harvey Ave.** in town, runs east-west across the lake and bisects the town. The floating bridge across the lake is one-of-a-kind in Canada.

Buses: Greyhound, 2366 Leckie Rd. (☎860-3835 or 860-2364), off Harvey Ave. next to the Best Western, runs buses to: **Calgary, AB** (10hr., 3 per day, $85); **Hope, BC** (3 hr., 5 per day, $37); **Penticton, OR** (1½hr., 6 per day, $13); and **Vancouver, BC** (6½hr., 6 per day, $58). Ticket office open 7am-7pm M-Su, depot open 7am-1am M-Su.

Public Transportation: Kelowna Regional Transit System (☎860-8121) services town. Runs M-F 6am-10pm, Sa 8am-10pm, Su 9am-5pm. Adults $1.25, students $1; day pass: $3.25, students $3.

Taxis: Kelowna Cabs, 1180 Graham St. (☎762-2222 or 762-4444). $1.60 base, $2.60 1st km., $1.45 per additional km. 24hr.

Car Rental: Rent-A-Wreck, 2787 N Hwy. 97 (☎763-6632) at McCurdy Rd., will supply your means about town. Must have a major credit card. 19+. From $30 per day, $0.12 per km over 100km. Open M-Sa 8am-5pm, Su 9am-4pm.

PRACTICAL INFORMATION

Tourist Office: Visitor Center, 544 Harvey Ave. (☎861-1515). Brochures, bathrooms, and a doggie watering trough. Open in the summer M-F 8am-7pm, Sa-Su 9am-7pm, and in the winter M-F 8am-5pm, Sa-Su 10am-3pm.

Equipment: Sports Rent, 3000 Pandosy St. (☎861-5699). City bikes $18 per day, mountain bikes $22 ($26 with shocks), in-line skates $11, kayaks $30, canoes $35, water skis $20 per day. Open May-Sept. daily 9am-6pm, Oct.-Apr. 9am-8pm.

Laundromat: Cullen's Cleaning Carousel, 2660 Pandosy St. Wash $2, dry $0.25 per 6min. Open M-Th 8:30am-8pm, F 8:30am-7pm, Sa 8:30am-6pm, Su 9am-5pm.

Emergency: ☎911.

Police: 350 Doyle Ave. (☎762-3300).

Hospital: 2268 Pandosy St. (☎862-4000), 7 blocks south of Harvey Ave.

Internet Access: Kelowna Public Library, 1380 Ellis St. (☎762-2800), offers 1hr. of free Internet access. Open M and F-Sa 10am-5:30pm, Tu-Th 10am-9pm; Oct.-May also Su 1-5pm. The **SameSun Hostel** charges $1 for 10min., and **Kelowna International Hostel** offers 30 min. for $2 (both see below.)

Post Office: Town Centre Postal Outlet, 101-591 Bernard St. (☎868-8480). Open M-F 8am-5:30pm, Sa 9am-5:30pm. **Postal Code:** V1Y 7G0.

ACCOMMODATIONS & CAMPING

Warm, dry summer days attract thousands of soggy Vancouverites, so be sure to make reservations (at campgrounds too) or you'll be stuck in a chain hotel 5km out of town.

Kelowna International Hostel (HI), 2343 Pandosy St. (☎763-6024). Only 1 block from the beach in a colorfully painted, restored home, this laid-back hostel is a budget paradise. Kitchen, free pancake and coffee breakfast, laundry ($1.25 wash, $1.25 dry), Internet access ($2 for 30min.), and pick-up from bus station. Reception 7am-11pm, checkout 11am. 30 dorm beds total. $17 with hosteling membership, passport, or student card; nonmembers $20. Private rooms $38, $40. ❶

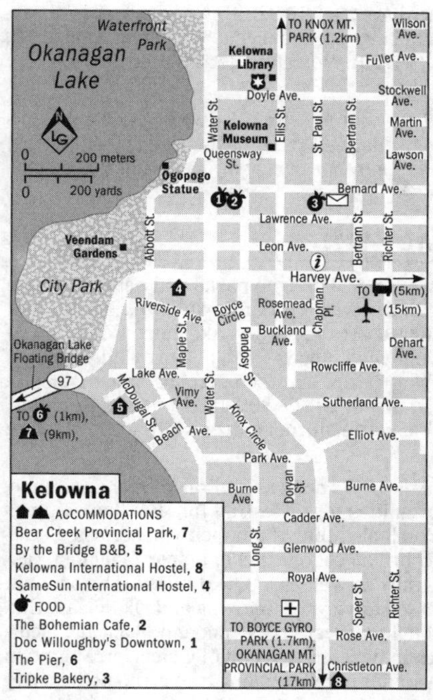

SameSun International Hostel, 245 Harvey Ave. (☎763-9814 or toll-free 1-877-562-2783). Just across the floating bridge, you'll find this brand-new youth hostel featuring keg parties and BBQs ($10 unlimited beer, $5 hamburgers) almost every summer night. For daytime fun, join a bike trip to Kettle Valley ($25, includes bike rental) or spend the day on the SameSun houseboat ($25 afternoon, $40 overnight). Huge kitchen, fresh linens .and laundry facilities. Key deposit $10. Reception 8am-11pm. Call ahead if you'll arrive after-hours. Pickup from bus terminal $5, from airport $10. Dorm beds $20; private rooms $49. ❶

By the Bridge B&B, 1942 McDougall St. (☎860-7518), at the east end of Okanagan Lake Bridge, minutes from the beach and downtown. Cozy rooms, private baths, and a continental breakfast including freshly baked bread, jam, and fruit. Checkout 11am. Singles $49-69; doubles $59-79; triples $79-89; quads $89-99. ❸

Bear Creek Provincial Park (☎1-800-689-9025 or ranger 494-6500), 9km north of Hwy. 97 on Westside Rd. Day use/picnic area and camping. Unique features include shaded lakeside sites, 400m of Okanagan lake shore, boat launch, and an Apple Triathlon in Aug. Lakeside sites go quickly in summer season. Toilets, water, and firewood. 122 sites, $18.50. Campground gate closed 10pm-7am. Free showers. ❶

FOOD

Kelowna overflows with fresh produce. Find juicy delights at the stands outside town along **Benvoulin Rd.** and **KLO Rd.**, or head south on **Lakeshore Dr.** to the u-pick cherry orchards. In town, the shelves groan beneath big carrots and cucumbers at **Safeway,** 697 Bernard Ave. (☎860-0332. Open daily 8am-midnight.) **Bernard Ave.** is lined with restaurants and cafes.

The Bohemian Cafe, 363 Bernard Ave. (☎862-3517). This cafe features delectable food in a comfortable atmosphere right on the main drag. Try the mango-chutney turkey salad ($5.95), homemade bread and soup ($4.75), or huge sandwiches (starting at $5). Open M-F 7:30am-3:30pm, Sa 9am-3pm. ❷

The Pier, Marine Pub, 2035 Campbell Rd. (☎769-4777), just across the floating bridge outside Kelowna. This unassuming joint serves up unbelievable daily specials: Tu 12oz. Sirloin steak ($7.50); Tu, W, Th $0.10 wings; Sa and Su seafood specials (Alaska King Crab $12.99). Nine beers on tap all the time ($3.75 pint). Take your meal outside to the patio for an incredible lake view. Open Su-W 11am-midnight, Th-Sa 11am-1am. ❸

Doc Willoughby's Downtown, 353 Bernard Ave. (☎868-8288). A new pub-style restaurant with live music ranging from Celtic to blues on F-Sa nights. Food starts around $8, W $0.25 wings, F double highballs ($4.95). Hostelers get 20% off. Open M-Su 11:30am-1am. ❷

Tripke Bakery Donditorei & Cafe, 567 Bernard Ave. (☎763-7666). You'll smell this European style bakery from across Lake Okanagan. Grab a loaf of health bread ($2.79) before taking off for an outdoor adventure. Or try one of their myriad pastries (cinnamon buns $0.85). Open M-Sa 8am-5:30pm. ❷

SIGHTS & OUTDOOR ACTIVITIES

The sun is Kelowna's main attraction, warming Okanagan parks and beaches for an average of 2000hr. per year. **City Park,** on the west end of downtown, is a popular hangout for locals and tourists alike. **Boyce Gyro Park,** on Lakeshore Rd. south of the Okanagan Bridge, features beach volleyball. **Sports Rent,** a short walk from the lake, rents camping, boating, and sporting equipment (see **Practical Information,** p. 304). **Kelowna Parasail Adventures,** 1310 Water St. (☎868-4838), at the docks of Grand Okanagan Resort north of City Park, transforms patrons into kites, floating them high above the lake.

HIKING, BIKING, & SKIING. While Kelowna's main attraction is Okanagan Lake, surrounding areas offer excellent opportunities for terrestrial fun. Ponderosa pines dominate this hot and dry landscape. You'll also find bluebunch wheatgrass, bitterroot (a pink flower) and balsamroot (a bright yellow flower). **Knox Mountain,** just north of the city, features many hiking trails as well as a paved road to the summit. Hike, bike, or drive to the top for a spectacular view of Kelowna and Okanagan. Hikers will also find trail opportunities throughout **Bear Creek Park** and **Okanagan Mountain Park.** Bikers head to **Wildhorse Canyon** in the southern end of Okanagan Mountain Park for technically challenging rides. Another popular biking trail is the **Kettle Valley Railbed** (12-41km, 2-8hr.), which passes through scenic Myra Canyon and then through the only desert in Western Canada. To access Myra Canyon from downtown, go east on the K.L.O. Rd. (off Pandosy) to McCulloch Rd., follow McCulloch to June Springs Rd., take June Springs to Little White Forest Service Rd., and follow Little White 4.5km to the parking lot. The railbed through Myra Canyon stretches 12km, but the bike trail continues all the way to Penticton. (Easy to moderate).

In the winter, downhill skiing is the most popular outdoor activity in the Okanagan Valley. **Big White Ski Resort,** on a clearly marked access road off Hwy. 33, east of town, offers over 100 trails throughout 7000 acres of terrain. With two hostels and plenty of cheap eats surrounding the slopes, Big White is a great place for skiers on a budget. (☎765-3101, snow report 765-7669; www.bigwhite.com. Open mid-Nov. to late Apr. Adult day pass $55, youth 13-18 $47. Night-skiing 5-8pm, $16. Multi-day discounts. Ski rental $26; snowboard $35.)

WINE & FRUIT. Over the past few years, the Okanagan valley has become the center of the British Columbian, and therefore Canadian, **wine** industry. Kelowna and the surrounding area is home to 12 of the valley's more than 25 wineries, all of which offer tastings, and many of which have tours. Contact the visitors centers or call ☎868-9463 for a complete list of tours. Wine and cheese parties are common at the **Okanagan Wine Festival** (☎861-6654; www.owfs.com) for 10 days in early October, for four days at its lesser counterpart in late April, and for three days at the new **Ice Wine Festival** in late January. **Mission Hill,** 1730 Mission Hill Rd., on the west bank of Okanagan Lake, is one of Kelowna's most respected local wineries. To get there, cross the bridge west of town, turn left on Boucherie Rd., and follow the signs. The winery overlooks Lake Okanagan. Free tours of a unique underground wine cavern, bell tower, and outdoor amphitheater. (☎768-7611. Open daily 10am-

5pm, July-Sept 10am-7pm. $5 tasting for those over 19.) The posh **Summerhill Estate Winery** lets you taste five sparklers and join a tour to get a peek into an aging replica of the Cheops pyramid. Take Lakeshore Dr. to Chute Lake Rd. (☎800-667-3538. Open daily 9am-6pm; tours every hr. on the hr. 1-4pm. Free.)

Kelowna Land and Orchard, 2930 Dunster Rd., off KLO Rd. on E Kelowna, is the town's oldest family-owned farm, and offers a 45min. hayride and a tour that explains farming techniques and technologies. Indulge in delicious produce at the end of the tour. (☎763-1091. Open May-Oct. daily 8am-5pm; call for winter hours. Tours run 11am, 1 and 3pm; $5.25, students $2, under 12 free.)

PENTICTON ☎250

Indigenous peoples named the region between Okanagan and Skaha Lakes Pen-tak-tin, "a place to stay forever." Today, Penticton (pop. 33,000) is known more commonly as the "Peach City." However, Penticton is more than an agricultural mecca. The city bustles with tourists during the summer months. With endless outdoor adventures and an inviting downtown, one is still tempted to stay forever, although the rise in prices due to the ever-encroaching tourist industry may strain the budget traveler's wallet.

TRANSPORTATION

Penticton lies 395km east of Vancouver at the junction of **Hwy. 3** and **Hwy. 97,** at the southern extreme of the Okanagan Valley. **Okanagan Lake** borders the north end of town, while smaller **Skaha Lake** lies to the south. **Main St.** bisects the city from north to south, turning into **Skaha Lake Rd.** as it approaches Skaha Lake.

Buses: Greyhound, 307 Ellis St. (☎493-4101), runs buses to **Kelowna** (1½hr., 7 per day, $12) and **Vancouver** (6-7hr., 6 per day, $52). Open M-Sa 6am-5pm, Su 7am-5pm.

Public Transportation: Penticton Transit System, 301 E Warren Ave. (☎492-5602), services town. $1.50, students and seniors $1.20; day pass $3.25, $2.75. Runs M-Sa 6:15am-10pm, Su 9am-6pm.

Taxis: Courtesy Taxi (☎492-7778). $2 base, $1.40 per km. 24hr.

Car Rental: Rent-a-Wreck, 130 W Industrial Ave. (☎492-4447), rents cars from $35 per day, then $0.12 per km over 100km. Major credit card required. Open M-Sa 8am-5pm.

PRACTICAL INFORMATION

Tourist Office: Penticton Wine and Information Center, 888 W Westminster Ave. (☎493-4055 or 800-663-5052; www.penticton.org), at Power St. The info center does not, unfortunately, serve wine. Open M-F 8am-8pm, Sa-Su 10am-6pm.

Equipment: Freedom: the Bike Shop, 533 Main St. (☎493-0686). Bikes $30 per day, $20 half day, $5 HI discount. Open M-Sa 9am-5:30pm.

Laundromat: The Laundry Basket, 976 W Eckhardt Ave. (☎493-7899), next to the golf course. Wash $1.50, dry $0.25 per 7min. Open daily 8am-8pm.

Hospital: Penticton Regional, 550 Carmi Ave. (☎492-4000).

Emergency: ☎911.

Police: 1101 Main St. (☎492-4300).

Crisis Line: ☎493-6622. **Women's Shelter:** (☎493-7233). 24hr.

Internet Access: Penticton Public Library, 785 Main St. (☎492-0024), offers free access for 30min. Open in summer M, W, F, and Sa 10am-5:30pm; Tu-Th 10am-9pm; in winter Su 1pm-5pm. **Mousepad Coffee Bar,** 320 Martin St. (☎493-2050), charges $3.50 per ½hr., $6 per hr. Open M-F 6am-10pm, Sa 8am-10pm, Su 8am-8pm.

Post Office: 56 W Industrial Ave. (☎492-5769). Open M-F 8:30am-5pm. **Postal Code:** V2A 6J8.

ACCOMMODATIONS & CAMPING

Penticton is a resort city year-round; cheap beds are few and far between, and it's essential to make reservations in summer. If possible, avoid the expensive yet decrepit hotels that lurk along Skaha Lake Rd., and benefit from the beautiful hostel. Campground sites along Skaha Lake are expensive and often tightly packed. If you're camping, head north to Okanagan Lake Provincial Park for a lakeside site.

Penticton Hostel (HI), 464 Ellis St. (☎492-3992). A large, well-maintained youth hostel with roof-top solar panels for hot water. Join a hostel bike tour ($44, includes bike), wine tour ($32), lake cruise ($10), or simply walk 10min. to the beach. Comfortable lounge, kitchen, TV room with cable, patio, free linen, and laundry facilities ($1 wash, $1 dry). Reception 8am-noon and 5-10pm. $16, nonmembers $20; private singles (without private bath) $36, $40. Ask about multi-day discounts. ❶

Riordan House, 689 Winnipeg St. (☎493-5997), rents lavishly decorated rooms with shared bathrooms in a Penticton heritage home. Scrumptious "Okanagan breakfast" of fresh muffins and fruit cobbler made from local peaches. Free pickup from Greyhound depot. Singles $50; doubles with TV/VCR and fireplace $60-85. ❶

Okanagan Lake Provincial Park, (☎494-6500 or 800-689-9025), 24km north of town on Hwy. 97. 168 sites total on 2 campgrounds (north and south). The north park is more spacious, and the beach is good for swimming. Reservations recommended. Free firewood, and toilets. $19. Free showers. ❶

Executive Inn, 333 Martin St. (☎492-3600). This newly renovated hotel is centrally located downtown just 2 blocks from Lake Okanagan. Indoor pool, fitness center and restaurant. Singles $109; doubles $119. ❺

FOOD

Find your staples at **Safeway,** 801-1301 Main St. (☎487-2103). The **Penticton Farmer's Market** sells local produce and baked goods. (In Gyro Park at the corner of Westminster and Main St. Open June-Oct. Sa 8:30am-noon.) You can also find **fruits and vegetables** at family stands (look for signs on the side of the road) both north and south of town of Hwys. 97 and 3A.

Il Vecchio Delicatessen, 317 Robinson St. (☎492-7610), just across the street from the Greyhound station. Locals, including the mayor, line up daily for delicious sandwiches that are an incredible value. Ask for the "mortadella capicollo," a 2-meat, 2-cheese sandwich for $2.95. Or try the vegetarian sandwich with sun-dried tomatoes and fresh pickles. Homemade soup $1.89. Open M-Sa 8:30am-6pm. ❶

The Dream Cafe, 74 Front St. (☎490-9012), is an organic oasis. Try the gypsy spring salad rolls ($4.95), the mango roasted chicken sandwich ($6.50), or szechuan prawns with rice and roasted veggies ($9.75). Live every week. Open M-Su 9am-10pm (closed M during winter). ❷

SIGHTS & OUTDOOR ACTIVITIES

To check out the history of Penticton's gold trails and the Kettle Valley Railway, head to the **Penticton Museum,** 785 Main St. (☎490-2451. Open M-Sa 10am-5pm.)

In the summer, the Penticton tourist trade revolves around both **Lake Okanagan** and **Lake Skaha.** Youths tend to gravitate toward Skaha Lake Park to the south. Floating down the Okanagan River canal from Lake Okanagan to Lake Skaha is an excellent way to cool down on a hot summer afternoon. **Coyote Cruises,** 215 Riverside, rents tubes for $10 and provides a free shuttle for the return. (☎492-2115.

Open in summer daily 10am-6pm.) **Pier Water Sports,** 45 N Martin St., rents more advanced water vessels for those with an active spirit and a few extra bucks. (☎493-8864. Jet skis $70 per hr., canoes $15 per hr., and kayaks $20 per hr.)

Although the lakes are the star attractions, those looking for land based adventures will not be disappointed. Visit **Munson Mountain,** an extinct volcano, for a bird's eye view of the valley. The mountain also has "PENTICTON" spelled out in letters 50 ft. high and 30 ft. wide. (Take Vancouver Ave. north of town, turn right on Tupper Ave. then left on Middle Bench Rd., to Munson Mt. Rd. The road takes you within minutes of the summit.

Bikers, walkers, and runners will enjoy the **Kettle Valley Railway,** which runs through Penticton. Traveling north, you'll pass through orchards, vineyards, and wineries, all with a fantastic view of Lake Okanagan. To access the KVR from downtown take Vancouver Ave. north to the intersection with Vancouver Pl. Those looking for a day trip from Penticton can travel 21 km at a gradual 2% ascent to Glenfir, or 41 km to Chute Lake. For shuttle service, contact **Vista Treks Tours and Shuttle** (☎496-5220; www.kettlevalleytrail.com).

The **Skaha Bluffs,** southeast of town on Valley View Rd., feature some of Canada's best sport and traditional rock-climbing. For hikers and spectators there are trails throughout the park. Check out *Skaha Rock Climbs*, by Howie Richardson (1997, Elaho Publishing), for detailed information on climbs. **Skaha Rock Adventures** (☎493-1765), 113-437 Martin St., offers guiding and instructional services. A resource for gear and advice is **Ray's Sports Den,** 101-399 Main St. They rent rock climbing shoes for $10, but not harnesses or other climbing equipment. In the winter, you can rent cross-country skis and snow-shoes for $13 per day. (☎493-1216. Open M-F 9:30am-6pm, Sa 9:30am-5pm, Su 10am-4pm.)

If you're visiting Penticton in the winter, **Apex Mountain Resort,** off an access road west of Penticton on Hwy. 3, offers the best downhill **skiing** in the area. Apex has downhill, cross-country, and night skiing (W and F-Sa 4:30-9:30pm) on over 60 runs with a 2000 ft. drop, and a new half pipe and terrain park for boarders. For a $12 round-trip bus ride from Penticton to Apex, contact Tim Horton's Magic Ski Bus (www.apexresort.com/skibus.htm). In the summer, ski slopes transform into a dream-come-true for mountain bikers. (☎292-8222 or 877-777-2739. Adult day pass $46, youth 13-18 $38, child 1-12 $29; night skiing $12. Adult rental equipment $29, youth $16, child $13.)

THE LOCAL STORY

LOCAL LEGEND: LOCH NESS LITE

First reported in 1872, Ogopogo the sea monster is said to have pre-dated the native people' inhabitancy of the Okanagan Lake area. Now affectionately dubbed "Ogie" by the people of Penticton and Kelowna, the monster is a whopping 50 ft. long with the head of either a horse, a bearded goat, or a sheep—discrepancies in the reports preclude certainty—and a worm-like body. Most of the Ogopogo sightings so far have been of several humps a few feet apart sticking out of the water. Between August of 2000 and September of 2001, a search for Ogopogo was conducted, with a prize of $2 million for a verifiable sighting of the monster in Okanagan Lake. To check the results of the hunt, or to join a potentially new race for the booty, head to www.ogopogosearch.com. If you don't become an instant millionaire with a sighting of the *real* Ogopogo, you can still enjoy its image on the signs, sculptures, and blow-up dolls peddled by the good people of the towns of Penticton and Kelowna.

NELSON ☎250

The history of Nelson is sobering, as it depicts the all too familiar disappearance of a native population in the wake of speculation, disease, and the mining industry. But today Nelson is not just another mining development, and tellingly, mining itself has become a very minor industry here. The town of just over 9,000 is a fascinating combination of Canadian culture, Bohemia, and the surrounding beauty of Kootenay Lake and its neighboring mountains. The sport of curling is all the rage for locals, granola devotees eat scrambled tofu for breakfast, and during summer and winter the town is awash with eager hikers and skiers in search of nature at its most extreme. But for all this, Nelson remains a mellow and alternative locale, one with a charm independent of its surrounding natural splendors.

TRANSPORTATION

Nelson lies at the junction of **Hwy. 6** and **3A,** 624km southwest of Calgary, 454km southeast of Kamloops, and 657km east of Vancouver. From Nelson, Hwy. 3A heads 41km west to Castlegar. Hwy. 6 leads 65km south to the US border, where it becomes Washington's Rte. 31 and continues 110 mi. south to Spokane.

Buses: Greyhound, 1112 Lakeside Dr. (☎352-3939), in the Chako-Mika Mall. Terminal open M-F 6am-8:30pm, Sa 6-11am and 4-8:30pm, Su 7:30-8:30am and 4:30-8:30pm. Runs buses to: **Banff, AB** (13½hr. with a 1-5am layover in Cranbrook, 1 per day, $73); **Calgary, AB** (12hr., 2 per day, $83); **Vancouver** (12hr., 2 per day, $94).

Public Transportation: Nelson Transit Systems (☎352-8201) has 5 bus lines that cover the city and lake. Runs M-F 7am-11:30pm, Sa-Su 8:30am-7:30pm. $1-3.

Taxis: Glacier Cabs (☎354-1111). 24hr. $2 base, $2 per km in Nelson.

Car Rental: Rent-a-Wreck, 524 Nelson Ave. (☎352-5122), in the Esso station. 18+. $40 per day, $0.12 per km after 200km.

PRACTICAL INFORMATION

Outdoor information is generally available at the **West Kootenay Visitor Centre** (☎825-4723), in Kokanee Creek Provincial Park, 20km east of Nelson on Hwy. 3A. Recent funding cuts, however, have made the Visitor Centre's hours (and existence) unpredictable. If the West Kootenay Centre is closed, some park information can be obtained from **BC Parks, Kootenay District** at ☎422-4200.

Tourist Office: Visitor Information, 225 Hall St. (☎352-3433; www.discovernelson.com), provides an unusually good map of the city and surrounding area. Open June-Aug. daily 8:30am-8pm; Sept.-Oct. daily 8:30am-5pm; Nov.-May, M-F 8:30am-5pm.

Equipment: The Sacred Ride, 213 Baker St. (☎354-3831), rents front suspension bikes for $35 per day and full-suspension bikes for $55-75. Maps sell for $5, and helpful trail advice is free. Open M-Sa 9am-5:30pm. **Gerick Cycle and Sports,** 702 Baker St. (☎354-4622; www.gericks.com), rents front-suspension bikes for $29 per day, $133 per week, and features cross-country ski packages for $15 per day. Hours vary from season to season and even month to month; call ahead for details.

Laundromat: Found at the **Esso Station,** 524 Nelson St. (☎352-3534). Open Su-F 7am-9:30pm. Wash $2-4, dryers free.

Showers: Nelson City Tourist Park (see below). $2 for non-campers.

Emergency: Dial ☎911.

Police: 606 Stanley St. (☎352-2266). Right next to the library.

Hospital: 3 View St. (☎352-3111). 24hr.

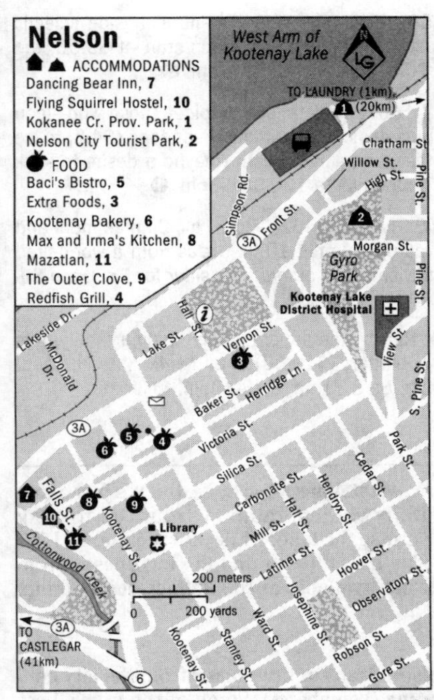

Internet Access: Nelson Library: 602 Stanley St. (☎352-6333). M, W, and F 1-8pm, Tu and Th 10am-6pm, Sa 11am-6pm. $2 per 30min. The **Dancing Bear Inn** (see below) charges $1 per 10min., as does the **Flying Squirrel Hostel** (see below).

Post office: 514 Vernon St. (☎352-3538). Open M-F 8:30am-5pm.

Postal Code: V1L4E0.

ACCOMMODATIONS & CAMPING

Flying Squirrel Hostel, 198 Baker St. (☎352-7285 or 866-755-7433; www.flyingsquirrelhostel.com). Superlatives abound here: younger, hipper, cooler. Catering, and catering well, to the more youthful outdoorsy crowd, this recent addition provides Nelson with a social scene unto itself. With foosball, a full kitchen, laundry, and free pickup from the bus station, they do it all. Internet access $1 per 10 min. Reception 8am-noon and 4-9pm. Checkout by 11am. $17-20, private rooms from $42. ❶

Dancing Bear Inn (HI), 171 Baker St. (☎352-7573 or 877-352-7573). This place just might remind you of grandma's house (don't forget to take off your shoes!) with its cozy, fire-warmed common room, art-decked and book-covered walls, full supply of board games and movies, and bountiful hospitality services. Super-helpful staff. Laundry, kitchen, free parking, and Internet access $1 per 10min. Reception 7-11am and 4-10pm. Reservations recommended June-Aug. Dorm rooms $17, nonmembers $20, under 10 half-price. Private rooms $34-45, nonmembers $40-54. ❶

Kokanee Creek Provincial Park, (☎825-4212; reservations ☎800-689-9025; www.discovercamping.ca). 20km north of town on Hwy. 3A. Shaded, spacious sites with decent privacy are near the lake. Flush toilets, running water. Wheelchair accessible. 166 sites; half for reservations, $25; half first come, first served, $19. ❷

Nelson City Tourist Park, (☎352-9031) on High St., is convenient for camping, backyard-style. Take Vernon St. to its eastern end and follow signs. Flush toilets. Wash $1, dry 50¢ for 30min. 40 sites. $15, power $18, with water $20; showers free. ❶

FOOD & NIGHTLIFE

Basic groceries can be found at **Extra Foods,** 708 Vernon St. (Open M-Sa 9am-9pm, Su 9am-6pm.) Fresh bread, vegan brownies, and organic goodies abound at the **Kootenay Bakery** on 295 Baker St. (☎352-2274. Open M-Sa 7:30am-6pm.)

Baci's Bistro, 445 Baker St. (☎354-0303). Founded and operated by a couple of native Nelson boys, Baci's is sure to appease even the most famished traveler with fresh dishes made entirely from scratch ($8-12). Regardless of why you came to Nelson, you can't leave without trying the Tiramisu ($4.50). Open daily 11am-10pm. ❷

Redfish Grill, 479 Baker St. (☎352-3456), offers an eclectic menu alongside eclectic local artwork. Both are in very good taste. Thai-influenced wraps start at $5.50; the unadventurous can try burgers that run $6-8. Open daily 7am-1am. ❷

The Outer Clove, 536 Stanley St. (☎354-1667). Vegetarians, rejoice! Those who sleep next to them, cringe! This "Garlic Cafe" puts garlic in everything from tapas ($4-8) to ice cream ($2). For those with problems other than garlic breath (maybe a desire to suck blood), the vampire-killer chili is only $7. Open M-Sa 11:30am-9pm. ❶

Max and Irma's Kitchen, 515 Kootenay St. (☎352-2332). More chic than its mom and pop name implies, Max and Irma's serves up gourmet 10 in. pizzas from a wood-fired oven ($10-13), and serves enticing sandwiches like *croque monsieur* for $8. Open Su-Th 11am-9pm, F-Sa 11am-10pm. ❷

Mazatlan, 198 Baker St. (☎352-1388). Run by the super-friendly Medina family, this place offers excellent (the salsa's green!) platters ($10-16) of authentic Mexican food. Tortilla está buena, eh? Open M-F 5-10pm, Sa 3-11pm, Su 3-10pm. ❷

OUTDOOR ACTIVITIES

Bordering Nelson on the north, the watery **West Arm** seems huge, but it's just a tiny segment of enormous **Kootenay Lake.** Dolly varden, rainbow trout (up to 14kg according to local legend), and kokanee cruise the lake, while sturgeon up to 1.5m long inhabit the nearby **Kootenay River.** The best time to find the big ones is from October to February. Licenses and bait are available at the **Balfour Dock,** 30min. north of town on Hwy. 3A.

HIKING

Hiking is plentiful in the hills around Nelson. Maps of brief hikes from the city center can be obtained at the **Dancing Bear Inn** (see above). Some of the area's best hiking can be found in **Kokanee Glacier Provincial Park,** which is generally uncrowded because it's so hard to reach. Various entrances off Hwy. 31 (which heads north off Hwy. 3A east of town) are not regularly maintained; these roads are not for the weak-willed driver or the low-riding vehicle and can be closed well into June. For a complete list of trails, check out *Don't Waste Your Time in the West Kootenays,* a worthwhile trail guide published by Voice in the Wilderness Press and available at most bookstores.

Old-growth Trail (2km, 1-2hr.) begins 12km up the Kokanee Creek Rd 20km out of town on Hwy. 31. Pass the Kokanee Creek campground turnoff on your right; the road is an unmarked, easily missable left turn about 500m further on. Trailhead on the left. Following the **Cedar Grove Loop,** this trail wanders through a cedar forest and offers views of the surrounding mountains and an old mining tramway. Easy.

Gibson Lake to Slocan Chief Cabin Trail (10km round-trip, 3-4hr.) lies another 4m up Kokanee Creek Rd. at the Gibson Lake Trailhead. If you're parking, wrap it with chicken wire to prevent porcupine damage (more info at the West Kootenay Visitor Center). From the trailhead, a 4km trail leads up and across the mountainside to **Kokanee Lake** and continues 3km to the **Kaslo Lake** campground, which consists of 10 sites that have pit toilets and good fishing. Another few kilometers and the path reaches the 12-person **Slocan Chief cabin** below **Kokanee Glacier.** (Campgrounds $5. Cabin $15 per person or $30 for group.) **Do not walk on any glacier without a guide.** Moderate.

Silver Spray Trail (8km, several hours). On Hwy 31, take the Woodbury Creek turnoff 10km north of Ainsworth Hot Springs (a few kilometers beyond Woodbury Creek itself) and drive 13km to the trailhead. This difficult trail passes through several avalanche areas and prime grizzly bear feeding zones en route to the Silver Spray Cabin (wood fireplace, sleeps 4-8) and the circa 1920s Violet mine and blacksmith shop. The views of the glacier are simply unbelievable. Strenuous.

HOT SPRINGS

Several kilometers northeast of Nelson, at 3609 Hwy. 31, the **Ainsworth Hot Springs** are a source of healing for the rheumatic and source of relaxation for everyone else. The water in the main swimming area hovers around body temperature and contains low levels of 10 healthful minerals. A second pool contains water 10 minutes melted from the glacier above (40° F). Jumping from pools of radically different temperatures is rumored to be good for the skin. Watching other swimmers jump from pool to pool is rumored to be wildly funny. The real highlights here are the humid limestone caves, naturally filled with water that reaches 112° F. It's like the batcave, only filled with steam and really hot water. (☎229-4212 or 800-668-1171. Open daily 10am-9:30pm. All day passes $11.)

SKIING

In winter, the soft powder of **Whitewater Ski Resort,** 12km southeast of town off of Hwy. 6, draws skiers and boarders to 32 well-maintained runs, some of Canada's best bowls, and 400m of vertical drop. With an average snowfall of 15m, Whitewater has over 12km of groomed cross-country trails. (☎354-4944 or 800-666-9420, snow report ☎352-7669; www.skiwhitewater.com. Lift tickets $37, ages 13-18 $28, ages 7-12 $21, under 7 free. Full package ski or snowboard rentals $25 per day.)

VALHALLA PROVINCIAL PARK ☎250

Valhalla stretches up from the enchantingly turquoise and trout-filled waters of Slocan Lake, then continues through a lush and temperate rain forest before arriving at a curtain of craggy alpine peaks. Once a homeland to the Sa-al-tkw't Indians, who left pictographs on the bluffs above the lake, the park has now been largely given over to feral pikas, mountain goats, and bears. Residents of nearby New Denver fought for countless years to have this treasure declared a park protected from logging interests before finally achieving success in 1983. Much of the park is accessible only by boat; the only roads to the park leave from the miniscule town of Slocan. Twenty-two separate camping areas, many with bear caches and pit toilets, are spread throughout the park. Motorists and cyclists beware—no mechanized vehicles of any kind, including mountain bikes, are allowed. Dogs must be leashed and are only allowed in certain areas of the park; fires also are allowed only in designated areas and must be made with driftwood from the beaches. Many trails require expert-level route-finding skills; others allow for a less strenuous journey through the amazing scenery. With cars, jet skis, and snowmobiles prohibited for miles, this is truly a place where the valiantly slain Norseman (or the odd traveler) can rest in peace.

ORIENTATION & PRACTICAL INFORMATION

Valhalla lies on the west shore of Slocan Lake, 150km south of Revelstoke and 286km east of Kelowna. In the south, a bridge from **Slocan** provides access to southern trailheads, most at the end of long and bumpy forest roads. In the north, the town of **New Denver** provides food and shelter to weary wanderers as well as water access to the northern trailheads. The towns are linked by Hwy. 6, which runs north from Nelson. Back in the 1940s, New Denver was one of many Japanese internment camps set up by the Canadian government during WWII. The **Nikkei Internment Memorial Center,** at 306 Josephine St. just off 3rd Ave., has exhibits on the living conditions and culture of the nearly 20,000 interned Japanese-Canadians. (☎358-7288. Open May-Sept. daily 9:30am-5pm. $4, students and seniors $3.)

Without a designated visitor's center, the best information about New Denver comes from the townspeople themselves. Many shops carry brochures on the area, but nothing seems to trump good old local know-how. For **outdoor info,** visit the folks who led the crusade to preserve Valhalla as a national park, the **Valhalla Nature Center/Valhalla Wilderness Society,** 307 6th Ave., in the building that says Valhalla Trading Post (☎358-2333. Open M-F 10am-5pm, Sa 11am-3pm.) If the office appears closed, knock anyway; someone working late may answer and provide you with their invaluable park trail guide ($4). To get to the park from New Denver, rent a kayak at **Sweet Dreams Guesthouse** ($40 per day, $25 for half day, or $180 per week; see **Accommodations,** below) or ask around about the local water taxi service. There is no 911 service for this area (which includes Valhalla park and New Denver). For emergencies call the **police:** 407 Slocan Ave. (☎358-2222), south of 6th St. **Post office:** 219 6th Ave. (☎358-2611. Open M-F 9am-5pm, Sa noon-4pm.) **Postal Code:** V0G 1S0.

ACCOMMODATIONS & FOOD

Those who don't wish to camp in the park can stay in luxury at the **Sweet Dreams Guesthouse ❸,** 702 Eldorado Ave. Take 6th Ave. toward the lake and turn left on Eldorado Ave. This B&B is located in a cozy country home with a beautiful view of the lake (Room 4 is famous for its view). Three-course dinners are available by reservation and run about $20. (☎358-2415. Singles $45-55, doubles $70-85, triples $85. Multiple-day rates are often available.) Another lodging option is the **Valhalla Inn ❷,** on Hwy. 6 in town, which offers spare but spacious and spotless motel rooms, as well as a restaurant (entrees run $6-15) and a pub with $4 pints. (☎358-2228. Singles $55, doubles $60, can accommodate up to seven in one room with an initial price of $70 for 2 people, $10 for each additional person.) Convenient but unaesthetic (aside from the view) camping is available at the **municipal campground ❷** at Centennial Park, on the south side of town by the lakeshore between 3rd and 1st Ave. Forty small sites, most filled with RV toting boaters, cluster around showers and a boat launch. (Tents $13, on the water $14, electricity and water $16.) **Valhalla Park ❶** itself is filled with free backcountry sites.

Basic supermarket goods can be found at **Eldorado Market,** 402 6th Ave. (☎358-2443. Open M-Sa 9am-6pm, Su 10am-5pm.) **Ann's Natural Foods,** 805 Kildare St., has a small selection of natural food products. (☎358-2552. Open M-Sa 9am-5:30pm.) Meals abound on 6th Ave., where you can find the renowned **Appletree Cafe ❶,** 210 6th Ave. The tiny cafe is home to a colorful local crowd promising, and honoring its promise of, "up to the minute gossip" and other essential small-town services including homemade soups ($3.50), and build-your-own $6-8 sandwiches. (☎358-2691. Open M-F 7am-4pm, Sa 11am-4pm.)

HIKING

Explorers of Valhalla's outdoor paradise must take a few important precautions. First off, Slocan Lake, while usually placid and eerily mirror-like, occasionally bears the brunt of winds funneled down the valley. Talk to locals about weather conditions and be sure to learn about "the black line" (talk about eerie). The temperate rain forest of Valhalla is often very wet, and hypothermia is a real concern, even in the summer. Extra layers of warm clothing are a good idea. Additional safety gear is always recommended when camping, and a whistle is particularly handy in Valhalla because it can be heard across the lake. Be aware of the possibility of bear encounters. Most camping areas provide bear-proof food caches, but if none are available, bear-bagging supplies are necessary. Finally, remember that forest roads may be impassable as late as June due to winter-like weather conditions. One popular activity, which arose in response to this problem, is kayaking along the lake's shore and camping near the beach.

Bannock Burn to Gimli Ridge (4km, 2-3hr.). Turn off Hwy. 6 at Slocan City, cross the river, and follow the gravel road 13km south. Turn right onto Bannock Burn Creek logging road and follow it to the parking lot. It is an unsurpassed hike with opportunities for world-class **rock climbing.** Camping is available along the trail. Moderate to strenuous.

Sharp Creek to New Denver Glacier (8.8km, day-long). The trail begins along the west shore of Slocan Lake, directly across from New Denver, and is accessible only by boat. A very steep climb through several hanging valleys of lush moss, monumental cascades, and old-growth forest. There's a campground about half way up and stunning views of the glacier and surrounding area from the top. Strenuous.

Evan's Creek Trail (8km, 2-3hr.). Park on the Slocan City side of the Slocan River bridge, walk across, then turn right to walk 200m to the trailhead. The trail passes along the lakeshore and past moss-carpeted waterfalls. A cabin and tent pads are available at the creek, and ample fishing awaits at Cahill and Beatrice Lakes. Easy to moderate.

OTHER ACTIVITIES

Newly constructed trails have made biking an increasingly common and popular activity. Pathways have been carved from old rail beds 50km in the direction of Nakusp to the north, and 50km to Kaslo to the east. Fairly flat, these trails offer a relaxing, leisurely, and quiet way to see the West Kootenays. Bike rental is a fairly informal affair usually run from someone's back porch. Ask locally for a map of the trails and rental information; **Sweet Dreams Guest House** (see above) is a good place to start. Kayaking, though often seen as a means of transportation by locals, is a perfect Slocan Lake recreation unto itself. Countless inlets are well worth exploration, filled with loons, wrecked ships, and pictographs. Winter sports are also available in the area. Cross-country skiing is the primary activity, but snowmobiling has also become popular.

FERNIE ☎250

Those willing to go the extra kilometer will be rewarded with the best snow around. A magnet for mountain bikers and snowboarders, Fernie combines the familiarity of small-town life with the commercialism of franchised strip malls, plus the breadth of outdoor activities found in Jasper and Banff. While not as familiar as Banff or Whistler, Fernie has begun to attract the attention of travel guides and snow-lovers alike. During the summer, Fernie offers everything you would expect from a city set in the Rockies: gorgeous hiking, superior mountain biking, and world-class trout fishing. Add to these a range of excellent, cheap hostels, and you have a locale that's destined for discovery.

ORIENTATION & PRACTICAL INFORMATION. Fernie is located on Hwy. 3, 1hr. east of Cranbrook and 3½hr. southwest of Calgary. Local services cluster along Hwy. 3 and in downtown Fernie, 5km north of the ski resort. The **Visitors Center,** with free pamphlets and a few free books, is set beneath a wooden oil rig 1km east of town on Hwy. 3. (☎423-6868. Open winter M-F 9am-5pm, summer daily 9am-7pm.) **Greyhound,** 742 Hwy. 3 (☎423-6871) in the Park Place Lodge, runs two buses per day to **Calgary** (6½hr.; $47, students $42) and **Vancouver** (18hr.; $100, students $90). **Kootenay Taxi** (☎423-4408) runs 24hr. and ferries powder-heads to the slopes in winter ($10 one-way). In an **emergency,** call ☎911 or contact the **police,** at 496 13th St. (☎423-4404). The **Fernie District Hospital** is at 1501 5th Ave. (☎423-4453). **Fernie Library,** 492 3rd Ave., offers **Internet access** for $5 per hr. (☎423-4458. Open T-Th 11am-8pm, Sa noon-5pm.) **Raging Elk Hostel** has access for $2 per 20 min. **Ski and See Adventure Lodge** offers free Internet access to guests. The **post office** is at 491 3rd Ave. (☎423-7555. Open M-F 8:30am-5pm.) **Postal Code:** V0B 1M0.

COAL-HEARTED ROMANCE Local Fernie legend holds that town founding father William Fernie had the hots for a local native princess. Being something of a shallow man, his interest was focused below her head—specifically, on the black stone in her necklace. When he finally discovered the valuable local coal deposits (the source of the necklace), he abandoned the woman. In retribution, a local medicine man placed a curse upon the entire valley. Two massive fires, a devastating flood, and a mining disaster later (all in the course of thirteen years), the curse seemed real enough. To exorcise the demons, local tribes were finally gathered in 1964. They lifted the hex, sharing a symbolic peace pipe with the mayor of the town. However, as tour guides are very ready to point out, on Mt. Hosmer, a peak to the west of town, afternoon shadows create the remarkably distinct image of a horse with two riders—the princess and her father still remind the residents of Fernie of the pain their ancestor caused.

ACCOMMODATIONS & FOOD. **Ski and See Adventure Lodge ❶,** 301 2nd Ave. above the Grand Central Hotel, is the latest addition to the Fernie travel scene. This new European-style hotel offers shared and private rooms, comfortable common areas, and a huge outdoor patio with a hot tub. (☎423-7367. In winter shared rooms $30, private rooms $60; in summer $19/30.) The **Raging Elk Hostel (HI) ❶,** 892 6th Ave., is a converted motel offering both dorm-style lodging and private rooms with a healthy dose of ski culture on the side. In addition to the cozy living quarters, it boasts private baths, a large common area, a kitchen, laundry, Internet access, and a free pancake breakfast. Reservations are crucial during the December to April ski season. (☎423-6811. Reception daily 8-11am and 5-11pm. In winter $18, private bath $22; in summer $15, nonmembers $18.) **Mount Fernie Provincial Park ❶** (☎422-4200), 3km south of town on Hwy. 3, offers 38 private and shaded sites as well as flush toilets and water for $12.

BRITISH COLUMBIA

Find groceries at **Overwaitea Foods** on 2nd Ave. (☎423-4607. Open Sa-Th 8am-8pm, F 8am-9pm.) **The Curry Bowl ❷,** 931 7th Ave., offers "enlightened Asian cuisine" like curry ($8-12) and large bowls of noodles for $5. (☎423-2695. Open Tu-F 5-11pm, Sa-Su 4-11pm.) **The Arts Station ❷,** 1st Ave. and 6th St., is a former train depot that now acts as a staging point for local artists; it also serves homemade soups ($3) and $7.50 sandwiches. (☎423-4842. Open daily 7am-2pm except W.) **Mug Shots Bistro ❷,** 592 3rd Ave., is a small cafe offering Internet access alongside its blueberry pancakes ($4.50), homemade (but homely) sandwiches ($5.50-8), and $8 bag lunches. (☎423-8018. Open daily 7am-4pm.) Unwind after snowboarding at **The Grand Central Hotel ❶,** 301 2nd Ave., with $4 pints, and on Monday nights, $0.15 wings. (☎423-3343. Open M-Sa noon-2am, Su noon-midnight.)

SKIING. The engine driving Fernie's expansion is the **Fernie Alpine Resort** and its 2500+ acres of feathery powder. With a 875cm/29 ft. annual snowfall, the Fernie Alpine Resort embarrasses the competition. Over 100 trails spread out across the Lizard Range, creating a winter wonderland of gullies, ravines, five alpine bowls, a terrain park, a vertical-drop, and tree-skiing. (☎423-4655, snow report 423-3555; www.skifernie.com. $56; students 18-24, ages 13-17 or 65+ $45; ages 6-12 $15.) **Fernie Sports,** 1191 7th Ave., on Hwy. 3, offers **ski and snowboard rental** packages for $22 and $25. (☎423-3611; www.ferniesports.com. Open in winter daily 8:30am-7pm; summer M-F 10am-6pm.)

OUTDOOR ACTIVITIES. The April thaw, while heralding the end of ski season, also uncovers Fernie's abundant hiking trails. Many trails leave from the Alpine Resort, where free maps are provided. The **Fernie Ridge Walk** (11 mi., at least 8hr.) begins in the parking lot of the ski resort and offers spectacular views of alpine meadows and jagged limestone peaks before returning to the valley floor. Cheaters can take the lift part way up the mountain in the summer ($8, bikes $3), but won't avoid the steep **Snake Ridge** or a 15m/50 ft. fixed-rope climb. (1000m/3300ft. gain. Strenuous.) Fernie and the mountain resort offer various trails. **The Guides Hut,** 671 2nd Ave., is happy to recommend equipment and trails, and rent front-suspension bikes. (☎423-3650 or 888-843-4885. Open in summer M-Sa 9:30am-6pm, Su noon-5pm; call for winter hours. $25 per day, $130 per week.) The **Bike Base,** 432 2nd Ave., and neighboring **Ski Base** rent trade-ins at great prices. (☎423-6464. Full-suspension $40 per day. Open Sa-Th 9:30am-5:30pm, F 9:30am-8pm.) The Elk river and its tributaries provide 180km of world-class **fly-fishing** for bulltrout and cut-throat. Follow the crowd and fish along Hwy. 3, or head off the beaten path and farther along the river. A good start, the **Kootenay Fly Shop and Guiding Company,** 821 7th Ave., rents rods for $20 per day and sells maps and books for $10-17. (☎423-4483. Open M-Sa 9am-5:30pm; July-Aug. also open Su.)

REVELSTOKE ☎250

In the 19th century, Revelstoke was a town straight out of an old west movie, complete with dust-encrusted misers maiming one another amid the gold-laden Selkirk and Kootenay Mountains. Located on both the Columbia River and the Canadian Pacific Railway, the town was born as a transfer station for boats and trains. Although still a stopover for travelers to the Rockies, Revelstoke is finally coming into its own. The first sign of excellent outdoor opportunities is that the town is empty during the day. Revelstoke's uniquely laid-back social life complements the physical rigors of the area. Excellent hostels, free and suprisingly lively outdoor entertainment in the town center, and extensive outdoor pursuits make Revelstoke a particularly welcoming destination.

ORIENTATION & PRACTICAL INFORMATION

Revelstoke is on the **Trans-Canada Hwy.** (Hwy. 1), 285km west of Banff, 210km east of Kamloops, and 565km east of Vancouver. The town is easily navigated on foot or by bike, as evidenced by the lack of traffic and abundance of parking spaces downtown. **Mount Revelstoke National Park** lies just out of town on Hwy. 1.

Buses: Greyhounds depart from 1899 Fraser Dr. (☎837-5874). To get there, turn away from the city center at the traffic lights on Hwy. 1 and take your 1st left. Open M-Sa 8am-7pm, Su 11am-1pm and 3-5pm. To **Calgary, AB** (6hr., 4 per day, $57); **Salmon Arm, BC** (1½hr., 5 per day, $17); and **Vancouver** (8-10hr., 5 per day, $69).

Taxi: ☎837-4000.

Visitors Info: Visitors Centre (☎837-3522; www.revelstokecc.bc.ca), located at junction of Hwy. 1 and Hwy. 23 N. Open daily July-Aug. 9am-6pm; May-June 9am-5pm. An additional, smaller information center is located at 204 Campbell Ave. in central Revelstoke (☎837-5345; open M-Sa 9am-5pm). **Parks Canada** (☎837-7500), at Boyle Ave. and 3rd St. Open M-F 8:30am-noon and 1-4:30pm.

Bike Rental: High Country Cycle and Sports, 118 Mackenzie Ave. (☎814-0090; fax 814-0091). $7-8 per hr., $35-40 per day. Open 9:30am-5:30pm.

BRITISH COLUMBIA

Laundry: Family Laundry, 409 1st St. W (☎837-3938), just behind the Samesun Hostel. $1.50 for single load wash, $4 for massive loads, dry $0.25 per 5min. Open M-Sa 8am-7pm, Su 9am-5pm.

Emergency: ☎911.

Police: 320 Wilson St. (☎837-5255).

Ambulance: ☎837-5885.

Hospital: Queen Victoria Hospital, 6622 Newlands Rd. (☎837-2131).

Internet Access: Free at the **library,** 600 Campbell Ave. (☎837-5095; open Tu and F 1-8pm, W and Sa 10am-4pm, Th 1-5pm). Also at **Woolsey Creek Cafe** (p. 319) and **Bertz Outdoor Equipment and Cafe** (p. 319).

Post Office: 307 W 3rd St. (☎837-3228). Open M-F 8:30am-5pm.

Postal Code: V0E 2S0.

ACCOMMODATIONS & CAMPING

Samesun Hostels Revelstoke, 400 2nd St. W (☎877-562-2783). The friendly staff successfully walks the fine line between providing a youthful hostel scene and offering decent private rooms to an older crowd. Several kitchens, full bathrooms, living room with TV, and a constant mellow soundtrack. Internet $1 for 10 min. Deals with some local restaurants and the Powder Springs Resort. 24hr. check-in. Dorms $20; singles $43, winter $39; groups of 6+ $18 per person. ❶

Daniel's Guest House, 313 1st St. E (☎837-5530), a 2min. walk from downtown. A home-turned-hostel, the comfortable beds, couch-filled common room, and porch make the place feel, well, homey. Kitchen, laundry ($1.50), satellite TV, 2 bathrooms, and pick-up from the bus station. 24hr. check-in. 20 beds in single-sex 6-person dorms and private rooms. Dorms $17; doubles $34; private rooms $30. HI discount; kids free. ❶

Williamson's Lake Campground, 1818 Williamson Lake Rd. (☎837-5512 or 888-676-2267), 5km southeast of town on Airport Way. Farther from the highway than competitors, it is next to a peaceful and popular swimming hole. Laundry and general store. Closed Nov. to mid-Apr. 41 sites, $14.50; 20 full RV sites, $18. Free showers. ❶

FOOD

The town's local market is **Cooper's Supermarket,** 555 Victoria St. (☎837-4372. Open daily 8am-9pm. On the east side of town lies **Southside Grocery,** 900 4th St. (☎837-3517. Open daily 9am-9pm.)

Luna Taverna, 102 2nd St. E (837-2499). Titanic helpings of Greek and Mediterranean fare. Meals like souvlaki dish up far more deliciously tender meat than the average mortal can handle. Appetizers run $4-8, full meals $11-16. Staying at Samesun Hostel earns free cheesecake. Open Tu-Sa 11am-2pm and 5pm-10pm; Su-M 5pm-10pm. ❷

Woolsey Creek Cafe, 212 Mackenzie Ave. (837-5500), offers three solid meals a day in a relaxed, toy-strewn atmosphere. Internet access $1 for 10min. Breakfast runs $1.50-9, lunch $3.50-8.50, dinner $6-15. Open Tu-Su 8am-10pm, but schedule varies. ❷

Chalet Deli and Bakery, 555 Victoria St. (☎837-5552), across the parking lot from Cooper's. The complete package for lunch and baked goods. Offers a hot deli, pizza by the slice ($2.50), and sandwiches on fresh bread ($4.50). Open M-Sa 6am-6pm. ❶

The Ol' Frontier Family Restaurant, 122 N Hwy. 23 (☎873-5119), at Hwy. 1 and 23 N, next to the visitors center. Serves ¼ lb. burger with the works and the "Ain't No Bull" mushroom-and-peppers veggie burger, each for $6. Open daily 5am-10pm. ❶

Bertz Outdoor Equipment and Cafe, 217 Mackenzie Ave. (☎837-6575), will supply you with food, outdoor equipment, and advice on local climbing and mountaineering. Large bagel sandwiches ($4.50). Internet access $4 for 30min., $7 per hr. Open in summer M-F 8am-5pm, Sa 9am-4pm, Su 10am-4pm; winter M-F 8am-5pm. ❶

SIGHTS & ENTERTAINMENT

Revelstoke Railway Museum, 719 W Track St. off Victoria Rd., tells of the construction of the Trans-Canada line, which was completed in 1885. Other exhibits include a real steam engine and a full passenger car. (☎877-837-6060; www.railwaymuseum.com. Open July-Aug. daily 9am-8pm; May-June and Sept. daily 9am-5pm; April and Oct. M-Sa 9am-5pm; Nov. M-F 9am-5pm; Dec.-Mar. M-F 1pm-5pm. $6, 60+ $5, ages 7-16 $3, under 7 free, family $13.) The quite interesting mechanical marvels of the **Revelstoke Dam,** 5km north of Hwy. 1 on Hwy. 23, along with the latest in utility company propaganda, are illustrated in a free talking-wand tour. Wheelchair accessible. (☎837-6515. Open May to mid-June and mid-Sept. to mid-Oct. daily 9am-5pm; mid-June to mid-Sept. 8am-8pm.) The town also boasts a **blues festival** in late June, a lumberjack competition in early July, and a railroad festival in August. Call the visitors center for dates. Also, from late June through August, the town's main square rings with quality bands from a cappella to ska. Weeknight shows tend to be more family oriented, while weekends rock a little harder.

OUTDOOR ACTIVITIES

SUMMER ACTIVITIES. Canyon Hot Springs, between Mt. Revelstoke National Park and Glacier National Park on Hwy. 1, sports two spring-fed pools that simmer at 26°C and 40°C. (☎837-2420. May-June and Sept. 9am-9pm; July and Aug. 9am-10pm. $6.50, seniors and under 14 $5.50, under 4 free.) The neighboring **Apex River** runs 2hr. and 4hr. whitewater rafting tours on the Illecillewaet's Class II-III rapids. (☎837-6376 or 888-232-6666. $69, under 17 $59.) A more relaxing aquatic experience can be found with **Revelstoke Kayaking Adventures.** (☎866-405-2925; www.revelstokekayaking.com. Open daily June-Sept. 9am-6pm. Double and single kayak rentals are available, as are half-day and weekend tours.) **Grizzly Country Tours** (☎837-3020 or 837-3010; reservations taken dawn to dusk) can take fisherfolk out on the Columbia to raft for various rates depending on numbers. The 140 bolted routes on Begbie Bluffs offer exceptional **sport climbing** (from the small parking area almost 9km down 23 South from Hwy. 1, the bluffs are a 10min. walk; take the left fork). Rogers Pass and the surrounding peaks offer a lifetime of year-round opportunity to hone one's **mountaineering** skills.

WINTER SPORTS. Winter in Revelstoke brings excellent **downhill skiing. Powder Springs Resort** (☎800-991-4455; www.catpowder.com) is only 5km outside town and maintains one chairlift and 21 trails (2000 ft. vertical drop) on the bottom third of Mt. MacKenzie. Tickets cost $28-32, but inquire about money-saving accommodation packages (see **Samesun Hostels Revelstoke,** p. 318). Local companies offer heli-skiing and cat-skiing on the upper two-thirds of this and other local mountains. Ask at the visitors center (see **Practical Information,** p. 317) for more information on where the cheapest equipment rentals can be found. Parks Canada offers excellent advice and brochures on area nordic trails and world-class backcountry skiing. They also provide information and brochures on area snowmobiling.

MT. REVELSTOKE NATIONAL PARK. Adjacent to town, Mt. Revelstoke National Park furnishes a quick and satisfying nature fix with its astounding scenery. It is a favorite of mountain bikers and hikers. **Summit Cycle Tours** drives customers to the summit of Mt. Revelstoke and provides bicycles and a guided tour on the 2hr., 27km descent. (☎888-700-3444; www.summitcycle.com. $54, under

16 $49; group discounts.) The park is too tiny to offer extensive backcountry opportunities, but does boast two **backcountry campgrounds** (permit $6); get details from the **Revelstoke Parks Canada** office or the **Rogers Pass** visitors center. For hiking, two boardwalks off Hwy. 1 on the east side of the park access the trails. **Skunk Cabbage Trail** (1.2km, 30min.) leads through acres of stinking perfection: skunk cabbage plants tower at heights of over 1.5m. **Giant Cedars Trail** (500m, 15min.) has majestic trees over 600 years old growing around babbling brooks. **Meadows in the Sky Parkway** (Summit Rd.) branches off Hwy. 1 about 1.5km east of town, leading to a 1km hike up Mt. Revelstoke to subalpine meadows. A wheelchair-accessible shuttle is available (summer only, 10am-4:20pm). The **Summit Trail** (10km one-way, full day) leaves from the trailer drop-off parking lot at the base of Summit Rd. and climbs steadily to the summit of Mt. Revelstoke, where the weary traveler will be joined by everyone who drove up. **Jade Lake Trail** (9km one-way, full day) cuts up from the Heather Lake parking lot on Summit Rd. to the parks most photographed, most jade-colored lakes.

GLACIER NATIONAL PARK ☎250

This aptly named national park is home to over 400 monolithic ice floes that cover one-tenth of its 1350 sq. km. area. The jagged peaks and steep, narrow valleys of the Columbia Range not only make for breathtaking scenery but also prevent development in the park. An inland rain (although it feels more like snow) forest, Glacier receives significant precipitation every other day in the summer, but the clouds of mist that encircle the peaks and blanket the valleys only add to the park's astonishing beauty. In late summer, brilliant explosions of mountain wildflowers offset the deep green of the forests. In the winter, brilliant explosions of Howitzer shells shake the calm of the valleys. Glacier is Canada's prime avalanche research and prevention area; scientists fire 105mm shells into mountain sides to create and observe controlled avalanches. This makes winter travel dangerous for multiple reasons, and consultation with park rangers is necessary. Roger's Pass, the park's main tourist attraction, has quite a history itself, as it was the last great obstacle of nature overcome by the Canadian Pacific Railroad in 1882.

ORIENTATION & PRACTICAL INFORMATION

Glacier is 350km west of Calgary and 723km east of Vancouver. **Greyhound buses** make one trip from Revelstoke. (☎837-5874. 1hr., $14.70.) For details on the park, including great trail suggestions, talk to the Parks Canada staff or buy a copy of *Footloose in the Columbias* ($2) at the **Roger's Pass Information Center,** on the highway in Glacier. (☎814-5232. Daily **park passes** cost $4, ages 65+ $3, 6-16 $2, group of 2-7 $10. Open daily Dec.-Mar. 7am-5pm, Apr. to mid-June, Sept.-Oct. 9am-5pm; mid-June to Aug. 8am-7pm; during Nov. Th-M 9am-5pm.) For more info, write to the Superintendent, P.O. Box 350, Revelstoke, BC V0E 2S0, or call ☎837-7500. In an **emergency,** call the **Park Warden Office.** (☎837-7500. Open daily 7am-5pm; winter hours vary; 24hr. during avalanche control periods.)

CAMPING

Glacier has 2 frontcountry campgrounds: **Illecillewaet** ❶ (ill-uh-SILL-uh-way-et), 3½km west of Roger's Pass (wheelchair accessible, 60 sites open mid-June to early Oct.), and **Loop Brook** ❶, another 3km west on Hwy. 1 (20 sites, open July-Sept.). Both offer toilets, kitchen shelters with cook stoves, and firewood. (Sites at both $14.) Backcountry campers must purchase a **backcountry pass** ($6 per day) from the Parks Canada office in Revelstoke (☎837-7500) or from the Rogers Pass Information Center. Food is limited; stock up in **Golden** or **Revelstoke.**

OUTDOOR ACTIVITIES

HIKING

More than 140km of rough, often steep trails lead from the highway, inviting mountaineers to conquer the unconquerable. While the highway works its way through the park's lush valleys, a majority of the area in the parkland lies above the treeline, providing for incredible high altitude, highly aesthetic hikes.

Meeting of the Waters Trail (2km one-way). A gentle hike that leads to the impressive confluence of the Illecillewaet and Asulkan Rivers. Easy.

Avalanche Crest Trail (8½ km round-trip, 6hr.) offers spectacular views of Roger's Pass, Hermit Range, and Illecillewaet River Valley. The treeless slopes below the crest attest to the destructive power of winter snowslides and endanger the highway. Moderate.

Balu Pass Trail (10km round-trip, 4hr.). Trailhead is at the west edge of Rogers Centre parking lot, near Roger's Pass info station. The Ursus Major and Ursus Minor peaks provide the best chance of seeing wildlife. (*Balu* is Inuit for bear, while *Ursus* is Latin for it.) This trail is prime bear habitat; check with park wardens before embarking. Difficult.

Copperstain Trail (16km, 6hr.). Beaver River Trailhead, 10km east of the Glacier Park Lodge uphill through alpine meadows. From early July to late August, the park staff run sporadic interpretive hikes at 8:30am. Contact the visitors center for details. Moderate.

Illecillewaet Trails (varies, 1km-6.5km one-way). A plethora of trails leave from the campground (see **Camping,** above) and climb to the retreating Illecillewaet and Asulkan Glaciers. Dramatic views of the valley behind and opportunities to extend the hikes to the toes of the glaciers make these trails well worth the rigorous climbs. Difficult.

OTHER ACTIVITIES

Biking and **fishing** in Glacier are prohibited. **Backcountry skiing** at Roger's Pass and Balu Pass is legendary. Contact the Roger's Pass Information Center for registration and info on areas and avalanche conditions. Glacier also boasts the **Nakimu Caves,** located off the Balu Pass Trail near the info center, an extensive limestone wonderland open only to experienced cavers. Access to the caves is granted a couple times per summer, depending on conditions, to groups led by a park officer; interested parties need to apply to the park superintendent (see **Orientation and Practical Info,** above) by early summer or hope for an empty spot at the last minute (not recommended).

YOHO NATIONAL PARK ☎250

A Cree expression for awe and wonder, Yoho is the perfect name for this small, superlative-laden park. It sports some of the most engaging names in the Rockies, such as Kicking Horse Pass, named after Captain John Hector who, struggling to find a mountain pass for the Canadian Pacific Railroad, was kicked in the chest by his horse. Driving down Yoho's narrow pass on Hwy. 1, visitors can see evidence of geological forces: massive bent and tilted sedimentary rock layers exposed in sharply eroded cliff faces, and natural rock bridges formed by water that has carved away the stone. Beneath these rock walls, Yoho overflows with natural attractions, including the largest waterfall in the Rockies—Takakkaw Falls—and paleontolologically illuminating 500 million-year-old fossils.

ORIENTATION & PRACTICAL INFORMATION

The park lies on the Trans-Canada Hwy. (Hwy. 1), next to Banff National Park. Within Yoho, the town of **Field** is 27km west of Lake Louise on Hwy. 1. **Greyhound** (☎800-661-8747) stops for travelers waving their arms on the highway at the Field junction as long as they call first. **Hostelling International** runs a shuttle connecting hostels in Yoho, Banff, and Jasper National Parks and Calgary ($8-65). The **Visitors Centre** in Field is on Hwy. 1. (☎343-6783. Open in summer daily 8am-7pm; spring and fall 9am-5pm; winter 9am-4pm.) Other services include **bike rentals** (see **Equipment Rental** for Banff) and **park pass** sales ($6, senior $4.50, child $3, groups $12. Valid for Glacier and Revelstoke.) In case of **emergency,** call ☎911 in the Field area; the **Park Warden Office** (☎343-6142, 24hr.; ☎762-1473 for non-emergencies); or the **RCMP** (☎344-2221) in nearby Golden. The **post office** is at 312 Stephen Ave. (☎343-6365. Open M-F 8:30am-4:30pm.) **Postal Code:** V0A 1G0.

ACCOMMODATIONS & CAMPING

With one of the best locations of all the Rocky Mountain hostels, the **Whiskey Jack Hostel (HI) ❶,** 13km off the Trans-Canada on the Yoho Valley Rd., perfectly blurs the line between civilization and nature. Located in one of Canada's most scenic spots, the hostel offers a kitchen, campfires, plumbing, propane light, easy access to Yoho's best high-country trails, and the splendor of the Takakkaw Falls right from the front porch. Reserve through the Banff Hostel. (☎403-762-4122. Open mid-June to mid-Oct., depending on snow. Su-Th $18, nonmembers $22; F-Sa $21, nonmembers $25.)

The four official **frontcountry campgrounds** offer a total of 200 sites, all easily accessible from the highway. All sites are first come, first served, but only Monarch and Kicking Horse fill up regularly in summer. **Takakkaw Falls Campground ❶** is situated beneath mountains, glaciers, and the magnificent falls 14km up curvy Yoho Valley Rd. It offers only pump water and pit toilets, and campers must park in the Falls lot and haul their gear 650m to the peaceful sites. (Open late June until the snow flies. 35 sites, $13.) **Hoodoo Creek ❶,** on the west end of the park, has kitchen shelters, running hot water, flush toilets, a nearby river, and a playground. (Open June-early Sept. 30 sites, $13.) **Monarch Campground ❶** sits at the junction of Yoho Valley Rd. and Hwy. 1. (Open late June-early Sept. 46 sites and 10 walk-ins, $13.) **Kicking Horse ❶,** another kilometer up Yoho Valley Rd., has toilets and is wheelchair accessible. (Open mid-May to mid-Oct. 86 sites, $18. Hot showers.) Reserve one of two backcountry **alpine huts ❶** through the Alpine Club of Canada. (☎403-678-3200. $16.) The group campground at splendid **Lake O'Hara ❶,** in the east end of the park, can only be reached by a 13km trail or on a park-operated bus. (Bus reservations ☎343-6433, up to 3 months in advance. Round-trip $12. Permit required for camping.)

FOOD

The most convenient food stop in Yoho, and potentially a sit-all-day-stop, is the **Truffle Pigs Cafe and General Store ❶,** on Stephen Ave. in Field. Sells basic foodstuffs, microbrews, wine, and camping supplies. Local crafts line the walls, and the owners peddle home-made sandwiches ($4.25), breakfast ($4.50-7), and eclectically delicious $8-15 dinners. (☎343-6462. Has the only **ATM** in the area. Open daily 8am-10pm; winter M-Sa 10am-7pm.)

OUTDOOR ACTIVITIES

HIKING

The park's six **backcountry campgrounds** and 400km of trail make for an intense wilderness experience, with countless quickly accessed trails exhibiting scenery equal to and beyond that of the larger parks. Before setting out, pick up **camping permits** ($6 per person per day), maps, and the free *Backcountry Guide to Yoho National Park* at the visitors center. Whiskey Jack Hostel (see above) is also well stocked with trail information. The park's finest terrain is in the Yoho Valley and is accessible only after the snow melts in mid- to late summer.

Iceline Trail (via Little Yoho 19.8km, via Celeste Lake 17km). Starts at the hostel. Takes hikers briefly through forests of alder, spruce, and fir before leading them on an extended trip above the tree line, over glacial moraines, and past the striated rock and icy pools of Emerald Glacier. Moderate.

Emerald Triangle (21.5km round-trip). The route travels through the Yoho Pass (see *Backcountry Guide*) to the Wapta Highline trail, Burgess Pass, and back to the start. Most of the journey is above treeline with breathtaking views over much of Yoho's diverse landscape. Moderate.

Mt. Hunter Lookout to Upper Lookout (12.8km). Cuts through Yoho's lush lower altitudes, but manages a nice view of Kicking Horse and Beaverfoot valleys. Moderate.

Wapta Falls (4.8km round-trip). The trailhead is not marked on Hwy. 1 for westbound traffic as there is no left-turn lane. Continue 3km to the west entrance of the park, turn around, and come back east. Highlights include seeing the Kicking Horse River drop 30m. The least ambitious and least spectacular of the Yoho hikes. Easy.

OTHER ACTIVITIES

The Great Divide is both the boundary between Alberta and BC as well as the Atlantic and Pacific watersheds. Here a stream forks with one arm flowing 1500km to the Pacific Ocean, and the other flowing 2500km to the Atlantic via Hudson's Bay. It is also the site of the **Burgess Shale,** a layer of sedimentary rock containing the world's most important animal fossils, imprints of the insect-like, soft-bodied organisms that inhabited the world's oceans prior to an intense burst of evolution known as the **Cambrian Explosion.** Discovered in 1909, the unexpected complexity of these 505 million-year-old specimens changed the way paleontologists thought about evolution. Larger, clumsier animals known as humans have since successfully lobbied to protect the shale from excessive tourism. Educational hikes led by the **Yoho-Burgess Shale Foundation** (☎800-343-3006) are the only way to see it. A full-day, 20km hike costs $45, under 12 $25. A steep 6km loop to the equally old and trilobite-packed **Mt. Stephen Fossil Beds** runs $25. (July to mid-Sept. only. Reservations required.) For easier sightseeing, follow the 14km of the Yoho Valley Rd. to views of the **Takakkaw Falls,** Yoho's most splendid waterfall, and the highest-altitude major falls in the Canadian Rockies.

KOOTENAY NATIONAL PARK ☎250/453

Kootenay National Park hangs off the Continental Divide on the southeast edge of British Columbia, bordering Alberta. Many visitors travel through Kootenay to get to or from Banff National Park on the majestic Banff-Windermere Hwy. (Hwy. 93), the first road to cross the Canadian Rockies. The federal government built the road in 1920 in exchange for the 8km of land on either side that now constitutes the park. Kootenay's biggest attraction is its lack of visitors: unlike Banff and Jasper, Kootenay has not been developed at all. The only civilization is found at the **Radium Hot Springs,** on the park's western border. The park's stately conifers, alpine meadows, and pristine peaks hide in Banff's shadow, allowing travelers to experience the true solitude of the Canadian Rockies while still in a national park.

ORIENTATION & PRACTICAL INFORMATION

Kootenay lies southwest of Banff and Yoho National Parks. **Hwy. 93** runs through the park from the **Trans-Canada Hwy.** in Banff to **Radium Hot Springs** (see **Hot Springs,** p. 325) at the southwest edge of the park, where it joins **Hwy. 95.** One **Greyhound bus** per day stops at the **Esso station,** 7507 W Main St. (☎347-9726; open daily 7am-11pm.), at the junction of Hwy. 93 and Hwy. 95 in Radium Hot Springs, on the way to **Banff** (2hr., $22) and **Calgary** (3½hr., $39). The **park information center** and **Tourism BC Info Centre** are both located at 7556 Main St. W in Radium. They supply free maps and a backcountry hiking guide. (Parks Canada: ☎347-9505; Tourism BC: ☎347-9331. Open July-Aug. daily 9am-7pm; Sept.-June approximately 9am-4pm.) The **Kootenay Park Lodge** operates another visitors center 63km north of Radium. (☎403-762-9196. Open July-Aug. daily 9am-8pm; reduced hours in June and early Sept.) The **Park Administration Office,** on the access road to Redstreak Campground, dispenses the backcountry hiking guide and is open in the winter. (☎347-9615. Open M-F 8am-noon and 1-4pm.) An **ambulance** can be reached at ☎342-2055. In an **emergency,** call the Banff Park Warden (☎403-762-4506) or the **police** in either Invermere (☎342-9292) or Radium Hot Springs (☎347-9393). **Windermere District Hospital** is in Invermere, 850 10th Ave. (☎342-9201), 15km south of Radium on Hwy. 95. The **post office** is on Radium Blvd in Radium Hot Springs. (☎347-9460. Open M-F 9am-5pm.) **Postal Code:** V0A 1M0.

ACCOMMODATIONS & FOOD

The **Misty River Lodge (HI)** ❶, 5036 Hwy. 93, is the first left after you exit the park's West Gate. Offers bike rentals for $10 per day. (☎347-9912. Dorms $17, nonmembers $22; private room with bath $42, nonmembers $65.) There's also a **B&B** ❹ upstairs. ($69-79, 10% HI discount.) Downtown, Radium features over 30 other motels, with high-season doubles starting at $40. The park's only serviced campground is **Redstreak** ❶, on the access road that departs Hwy. 95 near the south end of Radium Hot Springs, which boasts 242 sites, including 50 fully-serviced sites and 38 with electricity only. Features toilets, firewood, and playgrounds. Arrive early to secure a spot. (Open mid-May through mid-Oct. $17; full RV sites $22. Free showers.) **McLeod Meadows** ❶, 27km north of the West Gate entrance on Hwy. 93, offers more solitude and wooded sites on the banks of the very blue Kootenay River, as well as access to hiking trails. (Open mid-May to mid-Sept. 98 sites, $13.) From September to May, snag one of the seven free winter sites at the **Dolly Varden** ❶ picnic area, 36km north of the West Gate entrance, which boasts free firewood, water, toilets, and a shelter. Ask at the visitors centers for details on **Crooks Meadow** ❶, which is available for groups (75 people max.), and cheap ($8), unserviced camping in the nearby Invermere Forest District.

There is little affordable food in Kootenay, with the exception of a few basic staples at the **Kootenay Park Lodge.** Radium supports a few inexpensive eateries on Main St. The bst selection of groceries is at **Mountainside Market,** 7546 Main St. E. right next to the Visitor Centre. (☎347-9600. Open M-Sa 9am-9pm, Su 9am-8pm.)

OUTDOOR ACTIVITIES

The 95km **Banff-Windermere Highway (Hwy. 93)** forms the sinuous backbone of Kootenay. Stretching from Radium Hot Springs to Banff, the highway follows the Kootenay and Vermilion Rivers, passing views of glacier-enclosed peaks, dense stands of virgin forest, and green, glacier-fed rivers. The wild landscape of the Kootenay River Valley remains unblemished but for the ribbon of road.

HOT SPRINGS

The park's main attraction is **Radium Hot Springs,** named after the radioactive element detected there in trace quantities. The crowded complex is responsible for the traffic and towel-toting tourists just inside the West Gate. Natural mineral waters fill two swimming pools—a hot one for soaking at 40°C (open 9am-11pm) and a cooler one for swimming at 27°C (open noon-9pm). The hot pool is wheelchair accessible. (☎347-9485. Single entry $6.25, children and seniors $5.25; winter $5.25/$4.75; group and family rates available. Lockers $0.25, towel rental $1.25, swimsuit rental $1.50.) The **Lussier Hot Springs** in Whiteswan Lake Provincial Park offer a more natural alternative to Radium's lifeguards and ice-cream vendors. The springs flow directly from the riverbank into the Lussier River, and engineered rock walls form shallow pools that trap the water at varying temperatures. To find this diamond in the rough, turn onto the rough dirt logging road 66km south of Radium and follow it for 17km.

HIKING

The **Rockwall Trail** in the north of the park is the most popular backcountry area in Kootenay. All **backcountry** campers must stop at a visitors center (see **Orientation and Practical Info,** p. 324) for the hiking guide, which has maps, trail descriptions, and topographical profiles, and sells a mandatory **wilderness pass.** ($6 per person per night, $38 per year.) A number of shorter trails lead right off Hwy. 93 about 15km from the Banff border. Two fire roads, plus all of Hwy. 93, are open for **mountain biking,** but Kootenay lacks the extensive trail systems of its larger siblings. Icy water and rock flour from glaciers make for lousy fishing.

Marble Canyon Trail (750m, 15min.). Many tourists enjoy this path, which traverses a deep limestone gorge cut by Tokumm Creek before ending at a roaring waterfall. Easy.

Paint Pots Trail (1.6km, 30min.). 3.2km south of Marble Canyon on Hwy. 93. This partially wheelchair-accessible trail leads to springs rich in iron oxide. Tourist-heavy. Easy.

Stanley Glacier Trail (5.5km, 4hr.). Starts 3.5km from the Banff entrance and leads into a glacier-gouged valley, ending 1.6km from the foot of Stanley Glacier. One of the hot springs' most astounding and therapeutic powers is their ability to suck travelers out of the woods, leaving Kootenay's many longer hiking trails uncrowded. Considered the "best dayhike in the park." Moderately difficult.

Kindersley Pass (16.5km). The 2 trailheads at either end of the route, Sinclair Creek and Kindersley Pass, are less than 1km apart on Hwy. 93, about 10km inside the West Gate entrance. Trail climbs more than 1000m to views of the Columbia River Valley in the west and the crest of the Rockies in the east. Strenuous.

NORTHERN BRITISH COLUMBIA

Northern BC remains among the most remote and sparsely inhabited regions of North America. Averaging one person per 15 sq. km, the land's loneliness and sheer physical beauty are overwhelming. Native peoples have lived here for thousands of years, adapting their lifestyles and culture to patterns of animal migration and the uncompromising climate. White settlers began migrating West in the early 19th century, attracted by the wealth of natural resources. While furs were lucrative, it wasn't until several gold rushes hit, that stampedes rushed in to settle permanently. Since then, the lumber and mining industries have brought a steady flow eager to extract the wealth of the land. Despite some tell-tale signs of logging and mining, the land remains mainly unspoiled.

Unfortunately the area is often blown through by travelers hell bent on Alaska. Their loss; the stark mountains, yawning canyons, roaring rivers, and clear lakes are left all that more pristine for those who will stop to appreciate them.

ALONG HWY. 20: CHILCOTIN HWY.

WILLIAMS LAKE TO BELLA COOLA ☎250

The allure of the Chilcotin Hwy. lies not in its lackluster endpoint, Bella Coola, but in the rugged and scenic lands along the 457km highway (a 5-7hr. drive). Most of the drive is smooth sailing, but the unforgettable "Hill" is an unforgettably guard-rail-less 21km of gravel (see below). Leaving Williams Lake, the Chilcotin Hwy. heads west across the **Fraser River** and climbs briefly before flattening out through forests and pastures dotted with cattle ranches. Warning to unsuspecting travelers: cattle at large. Watch for them on roads to avoid unplanned barbecues.

Alexis Creek (Km 110), **Nimpo Lake** (Km 300), and **Anahim** (Km 305) are stops with gas, cafe, lodging, and a general store. **Bull Canyon Provincial Park ❶,** 8km past Alexis Creek, features fishing on the Chilcotin River as well as two dozen tent sites with pit toilets ($12). Lakeside resort turn-offs are sprinkled along the highway with a concentration worth visiting at **Puntzi Lake.** The best meal can be consumed around Nimpo Lake at the **Chilcotin's Gate ❷.** Burgers $7-8, sandwich and fries $7, steak dinner $13. (☎742-3720. Open daily June-Sept. 6am-9pm; winter 7am-7pm.)

Low-priced, convenient camping is across the highway at **Vagabond RVs ❶,** but bring earplugs to sleep through the early morning take-offs of floatplanes. (Tent $10, RV $15, free shower, coin laundry.) **Nimpo Towing** aids the Chilcotin-traveler in need (☎742-3484, M-Sa 8am-6pm) or feeds the hungered traveler at the bakery and cafe (open M-Sa 6am-6pm). **Chilko River Expeditions** runs **rafting** expeditions along the Chilcotin and Chilko Rivers from Williams Lake lodging. (☎354-2056 or 877-271-7626. $100 for daytrip.) Whatever you do and wherever you stay, bring enough insect repellant to permanently damage your skin.

PUNTZI LAKE. A 5km turn-off along a gravel road at Chilanko Forks (Km 175) leads to the 9km long **Puntzi Lake,** surrounded by several affordable resort options. Summer activities include fishing for kokanee and rainbow trout while watching white pelicans. Smiling owners dole out campsites, cabins, and canoe rentals at **Puntzi Lake Resort ❶** (☎481-1176 or 800-578-6804; sites $15; cabins $50-90; full RV sites $17-21) and **Barney's Lakeside Resort ❶** (☎481-1100; sites $15; cabins $45 for 2, $5 each additional person).

PARKS. South of the Chilcotin Hwy., **Tsylos Provincial Park** (sigh-LOSS) boasts Canada's first grizzly bear refuge, the glacier-fed, trout- and salmon-rich Lake Chilko. To reach the **Gwa da Ts'ih campground** on the north side of the park, turn off at Tatla Lake (Km 220) and drive 63km on washboard gravel roads (4-6hr. from Williams Lake). The highway enters the southern portion of **Tweedsmuir Provincial Park** (☎398-4414) at Heckman's Pass, 360km west of Williams Lake. The park protects the Atnarko River, Hunlen Falls, Monarch Glacier, and the colorfully streaked shield volcanoes of the Rainbow Mountains. Unfortunately, road trippers' introduction to the park is the final 21km of gravel road, commonly referred to as "The Hill": a one-lane, brake-burning, head-turning, windshield-cracking, free-falling, no-barrier, roller-coaster ride with steep (18%) grades and switch-backs exceptionally notable for their sharpness and susceptibility to avalanches, in addition to undeniably spectacular views (*Let's Go* always recommends that drivers keep both eyes on the road, but especially recommends it here) of the Coast Range and the valley below (road conditions ☎900-565-4997).

For decades, Hwy. 20 ended at **Anahim Lake,** 315km west of Williams Lake. In 1955, frustrated by inaction from a government that said the road to the sea could not, financially and physically, be completed, locals got two bulldozers, borrowed money, and finished the job themselves. The route's alternate name is the "Freedom Highway." After the hill, the highway is paved again for its most scenic 75km, following the **Bella Coola River** into town along the Hwy. 20 corridor through the rest of Tweedsmuir Park and into Bella Coola. Perhaps the biggest thing in Tweedsmuir is the terminus of the 25- to 30-day **Alexander Mackenzie Heritage Trail,** reserved for those hikers beyond hard-core and off the deep end. Its 420km stretch from **Blackwater River,** just west of Quesnel, across western British Columbia to **Burnt Creek Bridge** on Hwy. 20, traces the final leg of Mackenzie's 1793 journey across Canada to the West Coast. Mackenzie reached the Pacific more than a decade before Lewis and Clark, although the Americans continue to hog all the glory. The southern end of the park overflows with more hiking opportunities. One multi-day trip goes to **Hunlen Falls;** a difficult, grizzly inhabited 16.4km one-way (9hr.) hike. Trailhead access by 4WD next to the gate at the bottom of "The Hill." Depending on whom you ask, the cataract holds numerous records (is it second highest in BC? fourth highest in the Canada? the world? Locals disagree; but they are really, really big, loud, and supremely majestic in their misty descent).

After hiking into the falls, visitors can spend the night at **Turner Lake ❶** (all lake campsites $5) before renting canoes on the snow-capped-peak-studded **Turner Lakes Chain.** ($30 per day, 3-5 days. Canoe reservations, cabin rentals ($50), and flights for three people out to the lake ($210) are all available through **Tweedsmuir Air Services,** ☎800-668-4335, out of Nimpo Lake.) One can also walk the gorgeous alpine tundra wonderland up to and beyond **Ptarmigan Lake** (12km one-way, 5hr., two backcountry campsites). Summertime daytrippers can explore **Rainbow Ridge Trail** (trailhead before "the Hill," 8km one-way, 2-3hr.) or for a shorter trip follow the **Valley Loop/Burnt Bridge Trail** (5km round-trip, 1-2hr.) from the Mackenzie Heritage Trailhead (50km east of Bella Coola). The viewpoint overlooks the Bella Coola Valley. The park has two campgrounds along Hwy. 20; **Atnarko ❶,** right at the bottom of the hill (28 sites), and **Fisheries Pool ❶,** at the western end of the park (14 sites), both costing $10. Call the park for details (see above) and look for brochures in the Williams Lake Visitor Centre and at the campgrounds.

BELLA COOLA. The pot of pewter at the end of the Chilcotin rainbow is the coastal village of Bella Coola, homeland of the Nuxalk Nation. Salmon fishery restrictions and the pull-out of the logging industry over the last three years have severely depressed the local economy. This has made the town increasingly dependent on the tourism from the **BC Ferries'** *Discovery Passage* route, which links Bella Coola with Port Hardy, on the northern tip of Vancouver Island, from mid-June to mid-September. (☎888-223-3779. Adults $103, ages 5-11 $51, under 5 free. Car $205.) The **Shell Station,** across from the Valley Inn on McKenzie Rd., does repairs and has the only gas in town. (☎799-5314. Open daily 8am-8pm.) The **visitors center** is located in the *Tweedsmuir Travel* office (the place to make BC Ferries reservations) downtown. (☎799-5638, 800-515-8998. Open M, W, and F 9:30am-4:30pm, Tu and Th 9:30am-6pm, Sa 2-6pm.) Getting a room in town is expensive, but the **Bella Coola Motel ❹,** downtown, has **camping ❶** on its large back lawn. (☎799-5323; www.bcadventure.com/bellacoolamotel. Double rooms for $65. Tents $10; RV $12, no RV sites. Toilets, free showers.) For shaded and forested sites, head to **Gnome's Home Campground and RV Park ❶,** in Hagensborg 16km east of Bella Coola along the highway. (☎982-2504. Sites $12; full RV sites $15. Showers included.)

For a bite to eat, try the **Bay Motor Hotel ❶** coffee shop, on Hwy. 20 in Hagensborg, or the small grocery store across the street. (☎982-2212. Open daily 6am-9pm; F and Sa to 6am-10pm.) In Bella Coola, sit on the deck and enjoy pricier dinner options at the **Bella Coola Valley Inn ❸.** (☎799-5316. Open daily 7am-9pm.)

WILLIAMS LAKE TO QUESNEL ☎250

Williams Lake, 90km north of 100 Mile House, is the Cariboo's largest town, but certainly not its most appealing. Fortunately, it's easy to leave, with Hwy. 20 meandering 457km west to **Bella Coola** (see p. 326) and Hwy. 97 continuing north to the rough-hewn lumber towns of **Quesnel** and **Prince George.** The biggest thing happening in town is the celebration of its cowboy heritage over Canada Day weekend (July 1) with the **Williams Lake Stampede.** Festivities include a rodeo, mountain race, wild cow milking, barn dance, and live music. (☎800-717-6336. $11-15, cheaper if bought before June 14.) **Tourist information** in town is available on Hwy. 97. (☎392-5025. Open June-Aug. daily 9am-5pm; Sept.-May M-F 9am-4pm.) The town **library** at the corner of 3rd Ave. N and Proctor St. has free **Internet access** for 30min. (☎392-3630. Open Tu-Th 10am-8pm, F-Sa 10am-5pm.)

The **Slumber Lodge,** 27 7th Ave., is cheap with a small indoor pool, phones, and cable. (☎392-7116 or 800-577-2244. Singles $45; doubles $50.) For a cheap thrill, pitch tent on the **Stampede grounds** in the center of town. To get there, cross the bridge on Hwy. 20 from the junction with Hwy. 97 and take first right on Mackenzie Rd.; the grounds are on your right. (☎392-6585. $8, full RV sites $15.)

To escape the bustle, bask on the beach at **Blue Lake Holiday Campgrounds** (☎297-6505), turn off at Blue Lake Rd. 32km north of town and 3km up a gravel road. Campsites ($12) and canoes ($5 per hr.) on the bright blue-green lake are at your disposal. Corral your buckin' bronco and hightail it to the all-you-can-eat chock-full salad and hot entree buffet at **Fraser Inn,** Hwy. 97 north of intersection. (☎398-7055. Salad bar only $6, whole shebang $8. M-F 11am-1:30pm, Sa and Su 11am-4pm.) If looking to fill your saddlebag with an overflowing sub or wrap, the deli **Zesto's,** 86 3rd Ave. N, has every option under the western sun. (☎398-9801. Open M-Sa 8:30am-10pm, Su 10am-10pm.)

The 122km drive north to Quesnel can be a little dull, but those willing to subject their car to a little gravel can make it more interesting. About 35km north of Williams Lake, the **Soda Creek Townsite Rd.** splits from Hwy. 97 for 20km of rustic splendor alongside the **Fraser River.** The road returns to the highway several kilometers south of the free **Marguerite Ferry,** which shuttles drivers across the river to a gravel road paralleling Hwy. 97 for the remainder of the trip to Quesnel. (Open May-Oct. 5min., on demand 7-11:45am, 1-4:45pm, and 6-6:45pm.)

QUESNEL ☎250

The town of Quesnel, 123km north of Williams Lake and 116km south of Prince George, takes great pride in its gold-driven past and forestry-propelled present. The town itself has little to offer but provides relatively close access to other options. After being welcomed into town by the world's largest (and purplest) goldpan on the north end of town on Hwy. 97, it's only a 10min. drive to **Pinnacles Provincial Park:** cross the river on Marsh Rd., then turn right on Baker Dr., and follow it for 5km. Park at the gate walk 1km to the hoodoos—volcanic rock formations that look like giant sand dribble castles—and impressive views. Every third weekend of July, crowds flock to Quesnel for the wholesome family fun of **Billy Barker Days,** featuring a rodeo, live entertainment, and a "Crash-to-Pass" demolition derby. The logging industry maintains a very strong presence (and odor) in this industrial oasis.

ORIENTATION & PRACTICAL INFORMATION. Hwy. 97 becomes Front St. in Quesnel and wraps along the river. One block over the main road, Reid St., is the parallel Front St. in the "city centre." The **Greyhound** depot is on Kinshant between St. Laurent and Barlow. (☎992-2231 or 800-661-8747. Open M-F 6am-8pm,

Sa 6am-noon and 6-7:30pm, Su 6-10:30am and 6-7:30pm.) Buses run to **Prince George** (1½hr.; 3 per day; $19, students and seniors $17) and **Vancouver** (10hr.; 3 per day; $87, students and seniors $78). The **visitors center,** 705 Carson Ave., is just off Hwy. 97 at the south end of town. (☎992-8716 or 800-992-4922. Open July-Aug. daily 8am-6pm; mid-May to June and Sept.-Oct. daily 9am-4pm; Nov. to mid-May W-Su 9am-4pm.) **Market and pharmacy: Safeway,** 445 Reid St. (☎992-6477. Open daily 8am-10pm.) **Free Internet access** is at the **library,** 593 Barlow Ave. on two computers. Reserve in advance. (☎992-7912. Open Tu-Th 10am-8pm, F-Sa 10am-5pm.) Call ☎911 in an **emergency,** or contact the **police** at ☎992-9211. The **post office** is at 346 Reid St. (☎992-2200. Open M-F 8:45am-5:15pm.) **Postal Code:** V2J 2M0.

ACCOMMODATIONS & FOOD. With a nod to Quesnel's history, the **Gold Pan Hotel ❸,** 855 Front St., at the north edge of downtown, offers cheap rooms with dingy bedspreads but clean bathrooms, cable, coffee, and phones. (☎992-2107. Singles $40; doubles $44.) Treat yourself to the **Caribou Hotel ❸,** 254 Front St., downtown. Ten more bucks will land you a river view, continental breakfast, TV, phone, and whirlpool bath. Request rooms 1-3 when a live band plays downstairs in the **pub.** (☎992-2333 or 800-665-3200. Live music W-Sa. Open M-Sa 11am-1am, Su 11am-midnight. Check monthly calendar for nightly drink and food bargains. A **drive-in liquor store** keeps the place hoppin'.) For more ambience than the cheap RV parks on either end of town, try **Robert's Roost Campground ❷,** 3121 Gook Rd., 8km south of town and 2km off Hwy. 97, which offers elegantly landscaped lakeside sites. Features include coin showers, laundry, playground, and fishing; row boat and canoe rentals are $5. (☎747-2015. Sites $17; full RV sites $22.) Pub food can be found throughout Quesnel and south on Hwy. 97. A burlap-bag-ceilinged alternative for any meal, **Granville's Coffee ❶,** Reid St., bakes gigantic ham and cheese muffins ($1.50) and sells heaping sandwiches (under $6—try the Hungry Hobo) and $5 mac and cheese. (Open daily 7am-10pm.)

SIGHTS & OUTDOOR ACTIVITIES. The long-defunct mining town of **Barkerville,** 90km east of Quesnel along Hwy. 26, was established in 1862 after Billy Barker found gold on Williams Creek and sparked BC's largest gold rush. For the rest of the 19th century, Barkerville was the benchmark against which the rest of western Canada was measured. Since 1958 the town has been operated as an educational **"living museum,"** housing only residents who run the local B&Bs. (☎994-3332. Open daily 8am-8pm in summer. 2-day pass $8, students and seniors $6.25, youth $4.75, children $2.25, under 5 free. 30% off from late May to mid-June. Additional fee for shows and stagecoach rides.) Although brochures ask that you "plan to spend enough time to re-live a century of time," most modern folks find that one day is enough to see it all. However, those staying a while might find services 8km towards Quesnel in the mining town of **Wells.** The visitors center has the scoop on mill tours at **West Fraser Lumber** (times arranged on demand).

Bowron Lakes Provincial Park is a paddling paradise located 25km north of Barkerville. This necklace of lakes forms a 116km loop in the heart of the **Caribou Mountains,** which takes most canoers 10 days to complete. The park service charges $50 per person to canoe the circuit and $25 per person to canoe the westside to Unna Lake (three to four days) to help maintain the 54 lakeside camping areas. Reservations are required through **Super, Natural BC** (☎800-435-5622); two walk-ons per day. **Becker Lodge** rents canoes and kayaks (☎992-8864 or 800-808-4761; $130-230 for the circuit), as does the **Bowron Lake Lodge** (☎992-2733; $100-225). Both also offer camping and cabins within a stone's throw of the loop's starting point. **Tent sites ❶** overlooking the lake are more private at Becker (tents $15, RVs $20) while lodging in the **Bowron Lake Motel ❹** is the cheapest option with a hard roof ($60).

HOW MUCH WOOD DOES A CANUCK CHUCK? About 76 million cubic meters a year. That's enough to bring BC 15.3 billion loonies from exports, employ a group of people three times the population of the Yukon (nearly 100,000), and dole out $4 billion in wages and salaries. The majority of BC's chopped riches make their way to Canada's North American next-door neighbor–the USA–in the form of softwood lumber. Before you get your tree-hugging self heading to BC to tie yourself to a sapling in protest, note this: it's been done before and with some success. As a result of such a protest, stringent forest management laws were passed leading to careful planning and reforestation efforts. Over 200 million baby trees are plopped in the soil each year, and tree planters earn their wages by the tree. Eat your heart out, Johnny Appleseed.

Anyone traveling between Prince George and Quesnel on Hwy. 97 will live a better life for having stopped at **Cinema Second Hand General Store,** 32km north of Quesnel on Hwy. 97. Cash-strapped road warriors will find everything they need (except an actual cinema), plus a wide variety of things they could never possibly need, like old-fashioned snowshoes and disco LPs. The store also offers **free camping** with a pit toilet. (☎998-4774. Open daily 9am-9pm.)

PRINCE GEORGE ☎250

Prince George stands at the confluence of the Nechako and Fraser Rivers, the banks of which play host to the pulp and lumber mills that crowd the valley floor in an impressive display of industrial *forte*. Prince George is a crucial point of transport for goods and services heading in all directions, a true nerve center for the Northwest. But even with recent additions to the town—a civic center, a national university, and a Western League hockey team—Prince George is most definitely a stopover, not a destination.

TRANSPORTATION

Greyhound, 1566 12th Ave. (☎564-5454 or 800-661-8747; www.greyhound.ca), opposite the Victoria St. Visitors Center, is open M-Sa 6:30am-5:30pm and 8pm-midnight; Su 6:30-9:30am, 3:30-5:30pm, and 8:30pm-midnight. Buses to **Edmonton** (10hr., 2 per day, $101); **Dawson Creek** (6hr., 2 per day, $56); **Prince Rupert** (10hr., 2 per day, $96); and **Vancouver** (12hr., 3 per day, $104). **BC Rail,** 1108 Industrial Way (☎561-4033; www.bcrail.ca. Open M-F 3-11:30pm, Su 6-10pm and M, Th, Sa 6-10am), 2km south off Hwy. 97 at the end of Terminal Blvd., runs the scenic Cariboo Prospector to **Vancouver** (14hr.; M, Th, Sa at 7am; $247, over 59 $222 children $148; 3 meals included.

ORIENTATION & PRACTICAL INFORMATION

Hwy. 97 cuts straight through Prince George just to the west of the city center. **Hwy. 16** runs through the city center, becomes **Victoria St.** in town, and crosses Hwy. 97 to the south of town. Running the width of the city, **15th St.** is home to most of the shopping centers and terminates on the east end downtown.

Tourist Information: Visitors Center, 1198 Victoria St. (☎562-3700 or 800-668-7646; www.tourismpg.bc.ca), at 15th Ave. Open M-F 8:30am-6pm, Sa 9am-6pm. Another center (☎563-5493) is at the junction of Hwy. 16 and Hwy. 97 beneath a huge "Mr. P.G." logger. Open daily May-Sept. 9am-8pm.

Equipment Rental: Centre City Surplus, 1222 4th Ave. (☎564-2400), rents and sells outdoor gear at competitive prices. Open M-Sa 9am-6pm, Su 11am-4pm.

Market: The Real Canadian Superstore, 2155 Ferry Ave. (☎960-1335), at Hwy. 16, has loads of fresh produce, aisles of bulk bins, ethnic foods, a pharmacy, clothes, and gas. (Open M-F 9am-10pm, Sa 8am-10pm, Su 10am-8pm.)

Laundromat: Whitewash Laundromat, 231 George St. (☎563-2300). Wash $1.50, dry $0.25 per 8min. Open M-Sa 7:30am-6pm.

Emergency: ☎911.

Police: 999 Brunswick St. (☎561-3300).

Fire: ☎561-7664

Crisis Line: ☎563-1214. 24hr.

Hospital: 2000 15th Ave. (☎565-2000; emergency 565-2444).

Internet Access: Free 1hr. daily at the **library,** 887 Dominion St. (☎563-9251). 12 computers. Open in summer M-Th 10am-9pm, F-Sa 10am-5:30pm; winter Su 1-5pm. **Internet Cafe** (☎561-0011), inside London Drugs in the Parkwood Mall, at Victoria and 15th St. $3.20 per 30min. Open M-Sa 9am-10pm, Su 10am-8pm.

Post Office: 1323 5th Ave. (☎561-2568). Open M-F 8:30am-5pm. **Postal Code:** V2L 3L0.

ACCOMMODATIONS & CAMPING

During the summer, the **College of New Caledonia Student Residence ❶,** 3330 22nd Ave. (turn off Hwy. 97 west of downtown and take the second right), offers the best deal in town, boasting clean rooms and a young crowd. Rooms include a fridge and microwave. With kitchen, lounge, BBQ, sundeck, and cheap laundry, the price is unbeatable. (☎561-5849 or 800-371-8111. Linen $5. Wash $1.50, dry $0.50. Singles $20; doubles $25.) To upgrade to a queen bed and cable TV, a good bet is the **Queensway Court Motel ❸,** 1616 Queensway, one motel over from 17th Ave., close to downtown. Well-kept rooms come with fridges and cable. (☎562-5068. Singles $36; doubles $40.) The **Log House Restaurant and Kampground,** located on the shores of Tabor Lake, pleases adults with its impeccable grounds, proximity to fishing, and a costly German-owned steakhouse. To reach this slice of Europe, head out of town on Hwy. 16 E; after 3km, turn right on "Old Cariboo Hwy.," left on Giscome Rd. and follow the signs (15min. from downtown). Rowboats, canoes, and pedal boats can be rented. (☎963-9515. Boats all $8 per hr. Sites $15; full RV sites $22; cabins with kitchenettes $45; teepees $10 per person.) To secure a bed and breakfast room, call the helpful **B&B Hotline** (☎888-266-5555).

FOOD & NIGHTLIFE

While it is hard to escape chains and interchangeable pasta joints on George St., a few alternatives stand out. Freshness exudes from the **1085 Cafe ❷,** 1085 Vancouver St., tucked away at 11th Ave. near the mall. Enjoy vegetable pita pizzas ($6.75), wraps ($4-6), salads, or chai ($3.50) on the flowered patio. (☎960-2272. Open M 7am-4pm, Sa 9am-4pm, Tu-F 7am-7pm.) Hit up hip **Javva Mugga Mocha Cafe ❶,** 304 George St., for the best coffee in town. (☎562-3338. Open M-F 7am-5:30pm, Sa 8am-5:30pm.) An oasis for the big appetite, **Esther's Inn ❸,** 1151 Commercial Crescent, off Hwy. 97 near 15th Ave., has an all-you-can-eat spread laid out next to a waterfall in the tropical dining area. Main dish theme varies. Lunch $9, dinner M-Th $12, F-Sa $14. (Open for lunch 11am-2pm, dinner 4-10pm.)

There's no shortage of taps in Prince George. **JJ's Pub,** 1970 S Ospika off 15th Ave. heading from Hwy. 97 to UNBC, reminds its loyal Canadian crowd and visitors that "Canadians kick ass." (☎562-2234. Open daily 11am-midnight.) Cowboys congregate for live country rock at **Cadillac Ranch,** 1390 2nd Ave., and two-step under disco lights. (☎563-7720. Open M-Th 9pm-2am, F-Sa 8pm-2am.) Clubs and bars teem with college students during the academic year; in summer, twentysomethings line up outside **Sgt. O'Flaherty's,** 770 Brunswick at 7th Ave., under the Crest Hotel. Thursday nights, pints fill up for $3. Live music nightly, except for when the live acts are pre-empted by special events—then you'll see the crowds swell up even more than usual. (☎563-0121. Open M-Sa 4pm-1am.)

OUTDOOR ACTIVITIES & EVENTS

PARKS. **Fort George Park,** on the banks of the Fraser River off 20th Ave., offers an expansive lawn, beach volleyball courts, picnic tables, and barbecue pits. It also makes a perfect starting point for the 11km **Heritage River Trail,** which wanders through the city and along the Fraser and Nechako Rivers. After meandering through **Cottonwood Island Nature Park,** off River Rd., you'll get a sense of Prince George at its rawest and most industrial. For a bird's eye view of Prince George—the cement jungle—scramble up to **Connaught Hill Park,** with picnic tables and ample frisbee-throwing space. To reach the park, scale the yellow metal staircase across 15th Ave. from the visitors center or take Connaught Dr. off Queensway. **McMillan Regional Park** is right across the Nechako River, off Hwy. 97 N and features a deep ravine with a view of the city from the river's cutbanks. Two parks farther out of town have wide trails that are wheelchair accessible and double as cross-country skiing paths in the winter. The lush **Forests for the World,** only 15 min. away (take Hwy. 97 N, turn left on 15th Ave., right on Foothills Blvd., left onto Cranbrook Hill Rd., and finally left on Kueng Rd.), will pump the fresh woodsy air right back into your lungs. To take advantage of the web of trails, pick up a map at the Visitors Center first. The trails at **Esker's Provincial Park** (☎565-6340), off Hwy. 97 (12km north) and 28km down Ness Lake Rd., circle three lakes.

FISHING. With more than 1600 lakes within a 150km radius, fishing is excellent near Prince George. The closest spot is **Tabor Lake,** where the rainbow trout all but jump into boats in spring and early summer. Tabor is east on Hwy. 16; follow the directions to the Log House Restaurant and Kampground described above. For a complete listing of lakes and licensing information, contact the Visitors Center.

EVENTS. Imagine finding organic produce, baked goods, jams, salsas, and tofu concoctions in this town of chain food. Each Saturday these unexpected treats are available on tables at the **Farmers Market,** Courthouse Plaza on George Ave. (☎563-3383. Open May-Sept. 8:30am-1pm.) **Mardi Gras** (☎564-3737) lasts for 10 days in late February and features such events as snow golf, dog-pull contests, and bed races. You'll swear you're in New Orleans. **Sandblast** (☎564-9791) sends daredevils down the steep, snowless Nechako Cutbanks on the third Sunday in August. Anyone can participate, using almost any contraption—see how well your couch fares against the bikers, if you've got the guts.

JOHN HART (HWY. 97): PRINCE GEORGE TO DAWSON CREEK

For most travelers, the highlight of a stay in Prince George is departing for points elsewhere. To get to Mt. Robson, Jasper, or points farther east, take the Yellowhead Hwy. (Hwy 16) eastbound out of town. To connect to the Cassiar Hwy. (Hwy 37) and go to places like Prince Rupert or the Queen Charlotte Islands, take Hwy. 16 westbound out of Prince George. If Dawson Creek or the Alaska Highway is your thing, then roll north on Hwy. 97 (the 'Hart' or 'John Hart' Hwy.). Neon lights and strip malls become a distant memory a few kilometers into the 402km stretch from Prince George to Dawson Creek (Mile 0 of the Alaska Hwy.). The road cuts a lonely swath along a winding path through the forests of northern British Columbia. The first outpost of civilization is the micropolis of **Bear Lake,** 74km along Hwy. 97, which offers a motel, RV park, restaurant, and gas.

CROOKED RIVER & WHISKERS POINT PROVINCIAL PARKS

Situated on **Bear Lake,** 2km south of town, **Crooked River Provincial Park** ❶ offers a great beach for swimming and picnicking, as well as 90 secluded, wooded campsites. The trails around the lake make this park well-suited for winter activities such as tobogganing, snowshoeing, and cross-country skiing. For park conditions or ski and weather info, call ☎562-8288 during business hours. (Campground ☎972-4492. Toilets. Gates locked 11pm-7am. $15.) **Whiskers Point Park** ❶, 51km past Bear Lake, has the same lakefront charm and the same amenities as Crooked River on a slightly smaller scale. The park provides a boat launch for the large **McLeod Lake.** (Toilets. Gates locked 11pm-7am. $15.)

MACKENZIE

Blink and you'll miss **MacKenzie Junction,** 26km past Whiskers Point. From the junction, it's 149km to the next town of note, Chetwynd, and almost 80km to the next gas station, **Silver Sands Gas.** (☎788-0800. Open daily 9am-10:30pm.) The junction also provides a turn-off to the town of **MacKenzie,** 29km north on Hwy. 39, the largest town in the area and home to the closest hospital. Barring medical emergency, MacKenzie is probably not worth the detour unless it has been your life's dream to see the world's largest tree crusher.

CHETWYND

Pause to eat your picnic directly in front of the stubby but voluminous Bijoux Falls, 115km before Chetwynd at **Bijoux Falls Provincial Park.** 300km from Prince George, **Chetwynd** is the Chainsaw Sculpture Capital of the World. It's worth cruising downtown to see what's not visible from the highway. Ask at the **visitors center** for a town guide to see what chopped wood dreams are made of. (☎401-4100. Open daily 9am-5pm.) **Wildmare Campground** ❶, 5km before town along the highway, provides toilets, laundry facilities, and budget rates for basic sites. (☎788-2747. Tents $8; RV $18. Showers $2.) If clean and affordable is what you desire, head for the **Chetwynd Court Motel** ❸, 5104 North Access Rd. right off Hwy. 94, which offers TV and kitchenettes. (☎788-2271. Rooms $45.) After Chetwynd, Dawson Creek is 102km away.

MONKMAN PROVINCIAL PARK

The overlooked **Monkman Provincial Park** (☎787-3407) covers a gorgeous slab of the Rockies foothills and a few peaks as well. The park is home to the **Kinuseo Falls,** which are taller than Niagara Falls and totally surrounded by wilderness. Several dayhikes provide views and some easy paddling below the falls. The 4.5km Stone Corral Trail leads along a high cliff, past various fossils, to two caves. A 50km trail to Monkman Lake and ten spectacular waterfalls beyond takes 3 days and begins at the campground below. BC Parks volunteers maintain 42 sites at **Kinuseo Falls Campground** ❶ on Murray River. Pit toilets, water, and firewood. ($12). To reach Monkman, take Hwy. 29 south to the coal town of **Tumbler Ridge,** 94km from Chetwynd. Monkman is another 60km due south on a gravel road, past a huge anthracite coal mining operation.

ALONG HWY. 16: YELLOWHEAD HWY.

PRINCE GEORGE TO MT. ROBSON ☎250

East of Prince George, the pristine terrain that lines the 319km of road to Mt. Robson gives little indication of the logging that drives the regional economy, thanks to scenic, sightline-wide strips of forest left untouched alongside the route. Lakeside campsites can be found at **Purden Lake Provincial Park** ❶**,** 59km east of Prince George. (☎565-6340. Toilets and free firewood. Gate closed 11pm-7am. $15. One wheelchair-accessible site.) **Purden Lake Resort** ❶ (☎565-7777), 3km east, offers tent sites ($12), RV sites ($22-24), a cafe (open 7am-8pm), and the last gas before **McBride,** 140km east. Tenters find refuge, toilets, showers, and laundry at the **Beaverview Campsite** ❶**,** 1km east of McBride. (☎569-2513. $13; partial RV sites $17.)

From McBride, the Yellowhead weaves up the **Robson Valley,** part of the Rocky Mountain trench stretching north-south the length of the province. **Tête Jaune Cache** lies 63km east of McBride, where Hwy. 5 leads 339km south to Kamloops and the Okanagan beyond. **Tête Jaune Motel and RV Park** ❶ offers no-frills lodging right off the highway. (☎566-9815. Camping $12; RV sites $14. Showers $1.) Just 2km east of the intersection, the diminutive **Rearguard Falls** (a 20min. walk) marks the terminus of the chinook salmon's migration from the Pacific.

As Hwy. 16 continues east, the scenery reaches a crescendo at towering **Mt. Robson,** 84km west of Jasper and 319km east of Prince George. Standing 3954m tall, Robson is the highest peak in the Canadian Rockies; mountaineers reached its summit in 1913 only after five unsuccessful attempts. Less ambitious folk can appreciate the mountain's beauty from the parking lot and picnic site beside the **Mt. Robson Provincial Park Headquarters.** (☎566-4325, reservations 800-689-9025. Open June-Aug. daily 8am-8pm; May and Sept. 8am-5pm.) Sedentary types are accommodated at **Robson River Campground** ❶ and the larger **Robson Meadows Campground** ❶**,** both opposite the headquarters. (Toilets. $18. Free showers.). Five nearby **hiking trails,** ranging from 2km walks to 66km treks, are the park's main draws (backcountry camping permit $5 per person per night; under 13 free). The 22km trail to **Berg Lake** (two days; trailhead at the parking lot by Robson River, 2km from the visitors center) is a luscious, well-maintained path along the milky-blue Robson River past Lake Kinney and **Valley of a Thousand Falls.** Berg Lake is the highest of five campsites along the route, and can be used as a base to explore options from alpine ridge-running to wilderness camping.

PRINCE GEORGE TO TERRACE ☎250

As Hwy. 16 winds its way westward 575km (8hr.) toward Terrace from Prince George, towering timbers gradually give way to the gently rolling pastures and the tiny towns of British Columbia's interior **Lakes District.** To escape city camping, stop 1½hr. outside Prince George at **Beaumont Provincial Park** ❶**,** on Fraser Lake. There are 49 roomy sites, clean facilities, a playground, a swimming area, and firewood. (☎565-6340. $15).

NEW HAZELTON. The town of New Hazelton is 68km past Smithers. The **'Ksan Village & Museum,** 7km along Churchill Ave. towards Old Hazelton, displays a rich collection of totem poles, longhouses, and artwork of the Gitskan. Gitskan dancers perform every Friday at 8pm from July to August. (☎842-5544. Tours every 30min. Open July to mid-Aug. daily 9am-6pm; reduced hours in winter. Wheelchair accessible. $10, seniors and children 6-18 $6.50.) Another 44km west of New Hazelton is the junction with the Cassiar Hwy. (Hwy. 37; see p. 352), which leads 733km north to the Yukon Territory and the Alaska Hwy. (see p. 358). The **Petrocan** sells the last gas before Terrace. (☎849-5793. Open daily 7am-9pm.)

TERRACE ☎250

The site of a World War II army mutiny, Terrace is now known for its wildlife. The area is the habitat of the world's largest Chinook salmon (weighing in at 92½ lb.), and the infamous Kermodei bear, a member of the black bear family recognizable by a coat that ranges from light chestnut blond to steel blue gray in color. Terrace itself is a straightforward working-class town, but its backyard is the big wilderness. The locals will tell you all about the great fishing, but rodless hikers can still find their peace in the hills and on the curvy banks of the Skeena River.

PRACTICAL INFORMATION. Terrace is 144km east of Prince Rupert on the Yellowhead Hwy. (Hwy. 16) and 91km southwest of the junction of the Yellowhead and the Cassiar Hwy. (Hwy. 37). **VIA Rail** (☎800-561-8630), sends three trains per week to **Prince George** (10hr., $81) and **Prince Rupert** (2½hr., $19). **Greyhound,** 4620 Keith St. (☎635-3680), also runs twice daily to **Prince George** (8hr., $80) and **Prince Rupert** (2hr., $24). **Canadian Tire,** at 5100 Hwy. 16, will get your wheels back in action. (☎635-7178. Open M-F 7am-9pm, Sa 7am-6pm, Su 10am-5pm.)

The **visitors center,** 4511 Keith St., is off Hwy. 16 just east of town. (☎635-0832 or 800-499-1637. Open in summer daily 9am-5pm; winter M-F 8am-4:30pm.) The **24hr. ATM** is in the city center at **Bank of Montreal,** 4666 Lakelse Ave. (☎615-6150). The **Women's Resource Centre,** 4542 Park Ave., by the Aquatic Centre, has referral services, advocacy, lay counseling, and a library. (☎638-0228. Drop-in M-Th 10am-4pm.) **Richard's Cleaners,** 3223 Emerson St., has washers ($2) and dryers ($0.25 per 5min.). (☎635-5119. Open M-Sa 7:30am-9pm, Su 8am-9pm.) **Terrace Aquatic Center,** on Paul Clark Dr., has a pool, hot tub, saunas, and gym facilities. (☎615-3030. $4.50, students and seniors $2.50, ages 2-14 $1.75.) The **market** and **pharmacy** are at **Safeway,** 4655 Lakelse Ave. (☎635-7206. Open daily 8am-10pm.) For super cheap produce, and one-hour photo hit **The Real Canadian Wholesale Club,** located behind the visitors center off Hwy. 16. (☎635-0995. Open M-F 9am-9pm, Sa 9am-6pm, Su 10am-5pm.) **Mills Memorial Hospital:** 4720 Haugland Ave. (☎635-2211). **Emergency:** ☎911. **Police:** 3205 Eby St. (☎635-4911). **Sexual Assault Crisis Line:** ☎635-1911. (Staffed daily 8:30am-4:30pm.) **Internet access** is free at the **library,** 4610 Park Ave. for 1hr.; call ahead. (☎638-8177. Open M 1-9pm, Tu-F 10am-9pm, Sa 10am-5pm, Su 1-5pm; closed Su in July and Aug.) The **Post Office** is at 3232 Emerson St. (☎635-2241. Open M-F 8:30am-5pm.) **Postal Code:** V8G 4A1.

ACCOMMODATIONS & FOOD. Motels in the $45-75 range abound along the highway outside of the city centre. **Kalum Motel ❷,** 5min. west on Hwy. 16 is a bargain. (☎635-2362. Big TV, local phone calls, and coffee maker included. Singles or doubles $40. Kitchenettes $5 extra.) The **Alpine House Motel ❷,** 4326 Lakelse Ave., is also removed from noisy downtown. Take the Alternate Route across the one lane bridge as you enter on Hwy. 16 from the east. (☎635-7216 or 800-663-3123. Singles $45, doubles $55; Oct.-Apr. $10 less. Kitchenettes available for no extra charge.) **Ferry Island Municipal Campground ❶,** lies just east of Terrace on Hwy. 16 with big sites under big trees and lush walking trails. The island's prime fishing spot is a short walk away and is lined with eager anglers. The community pool is half-price for Ferry Island campers. (☎615-3000. Pit toilets, water, firewood. Sites $12; RV sites $14.) **Kleanza Creek Provincial Park ❶** is the site of an abandoned gold mine, 19km east of the town on Hwy. 16, with sites nestled in towering evergreens along the rushing creek. (Pit toilets, water, firewood. $12.)

Terrace offers a handful of welcome breaks from the dreariness of highway diner cuisine. **Don Diego's ❷,** 3212 Kalum St., is a fun, laid-back joint that serves Mexican, Greek, and whatever's in season. Fresh, new menu with each meal. (☎635-2307. Lunch $7-9. Dinner $10-15. Open M-Sa 11:30am-3pm and 5-9pm, Su 4:30-9pm.) For authentic and affordable Indian cuisine, drive 5min. west of town along Hwy. 16 to **Haryana's Restaurant ❷,** in the Kalum Motel. Vegetarian entrees cost $10-12 and succulent chicken tikka masala is $13. (☎635-2362. Open M-Th 5-9pm, F 5-11pm, Sa 11am-11pm, Su 11am-9pm.) Food, beer, and big TVs await at the **Back Eddy Pub,** 4332 Lakelse Ave., next to the Alpine House Motel. Chess boards and pool tables add class. (☎635-5336. Open daily 11am-midnight.)

SIGHTS. The **Falls Gallery,** 2666 Hwy. 37, just east of town, has an impressive collection of native masks and art. Take the Hwy. 37 turn-off south towards Kitimat, and turn in the driveway before the Volkswagen dealer. (☎638-0438. Open daily 10am-5pm.)

Gruchy's Beach, 13km south of Terrace on Hwy. 37, is a 1.5km hike from the parking lot and is big, sandy, and begging to be picnicked upon. Check out the locals cliff-jumping at **Humphrey Falls.** Take Hwy. 37 south towards Kitimat and after about 35km, turn left on a gravel road and then drive or walk to the water. The **Nisga'a Memorial Lava Bed,** Canada's youngest lava flow, lies 100km north of Terrace. To reach this 54 sq. km swath of moonscape, follow Kalum Lake Dr. (also called the Nisga'a Hwy.), which intersects Hwy. 16 just west of downtown, through the scenic valleys of the **Tseax** (T'SEE-ax) and **Nass Rivers.** At the end of the long trek, you can sleep amid the lava for $12 in a BC Parks **campground ❶** near the Lava Bed visitors center. **Hayatsgum Gibuu Tours** leads 4hr. hikes and guided tours of the lava bed. (☎633-2150. Hikes May-Aug. W-Su 10am and 3pm; reservation required. $12, students $10, children $5.)

OUTDOOR ACTIVITIES. The **Terrace Mountain Nature Trail** is a popular climb of moderate difficulty, beginning at Johnstone Ave. in the east end of town. The route (10km, 1½-2½hr.) offers spectacular views of plateaus and the surrounding valley. For an easy stroll, visit the **Redsand Lake Demonstration Forest,** 26km north on West Kalum Forestry Rd., a well-maintained gravel route found 200m past the Kalum River Bridge, west of town off Hwy 16. The three trails meander around beautiful Redsand Lake, and through a variety of forested areas. A steep, old skidder trail awaits mountain bikers who make it up to **Copper Mountain**—directions to the logging roads that lead up the mountain are complex. Get maps at visitors center.

Anglers can strap on their waders and try their luck on the east shore of **Ferry Island** (see above). Ask for tips at the **Misty River Tackle Shop,** 5008 Agar Ave. (☎638-1369. Open in summer M-Sa 7am-10pm, Su 8am-10pm; winter daily 7am-10pm.) A convenient eight-day angling license for non-Canadians costs $30 and can be purchased from any tackle shop or hardware store in town. To find the hottest fishing spots, watch for where the locals clump. The latest regulations are always posted at www.bcfisheries.gov.bc.ca. Click on the link for Skeena Region 6.

In winter, groomed **cross-country** trails stretch halfway to Kitimat (about 30km down Hwy. 37) around the enigmatic (depth-testing has yet to detect its bottom) **Onion Lake** (☎798-2227 or 615-3000). World-class **downhill skiing** is but

35km west on Hwy. 16 at **Shames Mountain.** Locals go nuts every winter on Shames' double chair and handle tow, the 18 trails on over 130 acres, and the 500m vertical drop.

PRINCE RUPERT ☎250

In 1910, railway magnate Charles Hays made a covert deal with the provincial government to purchase 10,000 acres of choice land at the western terminus of the Grand Trunk Pacific Railway. When the shady operation was exposed two years later, Hays was already under water—not drowned in his dire financial straits, but in the wreckage of the *Titanic*. The sole fruit of Hays' illegal labors was the town of Prince Rupert, victim of a nationwide naming contest lacking in creativity. Nowadays, the famous Cow Bay waterfront gets chicer by the month, while RV caravans blend much of the rest of town into strip-malled suburban mush. But that's a minor point. With exceptional hiking and sea kayaking available in the area, Prince Rupert offers a smooth blend of tasteful urbanism and access to the outdoors.

TRANSPORTATION

Prince Rupert is a gateway to Southeast Alaska. Both BC Ferries from Vancouver Island and the Alaska Marine Hwy. from Bellingham, WA have made this town a stop on their coastal routes, providing access to nearby villages like Metlakatla, and farther ports in the Inside Passage. The only major road into town is the Yellowhead Hwy. (Hwy. 16), known as **McBride St.** within the city. At the north end of downtown, Hwy. 16 makes a sharp left and becomes **2nd Ave.** At the south end, Hwy. 16 becomes **Park Ave.,** continuing to the **ferry docks.** Avenues run parallel to the waterfront with McBride splitting the east from west. Building numbers ascend from this central point as well. Streets run perpendicular and ascend numerically from the waterfront. Many of the city's businesses are located on 2nd and 3rd Ave. **Cow Bay** is off to the right as you enter town.

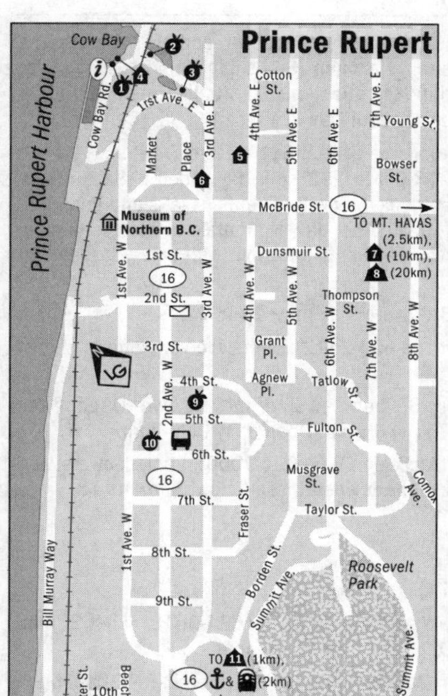

Flights: Prince Rupert Airport is on Digby Island. The ferry and bus to downtown costs $11 (seniors $7, children $4) and takes about 45min. **Air Canada** (☎888-247-22620) runs to **Vancouver** (2-3 per day; $401, under 25 $230). Book 14 days in advance.

Prince Rupert

ACCOMMODATIONS
- Andree's B&B, **5**
- Eagle Bluff B&B, **4**
- North Pacific Fishing Village, **7**
- Park Avenue Campground, **11**
- Pioneer Hostel, **6**
- Prudhomme Lake, **8**

FOOD
- Cow Bay Cafe, **1**
- Cowpuccino's, **2**
- Javadotcup, **9**
- Opa, **3**
- Rodho's, **10**

Trains: VIA Rail (☎627-7304 or 800-561-8630) at the BC Ferries Terminal. To **Prince George** (12hr., 3 per week, $78). A **BC Rail** (in BC ☎800-339-8752; elsewhere 800-663-8238 or 604-984-5500) train continues the next morning from Prince George to **Vancouver** (14hr., $247).

Buses: Greyhound, 6th St. at 2nd Ave. (☎624-5090). To **Prince George** (11 hr., 2 per day, $100) and **Vancouver** (24hr., 2 per day, $201). Station open M-F 8:30am-12:30pm and 4-8:45pm, Sa-Su 9-11am and 7-8:45pm.

Ferries: The docks are at the end of Hwy. 16, a 30min. walk from downtown. Ferry-goers may not park on Prince Rupert streets; check with the ferry company or visitors center for paid parking options. **Seashore Charter Services** (☎624-5645) runs shuttle buses between the terminal and the hotels and train station for $3. **Alaska Marine Hwy.** (☎627-1744 or 800-642-0066; www.akmhs.com) runs to **Ketchikan** (6hr., US$43) and **Juneau** (26hr., US$119). **BC Ferries** (☎624-9627 or 888-223-3779; www.bcferries.bc.ca). To **Port Hardy** (15hr.; every other day; $99, car $233) and **Queen Charlotte Islands** (6-7hr.; 6 per week; $23.50, car $86.50). Reserve for BC ferries well in advance. If the ferry is full, you can get on the standby list by phone.

Public Transportation: Prince Rupert Bus Service (☎624-3343) runs downtown Su-Th 7am-6:45pm, F until 10:45pm. $1, students $0.75, seniors $0.60; day pass $2.50, seniors and students $2. Buses from downtown leave from 2nd Ave. West and 3rd. About every 30min., the #52 bus runs to near the **ferry terminal.** Twice per day, a bus runs to **Port Edward** and the **North Pacific Cannery.** $2.50, students $2.

PRACTICAL INFORMATION

Tourist Information: (☎624-5637 or 800-667-1994) at 1st Ave. and McBride St., in a cedar building modeled after a traditional Tsimshian (SIM-shian) longhouse. Ask for maps and useful packets on accommodations, attractions, and trails. Open May 15 to Labour Day M-Sa 9am-8pm, Su 9am-5pm; Labour Day to May 14 M-Sa 10am-5pm.

Equipment Rental: Far West Sporting Goods (☎624-2568), on 3rd Ave. near 1st St., rents bikes, including lock and helmet. $8 per hr., $25 per day. Open M-Sa 9:30am-5:30pm. **Eco-Treks** (☎624-8311), on the dock in Cow Bay, rents **kayaks** and gear. Singles $35 per hr., double $45 per hr.; $40/$70 per day. No rentals to novices or soloists. 3hr. guided tours for any ability level leave at 1 and 6pm with safety lessons for novices ($45).

24hr. ATM: Banks line 2nd Ave. W and 3rd Ave. W; all have **24hr. ATM**s.

Market: Safeway, at 2nd St. and 2nd Ave. (☎624-2412), offers everything from a florist to a deli. Open daily 8am-10pm.

Laundromat: Mommy's Laundromat, 6th St. between 2nd and 3rd Ave. Offering the cheapest wash in the land: $1, dry $0.75 per 15min. Open daily 9am-9pm.

Showers and pool: Earl Mah Pool, 1000 McBride St. (☎624-9000). Pool, showers, and gym $4, students $3. Call for schedule. **Pioneer Hostel,** see below. Showers $3.

Emergency: ☎911.

Police: 100 6th Ave. (☎624-2136).

Hospital: 1305 Summit Ave. (☎624-2171).

Internet Access: Library, 101 6th Ave. W at McBride St. (☎624-8618). First 30min. free, then $2 per hr. Open M-Th 10am-9pm and F-Sa 10am-5pm.

Post Office: (☎624-2353), in the mall at 2nd Ave. and 5th St. Open M-F 9:30am-5pm. **Postal Code:** V8J 3P3.

ACCOMMODATIONS & CAMPING

Most of Prince Rupert's hotels nestle within the six-block area bordered by 1st Ave., 3rd Ave., 6th St., and 9th St. Everything fills to the gills when the ferries dock, so call a day or two in advance. Most motels are pricey—a single costs at least $60.

Andree's Bed and Breakfast, 315 Fourth Ave. E (☎624-3666). Set in a spacious 1922 Victorian-style residence overlooking the harbor and city—check out the sunsets from the deck. Singles $50; doubles $65; twins $70. $15 per extra person. ❸

Eagle Bluff Bed and Breakfast, 201 Cow Bay Rd. (☎627-4955 or 800-833-1550), on the waterfront in the loveliest part of town. Attractively furnished with bright rooms and private deck on the bay. Rooms come with TVs and a common kitchen area. Singles $45, doubles $55; $10 extra for private bath in single, $20 for double. ❸

Pioneer Hostel, 167 3rd Ave. E (☎624-2334 or 888-794-9998), 1 block east of McBride St. Rupert's only hostel keeps things simple and clean. Microwave, TV, gazebo, and BBQ. Laundry $3. Dorms $17; singles $25; doubles $35. ❶

North Pacific Historic Fishing Village (☎628-3538), at the Cannery Museum in Port Edward. Live for cheap in the renovated cannery workers' quarters, although it is inconvenient without wheels. Bunkhouse rooms $10; modest inn rooms with shared bath $45; small 1-bedroom units with kitchens $65. ❶

Prudhomme Lake, 20km east of town on Hwy. 16, run by BC Parks. Camp along the shore, under shady trees. Worth the drive to escape the RVs. Fishing, water, wood, and pit toilets. Sites $12. ❶

Park Avenue Campground, 1750 Park Ave. (☎624-5861 or 800-667-1994), 1km east of the ferry on Hwy. 16. An RV metropolis! Laundry. Sites $10.50; RVs $13.50, with RV sites $18.50. Showers free for guests. ❶

FOOD

Cow Bay Cafe, 201 Cow Bay Rd. (☎627-1212), shares the waterfront corner of Cow Bay with Eagle Bluff B&B. This popular hot spot switches the menu around on a whim but always keeps the lunches ($8-10) and dinners ($12-17) fresh. Lots of wine. Reservations necessary. Open Tu noon-2:30pm, W-Sa noon-2:30pm and 6-8:30pm. ❸

Opa, 34 Cow Bay Rd. (☎627-4560), upstairs. Pottery studio and sushi bar in old fishing net loft. Drink free tea out of handspun mugs. Spin a bowl at the in-house pottery studio, and while it's firing, hang out on the deck enjoying fresh sushi. Tuna rolls $3, miso soup $1.50. Open Tu-F 11:30am-2pm and 5-9pm, Sa noon-3pm and 5-9pm. ❸

Cowpuccino's, 25 Cow Bay Rd. (☎627-1395). Caffeinate while taking in the cow pics from around the world. Try colossal muffins ($1), bagel sandwiches ($4.50), or Sex in a Pan ($4.75). Open M-Sa 7am-10pm, Sa 8am-8pm. ❶

Rodho's (☎624-9797), on 2nd Ave. near 6th St. Huge menu of pleasing Greek entrees ($13-17), pastas ($9-10), and pizzas ($14 for a loaded medium). Open daily 4pm-1am. Free delivery in town. ❸

Javadotcup, 516 3rd Ave. W (☎622-2822). Internet cafe with speedy computers, coffee, and quick lunches ($3). Smoothies $3. Internet $1.75 per ½hr. Open M-Th 7:30am-10:30pm, F 7:30am-11pm, Sa 8am-11pm, Su 7:30am-10pm. ❶

SIGHTS & OUTDOOR ACTIVITIES

Prince Rupert's harbor has the highest concentration of archaeological sites in North America. Archaeologists have unearthed materials from Tsimshian settlements dating back 10,000 years. **Archaeological boat tours** leave from the visitors center. (2½hr. tours

BRITISH COLUMBIA

depart daily mid-June to early Sept. $28, children $15.) A local expert interprets several sites from the boat, with a stop at the village of **Metlakatla** across the harbor. The **Museum of Northern British Columbia,** in the same building as the visitors center, displays haunting Tsimshian artworks. (☎624-3207. Open late May-early Sept. M-Sa 9am-8pm and Su 9am-5pm; mid-Sept. to late May M-Sa 9am-5pm. $5, students $2, children 6-12 $1; includes guided tour of collection and totem pole and heritage walking tours.)

The best time to visit Prince Rupert may be during **Seafest** (☎624-9118), an annual four-day event planned for June 6-9, 2003. Surrounding towns celebrate the sea with parades, bathtub races, and beer contests. The **Islandman Triathlon** (☎624-6770), a 1000m swim, 35km bike, and 8km run, is also held around the time of Seafestivities and was won in 1997 by an intrepid *Let's Go* researcher. Later in June, Prince Rupert hops during the **National Aboriginal Day.**

A number of attractive small parks line the hills above Prince Rupert. Tiny **Service Park,** off Fulton St., offers views of downtown and the harbor beyond. An even wider vista awaits atop **Mt. Oldfield,** east of town, for serious hikers (8.4km, 5-6hr.). The trailhead is at Oliver Lake Park, about 6km from downtown on Hwy. 16. The **Butze Rapids trail** (5km, 2½-3½hr.) teaches walkers about plants and then plants them in front of rushing tidal rapids. The trailhead is across the highway.

Freshwater anglers can enjoy the great **fishing** in the Skeena and pull up big steelhead or salmon. Get permit and hotspot info at the visitor's center.

Prince Rupert is hemmed in by dozens of sandy little islands, and sea kayaking is a great way to explore them. **Eco-Treks** (see **Equipment Rental,** above) specializes in kayak introductions and rents to experienced paddlers, who can put in at Cow Bay, paddle north around Kaien Island—home to Prince Rupert—and brave the challenging **Butze Reversing Tidal Rapids.** One of the most incredible wilderness experiences in all of BC is the **Khutzeymateen/K'tzim-a-Deen Grizzly Bear Sanctuary.** Hiking is not permitted within the sanctuary, leaving the surrounding wilderness incredibly untouched. Access is through the Khutzeymateen River, and takes 6-10hr. from Rupert. For more information, contact BC Parks at ☎798-2277.

NIGHTLIFE

Drinking establishments in Prince Rupert compete for ferry tourists and fishing boat crews. Come sundown, the town is a-crawl with sea life come to shore. The **Surf Club,** 200 5th St., attracts a younger set later in the evening with space to dance and alternating nights of live music and karaoke. (☎624-3050. Open M, Th-Sa 10pm-2am.) The **Empress Hotel,** 716 3rd Ave. W (☎624-9917), has the best house band, but is not recommended for the pub-naive. **Shooters Bar and Grill** at The Commercial Inn, 901 1st Ave., and **Breaker's Pub,** 117 George Hills Way in Cow Bay overlooking the small boat harbor, are full of local color. (Shooters ☎624-6142. Open Su-M noon-midnight, Tu-Th noon-1:30am, F-Sa noon-2am. Breaker's ☎624-5990. Open M-Th 11:30am-midnight, F-Sa 11:30am-1am, Su noon-midnight.)

QUEEN CHARLOTTE ISLANDS/HAIDA GWAII

Nothing in Haida Gwaii is ever far from rainforest or foggy coast. A full 130km west of Prince Rupert, two principal islands and 136 surrounding inlets form the archipelago known as "the Canadian Galápagos." Graham, the northern island, is home to all but one of the islands' towns, a potent strain of hallucinogenic mushroom, and an eclectic population of tree-huggers, tree-cutters, First Nations people, and fishermen. Few tourist-huggers inhabit Haida Gwaii; in fact, locally drawn postcards poke fun at visitors. But the beaches and rainforests can't help but mellow folks out just a touch. To the south, hot springs steam from mountainous Gwaii Haanas (Gwaii-HAH-nus; Moresby Island on many maps), where the wooden totem poles of the islands' first inhabitants decay. Remote wilderness envelopes the kayakers and boaters who approach Haida Gwaii's lonely sandbars, outcroppings, coves, and shoals. The Islands' chief employer is the timber industry, edging out the Canadian government. In the 1980s, the Islands attracted global attention when environmentalists from around the globe joined the Haida Nation in demonstrations to stop logging on parts of Gwaii Haanas. In 1988, the Canadian government established the Gwaii Haanas National Park Reserve now managed co-operatively by the government of Canada and the Haida Nation.

TRANSPORTATION

The **BC Ferry** from Prince Rupert docks at Skidegate Landing on Graham Island, which is between **Queen Charlotte City** (4km west of the landing) and the village of **Skidegate** (SKID-uh-git), 2km to the northeast. All of the towns of Graham Island lie along Hwy. 16, which continues north from Skidegate through **Tlell, Port Clements,** and **Massett**. Be wary of deer while driving—they're everywhere, and they bolt at all the wrong times. Each town does its own thing. Hit Queen Charlotte City for eating and hostels, or trek north toward hikes and beaches near Tlell and Masset. To the south, Gwaii Haanas is home to **Sandspit** and the Islands' only commercial airport. From Skidegate Landing, 12 ferries per day make the 20min. crossing between the big islands. The lack of public transportation and the exorbitant cost of car rentals bankrupt backpackers, but residents are supposedly generous in picking up hitchhikers. *Let's Go* does not recommend hitchhiking.

QUEEN CHARLOTTE CITY ☎250

Queen Charlotte City's central location and size make it the base for exploring both main islands. "Size" is relative, however; this community of just over 1000 people is not the city its name claims it to be. Most locals either work the sawmills, the trawlers, or for the government.

TRANSPORTATION

Towns on the island line one waterfront road; in Charlotte that road is **3rd Ave.**

Ferries: BC Ferries (☎559-4485 or in BC 888-223-3779; www.bcferries.bc.ca), in Skidegate Landing, 3km east of Queen Charlotte City. To **Prince Rupert** (6hr.; July-Aug. 6 per week, Oct.-June 4 per week; $23.50, bike $6, car $86.50). Reserve at least 3 weeks in advance for cars; car fares do not include driver. Ferries also run between **Skidegate Landing** on Graham Island and **Alliford Bay** on Gwaii Haanas (20min.; 12 per day; round-trip $4.75, car $12.60, off-season car $9.50). No reservations.

Taxis: Eagle Cabs (☎559-4461). $8-11 between Charlotte and the ferry terminal. Open Su-W 7am-9pm, Th-Sa 7am-close.

Car Rental: Rustic Rentals (☎559-4641), west of downtown at Charlotte Island Tire. Must be 21+ with credit card. Will pick up at the ferry terminal in Skidegate. $41 per day, $0.15 per km. Office open daily 8am-7pm, but cars available 24hr.

Auto Repair: Charlotte Tire (☎559-4641), along Hwy. 33, provides 24hr. towing. Open daily 8am-7pm.

PRACTICAL INFORMATION

Tourist Information: (☎559-8316; www.qcinfo.com), on Wharf St. at the east end of town. Ornate 3D map of the islands and a creative natural history presentation. The free *Guide to the Queen Charlotte Islands* has detailed maps. Holds **mandatory orientations** for visitors to Gwaii Haanas Park every day at 8am and 7:30pm (see **Gwaii Haanas,** below). Open mid-May to mid-Sept. daily 10am-7pm; early May and late Sept. daily 10am-2pm.

Outdoor Information: Gwaii Haanas Park Information (☎559-8818; www.fas.sfu.ca/parkscan/gwaii), on 2nd Ave. off 2nd St. above city center. A trip-planning resource. Open M-F 8am-noon and 1-4:30pm. For registration info, see **Gwaii Haanas National Park Reserve,** p. 349. **Ministry of Forests** (☎559-6200), on 3rd Ave. at the far west end of town, has info on Forest Service campsites and logging roads on both islands. Open M-F 8:30am-4:30pm. Get a saltwater **fishing license** at **Meegan's Store,** 3126 Wharf St. (☎559-4428). Open M-Sa 9am-6pm. Freshwater licenses are available only from the **Government Agent** (☎559-4452 or 800-663-7867), 1½ blocks west of the city center.

Equipment Rental: Premier Creek Lodge has bikes. $15 per half-day, $30 per full day.

Bank: Northern Savings Credit Union (☎559-4407), on Wharf St., has a **24hr. ATM**. Many businesses don't take credit cards. Bank open Tu-Th 10am-5pm, F 10am-5:30pm, Sa 10am-3pm. The only other bank is in Massett.

Market: Food is more expensive on the islands. Stock up off-island. The only fully-stocked grocery in town is **City Centre Stores** (☎559-4444), in the City Centre Mall (open M-Sa 9:30am-6pm). **Isabel Creek Store,** 3219 Wharf St. (☎559-8623) opposite the visitors center, offers organic foods. Open M-Sa 10am-5:30pm.

Laundromat: 121 3rd Ave. (☎559-4444), in the City Centre Mall. Wash $1.50, dry $0.25 per 5min. Open daily 9am-9pm. At **Premier Creek Lodging,** $4 including soap.

Emergency: ☎559-8484. **No 911**. **Ambulance:** ☎800-461-9911.

Police: 3211 Wharf (☎559-4421).

Pharmacy: (☎559-4310), downstairs in the hospital building. Open M-Tu and Th-F 10:30am-12:30pm and 1:30-5:15pm, W 1:30-5:15pm.

Hospital: (☎559-4300), on 3rd Ave. at the east end of town.

Internet Access: Free at the **Library,** 138 Bay St. (☎559-4518), under the community hall. Open M and W 10:30am-12:30pm, 1:30-5:30pm, and 6:30-8:30pm., Sa 10:30am-12:30pm and 1:30-5:30pm. **Premier Creek Lodging,** $2 for 10min.

Post Office: (☎559-8349), in the City Centre Mall on 3rd Ave. Open M-F 9am-5pm, Sa noon-4pm. **Postal Code:** V0T 1S0.

ACCOMMODATIONS & CAMPING

Indoor accommodations in town cater to tourists who want to relax. During the summer, make reservations or arrive early in the day to secure a room.

The Premier Creek Lodging, 3101 3rd Ave. (☎559-8415 or 888-322-3388). Bunk beds in a creekside cottage behind the main hotel with shared kitchen, bath, common room, and campfire pit. Fresh breakfast $6-8. Laundry $4. Bed in hostel $20. Clean rooms in hotel $30, with kitchenette $45. Large rooms with kitchen and couches, overlooking the ocean $65 single, $75 double. Campsites $15. Credit cards accepted. ❶

Dorothy and Mike's Guest House, 3125 2nd Ave. (☎559-8439), centrally located up the hill behind the downtown Rainbow Gallery. A standing hammock chair, library, breakfast, and kitchen use. Call ahead. Singles $45; doubles $65. ❸

Joy's Campground (☎559-8890), halfway between the ferry terminal and Charlotte. Camp in Joy's waterfront backyard (which runs alongside 3rd Ave.), and drink from the spring. No toilets. To secure space, go to Joy's Island Jewelers, 3rd Ave., next to Sea Raven Restaurant. Tent sites $5; RV sites $9; electrical $15. ❶

Haydn-Turner Community Campground, 5min. drive west of town. Turn left down a short dirt road labeled "campground" as the main drag turns to gravel. Pleasant and forested. Water, firewood, pit toilets. 6 sites $10; walk-in beach front site $5. ❶

Sea Raven Motel, 3301 3rd Ave. (☎559-4423). Tidy rooms with TV, private bath, phones, and a central location overlook Bearskin Bay. Fishing licenses sold on premises. Singles $45; doubles $65. With kitchen $10 extra. ❸

FOOD

Hanging by a Fibre (☎559-4463), on Wharf St., beside the Howler's building. Hang out in this artsy, popular coffee shop. Take in the local art shows that change each month and a Starving Artist lunch ($4.50) of fresh bread and soup. Wraps or quiche with salad ($8). Lunch served 11:30am-4pm. Open M-Sa 9am-5:30pm and Su noon-4pm. ❶

Howler's Bistro (☎559-8602), on 3rd Ave. Dine on a deck overlooking the water. Fully loaded Howler burger or veggie burger $9. Sandwiches $7. Mexican dishes $8-10. Open in summer daily 11am-11pm; in winter 11am-10pm. **Howler's Pub,** downstairs, will get you good and liquored up. Open daily 1pm-2am. ❷

Oceana, 3119 3rd Ave. (☎559-8683), offers a huge menu of Asian cuisine ($10-14). Lunch specials $7-10. Open daily 11:30am-2pm and 5-10pm. ❷

Sea Raven, 3301 3rd Ave. (☎559-8583), offers an airy, sun-washed dining area and glimpses of the ocean through alder trees. Large seafood selection and the best salmon clam chowder on the island at $4.50 a bowl. Expensive at dinner ($15-22) but reasonable lunches ($8-10). Open daily 7am-2pm and 5-9pm. ❸

Summerland Pizza and Steakhouse (☎559-4588), west on 3rd Ave. about 1km from the center of town. A local pizza joint with Mediterranean and Greek mixed in. Pizza lunch special $6. Sandwiches with fries $6-9. Steak, seafood, or Greek dinners $14-20. Open daily 11am-3pm and 4:30-9pm. ❷

SIGHTS

Few Haidas survived the smallpox plague that hit the once-thriving villages in the southern islands in late 1800s. Still, today the Haida history of 10,000 years on the Queen Charlotte Islands, or "Haida Gwaii," which means "Islands of the People," remains alive. Six impressive cedar **totem poles** were raised in June 2001 on Second Beach, 1km east of the ferry landing on Hwy. 16, as a symbolic demonstration of the continuation of Haida culture. Traditionally, totem poles were built in Haida villages for a variety of reasons, spiritual and secular. The local poles represent each of the six southern Haida villages, now in ruins, which can be visited by boat in Gwaii Haanas Haida Heritage Site (see p. 350). Behind the poles, a shed protects a 50 ft. cedar canoe, the **Lootaas,** carved for Vancouver's Expo '86 by renowned Haida artist Bill Reid (open M-F 9am-4:30pm). Next door, the **Haida Gwaii Museum at Qay'llnagaay** houses totem poles alongside haunting Haida paintings. (☎559-4643. Open June-Aug. M-F 10am-5pm, Sa-Su 1-5pm; May and Sept. closed Su; Oct.-Apr. closed Tu as well. $4, students and seniors $3, children under 12 free.)

The Haida town of **Skidegate,** known as "the village," lies 1km beyond the museum. This community of 695 people is the nexus of Haida art and culture. Residents are sensitive to tourists and expect that visitors will exhibit discretion and respect concerning local culture and practices. Bald eagles often perch atop the totem pole out front of the **Skidegate Community Hall** near the water, a Haida long-house built in 1979 according to ancient design specifications. Visitors must get permission from the **Skidegate Band Council Office** (☎559-4496), between the Gwaii Coop on the main highway, to photograph the cemetery or to camp and hike in certain areas; ask for details from the receptionist at the **Haida Gwaii Watchmen,** next to the museum. (☎559-8225. Open M-F 9am-noon and 1-5pm.)

OUTDOOR ACTIVITIES

Queen Charlotte offers the easiest road access to the west coast of the island. Following 3rd Ave., it turns to gravel; multiple west coast destinations are listed on a sign less than a kilometer down the road. Multiple **forestry recreation sites** on Rennell Sound, 27km down feisty lumber roads, provide a true escape ($8 permit for overnight use). Watch out for the 22% grade as the road dips down toward the sound—if your brakes have given you any problems in the past, shy away.

Hiking the tangle of local logging roads is easier with a few good maps from the **Tlell Watershed Society** (see **Tlell,** below). Even on a two- or three-day hike, it's important to leave a **trip plan** with the visitors center before setting out. The visitors center issues crucial information on **tides** and **scheduled logging road activity.** It's very dangerous for hikers or 4x4s to vie for trail space with an unstoppable logging truck. For the most part, logging road use is restricted to industrial traffic from M-Sa 6am-6pm. Ignoring this restriction isn't just illegal, it's idiotic.

The **Spirit Lake Trail** network (several loops and 3km of trail, 1-2hr.) departs from a parking lot beside the George Brown Recreation Centre off Hwy. 16, in Skidegate. The network leads up a hill side and to the lake (1000m), where it breaks off into various loops that are all well maintained and clearly marked. A guide pamphlet is available at the visitors center. **Balance Rock** teeters on a roadside beach 1km north of Skidegate. A group of brawny loggers once failed in an attempt to dislodge the boulder, so it's unlikely to topple from its precarious perch.

Numerous outfitters rent boats and kayaks, with rates varying according to the length of your journey and your level of experience. **Queen Charlotte Adventures,** 34 Wharf St., offers a $125 guided day paddle of Skidegate Inlet perfect for island newcomers. It'll be tough to keep your mind on the paddling as otters, seals, salmon, and birds all sidle up alongside to investigate you. (☎559-8990 or 800-668-4288. Kayaks $40 per day, $200 per week.)

TLELL ☎250

Tlell (tuh-LEL), 40km north of Queen Charlotte City, is a line of houses and farms spread thinly along a 7km stretch of Hwy. 16. The quasi-town enjoys some of Graham Island's best beach vistas, plus a population of artisans who earn Tlell a reputation as the Charlottes' hippie zone. Tlell hosts its own Woodstock, **Edge of the World Music Festival,** in early July. Here, the rocky beaches of the south give way to sand, and the Tlell River offers fishing and water warm enough for swimming.

PRACTICAL INFORMATION. Visitors center, outdoors information, and flora and fauna displays are put together by the Tlell Watershed Society at **Naikoon Park Headquarters,** right before the campground. (Open Su-Th and Th-Sa 11am-5pm.) Tlell's **bookstore** is in the Sitka Studio (at the end of Richardson Rd.), which shows local art and sells art supplies. (☎557-4241. Open daily 10am-6pm.) **Wrench Tech,** on the Port Clements turnoff, offers some of the only auto service between Queen Charlotte and Masset. (☎557-4324. Open M-Sa 8am-6pm.) Other services include: **emergency/ambulance,** ☎800-461-9911, **no 911; police,** (☎559-4421) in Queen Charlotte City; and the **post office,** on Hwy. 16, 2km south of Wiggins Rd. (Open M-F 2:30-5:30pm.) **Postal Code:** V0T 1Y0.

FALL & RISE OF THE GOLDEN SPRUCE For years, oddity-seekers of the world drove, biked, hiked, and ran to Port Clements, where the planet's only Golden Spruce basked in singular glory. Due to a rare genetic mutation, the 300-year-old tree contained only a fraction of the chlorophyll present in an ordinary Sitka spruce, causing its needles to be bleached by sunlight. The striking 50m giant glowed fiery yellow in the sun, beaming its way into Haida creation myths and horticulturists' dreams. In January 1997, however, a disgruntled ex-forestry worker arrived at the site with an axe and a mission. To protest the logging industry's destruction of British Columbia's forests, he chopped down the tree. These actions won him no prize for logic, but certainly drew province-wide attention.

While islanders reacted with astonishment at their beloved tree's untimely demise, the University of British Columbia revealed another shocker: there had been not one but *three* Golden Spruces—two, created in 1977 from clippings of the original, were growing peacefully in the botanical gardens of the UBC Victoria campus. University authorities donated these golden saplings to the Haida nation, and their future looks good. Concurrent with the fall of the Golden Spruce, an albino raven was born on the island, an event that locals took as a sign foretelling a continuation of the Spruce's three-century history.

ACCOMMODATIONS & FOOD. Sea breezes and birds singing in the spruces await at **Cacilia's B&B/Hltunwa Kaitza ❸,** snuggled against the dunes just north of Richardson Ranch on the ocean side of the road. Friendly cats, driftwood furniture, and hanging chairs give character to the common living space. Rooms are skylit and comfortable. (☎557-4664. Singles $40; doubles $60; grassy tent site and campfire pit near dunes $15.) Pitch a tent or park an RV at the beautiful **Misty Meadows Campground ❶,** in Naikoon Provincial Park, 2km beyond Cacilia's, just south of the Tlell River bridge. (Pit toilets, water, picnic tables, beach access. 14-night max. stay. Sites $12.)

Lunch ($5-8) can be found at **Dress for Less ❶,** 1km south of Richardson Ranch in a pink building. Sidle up to the pink coffee bar nestled among racks of vintage clothing. Enjoy your pick of local artists' wares or sip coffee on the deck. (☎557-2023. Open daily 9am-5pm.) Turn off for Port Clements, 22km north of Tlell, for a good-sized dinner ($12-18) at a good old diner, the **Hummingbird Cafe ❹.** (Open Tu-Su 11am-3pm, 5-8pm.)

OUTDOOR ACTIVITIES. One of the most popular trails around Tlell leads to the **Pesuta Shipwreck,** the hulking remains of a 246 ft. lumber barge that ran aground during a gale in 1928. The 2hr. hike to the site leaves from the Tlell River picnic area off Hwy. 16, just north of the river. When the trail branches, follow the "East Beach" sign up the ridge, or walk the whole way at low tide along the river. Hwy. 16 cuts inland just north of Tlell, leaving over 90km of pristine beach exclusively to backpackers. Allow four to six days to reach the road access at the north end of the route, 25km east of Massett. Before setting out on the East Beach hike, register at **Naikoon Provincial Park Headquarters,** in a brown building on the right side of the highway, just before the Tlell River bridge. (☎557-4390; call ahead.) **Tlell Watershed Society** leads hikes throughout the island to local secret spots, such as Pretty John's Hike. Hikes are on island time so return time may be later than estimated. (Call Berry Wijdeven for information ☎557-4709; www.tlellwatershed.org.)

Visitors to Port Clements often mistakenly assume that the body of water surrounding town is a lake. It's actually the oceanic **Masset Inlet,** and has some of the most uncrowded fishing on the islands. Cast right off the docks or head down the rocky shore for total seclusion. Local shops along the Bayview Dr. waterfront can set you up with permits and whatever gear you need.

MASSETT ☎250

At Mile Zero of the Yellowhead Hwy. (Hwy. 16), Masset isn't a showy city. The mixture of loggers, Haidas, and hippies leads to the occasional culture clash and a sometimes volatile political and social scene. Spectacular scenery surrounds the town; the rainforest of Tow Hill and the expansive beachfront of the Blow Hole, east of town in Naikoon Provincial Park, more than justify the northward trek.

ORIENTATION & PRACTICAL INFORMATION

Massett is about 108km (1¼hr. on a good, although narrow and deer-filled, road) north of Skidegate on Hwy. 16. To get downtown, take a left off the highway onto the main bridge, just after the small boat harbor. After the bridge, **Delkatla Rd.** is on the left. **Collision Ave.,** the main drag, is the first right off Delkatla. To reach the campgrounds (see below), continue on Hwy. 16 without crossing the bridge.

Taxis: Vern's Taxi (☎626-3535). Open daily 8am-6pm.

Car Rental: Tilden Rentals, 1504 Old Beach Rd. (☎626-3318), at the Singing Surf Inn. From $40 per day; $0.25 per km. Must be 25+. Open M-Sa 7am-9pm, Su 8am-9pm.

Car Repair: TLC (☎626-3756), on Collision Ave. Open daily 8am-6pm. 24hr. towing.

Tourist Information: Tourist Information Centre, Old Beach Rd. (☎626-3982 or 888-352-9242), at Hwy. 16. History, maps for bird-watching, extensive Massett packet. Open daily July-Aug. 10am-8pm; Sept.-June F-M 9am-2pm. The **Village Office** (☎626-3955) has advice year-round. Open M-Th 9am-4pm, F noon-4pm.

Bank: Northern Savings (☎626-5231), Main St. north of Collision Ave. Only bank and **24hr. ATM** outside Queen Charlotte City. Open Tu-Th and Sa 10am-3pm, F noon-5pm.

Laundromat: (☎626-5007), just north of Collision on Orr St. Wash $1.75, dry $1.75. Open Tu-Sa 9am-9pm.

Pool: Massett Rec Centre (☎626-5507). Pay to use pool, fitness room, weights, and squash courts. Open M-F 8:30am-9pm, Sa noon-9pm, Su 3-9pm. $5, seniors and children under 18 $2.50.

Ambulance: ☎800-461-9911, **no 911.**

Police: (☎626-3991), on Collision Ave., at Orr St.

Hospital: (☎626-4700; emergency 626-4711). The clinic (☎626-4702 or 626-4703) is on Hodges Ave., on the right just over the main bridge into Massett. Call ahead.

Internet Access: Free at the **Library** (☎626-3663), at Collision Ave. and McLeod St. 30min. limit. Call ahead. Open Tu 2-6pm, Th 2-5pm and 6-8pm, Sa noon-5pm. Available daily but costly ($4 per 20min.) at **Tourist Information Centre** (see above).

Post Office: (☎626-5155), on Main St. north of Collision. Open M-F 9am-5:30pm, Sa 1-4pm. **Postal Code:** V0T 1M0.

BRITISH COLUMBIA

ACCOMMODATIONS & CAMPING

Massett campsites are scenic, cheap, and everywhere. There is **free beach camping** on North Beach, 1km past Tow Hill, 30km east of Massett, in Naikoon Provincial Park. Look for signs marking the end of Indian Reserve property. Call ahead for favored indoor lodging.

Rapid Richie's Rustic Rentals (☎626-5472; www.beachcabins.com), 18km east of Massett on Tow Hill Rd. Self-sufficient accommodation on a wild northern beach. 6 airy cabins with water collected from roof, propane lights, wood or propane heating, kitchen, cookstove, and pit toilets. Sleeps 2-4. Reservations recommended. $40-70 per day for 2; $15 per extra person. ❸

Singing Surf Inn, 1504 Old Beach Road (☎626-3318 or 888-592-8886), next to visitors center before crossing bridge into Massett. Revamped rooms are clean and modern. Attached bar and restaurant keep you fed and tipsy. TV, kitchenette, and queen bed in most singles. Singles from $59; doubles $65. ❹

Copper Beech House, 1590 Delkatla Rd. (☎626-5441), at Collision Ave. by small boat dock. Dine off Beijing china, share a bath with carved wooden frogs from Mexico, and snuggle under comforters from Finland. Singles $75; doubles $100; loft in the garden shed for $25 or make use of that shovel next to your pillow and stay for free. ❹

Village of Massett RV Site & Campground (☎888-352-9292), 2km east of town on Tow Hill Rd. The name belies nothing about this straightforward campground. The 22 sites crowd between forest and ocean. Sites $10-20. Electricity included. ❶

FOOD

Snag yourself a big crab for free on the North Beach. Razor clams are free too, but gathering them is a little more strenuous and the clams are potentially toxic. Call the **Department of Fisheries and Oceans** (☎626-3316) before harvesting mollusks and then stop by Christie St. behind the visitors center to pick up a free permit and harvesting tips. Lemons and seafood garnishes are sold at **Delmos Co-op,** on Main St., south of Collision Ave. (☎626-3933. Open M-Sa 10am-6pm.)

Moon Over Naikoon, 18km on the left on the Tow Hill Rd. Whale bones and other beachcomb finds decorate this small cafe. Edibles include whole wheat flaxseed bread ($5), melt-in-your-mouth butter tarts ($1), and marine-inspired lunch dishes. Open F-M 11am-7 or 8pm. ❷

Marj's (626-9344), on Main St. next to the post office. This little diner is the heart of Massett town and a local hangout where most of the village's problems are solved (or at least discussed) over all-day breakfast ($6-8), burgers ($6-8), NY steaks ($12), and gargantuan slices of fresh pie ($3). Open daily 7am-3:30pm. ❷

Sandpiper Gallery, 2062 Collision Ave. (☎626-3672). The owners happily *plaudern* with homesick Germans and serve *lecker* chicken burgers ($8). Open M-Sa 8:30am-9pm. ❷

Haidabucks (☎626-5548), on Main St. across from the Rec. Center. Haida art decorates this big, airy coffeehouse. Sandwiches run $5-7, but the big dessert pans behind the counter clinch repeat business. Open M-F 9am-5pm, Sa and Su 10am-4:30pm. ❶

SIGHTS & OUTDOOR ACTIVITIES

Tow Hill, an incredible outcrop of volcanic basalt columns about 26km east of town, rises out of nowhere at the far end of Agate Beach, and presides over Massett as the area's reigning attraction. Continue 1km past Agate Back Campsite to **Tow Hill Viewpoint trailhead.** Hustle up the tar paper-covered boards to a fabulous overlook (unless it's foggy) 100m above the rocky shoreline (30min. to ascend). On a clear day, miles of virgin beach and even the most southerly reaches of Alaska spread out below; slow summer sunsets hang in the horizon for hours. On the way back down (10min.), take a detour to loop past the **Blow Hole** (25min.), a small cave that erupts with 15ft. high plumes of water at mid-tide.

Two less-traveled trails depart from the Tow Hill Viewpoint parking lot: an 11km beach walk to **Rose Spit** (2½-3hr. one-way) at the island's northeast corner, and a 10km hike on the **Cape Fife trail** (3½-4hr. one-way), which passes through some of the island's most varied vegetation and accesses to the East Coast Beach and the long hiking route out of Tlell (see p. 344). A lean-to at the end of the Cape Fife trail allows tireless backpackers to link the two routes, exploring the entire island in a 4- to 6-day trek. Inform **Naikoon Park Headquarters** (☎557-4390 in Tlell; see p. 344) before multi-day trips, and contact them for advice. Across the Hiellen River, **North Beach** is where Raven discovered a giant clam containing the first men in the Haida creation myth and where clam and crab catchers congregate today.

Closer to town, red-breasted sapsuckers, orange-crowned warblers, glaucous-winged gulls, and binocular-toting bird-watchers converge on the **Delkatla Wildlife Sanctuary,** off Tow Hill Rd. The best paths for observing 113 local species begin at the junction of Trumpeter Dr. and Cemetery Rd. Continue on Cemetery Rd. past the sanctuary to reach **Oceanview Cemetery,** in a lush green forest on the beach.

Once the crabbing's done, grab your rod and permit (available at virtually any store in town) and **fish** off the docks. Locals regularly pull up bucketfuls of fresh catch in only a few hours. But be courteous—outsiders are too often rude when they visit town, and Massett folk won't take kindly to dock-hogs.

SANDSPIT ☎250

Sandspit is the only permanent community on Gwaii Haanas. The town sprawls alongside the beach, misting everything (people and bald eagles alike) with salty seaspray. Mother Nature buffets the community with a perpetual west wind and provides sprawling sunsets over a porpoise-filled bay each evening. This well-groomed hub houses the only commercial airport on the islands, and serves as a major launching point for kayak and boat trips to Gwaii Haanas National Park Reserve (see p. 350).

ORIENTATION & PRACTICAL INFORMATION. Having a car or bike is handy in Sandspit, since the town is spread over the long **Beach Rd.** parallel to the seashore. There isn't much traffic on the 13km road between Sandspit and **Alliford Bay,** where the ferry docks; those hitching to catch a late ferry report that it is often hard to find a ride. Bringing a bike over on the ferry is free, and the trip to town is an idyllic, easy 1hr. ride along the ocean.

Sandspit Airport is near the end of the spit on Beach Rd. **Air Canada** (☎888-247-2262) flies to **Vancouver** ($495, youth standby $180). **BC Ferries** (☎223-3779 or 888-559-4485; www.bcferries.bc.ca) runs between **Skidegate Landing** on Graham Island and **Alliford Bay** on Gwaii Haanas (20min.; 12 per day; round-trip $4.75, car $12.60, kayak or canoe $2). **Eagle Cabs** runs a shuttle from the airport across to Queen Charlotte City twice per day. (☎559-4461 or 877-547-4461. 1 shuttle Sa. $14 includes ferry. Reservations recommended.)

Tourist and outdoor information is available at the airport. Register and gather trail information or buy topographical maps here before heading into the park. **Park orientations** are held daily at 11am during the summer. (☎637-5362. Open mid-May to mid-Sept. daily 9am-6:30pm; May 1-16 and mid-Sept. to Sept. 30 daily 9am-1pm.) **Budget,** 383 Beach Rd., by the post office, rents autos. (☎637-5688 or 800-577-3228. $50 per day plus $0.35 per km. Must be 21+ with a credit card. **Bayview Sales and Services,** at the west end of town, pumps gas and sells camping fuel. (☎637-5359. Open M-F 9am-noon and 3-7pm, Sa 9am-noon and 1-6pm, Su 9am-1pm and 6-8pm.) **The Trading Post,** on Beach Front Rd., before the gas station when heading out of Sandspit, sells fishing licenses and outdoor gear. (Open M-Sa 9am-noon and 1-6pm.) The **Supervalu Supermarket,** 383 Alliford Bay, in the mini-mall near the spit, carries some produce and sells alcohol. (☎637-2249. Open M-Sa 9:30am-6pm, Tu 9:30am-7:30pm, Su 10am-4pm.) Call an **ambulance** at ☎800-461-9911. The **police** (☎559-4421) are in Queen Charlotte City. The **health clinic** is on Copper Bay Rd., in the school building. (☎637-5403. Open M-F 10am-noon.) After hours, call the **Queen Charlotte General Hospital** (☎559-4506). The **post office** is at Beach and Blaine Shaw Rd. (☎637-2244. Open M-F 9am-5pm, Sa 11am-2pm.) **Postal Code:** V0T 1T0.

ACCOMMODATIONS & CAMPING. Sandspit rooms are more affordable and less crowded than most on the islands. The **Seaport Bed and Breakfast ❷,** just up the road toward Spit Point, offers island hospitality with guest pickup at the airport. Rooms in two cottages with kitchens and cable TV common rooms. (☎637-5698. Reservations are essential in summer. Singles $35; doubles $40.) Identical accommodations are provided by Bonnie's daughter two blocks away on Beach Rd. at **Bayside Bed and Breakfast ❷** (☎637-2433). Not quite as homey but nearly as economical, **Moresby Island Guest House ❷,** on Beach Rd. next to the post office, has 10 rooms with shared washrooms, a kitchen, and coin-operated laundry facilities. Make-your-own-breakfast is provided, but further kitchen use costs $10. (☎637-5300. Singles $30; doubles from $60; cots $15.) **501 RV and Tent Park ❶,** 501 Beach Rd., has the only public showers on the island. (☎637-5473. Open daily 8am-9pm. 5 tent sites $8; 10 RV sites $10. Showers $1 per 2min.)

Along the west coast of the island, BC Parks and the Forestry Service maintain two campgrounds. The first at **Mosquito Lake ❶,** about 35km (1hr.) from Sandspit, is every tenter's dream with mossy sites in wooded seclusion. About another 7km down the road, **Moresby camp ❶** has mowed sites with fewer bugs but lots of loud boat traffic into Gwaii Haanas. Both require an $8 permit. Follow Alliford Bay Main past the ferry docks to South Bay Main to Moresby Rd. to get there. **Grey Bay,** 20km south of town (30min.), offers a virtually uninterrupted expanse of sand. Twenty primitive forestry **campsites ❶** line the long expanse of the beach and afford tons of privacy. Obtain directions and logging road activity updates at the visitors center. Arrive early on weekends. ($8 permit only.)

FOOD. For a nice, long round of golf ($20) and loaded burgers or veggie burgers ($7-9), head to **Willows Golf Course Clubhouse ❷,** near the end of Copper Bay Rd. (☎637-2388. Open W-Su 11:30am-8pm.) More pleasant inside than out, **Dick's Wok Restaurant and Grocery ❸,** 388 Copper Bay Rd., serves a heaping plate of fried rice ($9.50) next to a tank filled with monster goldfish. Dick also offers a limited selection of groceries. (☎637-2275. Open daily 5-10pm.) The **Sandspit Inn,** opposite the airport near the spit's end, houses the town's only **pub.** (☎637-5334. Open daily 11:30am-11pm, F-Sa 11:30am-1am.)

OUTDOOR ACTIVITIES & EVENTS. Spectacular sunrises and sunsets reward those who wander to the end of the **Spit,** where anglers surf-cast for silver salmon. Beachcombers should stay below the tide line if possible, since the spit is legally airport property. Several trails depart from the road between the ferry docks and the spit. In May take the easy stroll on **Onward Point trail** (30min.) to a grey whale watching outlook and a fossil bed. The **Dover Trail** (2hr.) begins 40m west of the Haans Creek Bridge across from the small boat harbor and passes giant cedars with ancient Haida markings. The **Skyline Loop** runs an hour to the shore over more difficult terrain. Although the trail system is marked, it goes through dense brush and crosses other trails, making the return trip more difficult.

Dirt logging roads lead south and west of town into some bogglingly scenic areas. If you plan on using **logging roads** between 6am and 6pm during the week, you must check in at the visitors center for active logging status; in winter call Teal Jones (☎637-5323). Ten kilometers past where Copper Bay Rd. turns into gravel are the rocky shores of **Copper Bay,** a haven for bald eagles.

The roads are perfect for **mountain biking.** The closest rentals are in Charlotte, and bikes are allowed free on ferries. The 24km Moresby Loop is a popular route that runs from Sandspit down to an old train trellis over Skidegate Lake and on to an abandoned Cumshewa Inlet logging camp. Logging in the area has slowed but locals still celebrate **Logger Sports Day** in July. The festival features pole-climbing, caber-tossing, axe-throwing, and other vigorous lumber-related activities.

GWAII HAANAS NATIONAL PARK RESERVE/HAIDA HERITAGE SITE

Roadless Gwaii Haanas corrals visitors with its haunting calm. Paddlers who reach the park's lonesome Haida villages, abandoned and rotting in the rainforest, clear nothing but mile and mile of quickening water and the steady thrum of ocean pounding the empty shore. Provincially owned Crown Land for most of the 20th century, the territory has been disturbed only by sporadic logging and occasional tourist visits to deserted Haida villages. In the mid-80s, the timber industry, the Haida nation, environmentalists, and the provincial government came to heads over land use on the island. In 1988, the federal government interceded, purchasing the southern third of the Queen Charlotte Islands to create a National Park Reserve. A 1993 agreement united the Haida Nation and the Government of Canada in the management of Gwaii Haanas. The Canadian Parks Ministry now patrols the islands, while the Haida Gwaii Watchmen guide visitors with the goal of protecting their cultural heritage.

ORIENTATION

By air or by sea, each summer a few thousand visitors make the long ocean journey south from Moresby Camp (about 25km). **No trails** penetrate Gwaii Haanas and most exploration remains close to the 1600km of shoreline. The seas on the rocky west coast pound, making travel treacherous. On the east coast, the serene, remote waters teem with marine life and birds, peaking in Burnaby Narrows with the highest density of animal and vegetable protein per square meter in the world. Gaze up to see bald eagle nests in dead trees and paddle silently along shore at dawn to spot the strong-jawed sub-species of **black bears** unique to Haida Gwaii.

The islands hold treasures as inspiring as the seascape. Old-growth forest stands tall in **Hik'yah (Windy Bay),** where Haida stood up to loggers. Chains of lakes and waterfalls span Gwaii Haanas. At **Gandll K'in (Hotsprings Island),** three pristine seaside pools steam, soothing ocean-weary muscles.

Haida Gwaii Watchmen share the history of their culture at settlements being permitted to "return to the land," in keeping with Haida tradition. Totem poles slowly decay at **K'uuna (Skedans)** on Louise Island, north of Gwaii Hanaas, and the UNESCO World Heritage site of **Nan Sdins (Ninstints).** Both Haida villages were deserted after late-19th-century epidemics of smallpox and tuberculosis. At **T'aanuu (Tanu),** a moss grown longhouse village can be envisioned from the depressions and fallen poles. The grave of the recently deceased, famous Haida carver Bill Reid can be visited on the point next to the grave of the anonymous "Charlie."

PRACTICAL INFORMATION

Three hundred people can enter the park without licensed tour operators each year; they face unique planning and preparation concerns. These experienced kayakers and small craft owners may reserve dates to enter and exit the park by calling **Super, Natural British Columbia.** (In Canada and the US ☎800-663-6000; elsewhere 250-387-1642. Reservations $15 per person.) The park also provides six standby entries daily, although if you secure one of these spots, you still may not be able to enter the park for another couple of days. All visitors must attend

SIREN'S CALL Pause from paddling or cut off your Zodiak engine. Break the silence with a bull kelp horn! Snatch a piece of the kelp and cut the kelp to a length of 1-2 meters. You should see daylight through the ends. Now hold your horn in a "U" shape, buzz as you would to play a brass instrument, and hear it echo! The kelp is freshest and most prevalent in the spring and early summer.

the 1½hr. **orientation session** before they depart: these are held daily from May to Sept. at 8am and 7:30pm at the **Queen Charlotte City visitor center** (see p. 342) and at 11am at the **Sandspit visitor center** (see p. 348). Call at least a day ahead to arrange sessions. Park user fees are $10 per day (under 17 free; $80 max.). For a **trip-planning** package with a list of charter companies, contact **Parks Canada** (☎250-559-8818). Ask the park management about camping locations to avoid traditional Haida sites. Kayakers venturing into the park alone should file a **sail plan** with the **Prince Rupert Coast Guard** (☎250-627-3081), but should be aware that rescue may not be possible for many hours after a distress incident due to the park's remoteness. Contact **Fisheries and Oceans** (☎559-4413) before sampling shellfish. Freshwater fishing is not allowed; saltwater licenses are available in Charlotte (see p. 341).

Weather reports are broadcast on VHF channel 21. Two **warden stations** are staffed from May to September, at Huxley Island (about halfway down the park) and at Rose Harbour (near the south tip of Gwaii Haanas). They can be reached on VHF channel 16. Five **watchmen sites** (VHF 6) are staffed during the same period, and will offer assistance upon request, although their role is not to act as tour guides. To visit a cultural site, contact the watchmen a day in advance. No more than 12 people are permitted ashore at any one time.

OUTDOOR ACTIVITIES

To avoid the exposed north portion of Gwaii Haanas and to begin your trip in shelter of coastal islands, **Moresby Camp,** on the west side of the island, is a logical place to enter the park. Check with the info center in Sandspit (see p. 348) before traveling the potentially hazardous logging roads to this access point. **Bruce's Taxi** will run you down the gravel roads to Moresby Camp. (☎637-5655. 1hr. one-way; $150; fits 7 people and 2 kayaks; pre-arranged pickup.) **Moresby Explorers** (☎800-806-7633) will transport kayakers, kayaks, and gear from Sandspit into Gwaii Hanaas ($125 per person to Juan Perez Sound) or to their float camp at the north edge of Gwaii Haanas to pickup rental kayaks ($320 per week to rent and be transported). **Queen Charlotte Adventures** (see p. 344), in Queen Charlotte City, offers sea kayak rentals (singles $40 per day, $200 per week) and marine transport ($135 from Queen Charlotte to Juan Perez Sound). A round-trip kayak voyage down the length of the Gwaii Haanas takes two weeks; a guided voyage all the way down and back will run you at least $3000.

To experience Gwaii Haanas quickly and easily, **tour operators** guide visitors and take care of all logistics for entering Gwaii Haanas. Guided visitors do not have to make independent reservations or attend an info session. Run by energetic Doug Gould, **Moresby Explorers,** on Beach Rd. in Sandspit, just west of Copper Bay Rd., offers chartered trips. (☎637-2215 or 800-806-7633; www.moresbyexplorers.com. Trips $125, 2 days with overnight at float camp $350.) **South Moresby Air Charters** (☎559-4222) flies over many of the heritage sites.

APPROACHING THE YUKON

If you want to drive up through the deep north of BC, you have two main options: the Alaska Hwy. and the Cassiar Hwy. The Alaska Hwy. will lead you and a few trillion RVs through eastern BC before curving west as it crosses into the Yukon. The less-developed Cassiar Hwy. runs straight up north into the Yukon through BC's western half. The Cassiar is accessed from the south from Hwy. 16. You'll still have to tussle with the motorhomes, though—the Cassiar's northern terminus is the Alaska Hwy. A smattering of small towns line each road.

ALONG HWY. 37: CASSIAR HWY.

A growing number of travelers prefer the Cassiar Hwy. to the Alaska Hwy., which has become an RV institution. Built in 1972, the Cassiar slices through charred forests and snow-capped ebony peaks, passing scores of alpine lakes on its way from the Yellowhead Hwy. (Hwy. 16) in British Columbia to the Alaska Hwy. in the Yukon. Three evenly spaced provincial **campgrounds ❶** right off the highway offer beautiful camping, and lodges in the provincial parks section in the middle provide resort-like accommodation at prices lower than highway motels on the Alaska Hwy. Any waiter or lodging owner along the Cassiar's 718km will readily list its advantages: less distance, consistently intriguing scenery, and fewer crowds. Be prepared, however, to sacrifice the frequent gas stations and hardtop pavement that come with tourists. Large sections of the road past Meziadin Junction are dirt and gravel and become slippery when wet, causing plenty of tire blowouts. Trucks often barrel up and down the highway; drive at dawn, dusk, and on Sundays to keep in sight of wildlife and out of the way of these gravel-spitting behemoths.

HWY. 16 TO MEZIADIN JUNCTION

Just north of the junction of Hwy. 37 and Hwy. 16 stand the totem poles of **Gitwengak,** which relate the history of the First Nation fort that stood on nearby **Battle Hill** until 1800. The 2.5km **Kitwanga Loop Rd.,** 4km north of the junction, leads through Kitwanga to the **National Historic Park,** where the Hill is located. Once a stronghold for the mighty warrior **Nekt,** Battle Hill has become demure. Its intricate tunnel system has given way to stairs and guided walkways. The totem poles in the small native village of **Gitanyom** lie another 19km to the north and 3km off the highway.

The first gas stop is 139km north at **Meziadin Lake General Store** (meh-zee-AD-in), where produce, deli sandwiches, mail, and fishing stuff can be found. (☎636-2657. Open in summer daily 7am-11pm; winter 7am-9pm.) **Postal Code:** V0J 3S0. **Meziadin Lake Provincial Park ❶** lies another 16km north, with plenty of fishing but tightly packed sites. (Water, free firewood, and pit toilets. 66 sites, $12.) The gravel sites are better geared to RVs, but tenters endure for the fishing; Meziadin Lake is one of three lakes in BC where salmon spawn. You might want to pick up a BC fishing regulations summary (available at nearly every BC visitors center) before you head out - unless you hire an outfitter, you'll have trouble finding one out in the wilderness. Violation fines are not trivial.

Make minor **tire repairs,** grab gas, and shoot the bull with truckers at **Meziadin Junction.** (☎636-2390. Open in summer daily 6am-10pm; winter 8am-7pm.) The nearby **cafe ❶** serves up inexpensive burgers and whatnot. (☎636-9240. Open daily in summer 7am-7pm.) Don't get confused by the "T" in the road. Turn right to **Whitehorse, YT,** which lies 953km (12-15hr. of solid driving) to the north. Or, turn left to **Stewart, BC,** and **Hyder, AK,** which are 62km (45min. on paved roads) west, along Hwy. 37A. The road to Stewart and Hyder is known as the "Glacier Highway"; sprawling, calving plates of pale blue ice spill off the mountains and nearly jam into the roadway, chilling the whole valley.

STEWART, BC & HYDER, AK ☎250

"It's the prettiest place on earth," profess most Hyderites. So as long as you keep your view trained above the dumpy townsite and toward the glacier-welted mountains on every side, you'll see why. **Stewart, BC** is positioned in the jaws of one of the world's longest fjords, among tidal flats. Its cross-border partner, the former ghost town of **Hyder, AK** looks like an old-west village plopped down in the mountains. Horses and townsfolk alike roam the unpaved streets. Although Hyder is technically in Alaska, its currency is Canadian (except at the US Post Office), its clocks tick to Pacific Standard Time, and its area code is 250. During International Days, from Canada Day to Independence Day (July 1-4), the two tiny communities erupt in an extravaganza of fellowship that is North America's longest birthday party, and visitors are heartily welcomed to bond in local bars. Stewart provides most modern amenities in contrast with Hyder, which sports frontier-style nightlife and dirt roads. Although the past economy has been based on the mining and timber industries, with attractions like the world's largest road-accessible glacier, Hyder and Stewart are becoming tourist centers. Visit before the tourist rush gets any more frenzied—the towns still don't depend tourists for most of their revenue, and the prevailing flavor is still local.

PRACTICAL INFORMATION

Hwy. 37A becomes **Conway St.** in Stewart. It intersects **5th Ave.,** which is the main drag on the waterfront, and leads along the bay into Hyder. On your return from Hyder, beware: Canadian customs patrols the border to curb smuggling. Be prepared to show ID and be asked how long you were in "America." Humorless officers don't flinch at the typical response of "about 5 minutes."

Airplanes: Taguan Air (☎636-2800) flies a mail plane that carries passengers to **Ketchikan** (45min., M and Th, $100). Call well ahead.

THE LOCAL STORY

ALL WORK, NO PLAY: INTERNATIONAL DAYS

Celebrated in Stewart, BC, and Hyder, AK, International Days run from Canada Day (July 1st), to American Independence Day (July 4th). The four days of wild festivities are kicked off with the wet t-shirt contest at the Sealaska. International Days features such events as the ax throw and the broom kick and culminates with the annual Bush Woman Classic. The strong-armed women of Hyder and Stewart come together to flex their muscles, trying to post the fastest time and highest accuracy over a course that includes hanging laundry, shooting a bear, chopping wood, diapering a baby, and finally sprinting while applying lipstick. Beware, these women take no prisoners, and spectators are often rallied into competing.

Local Transportation: Seaport Limousines (☎636-2622), in Stewart, drives to Terrace (4hr., daily 10am, $30) and takes sightseers to Salmon Glacier for $34 per person.

Auto Repair: PetroCan (☎636-2307, after hours ☎636-2456), at 5th Ave. and Conway, has the only gas in either town. Open daily 7:30am-8pm, repairs 8am-4:30pm. 24hr. road service.

Tourist Information: In **Stewart** (☎636-9224; www.stewartcassiar.com), on 5th Ave. heading to Hyder. Open June-Aug. daily 9am-7pm; in winter M-F 1-5pm. In **Hyder** (☎636-9148), at the **Hyder Community Association Building;** bear right at the Sealaska Inn downtown. Open June-Aug. M 10am-2pm, Th noon-4pm.

Outdoor Information: Forest Service (☎636-2367), down the hall from Hyder visitors center. Open May 1-Sept. 15, usually 10am-2pm. Call ahead.

Bank: Canadian Imperial Bank of Commerce (☎636-2235), on 5th Ave. in Stewart, has a **24hr. ATM.** Open M and W noon-3pm.

Laundromat and Public Showers: Shoreline Laundromat (☎636-2322), on Brightwell and 6th, behind the post office, in Stewart. Wash $1.75, dry $0.25 per 4min. Showers $1 per 1½min. Open daily 7am-11pm. In **Hyder**, beside the Sealaska Inn. Wash $2, dry $1.75. Showers $3 per 8min. Open 24hr.

Emergency: ☎911.

Police: (☎636-2233) at 8th Ave. and Conway St.

Ambulance: ☎800-461-9911.

Fire: ☎636-2345.

Health Centre: (☎636-2221), at Brightwell and 9th. Open M-F 9am-5pm.

Internet Access: A cheap $2 per hr. at **Stewart Public Library.** Turn left on 9th Ave. as you drive into Stewart from highway. Open in summer M-Th 1-4:30pm and 6-8pm, Su 1:30-4:30pm. **Toast Works,** see **Food,** below. $6 per hr.

Post Office: (☎636-2553) In Stewart, at Brightwell St. and 5th Ave. Open M-F 8:30am-5pm, Sa 9am-noon. In Hyder, 1 Hyder Ave. (☎636-2662), past the Community Building towards Fish Creek. US currency only. Open M-F 9am-1pm and 2-5pm, Sa 10:30am-12:30pm. **Postal Codes:** Hyder: 99923. Stewart: V0T 1W0.

BRITISH COLUMBIA

ACCOMMODATIONS & FOOD

Reasonably priced B&Bs are popping up all over Stewart and Hyder. **Kathi's B&B ❸**, at the corner of 8th and Brightwell, provides placid accommodations and a full breakfast. (☎636-2795. Singles $60; doubles $70.)

Stewart's **Rainey Creek Campground ❶,** located at the end of Brightwell St., is orderly, quiet, and woodsy, with putting-green quality grassy tent sites, forested sites with electricity, and impeccably clean showers. (☎636-2537. Tents $11 for 2 people, $3 per extra person. Dry RV sites $15, sites with electricity $18. Showers $1 per 4min.) Less appealing **Camp Runamuck ❶,** in Hyder, has tent-sites ($12) separated from a gravelly RV park (RV sites $18) with coin showers and laundry in the **Sealaska Inn ❷.** The Inn has **camping ❶** as well as cubicle-like "sleeping rooms" and regular rooms. (☎636-2486 or 888-393-1199. Tents $10; RV sites $18. Sleeping rooms with shared bath $36; singles $52; doubles $58.) It's upstairs from a night lounge famous for its wet t-shirt contests during **International Days.**

The **Bitter Creek Cafe ❶,** in Stewart on 5th Ave., keeps an array of thick, fresh sandwiches and sweets in a great building adorned with historical photos and frontier appliances. (☎636-2166. Open May-Oct. daily 11:30am-2pm and 5-8pm; July-Aug. 8am-9pm.) Across the street, **Toast Works ❶** has an interactive appliance bar and serves fruit smoothies. Two dollars will get you into toaster-lover's heaven, dedicated to the history of the toaster. (Open daily mid-May to mid-Sept.

noon-5:30pm.) **Rainey Mountain Bakery and Deli ❶,** also on 5th Ave. will tempt you with low-priced, fresh-baked treats and breads. (☎636-2777. Open daily 8am-8pm.) **Cut-Rate Foods,** on 5th Ave. in Stewart, lives up to its name. (☎636-2377. Open daily 9am-9pm. No credit cards.) **Wildflour Cafe ❷,** on Hyder's main drag, will feed you the vast Hungry Lumberjack breakfast for $12 or the merely enormous Country Road Special for $8. (☎636-2875. Open daily 6:30am-noon.)

SIGHTS & OUTDOOR ACTIVITIES

SIGHTS. The Stewart Historical Society runs a **museum,** on Columbia St. The classic horror flick *The Thing* was filmed in Stewart, and the museum's got the gory photos to prove it. (☎636-2568. In winter, call ☎636-9029 for appointment. Open mid-May to mid-Sept. daily 11am-7pm. $4, ages 6-12 $2, under 6 free.)

OUTDOOR ACTIVITIES. The chilling **Salmon Glacier,** 20 mi./32km from Hyder on the Salmon River Rd., is the fifth-largest glacier in Canada and the largest accessible by road. Beginning at Mile 19, the road creeps along a ridge almost directly above the glacier for several miles, providing eagle-eye views. The rocks above the road make for good hiking as the glacier lays beneath the setting sun. The road to the glacier is rocky and winding, but navigable for most vehicles. There are many scenic pull-outs. Check road conditions with the Forest Service and get a self-guided tour brochure. **Bear Glacier,** 35km east of Stewart, sits in plain and glorious view of Hwy. 37A. Most anglers let the bear population work the creeks and streams, but for a hefty sum, deluxe fishing boats can be chartered for the hour, day, or week. If you already possess boating prowess, you can rent your own craft.

Each year during the salmon spawning season (late July-Aug.), bears congregate at **Fish Creek,** 5 mi./8km down the road in Hyder, to feed on bloated, dying Alaskan chum salmon. Come early in the morning to avoid tourist crowds. The only maintained trail on the Hyder side is the **Titan Trail,** a challenging 16km (round-trip) hike up from the valley with creek crossings. It gains 1200m of elevation, becoming rocky and difficult toward the end (check with the Forest Service for trail conditions). Heading away from Hyder, the trailhead is on the right about half a mile past Fish Creek. Check with the forestry gang for trail conditions and bear density. 8 mi./13km north of Stewart along Hwy. 37A, the **Ore Mountain Trail** is a shorter, but still challenging 4 mi./7km (round-trip) climb to a viewpoint overlooking the Bear River Valley. Hunters near Hyder should note that the Canadian borderline is always very, very close—pay attention to topo maps to avoid huge fines.

NIGHTLIFE

The principal activity in Hyder is sidling up to the bar in the historic **Glacier Inn** and asking to be "Hyderized." Over $45,000 in signed bills line the tavern walls, where early miners would tack up cash to insure themselves against returning to town too broke to buy a drink. (☎636-9092. Open in summer 10am-close; winter 2pm-close.) If you want to catch a ballgame on TV or master the Grand Lizard pinball machine, head over to the **Sealaska.** (Take a left at the "intersection." ☎636-2486. Open 11am-close.)

MEZIADIN JUNCTION TO ISKUT ☎250

This stretch of the Cassiar Hwy. has hands-down the best lodging and roadside bear-viewing around and also closest access to the two provincial parks. The area around the small village of **Iskut,** 256km north of Meziadin Junction, presents a range of resorts, earning it the unremarkable title "Resort Capital of NW BC."

The first stop after the junction is 90km north at **Bell II Lodge ❷,** the posh heli-skiing jump-off point that caters to summer road-trippers searching for gas and food at reasonable prices. Big breakfasts are $8 and burgers are $6-8. (☎604-881-8530 or 800-655-5566. Sites $10; RV sites $22. Showers and dump station. Gas and coffee shop open daily 7am-10pm. Dining room open daily 7am-8pm.) Another 117km north is **Kinaskan Lake Provincial Park ❶,** where an immaculately kept campground includes water, pit toilets, firewood, and a boat launch onto the rainbow trout-stocked lake. (Wheelchair accessible. 50 lakeside sites, $12.) Pick up fishing permits before you arrive. At the far end of the lake is the head of a 24km hiking trail to **Mowdade Lake** in **Mount Edziza Provincial Park** (see below). There is gas, car repairs, lodging, boat rentals, and the last food for a long while among the moose antlers of the "wilderness oasis" of **Tatogga Lake Resort ❷,** another 25km north. (☎234-3526. Canoes $20 for 2hr., $40 per day. Boat and motor $65 per day. Meat lover's sandwich $4.75. Laundry $2.50 wash or dry. (Open May-Sept. daily 7am-10pm, winter 7am-7pm). Cabins with woodstoves $32, cabins with amenities $45 for 1 bed, $65 for 2 beds. Tent sites $10-12. RV sites $19. Showers $3.) A bit farther is the **Ealue Lake** (EE-lu-eh) turn-off on Spatsizi Rd., which leads to trailheads pointing deep into the virgin backcountry of the **Spatsizi Plateau Wilderness.**

Everyone heartily approves of **The Red Goat Lodge,** 3km south of Iskut on **Eddontenajon Lake.** The **hostel ❶** in the basement boasts a full kitchen, spacious common room, wood stove, coin showers, and laundry. The hosts' kids and llamas keep the place lively even when it's not packed. The **B&B ❸** upstairs is equally impressive. (☎234-3261. Wash $2, dry $1. Hostel $17; B&B singles $65, doubles $85. Cabins $90-105. Showers $1 per 3½min.) **Tent sites ❶** are on the loon-inhabited lake. (Canoes $10 per half-day. Rentals for trips on the **Stikine** and **Spatsizi Rivers** start at $35 per day. Sites $14; RV sites $20.)

At Iskut, travelers can get gas and groceries at **Kluachon Centre.** (☎234-3241. Open June-Aug. daily 8am-10pm; winter M-Sa 9am-6pm, Su noon-5pm.) It doubles as the **post office** (open M, W, and F 9am-4pm, Tu 1-4pm). **Postal Code:** V0J 1K0.

Just north of Iskut, **Mountain Shadow RV Park and Campground ❶** has lovely campsites nestled in the mountain forest near trails to the lake and hikes into the woods. (☎234-3333. Boat rental $15. Sleeping cabin with electricity $45, cabin with stocked kitchen and bathroom $65. Tent sites $15; RV electric RV sites $18; Full RV sites $20.)

DEASE LAKE ☎250

Dease Lake, 84km north of Iskut, became a Hudson Bay Company outpost in the late 1800s, although it had been long known by the local indigenous Tahltan as "Tatl'ah" ("Head of the Lake"). When the early gold rush glory petered out, so did the town's allure. There's little to draw road-trippers to Dease Lake besides gas and food. The traveler in search of accommodations should stay outside of Dease Lake in resort-like, lake-front accommodations in the **Iskut** area that cost less and have more character.

PRACTICAL INFORMATION. The **Dease Lake Tourist Information Office** is in the Northern Lights College, a small series of buildings on Cassiar in the middle of town (☎771-3900). The **Forest Service** (☎771-8100) occupies the building next door and offers info on local trails or campsites; call ahead. Fishing and camping supplies can be found at **McLeod Mountain Supply Ltd.,** on Boulder St. past **Tanzilla Bar.** (☎771-4699. Open M-Sa 9am-5pm, Su 10am-4pm.) The **TD Bank** is in the Government building across the highway from the college. (Open M, W, and

F 10am-noon and 1-3pm.) **Dease Gas Station** has **showers** ($4; includes towel, soap, and shampoo) and a **laundromat** (☎771-5600; wash $3, dry $0.25 per 5min.; open daily 7am-8pm). The **Stikine Health Center** is just off the Cassiar at the north end of town. (☎771-4444. Walk-in M-F 8:30am-4:30pm.) Other service include: **police,** ☎771-4111; and **ambulance,** ☎771-3333. Free **Internet access** is available at the Northern Lights College. (Open M-F 8:30am-noon and 1-4:30pm.) The **Post office** is in the Dease Gas Station. (☎771-5013. Open M-F 8:30am-1pm and 2-5pm.) **Postal Code:** V0C 1L0.

ACCOMMODATIONS & FOOD. The spacious, pine-furnished **Arctic Divide Inn ❹,** right on the Cassiar, features clean rooms with private bath, phones, TV, and access to a shared kitchen. (☎771-3119. Generous continental breakfast is included. Singles and doubles $68.) You can camp in town at **Allen Lake ❶.** From Boulder St., go left on 1st Ave. and follow it to the end ($8 camping permit only; no real sites, no water, pit toilets). Be warned—the road down to the lake is steep. For camping outside of town, head south to the **Tanzilla River Lion's Club Campground ❶** ($7 for a site with fire pit and pit toilets, $3 per bundle of wood) or drive an hour south for true camping paradise.

Northway Country Kitchen ❷, or "the restaurant," offers big portions in a spacious setting. Feel your arteries clog for only $9.50 with "pierogies & smokies," cheese-filled dumplings with four sizeable sausages. (☎771-4114. Open May-Oct. daily 7am-9pm.) Stock up on the best-priced and fullest selection of **groceries** for quite a distance at the **Supervalu.** (☎771-4381. Open mid-June to Sept. daily 8am-8pm; winter M-Sa 9am-7pm, Su 9am-6pm.)

NEAR DEASE LAKE: TELEGRAPH CREEK. Lying 119km from Dease Lake on Telegraph Creek Rd., Telegraph Creek is the only remaining settlement along the **Stikine River** (stuh-KEEN). The highest navigable point on the Stikine, the site was an important rendezvous for the coastal Tlingit and interior Tahltan people. Telegraph Creek's 400 residents are still mostly Tahltan.

The biggest attraction for thrill-seeking travelers is the 112km **Telegraph Creek Rd.** The gravel road is well maintained and offers magnificent views of the **Stikine Grand Canyon.** It is no place, however, to lug a clumsy RV or give a failed brake system a second chance. The second half of the road features 20% grades and hairpin turns along the steep obsidian outbanks of the Tuya and Stikine River canyons. Travelers should allow 2½hr. to drive each way, with time to de-frazzle in between. A rest stop, 88km from Telegraph Creek, offers a view of the canyon and a chance to stop and check on your car. If you don't know much about checking your car, learn the basics before tackling this road.

The modern village of Telegraph Creek revolves around the historic **Stikine RiverSong.** Today, the RiverSong acts as Telegraph Creek's **hotel ❸, cafe ❸,** gas station, and general store. Rooms are clean, with cedar finishing and a common kitchen. (☎235-3196. Showers $4. Open May-Sept. M-Sa 11am-7pm, Su noon-7pm. Singles $55, doubles $65; $10.50 per additional person.) Free **camping ❶** is available 15 mi. toward **Glenora** past Winter Creek. Outdoors adventurers need to be respectful of tribal lands, which have different access, fishing, and hunting regulations than the rest of BC. Tribal land holdings speckle the surrounding wilderness. Topo maps help identify their boundaries, but you'll need mapsheets anyway if you plan to do much hiking—there are few developed trails in the region.

The community welcomes its infrequent visitors, but those keen to explore should seek permission from the **Tahltan Band** (☎235-3151) before crossing onto tribal lands. For **tire repair,** contact **Henry Vance** (☎235-3300). Locals have been known to stop and help motorists stalled by the road. Call the **police** at ☎235-3111.

Follow signs for Glenora to find the **health clinic** (☎235-3212 or 235-3171). On your way into town from the south, the **post office** is on the right. (Open M and W 9:30-11:30am, Tu and Th 1-4pm, F 9:30-11:30am and 1-4pm.) **Postal Code:** V0J 2W0.

DEASE LAKE TO THE ALASKA HWY.

This stretch of highway follows the old Cassiar Gold Route, where some dredges are still in use. **Moose Meadow Resort ❶,** 85km north of Dease Lake, is a roomy lakeside campground with access to canoe routes. (Firewood, water. Sites $8; cabins from $25. Showers $2.50.) **Jade City ❶,** 113km past Dease Lake, offers free RV and tent sites in addition to an impressive jade stash. (Open daily 8am-9pm.)

Kididza Services, at Good Hope Lake, 23km past Jade City, is the last gas for 98km, when you hit the Alaska Hwy. (☎239-3500. Open M-Sa 8am-9pm, Su 10am-4pm.) **Boya Lake Provincial Park ❶** is 152km north of Dease Lake and the final campground before the Alaska Hwy. (85km later), situated on a magnificent turquoise lake with a boat launch and swimming dock. Grab some reading material at the book exchange box at the entrance. (Pit toilets, firewood, water. 45 sites, $12.) Having crossed into Yukon 3.5km back and reached the end of this 718km odyssey at the junction of the Cassiar Hwy. and the Alaska Hwy., travelers can find showers, munchies, gas, and minor repairs at the **PetroCan Station**, which doubles as the office for the **RV park ❶** and **motel ❷** next door. (☎536-2794. Sites $13-16, full RV sites $20. In motel, baths are shared. Singles and doubles $40. Showers free, $3 for non-guests.) If the office is closed, check in at the **saloon.** (☎536-2796. Open daily 11am-midnight.) The station also operates a **24hr. laundromat** (wash $1.50, dry $0.50 per 14min.). Travelers can chomp on a Junction Melt ($8) at the **Junction 37 Cafe ❷,** next to PetroCan. (☎536-2795. Open May-Oct. M-Sa 6am-midnight, Su 7am-10pm; winter daily 7am-10pm.) **Whitehorse** lies another 435km (5hr.) west on the Alaska Hwy. (see below).

BRITISH COLUMBIA

HWY. 97: ALASKA HWY.

Built during World War II in reaction to the Japanese bombing of Pearl Harbor and the capture of two Aleutian Islands, the Alaska Hwy. served to calm Alaskan fears of an Axis invasion. Due to the speed with which it was built, the highway stands as one of the most incredible engineering feats of the 20th century. Army troops and civilians pushed from both ends—Dawson Creek and Fairbanks—and bridged the 2451km at Mile 1202 (near Beaver Creek) in 8 months and 12 days.

While the original one lane dirt track has evolved into a "highway," the potholes that develop after the winter thaw and the patches of loose gravel give drivers a taste of the good old days. In recent years, the US Army has been replaced by an annual army of over 250,000 tourists and RV-borne senior citizens from the US and Europe. For those with the time to stop, there are countless opportunities to hike, fish, and view wildlife off the highway. However, if your priority is to beat the quickest path to the Yukon border, the **Cassiar Hwy.** (Hwy. 37; see p. 352) may be a better route for you. Another scenic option is on the far side of the Yukon border, on the **Campbell Hwy.** (Hwy. 4; see p. 415).

For daily Alaska Hwy. **road conditions** call ☎867-667-8215. Mileposts put up along the highway in the 1940s are still used as mailing addresses and reference points, although the road has been rebuilt and rerouted so many times that they are no longer accurate. Washouts sometimes occur in the spring, and other hazards include forest fires, falling rock, and construction delays. Motorists should always be aware of wildlife on the road, keep headlights on, carry spare tires and spare parts, and be prepared to slow down for graders, potholes, and general road breakup and gravel patches.

DAWSON CREEK ☎250

Mile 0 of the Alaska Hwy. is Dawson Creek, BC. First settled in 1890, it was just another pip-squeak frontier village of a few hundred people among the flaming canola fields of Peace River. Then the Alaska Highway came through, and so did nearly every senior citizen in North America with a motor home. The 13,000-odd residents are serious about their home's role as the womb of the Alaska Hwy., and visitors who pause to enjoy the town's history and hospitality can easily get caught up in the enthusiasm. Dawson draws a hardy Alaska-bound crew and caters more to the pure tourist than the outdoorsman.

ORIENTATION & TRANSPORTATION

There are two ways to reach Dawson Creek from the south. From Alberta, drive northwest from Edmonton along **Hwy. 43,** through Whitecourt to Valleyview; turn left on **Hwy. 34** to Grande Prairie, and continue northwest on **Hwy. 2** to Dawson Creek for a total journey of 590km. From Prince George, drive 402km north on the John Hart section of **Hwy. 97** (see p. 333). Both drives take the better part of a day.

Greyhound, 1201 Alaska Ave. (☎782-3131 or 800-661-8747), is open M-F 6am-5:30pm and 8-8:30pm; Sa 6-11am, 2:30-4:30pm, and 8-8:30pm; Su 6-10:30am, 3-4:30pm, and 8-8:30pm. Buses run to **Whitehorse, YT** (20hr.; June-Aug. M-Sa; $186); **Prince George** (6½hr., 2 per day, $58); and **Edmonton** (8hr., 2 per day, $78).

PRACTICAL INFORMATION

Tourist Information: Stop at the **visitors center,** 900 Alaska Ave. (☎782-9595), next to the big red grain elevator, for daily road reports, maps to just about everything in the city, and a small museum (donation requested). Open May 15-Labour Day daily 8am-7pm; winter Tu-Sa 9am-5pm.

Bank: CIBC (☎782-4816), 10200 10th St. **24hr. ATM.**

Markets: Groceries at **IGA,** 1100 Alaska Ave. (☎782-5766). Open daily 8am-11pm. **Safeway,** 1200 8th St. (☎800-723-3929). Open daily 8am-11pm.

Laundromat: King Koin Laundromat, 1220 103rd Ave. (☎782-2395). Wash $2.50, double load $3, dry $0.25 per 5min. Showers $2.75. Open daily 8am-9pm. At the **Mile 0 Campground,** loads are a buck apiece (see **Accommodations,** below).

Auto Repair: J&L Mechanical Services (☎782-7832) does **24hr. road service.**

Hospital: 1100 13th St. (☎782-8501). **Ambulance:** ☎782-2211.

Police: (☎782-5211), at Alaska Ave. and 102nd Ave.

Crisis Line: ☎877-442-2828

Internet access: Free 1hr. at the **library,** 10 St. and McKellar Ave. (☎782-4661). Open Tu-Th 10am-9pm, F 10am-5:15pm, Sa and Su 1:30-5:15pm; closed Su summer.

Post Office: (☎782-9429), at 104th Ave. and 10th St. Open M-F 8:30am-5pm. **Postal Code:** V1G 4E6.

ACCOMMODATIONS & CAMPING

Those willing to trade a few amenities for bargain prices, great location, and an offbeat aura should head straight for the historic **Alaska Hotel ❸.** It is located above the Alaska Cafe & Pub (see **Food,** below) on 10th St., 1½ blocks from the visitors center. The comfortable rooms are carefully decorated, some with pictures of Marilyn Monroe and Elvis. Shared bath; no TV or phone. (☎782-7998. Singles $32; doubles $37; winter $5 less.) The newer **Voyageur Motor Inn ❸,** 801 111th Ave., facing 8th Ave., offers motoring voyagers phones, cable TV, and fridges at no extra charge in sterile boxy rooms. (☎782-1020. Singles $45; doubles $50.) Folks willing to spend more can get all sorts of services at the **Inn On The Creek ❹,** 10600 8th St.: cable TV, fridge and microwave, and a location close to downtown. (☎782-8136. Singles $55-65; doubles $60-70.) The popular but RV-laden **Mile 0 Campground ❶** is 1km west of Alaska Hwy., adjacent to the Pioneer Village. (☎782-2590. Coin laundry $1.25. Sites $12; full RV sites $17. Free showers.) Campers can also head for the convenient **Alahart RV Park ❶,** 1725 Alaska Ave., at the intersection with the John Hart Hwy., for a dump station and laundry. The friendly owners rival the visitors center for maps and suggestions on entertainment and food. (☎782-4702. Sites $10; full RV sites $20. Free showers.)

FOOD

The **Alaska Cafe & Pub ❷,** "55 paces south of the Mile 0 Post" on 10th St., serves excellent burgers and fries from $7. The pub offers live music nightly at 9pm (mostly country), and travelers can sing at Monday night karaoke amidst stuffed cougars, elk, and marmots. (☎782-7040. Open Su-Th 10am-10pm, F-Sa 11am-11pm; pub open daily noon-3am.) Eating too many sandwiches ($5.50) at **PotBelly Deli ❶,** 1128 102nd. Ave., will give your tummy some chub too, but you won't regret it. Each night a new international cuisine inspires the chef. (☎782-5425. Open M-F 10am-7pm, Sa 10am-5pm.) Dine old-school style in **Mile One Cafe ❷.** Select your entree from the chalkboard as you relive 1940s Dawson Creek in the Pioneer Village. (See **Sights.** Open Tu-Su 8am-7pm.) Pick up a loaf for the road at the **Organic Farms Bakery,** 1425 97th Ave. From the visitors center, drive west along Alaska Ave. and take a right at 15th St. You can't miss it; the building is huge. Breads are baked fresh from local grain and start at $2; cakes and cookies are also available. (☎782-6533. Open F 9:30am-5:30pm, Sa 9am-4pm.)

SIGHTS & OUTDOOR ACTIVITIES

This town boomed during construction. Literally. On February 13, 1943, 60 cases of exploding dynamite leveled the entire business district save the **COOP** building, now Bing's Furniture, opposite the Mile 0 post. Travelers cruising through Dawson Creek can't miss the photo ops at **Mile 0 Cairn** and **Mile 0 Post** near the visitors center. Both commemorate the birth of the Alaska Hwy., and are within a stone's throw of the visitors center. The **Art Gallery** in the old grain elevator next door displays a photo essay on the Alaska Hwy. creation saga. (☎782-2601. Open daily June-Aug. 9am-5pm; winter Tu-Sa 10am-noon and 1-5pm.)

The **Pioneer Village,** 1km west of Mile 0, is an excellent re-creation of Dawson Creek life from the 1920s to the 40s, with antique (read: rusted) farm equipment, an antler carver hard at work, nine gardens tended by the Horticultural Society, and a play area for children. (☎782-7144. Open May-Aug. daily 8am-8pm. Donation requested.) In early August, the town plays host to the **Fall Fair & Stampede** (☎782-8911), with a carnival, fireworks, chuckwagon races, and a professional rodeo.

Travel 10km out of town to the highland marshes of **McQueen's Slough** and follow the trail to the left across a boardwalk and around the water. Take Hwy. 49 east from the visitors center, turn left onto Rd. 3. (Rolla Rd., not to be confused with Parkhill Dr., which is also marked "Rolla Rd.," and which is still in town), and take the second left at the driveway across from the binocular signpost. The slough is filled with a broad spectrum of birds.

FORT NELSON ☎250

Over 450km north of Dawson Creek and 210km east of Toad River is Fort Nelson, a bastion of natural resource extraction. The **visitors center,** in the Recreation Centre/Curling Rink on the west edge of town, provides **daily Alaska Hwy. road reports.** (☎774-6400. Open daily May-Sept. 8am-8pm.) The **Fort Nelson Heritage Museum,** across the highway from the visitors center, features an impressive collection of stuffed game, as well as remnants from the era of highway construction. (☎774-3536. Open daily 9am-6pm. $3, ages 6-16 and seniors $2.) The **First Nations Craft Center** is on 49th Ave. From 50th St., off 50th Ave. S, take a right on 49th Ave.; it's on the right. (☎774-3669. Open M-F 8:30am-4:30pm.)

Rest at the **Mini-Price Inn ❸,** 5036 51st Ave. W, one block off the highway near the visitors center. No phones. Cable TV. (☎774-2136. Singles $45; doubles $50; kitchenettes $5 extra.) The **Almada Inn ❹** is by the CIBC Bank off the Alaska Hwy. (☎774-2844. Free breakfast. Singles $69; doubles $79.) The **Westend Campground ❶,** across from the visitors center, has dusty sites in a pretty, wooded area, but the place is more RV-oriented than tent friendly. (☎774-2340. Laundry: wash $2, dry $1 per 30min. Sites $17; full RV sites $22. Showers $1 per 9min.)

There aren't many choices for dining in Fort Nelson. **Dan's Pub ❷,** at the southern end of town, offers nightly drink specials, pool, and an extensive menu in a dark pub. (☎774-3929. Open M-Th 11am-12:30am, F-Sa 11am-1:30am, Su 11am-midnight. After 8pm, 19+.) **Blue Bell Restaurant ❶,** opposite Dan's in the Blue Bell Inn, serves a $5 breakfast. (☎774-3550. Open M-Sa 6am-9pm, Su 8am-4pm.)

FORT NELSON TO BC/YUKON BORDER

Small towns, usually composed of one gas pump, one $50-60 motel, and one cafe, pock the remainder of the highway to Whitehorse. Fortunately for the glassy-eyed driver, highway scenery improves dramatically a few miles out of Fort Nelson.

STONE MOUNTAIN. About 150km north of Fort Nelson, the stark naked **Stone Mountain** appears. Next, **Summit Lake** lies below the highest summit on the highway (1295m). The neighboring **Stone Mountain Campground ❶** makes a superb starting point for hiking in the area. (New-fangled composting outhouse, firewood, water. Sites $12.) The steep **Summit Peaks Trail** begins across the highway from the campground, ascending 5km along a ridgeline to the breathtaking crest. A more moderate trail climbs 6km to the alpine Flower Springs Lake. Each hike takes about 5hr. round-trip. A 70km loop leads from km 632 of the Alaska Hwy. through the craggy MacDonald Creek Valley and back out the Wokkpash Valley Gorge. Gas and accommodations are available roadside 7km past the lake.

TOAD RIVER. The **Toad River Cafe ❷,** on the highway has some 5900 hats dangling from the ceiling. Tasty burgers from $7. (☎232-5401. Open in summer daily 6:30am-10pm; winter 7am-9pm.) An Alaska Hwy. odyssey—a grassy, RV- and tent-friendly campground with private, new sites—**Poplars Campground and Cafe ❶** springs up 5km after Toad River. (☎232-5465. Tents $14; full RV sites $20.)

MUNCHO LAKE. Fifty kilometers north of Toad River, Muncho Lake Provincial Park delights even the weariest drivers. Muncho ("big lake" in Tagish) is a 7 mi. long azure mirror. **Strawberry Flats Provincial Campground ❶** and **MacDonald Provincial Campground ❶,** 8km farther on, have the best camping in the area with sweet lakefront sites. (Pit toilets, fire wood, water. Sites $12.) If you don't want to camp, stay at the **Muncho Lake Lodge ❸,** 10km north of Strawberry Flats. Rooms are well-kept, and the service is good. (☎776-3456. Singles $45; tents $14; RV sites $16.)

LIARD RIVER HOT SPRINGS. Near the 775km mark are the Liard River Hot Springs. These two naturally steamy and sulfurous pools are a phenomenal place to sooth a driver's derriere. The park service manages campsites and free day-use of the springs. (Reservations ☎800-689-9025. Water, toilets, firewood. Gates closed 11pm-6am. Sites $15.) About 10km after Liard Hot Springs, a rough, 3km gravel road thwarts RVs and leads to the hidden and largely untouristed **Smith River Falls.** Watch carefully for the turn-off sign. A steep trail with rickety staircases leads right to the base of the huge cascade, and grayling can be fished from the Smith River with a permit. For permit info, contact BC Parks at ☎250-787-3407.

ALBERTA

ALBERTA FACTS & FIGURES
Capital: Edmonton. **Area:** 661,185 sq. km. **Population:** 2,907,882.
Alberta Provincial Tartan: Forest green, wheat gold, sky blue, rose pink, black.
Bird: Great Horny Owl. **Mammal:** Rocky Mountain Big-Horned Sheep.
World's Largest Mall: West Edmonton Mall. **Sales Tax:** 7%. **Drinking Age:** 18.

With its gaping prairie, oil-fired economy, and conservative politics, Alberta is often called the Texas of Canada by the Yanks to the south. (Historically speaking, Texas is actually the Alberta of the US.) Petrodollars have given birth to gleaming, modern cities on the plains. In 1988, the Winter Olympics temporarily transformed Calgary into an international mecca, and the city hasn't yet stopped collecting tourist interest off the legacy. Calgary is also the stomping grounds for the Stampede, the world's largest rodeo and meeting place for the most skilled cowboys in the West. The capital, Edmonton, is slightly larger than Calgary, its hockey rival to the south, and serves as the trusty transportation hub for the stunning national and provincial parks that line the Alberta-British Columbia border.

For adventurous outdoor enthusiasts, Alberta is a year-round playground. Hikers, mountaineers, and ice climbers will find a recreational paradise in the Canadian Rockies in Banff and Jasper National Parks and Kananaskis Country. The parks represent Alberta's most consistent draw, and with good reason: they pack enough scenic punch, exhilarating thrills, and luxurious hostels to knock travelers of all ages flat. The province boasts thousands of prime fishing holes, internationally renowned fossil fields, and centers of indigenous Canadian culture.

HIGHLIGHTS OF ALBERTA

MEANDER through breathtaking **scenery** between Banff and Jasper on the Icefields Parkway; this area is best seen from a bike (see p. 387).

SWAGGER into town for the **Calgary Stampede** (see p. 374).

DIG for dinosaur bones in the **Badlands** (see p. 375).

LEARN time-tested methods for killing tens of thousands of buffalo using only ingenuity and gravity at **Head-Smashed-In Buffalo Jump** (see p. 376).

HIT the slopes at **Lake Louise** (p. 386).

EDMONTON ☎780

The provincial capital of Alberta may not have claim to the amazing scenery of Banff and Jasper, or the spectacle that is the Calgary Stampede, but Edmonton has a variety of other things to offer a wide spectrum of tastes. This popular travel destination hosts the Canadian Finals Rodeo in November, and is home to the world's largest shopping mall. A plethora of museums attracts children and art lovers alike, while the Saskatchewan River valley draws hikers and bikers. A perpetual stream of music, art, and performance festivals brings summer crowds to the self-proclaimed "City of Festivals." A happening strip on Whyte Avenue transforms Edmonton into a pleasant urban oasis near the almost overpowering splendor of the neighboring Rockies.

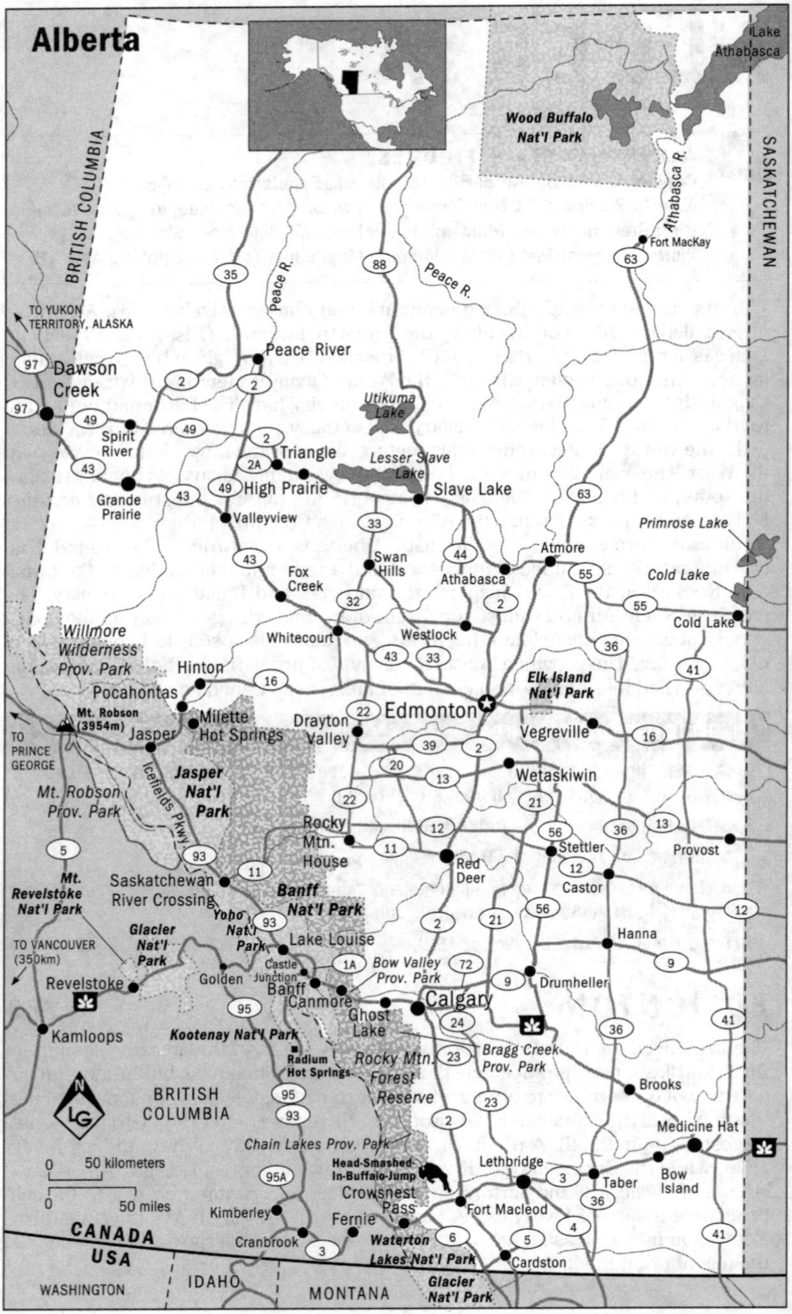

Alberta

Lake Athabasca
Wood Buffalo Nat'l Park
SASKATCHEWAN
BRITISH COLUMBIA
Athabasca R.
Fort MacKay
63
35
88
Peace R.
Peace R.
TO YUKON TERRITORY, ALASKA
Peace River
97
Dawson Creek
97
2
2
49
49
Spirit River
Utikuma Lake
2
Triangle
2A
Lesser Slave Lake
43
Grande Prairie
43
49
High Prairie
Slave Lake
63
Valleyview
33
Primrose Lake
43
Swan Hills
44
Atmore
Athabasca
55
Cold Lake
Fox Creek
32
2
55
Cold Lake
Whitecourt
Westlock
36
Willmore Wilderness Prov. Park
43
33
41
Hinton
16
Elk Island Nat'l Park
Pocahontas
22
Edmonton
Mt. Robson (3954m)
Milette Hot Springs
Drayton Valley
Vegreville
16
TO PRINCE GEORGE
Jasper
39
2
20
Wetaskiwin
Icefields Pkwy
Jasper Nat'l Park
13
Mt. Robson Prov. Park
22
21
Rocky Mtn. House
12
56
36
13
5
93
11
Red Deer
Stettler
Provost
Mt. Revelstoke Nat'l Park
Saskatchewan River Crossing
11
12
Castor
Banff Nat'l Park
Yoho Nat'l Park
93
56
12
Glacier Nat'l Park
2
21
Hanna
TO VANCOUVER (350km)
Lake Louise
Castle Junction
1A
Bow Valley Prov. Park
72
9
Drumheller
Golden
Banff
9
Revelstoke
Canmore
Calgary
Ghost Lake
95
24
41
Kamloops
Kootenay Nat'l Park
36
Radium Hot Springs
23
Rocky Mtn. Forest Reserve
Bragg Creek Prov. Park
Brooks
BRITISH COLUMBIA
95
93
23
2
Medicine Hat
Chain Lakes Prov. Park
0 50 kilometers
0 50 miles
Head-Smashed-In-Buffalo-Jump
Lethbridge
Bow Island
95A
3
Taber
Crowsnest Pass
36
Kimberley
Fort Macleod
Fernie
4
CANADA
41
Waterton Lakes Nat'l Park
6
5
Cranbrook
3
USA
Cardston
WASHINGTON
IDAHO
MONTANA
Glacier Nat'l Park

ALBERTA

TRANSPORTATION

The city lies 294km north of Calgary, an easy but tedious 3hr. drive on the **Calgary Trail (Hwy. 2).** Jasper is 362km to the west, a 4hr. drive on Hwy. 16. Edmonton's streets run north-south, and avenues run east-west. Street numbers increase to the west, and avenues increase to the north. The first three digits of an address indicate the nearest cross street: 10141 88 Ave. is on 88 Ave. near 101 St. The **city center** is quite off-center at 105 St. and 101 Ave.

Flights: Edmonton International Airport (☎890-8382) sits 29km south of town, a $35 cab fare away. The **Sky Shuttle Airport Service** (☎465-8515 or 888-438-2342) runs a shuttle downtown, to the university, or to the West Edmonton Mall for $13 ($20 round-trip). Cheapskates have been known to hop on free airport shuttle buses to downtown hotels.

Trains: VIA Rail, 12360 121 St. (800-842-7245) is a 10min. drive NW of downtown in the CN tower. 3 per week to **Jasper** (5hr.; $141, students $92) and **Vancouver, BC** (24hr.; $263, students $171). No train service to Calgary.

Buses: Greyhound, 10324 103 St. (☎420-2400). Open M-F 5:30am-1:30am, S 5:30am-midnight, Su and holidays 10am-6pm. To: **Calgary** (11 per day, $43); **Jasper** (5hr., 4 per day, $55); **Vancouver, BC** (16-21hr., 6per day, $148); **Yellowknife, NWT** (22-28hr.; 2 per day M-F, winter 3 per week; $203). Locker storage $2 per day. **Red Arrow,** 10010 104 St. (☎800-232-1958), at the Holiday Inn. Open M-F 7:30am-9pm, Sa 8am-9pm. 10% discount with hosteling card. To **Calgary** (4-7 per day, $51) and **Fort McMurray** (2 per day, $59).

Public Transportation: Edmonton Transit (schedules ☎496-1611, info 496-1600; www.gov.edmonton.ab.ca). Buses and **Light Rail Transit (LRT)** run frequently. LRT is **free downtown** between Grandin Station at 110 St. and 98 Ave. and Churchill Station at 99 St. and 102 Ave. Runs M-F 9am-3pm, Sa 9am-6pm. $2, over 65 or under 15 $1.50. No bikes on LRT during peak hours traveling in peak direction (M-F 7:30-8:30am and 4-5pm); no bikes on buses. Info booth open M-F 8:30am-4:30pm.

Taxis: Yellow Cab (☎462-3456). **Alberta Co-op Taxi** (☎425-0954). Both 24hr.

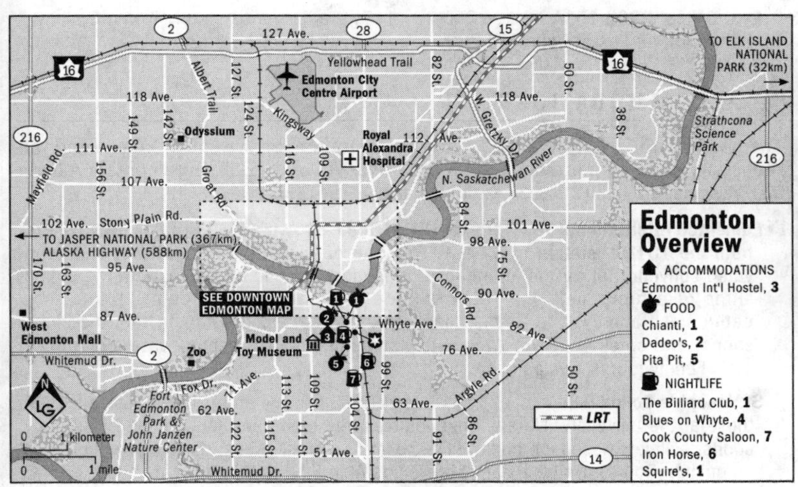

Car Rental: Budget, 10016 106 St. (☎448-2000 or 800-661-7027); call for other locations. From $46 per day, with unlimited km; cheaper city rates with limited km. 21+. Ages 21-24 $15 per day surcharge. Must have major credit card. Open M-F 7:30am-6pm, Sa 9am-3pm, Su 9am-2pm.

PRACTICAL INFORMATION

Tourist Information: Edmonton Tourism, Shaw Conference Centre, 9797 Jasper Ave. (☎496-8400 or 800-463-4667), on Pedway Level. Open M-F 8:30am-4:30pm. Also at **Gateway Park** (☎496-8400 or 800-463-4667), on Hwy. 2 south of town. Open summer daily 8am-8pm; winter M-F 8:30am-4:30pm, Sa-Su 9am-5pm. **Travel Alberta** (☎427-4321 or 800-252-3782) is open M-F 7am-7pm, Sa-Su 8:30am-5:30pm.

Equipment Rental: The **Edmonton International Youth Hostel** (see below) rents bikes. $7 per half-day, $12 per day. **Campus Outdoor Centre** (☎492-2767), NW corner of the Butterdome at U of A, rents a variety of equipment including cross-country skis ($7 overnight), camping gear, and bikes ($15 per day). Open Apr.-Aug. M-Tu 9am-7pm, W 10am-5pm, Th-F 9am-8pm, Sa-Su noon-4pm; call for hours in winter.

Gay and Lesbian Services: Gay/Lesbian Community Centre, Ste. 45, 9912 106 St. (☎488-3234). Open M-F 7-10pm. **Womonspace** (☎482-1794) is Edmonton's lesbian group. Call for a recording of local events.

Emergency: ☎911.

Police: ☎423-4567.

Crisis Line: ☎482-HELP (482-4357). **Sexual Assault Centre** ☎423-4121. Both 24hr.

Pharmacy: Shoppers Drug Mart, 11408 Jasper Ave. (☎482-1011), or 8210 109 St. (☎433-2424) by Whyte Ave. Open 24hr.

Hospital: Royal Alexandra Hospital, 10240 Kingsway Ave. (☎477-4111).

Internet Access: Dow Computer Lab, 11211 142 St. (☎451-3344), at the Odyssium (see **Sights,** below); free with admission. Free at the **library,** 7 Sir Winston Churchill Sq. (☎496-7000); 1hr. per day for a week. Open M-F 9am-9pm, Sa 9am-6pm, Su 1-5pm.

Post Office: 9808 103A Ave. (☎800-267-1177), adjacent to the CN Tower. Open M-F 8am-5:45pm. **Postal Code:** T5J 2G8.

ALBERTA

ACCOMMODATIONS

The hostel is the liveliest place to stay in Edmonton; St. Joseph's College and the University of Alberta provide a bit more privacy. For B&B listings, contact **Alberta B&B Association,** 3230 104A St. (☎438-6048).

Edmonton International Youth Hostel (HI), 10647 81 Ave. (☎988-6836). Bus #7 or 9 from the 101 St. station to 82 Ave. You'd never know that this hostel is in a renovated convent, but for the abundance of private 2-person bedrooms with the dimensions of a nun's cell. Facilities include a kitchen, game room, lounge, new bathrooms, laundry, and a small backyard. Just around the corner from the clubs, shops, and cafes of Whyte Ave. $20, nonmembers $25; semi-private rooms $22, $27. Family rooms available. ❶

St. Joseph's College, 89 Ave. at 114 St. (☎492-7681). The rooms here are smaller than those at the university. Library, huge lounges, rec room, and laundry, and close to U sports facilities. Reception open M-F 8:30am-4pm. Call ahead; the 60 dorms often fill up quickly. Rooms available early May to late Aug. Singles $33, with full board $43. ❷

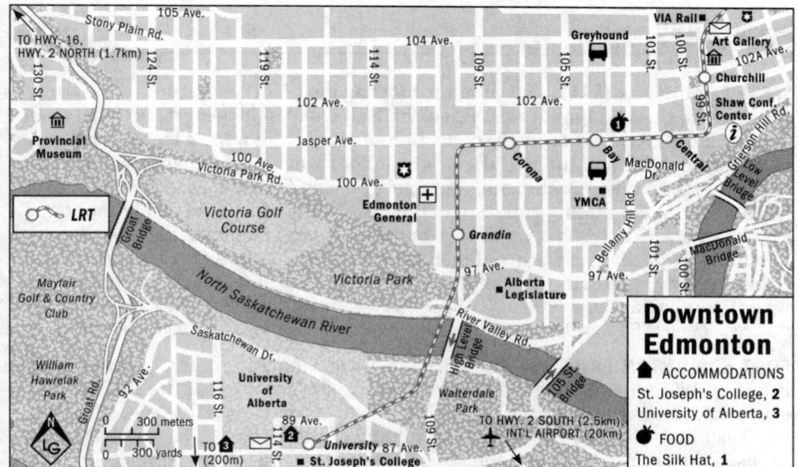

University of Alberta, 87 Ave. between 116 and 117 St. (☎492-4281). Generic dorm rooms. Dry cleaning, kitchen, Internet access ($1 for 10min.), convenience store, and buffet-style cafeteria downstairs. Check-in after 4pm. Reservations strongly recommended. Rooms available late May-Aug. Singles $33. Weekly and monthly rates available. ❷

FOOD

Edmonton locals tend to swarm into the coffee shops and cafes of the Old Strathcona area along Whyte (82) Ave., between 102 and 106 St.

Dadeo's, 10548 Whyte Ave. (☎433-0930). Cajun and Louisiana-style food away from the bayou at this funky 50s diner. Gumbo $4.50. M-Tu po'boys $7. Su $4 for a pint or a plate of wings. Spicy dishes make you sweat just right. Open M-Th 11:30am-11pm, F-Sa 11:30am-midnight, Su 10am-10pm. ❷

The Silk Hat, 10251 Jasper Ave. (☎425-1920). The oldest restaurant in Edmonton maintains enough character and sass to out-survive the competition. This diner in the heart of downtown serves a huge array of food, from seafood to veggie-burgers ($6.25) to breakfast all day. Happy Hour M-F 4-6pm. Open M-F 7am-8pm, Sa 10am-8pm. ❶

Chianti, 10501 Whyte Ave. (☎439-9829). Daily specials, desserts, and coffees accompany an expanse of pasta, veal, and seafood. Pastas $6.60-10; veal $10-13. M-Tu all pasta dishes $7. Open Su-Th 11am-11pm, F-Sa 11am-midnight. ❷

The Pita Pit, 8109 104 St. (☎435-3200), near Whyte Ave. Surprisingly delicious pitas, fast-food style. Souvlaki $5.25. Students don't pay sales tax. Open Th-Sa 11am-4am, Su noon-3am, M-W 11am-3am. ❶

Kids in the Hall Bistro, 1 Sir Winston Churchill Sq. (☎413-8060), in City Hall. This lunchroom is truly one-of-a-kind. Every employee, from waiter to chef, is a young person hired as part of a cooperative community service project. Various entrees ($5-10) and sandwiches ($5-7). Takeout available. Open M-F 8am-4pm. ❷

SIGHTS

WEST EDMONTON MALL. Yet another blow against Mother Nature in the battle for tourists, the $1.3 billion **West Edmonton Mall** engulfs the general area between 170 St. and 87 Ave. No ordinary collection of stores, the **world's biggest mall** contains water slides and the world's largest indoor wave pool, an amusement park with a 14-story roller coaster, miniature golf, dozens of exotic caged animals, over 800 stores, an ice-skating rink, 110 eating establishments, a full-scale replica of Columbus's *Santa Maria*, an indoor bungee jumping facility, a casino, a luxury hotel, a dolphin show, swarms of teenage mall rats, multiple movie theaters, and twice as many submarines as the Canadian Navy. One note of caution: remember where you park. *(Bus# 1, 2, 100, or 111. ☎444-5200 or 800-661-8890; www.westedmall.com. Open M-F 10am-9pm, Sa 10am-6pm, Su noon-6pm. Amusement park open later.)*

FORT EDMONTON PARK. At the park's far end sits the fort proper: a 19th-century office building for Alberta's first capitalists, the fur traders of the Hudson Bay Company. Between the fort and the park entrance are three streets—1885, 1905, and 1920 St.—bedecked with period buildings from apothecaries to blacksmith shops, all decorated to match the streets' respective eras. *(Park: On Whitemud Dr. at Fox Dr. Buses #2, 4, 30, 31, 35, 106, and 315 stop near the park. ☎496-8787; www.gov.edmonton.ab.ca/fort. Open mid-May to late June M-F 10am-4pm, Sa-Su 10am-6pm; late June to early Sept. daily 10am-6pm; rest of Sept. wagon tours only from M-Sa 11am-3pm, Su 10am-6pm. $8.25, seniors and ages 13-17 $6.25, ages 2-12 $4.50, family $26.)*

ODYSSIUM. The reincarnated Space and Science Centre still appeals to the curiosities of all ages with exhibits on the human body and the environment, including a **Gallery of the Gross** and a hands-on **Crime Lab.** Housed in a building shaped like an alien spacecraft, the largest **planetarium dome** in Canada uses a booming 23,000 watts of audio during its laser light shows. The **IMAX theater** makes the planetarium seem like a child's toy. *(11211 142 St. ☎451-3344; www.odyssium.com. Open summer daily 10am-9pm; winter Su-Th 10am-5pm, F-Sa 10am-9pm. Day pass includes planetarium shows and exhibits: $10, students and seniors $8, ages 3-12 $7, family $39. General admission and IMAX show $16, students and seniors $13, ages 3-12 $11, family $60.)*

RIVER VALLEY. The best part of Edmonton would have to be the longest stretch of urban parkland in Canada. Edmonton's **River Valley** boasts over 50km of easy to moderate paved multi-use trails and 69km of granular and chip trails for hiking and cycling. Any route down the river leads to the linked trail system; pick up a map at the Ranger Station. *(12130 River Valley Rd. ☎496-2950. Open daily 7am-1am.)*

FESTIVALS & ENTERTAINMENT

Edmonton proclaims itself "Canada's Festival City" (www.festivalcity.com); celebrations of some kind go on year-round. The **Jazz City International Music Festival** packs 10 days with club dates and free performances by top international and Canadian jazz musicians (☎432-7166; June 25-July 4, 2004). Around the same time is a visual arts celebration called **The Works.** (☎426-2122; June 25-July 7, 2004.) In August, the **Folk Music Festival,** considered one of the best in North America, takes over Gallagher Park (☎429-1899; Aug. 5-8, 2004). All the world's a stage in Old Strathcona for the **Fringe Theater Festival,** when top alternative music and theater pours from parks, stages, and streets. This is the high point of Edmonton's festival schedule, and 500,000 travelers come to the city just to find the Fringe. (☎448-9000; www.fringe.alberta.com. Mid-Aug.)

The Edmonton Oilers, the local NHL franchise, remain in an extended rebuilding period following their glorious Wayne Gretzky-led Stanley Cup runs of the 1980s. But this is Canada, and it is hockey. The Oilers play at 11230 110th St. (☎451-8000; www.edmontonoilers.com. Season runs Oct.-Apr.)

 NIGHTLIFE

Edmonton, like many big cities, has a variety of clubs; like other Alberta cities, many of them are cowboy-themed. The happening clubs are lined up along Whyte (82) Ave. in Old Strathcona. For club listings, see *Magazine*, published every Thursday and available in free stacks at cafes.

Squire's, 10505 82 Ave. (☎439-8594), lower level by Chianti. Popular with the college crowd. Specials include M $2.50 bottles of Canadian, Tu $2 highballs, and Th half-price from 7-11pm. Enjoy $0.09 wings on W. Open M-Tu 7pm-3am, W-Su 5pm-3am.

The Armory, 10310 85 Ave. (☎432-7300). This well-known dance club shows Edmonton's younger crowd how to party. Th $0.50 Coronas until 10pm, $2 everything all night; F $1-3 drinks. Sa offers $0.25 bottles of Canadian beer until 10pm. M is ladies' night, with male entertainers. Open M and Th-Sa 8pm-3am.

The Billiard Club, 10505 82 Ave. (☎432-0335), 2nd fl., above Chianti. A busy bar packed with a diverse crowd of young up-and-comers and some older already-theres. Pool tables and outdoor patio. Open Su-Tu 11:30am-1am, W 11:30am-2am, Th-Sa 11:30am-3am.

Blues on Whyte, 10329 82 Ave. (☎439-5058). If blues is what you want, blues is what you'll get. Live blues and R&B from top-notch performers every night; Sa afternoon jam 3pm-8:30pm. This joint may deserve its reputation as a biker bar; these blues are anything but sedate. 8 oz. glasses of beer for just $1. Open daily 10am-3am.

Cook County Saloon, 8010 103 St. (☎432-2665). Bring your hat and your best boots to Edmonton's rootinest, tootinest country bar. W night dance lessons. Happy Hour F-Sa 8-9pm. M oil wrestling. Hosts hot live concerts on many nights. Open W-Su 8pm-2am.

Iron Horse, 8101 103 St. (☎438-1907). A full restaurant turned Top 40 dance club at night. Live music Su, "Extreme Karaoke" Th, and "Love Train" (singles night) W. Popular with a younger crowd. Happy Hour M-F 4-8pm. Open daily 11:30am-2am.

CALGARY ☎403

Mounties founded Calgary in the 1870s to control Canada's flow of illegal whisky, but oil made the city what it is today. Petroleum fuels Calgary's economy and explains why the city hosts the most corporate headquarters in Canada outside of Toronto. As the host of the 1988 Winter Olympics, Calgary's dot on the map grew larger; already Alberta's largest city, this thriving young metropolis is the second fastest-growing in all of Canada. No matter how big its britches, however, the city still pays annual tribute to its original tourist attraction, the "Greatest Outdoor Show on Earth," the Calgary Stampede. For 10 days in July, the city dons cowboy duds for world-class bareback riding, country music, and Western art.

TRANSPORTATION

Calgary is 126km east of Banff along the Trans-Canada Hwy. (Hwy. 1). It is divided into quadrants (NE, NW, SE, SW): **Centre St.** is the east-west divider; the **Bow River** splits the north and south. Avenues run east-west, streets north-south. Cross streets can be derived by disregarding the last two digits of the street address: 206 7th Ave. SW would be on 7th Ave. at 2nd St.

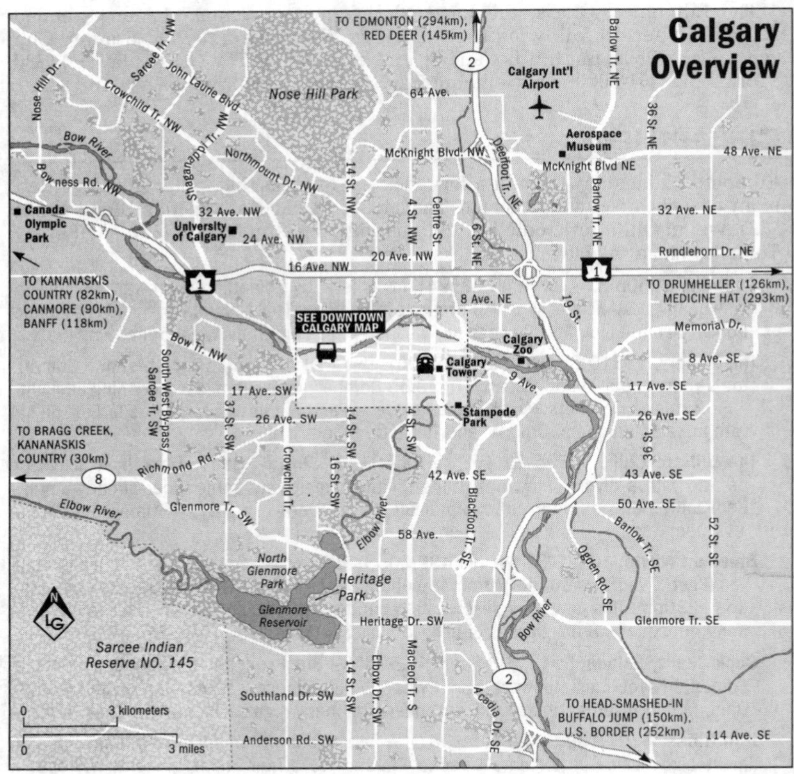

Flights: The **airport** (☎735-1200) is 17km northeast of the city center. Take Bus #57.

Buses: Greyhound, 877 Greyhound Way SW (☎260-0877 or 800-661-8747). To: **Banff** (1¾hr., 4 per day, $23); **Drumheller** (2hr., 3 per day, $25); **Edmonton** (3½-5hr., 10-11 per day, $44), with lower student rates. Free shuttle from Calgary Transit C-Train at 7th Ave. and 10th St. to bus depot (every hr. near the ½hr. 6:30am-7:30pm). **Red Arrow,** 205 9th Ave. SE (☎531-0350), goes to **Edmonton** (4-7 per day, $51) and points north. 10% HI discount; student and senior rates. **Brewster Tours** (☎221-8242), from the airport to **Banff** (2hr., 2 per day, $42) and **Jasper** (8hr., 1 per day, $80). 10% HI discount.

Public Transportation: Calgary Transit, 240 7th Ave. SW (☎262-1000). Open M-F 8:30am-5pm. C-Trains free in downtown zone on 7th Ave. S from 3rd St. E to 10th St W. Buses and C-Trains outside downtown $2, ages 6-14 $1.25, under 6 free. Day pass $5.60, ages 6-14 $3.60. Book of 10 tickets $17.50, ages 6-14 $10. Runs M-F 6am-midnight, Sa-Su 6am-9:30pm. Tickets at stops, the transit office, or Safeway stores.

Taxis: Checker Cab (☎299-9999). **Yellow Cab** (☎974-1111).

Car Rental: Rent-A-Wreck, 113 42nd Ave. SW (☎287-1444). From $40 per day. $0.12 per km over 250km. 21+ need credit card. Open M-F 8am-6pm, Sa-Su 9am-5pm.

PRACTICAL INFORMATION

Tourist Information: 220 8th Ave. SW (☎800-661-1678; www.tourismcalgary.com). Open in summer daily 9am-5pm; winter 9:30am-5:30pm.

American Express: Boulevard Travel, 1322 15th Ave. SW (☎237-6233). Open M-F 8am-5:30pm.

Equipment Rental: Outdoor Program Centre, 2500 University Dr. (☎220-5038), at U of Calgary, rents tents (from $10), canoes ($18), and downhill skis ($21). Open daily 8am-8pm. **Mountain Equipment Co-op,** 830 10th Ave. (☎269-2420) rents watercraft ($15-55 per day, including all safety equipment and paddles), camping gear ($4-21), rock- and ice-climbing gear ($4-22), and snow sports equipment ($8-35). Both companies have weekend specials. Be prepared to shell out a large deposit.

Laundromat: Inglewood Laundromat, 1018 9th Ave. SE (☎269-1515). Wash $2, dry $0.35 for 7min. Open daily 8am-5:30pm.

Gay and Lesbian Services: Events and clubs ☎234-9752. Counseling ☎234-8973.

Weather: ☎299-7878.

Emergency: ☎911.

Police: 133 6th Ave. SE (☎266-1234).

Pharmacy: Shopper's Drug Mart, 6455 Macleod Trail S (☎253-2424). Open 24hr.

Hospital: Peter Lougheed Centre, 3500 26th Ave. NE (☎943-4555).

Internet Access: At the **library,** 616 Macleod Trail SE (☎260-2600). $2 per hr. Open M-Th 10am-9pm, F-Sa 10am-5pm; mid-Sept. to mid-May also Su 1:30-5pm.

Post Office: 207 9th Ave. SW (☎974-2078). Open M-F 8am-5:45pm. **Postal Code:** T2P 2G8.

ACCOMMODATIONS

Lodging prices skyrocket when tourists pack into the city's hotels for the July Stampede; call far in advance. Calgary's downtown lacks cheap places to sleep; finding a hotel bed for under $100 is virtually impossible. As a result, hostels and alternative accommodations are undoubtedly the way to go. For a more homey feel, contact the **B&B Association of Calgary** for info and availability. (☎543-3900. Singles from $30; doubles from $50.)

Calgary International Hostel (HI), 520 7th Ave. SE (☎269-8239), near downtown. Walk east along 7th Ave. from the 3rd St. SE C-Train station; the hostel is on the left just past 4th St. SE. Busy and sometimes impersonal, this urban hostel has some nice accessories; the clean kitchen, lounge areas, laundry, and backyard with barbecue are pluses. Information desk, occasional guest activities. Wheelchair-accessible. 120 beds. $22, nonmembers $26; Oct. 16-May 1: $17, $21. Private rooms $75, nonmembers $83. ❶

University of Calgary, the ex-Olympic Village in the NW quadrant, far from downtown if you're walking. Accessible by bus #9 or a 12min. walk from the University C-Train stop. Popular with conventioneers and often booked solid. Coordinated through **Cascade Hall,** 3456 24th Ave. NW (☎220-3203). Rooms available May-Aug. only. Shared rooms $25 per person; singles $34-100. Rates subject to change; call ahead. ❶

YWCA, 320 5th Ave. SE (☎232-1599). Walk 2 blocks north of the 3rd St. SE C-Train station. 2 newly renovated residential floors. **Women only.** 150 beds available. Singles from $40; doubles from $50; triples $130; quads $140. Seniors 10% discount. ❸

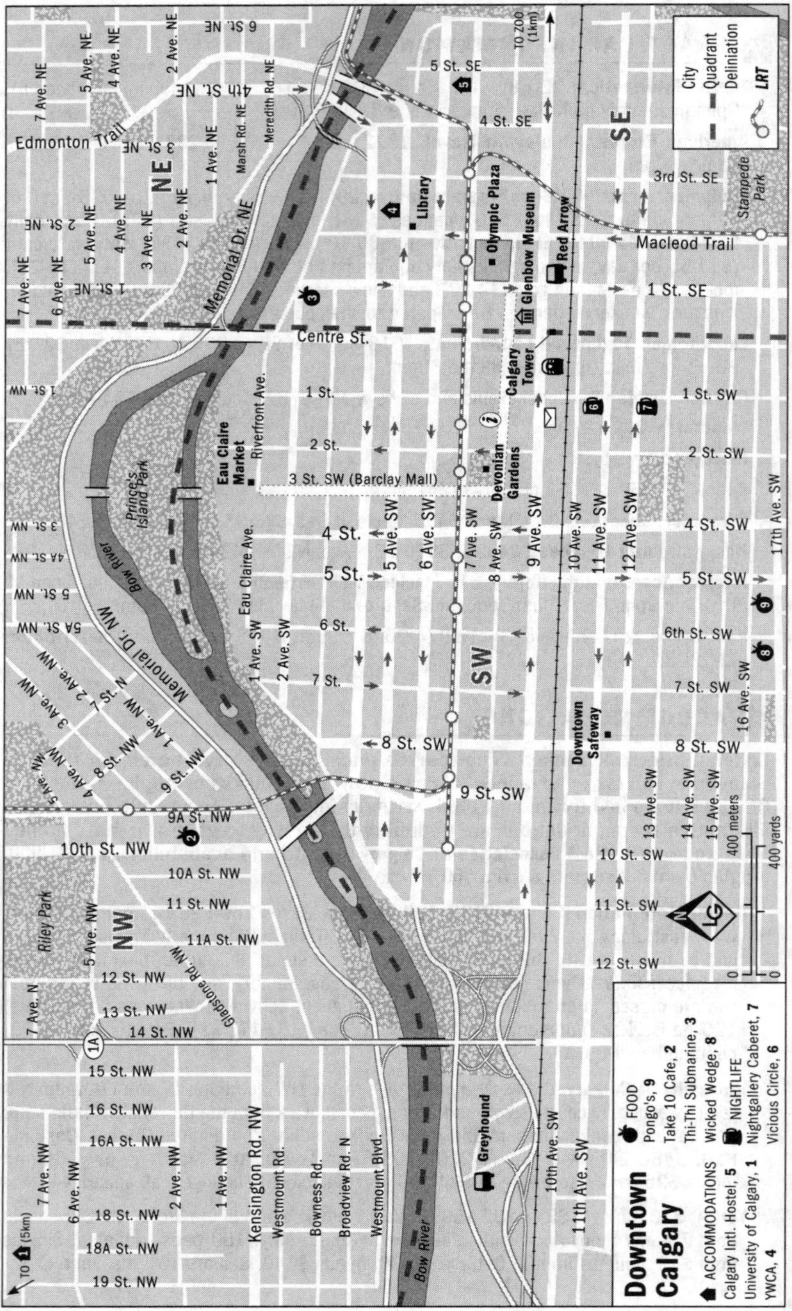

Downtown Calgary

ACCOMMODATIONS
Calgary Intl. Hostel, 5
University of Calgary, 1
YWCA, 4

FOOD
Pongo's, 9
Take 10 Cafe, 2
Thi-Thi Submarine, 3
Wicked Wedge, 8

NIGHTLIFE
Nightgallery Caberet, 7
Vicious Circle, 6

City Quadrant Delineation
LRT

FOOD

It seems fitting that most of the affordable restaurants with good food in Calgary are not found downtown. The most gloriously satisfying and cheap eats are located in **Chinatown,** concentrated in a four block area at the north end of Centre St. S and 1st St. SE. Six dollars gets you a feast in any Vietnamese noodle-house or Hong Kong-style cafe, many of which don't even close until the wee hours. Some budget chow-houses also hide out among the trendy, costlier spots in the popular **Kensington District,** along Kensington Rd. and 10th and 11th St. NW; still others can be found on **17th Ave.** between 2nd St. SW and 14th St. SW. **Downtown Safeway** (☎800-723-3929), 813 11th Ave. SW, sells groceries. (Open daily 8am-11pm.) Restaurants, produce, international snack bars, and flowers grace the plaza-style, upscale **Eau Claire Market** mall, at the north end of 3rd St. SW.

Thi-Thi Submarine, 209 1st St. SE (☎265-5452). Some people have closets larger than Thi-Thi, but this place manages to pack in 2 plastic seats, a bank of toaster ovens, and the finest Vietnamese submarines in Calgary. Most meaty subs are sub-$5; the veggie sub is an unreal $2.25. Open M-F 10am-7pm, Sa-Su 10:30am-5pm. ❶

Peter's Drive In, 219 16th Ave. NE (☎277-2747). Peachy keen! A generational anomaly and worthy destination, Peter's is one of the city's last remaining drive-ins. Hordes of chummy patrons attest to the swell quality. Drive-in or walk to the service window. Famous milkshakes under $3 and burgers under $4. Open daily 9am-midnight. ❶

Pongo's, 524 17th Ave. SW (☎209-1073). Pongo's sterile, futuristic decor seems at odds with the large portions of quality Asian food they serve. Huge helpings of pad thai are $8. Takeout available. Open Su-Th 11:30am-midnight, F-Sa 11:30am-4am. ❷

Take 10 Cafe, 304 10th St. NW (☎270-7010). Take 10 became a local favorite by offering dirt-cheap, high-quality food. All burgers are under $5.75, and the menu also sports some sizzling Chinese food (under $8). Open M-F 9am-4pm, Sa-Su 8:30am-3pm. ❷

Wicked Wedge, 618 17th Ave. SW (☎228-1024). Serves large, topping-heavy slices of pizza ($3.75) to Calgary's post-party scene. 3 varieties of pie dished out nightly. Open M-Th 11am-midnight, F-Sa 11am-3am, Su 11am-midnight. ❷

SIGHTS

OLYMPIC LEFTOVERS. For two glorious weeks in 1988, the world's eyes were on Calgary for the Winter Olympics. Almost fifteen years later, the world has moved on, but the city still has some very exciting facilities, and relentlessly clings to its two weeks of Olympic stardom. Visit the **Canada Olympic Park** and its looming ski jumps and twisted bobsled and luge tracks. The **Olympic Hall of Fame,** also at Olympic Park, honors Olympic achievements with displays, films, and a **bobsled simulator.** In summer, the park opens its hills and a lift to **mountain bikers.** *(A 10min. drive northwest of downtown on Hwy. 1. ☎247-5452. Open summer daily 8am-9pm; winter M-F 9am-9pm, Sa-Su 9am-5pm. $10 ticket includes chair-lift and entrance to ski-jump buildings, Hall of Fame, and ice-house. Tour $15; families $45. Mountain biking open May-Oct. daily 9am-9pm. Roadway pass $9 for cyclists. Front-suspension bike rental $12 per hr., $31 per day.)* Keep an eye out for ski-jumpers, who practice at the facility year-round. The miniature mountain (113m vertical) also opens up for recreational **downhill skiing** in winter. *(Snow report ☎289-3700. $21.)* The **Olympic Oval,** an enormous indoor speed-skating track on the University of Calgary campus, remains a major international training facility. Speedskaters work out in the early morning and late afternoon; sit in the bleachers and observe the action for free. *(☎220-7890; www.oval.ucalgary.ca. Public skating hours vary, so call ahead. $4.75, children and seniors $2.75, family $10.50, under 6 free. Skate rental under $5.)*

PARKS & MUSEUMS. Footbridges stretch from either side of the Bow River to **Prince's Island Park,** a natural refuge only blocks from the city center. In July and August, Mount Royal College performs **Shakespeare in the Park.** *(☎240-6908. Various matinees and evening shows; call for shows and times.)* Calgary's other island park, **St. George's Island,** is accessible by the river walkway to the east or by driving. It houses the **Calgary Zoo,** including a botanical garden and children's zoo. For those who missed the wildlife in Banff and Jasper, the **Canadian Wilds** exhibit has recreated animal habitats. For those who missed the Cretaceous Period, life-sized plastic dinosaurs are also on exhibit. *(Parking is off Memorial Dr. on the north side of the river. ☎232-9300. Open daily 9am-5pm. $15, seniors $13, ages 13-17 $9, ages 3-12 $6.50.)*

STAMPEDE. The more cosmopolitan Calgary becomes, the more tenaciously it clings to its frontier roots. The **Stampede** draws one million cowboys and tourists each summer, in the first couple weeks of July, when the grounds are packed for world-class steer wrestling, bareback and bull-riding, pig and chuck wagon races. Check out the livestock shows, cruise the midway and casino, ride the roller coaster, or hear live country music and marching bands. The festival spills into the streets from first thing in the morning (free pancake breakfasts all around) through the night. Depending on your attitude, the Stampede will either be an impressive spectacle rekindling the Western spirit or an overpriced, slick carnival where humans assert their hegemony over lesser animals. *(Stampede Park is just southeast of downtown, bordering the east side of Macleod Trail between 14th Ave. SE and the Elbow River. The C-Train features a Stampede stop. Tickets ☎269-9822 or 800-661-1767; www.calgarystampede.com. $11, ages 65+ and 7-12 $6, under 7 free. Rodeo and evening shows $22-63, rush tickets on sale at the grandstand 1½hr. before showtime.)*

NIGHTLIFE

Nightclubs in Alberta only became legal in 1990, and Calgary is making up for lost time. The city is crawling with bars and nightclubs that cater to waves of visitors and young locals. Live music in Calgary ranges from national acts and world-famous DJs to some guy with a guitar. The best areas in town for finding pubs, clubs, and live music are the **Stephen Ave. Walk** (8th Ave. SW), **17th Ave. SW,** and **1st and 4th St. SW.** Wherever you head, finding cheap liquor is not a problem; many bars in town offer unbelievable drink deals. Last call in Alberta is at 2am, and is strictly observed. For listings of bands and theme nights, check *The Calgary Straight* or *Calgary's Ffwd.* Both come out on Thursday and are free. *Outlooks*, the city's gay and lesbian events publication, offers information on different bars. All are available at local clubs and cafes.

Nightgallery Cabaret, 1209B 1st St. SW (☎264-4484, www.nightgallerycabaret.com). A large dance floor, a bar, and a diverse program attract clubbers. Has the best House in town on Th and at "Sunday Skool." Reggae-Dub on M draws a slightly older crowd. Live music F and Sa. $1.50 highballs before 11pm. Cover $5. Open daily 8pm-3am.

Vicious Circle, 1011 1st St. SW (☎269-3951). A very relaxing bar, "The Vish" offers a solid menu, colored mood lights, and a disco ball, plus pool tables, couches, eclectic local art, and TV. All kinds of coffee, a full bar, and 140 different martinis. Summer patio seating. Happy Hour all night Su, live music W. Open M-Th 11:30am-1am, F 11:30am-2am, Sa-Su noon-2am.

Eau Claire Market IMAX, 132 200 Barclay Parade SW (☎974-4629). Pit your imagination against a large-screen feature that claims to be bigger. Box office open M-F 11:30am-10pm, Sa-Su 10:30am-10pm. IMAX films $10.50, ages 65 and up $8.50, under 13 $7.50, night double feature $15. Also at Eau Claire, Cineplex Odeon shows regular films; call for times (☎263-3166).

DAYTRIP: ALBERTA BADLANDS

Once the fertile shallows of a huge ocean, the Badlands are now one of the richest dinosaur fossil sites in the world. After the sea dried up, wind, water, and ice molded twisting canyons into sandstone and shale bedrock, creating the desolate splendor of the Alberta Badlands. The **Royal Tyrrell Museum of Paleontology** (TEER-ull), with its remarkable array of dinosaur exhibits and hands-on paleontological opportunities, is the region's main attraction. **Greyhound** runs from Calgary to **Drumheller** (1¾hr., 2 per day, $24), which is 6km southeast of the museum.

ROYAL TYRRELL MUSEUM OF PALEONTOLOGY. The world's largest display of dinosaur specimens is a forceful reminder that *Homo sapiens* missed out on the first 2½ billion years of life on earth. From the Big Bang to the present, the museum celebrates evolution's grand parade with quality displays, videos, computer activities, and towering skeletons, including one of only 12 reconstructed *Tyrannosaurus rex* skeletons in existence. You cannot miss the Predator Room, which features cunning dinosaurs and creepy background lighting. It does not, at any point in earth's evolution, ever get cooler than this. *(6km northwest of Drumheller, which itself lies 138km northeast of Calgary. Get there by driving east on Hwy. 1 from Calgary, then northeast on Hwy. 9. ☎403-823-7707 or 888-440-4240; www.tyrrellmuseum.com. Open Victoria Day-Labour Day daily 9am-9pm; Labour Day-Thanksgiving daily 10am-5pm; Thanksgiving to Victoria Day Tu-Su 10am-5pm. $10, seniors $8, ages 7-17 $6, under 7 free, families $30.)*

DIGS. The museum's hugely popular 12-person **Day Digs** include instruction in paleontology and excavation techniques, and a chance to dig in a fossil quarry. The fee includes lunch and transportation; participants must also agree that all finds go to the museum. *(July-Aug. daily; June Sa-Su. Digs depart 8:30am, returning 4pm. $90, ages 10-15 $60. Reservations required; call the museum.)*

DINOSAUR PROVINCIAL PARK & BADLANDS BUS TOUR. The Badlands, a UNESCO World Heritage Site, are the source of many finds on display at the Tyrrell Museum; more fossil species—over 300, including 35 species of dinosaurs—were discovered here than anywhere else in the world. The museum's **Field Station,** 48km east of the town of **Brooks** in **Dinosaur Provincial Park,** contains a small museum, but the main attraction is the **Badlands Bus Tour.** The bus chauffeurs visitors into a restricted hotspot of dinosaur finds. Many fossils still lie within the eroding

IN RECENT NEWS

THE BUSK STOPS HERE

Being a good citizen in Calgary doesn't mean giving the corner guitarist a dollar—it means turning him in to the police. Busking (giving street performances) is illegal, and has been since the government tightened its policy on performers in 2002. The move was innocently designed to ease major congestion problems on the city's byways, but it has infuriated supporters of Calgary's open music scene. Designated "Busk Stops," or spots performers can sign up for in advance, have eased the tension somewhat; still, police maintain a zero-tolerance policy toward buskers who are caught anywhere that is not the south side of Olympic Plaza or the Eau Claire Market Amphitheater. People on both sides of the issue claim that the system is imperfect and will require additional modifications. The city makes references to opening more Busk Stops, but where and when they'll do it is not entirely clear. So, the future of public music in Calgary hangs in the balance. For now, most of the streets of downtown Calgary lack music and life beyond the drone of passing cars.

HEAD-SMASHED-IN Some 5700 years ago, plains-dwelling Blackfoot began using gravity to kill bison. Disguised as calves, a few men would lure a herd of the short-sighted animals into lanes between stone cairns. Hunters at the rear, dressed as wolves, then pressed forward, whipping the bison into a frenzy. When the front-running bison reached the cliff and tried to stop, the momentum of the stampede pushed their one-ton bodies over the edge. Each year, the communities obtained food, tools, and clothing from the bodies of the bison. The particular cliffs of Head-Smashed-In Buffalo Jump were an active hunting site for nearly 8,000 years, but only earned their modern name at one of the site's final jumps 150 years ago when a thrill-seeking warrior watching the massacre from under the cliff ledge was crushed. As European settlement spread over the plains, the bison that once numbered 60 million continent-wide were nearly extinct in 1881. A century later, the United Nations named Head-Smashed-In a UNESCO World Heritage Site; ten-meter-deep beds of bone and tools make this one of the best-preserved buffalo jumps in North America. The magnificent **interpretive center** explores the hunting, history, and rituals of the Plains people. (☎553-2731. Open daily May 15 to Labour Day 9am-6pm; off-season 10am-5pm. $6.50, seniors $5.50, ages 7-17 $3, family $15, under 7 free.) Head-Smashed-In Buffalo Jump lies 175km south of Calgary and 18km northwest of Fort Macleod, on Secondary Rd. 785 off Hwy. 2.

rock. The park's **campground** ❶ is shaded from summer heat, and grassy plots cushion most sites. Although it stays open year-round, the campground only has power and running water in summer. *(To reach the Field Station from Drumheller, follow Hwy. 56 south for 65km, then take Hwy. 1 about 70km to Brooks. Once in Brooks, go north along Hwy. 873 and east along Hwy. 544. Field Station ☎378-4342. Field Station Visitor Centre exhibits $3, seniors $2.50, ages 7-17 $2. Open mid-Oct. to mid-May M-F 9am-4pm; mid-May through Aug. daily 8:30am-9pm; Sept. to mid-Oct. daily 9am-5pm. Tours $6.50, ages 7-17 $4.25. Reservations ☎378-4344. Sites $15; with power $18.)*

DINOSAUR-FREE ACTIVITIES. The Badlands also offer a variety of other recreational activities. The staff of **Midland Provincial Park** (☎823-1749), located halfway between the Tyrrell Museum and Drumheller, leads free 75min. natural history walking tours, departing from the museum one or two times per day. To see **hoodoos** in the making, go 15km east on Hwy. 10 from Drumheller. These limestone columns are relatively young: the stone caps on their tops have not yet eroded away. In **Horseshoe Canyon,** about 20km west of Drumheller on Hwy. 9, **hiking and biking trails** wind below the prairie through red rock layers carved into bizarre, rounded formations. Several trails located in Dinosaur Provincial Park take hikers over and through the eroded landscape, including the **Coulee Viewpoint Trail** (1km, 45min., moderate) and the **Cottonwoods Flats Trail** (1.4km, 2hr., easy), which weaves around Deer River. Carry plenty of water during hot weather, and be sure not to hop fences onto private property. Stock up on groceries at **IGA Market,** at N Railroad Ave. and Centre St. (☎823-3995. Open daily 24hr.)

CANADIAN ROCKIES

The five national parks of the Canadian Rockies comprise one of Canada's top tourist draws, and with excellent reason. Every year, some five million visitors make it within sight of the parks' majestic peaks, stunning glacial lakes, and myriad varieties of wildlife. Thankfully, much of this traffic is confined to highway-

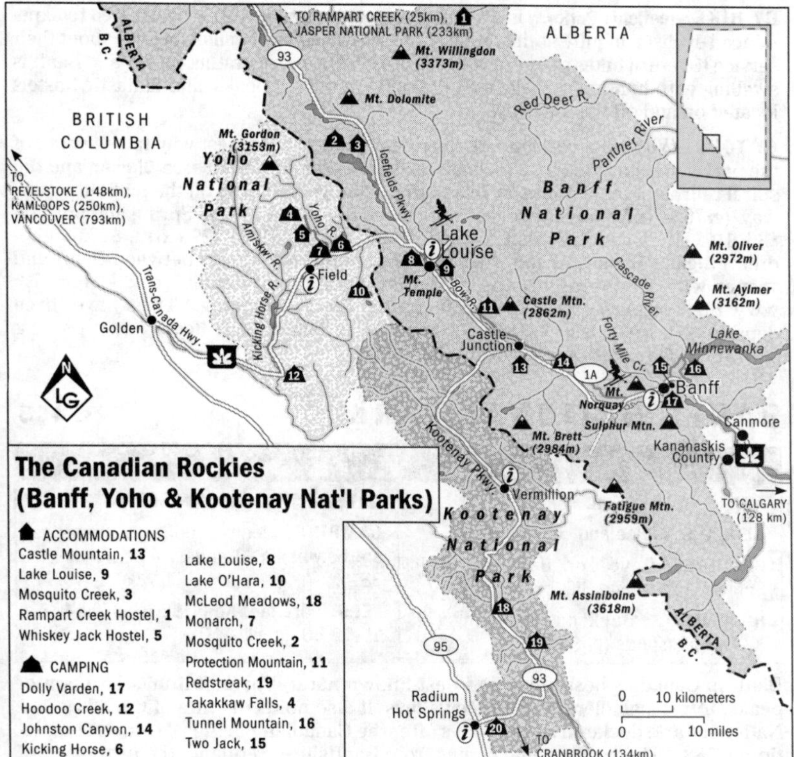

side gawkers, leaving infinite backcountry trails and mountains where one can escape the flocks of tourists. Of the big two parks—Banff and Jasper—the latter feels a little farther removed from the droves of tourists. The hostels that line both parks are among the country's best, and are usually booked up as a result. It's also well worth diving into the quieter Yoho (see p. 321), Glacier (see p. 320), and Kootenay National Parks (see p. 323), as well as Kananaskis Country (see p. 376), the locals' free playground that separates Calgary from the Rockies.

TRANSPORTATION

BY CAR, BUS, & TRAIN. Alberta's extensive highway system makes travel between major destinations easy, and provides the traveler with beautiful roadside scenery. The north-south **Icefields Parkway (Hwy. 93)** runs between **Banff** and **Jasper.** The east-west **Yellowhead Hwy. (Hwy. 16)** connects **Edmonton** with **Jasper,** and continues across British Columbia. The **Trans-Canada Hwy. (Hwy. 1)** completes the loop, linking **Calgary** with **Banff.** The easiest way to get here is to drive yourself or explore the bus options. **Buses** (Greyhound, Brewster, and Red Arrow) travel all of these routes; VIA Rail **trains** run from **Edmonton** to **Jasper.**

BY BIKE. Icefields Parkway is a popular trail, although the trip is best suited to experienced cyclists. Inquire at the rental shops (see **Equipment Rental,** below) about their service to return bikes after one-way trips. The 291km separating Jasper and Banff is swelling with hundreds of glaciers, dramatic mountain peaks, and fantastic hostels located on and off the highway.

BY TOUR. Without a car, guided bus rides may be the easiest way to see some of the park's main attractions, such as the **Great Divide,** the **Athabasca Glacier,** and the spiral railroad tunnel. **Brewster Tours** offer 9½hr. guided trips on the Icefields Parkway. (☎762-6767. Mid-May to Oct. at 8:10am. $57, child $47.50. Spring and fall $72/$36. 10% HI discount. A visit to the Columbia Icefields is $27 extra, $13.50 children.) **Bigfoot Tours** runs fun, two-day, 11-passenger van trips between Banff and Jasper with an overnight stop at the **Mt. Edith Cavell Hostel.** (☎888-244-6673; www.bigfoottours.com. $95, not including food or lodging.) Trips have three departures a week; trips east stop at the **Squilax General Store Hostel** and trips west stop at the **Old Courthouse Hostel** in Kamloops.

BANFF NATIONAL PARK ☎403

AT A GLANCE	
AREA: 6641 sq. km. **CLIMATE:** Alpine and subalpine. **FEATURES:** Cave and Basin Mineral Springs, Tunnel and Sulphur Mountain. **HIGHLIGHTS:** Backcountry hiking (p. 384), watersports (p. 385).	**GATEWAYS:** Calgary (p. 369). **CAMPING:** Plenty of options. Most sites are between $10 and $17 per night. (p. 382). **FEES:** Park fee: Adult $5, senior $4, 6-16 $2.50, family $10.

Banff is Canada's best-loved and best-known natural park, with 6641 sq. km of peaks, forests, glaciers, and alpine valleys. It also holds the title of Canada's first National Park, declared so only days after the Canadian Pacific Railway's completion in 1885. The park's name comes from Banffshire, Scotland, the birthplace of a certain two Canadian Pacific Railway financiers. These men convinced Canada's first Prime Minister that a "large pecuniary advantage" might be gained from the region, telling him that "since we can't export the scenery, we shall have to import the tourists." Their plan worked to a fault, but even streets littered with gift shops and chocolatiers cannot mar the beauty of the wilderness outside of the Banff townsite. Outdoors lovers arrive with mountain bikes, climbing gear, and skis, but a trusty pair of hiking boots remains the park's most widely-used outdoor equipment. Banff's natural beauty, along with the opportunities for excitement and laid-back attitude it affords, have turned Banff into one of Canada's youngest towns.

TRANSPORTATION

Banff National Park hugs the Alberta side of the Alberta/British Columbia border 128km west of Calgary. The **Trans-Canada Hwy. (Hwy. 1)** runs east-west through the park, connecting it to Yoho National Park in the west. The **Icefields Parkway (Hwy. 93)** connects Banff with Jasper National Park to the north and Kootenay National Park to the southwest. Civilization in the park centers around the towns of **Banff** and **Lake Louise,** 58km apart on Hwy. 1. The more serene **Bow Valley Parkway (Hwy. 1A)** parallels Hwy. 1 from Lake Louise to 8km west of Banff, offering excellent camping, hosteling, sights, and wildlife. The

FLOUR POWER Passing by the many lakes and streams in the Rockies, you may notice that they have an unusual color. When looking at the swimming-pool turquoise or glowing blue color of these bodies of water, you might wonder if this is some kind of gimmick perpetuated by the park wardens to bring in the tourists. Many years ago, one visitor to Lake Louise claimed that he had solved the mystery of the beautiful water: it had obviously been distilled from peacock tails. Turns out he was a bit off the mark. The actual cause of the color is "rock flour." This fine dust is created by the pressure exerted by the glacier upon rocks trapped within the ice; the resulting ground rock is washed into streams and lakes in the glacial meltwater. Suspended particles trap all colors of the spectrum except for the blues and greens that are reflected back for your visual pleasure.

southern portion of Hwy. 1A is restricted at night in the late spring and early summer to accommodate the wildlife on the road. All listings apply to Banff Townsite, unless otherwise specified.

Buses: Brewster Transportation, 100 Gopher St. (☎762-6767). Depot open daily 7:45am-9pm. To: **Calgary** (2hr., $42); **Jasper** (5hr., $57); **Lake Louise** (1hr., $13.50). Ages 6-15 half-price. See **The Rockies,** p. 376, for info on tours to, from, and within parks. **Greyhound** (☎800-661-8747) uses Brewster's station. 4 per day to **Lake Louise** (1hr., $12) and **Vancouver, BC** (12½-15hr., $118); 5 per day to **Calgary** (1½hr., $23).

Public Transportation: Banff Transit runs between the Banff Springs Hotel, the RV parking area, and Banff Hostel on Tunnel Mountain Rd., as well as between the Tunnel Mountain Campground, downtown, and the Banff Park Museum. $1, children $0.50. Mid-May to Sept. 7am-midnight; late Apr. to early May and Oct.-Dec. noon-midnight.

Taxis: Banff Taxi (☎726-4444). 24hr. **Lake Louise Taxi** (☎522-2020). Runs 6am-2:30pm.

Car Rental: Available from several establishments with rates ranging from $50-60 per day, with 100-150 free km. Ask at the visitors center for a comparison chart.

Tours: Bigfoot Adventure Tours (☎888-244-6673; www.bigfoottours.com) runs fun 10-day trips from Vancouver to Jasper and Banff. Passengers can get on and off any of their 3 tour vans. (Daily from July-Sept.) A $410 ($400 with ISIC card) fee covers transportation and park fees, but not the HI accommodations, food, or entertainment.

PRACTICAL INFORMATION

Tourist Information: Banff Visitor Centre, 224 Banff Ave. Includes **Banff/Lake Louise Tourism Bureau** (☎762-8421; www.banfflakelouise.com) and **Parks Canada** (☎762-1550). Open June-Sept. daily 8am-8pm; Oct.-May 9am-5pm. **Lake Louise Visitor Centre** (☎522-3833), at Samson Mall on Village Rd. Open June-Sept. daily 9am-7pm; Oct.-May 9am-4pm.

Equipment Rental:

Mountain Magic Equipment, 224 Bear St. (☎762-2591) is one of the few places in Banff to rent packages for Telemark ($25 per day) and mountaineering ($50 per day). They also offer the usual bike, ski, and snowboard rentals. Open Dec.-Mar. daily 8am-9pm; Apr.-Nov. 9am-9pm.

Bactrax Rentals, 225 Bear St. (☎762-8177), rents mountain bikes for $6-10 per hr., $22-36 per day. Bike tours $15 per hr. including all equipment. Ski packages from $16 per day, snowboard packages $28. 20% HI discount. Open Apr.-Oct. daily 8am-8pm; Nov.-Mar. 7am-10pm.

Performance Sports, 208 Bear St. (☎762-8222), rents tents ($20-26 per day), fishing gear ($16-30 per day), cross-country ski or snowshoe packages ($12 per day, $31 for 3 days), avalanche packages ($23 per day), and snow or rainwear ($8-17 per day). 10% HI or Real Big Adventures discount. Open daily July-Aug. 9:30am-8pm; Sept.-June 10am-6pm.

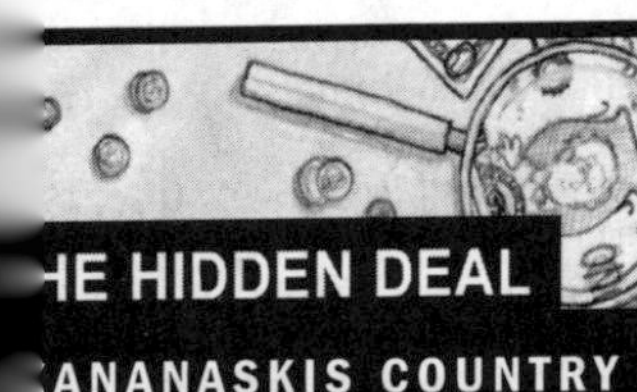

HE HIDDEN DEAL

ANANASKIS COUNTRY

Between Calgary and Banff lie 4200 sq. km of provincial parks and multi-use recreational areas collectively known as **Kananaskis Country** (KAN-uh-NASS-kiss). The landscape rolls down from the Canadian Rockies through undulating foothills less than an hour from Banff. Kananaskis has a majesty comparable to the national parks, but thankfully with few of their crowds and none of their entrance fees. This is truly a gem of the Rockies—don't mention it to anyone.

Though harmed by recent budget cuts, the best info source is **Barrier Lake Visitor Centre,** 6km south of Hwy. 1 on Hwy. 40. (☎673-3985. Call for hours.) **Ribbon Creek Hostel (HI)** ❶ is 24km south of the Trans-Canada Hwy. (Hwy. 1) on Hwy. 40. The common room has a fireplace and comfy couches. Firepit, BBQ, volleyball court, and huge kitchen. (Reservations ☎866-762-4122. $15, nonmembers $19. Private rooms $42, nonmembers $50. Free showers.) The hostel has winter-time lift ticket and lodging deals with nearby Nakiska. Over 38 **campgrounds** ❶ are accessible via K-Country roads (there are also many group camps).

The area is divided into nine provincial parks. The three most popular are the forests of **Bow Valley Provincial Park** (☎673-3663), the grasslands of **Elbow River Valley** (☎949-3754) on Hwy. 66 near Bragg Creek, and the towering peaks of **Peter Lougheed Provincial Park** (☎591-6322), 1hr. south on Hwy. 40

Wilson Mountain Sports (☎522-3636) in the Lake Louise Samson Mall, rents bikes ($15 per hr., $35 per day) and camping and fishing gear. They also offer mountaineering packages ($35 per day), rock climbing packages ($15 per day) and sell fishing permits. Open daily mid-June to Sept. 9am-9pm; Oct. to Apr. 8am-8pm; May to mid-June 9am-8pm.

Laundry: Johnny O's, 223 Bear St. (☎762-5111). $2.75 for regular wash, $6 for huge load (more than 2 regular loads). $2.50 for dry. Open in summer daily 9am-10pm, until 9pm in winter.

Weather: ☎762-2088.

Road Conditions: ☎762-1450.

Emergency: ☎911.

Police: Banff Police (☎762-2226. Non-emergency 762-2228). On Lynx St. by the train depot. **Lake Louise Police** (☎522-3811. Non-emergency 522-3812). **Banff Park Warden** (☎762-4506. Non-emergency 762-1470). 24hr. **Lake Louise Park Warden** (☎522-1200).

Hospital: Mineral Springs, 301 Lynx St. (☎762-2222), near Wolf St. in Banff.

Internet Access: Library, 101 Bear St. (☎762-2611). Sign up in advance. Open daily 10am-8pm. Closed Su from late May-early Sept. **Cyber Web** (☎762-9226), 215 Banff Ave. $3 per 15min., $8 per hr., $5 per hr. from 9:30pm-close. Open daily 10am-midnight. For laptops, open M-Th 10am-8pm, F 10am-6pm, Sa 11am-6pm, Su 1-5pm. $1 per 15min.

Post Office: 204 Buffalo St. (☎762-2586). Open M-W 8:30am-5:30pm, Th-F 8:30am-7pm, Sa 8:30am-5pm. **Postal Code:** T0L 0C0.

ACCOMMODATIONS

Finding a cheap place to stay in Banff has become increasingly difficult; the number of visitors soars into the millions every year. Townsite residents offer rooms in their homes, occasionally at reasonable rates ($75-140, winter $60-100). Check the list at the back of the *Banff and Lake Louise Official Visitor Guide*, available free at the visitors centers.

Mammoth **modern hostels** at Banff and Lake Louise anchor a chain of cozier hostels from Calgary to Jasper. **Rustic hostels** provide more of a wilderness experience (read: no electricity or flush toilets), and often have some of the park's best hiking and cross-country skiing right in their backyards. HI runs a **shuttle service** connecting all the Rocky Mountain hostels and Calgary ($8-90). Wait-list beds become available at 6pm, and the larger hostels try to save a few standby beds for shuttle arrivals. Beds go quickly, especially during the summer, so make your reservations as early as possible. The hostels below are listed from south to north, and all reservations are made through the southern Alberta HI administration at ☎866-762-4122 or online at www.hostellingintl.ca. Free reservations are held until 6pm, but can be guaranteed until later with a credit card. Because of a recent move towards centralizing the administration of these hostels, information regarding prices, closures, and facilities will be in flux for some time.

Lake Louise Alpine Centre (HI) (☎670-7580), 500m west of the Info Centre in Lake Louise Townsite, on Village Rd. toward the Park Warden's office. Ranked 4th in the world by HI, and rightly so. More like a resort than a hostel, it boasts a reference library, a stone fireplace, 2 full kitchens, a sauna, and a quality cafe. Internet access $2 per 20min. Hub for mountaineering tours. Check-in 3pm, check-out 11am. Dorms $24-34, nonmembers $28-38; private rooms available. ❶

Rampart Creek Wilderness Hostel (HI), 34km south of the Icefield Centre. Close to several world-famous ice climbs (including Weeping Wall, 17km north), this hostel is a favorite for winter mountaineers and anyone who likes a rustic sauna after a hard day's hike. Wood-burning sauna, full-service kitchen. A steep climb behind the hostel leads to a hammock with free access to the visual orgy of the entire valley. 2 co-ed cabins with 12 beds each. $18, nonmembers $22; F-Sa $21, nonmembers $25. ❶

Castle Mountain Wilderness Hostel (HI), in Castle Junction, 1.5km east of the junction of Hwy. 1 and Hwy. 93 south, between Banff and Lake Louise. One of the hardest hostels to find, Castle Mountain offers a smaller, quieter alternative to the hubbub of its big brothers. Comfortable common area with huge bay windows. A library, collection of games, and fireplace. Friendly staff, hot showers, kitchen, laundry, electricity, and volleyball. Check-in 5-10pm; check-out 10am. Sleeps 28. Su-Th $19, nonmembers $23; Fr-Sa $21, nonmembers $25. ❶

Mosquito Creek Wilderness Hostel (HI), 103km south of the Icefield Centre and 26km north of Lake Louise. Across the creek from the Mosquito Creek campground. Close to the Wapta Icefield. Enormous living room with wood stove, wood-burning sauna, kitchen, and pump water. 2 co-ed cabins of 16 beds each. $18, nonmembers $22; F-Sa $21, nonmembers $25. ❶

Banff International Hostel (HI) (☎762-4122), 3km uphill from Banff Townsite on Tunnel Mountain Rd. Walk or take Banff Transit from downtown ($1). This monster hostel has 3 lounges and kitchens. Check-in 3pm. Check-out 11am. Laundry and hot showers. Sleeps 215. $26 nonmembers $30; for better rooms in new building add $1.50. ❷

(Continued from previous page)

Descriptions of Kananaskis Country's abundant activities give outdoor enthusiasts goose bumps. With over 1000km of trails, hiking in K-Country can provide anything from a 1hr. quick fix to a full-blown Rocky Mountain High. Pick up the $1 trail guide at one of the visitor centers. Gillean Dafferns's *Kananaskis Country Trail Guide* ($17), published by Rocky Mountain Books and available at any area information center, is a definitive, detailed source of information on longer trails. **1982 Canadian Mt. Everest Expedition Trail** (2km) starts at the White Spruce parking lot in Peter Lougheed Park 10km south of the visitors center. Climb through forest to a lookout point that provides a majestic view of both Upper and Lower Kananaskis Lakes. **Upper Lake Trail** (15km loop, 4.5km to campsite) circumnavigates the Upper Lake and provides incredible views of the surrounding mountains, reflected in the Lake's still waters. **Ribbon Creek Trail** (8km to falls, 10km to lake; 350m gain) starts half a kilometer south of the hostel parking lot and passes through the waterfall-rich canyon land between **Mt. Kidd** and **Mt. Bogart,** arriving at the Ribbon Falls campground.

Cliffs throughout the park offer excellent climbing opportunities. **Barrier Bluffs** has dozens of bolted routes up the wall. The foothills of the **Sibbald Area** in the northeast of K-country (30min. off Hwy. 1) offer wide expanses of terrain to horseback riders, hikers, and cyclists.

CAMPING

A chain of campgrounds stretches between Banff and Jasper. Extra-large, fully hooked-up grounds lie closer to the townsites; for more trees and fewer vehicles, try the more remote sites farther from Banff and Lake Louise. At all park campgrounds, a campfire permit (includes firewood) is $4. Sites are first come, first served; go early. The sites below are listed from south to north and have wheelchair access but no toilets or showers unless otherwise noted.

Tunnel Mountain Village, 4km from Banff Townsite on Tunnel Mountain Rd. With nearly 1200 sites, this facility is a camping metropolis. Trailer/RV area has 321 full RV sites, Village 2 has 188 sites, and Village 1 houses a whopping 618 sites. Fires allowed in Village 1 only; all villages have showers. Village 2 is open year-round; 1 and 3 closed Oct.-early May. $17; power only $21; full RV sites $24. ❶

Two Jack, 13km northeast of Banff, across Hwy.1. Open mid-May to Aug. The 381 sites in the main area ($13) have no showers or disabled access, while the 80 lakeside sites ($17) do. ❶

Johnston Canyon, 26km northwest of Banff on Bow Valley Pkwy. Access to Johnston Canyon Trail (see below). Open mid-June to mid-Sept. 140 sites, $17. Showers. ❶

Protection Mountain, 15km east of Lake Louise and 11km west of Castle Junction on the Bow Valley Pkwy. (Hwy. 1A). 89 spacious and wooded sites (14 trailer) in a basic campground. Open late June-early Sept. Sites $13. ❶

Lake Louise, 1½km southeast of the visitors center on Fairview Rd. On Bow River, not the lake. Plenty of hiking and fishing awaits near this tent city. 189 trailer sites with electricity, open year-round; $21. 220 tent sites, open mid-May to Sept.; $17. Showers. ❶

Mosquito Creek, 103km south of the Icefield Centre and 26km north of Lake Louise. 32 sites with hiking access. Pit toilets. Sites $10. ❶

Rampart Creek, 147km north of Banff, 34km south of the Icefield Centre, across the highway from Rampart Creek hostel and amazing ice climbing. Pit toilets. Open late June-Aug. 50 sites, $10. ❶

FOOD & NIGHTLIFE

Like everything else in the park, Banff restaurants tend toward the expensive. The Banff and Lake Louise hostels serve affordable meals in their cafes ($3-10). Groceries await at **Safeway,** at Marten and Elk St. just off Banff Ave. (☎762-5378. Open daily 8am-11pm.) Bartenders maintain that Banff's true wildlife is in its bars. Check the paper or ask at the visitors center to find out which nightspots are having "locals' night," featuring cheap drinks. Banff Ave. hosts more bars, restaurants, kitschy gift shops, ATMs and banks than there are mountains. The fun doesn't stop after Saturday night, either: Banff Sundays boast great nightlife.

Rose and Crown, 202 Banff Ave. (☎762-2121), upstairs on the corner of Banff and Caribou. Ample room for dancing, and pool-playing ($1.25), even on busy nights. Couch-adorned living room for watching sports and live music every night at 10pm. Happy hour M-F 3:30-6:30pm. $2 cover Sa, Jam Night Su with happy hour 9pm-close. Open daily 11am-2am. ❷

Laggan's Deli (☎522-2017; fax 522-3299), in Samson Mall in Lake Louise. Always crowded. Thick sandwiches ($4-5) or fresh-baked loaves ($3). Open June-Sept. daily 6am-8pm; Oct.-May 6am-7pm. Cash or traveler's checks only. ❶

Sunfood Cafe, 215 Banff Ave. (☎760-3933), 2nd floor of the Sundance Mall. A very relaxed vegetarian cafe hidden upstairs in a touristy mall. Veggie burger with the works $6.25. Daily specials, takeout available. Beer and wine. Open M-Sa 11am-9pm. ❶

Aardvark's, 304A Caribou St. (☎762-5500 or 762-5509). Does big business after the bars close. Skinny on seating. Small-ish slices of pizza $3. Small pie $6-9; large $13-21; buffalo wings $5 for 10. Open daily 11am-4am. ❸

Aurora, 110 Banff Ave. (☎760-5300). This neon-lit, ultra-modern club caters to the 25+ crowd with a martini and cigar bar in back. House, hip-hop, and trance dance floor; sports area with big-screen; 5 bars. Highballs and beer Sa. Open daily 9pm-2am.

Lux Cinema Centre, 229 Bear St. (24hr. cinema info ☎762-8595). Fun for the whole family. Call for movies and times.

St. James's Gate, 205 Wolf St. (☎762-9355). A laid-back Irish Pub with friendly staff. Ask the bartenders which of the 32 beers on tap to try. Live jigs and reels F-Sa completes the Irish ambience. Open daily 11am-2am.

SIGHTS

MUSEUMS. Visitors can purchase a pass to gain admission to all of the following sites for $9, seniors and students $6.50, family $20. The **Whyte Museum of the Canadian Rockies** explores the history and culture of the Canadian Rockies over the last two centuries in the Heritage Gallery, while temporary exhibits focus on the natural history of the region. Displays include works done by Canadian painters. *(111 Bear St. ☎762-2291. Open daily 10am-5pm. $6, students and seniors $4, 5 and under free.)* The **Banff Park Museum National Historic Site** is western Canada's oldest natural history museum, with rooms of stuffed specimens dating to the 1860s. *(☎762-1558. Open mid-May to Sept. daily 10am-6pm; Oct. to mid-May 1-5pm. Tours in summer daily 3pm, weekends in winter. $2.50, seniors 65 $2, children $1.50.)* Banff National Park would not exist if not for the **Cave and Basin Mineral Springs,** once rumored to have miraculous healing properties. The **Cave and Basin National Historic Site,** a refurbished bath house built circa 1914, is now a small museum detailing the history and science of the site. Access to the low-ceilinged cave containing the original spring is inside the building. Five of the pools are the only home of the park's most endangered species: the small Banff Springs snail—*Physella johnsoni*. *(☎762-1566. Open in summer daily 9am-6pm; winter M-F 11am-4pm, Sa-Su 9:30am-5pm. Tours at 11am. $4, seniors $3.50, ages 6-18 $3.)* The **springs** are southwest of the city on Cave Ave. For an actual dip in the hot water, follow the egg smell to the Upper Hot Springs pool, a 40°C (104°F) sulfurous cauldron on Mountain Ave. *(☎762-1515. Open mid-May to mid-Oct. daily 9am-11pm; mid-Oct. to mid-May Su-Th 10am-10pm, F-Sa 10am-11pm. Summer rates $7.50, seniors and children 3-17 $6.50, families $21.50. Winter $5.50, $4.50, $15. Swimsuits $1.50, towels $1.25, lockers $0.50.)*

EVENTS. In summer, the **Banff Festival of the Arts** keeps tourists occupied. A wide spectrum of events, from First Nations dance to opera, are performed from May to mid-August. Some shows are free; stop by the visitors center for a schedule. The **Banff Mountain Film Festival,** in the first week of November, screens films and videos that celebrate mountains and mountaineers. *(For times and info, call ☎762-6301.)*

OUTDOOR ACTIVITIES

A visitor sticking to paved byways will see only a tiny fraction of the park and the majority of the park's visitors. Those interested in the seemingly endless outdoor options can hike or bike on more than 1600km of trails. Grab a free copy of the "Mountain Biking and Cycling Guide" or "Dayhikes in Banff" and peruse park maps and trail descriptions at information centers. For still more solitude, pick up "The Banff Backcountry Experience" and an **overnight camping permit** at a visitors center and head out to the backcountry ($6 per person per day, up to $30; $38 per year). Be sure to check with the park rangers at the information center for current weather, trail, and wildlife updates.

BANFF TOWNSITE AREA

HIKING

Two easy trails are within walking distance of Banff Townsite, but longer, more rigorous and escapist trails abound farther away. The best escapes and incomparable experiences are found in the backcountry.

Fenland (2km, 1hr.). Follow Mt. Norquay Rd. to town outskirts, look for signs across the tracks on road's left side. The trail winds through a flat area shared by beaver, muskrat, and waterfowl, but is closed for elk calving in late spring and early summer. Easy.

Tunnel Mountain (2.5km, 2hr.). Follow Wolf St. east from Banff Ave., and turn right on St. Julien Rd. to reach the head of the steep trail. Provides a dramatic view of the **Bow Valley** and **Mt. Rundle.** Tunnel Mountain has the unfortunate distinction of being the Rockies' smallest mountain. Not that it matters. Easy to moderate.

Aylmer Pass (26.5km round-trip, 8hr.) The trail leaves from the shore of Lake Minnewanka on Lake Minnewanka Rd. (the extension of Banff Ave. across the Trans-Canada from town). Parking just above tour boat area. A steep climb to the summit yields a panoramic view of the lake and surrounding scenery. The trail can be abridged by hiking only 11.6km to the lookout, cutting the final 250m ascent. Strenuous.

Johnston Canyon (5.5km). West of the Norquay Interchange on Hwy. 1, then 18km along the Bow Valley Pkwy. (Hwy. 1A). A very popular half-day hike. A catwalk along the edge of the deep limestone canyon runs 1.1km over the thundering river to the canyon's lower falls, then another 1.6km to the upper falls. The trail continues for a more rugged 3.2km to seven blue-green cold-water springs, known as the **Inkpots,** in an open valley above the canyon. More than 42km of trails beyond the Inkpots are blissfully untraveled and punctuated with campgrounds roughly every 10km. Moderate to strenuous.

Sulphur Mountain (5.5km, 2hr.). Winds along a well-trodden trail to the peak, where a spectacular view awaits; the **Sulphur Mountain Gondola** doesn't charge for the 8min. downhill trip. (☎762-2523. Uphill $19, ages 6-15 $9.50, under 6 free.) The **Panorama Restaurant** (☎762-7486), perched atop the mountain, serves breakfast ($10) and lunch buffets ($13) from mid-May to mid-August. Moderate.

BACKCOUNTRY

Backcountry trekking is the way to see Banff as the masses of travelers cannot. Banff's backcountry, replete with picture-postcard, mind-boggling scenery, belies the kitschy tourist trap that the townsite has become. Amateurs and experts alike should beware of dangerous and changing conditions on strenuous trails that do not receive as much maintenance as more accessible routes; consult park rangers for information. Trails to ask about include **Egypt Lake** (12.5km one-way, 2 days), **Twin Lakes** (9km one-way, 2 days), **Mystic Pass** (37km, 3 days), **Skoki Loop** (34km, 3 days), **Assiniboine Loop** (55km, 4 days), **Sunshine-Assiniboine-Bryant Creek Trail** (56km, 4 days, two cars recommended), **Sawback Trail** (74km, 5 days), and **Mystic Pass-Flint's Park-Badger Pass Trail** (76km, 5 days).

BIKING

Biking is permitted on public roads, highways, and certain trails in the park. Spectacular scenery and a number of hostels and campgrounds make the **Bow Valley Parkway (Hwy. 1A)** and the **Icefields Parkway (Hwy. 93)** perfect for extended cycling trips. Every other store downtown seems to rent bikes; head to **Bactrax** or **Performance Sport** (see **Equipment Rental,** p. 379) for HI discounts. Parks Canada publishes a "Mountain Biking and Cycling Guide" that describes trails and roadways where bikes are permitted (free at bike rental shops and visitors centers).

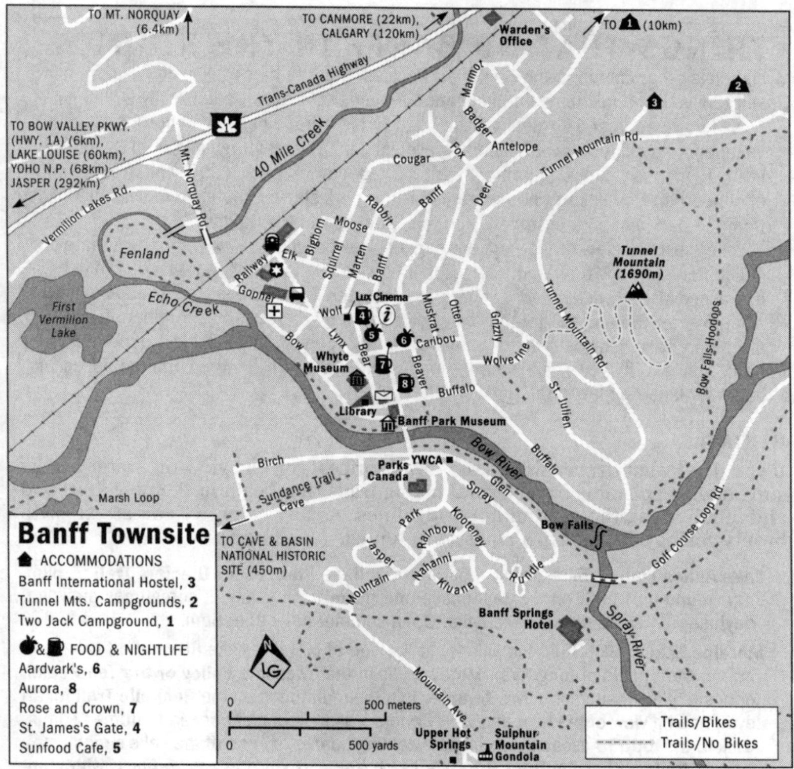

WATERSPORTS

Fishing is legal in most of the park's bodies of water during specific seasons, but live bait and lead weights are not. Get a **permit** and check out regulations at the info center. (7-day permit $6, annual permit valid in all Canadian National Parks $13.) **Bourgeau Lake,** a 7km hike in, is home to a particularly feisty breed of brook trout. Closer to the road, try **Herbert Lake,** off the Icefields Pkwy., or **Lake Minnewanka,** on Lake Minnewanka Rd. northeast of Banff. Lake Minnewanka Rd. passes **Johnson Lake,** where shallow warm water makes a perfect **swimming hole.**

Hydra River Guides runs **whitewater rafting** trips along the **Kicking Horse River.** (☎762-4554 or 800-644-8888; www.raftbanff.com. 22km, 2½hr; 6hr. including transportation. Up to Class IV+ rapids. $90, includes lunch, transportation, and gear; HI members $76.) **Blast Adventures** leads half-day, 1- to 2-person **inflatable kayak** trips on the rowdy Kananaskis River. (☎609-2009 or 888-802-5278; www.blastadventures.com. $64 per person including transportation, gear, and snacks.)

LAKE LOUISE TOWNSITE AREA

The highest community in Canada (1530m), Lake Louise and the surrounding glaciers have often passed for Swiss scenery in movies and are the emerald in the Rockies' tiara of tourism. Once at the lake, the hardest task is escaping fellow gawkers at the posh, though aesthetically misplaced, **Chateau Lake Louise.** The chateau's canoe rentals are an unheard of $30 per hr.

THINGS THAT GO BANFF IN THE NIGHT Bear sightings are common in the Canadian Rockies, but one black bear took it upon himself to give Banff residents an uncommon reminder of whose park it really is. Imaginatively known as Bear 16 (numbers are used to discourage personification), this ursine vagabond moved into town, disrupting everyday activity by foraging in front lawns and lazing in the road, blocking traffic. Bear 16 crossed the line when the scent from a bakery lured him too close to human territory. The park staff ultimately removed Bear 16 from the park, had him castrated, and relocated him to the Calgary Zoo.

While most travelers to the park are eager to see its wildlife, few want as intimate an encounter as Bear 16 offered. The safest bet is to talk, sing, or yodel loudly while hiking, especially on windy days or near running water. The number of bear attacks actually ranks low among the total number of attacks by park animals; dozens of visitors are bitten each year by rodents pursuing human food. By far the most dangerous of Banff animals, however, are people—road accidents are the most common cause of death for large wildlife in the park.

HIKING

If you don't want to succumb to the town's prices, you can view the water and its surrounding splendor from several hiking trails that begin in the neighborhood and climb along the surrounding ridgelines. As any celebrity can attest, with beauty comes crowds; expect masses of tourists (and bears).

Lake Agnes Trail (3.5km, 2½hr. round-trip), and the **Plain of Six Glaciers Trail** (5.5km, 4hr. round-trip) both end at teahouses and make for a lovely, if sometimes crowded, dayhike with views down to the Lake. Open summer daily 9am-6pm.

Moraine Lake, 15km from the village, at the end of Moraine Lake Rd. and off Lake Louise Dr. (no trailers or long RVs). Moraine lies in the awesome **Valley of the Ten Peaks,** opposite glacier-encrusted **Mt. Temple.** Join the multitudes on the **Rockpile Trail** for an eye-popping view of the lake and valley and a lesson in ancient ocean bottoms (10min. walk to the top). To escape the camera-wielding hordes, try one of the Lake's more challenging trails, either **Sentinel Pass** via Larch Valley (6km one-way, 5-6hr.), with stunning views from flower studded meadows, or **Wenkchemna Pass** via Eiffel Lake (10km one-way, full day), which carries hikers the length of the Valley of the Ten Peaks with incredible views in both directions. Moraine packs more scenic punch than its sister Louise; be sure to arrive before 10am or after 4pm to see the view instead of the crowds. If you don't visit Moraine, just get your hands on an old $20 bill; the Valley of Ten Peaks is pictured on the reverse.

Paradise Valley, depending on which way you hike it, can be an intense dayhike or a relaxing overnight trip. From the **Paradise Creek Trailhead,** 2.5km up Moraine Lake Rd., the loop through the valley runs 18.1km through subalpine and alpine forests and along rivers (7½hr., elevation gain 880m). One classic backpacking route runs from Moraine Lake up and over **Sentinel Pass,** joining the top of the Paradise Valley loop after 8km. A **backcountry campground** marks the mid-point from either trailhead. Campers aren't the only admirers of the scenery: grizzly activity often forces the park wardens to close the area in summer. Check with the wardens before hiking in this area.

WINTER SPORTS

Winter activities in the park range from world-class ice climbing to ice fishing. Those 1600km of hiking trails make for exceptional **cross-country skiing** (**Moraine Lake Rd.** is closed to vehicle traffic in the winter, and is used for cross-country skiing, as are the backcountry trails), and three allied resorts offer a range of **skiing and snowboarding** opportunities from early Nov. to mid-May. All have terrain parks for snowboarders. Shuttles to all the following three resorts leave from most big hotels in the townsites, and Banff and Lake Louise hostels typically have ticket and transportation **discounts** available for guests. Multi-day passes good for all three resorts are available at the **Ski Banff/Lake Louise** office, 225 Banff Ave., lower level, and at all resorts. Passes include free shuttle service and an extra night of skiing at Mount Norquay. (☎762-4561; www.skibanfflakelouise.)

Sunshine Mountain (☎762-6500, snow report 760-7669, in Calgary 277-7669; www.skibanff.com). Spreading across 3 mountains, with the most snowfall (9.9m) in the area, this mountain attracts loyal followers to its 3168 acres. $59; students under 24, ages 13-17, and over 65 $46; ages 6-12 $20.

Lake Louise (☎522-3555, snow report in Banff 762-4766, in Calgary 244-6665; www.skilouise.com). The 2nd-largest ski area in Canada (4200 ski-able acres), with amazing views, over 1000m of vertical drop, and the best selection of expert (double-black) terrain. Some simpler slopes cover plenty of the mountain. $58; students under 25 and adults over 65 $47; ages 6-12 $15.

Mt. Norquay (☎762-4421). A local's mountain: smaller, closer to town, and less manic. Draws like F night-skiing and 2-5hr. tickets. ($49; students, ages 13-17 and 55+ $37; ages 6-12 $16. Night-skiing $23; students, youth, and seniors $21; ages 6-12 $12.)

SIGHTSEEING

The **Lake Louise Sightseeing Lift,** up Whitehorn Rd. and across the Trans-Canada Hwy. from Lake Louise, cruises up **Mt. Whitehorn.** (☎522-3555; www.skilouise.com. Open daily May 9am-4pm; June and Sept. 8:30am-9pm; July and Aug. 8am-6pm. $19, students and seniors $17, ages 6-12 $9, under 6 free. To enjoy breakfast at the top, add $2; for lunch, add $6, under 6 $2.)

BANFF TO JASPER: ICEFIELDS PARKWAY (HWY. 93)

The Icefields Parkway began in the Great Depression as a work relief project. The 230km Parkway is one of the most beautiful rides in North America, heading north from Lake Louise in Banff National Park to Jasper Townsite in Jasper National Park. Drivers may struggle to keep their eyes on the road as they skirt stunning peaks, aquamarine glacial lakes, and highwayside glaciers, not to mention all the wonders of Rocky Mountain fauna, visible from the safety of a car window.

PRACTICAL INFORMATION Parks Canada manages the parkway as a scenic route, so all users must obtain a **Park Pass,** available at entrance gates and information centers. ($10 per day, seniors $8; $38 per year, $70 for 2-7 persons. Valid at all Canadian national parks.) Free maps of the Icefields Parkway are available at park visitors centers in Jasper, Lake Louise, and Banff. They are also available at the **Icefield Centre,** at the boundary between the two parks, 132km north of Lake Louise and 103km south of Jasper Townsite. (☎780-852-6288. Open May to mid-Oct. daily 9am-5pm; July and Aug. 9am-6pm.) Although the center is closed in winter, the Parkway is only closed for plowing after heavy snowfalls. Thanks to the extensive campground and hostel networks that line the Parkway, longer trips between Banff and Jasper National Parks are convenient and affordable. Cyclists should be prepared to face rapidly changing weather conditions and some very steep hills.

OUTDOOR ACTIVITIES. The Icefields Parkway has 18 trails into the wilderness and 22 scenic points with spectacular views. **Bow Summit,** 40km north of Lake Louise, is the Parkway's highest point (2135m); there, a 10min. walk leads to a view of fluorescent, aqua **Peyto Lake.** The Icefield Centre (see above) lies in the shadow of the tongue of the **Athabasca Glacier.** This gargantuan ice floe is one of six major glaciers that flow from the 200 sq. km **Columbia Icefield,** the largest accumulation of ice and snow in the Canadian Rockies. The icefield's runoff eventually flows to three oceans: the Pacific, Atlantic, and Arctic.

Columbia Icefield Snocoach Tours carry visitors over the Athabasca Glacier in monster-truck-like buses for an 80min. trip. (☎877-423-7433; www.columbiaicefield.com. Open mid-Apr. to mid-Oct. daily 9am-5pm; $28, ages 6-15 $14.) Visitors can also drive close and take a 10min. walk up piles of glacial debris onto the glacier's mighty toe. Dated signposts mark the glacier's speedy retreat up the valley over the last century. The trail onto the glacier is limited to a very small "safe zone," and all hikers are warned that glacial crevices are a very real concern; two people have died on Athabasca in the last decade. For more geological tidbits, sign up for an **Athabasca Glacier Icewalk.** The daily "Ice Cubed" hike provides 3hr. of fun and education on the ice. ($45, ages 7-17 $23.) Sunday and Thursday at 11am, the "Icewalk Deluxe" hike takes the eager out for a 5-6hr. tour higher up on the glacier, though snow may limit these trips to July and August. ($50, ages 7-17 $25.) Contact the Icefield Centre. (☎780-852-3803. Tours run mid-June to mid-Sept.)

The **Wilcox Pass Trail** begins 3km south of the Icefield Centre at **Wilcox Creek Campground** (see p. 390). After 2.5km, the path reaches a ridge with astounding views of Athabasca Glacier and Mt. Athabasca. Considered one of the best hikes in Jasper, it's 8km to the pass and back, and 11km one-way from the trailhead to a later junction with the Icefields Parkway, requiring either two vehicles or good hitchhiking skills. *Let's Go* does not recommend hitchhiking. The **Parker Ridge Trail** leads 2.5km away from the road and up above treeline, where an impressive view of the **Saskatchewan Glacier** awaits. The trailhead is 1km south of the **Hilda Creek Hostel's** burned down remains, and 8.5km south of the Icefield Centre.

JASPER NATIONAL PARK ☎780

AT A GLANCE

AREA: 10,878 sq. km **CLIMATE:** Alpine, subalpine **FEATURES:** Columbia Icefields, Maligne Lake **HIGHLIGHTS:** Hiking the 2 Mt. Edith Cavell trails, visiting the Athabasca Glacier	**GATEWAYS:** Banff (p. 378), Edmonton (p. 363) **CAMPING:** First come, first served (p. 391) **FEES:** Day pass $6, $4.50 senior, $3 ages 6-16

Northward expansion of the Canadian railway system led to further exploration of the Canadian Rocky Mountains and the 1907 creation of Jasper, the largest of the National Parks in the region. The area went virtually untouristed until 1940, when the Icefields Parkway paved the way for the masses to appreciate Jasper's astounding beauty. The Parkway is popular with cyclists, making for a remarkable, albeit long, bike journey. In summer, caravans of RVs and charter buses line the highway jostling for the chance to take photos of surprisingly fearless wildlife. Because 40% of the park is above the treeline, most visitors stay in the sheltered vicinity of Jasper Townsite, smaller than its nearby counterpart, Banff. Every summer, the tourists quadruple the town's population to over 20,000. In the face of this annual bloat, Jasper's permanent residents struggle to keep their home looking and feeling like a small town. In the winter, crowds melt away, snow descends, and a modest ski resort welcomes visitors to a slower, more relaxed town.

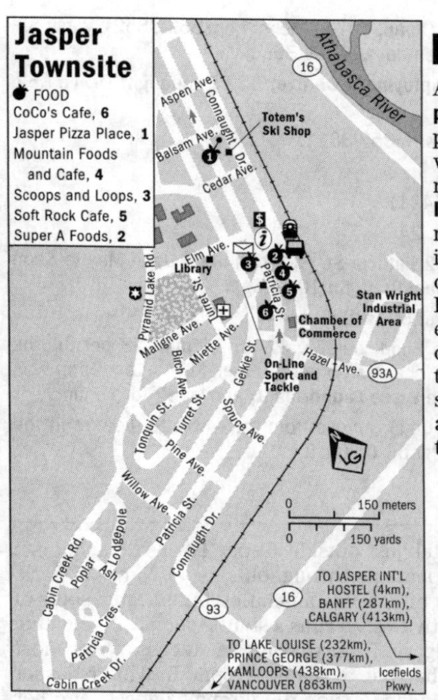

TRANSPORTATION

All of the addresses below are in **Jasper Townsite,** near the center of the park at the intersection of **Hwy. 16,** which runs east-west through the northern reaches of the park, and the **Icefields Parkway (Hwy. 93),** which connects Jasper with Banff National Park in the south. Many bike shops rent one-way between the two parks. Hitching is popular and reportedly easy along the Parkway, but *Let's Go* does not recommend hitchhiking. The two front streets in Jasper hold all the shops and stores, while the hostels and campgrounds are several kilometers out from town.

Trains: VIA Rail, 607 Connaught Dr. (☎800-561-8630). 3 per week to **Edmonton** (5hr., $142), **Vancouver, BC** (17hr., $198), and **Winnipeg, MB** (1 day, $288).

Buses: Greyhound (☎852-3926), in the train station. To **Edmonton** (4½hr., 3 per day, $54) and **Vancouver, BC** (10½hr., 2 per day, $106), via **Kamloops, BC** (5hr., 2 per day, $60). **Brewster Transportation** (☎852-3332), in the movie theater, across the street from the train station. To **Calgary** (8hr., $75) via **Banff** (6hr., $54).

Taxis: Heritage Cabs (☎852-5558). Metered for short local trips. 24hr.

Car Rental: Hertz (☎852-3888), in the train station. $50 per day, $0.23 per km after 150km. Must be 24+ with credit card. Open M, W, F 9am-7pm, and Tu, Th, Sa-Su 9am-5pm. **Budget,** 638 Connaught Dr. (☎852-3222), in the Shell Station. $53 per day, $0.23 per km after 150km; $33 per 6hr. with 50km free and $0.23 per km thereafter. Open daily 8am-7pm.

Car Repair: Petro Canada, 300 Connaught Dr. (☎852-3366).

Tours: Bigfoot Adventure Tours (see p. 379) run between Vancouver, Jasper, and Banff.

ALBERTA

PRACTICAL INFORMATION

Tourist Information: Park Information Centre, 500 Connaught Dr. (☎852-6176), has trail maps, trail reports, and backcountry permits. Lists local accommodations, homestay and activity options. Offers free local calls. Open mid-June to early Sept. daily 8am-7pm; early Sept. to late Oct. and late Dec. to mid-June 9am-5pm.

Bank: CIBC, 416 Connaught Ave. (☎852-3391), by the visitors center. Open M-Th 10am-3pm, F 10am-5pm. **24hr. ATM.**

Equipment Rental: Freewheel Cycle, 618 Patricia Ave. (☎852-3898; www.freewheeljasper.ca). Hi-end mountain bikes $8 per hr., $24 per day, $32 overnight. Snowboards $28 per day. Watch for twin-tip ski demo deals. Open summer daily 9am-9pm; spring and fall 9am-6pm; call for winter hours. **Jasper International Hostel** rents mountain bikes. $8 per half-day, $15 per day. Snowshoes $8 per day.

Laundromat and Public Showers: Coin Clean, 607 Patricia St. (☎852-3852). Wash $2, dry $1.50. Showers $2 per 10min. Open daily 8am-9:30pm.

Local Work Opportunities: Jasper Employment Centre, 622 Connaught Dr. (☎852-5982). Open M-F 10am-4pm.

Weather: ☎852-3185. **Road Conditions:** ☎852-3311.

Emergency: ☎911.

Police: 600 Pyramid Lake Rd. (☎852-4421).

Women's Crisis Line: ☎800-661-0937. 24hr.

Pharmacy: Cavell Value Drug Mart, 602 Patricia St. (☎852-4441). Open May to Sept. daily 9am-11pm; Sept. to May M-Sa 9am-9pm, Su 10am-6pm.

Hospital: Corner of Miette Ave. and Turret St. (☎852-3344).

Internet Access: Soft Rock Cafe (see **Food,** below). $2 for 15 min, $8 per hr. The **library,** 500 Robson St. (☎852-3652), charges $5 per hr. Open M-Th 11am-9pm, F-Sa 11am-5pm. Also available at **Coin Clean,** see **Laundromat,** above, $2 for 15min.

Post Office: 502 Patricia St. (☎852-3041), across from the townsite green and the visitors center. Open M-F 9am-5pm. **Postal Code:** T0E 1E0.

ACCOMMODATIONS

The modern Jasper International Hostel, just outside Jasper Townsite, anchors a chain of **Hostelling International (HI)** locations throughout Jasper National Park. The rustic hostels farther into the park offer fewer amenities, but lie amid some of Jasper's finest scenery and outdoor activities. HI runs a shuttle service connecting the Rocky Mountain hostels with Calgary. Reservations are necessary for most hostels in summer, but wait-list beds become available at 6pm. In winter, Jasper International, Athabasca Falls, and Maligne Canyon run normally; guests at other hostels must pick up the key at Jasper International and give a deposit. For couples or groups, a B&B may prove more economical (doubles summer $40-130; winter $30-95). Many are in town near the train station; ask for a list at the park information center or the bus depot.

Jasper International Hostel (HI) (☎852-3215 or 877-852-0781), known as Whistlers Hostel, is 3km up Whistlers Rd. from its intersection with Hwy. 93, 4km south of the townsite. Closest hostel to the townsite. Attracts a gregarious breed of backpackers and cyclists. 88 often-full beds (get ready for some sharing–it's possible to have as many as 43 roommates). 2 private rooms available with at least 2 people. 2am curfew. Sun Dog Shuttle (☎852-4056) runs from train station to hostel en route to Jasper Tramway ($3). $18, nonmembers $23. ❶

Maligne Canyon Hostel (HI), on Maligne Lake Rd. north of the Maligne Canyon parking lot, 11km east of town off Hwy. 16. Small, recently renovated cabins sit on bank of Maligne River, with access to the Skyline Trail and the Maligne Canyon. Manager is on a first-name basis with several local bears. Electricity, fridge, pay phone, potable water. Check-in 5-11pm. Closed W Oct.-Apr. 24 beds. $13, nonmembers $18. ❶

Mt. Edith Cavell Hostel (HI), 12km up Edith Cavell Rd., off Hwy. 93A. Cozy quarters heated by wood-burning stoves. A postcard view of Mt. Edith Cavell and her glaciers, with easy access to the mountain and trails. Propane light, spring water (filter in the newly-painted kitchen), private wash area, firepit, and the best smelling outhouses in the park. Road closed in winter, often until late June, but the hostel is open to anyone willing to pick up the keys at Jasper International Hostel and ski uphill from the highway. Check-in 5-11pm. 32 beds $13, nonmembers $18. ❶

Athabasca Falls Hostel (HI), on Hwy. 93 just south of the 93-93A junction, 32km south of the townsite. A hostel in a quiet setting that still has the comforts of town—electricity, e-mail, and ping pong. However, the only running water around is the beautiful Athabasca Falls, which are a 500m stroll away. Propane heat. 40 beds in 3 cabins. $13, nonmembers $18. ❶

Beauty Creek Hostel (HI), on Hwy. 93, 87km south of the townsite. On the banks of the glacier-fed Sunwapta River and close to the Columbia Icefields. ½km south of the 3.2km Stanley Falls trailhead. Poetry on the outhouse walls and views of the whole valley from the solar shower. Check-in 5pm-11pm. 22 beds, $12; nonmembers $17. ❶

CAMPING

These government-run campgrounds are listed from north to south. Most are primitive sites with few facilities. All are first come, first served, and popular. Call the park info center (☎852-6176) for details. Fire permits are $4. All campgrounds except for Pocahontas also offer kitchen shelters.

Pocahontas, on Hwy. 16 at the northern edge of the park, 44km northeast of the townsite. Closest campground to Miette Hot Springs. Flush toilets. Open mid-May to mid-Oct. 130 sites and 10 walk-in tent sites. $13. ❶

Snaring River, on Hwy. 16, 16km north of Jasper Townsite. Right on the river. Come early for choice spots. 56 sites and 10 walk-in tent sites, dry toilets. Open mid-May to late Sept. $10. ❶

Whistlers, on Whistlers Rd., 3km south of the townsite off Hwy. 93. This 781-site behemoth is the closest campground to Jasper Townsite and has all the amenities. Public phones, dump station. Wheelchair accessible. Open early May to mid-Oct. Sites $15; full RV sites $24. Free showers. ❶

Wapiti, on Hwy. 93, 3.8km south of Whistlers, along the Athabasca River. Plentiful brush separates tenters from RVers. Pay phone, sani-dump, and electric RV site. Wheelchair accessible. Mid-June to early Sept.: 362 sites, $15-18. Oct.-early May: 91 sites, $13-15. Coin showers. ❶

Columbia Icefield, 109km south of the townsite. Lies close enough to the Athabasca Glacier to intercept an icy breeze and even a rare summer night's snowfall. Difficult and steep access road makes sites tents-only. Dry toilets and pay phones. Open mid-May to mid-Oct. 22 sites and 11 walk-ins. $10. ❶

FOOD

Food prices in Jasper range from the affordable to the outrageous. However, cheap options can be found and lots of places offer good lunch deals. **Super A Foods,** 601 Patricia St., satisfies basic grocery needs. (☎852-3200. Open daily 8am-10pm.) A larger selection and the bakery at **Robinson's IGA Foodliner,** 218 Connaught Dr., is worth the 5min. walk. (☎852-3195. Open summer daily 9am-9pm.) **Nutter's Bulk Foods,** 622 Patricia St., offers bulk snacks, vitamins, and fresh $5 sandwiches. (☎852-5844. Open daily 8am-11pm.)

Mountain Foods and Cafe, 606 Connaught Dr. (☎852-4050). Offers a wide selection of sandwiches, salads, home-cooked goodies, and take-out lunches for the trail. Turkey focaccia sandwich and assorted wraps $7.50. Fantastic breakfast special for $5.50. Open daily 8am-6pm. ❷

Jasper Pizza Place, 402 Connaught Dr. (☎852-3225). Has both draft and bottle beer. Free delivery in Jasper area (min. order $5). Large wood-oven pizzas $9-13, sandwiches $3-8. Open daily 11am-midnight. ❷

Coco's Cafe, 608 Patricia St. (☎852-4550). A small, vegetarian-friendly cafe downtown. Homemade items include tasty soups, baked goods, and smoothies ($3.50). Breakfast wraps are served all day ($5.25). A variety of tasty sandwiches from $4.75. Open in summer daily 7am-8pm; winter 7am-6pm. ❶

Scoops and Loops, 504 Patricia St. (☎852-4333). Not just an ice-cream parlor. Sandwiches ($3-4), sushi ($3-7), *udon* ($8). Open M-Sa 10am-11pm, Su 11am-11pm. ❶

Soft Rock Cafe, 622 Connaught Dr. (☎852-5850). Internet access, but no trademark t-shirts. Baguette sandwiches $4.25-8. Breakfast all day: sizable omelette, homefries, and thick toast $8. Open summer daily 7am-11pm; winter 7am-7pm. ❷

OUTDOOR ACTIVITIES

HIKING

Jasper National Park offers excellent dayhiking. This means nature writ large and exotic wildlife that includes bears and bighorn sheep. Remember, it's illegal to feed wildlife. Short, aesthetically mind-boggling walks make the postcard-perfect scenery of the Canadian Rockies easily accessible. For more info, stop by the Information Centre for a copy of their "Summer Hiking" pamphlet and trail condition updates. As a supplement to hiking, check out **The Jasper Tramway** (☎852-3093), just past the hostel on Whistlers Rd., 4km south of the townsite on Hwy. 93. Climbing 973m up Whistlers Mountain, the tramway leads to a panoramic view of the park and, on clear days, far beyond it. From the upper station, you can join hikers on the Whistlers Trail for the last 200m elevation gain to the summit. ($19, ages 5-14 $9.50, under 5 free. Open daily Apr. 13-May 17 and Oct. 9:30am-4:30pm; May 18-June 25 and Sept. 9:30am-9pm; June 26-July 8:30am-10pm.) **Sun Dog Tours** (☎852-4056; fax 852-9663) offers a shuttle from town and tram ride to the top ($24).

Path of the Glacier Loop (1.6km, 45min.). The trailhead is 30km south of the townsite; take Hwy. 93 to 93A to the end of the bumpy, twisty, and quite often closed (see Mt. Edith Cavell Hostel) 15km Mt. Edith Cavell Rd. One of the 2 paths features **Mt. Edith Cavell,** the glacier-laden peak named after an English nurse executed by the Germans for providing aid to the Allies during World War I. An easy path leads to a rewarding view of a glacier receding into a lake littered with icebergs. Open June-Oct.; no trailers or vehicles over 6m long.

Cavell Meadows Loop (8km, 3-6hr.). Trailhead is same as Path of the Glacier Loop. A more strenuous ascent past the treeline and through a carpet of wildflowers (from mid-July to Aug.), with striking views of the towering north face and the Angel Glacier. Be careful to stay on the trail as steep cliffs make for dangerous slide conditions. 400m gain. Open June-Oct.; no trailers or vehicles over 6m long.

Sulphur Skyline Trail (9.6km round-trip, 4-6hr.). This challenging hike enables the hardy to summit a peak in a day and attain views of the limestone Miette Range and Ashlar Ridge. The trail leaves from the parking lot of the Miette Hot Springs. If you have lunch at the peak, guard it from the courageous golden-mantled ground squirrels. Beware afternoon thunderstorms and serious wind gusts at the peak. 700m gain.

Maligne Canyon (2.1km one-way, 1-2hr.). The spectacular, over-touristed Maligne Canyon (mah-LEEN) is 8km east of the townsite on the Maligne Lake Rd. The best way to view the Canyon is by parking at the 5th Bridge parking area, crossing the bridge, and bearing right at every possible opportunity. From the trailhead, the path follows the Maligne River as it plunges through a narrow and intricately sculpted limestone gorge. Be sure to make it all the way to the first Bridge for views of the ground-shaking, breathtaking upper waterfall—truly a must-see. Along the walk, look for springs pouring into the Canyon. The water flows underground from Medicine Lake, 15km away, making this the longest underground river in North America.

Whistlers Trail (7.9km one-way; 3-5hr. up, 2-3hr. down) is a strenuous hike beginning next to the Jasper International Hostel basketball court. Bring extra layers, as weather conditions change rapidly at the 2470m summit. Worth the effort; the summit features an incredible 360-degree view of mountain range after mountain range. 1200m gain.

MALIGNE LAKE

Maligne Lake, at the end of the road, is the longest (22km) and deepest (97m) lake in the park. A flotilla of water vessels allows escape from fellow tourists (except those who also rent a boat) and the plastic geraniums of Maligne Lake Chalet. **Maligne Tours,** 627 Patricia St. (☎852-3370), rents kayaks ($70 per day) and leads canoe trips ($15 per hr.) and narrated scenic cruises (90min.; $35, seniors $29.75, children $17.50). Free maps to hiking trails are available at the Maligne Tours office or by the lake; bookings for whitewater and sightseeing trips are available at the office. Perhaps the best way to see the Lake's scenery is to escape into the surrounding hills on foot. The **Opal Hills Trail** (8.2km round-trip, 4-6hr.), which starts at the northeast corner of the first parking area, winds through subalpine meadows and ascends 460m in only 3km to views of the lake. The truly strong of stamina and mammoth of calf muscle can follow one of the drainages away from the lake at the halfway point of the hike in the high, tundra valley. At the ridge overlooking the valley, follow the rough footpath (avoid trampling the delicate alpine tundra) that leads up to **Opal Peak,** the highest in the vicinity. Note that this is not a maintained trail, and the loose shale makes for dangerous hiking, but the champion of the mountain will be rewarded with a view hard to surpass in this or any region. **Shuttle service** from Jasper to the area is available from Maligne Tours. (To the canyon $8; to the lake $12; round-trip with cruise $56; 3-6 per day, 8:30am-5:30pm.)

BACKPACKING

An extensive network of trails weaves through the park's backwoods, providing respite from tourist-land. The trails cover three different ecological regions. The **montane zone,** which includes Jasper Townsite, blankets valley floors with lodgepole pine, Douglas fir, white spruce, and aspen; it hosts elk, bighorn sheep, and coyotes. Subalpine fir and Engelmann spruce share the **subalpine zone** with porcupines and marmots, while fragile plants and wildflowers struggle against mountain goats and pikas in the uppermost **alpine zone.** To avoid trampling endangered plant species, hikers should not stray from trails in the alpine area.

Kick off any foray into the wilderness with a visit to the visitors center in the townsite, where rangers distribute the free *Backcountry Visitors' Guide* and plentiful advice. Overnight hikers need to register and pay the $6 per night fee, either at the Visitor Centre or by calling ☎852-6177; many buy *The Canadian Rockies Trail Guide* ($15). Before hitting the trail, ask about road and trail closures, water levels (some rivers cannot be crossed at certain times of the year), and snow levels at high passes. The Icefield Centre (see p. 387), on Hwy. 93 at the southern entrance to the park, provides similar services.

Trails particularly worthy of recommendation include the **Skyline Trail** (45km, 3 days), **Maligne Pass** (48km, 3 days), **Tonquin Valley** (42km, 3 days), **Jonas Pass** (53km, 4 days), **Athabasca Pass** (51km one way, 7 days), **North Boundary Trail** (192 km, 10 days), and **South Boundary Trail** (176km, 10 days). Backpackers should know their skill level and recognize the dangers that accompany trips of these durations in such mountainous conditions.

HOT SPRINGS

The **Miette Hot Springs,** 42km north of the townsite on Hwy. 16 and 15km along Miette Hot Springs Rd., blends heat therapy with a panoramic view of the surrounding limestone mountains. Once a rudimentary log bath-house in 1913, the waters—the hottest in the Canadian Rockies—are now chlorinated, filtered, and cooled before they arrive in three outdoor swimming pools at temperatures ranging from 39-41°C or 6-22°C. The road to Miette is, sadly, closed in winter. (☎866-3939. Open early May to mid-Oct. daily 8:30am-10:30pm. $6, children and seniors $5. Mid-Oct to Apr. open 10:30am-9pm, $1 cheaper. Swimsuit $1.50, towel $1.25.)

SKIING

Winter brings 4m of snowfall and plenty of skiing opportunities to the slopes of **Marmot Basin,** 19km south of Jasper via Hwy. 93, 93A, and the Marmot Basin Rd. The upper half of the slope's 897m vertical drop is above the treeline, creating room for bowls and a modest snowboard park. (☎852-3816; www.skimarmot.com. Full-day lift ticket $49, 65 and over $35, ages 13-17 and students up to age 25 $41, ages 6-12 $20, under 6 free.) Bargain **ski rental** is available at **Totem's Ski Shop,** 408 Connaught Dr. (☎852-3078. Open winter daily 8am-6pm; summer 9:30am-10pm. Ski package $9-20; snowboard package and boots $25; cross country skis from $9 per day.) **The Sports Shop,** 406 Patricia St., offers the same hours and ski rental prices and rents ice skates as well as camping and fishing equipment. (☎852-3654. Skates $4 per hr., $10 per day.) Maligne Lake offers **cross-country ski trails** from late November through May. **Everest Outdoor Stores,** 414 Connaught Dr., also has ski rentals. (☎852-5902. Open daily 9:30am-10pm, winter 8am-6pm. Cross-country skis from $12 per day, downhill skis and boots $25-35 per day, snowshoes $10 per day.)

OTHER OUTDOOR ACTIVITIES

Paul Valiulis teaches half-day ($59) and full-day ($89) **rock climbing** courses (☎852-4161; www.icpeaks.com). **Peter Amann** teaches 2-day introductory climbing classes for $150 as well as 2-3 day ice climbing classes for $220-300. (☎852-3237. May-June and Sept.) Both companies lead ice climbing and mountaineering trips. **Gravity Gear,** 618 Patricia St. (☎888-852-3155), has rentals for mountain adventures and offers multi-day discounts. **Rocky Mountain Unlimited,** 414 Connaught Dr., serves as a central reservation service for most local outdoor businesses. They provide prices and recommendations for rafting, fishing, horseback riding, wildlife safaris, and all your outdoor pursuits. (☎852-4056. Open summer daily 8:30am-9pm; winter 9am-6pm.) **Whitewater** leads two trips on the Athabasca River and one on the faster Sunwapta River. (☎852-7238. 2-3½hr. From $43. Register by phone.) **Rocky Mountain River Guides,** 626 Patricia St., offers similar rides. (☎852-3777. 2-3hr. $40.) **Boat rentals** are available at **Pyramid Lake Resort,** 7km from town off Pyramid Ave. from Connaught Dr. (☎852-4900. Open daily 8am, last boat out at 8:30pm. Canoes $15, pedal boats $24 for 1hr., both $15 per additional hr.)

YUKON TERRITORY

YUKON TERRITORY FACTS & FIGURES
Capital: Whitehorse. **Area:** 478,970 sq. km. **Drinking Age:** 19.
Human Population: 32,635. **Caribou Population:** 145,290.
Bird: Raven. **Flower:** Fireweed. **Holiday:** Discovery Day (3rd M in Aug.).
☎**911** may not work outside Whitehorse; call local police or ☎867-667-5555.

If you want to be alone with the land, the Yukon is where you ought to be. Yukon vistas cross glaciated, sawtooth mountain ranges and ease down into lakes, tundra, gigantic forests, and arid plateaus. And best of all for many travelers, the area is all but unpopulated. Glaciation left much of the Yukon untouched, creating an ice-free corridor for vegetation, wildlife, and early hunters. Although summer here is spectacular, Yukoners have been suffering payback for the ancient fair weather ever since, enduring what's often described as "nine months of winter and three months of bad snowmobiling." Fur traders in the 1800s came looking for faster routes and new partners. The gold seekers of 1898 came charging to Carcross from Skagway, then down the Yukon River to Whitehorse, Dawson City, and the goldfields beyond. A second territorial rush occurred during the construction of the Alaska Highway. These days, logging, mining, and the federal government support the region's economy. Yukon First Nations are presently negotiating with the federal government for land, self-government, and funding for innovative projects to rebuild their communities. But the human footprint on the land evaporates meters away from any Yukon road, and the highway system is but a tiny skeleton laid over a huge area. It's an intimidating area, but one that demands exploration.

HIGHLIGHTS OF THE YUKON TERRITORY

JAM with musicians at the **Dawson City Music Festival** (see p. 415).

DIP your toes in the Arctic Ocean after driving up the **Dempster Hwy.** (see p. 417).

FLY over **Kluane National Park** (see p. 405) to enjoy all its splendor.

RETRACE prospectors' foot steps on the **Chilkoot Trail** (see p. 405).

BASK under the **aurora borealis** in the winter (see p. 403), and the **midnight sun** in the summer.

WHITEHORSE ☎867

Whitehorse was born during the Klondike Gold Rush, when the gold-hungry used it as a layover on their journey north. Miners en route to Dawson coined the name, claiming that whitecaps on the rapids downstream resembled galloping white stallions. With a population of 24,000, Whitehorse is home to 70% of the territory's population. The capital of the Yukon shifted from Dawson to here in 1953, and now the majority of government employees call Whitehorse home. The town itself is clogged with acres of RVs during the summer, and an adventure traveler's best bet is to head on out into the surrounding wilds—the drone of city life disappears just a kilometer or two outside city limits.

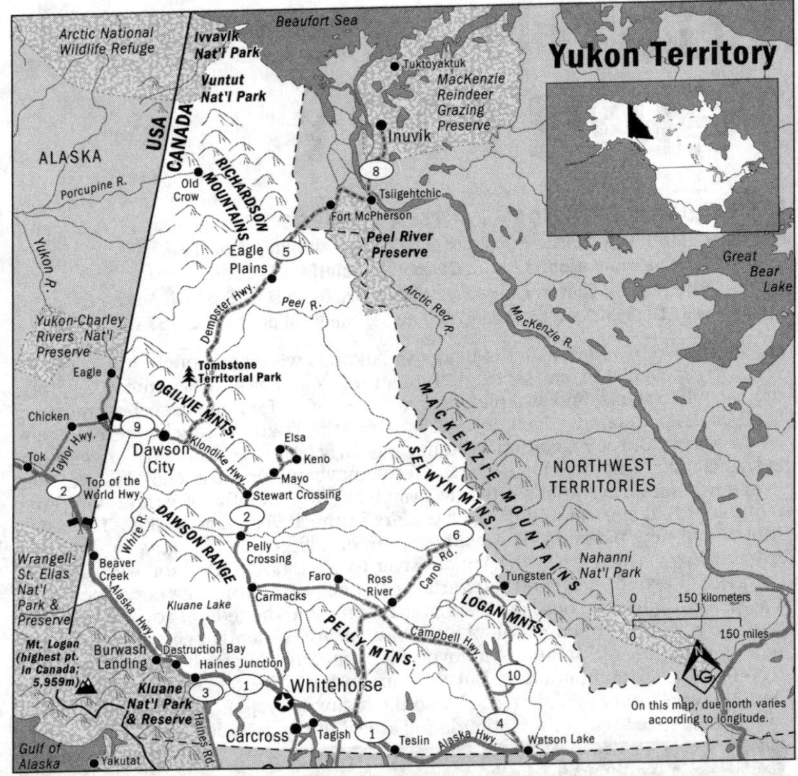

TRANSPORTATION

Whitehorse lies 1500km northwest of Dawson Creek, BC, along the **Alaska Hwy.** and 535km south of Dawson City. The city is an oblong grid of numbered avenues running north-south and streets running east-west.

Flights: The **airport** is off the Alaska Hwy., southwest of downtown. **Air Canada** (☎888-247-2262 or 668-4466) flies to **Calgary** and **Edmonton, AB** via **Vancouver, BC** (3 per day; prices fluctuate between $400 and $1100, so call ahead). Expect to pay through the roof for short-notice flights, especially in the summer.

Buses: The bus station is on the northeast edge of town. **Greyhound,** 2191 2nd Ave. (☎667-2223; www.greyhound.ca), runs to: **Dawson Creek, BC** (18hr., $187) and **Vancouver, BC** (41hr., $340). A **Dawson City** route (5hr.) is run by **Dawson City Courier** (☎393-3334; open M-F 8am-5pm, Sa 4-8am). No service to AK. Buses run daily from late June to early Sept.; rest of year M, W, and F departures. **Alaska Direct,** 509 Main St. (☎668-4833 or 800-770-6652), runs to: **Anchorage, AK** (15hr., 3 per week, $165); **Fairbanks, AK** (13hr., 3 per week, $140); and **Skagway, AK** (3hr.; reservation only; M, Th, and F; $50). In winter, 1 bus per week to above destinations.

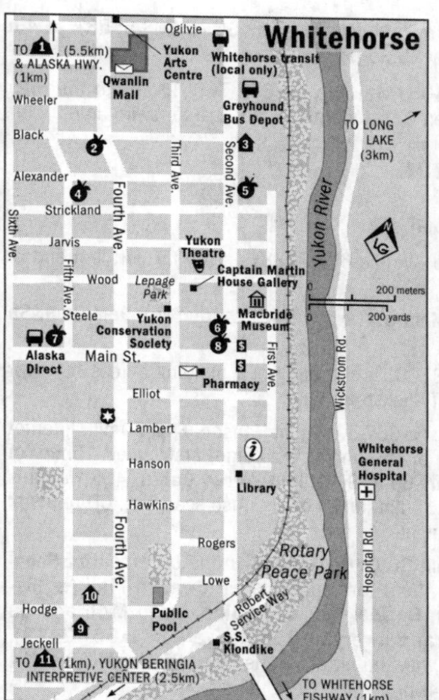

Public Transportation: Whitehorse Transit (☎668-7433). Limited service to downtown, the airport, Robert Service campground, and Yukon College. Buses arrive and depart next to the Canadian Tire on Ogilvie St. $1.50. Runs M-Th 6:15am-7:30pm, F 6:15am-10:30pm, Sa 8am-7pm.

Taxis: Yellow Cab (☎668-4811) or **Global Taxi** (☎633-5300). Both 24hr.

Car Rental: Norcan Leasing, Ltd., 213 Range Rd. (☎668-2137; from western Canada 800-661-0445; from AK 800-764-1234; www.norcan.yk.ca). Cars from $50 per day, winter prices lower, $0.25 per km after 100km per day. Must be 21+ with credit card.

Auto Repair: Petro Canada, 4211 4th Ave. (☎667-4003 or 667-4366). Full service. Oil and lube approx. $45. Open daily 7am-10pm; gas pumps open 24hr.

PRACTICAL INFORMATION

TOURIST, LOCAL, & FINANCIAL SERVICES

Whitehorse

ACCOMMODATIONS
Beez Kneez Bakpakers, **10**
Hide on Jeckell Guesthouse, **9**
Roadhouse Inn, **3**
Robert Service Campground, **11**
Takhini Hot Springs, **1**

FOOD
Alpine Bakery, **4**
Klondike Rib & Salmon, **6**
Little Japan, **5**
Midnight Sun Coffee Roaster, **2**
Sam and Andy's, **7**
The Talisman Cafe, **8**

Tourist Information: 100 Hanson St. (☎667-3084) off 1st Ave., in the Tourism and Business Centre at 2nd Ave. Free 15min. film every ½hr. daily. English, German, French, and Dutch spoken. Open mid-May to mid-Sept. daily 8am-8pm; winter M-F 9am-5pm.

Outdoor Information: Yukon Conservation Society, 302 Hawkins St. (☎668-5678; www.yukonconservation.org), offers maps and great ideas for area hikes along with titles such as *The Yukon Hiking Guide* ($20). Open M-F 10am-2pm.

Equipment Rental: Several upscale equipment shops line Main St. between 2nd and 3rd Ave. **Kanoe People** (☎668-4899), at Strickland and 1st Ave., rents mountain bikes ($15 per half-day), canoes ($25 per day, $150 per week), and kayaks (plastic $35 per day, fiberglass $45). Pick-up 20km downstream $30. Open daily 9am-6pm.

Bank: Bank of Montreal (☎668-4200) or **CIBC** (☎667-2534), at the corner of Main St. and 2nd Ave. **24hr. ATM.**

Bookstore: Mac's Fireweed Bookstore, 203 Main St. (☎668-2434). Open daily 8am-midnight. Used books, CDs, and videos across from library at **Zack's New & Used Books,** 2nd Ave. and Hawkins (☎393-2614). Open M-Sa 11am-6pm.

Market: Extra Foods, 4th Ave. and Ogilvie St. (☎667-6251), in the Qwanlin Mall. Open M-W and Sa 8:30am-7pm, Th-F 8:30am-9pm, Su 10am-6pm.

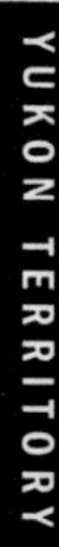

Laundromat: Public Laundromat at Family Motel, 314 Ray St. (☎668-5558), at 4th Ave. next to Qwanlin Mall. Wash $2, dry $0.25 per 5min.

Public Pool: Whitehorse Lions Pool, 4051 4th Ave. (☎668-7665), next to the High Country Inn. $4.50, seniors and children $2, students $3.50. Call for swim times.

EMERGENCY & COMMUNICATION

Emergency: ☎911.

Police: 4100 4th Ave. (☎667-5555). 24hr.

24hr. Refuge: Tim Horton's, 2210 2nd Ave. (☎668-7788), at the far northern end of downtown, 1 block from river.

Pharmacy: Shoppers Drug Mart, 211 Main St. (☎667-2485). Open M-F 9am-9pm, Sa 9am-6pm, Su 10am-6pm.

Hospital: Whitehorse General (☎393-8700) is the big green building across the river from downtown on Hospital Rd., just off Wickstrom Rd.

Internet Access: Library, 2071 2nd Ave. (☎667-5239), at Hanson. Free 30min. Internet access twice daily; reserve in advance or stop in for first-come, first-served 15min. of access. Open M-F 10am-9pm, Sa 10am-6pm, Su 1-9pm. **Wired Cabin,** 402 Hawkins (☎250-309-1225), at 4th Ave. $2 per 10min. or $5 per hr. Also scanning, CD burning, and color copies. Open daily 8am-midnight.

Post Office: General services, 211 Main St. (☎667-2485), in the basement of **Shopper's Drug Mart.** Open M-F 9am-6pm, Sa 11am-4pm. Also in **Qwanlin Mall** (☎667-2858) at 4th Ave. and Ogilvie St., in **Coffee, Tea and Spice.** Open M-Th and Sa 9:30am-6pm, F 9:30am-8pm. **General delivery** at 300 Range Rd. (☎667-2412). **Postal Code** for last names beginning with the letters A-L is Y1A 3S7; for M-Z it's Y1A 3S8. Open 10am-1:40pm and 2:15-4:45pm.

ACCOMMODATIONS & CAMPING

Interchangeable motels around town charge upwards of $70, but fear not; the hostel and campground options are superb.

Hide on Jeckell Guesthouse, 410 Jeckell (☎633-4933), between 4th Ave. and 5th Ave., 1 block from Robert Service Way. Stay in the continent-themed room of your choice and pick your endangered species-labeled bed. Amenities include coffee, kitchen, bikes, Internet, local calls, linens, lockers, and BBQ night. No curfew. 22 beds, 6 rooms. $20. 10% discount for cyclists, 20% for tandem. ❷

Beez Kneez Bakpakers Hostel, 408 Hoge St. (☎456-2333), off 4th Ave., 2 blocks from Robert Service Way. Weary backpackers find refuge in this hostel equipped with Internet, BBQ deck, washer ($2) and dryer ($2). 8 bunks, $20 each. Private rooms $50. ❷

Robert Service Campground (☎668-3721), 1km from town on Robert Service Way along the Yukon River. A home for university students who tan on the lawn and gear up for the outdoors. Food trailer, firewood ($2), drinking water. Gates open 7am-midnight. Open late May to early Sept. 68 sites. $14 per tent. Showers $1 per 5min. ❶

Takhini Hot Springs (☎633-2706). Follow the Alaska Hwy. northwest from downtown about 10km, turn right on North Klondike Hwy., and left after 6.5km onto Takhini Hot Springs Rd. Drive 10km to the end for tent camping and thermal relief. Separate $4-5.50 admission charge for daily pool use in winter or summer. Restaurant, horseback riding ($20 per hr.). Pools open May-Sept. daily 10am-10pm. 88 sites. $12.50, with electricity $15. Showers. ❶

Roadhouse Inn, 2163 2nd. Ave. (☎667-2594), at Black St. An affordable downtown alternative to pricier tourist havens. Rooms are straightforward and simple; the saloon next door keeps the taps flowing until 2am. Phones and private bathrooms. Motel units start at $45 for singles; from $50 for doubles. Hotel units with cable TV $10 more. ❹

FOOD & ENTERTAINMENT

While Whitehorse gives the impression of catering only to the fast food-craving Alaska Hwy. driver, hip musicians and tourists hungering for the frontier will find good grub, too. An excellent selection of top-quality fruits and veggies can be found at **The Fruit Stand,** at 2nd Ave. and Black St. (☎393-3994. Open in summer M-Sa 10:30am-7pm.) **Alpine Bakery,** 411 Alexander St., between 4th and 5th Ave., turns out exquisite bread. (☎668-6871. Open M-Sa 8am-6pm; winter closed M.) Those looking for bars can choose from a wide variety on Main Street. Most have nightly live music, and the scene varies from 20-year-old pop fans at **Lizard Lounge** to classic rock at the **Roadhouse Saloon** to Canadian rock at **Capitol Hotel.**

The Talisman Cafe, 2112 2nd Ave. (☎667-2736). Decorated with local First Nations and local art. Vegetarians, ethnic food lovers, and carnivores will all leave happy and full. Serves heaps of fresh food ranging from Mexican to Middle Eastern for $10-14. Open daily 9am-8pm. ❸

Klondike Rib and Salmon Barbecue, 2116 2nd Ave. (☎667-7554). In an old wall-tent structure, these down-home folks will call you "sweetie" and serve you friendly-like. Worth its weight in (Yukon) gold, the rich salmon-dip lunch ($13) comes with a big ole hunk of homemade bread. The dinner menu is pricey. Open May to Sept. M-F 11:30am-9pm, Sa-Su 5-9pm. ❸

Sam and Andy's, 506 Main St. (☎668-6994), between 5th and 6th. Tex-Mex on a jumpin' patio. Generous build-your-own fajitas are mid-range entrees ($13). You can save money by ordering the veggie version. Thrifty Thursdays mean $1 drafts, $2 pints. Open M-Sa 11am-11pm, Su 11am-10pm. ❷

Midnight Sun Coffee Roaster, 4168 4th Ave. (☎633-4563). Offers every coffee drink under the sun ($3-8) to sip among stained-glass art in comfy chairs or in funky outdoor booths. Internet $3 for 30min., $5 per hr. Open M-F 7am-10pm, later on weekends. ❷

Little Japan, 2157 2nd Ave. (☎668-6620). Offers affordable sushi (five salmon rolls $6.50) and western fare for the squeamish (small $15 "Meatzza" pizzas are not that small). Open M-F 6:30am-9pm, Sa-Su 11am-9pm. ❷

SIGHTS

YUKON BERINGIA INTERPRETIVE CENTRE. Huge woolly mammoths, saber-toothed tigers, and other reconstructed Ice Age critters make you realize how rough the north's first settlers had it. Even the bears were bigger back then—see for yourself. *(On the Alaska Hwy., 2km northwest of the Robert Service Way junction. ☎667-8855; www.beringia.com. Open mid-May to June, and Sept. daily 9am-6pm; July-Aug. daily 8:30am-7pm; winter Su 1-5pm and by appointment. $6, seniors $5, students $4.)*

WHITEHORSE FISHWAY. If you think you're a weary traveler, meet the chinook salmon who swim 27,740km upstream before reaching the fish ladder—designed to save them from death by dam. You're most likely to see them climbing the 370m ladder from late July through August. *(2.4km from town, over the bridge by the S.S. Klondike. ☎633-5965. Open June W-Su 10am-6pm. Open early July to early Sept. daily 8:30am-9pm. Wheelchair accessible. Admission by donation.)*

VISUAL ARTS. Government patronage and an inspired population make Whitehorse a northern epicenter of the arts. The Yukon Government's **permanent collection** is housed throughout the administrative and public spaces of the capital. *(☎667-5264.)* Pick up a free **ArtWalk** brochure at the **visitors center,** or at the nonprofit, Yukon-artwork-adorned **Captain Martin House Gallery.** *(305 Wood St. ☎667-4080. Open summer M-F 10am-8pm, Sa 10am-5pm, Su noon-5pm; winter M-Sa 11am-5pm; closed Jan.)* The Yukon's only public art museum, the **Yukon Arts Centre Art Gallery,** typically shows Canadian contemporary art every 6-10 weeks. *(300 College Drive, Yukon College. ☎667-8578. Open June-Aug. M-F 11am-5pm, Sa-Su noon-5pm; Sept.-May Tu-F 11am-5pm, Sa-Su 1-4pm. Adult $3, students and seniors $2, children under 12 free. Su free.)*

EVENTS. Two Whitehorse festivals draw crowds from all over the world: the **Yukon International Storytelling Festival** *(☎633-7550),* to be held May 30-June 2 2003, and the **Frostbite Music Festival** *(☎668-4921),* in February. The **Commissioner's Potlatch** gathers indigenous groups and visitors in June for traditional dancing, games, artistry, and a feast. Locals, transients, and native artists perform for free at noon with **Arts in Lepage Park** on weekdays. *(At Wood St. and 3rd Ave. ☎668-3136. From June to mid-Aug.)* Call the **Yukon Arts Centre Theatre** for stage updates. *(☎667-8574; www.yukonartscentre.org.)* The **Yukon River** hosts the popular **Rubber Duckie Race** on Canada Day, July 1. *(☎668-7979. $5 per duck. Proceeds go to charity.)*

OUTDOOR ACTIVITIES

HIKING

There seem to be more trails than people around Whitehorse. Seasoned hikers can simply wander (respecting the bear population, of course). **Kluane National Park** (see p. 405) beckons from the west, but there is plenty of accessible dayhiking near town. *Whitehorse Area Hikes and Bikes* ($19), published by the **Yukon Conservation Society,** and the *Whitehorse Area Hikes* map ($10) are both available at Mac's Fireweed Books (see **Practical Information,** p. 397). Discover where to spot a golden eagle or the boreal birds with the aid of the **Yukon Bird Club** (☎667-4630) or take a leisurely free birding trip into the wetlands in summer.

Grey Mountain. Take Lewes Blvd. across the bridge by the S.S. Klondike, then take a left on Alsek Ave. Turn left again at the Grey Mt. Cemetery sign and follow the gravel road to its end. Partially accessible by gravel road, Grey Mountain is a fairly vigorous dayhike. Moderate to difficult.

Miles Canyon Trail Network. Take Lewes Blvd. to Nisutlin Dr. and turn right; just before the fish ladder, turn left onto the gravel Chadburn Lake Rd. and continue 4km up to the parking area. The Network parallels the Yukon River and is frequented by joggers, bikers, and cross-country skiers alike. The Conservation Society leads free hikes daily July-Aug. Schedule available at office. (Open M-F 10am-2pm). Easy to moderate.

Lookout Hill. Go down to the Whitehorse Fishway on Nisultin Dr.; the trailhead is across from the fishway's information building. This short 1.5km trail takes you to an outstanding lookout over Schwatka Lake and surrounding mountains. Easy.

WATER

The **M.V. Schwatka,** on Miles Canyon Rd. off Robert Service Way, floats folks on a relaxing, historical ride through Miles Canyon. (☎668-4716. 2hr. cruises. 2pm daily from June to early Sept. 7pm tour added in July. $21, ages 2-10 $10.50, under 2 free. Wheelchair accessible.) **Up North Boat and Canoe Rentals,** 103 Strickland St., lets you paddle 25km to Takhini River or take a longer trip. (☎667-7035; www.upnorth.yk.ca. 4hr. $30 each for 2 or $60 solo, including transportation.) An

JUSTICE TO GO, TRIBAL STYLE As in many remote regions, law in the Yukon is administered with a long arm. While Whitehorse is the seat of the territorial government, the work of frontier justice is carried out on the frontier: once a week a judge, a clerk, and a recorder climb into a single-engine plane and depart for outlying towns, where a prosecuting and defending attorney will meet them, themselves arriving by car in long, cross-country odysseys between clients. Court is then set up in community centers and recreation halls. This system has evolved in recent years from a transplanted version of a courthouse's formal proceedings to a truer reflection of the traditions of the mostly indigenous communities it serves. Increasingly, elements of traditional justice are changing how community members are punished: friends and family are in more and more cases invited to sit down in a "sentencing circle," in which everyone has a say in how the criminal can be cared for and reintegrated into society. The circle has done amazing work, greatly reducing recidivism, and creating a team-building attitude in the makeshift halls of justice.

8-day trip on the Teslin River costs $200, but you can rent sea kayaks and canoes by the day ($30-35). The waterways around **Sanfu Lake** (1½hr. south of Whitehorse on Atlin Rd.) are ideal for kayaking among tiny islands. **Tatshenshini Expediting,** 1602 Alder St., leads intense whitewater rides. (Take the Alaska Hwy. north 2km, turn left on Birch, and left again on 15th St., which becomes Alder. ☎633-2742. Full day $115.)

WINTER ACTIVITIES

In winter, the Whitehorse area is criss-crossed by 300km of groomed and ungroomed **snowmobile trails. Up North Boat and Canoe Rentals** (see above) rents snowmobiles and skis. Whitehorse is also a **cross-country skiing** paradise. The **Whitehorse Cross Country Ski Club,** beside Mt. McIntyre, off Hamilton Blvd. near the intersection of Two Mile Hill and the Alaska Hwy., grooms 50km of world-class trails; 5km of trails are lit at night. Club facilities include saunas and showers. (☎668-4477. Day passes $9, under 19 $4; 3 days $22; 5 days $35.) In February, "the toughest race in the world," the **Yukon Quest 1000 Mile International Sled Dog Race** (☎668-4711), follows gold rush routes between Whitehorse and Fairbanks.

ALASKA HWY.: BC TO WHITEHORSE

WATSON LAKE ☎867

Switchbacking between the Yukon and British Columbia, the Alaska Hwy. winds through tracts of young forest that stretch in all directions. Just after it crosses into the Yukon for the second time, at km 1021, the highway runs through **Watson Lake,** site of the zany **Sign Post Forest.** In the 1940s, a homesick WWII Army G.I. posted the mileage from Watson to his hometown of Danville, Illinois. The 50,000 signs that subsequent travelers put up make this site a gigantic, mind-boggling oddity than should not be missed. Find the distance to your hometown buried somewhere in the wacky forest. The **visitors center** is hidden inside this forest of signs, along the Robert Campbell Hwy. (☎536-7469. Open May-Sept. daily 8am-8pm.) If finding the distance to your hometown fails to smother your homesickness, email your pals for free on one of the computers at the new **library,** in the town office on Adela Trail. (☎536-7517. Open Tu-F 10am-8pm, Sa noon-6pm.)

Scan for mountain bluebirds on **Wye Lake** from the 3km boardwalk trail running from the Town Center to **Wye Lake Park.** Watson Lake also lures passers-by with the **Northern Lights Centre** opposite the visitors center, which dispenses scientific

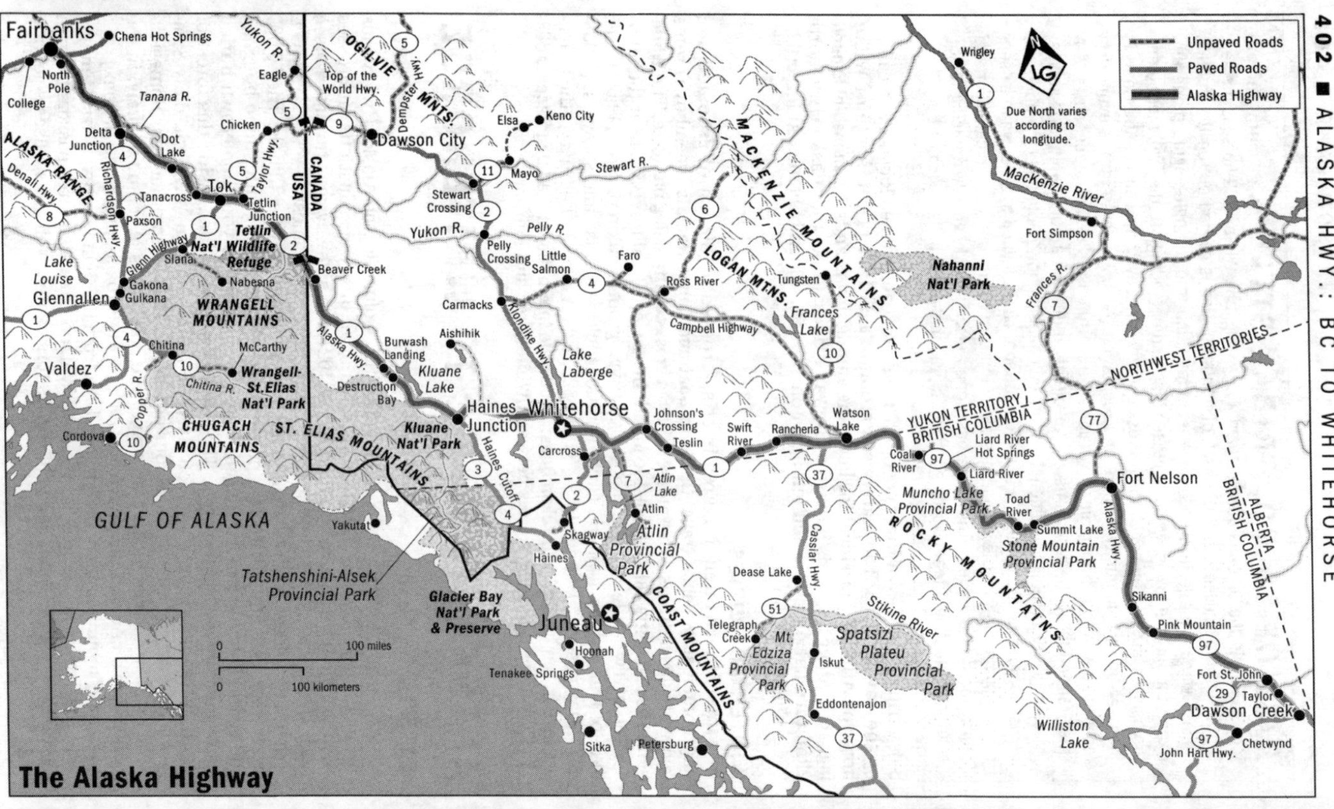
The Alaska Highway
Unpaved Roads
Paved Roads
Alaska Highway
Due North varies according to longitude.
100 miles
100 kilometers
ALBERTA
BRITISH COLUMBIA
NORTHWEST TERRITORIES
YUKON TERRITORY
CANADA
USA
GULF OF ALASKA
MACKENZIE MOUNTAINS
LOGAN MTNS.
OGILVIE MNTS.
ROCKY MOUNTAINS
COAST MOUNTAINS
ST. ELIAS MOUNTAINS
CHUGACH MOUNTAINS
WRANGELL MOUNTAINS
ALASKA RANGE
Fairbanks
Whitehorse
Juneau
Fort Nelson
Dawson Creek
Dawson City
Haines Junction
Watson Lake
Glennallen
Valdez
Tok
Delta Junction
Nahanni Nat'l Park
Kluane Nat'l Park
Wrangell-St.Elias Nat'l Park
Glacier Bay Nat'l Park & Preserve
Tatshenshini-Alsek Provincial Park
Spatsizi Plateu Provincial Park
Mt. Edziza Provincial Park
Atlin Provincial Park
Stone Mountain Provincial Park
Muncho Lake Provincial Park
Tetlin Nat'l Wildlife Refuge
Alaska Hwy.
Cassiar Hwy.
Klondike Hwy.
Campbell Highway
Haines Cutoff
Top of the World Hwy.
Dempster Hwy.
Taylor Hwy.
Richardson Hwy.
Glenn Highway
Denali Hwy.
John Hart Hwy.
MacKenzie River
Yukon R.
Stewart R.
Pelly R.
Tanana R.
Copper R.
Chitina R.
Stikine River
Frances R.
Kluane Lake
Lake Laberge
Atlin Lake
Frances Lake
Lake Louise
Williston Lake
Wrigley
Fort Simpson
Tungsten
Ross River
Faro
Little Salmon
Carmacks
Pelly Crossing
Stewart Crossing
Mayo
Elsa
Keno City
Aishihik
Burwash Landing
Destruction Bay
Beaver Creek
Carcross
Johnson's Crossing
Teslin
Swift River
Rancheria
Coal River
Liard River Hot Springs
Liard River
Toad River
Summit Lake
Sikanni
Pink Mountain
Fort St. John
Taylor
Chetwynd
Dease Lake
Telegraph Creek
Iskut
Eddontenajon
Atlin
Skagway
Haines
Hoonah
Tenakee Springs
Sitka
Petersburg
Yakutat
Cordova
Chitina
McCarthy
Nabesna
Slana
Gakona
Gulkana
Paxson
Tanacross
Dot Lake
Tetlin Junction
Chicken
Eagle
North Pole
College
Chena Hot Springs

BRIGHT LIGHTS, NO CITY Many travelers come to Alaska to get away from all the bright lights and noise of the big city, only to find themselves falling under the spell of the most awesome of natural light shows: the aurora borealis (northern lights). Some bands of Native Americans believed these Christmas-colored clouds and arcs were the torches of spirits, lighting the way to heaven for those who had died a voluntary or violent death. Scientists, however, point the finger at violent solar flares which hit the earth, sweeping streams of electrically charged particles into the atmosphere. As the earth's magnetic field deflects these particles away from the Equator and up toward the poles, the particles enter the atmosphere and begin to glow. Oxygen atoms create either the brilliant yellow-green, or if higher in the atmosphere, a burning red. Ionized nitrogen particles cast a blue hue, while neutral nitrogen creates a cloud of purplish-red. But such scientific mumbo-jumbo can't detract from the supernatural mystery of the northern lights. A few onlookers claim to be able to even *hear* the lights overhead, although no scientist has yet to record these sounds or come up with an explanation. Some Inuit tribes interpreted these noises as the whisperings of the spirits. So prick up your ears as you next stare skyward, and you may discover that no matter how far away you think you've gotten from civilization, there might still be someone to spoil your quiet.

and cultural explanations for the aurora borealis. (☎867-536-7827; www.watsonlake.net. Call ahead for hours. 50min. shows 6 times daily. $10; seniors and students $9; children $6. Exhibits free.)

The **Liard Canyon Recreation Site** on **Lucky Lake,** 8km before town, makes for great picnicking and swimming. A 2km trail down the canyon is a relaxing and scenic stroll. Accommodations in Watson Lake are plentiful but pricey. A budget traveler's best bet is the **Watson Lake Campground ❶,** 3km west of town along the highway and then 4km down a well-marked gravel road, with primitive private sites ideal for tenting. ($8 camping permit only.) Campers can swim on the lake and hike several trails of varying difficulty. If you continue out of Watson Lake 21km northwest, you'll find accommodations at the **Cassiar Hwy.** junction. Dining options in town are restricted to highway fare. The **Pizza Place ❸,** at the **Gateway Motor Inn,** is a somewhat pricey gem. Medium specialty pies start at $15, but ambitious eaters go right for the $22 "Yukoner," loaded with all manner of meats and vegetables. For the tighter budget, meals from the grill range from $6.50 to $9. (☎536-7722. Open daily 6:30am-10pm.) **Groceries** and an **ATM** can be had at **Tags Foods,** by the visitors center. (☎536-7422. Open daily 6am-midnight.) Gas pumps and convenience store open 24hr. CIBC Banking Center (☎536-7495) in the shopping center on the east side of the visitors center has a **24hr. ATM.** Next door is the **post office.** (Open M-F 8:30am-5:30pm, Sa 8:30am-12:30pm.) **Postal Code:** Y0A 1C0.

Hardcore travelers **fish** for dinner. In mid-summer, grayling swim in the back eddies of tiny streams west along the Alaska Hwy., and both **Lucky Lake** (5½km east of town) and **Hour Lake** (at the east end of town behind the RCMP) are full of rainbow trout. Check in at the visitors center to purchase the appropriate permits.

Here at Watson Lake, the **Campbell Hwy.** (Hwy. 4) begins an alternate route into the Yukon Territory toward Whitehorse via Ross River and Johnson's Crossing, or to Dawson City via Ross River, Little Salmon, and Carmacks. For coverage of this wonderful side track, see p. 415. Km 1043 (or Mile 649) marks the Alaska Hwy.'s junction with the **Cassiar Hwy** (Hwy. 37; see p. 352), which leads south to the **Yellowhead Hwy.** (Hwy. 16; see p. 334). For coverage of this junction, see p. 358.

TESLIN LAKE ☎867

About 260km west of Watson Lake, the **Dawson Peaks Resort** on **Teslin Lake** dishes up delectable burgers in its restaurant ($7) and offers a number of accommodation choices. (☎390-2244. Open daily 7:30am-10pm. Showers $2. Toilets, firewood, water. Sites $10; full RV sites $18; canvas tent platforms $35; private cabins $82.) The friendly hosts lead **river runs,** (4-5 days, $400) organize guided **fishing charters,** ($50 per hr.) and rent canoes ($8 per hr.) and powerboats ($25 per hr.).

Teslin, 11km west of the resort, tells its story at the duly acclaimed **George Johnston Museum,** on the Alaska Hwy. at the west end of town. Born in Alaska in 1889, George Johnston was a Tlingit man who ran a trap line and a general store while experimenting with photography on the side. Johnston left a series of stunning photographs documenting Tlingit life in Teslin from 1910 to 1940. The museum also displays a moose skin boat, Teslin's first automobile (bought by Johnston when the town was roadless), and an excellent video about the Alaska Hwy.'s effect on native culture. (☎390-2550. Open daily mid-May to early Sept. 9:30am-5:30pm. $4, students and seniors $3.50, children 6-15 $2, families $10. Wheelchair accessible.) RV travelers bond over food and the free house boat rides at **Muklak Annie's ❹,** 7km east of Teslin. There's nothing miniature about a mini-salmon plate ($15) or kids' portion ($9), but the big-eaters can pay $19 for loads of salmon, all-you-can-eat salad, fresh rolls, coffee, and dessert. Ribs, pork chops, and burgers are also served on the checked cloths in the gift shop decor dining hall. (☎667-1200. Open daily 7am-9pm. Free campsite, house boat ride, RV wash, dump station, and water fill-up with meal. Showers $4, cabins with shared bath $40, motel $50.) From Teslin, the 183km (2hr.) drive to Whitehorse is interspersed with a few **gas stops** and **provincial campgrounds**.

CARCROSS ☎867

Carcross, shortened from "Caribou Crossing," perches on the narrows between Bennett and Nares Lakes, surrounded by snow-capped peaks and pristine waterways. At the turn of the century, Carcross served as a link in the gold seekers' treacherous route between Skagway and the Yukon River, and during the 1940s Carcross was a supply depot for the construction of the Alaska Hwy. But the heyday passed decades ago, and recent years have roughed the town up quite a bit. The few shops in town now cater to tour buses from the Skagway cruise ships, and the best attractions are outside the town, in the nearby wildlands.

TRANSPORTATION & PRACTICAL INFORMATION. Carcross lies 74km south of Whitehorse, YT, and 106km north of Skagway, AK, on the **Klondike Hwy.** (Hwy. 2). Turn right off the highway into town. **Atlin Express Buses** (☎250-651-7575) run to **Atlin, BC** (2hr.; $23, seniors $20, ages 5-11 $11.50, under 5 free) and **Whitehorse** (1¼hr.; $17, seniors $15, ages 5-11 $8.50, under 5 free). **Tourist information** and daily highway or weather reports are available inside the depot. (☎821-4431. Open daily mid-May to mid-Sept. 8am-8pm.) **Montana Services,** in the Shell Station on Hwy. 2, has **laundry, public showers,** and the only **ATM** in town. (☎821-3708. Open daily 7am-11pm, winter 8am-8pm. Wash $2.25, dry $0.25 per 4min. Shower $3.) A **health station** (☎821-4444) is inside the two-story red building behind the Caribou Hotel. For an **ambulance,** call ☎821-3333; for the **police,** call ☎821-5555 or 667-5555. The **library** on Tagish St. has free **Internet access.** (☎821-3801. Open summer M-Th noon-4:30pm.) The **post office,** with a free paperback exchange, is in the red-trimmed white building on Bennett Ave. (☎821-4503. Open M, W, and F 8am-noon and 2:30-4pm, Tu and Th 10-11:45am.) **Postal Code:** Y0B 1B0.

CHILKOOT TRAIL A valuable coastal trade route protected by the Tagish and Tlingit for thousands of years, the Chilkoot Trail bore the great torrent of gold-seekers hungering for the Yukon interior in the late 1890s. First led by native packers and later accompanied by hordes of their fellow stampeders, north-country novices slogged back and forth 33 mi. between Skagway, Dyea, and Lake Bennett, transporting 1000 pounds of provisions each to satisfy Canadian officials that they were prepared for the country ahead. Hikers take to the trail today for a rigorous 3-5 dayhike past the horse skeletons and gold-rush relics that still litter the precipitous pass. The trail departs from the coast and travels through a dramatic variety of climate, terrain, and vegetation, both above and below the timberline, before descending into the forests of northern British Columbia within reach of Lake Bennett and Carcross.

ACCOMMODATIONS & FOOD. The Yukon Government maintains 14 **campsites ❶** by the airstrip across Hwy. 2 from the Shell station with potable water, firewood, and pit toilets. (Requires an $8 Yukon government camping permit.) **Spirit Lake Wilderness Resort ❶,** 10km north of town on Hwy. 2, has lakeside accommodations and rents canoes for $8 per hour. (☎821-4337. Toilets, coin laundry. Tent sites $14, with power $20; cabins on the jade-colored lake $72 for 1-2 people, $81 for 3-4 people. Free showers.) If you don't mind parking lots, stay at **Montana Services ❶**, which offers RV hook-ups ($12) and car tent sites ($7).

Just up the road from the Spirit Lake Resort (9km north of town), the **Cinnamon Cache ❶** is a gem among Dall sheep and bluebirds. Homemade cinnamon buns, survival cookies for the trail (both $2.50), hot pies, and soup and sandwiches make tummies happy. (☎821-4331. Open Feb.-Sept. daily 7am-7pm.) Another choice is the small **Koolsen Place ❷.** Watch the river wash by and munch on one of the few items on the menu. (Open daily 10am-7pm.)

OUTDOOR ACTIVITIES. Legendary big-game guide Johnny Johns led countless trips out of the Carcross area in the direction of the Yukon Mountains, the Upper Rockies, and the Coastal Range, which are all visible from town. While outfitting companies such as his no longer operate, hiking in the Carcross area garners justifiable acclaim. Pick up a copy of *Whitehorse Area Hikes and Bikes* at the visitors center or in Whitehorse before setting out. The most popular hike in the area is the **Chilkoot Trail** (see p. 405), a moderately difficult 3-5 day adventure beginning at Skagway and ending at the far end of Lake Bennett. The lake's two sandy beaches are understandably popular with locals in July and August. Overlooking the town, **rough mining roads** snake around Montana Mountain. To access them, follow Hwy. 2 south and take the first right after crossing the bridge. Take the first left and drive until you reach the washout. From there, it's all on foot to astounding views. (Round-trip 21km, 8hr. including drive; 1000 ft. gain.) The adventurous can play in the sand of an exposed glacial lake bottom in the world's smallest desert, **Carcross Desert,** 3km north of town on the highway.

KLUANE NATIONAL PARK ☎867

Dizzyingly massive glaciers spill off of huge mountains and keep going for dozens of kilometers, wedging into the surrounding forests like waves of cold crystal. Lakes thick with fish ("Kluane" means "place of many fish" in the Southern Tutchone language) speckle unbroken tracts of raw forest wilderness, and bears mingle with Dall Sheep beneath soaring eagles. Kluane doesn't shy from natural spectacle. Together with Glacier National Park, the adjacent Wrangell-St. Elias National Park in Alaska, and Tatshenshini/Alsek Provincial Park in BC, Kluane is part of one of

AT A GLANCE

AREA: 22000 sq. km **CLIMATE:** Cool and dry; often extreme cold in winter. **FEATURES:** Mt. Logan (Canada's highest peak), Kathleen Lake.	**GATEWAYS:** Haines Junction, Klukshu. **CAMPING:** No limit on length of stay. **FEES AND RESERVATIONS:** Wilderness permit $5 per day. Fishing permit $5 per day.

the world's largest protected wilderness areas. Canada's massive mountain range, the St. Elias Mountains, divides into two separate ranges within the park. The smaller Kluane Range runs right along the Alaska Hwy. (p. 358). The soaring giants of the Icefield Range, including Canada's highest peak, Mt. Logan (5959m), and the most massive non-polar ice fields in the world are separated from the Kluane range by the Duke Depression. The ice-blanketed mountains of Kluane's interior are a haven for experienced expeditioners, but their remoteness renders two-thirds of the park inaccessible (except by plane) to humbler hikers. Fortunately, the northeastern section of the park (bordering the Alaska Hwy.) offers splendid, easily accessible backpacking, rafting, biking, fishing, and dayhiking. Many routes follow original Southern Tutchone and Tlingit trails and old mining roads left over from Kluane's brief and disappointing fling with the gold rush in 1904-05. Most ventures into Kluane begin from **Haines Junction.**

ORIENTATION & PRACTICAL INFORMATION

Kluane's 22,015 sq. km are bounded by the **Kluane Game Sanctuary** and the **Alaska Hwy.** (Hwy. 1; see p. 358) to the north, and the **Haines Hwy.** (Hwy. 3) to the east. **Haines Junction** (pop. 800), 158km west of Whitehorse at the park's eastern boundary, is the gateway to the park. There is also access to trails in the north of the park from **Sheep Mountain,** 72km northeast of Haines Junction on the Alaska Hwy.

Buses: Alaska Direct (☎800-770-6652, in Whitehorse ☎668-4833) runs a summer schedule from **Haines Junction** on Su, W, and F to **Anchorage, AK** (13hr., US$145); **Fairbanks, AK** (11hr., US$125); **Skagway, AK** (16hr., 12hr. overnight in Whitehorse, US$90, reservations required); and **Whitehorse, YT** (2hr., US$40).

Auto Repair: Source Motors Ltd. (☎634-2268), 1km north of Haines Junction on the Alaska Hwy. Does just about everything and offers 24hr. emergency road service. Open M-F 7am-9pm, Sa-Su 9am-9pm.

Tourist Information:

Kluane National Park Visitor Reception Centre (☎634-7207; www.parkscanada.gc.ca/kluane), on Logan St. in Haines Junction (Km 1635 on the Alaska Hwy.). Provides **wilderness permits** ($5 per night, $50 per season); **fishing permits** ($5 per day for non-Yukoners, $25 per season for Canadians, $35 for non-Canadians); **topographical maps** ($12); **trail and weather info,** and registers overnight visitors to the park. Open May-Sept. daily 9am-7pm; Oct.-Apr. M-F 10am-noon and 1-5pm.

Yukon Tourism (☎634-2345) gives information on activities inside and outside the park. Open mid-May to mid-Sept. daily 8am-8pm. Inquire about guided tours in late June and Aug.

Sheep Mountain Information Centre lies 72km north of town at Alaska Hwy. Km 1707. Registers hikers headed for the northern area of the park, sells hiking guides for $1, and rents bear canisters. Open daily May-Labour Day 9am-5pm. Overnight registrations until 4:30pm only.

Bank: Toronto Dominion (☎634-2820), in Madley's Store. Exchanges foreign currency and cashes traveler's checks. Open M-F 12:30-4:30pm. **ATM** available 8am-9pm daily.

Laundromat and Showers: Gateway Motel (☎634-2371), at the junction. Wash $2, dry $0.25 per 6 min. Shower $4. Open daily 8:30am-10pm. Comparable prices at **Kluane**

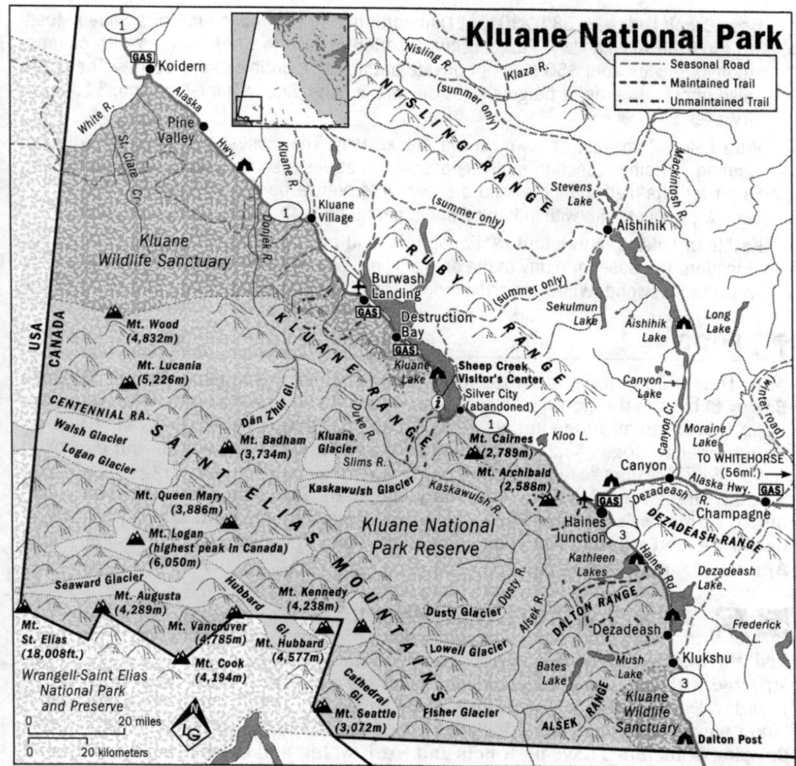

RV Kampground (☎634-2709), north from the junction on the Alaska Hwy. 24hr. access to laundry and showers on the meter.

Emergency and Police: ☎634-5555; **no 911.**

Fire: ☎634-2222.

Ambulance/Health Clinic: ☎634-4444. By Madley's. Open M-F 9am-noon and 1-5pm.

Internet Access: Free at the **library** (☎634-2215), located next door to Madley's. Book ahead if possible. Open Tu-F 1-5pm and Sa 2-5pm. Better hours but a fee at **Village Bakery.** (☎634-2928). $3 per 30 min. Open in summer daily 7am-9pm.

Post Office: (☎634-3802), in Madley's. Open M-F 8:15am-noon and 1-5pm. **Postal Code:** Y0B 1L0.

ACCOMMODATIONS & CAMPING

Camping by a gorgeous lakeside beats staying at a clean-but-forgettable highway motel or RV park any day (see below).

Stardust Motel, (☎634-2591), 1km north of town on the Alaska Hwy. The Stardust offers spacious rooms with satellite TV and private bath. No phones. Kitchenettes extra. Reservations recommended. Open mid-May to mid-Sept. Singles $55; doubles $65. ❸

Bear Creek Lodge (☎634-2301), 11km north of Haines Junction towards Sheep Mountain on the Alaska Hwy. Forgoing the location in town rewards visitors with cheaper rooms. Singles from $50 (without private bathrooms); doubles from $60. ❸ The Lodge also offers **camping** at bargain rates on simple sites. Sites $5 for 1 person, $10 for 2. RV sites $15. ❶

Pine Lake, 7km east of town on the Alaska Hwy. The closest government-run campground to Haines Junction and very popular. Features a sandy beach with a swim float, a pit for late-night bonfires, and a snazzy interpretive trail along the river. Water, firewood, pit toilets. $8 with Yukon camping permit only. ❶

Kathleen Lake Campground, National Park land off Haines Rd. 27km south of Haines Junction. The base for many of the area's hikes. Water (boil before drinking), toilets, fire pits, and firewood. Wheelchair accessible. Open mid-May to mid-Sept. 39 sites, $10. ❶

FOOD

Most Haines Junction restaurants offer standard highway cuisine. But the **Village Bakery** ❷ breaks the trend, offering fresh veggie dishes, beefy sandwiches, and tray upon tray of novel fudge and sweets. Substantial soups with bread ($3.50), sourdough cheese dogs ($2.25), sushi (on F only; $4.50 for 5 pieces), and espresso fudge ($1.75). Make reservations to enjoy live music and salmon-BBQs ($13.50) on Monday nights. (☎634-2867. Open daily May-Sept. 7am-9pm.) "We got it all"—the motto of **Madley's General Store**—is an understatement. Find star fruit, tackle, hardware, and a butcher block. (☎634-2200. Open May-Sept. daily 8am-9pm; Oct.-Apr. daily 8am-6:30pm.)

SIGHTS & ENTERTAINMENT

Visit the **Kwaday Dan Kenji** traditional camp of the Champagne people, recently constructed with the help of local elders, and enjoy a mug of fresh brewed tea ($1.25). Kwaday Dan Kenji is a few minutes east of the village of Champagne, situated 70km west of Whitehorse and 88km east of Haines Junction on the Alaska Hwy. **Camping** ❶ facilities have pit toilets and fresh water, and there is a guided tour of the traditionally-made shelters and animal traps. (Shop with artifacts and local crafts open daily May-Oct. 9am-7:30pm. $10, children $6. Sites $10.)

Reserved little Haines Junction lets it all hang out in late June for back-to-back festivals. During the second weekend in June, music-loving rowdies from all over the area gather for "the function at the junction" to hear northern artists perform at the **Alsek Music Festival.** (☎634-2520; ask about the Kidzone for children.)

HIKING

Kluane's trails are varied and very accessible. The visitors centers are great sources for trail maps, information, and conditions. A $1 pamphlet lists about 25 trails and routes ranging from 500m to 96km. Routes, as opposed to trails, are not maintained, do not have marked paths, are more physically demanding, and require backcountry navigation skills. Overnight visitors must register and pay at one of the visitors centers ($5 per night for adults), and use bear-resistant food canisters, which the park rents for $5 per night (with $150 cash or credit refundable deposit).

Dezadeash River Loop (DEZ-dee-ash, 5km). The trailhead is downtown at the day-use area across from Madley's on Haines Rd. This flat, forested trail will disappoint anyone craving steepness, but it makes for a nice stroll. As always when in bear country, use a noise-maker or belt out tunes to warn bears that you're coming. Easy.

Auriol Loop (15km, 4-6hr., 400m gain). The trail begins 7km south of Haines Junction on Haines Rd. and cuts through boreal forest, leading to a subalpine bench just in front of the Auriol Range. Divided by a primitive campground halfway along, this is a popular overnight trip, although it can easily be hiked in a day without heavy packs. Moderate.

King's Throne Route (10km round-trip, 1220m gain). This rewarding dayhike with a panoramic view begins at the Kathleen Lake day-use area (see p. 408). Difficult.

Sheep Creek Trail (10km round-trip, 430m gain). Down a short gravel access road just north of the visitors center for **Sheep Mountain.** This satisfying dayhike gives you a good chance to see Dall sheep during the summer months. Sheep Mountain boasts more excellent hiking near the park's northern section. An easy 500m jaunt up to **Soldier's Summit** starts 1km north of the Sheep Mountain Info Centre and leads to the site where the Alaska Hwy. was officially opened on Nov. 20, 1942. Moderate.

The Deep Backcountry. Backcountry hiking can quickly become a dangerous and challenging enterprise in the undeveloped, glaciated Kluane interior. Be sure to carry twice as much food as you expect to need, buy the proper topographic maps, and always consult rangers before you head out. Don't underestimate the bears, either. **Donjek** and **Kaskawulsh** glaciers are the most accessible to backcountry travelers–consult the visitor's center for more detailed advice on specific approaches. Extreme.

OTHER OUTDOOR ACTIVITIES

WATER. Anglers can readily put the park's many-fished reputation to the test at **Kathleen Lake** (see p. 408), home to lake and rainbow trout (catch and release only), grayling, and rare freshwater Kokanee salmon (usually in season mid-May to early June). Less-crowded **St. Elias Lake** is an easy 3.5km hike from the trailhead, 60km south of Haines Junction on Haines Rd. **Pine Lake,** the popular territorial campground, is a good spot to put in a canoe for a paddle, as it is less windy than Kathleen Lake. Fishing here requires a Yukon permit from Madley's, while Kluane waters require a National Parks **fishing permit,** available at the visitors center in Haines Junction (see p. 406). Be sure to pick up the essential **Yukon Fishing Regulations Summary Booklet** for free from the visitor's center to avoid any uncomfortable incidents with the law and fines.

TOURS. If you've got the cash, guides are invaluable for area information, bear security, and navigation skills. In addition to guiding services, **PaddleWheel Adventures,** directly down the road from the Village Bakery, arranges flightseeing over the glaciers, hike-out helicopter rides to the **Kluane Plateau,** and full-day rafting trips on the Class III and IV rapids of the **Blanchard** and **Tatshenshini Rivers.** They also rent the gear you'd need to explore the park on your own, including tents, packs, and bear spray. (☎634-2683. Flightseeing $95 per person for 30min. flight over the Kaskawulsh. Rafting $100 per person including lunch. Helicopter rides vary depending on what you want to see. Bikes $25 per day, canoes $25. Guides $150 per day for up to 6 people and $25 per additional person; fishing guides $150 per day for one person.) Call **Kluane Ecotours** for custom-fitted hiking, canoeing, or kayaking guides. (☎634-2626. $85 per person; minimum $150 per day.)

MOUNTAIN BIKING. The **Alsek River Valley Trail,** which follows a bumpy old mining road for 14km from Alaska Hwy. Km 1645 to Sugden Creek, is popular with mountain bikers who crave rugged terrain. The rocky road crosses several streams before gently climbing to a ridge with a stellar view of the Auriol Mountains. More insider tips on the park's bike-friendly trails are available from PaddleWheel Adventures (see above).

WINTER ACTIVITIES. For winter use of the southern portion of the park, call ahead for snow conditions (☎634-7207) and stop by the visitors center for free, detailed maps of **cross-country ski routes.** The **Auriol, Dezadeash,** and **St. Elias trails** (see above) are all local favorites. Bound through the trails with snowshoes, or pick up dogmushing regulations at the information center and round up a team. Camping is available at day-use area in town in the winter.

SHEEP MOUNTAIN TO ALASKA

KLUANE LAKE. The drive northwest from Haines Junction to the Alaska border is broken up by a smattering of tiny pit stops, the most scenic of which lie along Kluane Lake. The lake's spectacular aquamarine color is due to suspended "glacier flour" particles in the water that reflect blue light waves. Spanning 478 sq. km, Kluane Lake is the largest in the Yukon. **Congdon Creek Campground ❶,** at Km 1723 on the Alaska Hwy., is the nicest campground before the US border, with a long stone beach for evening strolls and romantic mountain views. Prime lakeside sites fill up early. Be warned—sometimes the camp shuts down from mid-July to September due to the ripening soapberries and the bears which eat them. (Water, pit toilets, firewood. 80 sites, $8 with Yukon camping permits.) If lake spots at the territorial campground are all taken or you prefer showers and laundry, stop 6km short of Congdon at the beautiful **Cottonwood RV Park and Campground ❶.** Melt away your woes in the hottub ($4 for 30min.) or tool around on the mini-golf course. (No phone. Full RV site $24; dry site $18.)

BURWASH LANDING. Sixteen kilometers north of Destruction Bay is Burwash Landing, home to the world's largest gold pan at the **Kluane Museum of Natural History.** This noisy museum plays animal sound effects to accompany the Yukon's largest wildlife display and a collection of Southern Tutchone garb. The mammoth teeth are enormous. (☎841-5561. Open daily late May and early Sept. 10am-6pm; June-Aug. 9am-9pm. $3.75, seniors $3.25, children 6-12 $2.) Stop at Kluane First Nation's **Dalan Campground ❶** for secluded campsites on the lake. (☎841-4274. Wood, water, pit toilets. 25 sites, $10.) The **Burwash Landing Resort ❹** offers rooms with TV and private bath. **Tenting ❶** or dry RV is free on the lawn or parking lot. The lakeside resort houses a **diner ❷** in the lodge that serves up hefty $7 sandwiches. (☎841-4441. Open in summer daily 7am-11pm. Singles $70; doubles $80. RV sites $18. Showers $4.)

Between Burwash and Beaver Creek, break up the monotonous mountain-viewing miles at **Pine Valley Bakery and RV ❸** (Km 1845) and grab some grub, shower, gas, tire repair, or relatively cheap ($50 and up) lodging at this busy jack-of-all-trades stop. (☎862-7407. Open mid-May to mid-Sept. 24hr.)

BEAVER CREEK. The westernmost community (Km 1935) in Canada is by far the liveliest of all these roadside wonders. Get a sales pitch about Beaver Creek offerings, such as the oddly shaped historic church, at the **visitors center.** (☎862-7321. Open daily in summer 8am-8pm.) Most of what you need can be found at the log **1202 Motor Inn,** from **camping ❶** (dry sites $10; RV sites $15) and **motel rooms ❷** ($35 for "plain jane" with shared bath, $65 for the works) to a grocery store, **restaurant ❷** with giant sandwiches ($6.50-8), and an **ATM.** (☎800-661-0540. Open daily 6:30am-1am.) A heated indoor public **pool** is open June-Aug. (☎862-7702). Lodging is a steal at the **Beaver Creek Hostel** in the **Westmark Inn ❶,** which has a bar and rec room for fun. (☎862-7501. Open May-Sept. Rooms $22.)

ENTERING THE US. Past Beaver Creek, 20 mi. of highway and prime moose-viewing wilderness separate US and Canadian customs and immigration, although several signs and landmarks can be found at the official border on the 141st meridian. Alaska time is 1hr. behind Pacific time, and gas a few miles into US territory is considerably cheaper than anything in Canada. From the border it's 80 mi. (1½hr.) to Tetlin Junction, where the Alaska Hwy. meets the Taylor Hwy., and 92 mi. (2hr.) to Tok (see below).

ALONG HWY. 9: TOP OF THE WORLD HWY.

The majestic 127km (1½hr.) highway earns its name--visit and see. Starting across the Yukon River from Dawson City, it climbs for several kilometers and then follows the spine of a series of mountains. The trip affords staggering views of the Southern Ogilvies and the North Dawson Range before connecting with the Taylor Hwy. at **Jack Wade Junction** in Alaska. Unmarked trails head into the bush from rest stops, and the bare hills make for simple climbs up to expansive views. The road is open May-September, although the mountainous Yukon-Alaska border crossing at Km 108 is only open 9am-9pm Pacific (i.e., Yukon) time. The only services on the Canadian side are the links at the **Top of the World Golf Course** (☎867-667-1472), about 10km past the ferry. The 5min. ferry runs 24hr. from June to July (peak traffic 7-11am from Dawson and 2-8pm to Dawson). The US side of the road is full of pocks in the gravel, while the Canadians lay down some asphalt in between their pocks. Just over the border in the US, the **Boundary Cafe** sells snacks and will trade a gallon of gasoline for US$2.

DAWSON CITY ☎867

Born in a frenzied lust for dust, Dawson City booms today by telling its own history. On August 17, 1896, three men stumbled upon thick ribbons of gold in a stream outside of today's Dawson City. Within weeks, gold-diggers flooded town. Shops, saloons, and hotels quickly sprung up all over the boomtown. For 12 boggling months from 1898-1899, this was the largest Canadian city west of Toronto, known as "the Paris of the North." After that year of frenzied claim-staking and legend-making, most of the gold seekers realized that the early birds had scooped up all the prime claims before their arrival; they packed up and headed to Nome. Dredges took over and corporate mining trudged on from its center in Bear Creek, 13km south of Dawson, until sputtering out in 1966. In the early 1960s the Klondike Visitors Association and the Canadian government set out to return Dawson City to its gold-rush glory, restoring dirt roads, long boardwalks, and wooden store fronts, and in the process transforming the town into the lively summer RV and college student destination that it is today.

TRANSPORTATION

To reach Dawson City, take the **Klondike Loop (Hwy. 2)** 533km (6hr.) north from **Whitehorse,** or follow the majestic **Top of the World Hwy. (Hwy. 9)** 108km east from the Alaska border.

Buses: Dawson City Taxi and Courier Service (☎993-6688, www.dawsonbus.ca), at the corner of 2nd and York. To **Whitehorse** (7½hr., June-Aug. M-F, $82.50). **Parks Hwy. Express** (☎888-600-6001, www.alaskashuttle.com) will take you across the "top of the world" and to **Fairbanks** (11hr., 3 daily, $145).

Cruise: Yukon Queen II River Cruises (☎993-5599), on Front St. next to the Keno. Office open daily 8am-8pm. Departs daily at 9am for **Eagle, AK** along the Yukon River. Includes hot meals. (10-11hr. round-trip. One-way standby US$91, CDN$130; round-trip US$149, CDN$215. Returns canoes from Eagle for US$50.

Car Rental: Budget, 451 Craig St. (☎993-5644), in the Dawson City B&B. $60 per day, $0.20 per km after 100km. Free pick-up and delivery. Must be 21+ with a credit card.

Auto Repair: Esso (☎993-5142) on the Klondike Hwy. (Hwy. 2) immediately before town. Open in summer daily 7am-11pm.

PRACTICAL INFORMATION

Tourist Information: (☎993-5566), at Front and King St. Movies, inexpensive tickets and pick-a-pack tour tickets (see **Sights,** below). Open mid-May to mid-Sept. daily 8am-8pm. The **Northwest Territories Visitors Centre** (☎993-6167) opposite, knows the Dempster Hwy. Open May-Sept. daily 9am-8pm.

Bank: Canadian Imperial Bank of Commerce, at 2nd Ave. and Queen. St. has a **24hr. ATM.** Open M-Th 10am-3pm, F 10am-5pm.

Equipment Rental: Dawson City River Hostel (see **Accommodations,** p. 413). Bikes $20 per day, canoes $20. Non-hostelers must use passport as deposit.

Bookstore: Maximilian's Goldrush Emporium (☎993-5486), on Front near Queen St., stocks every word ever written by local stars Jack London and Robert Service. Open in summer M-Sa 9am-8pm, Su 10am-8pm; winter M-Sa 9am-6pm, Su noon-6pm.

Laundromat and Public Showers: The Wash House Laundromat (☎993-6555), on 2nd Ave. between Princess and Queen. Wash $2.50, dry $0.25 per 4min. Showers $1 per 4min., towels $0.50. Open in summer daily 9am-9pm; winter 10am-6pm.

Pool: (☎993-7412), on 5th next to Museum. Adults $4, college students $3.50, youth and seniors $3, child $2, family $9. Reduced after 8pm. Call for exact hours.

Weather: ☎993-8367.

Women's Shelter: (☎993-5086). 24hr.

Police: (☎993-5555 or 667-5555), at Front St. and Turner St., in the south of town.

Ambulance: ☎993-4444.

Medical Services: Nursing Station (☎993-4444), at 6th Ave. and Church. Open M-F 8:30am-5pm.

Internet Access: Free 30min. at the **Library** (☎993-5571), in the school at 5th Ave. and Princess St. Call ahead. Open in summer Tu-Th 10am-9pm, F-Sa 10am-5pm; winter Tu-Th 1-9pm, F-Sa noon-5pm. Also at **Grubstake** (☎993-6706), 2nd Ave. between King St. and Queen St. $5 per hr. Open Su-Th 10am-10pm, F-Sa 10am-11pm.

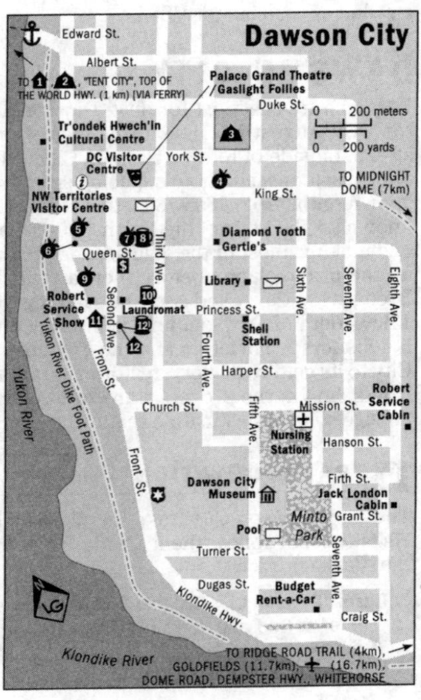

Post Office: (☎993-5342), 5th Ave. near Princess St. and Queen St. Open M-F 8:30am-5:30pm, Sa 9am-noon. The **Historical Post Office,** at 3rd and King St., gives historical service nearer downtown. Open daily noon-3pm and 3:30-6pm. **Postal Code:** Y0B 1G0.

ACCOMMODATIONS & CAMPING

The hostel and campground on the west side of town, across the Yukon River, are by far the most attractive options in town. A hotel room in town will rarely go for much less than $90. The ferry to float you and your wheels across the river is free and runs 24hr. Hop on at Front and Albert St., in the north end of town. The **tent city,** in the woods next to the hostel, remains popular with the town's summer college crowd, despite the $100 per person per summer price tag. Contact the Northern Network of B&Bs (☎993-5644) for the town's listings.

Dawson City River Hostel (**HI;** ☎993-6823), across the Yukon River from downtown; take the first left off the ferry. Sun on lounge chairs overlooking the Yukon, bathe in wood-stove-heated creek water, stir-fry in the outdoor kitchen, or snuggle in the cozy lounge. Open mid-May to Sept. Beds $15, nonmembers $18; tent sites $10, additional tent occupants $7 per person; private rooms $38. No credit cards. ❶

The Bunkhouse (☎993-6164), on Princess at Front St. Basic, clean wood-planked rooms with comfy firm beds. Best option actually *in* town. Open mid-May to mid-Sept. Singles $50, with bath $80; doubles $60, $90; quads with bath $120. ❸

Bombay Peggy's (☎993-6969), on Princess at 2nd St. Each of the rooms in this historic restored brothel has its own distinct decoration and ambience. Though the madame and her ladies are long gone, the pub below will mellow you out long past the midnight sun. Reservations recommended. Rooms $89-$109; most are doubles. ❺

Yukon River Campground, first right off the ferry. Roomy, secluded sites are a haven for nature-lovers, who can peer at the peregrine falcons nesting across the river. An escape from the RV-mania across the river. Water, pit toilets. Requires $12 Yukon Camping Permit available from local vendors or the visitors center. ❶

Gold Rush Campground (☎993-5247), at 5th and York St. Right downtown. Pure RV, baby. Laundry $3, dry $1.50. Dump station. Gravel tent sites $14; RV sites $23-26; pull-through sites $22. Shower $2 per 6min. ❶

FOOD

On Thanksgiving Day in 1898, a turkey in Dawson City cost over $100. Snag one today (or any other grocery product) for much less at the **Dawson City General Store,** on Front St. (☎993-5475. Open M-Sa 8am-8pm, Su 10am-7pm.)

Riverwest Bistro (☎993-6339), Front St. between Princess and Queen. Dawson's artists, tourists, and hipsters converge here for fresh sandwiches ($4.95) and specialty sweets like pecan streusel ($1.50). Open M-Sa 7am-7pm, Su 8am-6pm. ❶

Klondike Kate's (☎993-6527), at 3rd and King St. A favorite of Dawson Sourdoughs. Daily specials add to the full menu of pita wraps ($6), salads ($6-8), burgers ($8), and a hummus plate ($6). Vegetarians and martini connoisseurs ($5.75) rejoice. Open mid-May to mid-Sept. daily 6:30am-11pm. ❶

Dawson City

ACCOMMODATIONS
The Bunkhouse, **11**
Bombay Peggy's, **12**
Dawson City River Hostel, **1**
Gold Rush Campground, **3**
Yukon River Campground, **2**

FOOD
General Store, **6**
Klondike Kate's, **4**
Midnight Sun Hotel Restaurant, **7**
Riverwest Bistro, **9**
Rio, **5**

NIGHTLIFE
Bombay Peggy's, **12**
Pit Tavern & Lounge, **10**
Sun Tavern & Lounge, **8**

Rio (☎993-4683), on Front St. between King and Queen. A burger shack that attracts the summer college crowd with its patty creations and tasty fries ($8-9) and pool table on the deck. The best milkshakes in the north run $4.50. Open daily 11am-10pm. ❷

Midnight Sun Hotel Restaurant (☎993-5495), at 3rd and Queen St. Chinese entrees from $11. Burgers and more $6-8. Lunch smorgasbord on F $10. Close enough to the lounge to hear locals belting out their favorite tunes at the hottest karaoke joint in town (see **Debauchery,** p. 414). Open Su-Th 6am-1am, F-Sa 6am-3am. ❷

SIGHTS

Parks Canada looms large, overseeing the sights in town. Scope information and buy ticket packages at the visitors center (see **Practical Information,** p. 412).

GOLD. Nearly 16km of maintained gravel road follow Bonanza Creek to the former site of **Grand Forks,** which was chewed up when the dredges came through, leaving monster-size gopher tunnels. Along the way are **Gold Dredge #4,** a gigantic machine used to exhaust Bonanza Creek when corporate mining replaced hand-mining, and **Discovery Claim,** the site of the first discovery of gold in Dawson. *(Gold Dredge #4: gold-info rich tours on the hour daily 9am-4pm, except 11am; $5. Discover Claim: interactive gold-staking program daily 11am. $5.)* **Goldbottom Mining Tours and Gold Panning,** 30km south of town, offers a tour of an operating mine and an hour of panning. *(☎993-5023. Open June to freeze-up daily 11am-7pm. $12.)* Pan for free at the confluence of the Bonanza and Eldorado Creeks beyond the Discovery Claim site; panning anywhere else could lead to an unpleasant encounter with the owner of the claim you're jumping. Pans sold at local hardware stores for about $10.

ROBERT SERVICE. Before stopping by Robert Service's cabin for an animated account of his life and poetry, catch the Robert Service Show given by the magnificent Tom Byrne, who recounts the life of Robert Service as he weaves in Service's famous poems, "The Cremation of Sam McGee" and "The Shooting of Dan McGrew." The poems' wit and Byrne's story-telling make the show a feature attraction in Dawson. *(Cabin on 8th near Hanson. Free viewing daily 9am-noon and 1-5pm. Shows at 10am and 1:30pm. $5 includes Jack London talk. Robert Service Show at corner of Front St. and Prince. Shows June-Aug. daily at 3pm and 8pm. $8, 10-16 $4, under 10 free.)*

JACK LONDON. Examine the traces of frontier literary genius Jack London at his **cabin,** where the great California author's life and brief stint in the Yukon are described in letters, photographs, and a talk by London fanatic and Canadian author Dick North. *(On 8th Ave. and Firth St. Open daily 10am-1pm and 2-6pm. 30min. tours daily 11:15am and 2:45pm. Exhibit and talk $2 or free with Robert Service cabin talk.)*

DEBAUCHERY. **Diamond Tooth Gertie's** was Canada's first legal casino and the stuff movies are made of. Gamblers fritter the night away with roulette, blackjack, and Texas Hold 'em against local legends such as Johnny Caribou and No Sleep Filippe. Madame Gertie belts out tunes and can-can dancing at 8:30pm, 10:30pm, and midnight. *(☎993-5575. At 4th and Queen St. 19+. Open nightly 7pm-2am. $6 cover or $20 season pass. No cover after 11pm. Happy hour midnight-2am. On-site ATM for those who need to really clean out their nest eggs.)* The **Gaslight Follies,** a high-kicking vaudeville revue, is held in **Palace Grand Theatre.** *(King St., between 2nd and 3rd. ☎993-6217. Up to 2 shows nightly. Reservations available. Box office open daily 11am-9pm. $15-17, under 12 $7.50.)* As the night winds down, karaoke winds up at the **Sun Tavern and Lounge.** Young and old alike pack in to check out the local talent. Though no longer Dawson's roughest bar, the Sun is still no place to sip fruity drinks. Pints are $4. *(3rd St. and Queen. ☎993-5495. Open daily noon-2am.)* See grown men cry to home-spun country tunes at **The Pit Tavern and Lounge.** Barnacle Bob plays the tavern from 4pm, and the much-acclaimed country and blues house band plays the lounge Wednesday-Saturday at 10pm. *(At the old Westminster Hotel on 3rd. ☎993-5339. Tavern open 9am-11pm; lounge open noon-2am. Happy hour 4:45-5:45pm.)* For a less rowdy glass of sangria, head to **Bombay Peggy's.** Sangria pitchers are $12 from 7-9pm. *(2nd St. and Princess. ☎993-6969. Happy hour 5-6pm, sangria pitchers $12 7-9pm. Open in summer 2pm-1:30am; winter 4pm-1am.)*

TR'ONDEK HWECH'IN CULTURAL CENTRE. The **Tr'ondek Hwech'in Cultural Centre,** celebrated for its architecture since its completion in 1998, is a striking and innovative home for exhibits on First Nations culture. The center is open for visitors to browse displays, watch videos, or participate in various cultural activities and demonstrations. *(On Front St. ☎993-6564. Open daily 10:30am-6pm. Donations welcome. Tours of gallery and slide show Offered 3 times a day. $5, under 5 free.)*

OUTDOOR ACTIVITIES. Dawson is a jungle-gym for outdoors-lovers. Find trail maps for **Moosehead Slide** and **Midnight Dome** at the visitors center. The Dawson region is surrounded by a network of loop roads and trails perfect for hiking and biking (but watch out for jeeps and ATVs on the wider ones). The trailhead for the **Ridge Road Trail** (32km), which runs up some wilderness hills before connecting with Bonanza Creek Rd., is located by the Callison Industrial Area—the visitors center has essential maps. **Hunker, Dominion,** and **Sulphur Creek Rds.** also provide hiking challenges—but pack well, because the full loop is 164km. Fishers will find angling on the Yukon or its tributaries difficult without the *Regulations Summary.* Pick it up for free at the visitors center. The Dawson City River Hostel (see p. 413) sells topographic maps of the region ($12) and arranges four-day **canoe rentals** to Eagle, AK (US$110), or ten-day trips to Circle, AK .

EVENTS

A trip up the **Midnight Dome,** 7km along Dome Rd., just past the Esso gas station on the way into town, is a Yukon-wide tradition on the **summer solstice,** on which the sun dips below the horizon for just 20min. around 12:30am. The Midnight Dome makes for a panoramic picnic spot or sunset photo op. Drive up or take the steep 7km trail that ascends over 600m leaving from the end of King St. (2hr. one-way, map at visitors center). Race it on the Saturday of Music Fest and then head riverside for a salmon barbecue.

During the third weekend of July, Gold Fever becomes Dance Fever as Canadians bust their move at the **Dawson City Music Festival** for three days of fantastic music and energy. Kid Fest events thrill the younger crowd. Tickets to see 20-plus pop, rock, and folk bands, go on sale in April, and usually sell out by mid-June. The ticketless eavesdrop outside venues and in the beer garden. (☎993-5584; www.dcmf.com. July 18-20, 2002. $70 for 3 days of workshops, performances, and dancing.) Mid-August sees Dawson explode in Sourdough charm during **Discovery Days,** with a parade, pancake breakfasts, and an entire town in gold-rush period costume. Be prepared to face down the columns of tourist RVs. Labour Day visitors will not want to pass up watching the **Great International Outhouse Race.** Teams of contenders tow occupied outhouses on wheels through the streets of Dawson. (Visitors Association ☎993-5575. Sept. 1, 2003.)

ALONG HWY. 4: CAMPBELL HWY. ☎867

Unlike drivers on the Alaska Hwy., those who travel the Campbell Hwy. (Hwy. 4) feel like they are truly penetrating the wild and powerful north alone. They are following the footsteps of the highway's namesake, Robert Campbell, the first white man to brave the Yukon. From the south, the Campbell Hwy. runs 602km from **Watson Lake** to **Carmacks** (8hr.). Faltering mining ventures have turned the towns along the highway into ghost-towns. Only anglers, solitude-seekers, and wildlife buffs lured by Faro's eco-tourism venture on the road, and the land is devoid of RVs. From the tiny, largely native community of Ross River (originally a 19th-century fur-trading post), a finger of road cuts off towards the Northwest Territories (NWT) wilderness. Other roads off the Campbell service smaller mining and prospecting operations. Indeed, much of the activity and sparse settlement found along the Campbell seems to be dedicated to its maintenance; the 383km (5-5½hr.; no services on this stretch) of graded dirt road from Watson Lake in the south (on the Alaska Hwy.) to Ross River runs through wilderness broken only by year-round highway servicing camps. **This stretch is not to be taken lightly:** tires are sliced and windshields are cracked at high speeds. Unless you want to be stranded roadside for hours, carry extra auto-fixing gear with you. As you get closer to Ross River, you start to catch views of the velvet-puckered green Pelly Range to the south and strange, rounded, high dirt cliffs. On the way to Carmacks from Faro, the greatly improved road continues on high bluffs and eventually follows the Yukon River with some forceful views approaching town. Five government campsites lie on the route (Kms 80, 177, 376 at the turn-off for Ross River, 428 up toward Faro, and 517 on Little Salmon Lake; $8 permit camping only), and three more on the short Frenchman Rd. This road branches off the Campbell at Km 551, near Carmacks, and leads 60km to the **Klondike Hwy.**

ROSS RIVER. Ross River is 370km of gravel road and two campsites away from Watson Lake and the Alaska Hwy. Camping awaits just beyond the Ross River at **Lapi Canyon Territorial Campground ❶,** above the river that flows between the sandy cliffs of the canyon. (Pit toilets, firewood, water. $8.) The sole **gas station** doubles as a **general store** with groceries. (☎969-2212. Open daily 8am-6pm.) **Medical emergencies:** ☎969-4444. **Police**: ☎867-667-5555.

FARO. One hour northeast of Ross River and a jaunt down 10km of road will land you in the almost-ghost-town of **Faro.** When active, the town's mine held the world's largest open-pit lead and zinc production complex. If you do make the trip to Faro, there is spectacular wilderness fit for **fishing** and **hiking.** The underdeveloped nature of the land means that most hiking ventures will become backcountry treks—bring appropriate gear and maps.

You may catch a view of rare black-and-white **Fannin sheep** from one of the town's specially constructed **viewing platforms.** The closest platform to town is at the corner of Blind Creek Rd. and Lorna Blvd.; ask at the visitors center for directions to others. Take the short hike from the visitors center over to **Van Gorder Falls,** a beautiful spot not requiring backcountry hiking. To reach the **nursing station,** take a left on Bell Ave. of Campbell St. For the **police,** (☎994-5555), turn right immediately upon entering town. The **post office** is on the left past Hoang's. (open M-F 8:30am-5:30pm, Sa 8:30am-noon). If you need car repair, try **Shell.** (☎994-2538. **24hr. road service** ☎994-3019 or 994-2538).

The **Johnson Lake Territorial Campground ❶** lies 6.5km back toward the highway. (Pit toilets, pump water, and firewood. $8.) Down the road from the visitors center, **Redmond's Hotel ❹** has the only rooms in town. **Hoang's ❷** is the only restaurant in town, attached to the hotel on your left past the visitors center. Meals $6-13. (Open M-Sa 11am-8pm).

CARMACKS. **Little Salmon Lake ❶** lies 85km before Carmacks and offers awesome lakeside campsites. (Permit required. Pit toilets, firewood, water. $8.) Signs from here will guide you down the Campbell's paved 180km (2hr.) to

Faro. Stop at **Eagle's Nest Bluff,** about 30km from Carmacks, to hear the aspens rustle and get a wide-ranging view of the wide Yukon River and its surroundings. The end of the Campbell meets the North Klondike Hwy. (Hwy. 2); turn left for Carmacks. The final approach to Carmacks delivers in-town **camping** along the Nordenskiold River at the popular **Tantalus Public Campground ❶,** and a meandering stretch of riverside boardwalk. (Pit toilets, water. $12.) Eat with local characters at the **Gold Panner Cafe ❷,** part of the Hotel Carmacks complex below the highway. (☎863-5221. Open daily 6am-10pm; winter reduced hours.) North of town, the new **Tage Cho Hudan Cultural Centre** preserves the Tutchone culture and displays the world's only mammoth snare model. (☎863-5830. Open daily 9am-5pm. Donation requested.) The **visitors center** is beside the campground (☎863-6330. Open M-F 8:30am-5pm.) Other services include: **police,** ☎863-5555 and **ambulance/health clinic,** ☎863-4444. From **Carmacks,** the smooth **North Klondike Hwy.** (Hwy. 2) runs 175km south to Whitehorse and 360km north to Dawson City.

MT. HALDANE. 179km north of Carmacks on Hwy. 2, Hwy. 11 branches off to the mining towns of **Mayo, Elsa,** and **Keno.** A 76km detour down the rough, gravel-surfaced Hwy. 11 leads hikers toward the Mt. Haldane trailhead—the trail winds steeply toward the mountain's nearly 2000m summit and some of the best lookouts in all of the central Yukon, since Haldane juts starkly alone out of the vast McQuesten Valley. The trail's remoteness keeps it largely off the tourist track, and weeks often pass without any hiker traffic. Plan to spend 3hr. each way on the 6km trail. To get to the trailhead, look for the Mt. Haldane Trail sign after heading north from Mayo toward Elsa—it is about 26km from Mayo.

APPROACHING THE NORTHWEST TERRITORIES: DEMPSTER HWY. ☎867

If you have ever dreamed of a day in which the sun never sets, or a sunset that lasted for hours before slowly flowing into a gorgeous sunrise, then the Dempster Hwy. will fulfill your Arctic Circle fantasies. The residents of the towns above the Arctic Circle shed their watches during the summer; while it may be perfectly fine to knock on your neighbors door at 2am, 10am may be late in the day. The experience is entirely worthwhile, but be prepared to pay for it—prices on everything rise along with the latitude.

THE ROAD. The Dempster Hwy. begins in the Yukon as Hwy. 5. It winds a spectacular 734km toward Inuvik, becoming Hwy. 8 when it crosses into the Northwest Territories (Km 465). Construction of the highway began in the 1950s when oil and gas were discovered near the Arctic Circle at Eagle Plains. It was not until 1979, however, that Canada's isolated Mackenzie River Delta towns of **Fort McPherson, Tsiigehtchic,** and **Inuvik** (ih-NOO-vik) finally had road access. These communities are largely indigenous Inuvialuit and Gwich'in.

THE REALITY. The Dempster presents its drivers with naked wilderness, huge tracts of wholly undeveloped forest, plains, and tundra. Though recent improvements have made it easier to drive close to the 90km speed limit most of the way, you won't want to—amazing vistas await at every curve and pass. The road is not to be taken lightly. Part of the Dempster is built on a bed of sharp, graded shale, which pops right up through the toughest 18-ply truck tires. The drive should be approached with careful planning. Services are limited to Klondike River Lodge (Km 0), Eagle Plains (Km 369), Fort McPherson

DESTRUCKTION (deh-STRUK-shun) n. the act of semis racing along the Dempster Highway at high speeds, spitting gravel at the windshields of oncoming vehicular traffic. Vehicles can best avoid cracks from destrucktion by playing Dempster Chicken. Hug the center of the road and begin braking as the truck approaches, thus encouraging the steamroller to slow down. Before the truck passes, pull to the side of the road and stop so flying gravel will be less likely to crack the windshield.

(Km 550), and Inuvik (Km 734), Although a trip to Tombstone makes a pleasant overnight, the full drive takes around 12hr. (two days each way to be fully and safely appreciated). The weather is erratic. Quick rainstorms or high winds can make portions of the route impassable (watch for flashing red lights that denote closed roads) and can disrupt ferry service to Inuvik for as long as two weeks, leaving travelers stranded.

ORIENTATION. The spectacular first 150km of the Dempster pass through the crags of the **Ogilvie Mountains,** whose curvy, barren slopes are shaped like glaciers. The dramatic peaks of the southern ranges gradually round out to the gentler, gravel-covered, unglaciated **Northern Ogilvies** near Engineer Creek (Km 194). The road then descends into forests and velvet tundra as it approaches the **Arctic Circle** (Km 405). The northernmost stretch of the Rockies, the Richardson Mountains, parallel the road in the distance. The trees become more stunted the farther north you go, due to the permafrost that covers much of the Yukon. The trees are forced to dig their roots in the "active layer" above the ice. There are only a handful of settlements to distract drivers from the wonder of gazing.

PRACTICAL INFORMATION. Road and Ferry Report (☎800-661-0752; in Inuvik 777-2678) provides up-to-date road info. The **NWT Visitor Centre** (see p. 411) in Dawson City has free regional brochures, a map of the highway, a short video, and reports from recent drivers. A full tank of gas, dependable tires (6-ply or better), a good spare or three, extra oil and coolant, and emergency supplies (food, water, clothes, a first aid kit, and a can of gas) are necessary Dempster companions. The **Klondike River Lodge** (☎993-6892; open daily 7am-10:30pm, garage services limited to tire repair on Su) has full services and will rent you a gas can for $5 with a $15 deposit. Bring powerful bug repellant—even 100% DEET won't thwart every skeeter bite—and some form of netting if camping. If you lack wheels or doubt yours will survive the trip, **Dawson City Courier** (☎993-6688) drives up Mondays and Fridays and returns Wednesdays and Sundays for $230 each way.

TOMBSTONE. Some drivers from Dawson stay in Tombstone, a beautiful range of igneous rock, overnight. The **Interpretive Centre** at **Tombstone Campground** (Km 72) has wise staff, trails, and expansive displays including real specimens of local flora and fauna. The migrating **Porcupine caribou herd** north of Tombstone is, at 150,000 head, the largest in North America.

CAMPING. Several Yukon **government campgrounds** ❶ ($8) line the route north to Inuvik (Km 72, 194). At the foot of Sapper Hill and Rock River, **Engineer Creek** ❶ (Km 194) provides the most scenic camping. In **Nitainlii** (just before Ft. McPherson at Km 541), there is an excellent Gwich'in **interpretive center** and **campground** ❶. (Center open June-Sept. daily 9am-9pm. Sites $15.)

BACKCOUNTRY. The mesmerizing landscape tempts **backcountry** trippers but does not play kindly with the under-prepared. The Ogilvie and Blackstone Rivers are favored by backcountry paddlers. *Paddling the Yukon* ($24, available at **Max-**

imillian's, see p. 412) is a comprehensive guide. Only a handful of paths access this wilderness. The road guide *Along the Dempster* describes routes accessible from the highway. Updated descriptions of routes that have become trails due to use, *Yukon's Tombstone Range and Blackstone Uplands: A Traveler's Guide* is well-worth the $20. Backcountry hikers should carry maps of where they intend to travel, however—much of the terrain lining the highway is Vuntut Gwich'in settlement land, and hiking, hunting, fishing, or camping on it requires tribal authorization. If the visitors centers can't answer your questions, you can contact the **Gwich'in Land Administration** directly. (☎867-777-4869, fax 867-777-4538.)

DAYHIKES. At Km 58, a small road behind the gravel pit becomes the **Grizzly Valley** trail (3hr. one-way), leading through spruce forest to an alpine ridge with a fine view. The hike to **Tombstone Mountain** (known in Gwich'in as **Ddhah Ch'aa Tat,** "among the sharp, ragged, rocky mountains") begins just north of the interpretive centre or at Grizzly Creek, takes three to four days, and requires self-reliance, a compass, and topo maps. For a day-long adventure in the Northern Ogilvies, try the **Mt. Distincta trail** ("Windy Pass") at Km 154, which heads over craggy boulders to one of the area's highest peaks (1800m). From the highway, walk southeast across a narrow ribbon of tundra to the ridge base. Follow the ridge south 6km, past a radio tower, and up a slope to the west to the true summit. From there, hike north 6km and then descend back to the highway where you'll emerge 5km west of the trailhead. This trail rises about 1000m/3274 ft. **Sapper Hill,** with its yellow-gray ridge, is one of the best half-day hikes along the highway. It begins just after Engineer Creek (Km 194) and takes 4hr. Avoid walking along the fishbone crest of the ridge; the chunky limestone near the summit can be tricky to navigate. Once the road descends into the river delta lowlands of the Northwest Territories, hiking becomes nearly impossible due to the swampy top layer of permafrost—even worse, the mosquitoes will sap pint after pint out of any hiker unbowed by soggy feet.

EAGLE PLAINS HOTEL. Gas, food, a coin laundry and showers, and accommodations are available at the well-kept **Eagle Plains Hotel ❺,** halfway to Inuvik at Km 369—rooms have monopoly pricing and a comfy 70s decor. Parking lot-style camping is available. Gas in the summer of 2002 topped out at over a buck a liter, but driving through the middle of nowhere is no time to be picky. The next pump is 197km away and the price is not much better. (☎993-2453. Singles $112; each extra person $14. Sites $10. Electricity $15.) **Food ❷** at the hotel is of disarmingly good value. A Bushfire burger (onions, hot peppers, and horseradish) with thick fries costs $8. (Restaurant open daily 7am-9pm. Lounge open daily 4:30pm-2am.)

ARCTIC CIRCLE. Just past Eagle Plains at Km 405, the Dempster crosses the Arctic Circle. Here lies an imaginary dotted line in the tundra. A sign provides photographic proof that you've reached the **Land of the Midnight Sun.**

NORTHWEST TERRITORIES. Set your watch to **Mountain Time** upon entering the Northwest Territories at Km 465. From mid-June to mid-October, **free ferries** cross **Peel River** (Km 539; runs daily on demand) and **Arctic Red River/MacKenzie River** (Km 608; departs daily from south shore 25min. past the hour 9am-12:25am). In winter, cars can drive across the thick ice. No crossing is possible during fall freeze or spring thaw. Call ☎800-661-0752 for ice status. Travelers who wish to visit the community of Tsiigehtchic should note that the MacKenzie River ferry does not dock there by default (the Dempster skirts Tsiigetchic by a few hundred meters), and that ferry operators must be notified to make a landing at Tsiigetchic.

FORT MCPHERSON. The small community of Ft. McPherson doesn't have a lot to offer travelers, but it does have the only **ATM** and auto repair between Eagle Plains and Inuvik. Pick up some groceries or an axe at the **Tetlit Co-op,** located in the big white building on the right a ways down the Ft. McPherson turnoff. (☎952-2417. Open M-Sa 10am-6pm; **public phone** available.) Thank God for **Wolf Creek Services** and their $25 tire repair, along with garage, wash, and tow services. To get there, drive a few dozen meters down the Ft. McPherson turnoff to the intersection with C Wilson St.—it's the garage building on the right. If you get to the Co-op, you've driven too far. (☎867-952-2139. Open daily 9am-9pm.) In emergencies, call the **police** ☎952-2551, **fire** ☎952-5555, or **Health Center** ☎952-2586.

INUVIK, NT ☎867

Inuvik ("living place") has 3600 residents, mostly from two Arctic tribes: Inuvialuit of the Beaufort Sea coast and the Gwich'in of the Mackenzie River Delta. During the long winter, Inuvik's houses are painted bright colors, and during the summer, the community hosts a renowned 10-day Great Northern Arts Festival. A recent upsurge in petroleum exploration has caused traffic jams and sent housing prices even farther north. While most shops try to operate on a night and day schedule, the town is usually out and about for the sun's lowest point in the sky (2:30am).

PRACTICAL INFORMATION. Just about everything in town is on Mackenzie St., starting with the welcoming **Western Arctic Visitor Centre.** (☎777-4727. Open daily 9am-8pm.) Stop here on arrival and receive your **free Arctic Adventurer certificate** for driving the Dempster and visit its extensive display for a crash course on the area. **Arctic Tire,** 80 Navy Rd., offers 24hr. road service and 24hr. gas pumps. (☎777-4149. Open M-Sa 8am-6pm.) Both the **CIBC bank** and the **post office** have **24hr. ATMs.** A great book selection and amazing topo maps are available at **Boreal Books,** 181 Mackenzie Rd. They also carry the coveted "We drove the Dempster Highway" bumper stickers. (☎777-3748. Open daily 10am-6pm.) Other services include: **police** (☎777-2935); **ambulance** (☎777-4444); and **Inuvik Regional Hospital** (☎777-8000). Free **Internet** access is available at the **library,** 100 Mackenzie Rd., for 1hr. (☎777-2749. Open M-Th 10am-6pm and 7-9pm, F 10am-6pm, Sa-Su 2-5pm.)

ACCOMMODATIONS AND FOOD. The four hotels in town charge prices north of outrageous. For an unparalleled Arctic experience, stay with twenty sled dogs at the **Arctic Chalet ❷.** Walk your favorite dog in the summer or pay for a thrilling sled ride in the winter. (Single cabin $45; large cabins with kitchen, private toilet, and shared bathhouse from $85.) **Robertson's Bed and Breakfast ❹,** 41 Mackenzie Rd., offers the cheapest rooms in town. (☎777-3111. Singles $70; doubles $80.) Pretty camping awaits at **Chuk Campground ❶,** right outside town. (☎777-3613. Toilets. Sites $15, day use $5, electric RV sites $20. Free showers.)

While in town, eat up like the natives do. The cheapest caribou and musk-ox burgers ($6-8) and greasy food are at **To Go's,** 71 Mackenzie St. (☎777-3030. Open M-Th 7am-midnight, F and Sa 9am-3am, Su 11am-11pm.) Get Inuvik's best falafel ($6.95) and *shwarma* ($9.95) at the diverse **Fast Food Cafe ❷,** across from the Igloo Church (☎777-2020. Open daily 11:30am-2:30am.) The **Cafe Gallery ❷** serves baked goods (big muffins $2.50) and light lunches (sandwich and soup $10) in a studio with comfy chairs. (☎777-2888. Open M-Sa 8am-6pm, Su noon-6pm.) On a late night hit **The Zoo,** the Arctic's rowdy hot spot in the Mackenzie Hotel. (Open daily 11am-2am. Dance party F and Sa.) Recently-opened **Frosty's Arctic Pub,** also across from the Igloo Church, draws crowds with its live music and freewheeling party atmosphere. (☎777-5194. Open daily 11:30am-2am.)

EVENTS & OUTDOOR ACTIVITIES. Begun in 1989, the **Great Northern Arts Festival** brings over 100 artists and entertainers to Inuvik for performances, workshops, and a world-class art sale. (☎777-3536. Mid-July, 2003.) The **Midnight Sun Tundra Nature Hike** (2hr. one-way) begins at the Marine Bypass Rd. on the north side of Inuvik and follows mountain ridges for 6km to **Three Mile Lake.** The ridges are a perfect spot to watch the sun in its lowest arc and to survey the **Richardson Range.** To explore the Mackenzie Delta, contact **Western Arctic Adventures and Equipment,** 38 Sprucehill Dr. (☎777-2594), for canoes, kayaks, air charters, and trip-planning help. Canoes and kayaks can be put in behind the house for $35 a day with paddles, jackets, and friendly advice. **Arctic Nature Tours** (☎777-3300; www.arcticnaturetours.com), beside the Igloo church, mobilizes outfitters and community contacts to lead nature and culture tours. Explore Inuvik (1½hr., $25); cruise the Mackenzie River and visit an Inuvialuit camp (4hr., 1hr. tour in camp, $75); have tea and bannock with an elder (3½ hr., $65); or fly to Herschel Island Territorial Park to see abandoned whaling towns (5hr., $228). **Aurora Research College Research Centre** offers a naturalist's canoe tour of the Delta. At the research station, at Duck Lake St. and Mackenzie Rd., you can peruse the arctic library, browse the **Internet** for free, or catch a free slideshow on the region. (☎777-3838. Open M-F 8:30am-noon and 1-5pm. Tour 4hr.; summer M 6pm, Th 1pm; $32.)

INDEX

S

Y

Z

MAP INDEX

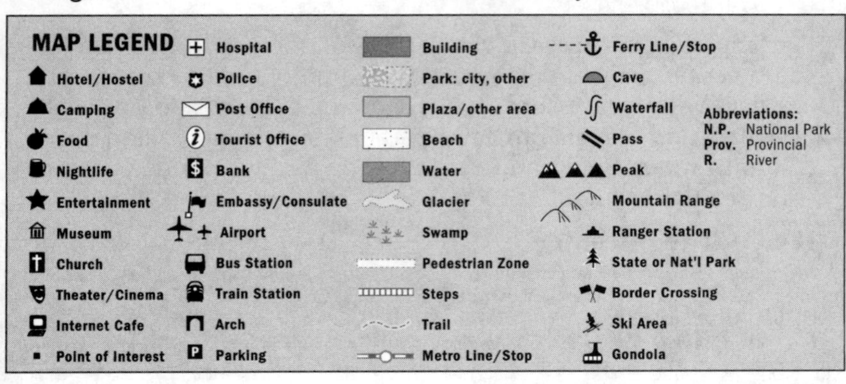
MAP LEGEND
Hotel/Hostel
Camping
Food
Nightlife
Entertainment
Museum
Church
Theater/Cinema
Internet Cafe
Point of Interest
Hospital
Police
Post Office
Tourist Office
Bank
Embassy/Consulate
Airport
Bus Station
Train Station
Arch
Parking
Building
Park: city, other
Plaza/other area
Beach
Water
Glacier
Swamp
Pedestrian Zone
Steps
Trail
Metro Line/Stop
Ferry Line/Stop
Cave
Waterfall
Pass
Peak
Mountain Range
Ranger Station
State or Nat'l Park
Border Crossing
Ski Area
Gondola
Abbreviations:
N.P. National Park
Prov. Provincial
R. River